Multilateralism Matters

New Directions in World Politics

Helen Milner and John Gerard Ruggie,

GENERAL EDITORS

Columbia University Press
New York   Chichester, West Sussex
Copyright © 1993 Columbia University Press

The following chapters have appeared in *International Organization*. They are reprinted by permission of the MIT Press Journals and the copyright holders, The World Peace Foundation and the Massachusetts Institute of Technology.

Chapter 1, John Gerard Ruggie, "Multilateralism: The Anatomy of an Institution." Volume 46(2). Spring 1992.

Chapter 2, James A. Caporaso, "International Relations Theory and Multilateralism: The Search for Foundations." Volume 46(3). Summer 1992.

Chapter 3, Lisa M. Martin, "The Rational State Choice of Multilateralism." Volume 46(4). Autumn 1992.

Chapter 7, Steve Weber, "Shaping the Postwar Balance of Power: Multilateralism in NATO." Volume 46(3). Summer 1992.

Chapter 8, Miles Kahler, "Multilateralism with Small and Large Numbers." Volume 46(3). Summer 1992.

Chapter 10, Geoffrey Garrett, "International Cooperation and Institutional Choice: The European Community's Internal Market." Volume 46(2). Spring 1992.

Library of Congress Cataloging-in-Publication Data

Multilateralism matters :
the theory and praxis of an institutional form /
John Gerard Ruggie, editor.
p.   cm. — (New directions in world politics)
ISBN 0–231–07980–X (cloth). — ISBN 0–231–07981–8 (pbk.)
1. International cooperation,   2. International organization.
3. International economic relations.
I. Ruggie, John Gerard, 1944–.   II. Series.
JC362.M74 1993   327.1'7—dc20   92–31586
                              CIP

Printed in the United States of America

c 10 9 8 7 6 5 4 3 2 1
p 10 9 8 7 6

Contents

❖

Part 4. INTERNATIONAL CHANGE 293

Part 5. THEORETICAL REPRISE 441

Contributors

John Gerard Ruggie is Dean of the School of International and Public Affairs, as well as Professor of Political Science, at Columbia University in New York.

James A. Caporaso is the Virginia and Prentice Bloedel Professor of Political Science at the University of Washington in Seattle.

Lisa L. Martin is Associate Professor of Government at Harvard University.

Anne-Marie Burley is Assistant Professor of Law and International Relations at the University of Chicago Law School.

Peter F. Cowhey is a Professor at the University of California, San Diego, with a joint appointment in the Graduate School of International Relations and Pacific Studies and the Department of Political Science.

Judith Goldstein is Associate Professor of Political Science at Stanford University.

Steve Weber is Assistant Professor of Political Science at the University of California, Berkeley.

Miles Kahler is Professor in the Graduate School of International Relations and Pacific Studies, University of California, San Diego.

Patrick M. Morgan is the Thomas and Elizabeth Tierney Professor of Peace Research at the University of California, Irvine.

Geoffrey Garrett is Assistant Professor of Political Science at Stanford University.

Mark W. Zacher is Professor of Political Science, University of British Columbia.

Friedrich Kratochwil is Professor of Political Science at the University of Pennsylvania.

Preface

❖

PARTS of the international institutional order today appear quite robust and adaptive. This is true not only in economic but also in security affairs, and it is true not only in Europe but also at the global level. The reasons go beyond the fact that these are institutions and that institutions are "in demand." A core feature of the current international institutional order is its multilateral form. The multilateral form, under certain circumstances, appears to have characteristics that enhance its durability and ability to adapt to change. Yet the concept of multilateralism is poorly defined, and therefore poorly understood, in the literature. This volume recovers its principled meanings from historical practice, shows how and why these principled meanings have come to be institutionalized, and suggests why multilateralism may continue to play a significant role today even as some of the postwar conditions that gave rise to it have changed.

In doing so, the essays in this volume also engage a number of central theoretical debates in our discipline: Is the relative neglect of multilateralism in the literature due to the atomistic ontology and instrumental-rationalist epistemology that characterize prevailing modes of theorizing? Is it possible to reconcile and perhaps even mutually enrich the so-called rationalist and reflectivist approaches to the study of international institutions? What is the balance of systemic vs. domestic factors in explaining the shape of the international order? Of structural factors vs. ideas, norms, and institutions?

This volume is the product of the West Coast Workshop on Multilateralism, sponsored by the Ford Foundation, which met from 1989 to 1991. Ford's rekindled interest in this subject goes back at least to 1984, long before it became fashionable again. At that time, Dr. Enid C. B. Schoettle, who headed Ford's international affairs programs, convened a meeting in New York City on the sorry state of mainstream scholarship and policy as it concerned the domain of multilateralism. I was asked to prepare one of the discussion papers for that meeting, a paper that was subsequently substantially expanded and published as Friedrich Kratochwil and John Gerard Ruggie, "International Organization: A State of the Art on an Art of the State," *International Organization* (Autumn 1986), vol. 40.

One follow-up to that 1984 meeting was a set of grants by Ford to a Harvard–MIT group and a Berkeley–Stanford group, designed to encourage the revival of scholarly interest in the subject by convening a series of seminars in both locations. On the West Coast, these exploratory seminars were succeeded by the focused workshop that produced this volume.

Our first debt of gratitude is to the Ford Foundation, for their vision and their financial support; the study and practice of multilateralism is stronger and more vibrant today as a result of their multifaceted efforts to make it so. In the conduct of the workshop itself, I gratefully acknowledge the assistance of the University of California Institute on Global Conflict and Cooperation, of which I was then the Director, for orchestrating the entire project, including organizing the two La Jolla meetings—Trudy Elkins deserves special mention. Additional thanks go to Stephen Krasner and Stanford University as well as Mark Zacher and the University of British Columbia for hosting the other two sessions and to Jeff Frieden and Robert O. Keohane, who served as commentators when we discussed the penultimate drafts of our papers.

In the attempt to share the product of our labors as widely as possible, we have also published several of these essays in the journal *International Organization*. Those by Ruggie, Caporaso, Kahler, and Weber appeared as a special symposium on "Multilateralism" in vol. 46 (Summer 1992); Garrett's paper was published as a free-standing article in vol. 46 (Spring 1992), and Martin's in vol. 46 (Autumn 1992). We thank the editors of *International Organization* and the MIT Press for permission to include these articles here.

Finally, I want to express my sincerest appreciation to the other contributors to this volume for proving beyond any doubt that multilateral cooperation under anarchy not only is feasible but also can be mutually profitable and fun.

John Gerard Ruggie
New York City

Multilateralism
Matters

Part 1

❖

THE

CONCEPT

❖

1. Multilateralism: The Anatomy of an Institution

❖

John Gerard Ruggie

I N 1989, peaceful change, which a leading realist theorist had declared a very low probability event in international politics less than a decade before,[1] accommodated the most fundamental geopolitical shift of the postwar era and perhaps of the entire twentieth century: the collapse of the Soviet East European empire and the attendant end of the cold war. Many factors were responsible for that shift. But there seems little doubt that multilateral norms and institutions have helped stabilize their international consequences. Indeed, such norms and institutions appear to be playing a significant role in the management of a broad array of regional and global changes in the world system today.

In Europe, by one count at least fifteen multilateral groupings are involved in shaping the continent's collective destiny.[2] The European Community (EC) is the undisputed anchor of economic relations and increasingly of a common political vision in the West. And the former East European countries want nothing so much as to tie their economic fate to the Community, a goal that the Community members have facilitated through the creation of the European Bank for Reconstruction and Development and, in some cases, through the prospect of association agreements. Yet the author of another influential realist treatise published a decade ago gave the EC only a few fleeting references—and then only to argue that it would never amount to much in the international "structure" unless it took on the form of a unified state, which it shows no signs of doing even now.[3]

In the realm of European security relations, the central policy issue of the day concerns the adaptation of the North Atlantic Treaty Organization (NATO) to the new European geopolitical realities and the question

I am very grateful to Robert O. Keohane for his extensive and helpful critiques of an earlier draft, which forced me to rethink and clarify several key issues; to Ernst B. Haas for his constructive comments; and to David Auerswald for research assistance.

of whether supplementary indigenous West European or all European multilateral security mechanisms should be fashioned.[4] The Soviet Union, contrary to most predictions, posed no obstacles to German reunification, betting that a united Germany firmly embedded in a broader Western institutional matrix would pose far less of a security threat than a neutral Germany tugged in different directions in the center of Europe.[5] But perhaps the most telling indicator of institutional bite in Europe today is the proverbial dog that has not barked: no one in any position of authority anywhere is advocating, or quietly preparing for, a return to a system of competitive bilateral alliances—which surely is the first time that has happened at any comparable historical juncture since the Congress of Vienna in 1815![6]

Security relations in the Asia–Pacific region make the same points in the negative. It was not possible to construct multilateral institutional frameworks there in the immediate postwar period. Today, the absence of such arrangements inhibits progressive adaptation to fundamental global shifts. The United States and Japan are loath to raise serious questions about their anachronistic bilateral defense treaty, for example, out of fear of unraveling a fragile stability and thereby triggering arms races throughout the region. In Asia–Pacific there is no European Community and no NATO to have transformed the multitude of regional security dilemmas, as has been done in Europe with Franco–German relations, for example. Indeed, no Helsinki-like process through which to begin the minimal task of mutual confidence building exists in the region.[7] Thus, whereas today the potential to move beyond balance-of-power politics in its traditional form exists in Europe, a reasonably stable balance is the best that one can hope to achieve in the Asia–Pacific region.[8]

At the level of the global economy, despite sometimes near-hysterical predictions for twenty years now of imminent monetary breakup and trade wars that could become real wars, "just like in the 1930s,"[9] the rate of growth in world trade continues to exceed the rate of growth in world output; international capital flows dwarf both; and the eighth periodic round of trade negotiations, which had been prematurely pronounced dead, is moving toward completion—this time involving difficult domestic and new transnational issues that the originators of the regime never dreamed would become subject to international rules. And despite considerable tension between them, the United States and Japan continue, in Churchill's phrase, to "jaw-jaw" rather than "war-war" over their fundamental trade differences.[10]

Limited multilateral successes can be found even in the global security realm. One is in the area of nuclear nonproliferation. Many responsible officials and policy analysts in the 1960s predicted that by the 1980s there would exist some two dozen nuclear weapons states.[11] As it has turned out, the total set of actual *and potential* problem states today consists of only half that number, at least in part due to the nonproliferation treaty (NPT) regime.

> Virtually every nonproliferation initiative has turned out to be much more effective than expected when it was proposed or designed, and nonproliferation success has been cheaper than expected. The fact that the nuclear proliferation problem has been "bounded" by the NPT regime means that policy initiatives can be focused on a handful of states.[12]

Moreover, after years of being riveted by the cold war, the United Nations has been rediscovered to have utility in international conflict management: its figleaf role proved useful in Afghanistan, and its decolonization function aided Namibia. It serves as one means by which to try to disentangle regional morasses from Cambodia to the Western Sahara. And perhaps of greatest importance for the new, postcold war era, the posture adopted by the U.N. Security Council to sanction Iraq for its invasion and annexation of Kuwait constituted the organization's most comprehensive, firm, and united response ever to an act of international aggression.[13]

Seen through the lenses of conventional theories of international relations, which attribute outcomes to the underlying distribution of political or economic power, the roles played by normative constraints and institutions in the current international transformation must seem paradoxical. Norms and institutions do not matter much in that literature to begin with; they are viewed as byproducts of, if not epiphenomenal adjuncts to, the relations of force or the relations of production. What is more, insofar as the conventional literature has any explanation at all of extensive institutionalization in the international system, the so-called theory of hegemonic stability is it. But in addition to all the other historical and logical problems from which that theory suffers,[14] merely finding the hegemony to which the current array of regional and global institutional roles could be ascribed is a daunting, if not insurmountable, challenge.

The fact that norms and institutions matter comes as no surprise to the "new institutionalists" in international relations; after all, that has long been their message.[15] But, curiously, little explicit and detailed analytical attention has been paid in this literature to a core feature of current international institutional arrangements: their multilateral form. A literature search keyed on the concept of multilateralism turns up relatively few entries, and only a tiny number of these are of any interest to the international relations theorist. The focus of the new institutionalists has been on "cooperation" and "institutions" in a generic sense, with international regimes and formal organizations sometimes conceived as specific institutional subsets.[16] For example, no scholar has contributed more to the new institutionalism in international relations than Robert Keohane. Yet the concept of multilateralism is used sparingly in his work, even in a literature survey on that subject. And the definition of multilateralism that he employs is purely nominal: "the practice of coordinating national policies in groups of three or more states."[17]

The nominal definition of multilateralism may be useful for some purposes. But it poses the problem of subsuming institutional forms that traditionally have been viewed as being expressions of bilateralism, not multilateralism—instances of the Bismarckian alliance system, for example, such as the League of the *Three* Emperors. In short, the nominal definition of multilateralism misses the *qualitative* dimension of the phenomenon that makes it distinct.[18]

In a superb discussion of this issue, attempting to sort out the enormous variety of trade relations in the world today, William Diebold insists for starters on the need to distinguish between "formal" and "substantive" multilateralism—by which he means roughly what I mean by nominal vs. qualitative. "But that is far from the end of the matter. The bilateral agreements of Cordell Hull were basically different from those of Hjalmar Schacht."[19] That is to say, the issue is not the number of parties so much, Diebold suggests, as the *kind of relations* that are instituted among them. It is this substantive or qualitative characteristic of multilateralism that concerns me in the present essay, not only for trade, but also for the institutional dimension of international relations in general.

Nor is the missing qualitative dimension captured entirely by the concepts of international regimes or intergovernmental organizations. Instances of international regimes exist that were not multilateral in form, such as the Nazi trade and monetary regimes, to which we will return momentarily. As for multilateral formal organizations, although they entail no analytical mystery, all practitioners of the new institutionalism agree that these organizations constitute only one small part of a broader universe of international institutional forms that interest them.

The missing qualitative dimension of multilateralism immediately comes into focus, however, if we return to an older institutionalist discourse, one informed by the postwar aims of the United States to restructure the international order. When we speak here of multilateralism in international trade we know immediately that it refers to trade organized on the basis of certain principles of state conduct, above all, nondiscrimination.[20] Similarly, when we speak here of multilateralism in security relations we know that it refers to some expression or other of collective security or collective self-defense.[21] And when President George Bush today enunciates a "new world order" for the Middle East and elsewhere—universal aspirations, cooperative deterrence, joint action against aggression[22]—whether it constitutes vision or rhetoric, the notion evokes and is entirely consistent with the American postwar multilateralist agenda, as we shall see below. In sum, what is distinctive about multilateralism is not merely that it coordinates national policies in groups of three or more states, which is something that other organizational forms also do, but additionally that it does so on the basis of certain principles of ordering relations among those states.

Thus, a compound anomaly exists in the world of international relations theory today. An institutional phenomenon of which conventional theories barely take note is both widespread and significant, but at the same time, the particular features that make it so are glossed over by most students of international institutions themselves. This essay is intended to help resolve both parts of the anomaly.

The premise of the present paper is that we can better understand the role of multilateral norms and institutions in the current international transformation by recovering the principled meanings of multilateralism from actual historical practice, by showing how and why those principled meanings have come to be institutionalized throughout the history of the modern interstate system, and by exploring how and why they may perpetuate themselves today even as the conditions that initially gave rise to them have changed.

My "grounded" analysis of the concept suggests a series of working hypotheses, which require more extensive testing before strong validity claims can be made for them. Nevertheless, we believe that they are sufficiently interesting, and that the case we make for them is sufficiently plausible, to warrant such further study, and we present them here in that spirit. The argument, in brief, goes something like this. Multilateralism is a generic institutional form of modern international life, and as such it has been present from the start. The generic institutional form of multilateralism must not be confused with formal multilateral organizations, a relatively recent arrival and still of only relatively modest importance. Historically, the generic form of multilateralism can be found in institutional arrangements to define and stabilize the international property rights of states, to manage coordination problems, and to resolve collaboration problems. The last of these uses of the multilateral form historically is the least frequent. In the literature, that fact traditionally has been explained by the rise and fall of hegemonies and, more recently, by various functional considerations. Our analysis suggests that a permissive domestic environment in the leading powers of the day is at least as important. Looking more closely at the post-World War II situation, for example, it was less the fact of American *hegemony* that accounts for the explosion of multilateral arrangements than of *American* hegemony. Finally, we suggest that institutional arrangements of the multilateral form have adaptive and even reproductive capacities which other institutional forms may lack and which may, therefore, help explain the roles that multilateral arrangements play in stabilizing the current international transformation.

The Meanings of Multilateralism

At its core, multilateralism refers to coordinating relations among three or more states in accordance with certain principles. But what, precisely, are those principles? And to what, precisely, do those principles pertain? To facilitate the construction of a more formal definition, let us begin by examining a historical instance of something that everyone agrees multilateralism is not: bilateralism.

Earlier in this century, Nazi Germany succeeded in finely honing a pure form of bilateralism into a systemic organizing principle. Now, as Diebold notes, the everyday term *bilateral* is entirely neutral with regard to the qualitative relationship that is instituted among countries.[23] So as to give expression to its qualitative nature, the Nazi system therefore typically has been referred to as bilatera*list* in character, or as embodying bilatera*lism* as its organizing principle. In any case, once the New Plan of the Nazi government took effect in 1934, Hjalmar Schacht devised a scheme of bilateralist trade agreements and clearing arrangements.[24] The essence of the German international trade regime was that the state negotiated "reciprocal" agreements with its foreign trading partners. These negotiations determined which goods and services were to be exchanged, their quantities, and their price. Often, Germany deliberately imported more from its partners than it exported to them. But it required that its trading partners liquidate their claims on Germany through reinvestment there or by purchasing deliberately overpriced German goods. Thus, its trading partners were doubly dependent on Germany.

This trade regime in turn was linked to bilateralist monetary clearing arrangements. Under these arrangements, a German importer would, for example, pay marks to the German Reichsbank for its imports rather than to the foreign source of the goods or services, while the foreign counterpart of the transaction would receive payment in home country currency from its central bank—and vice versa for German exports. No foreign exchange changed hands, the foreign exchange markets were bypassed, and artificial exchange rates prevailed. The permissible total amounts to be cleared in this manner were negotiated by the two states.

German bilateralism typically but not exclusively focused on smaller and weaker states in East-Central Europe, the Balkans, and Latin America, exchanging primary commodity imports for manufactured exports. But the scheme had no inherent limit; it could have been geographically universalized to cover the entire globe, with an enormous spiderweb of bilateralist agreements radiating out from Germany.[25]

The nominal definition of multilateralism would not exclude the Schachtian bilateralist device: it coordinated economic relations among more than three states. Nor is the fact decisive that negotiations took place bilaterally: after all, many tariff reductions in the General Agreement on Tariffs and Trade (GATT) are also negotiated bilaterally. The difference is, of course, that within GATT bilaterally negotiated tariff reductions are extended to all other parties on the basis of most-favored nation (MFN) treatment, whereas the Schachtian scheme was inherently and fundamentally discriminatory, so that bilateral deals held only on a case-by-case and product-by-product basis *even if* they covered the entire globe in doing so.

Let us examine next an institutional arrangement that is generally acknowledged to embody multilateralist principles: a collective security system. None has ever existed in pure form, but in principle the scheme is quite simple. It rests on the premise that peace is indivisible, so that a war against one ipso facto is considered a war against all. The community of states is therefore obliged to respond to threatened or actual aggression, first by diplomatic means, then through economic sanctions, and finally by the collective use of force if necessary. Facing the prospect of such a community-wide response, any rational potential aggressor would be deterred and would desist. Thus, the incidence of war would gradually decline.

A collective-security scheme certainly coordinates security relations among three or more states. But so too, as noted above, did the League of the Three Emperors, which was nothing more than a set of traditional alliances.[26] What is distinct about a collective-security scheme is that it comprises, as Sir Arthur Salter put it a half-century ago, a permanent potential alliance "against the *unknown* enemy"[27]—and, he should have added, in behalf of the *unknown* victim. The institutional difference between a bilateral alliance and a collective-security scheme can be simply put: in both instances, state *A* is pledged to come to the aid of *B* if *B* is attacked by *C*. In a collective-security scheme, however, *A* is *also* pledged to come to the aid of *C* if *C* is attacked by *B*. Thus,

> A cannot regard itself as the ally of B more than of C, because theoretically it is an open question whether, if an act of war should occur, B or C would be the aggressor. In the same way B has indeterminate obligations towards A and C, and C towards A and B, and so on with a vast number of variants as the system is extended to more and more states.[28]

It was precisely this difference between a collective-security system and alliances that ultimately doomed the fate of the League of Nations in the U.S. Senate.[29]

The United States frequently invoked the collective-security model in leading the anti-Iraq coalition in the Persian Gulf crisis and then war, though what if any permanent institutional consequences will follow from that effort remains to be seen.[30] NATO reflects a truncated version of the model, in which a subset of states organized a collective self-defense scheme of indefinite duration, de jure against any potential aggressor though de facto against one. Nevertheless, internally the scheme was predicated on the indivisibility of threats to the collectivity—that is, it did not matter whether Germany or Great Britain, or the Netherlands, or Norway was attacked, nor in theory by whom—together with the requirement of an unconditional collective response.[31]

We are now in a position to be more precise about the core meaning of multilateralism. Keohane has defined institutions, generically, as "persistent and connected sets of rules, formal and informal, that prescribe behavioural roles, constrain activity, and shape expectations."[32] Very simply, the term *multilateral* is an adjective that modifies the noun *institution*. Thus, multilateralism depicts a *generic institutional form* in international relations. How does multilateral modify institution? Our illustrations suggest that multilateralism is an institutional form that coordinates relations among three or more states on the basis of generalized principles of conduct: that is, principles which specify appropriate conduct for a class of actions, without regard to the particularistic interests of the parties or the strategic exigencies that may exist in any specific occurrence. MFN treatment is a classic example in the economic realm: it forbids discrimination among countries producing the same product—full stop. Its counterpart in security relations is the requirement that states respond to aggression whenever and wherever it occurs—whether or not any specific instance suits their individual likes and dislikes. In contrast, the bilateral form, such as the Schachtian device and traditional alliances, differentiates relations case-by-case based precisely on a priori particularistic grounds or situational exigencies.

Bilateralism and multilateralism do not exhaust the institutional repertoire of states. Imperialism can be considered a third generic institutional form. Imperialism is also an institution that coordinates relations among three or more states, though, unlike bilateralism and multilateralism, it does so by denying the sovereignty of the subject states.[33]

Two corollaries follow from our definition of multilateralism. First, generalized organizing principles logically entail an indivisibility among the members of a collectivity with respect to the range of behavior in question. Depending on circumstances, that indivisibility can take very different forms, ranging from the physical ties of railway lines that the collectivity chooses to standardize across frontiers, all the way to the adoption by states of the premise that peace is indivisible. But note that indivisibility here is a *social construction,* not a technical condition: in a collective-security scheme, states *behave as though* peace were indivisible, and thereby make it so. Similarly, in the case of trade, *adherence to* the MFN norm makes the system of trade an indivisible whole among the member collectivity, not some inherent attribute of trade itself.[34] Bilateralism, in contrast, segments relations into multiples of dyads and compartmentalizes them. Second, as we shall see below, successful cases of multilateralism in practice appear to generate among their members what Keohane has called expectations of "diffuse reciprocity."[35] That is to say, the arrangement is expected by its members to yield a rough equivalence of benefits in the aggregate and over time. Bilateralism, in contrast, is premised on specific reciprocity, the simultaneous balancing of specific quids pro quos by each party with every other at all times.[36]

What follows from this definition and its corollaries is that multilateralism is a highly demanding institutional form. Its historical incidence is, therefore, likely to be less frequent than that of its alternatives, and if its relative incidence at any time were to be high, that fact would pose an interesting puzzle to be explained.

The obvious next issue to address is the fact that, as Keohane points out, the generic concept of international institution applies in practice to many different types of institutionalized relations among states.[37] So too, therefore, does the adjective *multilateral:* the generic attribute of multilateralism, that it coordinates relations among three or more states in accordance with generalized principles of conduct, will have different specific expressions depending on the type of institutionalized relations to which it pertains. Let us examine some instances. Common usage in the literature distinguishes among three institutional domains of interstate relations: international orders, international regimes, and international organizations. Each type can be, but need not be, multilateral in form.

The literature frequently refers to international economic orders, international security orders, international maritime orders, and so on. An "open" or "liberal" international economic order is multilateral in form, as is a maritime order based on the principle of *mare liberum.* The New Economic Order of the Nazis was not multilateral in form, for reasons I have already suggested, and neither was the European security order crafted by Bismarck. The concept of multilateralism here refers to the constitutive rules that order relations in given domains of international life—their architectural dimension, so to speak. Thus, the quality of "openness" in an international economic order refers to such characteristics as the prohibition of exclusive blocs, spheres, or similar barriers to the conduct of international economic relations. The corresponding quality in an international security order—which would cause it to be described as "collective"—is the condition of equal access to a common security umbrella. To the extent that these conditions are met, the order in question may be said to be multilateral in form. In short, multilateralism here depicts the character of an overall order of relations among states; definitionally it says nothing about *how* that order is achieved.

Regimes are more concrete than orders: typically, the term refers to functional or sectoral components of orders. Moreover, the concept of regime encompasses more of the "how" question than does the concept of order in that, broadly speaking, the term "regime" is used to refer to common, deliberative, though often highly asymmetrical means of conducting interstate relations. That much is clear from common usage. But while there is a widespread—assumption in the literature that all regimes are, ipso facto, multilateral in character, this assumption is egregiously erroneous. For example, there is no reason not to call the Schachtian schemes for organizing monetary and trade relations international regimes; they fully meet the standard criteria specified by Stephen Krasner and his colleagues.[38] Moreover, it is entirely possible to imagine the emergence of regimes between *two* states—superpower security regimes, for example, were a topic of some discussion in the 1980s[39]—but such regimes by definition would not be multilateral either. In sum, what makes a regime a *regime* is that it satisfies the definitional criterion of encompassing principles, norms, rules, and decision-making procedures around which actor expectations converge. But in and of themselves, those terms are empty of substance. What makes a regime *multilateral* in form, beyond involving three or more states, is that the substantive meanings of those terms roughly reflect the appropriate generalized principles of conduct. By way of illustration, in the case of a multilateral trade regime, these would include the norm of MFN treatment, corresponding rules about reciprocal tariff reductions and the application of safeguards, and collectively sanctioned procedures for implementing the rules. In the case of a collective-security regime, they would include the norm of nonaggression, uniform rules for use of sanctions to deter or punish aggression, and, again, collectively sanctioned procedures for implementing them.

Finally, formal international organizations are palpable entities with headquarters and letterheads, voting procedures, and generous pension plans. They require no conceptual elaboration. But, again, their relationship to the concept of multilateralism is less self-evident than is sometimes assumed. Two issues deserve brief mention. The first, though it may be moot at the moment, is that there have been international organizations that were not multilateral in form. The Comintern and later Cominform come to mind; they were based explicitly on Leninist principles of organization, which were quite different from their multilateral counterparts.[40] Along the same lines, the recently collapsed Soviet–East European system of organizations differed from multilateral forms in ways that students of international organization never fully came to grips with.[41] The second issue is more problematic even today. A common tendency exists in the world of actual international organizations, and sometimes in the academic community, to equate the very phenomenon of multilateralism with the universe of multilateral organizations or diplomacy. The preceding discussion makes clear why that view is in error. It may be the case empirically that decisions concerning aspects of international orders or, more likely, international regimes are in fact made in multilateral forums. The European Community exhibits this empirical pattern most extensively; the failed quest by developing countries for a New International Economic Order in the 1970s exhibits the desire to achieve it; and decisions on most international trade and monetary matters fall somewhere in between. But definitionally, "multilateral organization" is a separate and distinct type of institutionalized behavior, defined by such generalized decision-making rules as voting or consensus procedures.

In sum, the term *multilateral* is an adjective that modifies the noun *institution*. What distinguishes the multilateral form from others is that it coordinates behavior among three or more states on the basis of generalized principles of conduct. Accordingly, any theory of international institutions that does not include this qualitative dimension of multilateralism is bound to be a fairly abstract theory and one that is silent about one of the most crucial distinctions within the repertoire of international institutional forms. Moreover, for analytic purposes it is important not to (con)fuse the very meaning of multilateralism with any one particular institutional expression of it, be it an international order, regime, or organization. Each can be, but need not be, multilateral in form. In addition, the multilateral form should not be equated with universal geographical scope; the attributes of multilateralism characterize relations within specific collectivities that may and often do fall short of the whole universe of nations. Finally, it should be kept in mind that these are formal definitions, not empirical descriptions of actual cases, and we would not expect actual cases to conform fully to the formal definitions. But let us turn now to some actual historical cases exhibiting the multilateral form.

Multilateralism in History

The institutional form of multilateralism has now been defined. What can we say about its specific expressions over time, their frequency distribution, and some possible correlates? A brief historical survey will situate the phenomenon better and help us begin to answer these questions. To organize the discussion, I adapt a standard typology of institutional roles from the literature: defining and stabilizing international property rights, solving coordination problems, and resolving collaboration problems.[42]

PROPERTY RIGHTS

Not surprisingly, the earliest multilateral arrangements instituted in the modern era were designed to cope with the international consequences of the novel principle of state sovereignty. The newly emerged territorial states conceived their essence, their very being, by the *possession* of territory and the *exclusion* of others from it. But how does one possess some thing one does not own? And, still more problematical, how does one exclude others from it?

The world's oceans posed this problem. Contiguous waterways could be shared, administered jointly, or, more than likely, split down the middle; the international property rights of states were thereby established bilaterally. The oceans were another matter. States attempted to project exclusive unilateral jurisdiction, but they failed. Spain and Portugal tried a bilateral solution, whereby Spain claimed a monopoly of the western trade routes to the Far East and Portugal claimed the eastern routes. But they, too, failed. All such efforts failed for the simple reason that it is exceedingly difficult if not impossible in the long run to vindicate a property right that is not recognized as valid by the relevant others in a given community, especially when exclusion is as difficult as it was in the oceans. Attempts to do so lead to permanent challenge and recurrent conflict. A multilateral solution to the governance of the oceans was, therefore, inescapable. The principle that was first enunciated by Hugo Grotius at the beginning of the seventeenth century, and that states slowly came to adopt, defined an international maritime order in two parts: a territorial sea under exclusive state control, which custom eventually set at three miles because that was the range of land-based cannons at the time; and the high seas beyond, available for common use but owned by none.[43] Under this arrangement, all states were free to utilize the high seas, provided only that they did not thereby damage the legitimate interests of others.[44] And each state had the same rules for all states, not one rule for some and other rules for others.

An even more profound instance of delimiting the property rights of states—more profound because it concerned *internal,* as opposed to *external,* space—was the invention of the principle of extraterritoriality as the basis for organizing permanent diplomatic representation. As Garrett Mattingly put it in his magisterial study of the subject:

> By arrogating to themselves supreme power over men's consciences, the new states had achieved absolute sovereignty. Having done so, they found they could only communicate with one another by tolerating within themselves little islands of alien sovereignty.[45]

Instituting those little islands of alien sovereignty in the end required a multilateral solution, though differential arrangements based on the religious preferences and social status of rulers were tried first. And their maintenance came to be seen as necessary to the very existence of a viable political order among states.[46] As a result, grave breaches of the principle of extraterritoriality are, ipso facto, deemed a violation against the entire community of states.[47]

Until quite recently, neither regimes nor formal organizations played significant roles in the definition and stabilization of international property rights. Conventional practice and episodic treaty negotiations sufficed to establish multilateral orders of relations.

COORDINATION PROBLEMS

States have strong and conflicting preferences about international property rights. In the case of the oceans, for example, coastal states were favored over landlocked states by the allocation of *any* territorial sea; different coastal states ended up with differentially sized territorial seas by virtue of the length of their coastlines; but coastal states would have preferred *no* limit at all to the territorial sea. And so on. There also exists a class of problems in international relations wherein states are more or less indifferent in principle about the actual outcome, provided only that all accept the same outcome. These are typically referred to as coordination problems.[48]

A paradigmatic case of a coordination problem in the mid-nineteenth century was posed by electronic telegraphy, and concerned what would happen to a message as it came, for instance, to the border between France and the Grand Duchy of Baden.

> A common station was established at Strasbourg with two employees, one from the French Telegraph Administration, the other from Baden. The French employee received, for example, a telegram from Paris, which the electric wires had transmitted to him with the speed of light. This message he wrote out by hand onto a special form and handed it across the table to his German colleague. He translated it into German, and then sent it again on its way.[49]

With the intensification of trade, the desire for the latest stockmarket information from London, Paris, and Berlin, and important diplomatic messages that governments wished to send to one another, this arrangement became untenable. Its costs in profits lost, opportunities forgone, and administrative resources expended mounted rapidly. The initial response was to negotiate a series of bilateral treaties. But in the dense communications complex of the European continent, bilateral solutions also soon proved inadequate. Several multilateral arrangements were therefore constructed and were subsequently combined in 1865, when the International Telegraph Union was established.

This multilateral arrangement consisted of three parts. First, rules of the road were devised in regard to the network of telegraph lines that were to connect countries within Europe (and, later, in other parts of the world), the codes to be used, the agreed priorities of transmission, the languages that were permissible, the schedule of tariffs levied, and the manner in which proceeds would be divided, and so on. Second, a permanent secretariat was established to administer the day-to-day implementation of these rules and to coordinate the technical operations of the system. Third, periodic conferences of plenipotentiaries were convened, to make any such revisions in the basic system as became necessary over time.

Much the same kind of arrangement had already been anticipated in the domain of European river transport, as on the Rhine and the Danube, typically consisting of commissions, secretariats, and judicial bodies—and in some instances even uniforms for officials.[50] Later in the nineteenth century, similar multilateral arrangements were instituted in the field of public health.[51]

In situations exhibiting coordination problems, the incentives are high for states to order their relations on the basis of generalized principles of conduct. At least in the long run, therefore, the desire to reduce transaction costs tends to become a driving factor. Not surprisingly, historically the highest incidence of multilateral regimes and organizations is found in this domain.

COLLABORATION PROBLEMS

Where the definition and stabilization of at least some international property rights is concerned, an ultimate inevitability to multilateral solutions appears to exist, although "ultimate" may mean after all possible alternatives, including war, have been exhausted. In cases of coordination problems, an ultimate indifference appears to exist about which one of several outcomes is selected, although "ultimate" here may mask such concrete problems as sunk investments that individual states may have in the "equally acceptable" outcome that did not get adopted.

Between the two extremes of inevitability and indifference lies the domain of mixed-motive, conflict-of-interest situations. Even in this domain, however, cooperation occurs. And sometimes it occurs on a multilateral basis. Before 1945, however, it did not do so very often.

In the security realm, the most celebrated case is the Concert of Europe, a case in which students of international relations have paid far more attention to the issue of whether or not the Concert constituted a security *regime* than to the fact that it exhibited elements of the *multilateral form*. Charles and Clifford Kupchan have recently provided us with a useful continuum of collective-security arrangements, with the "ideal" form at one end, and concerts at the other. We have already examined the formal attributes of the "ideal" model. According to the Kupchans, the concert version is characterized by the dominance of the great powers, decisions taken by informal negotiations and consensus, and no explicit specification of the mechanisms for implementing collective action. But— and this is what puts it in the class of collective-security mechanisms—a concert nevertheless is "predicated on the notion of all against one"[52]— that is, on the indivisibility of peace among the members of the concert, and their nondiscretionary obligation to respond to acts of aggression.

Between the Napoleonic and the Crimean wars, from 1815 to 1854, peace in Europe was maintained, in Henry Kissinger's words, by an institutional "framework" that was regarded by participants as "legitimate," so that "they sought adjustment within [it] rather than in its overthrow."[53] In doing so, according to Robert Jervis, they "behaved in ways that sharply diverged from normal 'power politics.' "[54]

As Jervis describes it, the five leading powers—Austria, Great Britain, Prussia, Russia, and a French monarchy restored with the aid of the other four—refrained from seeking to maximize their relative power positions vis-à-vis one another, instead moderating their demands and behavior; they refrained from exploiting one another's temporary weaknesses and vulnerabilities, and they threatened force sparingly and used it rarely as a means of resolving differences among them—except, Kal Holsti adds, that they "were clearly of the opinion that force could be used individually or collectively for enforcing certain decisions and for coercing those who threatened the foundations of the order or the system of governance."[55]

How were these feats achieved? The five powers constituted themselves as "an executive body" of the European international system,[56] convening extensive multilateral consultations through which they acted on matters that could have undermined the peace. For example, they collectively created and guaranteed the neutrality of Belgium and Greece, thereby removing those territories from the temptations of bilateral partition or competition. The "Eastern Question" in general, Albrecht-Carrie has argued—that is, the problem of how to secure orderly change and national independence in the wake of the irreversible decay of the Ottoman Empire—"provides many illustrations of an authentic common preference for orderly and peaceful procedure, more than once successfully implemented."[57]

What could account for this unusual institutional development? It seems that the threat posed by Napoleon's imperial ambitions to the very principle of the balance of power proved weightier than the usual risks and uncertainties that plague cooperation in the security realm. Moreover, the threat posed by the French revolutionary wars to the very principle of dynastic rule seems to have proved weightier than the differences in domestic social formations, such as those existing between liberal and protestant England, on the one hand, and the more conservative and catholic Austria and orthodox Russia, on the other. These two threats helped crystallize the norm of systemic stability—the "repose" of Europe was the term the five preferred[58]—that the Concert was geared to sustain. They emboldened states to place a *collective* bet on their future. And the multilateral consultations instituted via the Concert limited the extent of cheating on that bet by providing a forum within which intelligence could be shared, actor intentions questioned, and justifications for actions proferred and assessed.

The Concert of Europe gradually eroded, not only because the memory of the initial threats faded, which it did, but also because over time the parameters of the situation were transformed. Above all else, the revolutions of 1848 seriously shook the prevailing concept of legitimate political order from within, and the sense of international cohesion diverged sharply thereafter. "I do not see Europe anymore,"[59] a French Foreign Minister lamented at the time. In the second half of the nineteenth century, multilateral consultation and self-restraint yielded to the striving for unilateral advantage checked only by external constraints, while bilateral alliance formation was raised to a new level of sophistication by Bismarck.

In the economic realm, the nineteenth century witnessed what economists consider to be paradigms, if not paragons, of multilateralism: free trade and the gold standard. By free trade is meant two things: a minimum of barriers to trade, including tariff and nontariff barriers; and nondiscriminatory treatment in trade. An international gold standard exists when two sets of conditions are approximated. First, the major countries must maintain a link between their domestic money supply and gold at substantially fixed ratios. Second, in principle they must allow the outflow of gold to liquidate an adverse balance of current obligations, and they must accept a corresponding inflow in case of a favorable balance. These conditions also establish the convertibility of currencies into one another at relatively fixed rates, and they facilitate international adjustment insofar as the initial imbalance in the current account in principle will be rectified automatically in both surplus and deficit countries by the appropriate domestic measures that follow from the inflow and outflow of gold.

By the mid-nineteenth century, Great Britain—the frontrunner in the Industrial Revolution, the foremost importer of raw materials and exporter of manufactured products, and the enthusiastic occupant of the doctrinal house built by Adam Smith and David Ricardo—was prepared to move toward free trade on a unilateral basis. Prime Minister Robert Peel declared in Parliament that "if other countries choose to buy in the dearest market, such an option on their part constitutes no reason why we should not be permitted to buy in the cheapest."[60] Indeed, Britain did liberalize trade unilaterally, culminating in the abolition of the Corn Laws in 1846. Others, however, did not follow the British example as Britain had expected. Reluctantly, therefore, and in part also inspired by broader diplomatic considerations, Britain commenced with a series of bilateral tariff negotiations with other countries, and those other countries did the same with third parties, which had the effect of significantly lowering tariff barriers. The model was the Cobden–Chevalier Treaty between Britain and France, concluded in 1860.[61] Although this was a bilateral treaty, it had multilateral *consequences* because it contained an unconditional most-favored-nation provision: it committed Britain and France to extend to each other any subsequent concessions obtained from agreements with any third party. Bismarck, Louis Napoleon, and Cavour all viewed such trade treaties primarily as instruments of traditional bilateral diplomacy and less as the means to multilateralize trade. But they negotiated them, and they included the MFN provision. The inclusion of this provision in a series of trade treaties had the effect of multilateralizing the trading order.[62]

As it did in international trade, Britain followed the rules of the gold standard more closely than anyone else. It thereby provided the world economy with a pillar of financial stability in the pound sterling, making multilateral convertibility and adjustment that much easier to achieve.[63]

Britain's policies may have been conducive to multilateralism in two other ways as well. As the world's largest creditor country, Britain did not exploit its position to accumulate large gold stocks but instead made those surpluses available for additional overseas investments and loans. The international economy as a result functioned more smoothly and grew more steadily than would otherwise have been the case. In addition, Britain always allowed debts to Britain incurred by other countries to be canceled by credits they earned elsewhere. That in turn facilitated the multilateral clearing of payments balances.[64]

The multilateralism of free trade and the international gold standard appears to have been created and sustained by two sets of factors. Although it may appear paradoxical, these paragon cases of multilateralism were not achieved by multilateral means. The decisive factor seems to have been Britain's unilateral move toward free trade and the gold standard and its bilateral dealings to achieve both goals. Britain thereby signaled its willingness to bear the costs of an open trading order and a stable monetary order and thus reduced the distributive and strategic uncertainties for others.[65] In that sense free trade and the gold standard can be said to have been less "regime-ish" than was the Concert of Europe. Another critical factor was a permissive domestic political environment. As Arthur Bloomfield has pointed out with regard to the monetary realm:

> The view, so widely recognized and accepted in recent decades, of central banking policy as a means of facilitating the achievement and maintenance of reasonable stability in the level of [domestic] economic activity and prices was scarcely thought about before 1914, and certainly not accepted, as a formal objective of monetary policy.[66]

Indeed, many countries lacked the institutional capacity to pursue such a monetary policy, in some cases including even a central bank itself. The second of these conditions collapsed well before the first.[67]

This brief overview of multilateralism prior to the twentieth century suggests several broad generalizations that shed further light on the character of the multilateral institutional form. The first concerns the impact of the strategic task environment. Defining and delimiting the property rights of states is as fundamental a collective task as any in the international system. The performance of this task on a multilateral basis seems inevitable in the long run, although in fact states appear to try every conceivable alternative first. Moreover, in the past the multilateral arrangements that did emerge in this domain were monopolized by states and essentially codified state practice into prevailing orders of relations. At the other extreme, limiting transaction costs by solving coordination problems is institutionally neither complex nor particularly demanding, and it was the domain in which multilateralism in all three institutional expressions—orders, regimes, and organizations—flourished in the nineteenth century. Between these two lies the problematic terrain of significant conflict-of-interest situations, in which states *sometimes,* albeit rarely prior to the twentieth century, construct multilateral arrangements *even though* alternatives are available and viable. The major powers could have selected bilateral alliances in the early nineteenth century and discriminatory economic arrangements in the mid-nineteenth century—as they had done before, and as they would do again subsequently. But at those particular points in time they did not. Why not? Presumably, multilateralism was in their interest. But what, concretely, does that mean? How and why did states come to define their interests in a manner that yielded such an unusual institutional outcome? As noted above, it seems that the Concert of Europe was due in part to exogenous shocks to both the international system and the system of domestic rule. Free trade and the gold standard in part seem to have been due to the willingness and the capability of Great Britain to take the lead. Both cases also were made possible by the existence of compatible or least permissive domestic settings.

Second, as was alluded to earlier, it seems that successful instances of multilateralism come to exhibit "diffuse reciprocity."[68] For example, what was crucial to the success of the Concert of Europe, according to Jervis, "is that 'self-interest' was broader than usual [and] also longer-run than usual . . . . For this system to work, each state had to believe that its current sacrifices would in fact yield a long-run return, that others would not renege on their implicit commitments when they found themselves in tempting positions."[69]

Third, the record shows that before the twentieth century very few instances of multilateralism generated formal organizations. The Concert of Europe never went beyond great power consultations, while free trade and the international gold standard were instituted and sustained by even more ad hoc bilateral and unilateral means. The multilateral organizations that did exist functioned exclusively in the domain of coordination problems, where the task at hand was to devise mutually acceptable rules of the road and to change them as technology and other such factors changed. And the role of these organizations was strictly circumscribed by the overall normative structure within which they existed.

THE TWENTIETH-CENTURY DISCONTINUITY

An important break in this third pattern occurred with the twentieth-century "move to institutions," as the critical legal theorist, David Kennedy, has described it—by which he means a move to formal organizations.[70]

Above all, a completely novel form was added to the institutional repertoire of states in 1919: the multipurpose, universal membership organization, instantiated first by the League of Nations and then by the United Nations. Prior international organizations had but limited membership, determined by power, function, or both, and they were assigned specific and highly circumscribed tasks. In contrast, here were organizations based on little more than shared aspirations, with broad agendas in which large and small had a constitutionally mandated voice. Moreover, decision making within international organizations increasingly became subject to the mechanism of voting, as opposed to treaty drafting or customary accretion, and voting itself subsequently shifted away in most instances from the early unanimity requirement that was consistent with the traditional mode of conducting international proceedings. Finally, the move amplified a trend that had begun in the nineteenth century, a trend toward multilateral as opposed to merely bilateral diplomacy, especially in the form of "conference diplomacy."[71]

This move to institutions produced several important consequences for the status of multilateralism. First, it complicated, and in some instances actually reversed, the straightforward ends-means relation that previously prevailed between the goals embodied in multilateral arrangements and whatever formal organizational mechanism may have existed to serve them. Or, to put it differently, it created principal–agent problems that had not existed before. Any form of organizational mediation is capable of affecting outcomes, of introducing elements into the substance or process of decision making that previously were not present. A multipurpose, universal membership organization complicates that situation by involving itself even in areas where no normative consensus exists; aspects of both the League of Nations and the United Nations illustrate that problem in spades. Second, multilateral forums increasingly have come to share in the agenda-setting and convening power of states. For example, such forums increasingly drive the international conference diplomacy game. Third, and perhaps most important, multilateral diplomacy has come to embody a procedural norm *in its own right*—though often a hotly contested one—in some instances carrying with it an international legitimacy not enjoyed by other means.

In short, as a result of the twentieth-century move to institutions, at least to some extent a multilateral political order has emerged "which [is] capable of handling at least some collective tasks in an *ex ante* co-ordinated manner."[72] I might add in conclusion that while numerous descriptions of this "move to institutions" exist, I know of no good explanation in the literature of why states should have wanted to complicate their lives in this manner. And I would think it particularly difficult to formulate any straightforward explanation within the currently ascendant logic of instrumental rationality.

The United States and Postwar Multilateralism

The preceding discussion makes it abundantly clear that multilateralism was not invented in 1945. It is a generic institutional form in the modern state system, and incipient expressions of it have been present from the start. However, the breadth and diversity of multilateral arrangements across a broad array of issue areas increased substantially after 1945. Quite naturally, therefore, one associates the change with the postwar position of the United States.

According to the theory of hegemonic stability, hegemonic powers are alike in their quest to organize the international system. Hegemonic stability theory is right only up to a point. To the extent that it is possible to "know" these things, historical counterfactuals suggest that the likeness among hegemons stops short of the *institutional form* by which they choose to organize the system.[73] For instance, had Nazi Germany or the Soviet Union ended up as the world's leading power after World War II, there is no indication whatsoever that the intentions of either country included creating anything remotely like the international institutional order that came to prevail. Politically, Germany pursued an imperial design in the European core, complete with tributary states on the periphery. Economically, the Nazi scheme of bilateral, discriminatory, and state-controlled trade pacts and monetary clearing arrangements would no doubt have been extended geographically to complement Germany's political objectives. The Soviet Union presumably would have sought political control through a restored Comintern while causing the modes of production in its subject economies to be socialized and relations among those economies to be administered on a planned and discriminatory basis.

In point of fact, and this we can say with greater assurance, even if

Britain had become hegemon, things would have differed in some respects. Colonialism as a political institution would have continued longer. And while monetary relations probably would have been organized similarly, merely based on sterling instead of the U.S. dollar,[74] British imperial preferences would have remained a central feature of international trade, possibly forcing others to carve out regional trading blocs for themselves.[75]

Finally, Europe certainly would have been "integrated" by a German or a Soviet hegemony—but in a very different fashion that exists via the European Community today. And in a British-run system, Europe most probably would have returned to prewar multipolarity and the continued existence of separate national economies.

Thus, all hegemonies are not alike. The most that can be said about a hegemonic power is that it will seek to construct an international order in *some* form, presumably along lines that are compatible with its own international objectives and domestic structures. But in the end, that really is not saying very much.

For American postwar planners, multilateralism in its generic sense served as a foundational architectural principle on the basis of which to reconstruct the postwar world. Take first the economic realm. During the war, when planning for the postwar era began, the Nazi economic order was the focal point of American antipathy.[76] It had effectively excluded nonparticipants, which not only limited U.S. trade opportunities but also, U.S. officials believed, triggered economic conflicts that spilled readily over into the security realm. "Nations which act as enemies in the market-place cannot long be friends at the council table," warned Assistant Secretary of State for Economic Affairs, William Clayton, echoing a favorite refrain of his boss Cordell Hull.[77]

The defeat of Germany and the allied occupation of its Western sector afforded the United States an opportunity to help implant the domestic social bases for a markedly different form of foreign economic policy by the new West German state. Much of the negotiating energy expended by the United States on the creation of the postwar economic order was, therefore, directed toward undoing the more benign but still vexing British position. It consisted of a commitment to imperial preferences on the part of the Tories and to extensive controls on international economic transactions by Labor as part of its objective to institute systematic national economic planning. Both were inherently discriminatory. The United States sought to substitute in their place a global version of the "open door."[78] Discriminatory trade barriers and currency arrangements were to be dismantled, tariffs reduced, and decolonization supported. But nowhere would domestic politics sustain a mere return to the nineteenth-century laissez-faire of unrestricted trade and the gold standard, wherein the level of domestic economic activity was governed by the balance of payments. Even for the relatively more liberal United States, the international edifice of the "open door" had to accommodate the domestic interventionism of the New Deal.[79]

Little dispute is found in the literature about the role of multilateralism in organizing the postwar economic order; the consensus is that its role was substantial. Little dispute exists about its role in the security domain either—but here for the very different reason that students of international relations have assumed that multilateralism played no role. That interpretation is not supported by the historical record *if* we think of multilateralism in its broad generic sense rather than merely in the form of multilateral organizations.

As World War II drew to a close, President Roosevelt faced an institutional problem. The United States must not retreat into a "fortress America," Roosevelt insisted, or else it would once again have won the war only to lose the subsequent peace. Winning the peace, Roosevelt felt, would require active U.S. international involvement. But at the same time, the American public would not accept international involvement via "entangling alliances."[80] Hence, some other form would have to be found. To complicate matters further, as John Gaddis puts it, Roosevelt favored a policy of "containment by integration" toward the Soviet Union and felt that a stable postwar security order required "offering Moscow a prominent place in it; by making it, so to speak, a member of the club."[81] That in turn required a club to which both belonged.

Given that combination of objectives, Roosevelt had little alternative but to move toward some form of collective-security organization. But it was to be a modified form in the sense that it stripped away the Wilsonian aspiration that collective security somehow be *substituted for* balance of power politics. That was too wild and wooly a notion for depression-and-war-hardened U.S. officials in 1945. Instead, they sought to make the two compatible, so that the collective-security mechanism would have a basis in the balance of power but also mute the more deleterious effects of balance-of-power politics. Thus was the United Nations born: at its core, an enforcement mechanism "with teeth," but subject to great-power veto.[82]

Once the iron curtain went down and Europe was split, containing

Moscow by exclusion became the dominant U.S. objective, and the United Nations became marginalized to core U.S. security concerns.[83] But the American problem of simultaneously avoiding both a retreat into fortress America *and* an embrace of entangling alliances still had to be resolved vis-à-vis a threatened Europe. As Steve Weber reminds us in this volume, the United States repeatedly turned back requests from its European friends to form bilateral alliances with them. Instead, the United States initially pursued a strategy of "economic security," of providing the Europeans with the economic wherewithal to take care of their own security needs.[84] By 1947, bilateral economic assistance to Europe gave way to the more comprehensive Marshall Plan, which required the Europeans to develop a multilateral framework for their own postwar reconstruction in return for receiving aid. Moreover, the United States was an early advocate and strong supporter of European efforts to achieve economic and political integration.[85]

But European security demanded more. Driven by *"la grande peur"* of 1948, the Europeans came to feel that "it was [also] necessary to have some measure of military 'reassurance.' "[86] Still the United States continued to resist bilateral deals and military commitments of any kind.[87] Eventually, the State Department relented, but not until succeeding in its insistence that the United States would aid only a European-initiated collective self-defense effort. The Belgians under Paul-Henri Spaak took the lead. In March 1948 the Benelux countries, France, and Britain signed a mutual-assistance treaty. But how to tie the United States to this framework? The British played the critical swing role in defining an indivisible security perimeter from Scandinavia to the Mediterranean and, with Canadian help, getting it to reach across to the Western hemisphere.[88] The concept of the "North Atlantic" emerged as the spatial image that helped tie the knot. Its formulation and acceptance were perhaps facilitated by the recent revolution in military cartography, whereby the "airman's view," and thus the polar proximity of the Soviet Union to the United States, came to shape U.S. strategic planning.[89] The North Atlantic Treaty was concluded in 1949. "The signing of the NATO Alliance," Sir Michael Howard has said, "provided a sense that now at last all were for one and one was for all. . . ."[90]—which of course is what the notion of collective security has always meant.

Indeed, NATO was conceived and justified as an expression of the collective self-defense provision of the U.N. Charter. There is a direct path from the negotiations over Article 51 of the U.N. Charter, endorsing an inherent right of individual and collective self-defense, to the drafting of the North Atlantic Treaty.[91] The same cast of characters who negotiated the U.N. provision at San Francisco, Gladwyn Jebb on the British side and Senator Arthur Vandenberg on the American, also sought to ensure that the North Atlantic Treaty was compatible with it. That accomplishment allowed the United States to operate "within the Charter, but outside the [Soviet] veto," as the Senator liked to say.[92] What is more, Article 51 was *not* drafted with a future NATO in mind; it was instigated by the Latin Americans to allow for a Latin American regional security organization that was beyond the reach of the U.S. veto in the U.N. Security Council.

To underscore the obvious, the United States did not seek to endow formal international organizations with extensive independent powers; that was *not* its multilateralist agenda. The United States insisted on a veto in the U.N. Security Council every bit as much as the Soviets did. Voting in the international financial institutions was and remains weighted, the United States still having the largest single share. The GATT barely exists as a formal organization (it was supposed to have been folded into the International Trade Organization that never came into being), and until recently State Department funding for it came out of an account for ad hoc international conferences. And the "O" in NATO never has and does not now determine the collective security of its members.

The American postwar multilateralist agenda consisted above all of a desire to restructure the international order along broadly multilateral lines, at the global level, and within Western Europe and across the North Atlantic. (In East Asia, on the other hand, the potential was lacking to construct anything but the bilateral security ties on which the United States turned its back in Europe.[93]) Secondarily, the United States occasioned the creation of several major multilateral regimes, as in the fields of money and trade. Lastly, the United States helped to establish numerous formal international organizations to provide technically competent and/or politically convenient services in support of those objectives.[94]

To be sure, the United States hardly acted against its self-interests. But the fact that U.S. behavior was consistent with its interests does not explain the behavior. Nor was multilateralism what some would call "a consumption good" for the United States, an end in itself. So how does one explain U.S. actions? One possible source of explanation for the American multilateralist agenda is the international system itself. System-level theories of international relations, much favored in the discipline at the moment, are essentially of two sorts. One is structural, the other functional. Both offer parsimonious and often powerful first-cut explanations. Structural accounts of the postwar multilateralist posture of the United States would focus either on U.S. hegemony or on strategic bipolarity as independent variables.[95] The problem with using hegemony—*tout court*—as an explanation has already been addressed: other hegemons would have done it differently, and so subsequent history would have been different. Hence we still require insight into why this particular hegemon did things in this particular way.

Invoking bipolarity as an explanation is much more promising—*once bipolarity exists*.[96] But it is not without problems for the earliest postwar years, when bipolarity was just in the process of becoming, *even as* some of the multilateral developments described above were taking place. Indeed, it took policymakers and analysts quite some time to grasp the fact of bipolarity. Serious postwar planning by the United States began in 1942. William Fox's book, *The Super-Powers,* published in 1944, still assumed that there would be three of them.[97] The Bretton Woods conference was held that year, with the Soviets in attendance. Moreover, the option of dividing the world into three spheres of influence for the purposes of conflict management had not yet been entirely discarded in 1944; by 1945 it had been, but in favor of the universal United Nations.[98] In his 1946 "long telegram," and again in the 1947 "Mr. X" article, George Kennan warned about the emerging Soviet sphere of influence, but he explicitly expected multipolarity to reemerge from the devastation of the war before long, and he designed his proposed containment strategy in order to achieve that goal.[99] Moreover, as late as 1947, trade negotiators were trying to square circles to devise a multilateral trade regime that could accommodate socialist state-trading countries.[100] Even more important, also in 1947, Lucius Clay, the U.S. Military Governor in Germany, initially blamed the French, not the Soviets, for impeding quadripartite government there when it was still doable; the failure to achieve it resulted ultimately in the bizonal division of Germany that became emblematic of the cold war.[101]

Admittedly, actor perceptions do not matter much in structural theories. Nevertheless, it does seem more than a little awkward to retroject as incentives for actor behavior structural conditions that had not yet clearly emerged, and were not yet fully understood, and that in some measure only the subsequent behavior of actors helped to produce![102]

Functional theories of international institutions, as I noted at the outset, thus far have focused largely on undifferentiated "cooperation" and "institutions," not the specific form of multilateralism. Their limited utility on this count has already been commented on. Moreover, functional theories have been concerned largely with such factors as the desire to minimize transaction costs, information costs, and similar institutional inefficiencies. This rationale too has limits. First, although our historical cases are too few to make a strong case, they do suggest that the drive to limit institutional inefficiencies of this kind is most decisive in the realm of coordination problems. When it comes to shedding blood or institutionalizing hopes for lasting peace, the calculus of countries appears to draw on a different universe of discourse. Second, it also seems that what constitutes institutional inefficiencies or costs is not entirely independent of the attributes of the states making the calculation. For example, it is difficult to imagine an institutional arrangement that imposed higher transaction costs on all concerned than the Nazi trade and monetary regimes. But given the overall strategic objectives of the German state at the time, the price of administering those arrangements was seen as an investment, not an expenditure to be minimized. The domestic mechanisms that shape the Japanese foreign trade posture today, with all their reputed institutional "inefficiencies," may pose an analogous conceptual problem.[103]

In short, to determine why *this* particular institutional agenda was pursued, it is inescapable at some point to look more closely at *this* particular hegemon. That in turn requires not only examining the hegemon's international situation but also delving into its domestic realm.

It seems clear that across a broad array of social and economic sectors, the United States after World War II sought to project the experience of the New Deal regulatory state into the international arena.[104] According to Burley, in this volume, this endeavor entailed two distinct dimensions. The first was a belief that the long-term success of domestic reform programs required a compatible international order, if those programs were to be sustained. The second was a commitment at the international level to institutional means that had already been tried domestically and that grew out of the legal and administrative revolution that accompanied the New Deal. The combination of the two translated into an active U.S. effort to institutionalize a multilateral international economic and social order.

In the security realm, a count of the domestic political noses led President Roosevelt to believe that isolationist tendencies could not be neutralized by having the United States form bilateral alliances with or against the very European states that kept dragging it into war—which is how the isolationists viewed the world. Accordingly, the notion was foremost in Roosevelt's mind that only by binding the United States to a more permanent multilateral institutional framework, which promised to *transform* traditional international politics, could a relapse into isolationism be avoided.[105] By 1947, the Truman administration discovered anticommunist rhetoric to be a useful tool toward that same end.[106]

More generally, Peter Cowhey in his contribution to this volume advances the provocative thesis that the very structure of the U.S. polity enhanced the credibility of America's postwar commitment to multilateralism. The problem of "defection" that is explored at length in the literature focuses not on the hegemon but, rather, on the other states, considered potential free riders one and all. But multilateralism is an extremely demanding institutional form, and the fact is that the hegemon has far more unilateral and bilateral options available to it than any other state. So how does it make its own commitment to multilateralism credible? How can others be assured that the *hegemon* will not defect, if it should change its mind or recalculate its short-term interests, leaving *them* in the lurch? Ironically, Cowhey attributes the credibility of the American commitment to multilateralism to the very features of the U.S. polity that are often said to hamper its effective conduct of foreign policy. These include the institutional consequences of an electoral system geared to the median voter; a division of powers making reversals of fundamental policy postures difficult; and greater transparency of, and access to, the domestic political arena even on the part of foreign interests. No potential *Pax Nipponica* today, Cowhey concludes, would instill a sufficient level of confidence; it lacks the appropriate domestic base. Cowhey's thesis, and the comparison, deserve more extensive study.

In sum, in one crucial sense the origins of multilateralism in the postwar era reiterate the record of prior periods. Between the very deep level of defining and stabilizing the international property rights of states and the relatively superficial level of solving coordination problems, a pronounced shift toward multilateralism in economic and security affairs requires a combination of fairly strong international forces and compatible domestic environments. If that is so, then it was the fact of an *American* hegemony that was decisive after World War II, not merely American *hegemony*. And that in turn makes the role of multilateralism in the current international transformation of even greater interest.

Multilateralism and Transformation

The issue of whether the United States is in relative decline and, if so, whether it is taking the international order along with it, has been debated in the literature for nearly two decades.[107] More recently, the end of bipolarity has been adduced as a cause for similar alarm.[108] The new institutionalists were the first to question any direct relationship between international power shifts and institutional unraveling. They provided several functional reasons why states would, under some circumstances, remain committed to existing institutions even "beyond hegemony," focusing on such factors as institutional inertia, sunk costs, the services institutions continue to provide, and the common objectives they may continue to pursue.[109]

But as we saw at the outset of our discussion, the situation today, especially but not exclusively in Europe, is not simply one of past multilateral arrangements hanging on for dear life. Numerous instances exist of active institutional adaptation and even creation. Again, not much in the theoretical literature provides ready explanations. Our definitional and historical analysis of multilateralism does, however, suggest several factors that may be at work.

One such factor is logically implied by the definition of multilateralism itself. Ironically, the very features that make it strategically difficult to establish multilateral arrangements in the first place may enhance their durability and adaptability once in place. I pointed out earlier that successful multilateral arrangements in the past have come to exhibit expectations of diffuse reciprocity. It seems plausible to hypothesize that so long as that expectation continues to hold, so long as each party does not insist on being equally rewarded on every round, the sustainability of the arrangement should be enhanced because it makes both cross-sectoral and intertemporal trade-offs and bargains feasible. Cooperation with the European Community seems most clearly to exhibit this pattern. It may have benefited from, or perhaps even required, active U.S. encouragement at the start, but obviously it has long since taken off on a self-sustaining industrial path. Garrett in this volume argues that the adoption and implementation by the European Community of the Single European Act is entirely consistent with a "rationalist" view of institutions. Thus, if he is correct, it would suggest that, given a certain institutional framework for collaboration, and given a certain set of incentives to collaborate, beyond some point no extra push from any "extraneous" integrationist aspirations or symbols may be necessary to achieve integrative solutions.

Similarly, all other things being equal, an arrangement based on generalized organizing principles should be more elastic than one based on particularistic interests and situational exigencies. It should, therefore, also exhibit greater continuity in the face of changing circumstances, including international power shifts. A collective-security arrangement more readily absorbs such shifts, as does a trade regime based on MFN treatment. It is, however, hard to imagine the discriminatory order of the Nazis surviving the hegemony of the Third Reich. And even in the case of traditional alliances, the major means of adjustment is simply to abandon the prevailing dyadic ties. Although the cases are no doubt overdetermined, the ready adaptation of NATO at least as a transitional arrangement vs. the total collapse of the Warsaw Pact may nevertheless help illustrate this point.

The durability of multilateral arrangements, our analysis suggests, is also a function of domestic environments. For example, no shift occurred in multipolarity around the mid-nineteenth century that could have accounted for the final collapse of the Concert of Europe and the reemergence of competitive alliances, but domestic environments did diverge sharply after the revolutions of 1848. The erosion of the gold standard and free trade to some extent may be overdetermined in that both sets of factors changed, but even before Britain declined appreciably as a world power, governments were politically compelled to intervene in their domestic economies in ways that were incompatible with the two multilateral arrangements. In fact, even Kindleberger's climacteric case of the 1933 London Economic Conference—when "the British couldn't and the United States wouldn't"—does not lend itself to a straightforward systemic account. What the United States "wouldn't" was to support *the prevailing form* of economic multilateralism: the laissez-faire kind, the London and New York bankers' kind, Herbert Hoover's kind. But no one, including President Roosevelt, had yet figured out a viable and mutually acceptable alternative.[110] As Arthur Schlesinger notes in his classic account: "This difference [between the U.S. and the U.K.] was too great to be bridged by any form of economic or diplomatic legerdemain. The London Conference did not create the difference. It simply came along too late—or too early—to do anything about it."[111] No domestic divergence that stark exists among the major powers today. The implosion of the Soviet Union, and domestic changes in Eastern Europe, have eliminated the international significance of the socialist economic model. The domestic economic structure of Japan may pose a somewhat comparable problem, but it is hardly of the same magnitude.[112]

Furthermore, by and large, actual multilateral arrangements with well-defined tasks simply have not lived up to the bad billing they get in some of the literature as unwieldy expressions of the law of large numbers. This is so for several reasons. First of all, most major multilateral arrangements in practice are governed by subsets of states—the "k-groups" that Snidal, following Hardin, suggests attenuate many international collective-action problems.[113] Kahler, in his article in this volume, shows empirically what Snidal postulates theoretically: the major postwar global regimes have been governed by what he terms "minilateralist" groupings within them. Thus, the regimes were not mere expressions of hegemony, and they thereby avoided obvious legitimacy problems. Nor did they operate, however, purely on the basis of egalitarian decision-making rules. Decolonization began to strain this "minilateralist" solution in the 1960s and 1970s. Nevertheless, whether in the subsequent Law of the Sea negotiations, GATT rounds, or drafting of global environmental conventions, Kahler finds little evidence that states have encountered insuperable difficulties in devising institutional mechanisms that, at one and the same time, accommodate larger numbers of participants while retaining their capacity to reach decisions. Even in the extraordinarily complex and more "democratic" context of the UN Conference on the Law of the Sea, as Buzan has shown in great detail, the institutional inventiveness of states to accommodate large numbers were impressive, and the failure to obtain a ratified treaty resulted from fundamental conflicts of interests, not from any mechanical problem of size.[114]

A final factor to be considered is that in some instances the twentieth-century "move to institutions" clearly has kicked in. Indeed, much of the institutional inventiveness within multilateral arrangements today is coming from the institutions themselves, from platforms that arguably represent or at least speak for the collectivities at hand. Again the European Community offers the most dramatic illustrations, whether it concerns plans for orchestrating EC relations with the European Free Trade Area and the East European states, or plans for the future of the community itself.[115] Patrick Morgan's analysis of European security prospects, in this volume, goes so far as to argue that West European actors today are explicitly applying to Eastern Europe some of the institutional lessons they derived from their own earlier postwar experience with the United States, not only in the economic but also in the security realm. Beyond Europe, the convening and agenda-setting power of multilateral organizations is perhaps best illustrated in the area of the commons. There would be no plan to try to salvage the Mediterranean if it were not for multilateral players, as Peter Haas has shown.[116] Similarly, multilateral players kept first the ozone issue and now global warming on the negotiating table even when major powers, including the United States, were reluctant participants at best.[117] Mark Zacher, in this volume, explores the consequences of the move to institutions for the governance of a variety of nonterrestrial spaces.

In sum, parts of the international institutional order today appear quite robust and adaptive. Our discussion suggests that the reason is not simply that these are institutions and that institutions are "in demand." The reason is also that these institutions are multilateral in form, and that this form, under certain circumstances, has characteristics that may enhance its durability and ability to adapt to change. This, at any rate, is the central notion that our exploration of the concept of multilateralism advances for further scrutiny. Discovering precisely what those circumstances are, and why the picture is far from being uniform across issue areas, is clearly a necessary next step in this line of inquiry.

Conclusion

This essay was written with two sets of protagonists in mind. The first are those theorists of international relations for whom institutions matter little. It may be true, as these theorists insist, that they do not purport to explain everything but that what they do explain is important.[118] It does not follow, however, that what they leave unexplained is unimportant. And institutions, clearly, are not unimportant.

The second set of protagonists are those of my fellow institutionalists for whom the form that institutions take is left unexplored. Their focus is on institutions in a generic sense or on cooperation even more generally. Much can be learned about international relations from that perspective. But at the same time, too much is left unsaid. And what is left unsaid—the form that institutions assume—affects vitally the role which institutions play on the world stage today. Above all else, policymakers groping for alternatives amid rapid change, hoping to grasp the flow of events and channel it in desirable directions, do not deal in generic choices; theirs are palpably concrete.

A core and concrete feature of current international institutional arrangements is in their multilateral form. Why both the conventional literature on international relations and the literature on institutions should remain relatively silent on it may well have something to do with the atomistic ontology of the one and the instrumental-rationalist epistemology of the other, as James Caporaso and Friedrich Kratochwil, in different ways, suggest in their contributions to this volume. Or, as Martin counters, the limitations may be, not inherent to those approaches, but simply the product of past neglect that future practice can and will rectify. Be that as it may, I hope I have established, at minimum, that the effort is worthwhile: form matters.

No theory has been advanced in the present essay; no theory was vindicated or even tested. We cannot explain what we have not first described. And conceptual explication is a requisite for theoretically informed description, leading ultimately to theory building itself. My main objective here has been to explicate the concept of multilateralism, both analytically and historically, and to offer some preliminary guiding hypotheses about what may and may not explain its incidence and correlates, about how and why it matters.

NOTES

1. Robert Gilpin, *War and Change in World Politics* (New York: Cambridge University Press, 1981), p. 15:

> Although . . . peaceful adjustment of the systemic disequilibrium is possible, the principle mechanism of change throughout history has been war, or what we shall cal hegemonic war (i.e., a war that determines which state or states will be dominant and will govern the system).

2. William M. Clarke, "The Midwives of the New Europe," *Central Banker* (Summer 1990), vol. 1; see also Bruce Stokes, "Continental Shift," *National Journal* (August 18, 1990), no. 33–34.

3. Kenneth N. Waltz, *Theory of International Politics* (Reading, Mass.: Addison–Wesley, 1979); see the references to a united Europe on p. 180 and pp. 201–202.

4. Moreover, Hungary and Czechoslovakia have already joined the Council of Europe, and both have raised the issue of forging some type of affiliation with NATO. "Prague Courts NATO," *Los Angeles Times* (March 19, 1991).

5. Those who discount the efficacy of institutions have drawn dire inferences from the end of the cold war for the future of European stability, whereas those who take institutions seriously are much more likely to see an adaptive political order ahead. See, respectively, John J. Mearsheimer, "Back to the Future: Instability in Europe After the Cold War," *International Security* (Summer 1990), vol. 15; Jack Snyder, "Averting Anarchy in the New Europe," *International Security* (Spring 1990), vol. 14; and Stephen Van Evera, "Primed for Peace: Europe After the Cold War," *International Security* (Winter 1990/91), vol. 15.

6. As described by Steve Weber, in 1989

some foreign policy thinkers in Paris reverted to old ideas, suggesting a new alliance with Poland, the emerging Eastern European states, and perhaps the Soviet Union as well in opposition to Germany. These flirtations with bilateral treaties and a new balance of power have been mostly left by the wayside.

Weber, "Security After 1989: The Future with Nuclear Weapons," in Patrick Garrity, ed., *The Future of Nuclear Weapons* (New York: Plenum Press, forthcoming), p. 29 of ms. By comparable historical junctures I mean 1848, 1919, and 1945. After 1848 what was left of the Concert system rapidly degenerated into a system of competitive alliances; after World War I France in particular sought the protection of bilateral alliances against Germany, and after World War II several West European countries sought bilateral alliances with the United States and with one another. Among useful sources for the two earlier periods are Rene Albrecht-Carrie, *A Diplomatic History of Europe Since the Congress of Vienna* (New York: Harper & Row, 1958), E. H. Carr, *International Relations Between the Two World Wars* (New York: St. Martin's Press, 1961), Henry W. Degenhardt, *Treaties and Alliances of the World*, 3rd ed. (Essex, England: Longmans, 1981), and A. J. P. Taylor, *The Struggle for Mastery of Europe: 1848–1918* (New York: Oxford University Press, 1971).

7. Some proposals along these lines may be found in Stuart Harris, " 'Architecture for a New Era' in Asia/Pacific," *Pacific Research* (May 1990), vol. 3.

8. Latin America seems to fall somewhere in between. According to one recent assessment, "while the United States was ignoring and undermining multilateralism in the Western hemisphere, the Latin American nations themselves were moving towards greater co-operation, or *concertacion,* as they call it, to some degree as a response to United States policy." Richard J. Bloomfield and Abraham F. Lowenthal, "Inter-American Institutions in a Time of Change," *International Journal* (Autumn 1990), 45:868.

9. This refrain was begun by C. Fred Bergsten, "The New Economics and U.S. Foreign Policy," *Foreign Affairs* (January 1972), vol. 50; for a recent rendition, see "Echoes of the 1930s," *The Economist* (January 5, 1991).

10. On recent developments in the GATT, consult Gilbert R. Winham, "GATT and the International Trade Regime," *International Journal* (Autumn 1990), vol. 45. One real problem is that the variety of extant trade arrangements today is well beyond the scope of the traditional GATT terminology, and no new consensus exists about what types of unilateral, bilateral, and other measures are compatible or not with the underlying multilateral character of the GATT— thereby giving added relevance to the type of conceptual clarification we are proposing here.

11. Mitchell Reiss, *Without the Bomb: The Politics of Nuclear Nonproliferation* (New York: Columbia University Press, 1988), ch. 1.

12. Thomas W. Graham and A. F. Mullins, "Arms Control, Military Strategy, and Nuclear Proliferation," paper presented at the conference on "Nuclear Deterrence and Global Security in Transition," University of California, Insti-

tute on Global Conflict and Cooperation, La Jolla, Calif., February 21–23, 1991, p. 3. Graham is a former official of the U.S. Arms Control and Disarmament Agency, and Mullins an analyst at the Lawrence Livermore National Laboratory. As the authors point out, of late, states have left the "problem" list more rapidly than they have joined it. See also Joseph F. Pilat and Robert E. Pendley, eds., *Beyond 1995: The Future of the NPT Regime* (New York: Plenum Press, 1990).

13. As Francois Heisbourg has suggested, it is also quite possible, though difficult to prove, that

> Without the decisions of the U.N. Security Council, there would have been no [international] coalition capable of weathering close to seven months of crisis and war [and] that the U.S. Congress would not have approved offensive military operations in the absence of the Security Council's Resolution 678, which authorized the use of force. Heisbourg, "An Eagle Amid Less Powerful Fowl," *Los Angeles Times* (March 10, 1991).

14. Robert O. Keohane, "The Theory of Hegemonic Stability and Changes in International Economic Regimes, 1967–1977," in Ole R. Holsti, Randolph M. Siverson, and Alexander L. George, eds, *Change in the International System* (Boulder, Colo.: Westview Press, 1980); Arthur A. Stein, "The Hegemon's Dilemma: Great Britain, the United States, and the International Economic Order," *International Organization* (Spring 1985), vol. 38; Duncan Snidal, "The Limits of Hegemonic Stability Theory," *International Organization* (Autumn 1985), vol. 39; and John A. C. Conybeare, *Trade Wars: The Theory and Practice of International Commercial Rivalry* (New York: Columbia University Press, 1987).

15. I mean to include here both stands of theorizing identified by Robert O. Keohane: the rationalist and the reflectivist. "International Institutions: Two Approaches," *International Studies Quarterly* (December 1988), vol. 32.

16. Stephen D. Krasner, ed., *International Regimes* (Ithaca, N.Y.: Cornell University Press, 1983); Kenneth A. Oye, ed., *Cooperation Under Anarchy* (Princeton: Princeton University Press, 1986); and Robert O. Keohane, *After Hegemony* (Princeton: Princeton University Press, 1984).

17. Robert O. Keohane, "Multilateralism: An Agenda for Research," *International Journal* (Autumn 1990), 45:731. After introducing the concept and defining it in this manner, Keohane essentially goes on to discuss international institutions in the generic sense. See also Keohane, *After Hegemony,* in which there are but two fleeting references to multilateralism, both to specific agreements in trade; and Keohane, *International Institutions and State Power* (Boulder, Colo.: Westview Press, 1989), which contains no entry under multilateralism in its index. I must admit that this is equally true of my own writings on the subject of institutions. Keohane has kindly referred to a 1975 paper of mine as having "foreshadowed much of the conceptual work of the next decade." Alas, it also foreshadowed this blind spot, my having been concerned primarily with differentiating the study of international organization from the study of formal

international organizations—hence the introduction of the concept of "regimes." Keohane, "Multilateralism," p. 755, fn. 44, referring to Ruggie, "International Responses to Technology: Concepts and Trends," *International Organization* (Summer 1975), vol. 29.

18. In the United Nations context, what Keohane defines as multilateral is called multi*national*—for example, the multinational (non-U.N.) observer team in the Sinai. In the United Nations, only that is considered multilateral which is duly authorized by a multilateral forum. But if Keohane's definition is analytically too loose, the U.N. conception is too limiting, as will be discussed below.

19. William Diebold, Jr., "The History and the Issues," in Diebold, ed., *Bilateralism, Multilateralism and Canada in U.S. Trade Policy* (Cambridge, Mass.: Ballinger, for the Council on Foreign Relations, 1988), p. 1. Diebold seeks to formulate some principled basis for distinguishing what kind of recent trade measures—unilateral, bilateral, and what he calls plurilateral—are consistent with, and what kind undermine, the principles of multilateralism on which the GATT regime is based.

20. Diebold, "The History and the Issues;" Richard N. Gardner, *Sterling-Dollar Diplomacy in Current Perspective*, rev. ed., (New York: Columbia University Press, 1980); Jacob Viner, "Conflicts of Principle in Drafting a Trade Charter," *Foreign Affairs* (January 1947), vol. 25; Herbert Feis, "The Conflict Over Trade Ideologies," *Foreign Affairs* (July 1947), vol. 25; and Robert Pollard, *Economic Security and the Origins of the Cold War* (New York: Columbia University Press, 1985).

21. Robert Dallek, *Franklin D. Roosevelt and American Foreign Policy* (New York: Oxford University Press, 1979); John Lewis Gaddis, *The Long Peace* (New York: Oxford University Press, 1987), chs. 1, 2; and Pollard, *Economic Security*.

22. See the text of "President Bush's Address to Congress on End of the Gulf War," *New York Times* (March 7, 1991).

23. William Diebold, "The History and the Issues."

24. The classic, and appropriately titled, study of the Nazi system is Albert O. Hirschman, *National Power and the Structure of Foreign Trade* (Berkeley and Los Angeles: University of California Press, 1945; 1980); see also Leland B. Yeager, *International Monetary Relations: Theory, History, and Policy* (New York: Harper & Row, 1976), ch. 18.

25. Several major states, including Great Britain and the United States, had limited *Sondermark* agreements with Germany—marks that foreigners could earn through the sale of specified products to Germany but that Germany in turn restricted to particular purchases from Germany.

26. Taylor, *The Struggle for Mastery in Europe*, ch. 12.

27. Sir Arthur Salter, *Security* (London: Macmillan, 1939), p. 155, emphasis in original.

28. G. F. Hudson, "Collective Security and Military Alliances," in Herbert

Butterfield and Martin Wight, eds, *Diplomatic Investigations* (Cambridge, Mass.: Harvard University Press, 1968), pp. 176–177. See also Charles A. Kupchan and Clifford A. Kupchan, "Concerts, Collective Security, and the Future of Europe," *International Security* (Summer 1991), vol. 16.

29. Contrary to folklore, Woodrow Wilson was not prepared to commit the United States to specific and automatic military obligations under the League of Nations; his collective-security scheme would have relied on public opinion, arms limitations, and arbitration more than on enforcement mechanisms. Senator Henry Cabot Lodge's fundamental objection to the League was its permanence and universalism and the limitless entanglements he saw that entailing for the United States, as well as his fear that it would violate the Monroe Doctrine and allow European meddling even in U.S. internal affairs. Lloyd E. Ambrosius, *Woodrow Wilson and the American Diplomatic Tradition* (New York: Cambridge University Press, 1987).

30. The key shortcoming of collective security U.N. style is, of course, that the United Nations has no means of its own to implement a military response to aggression, because no state has ever negotiated an Article 43 agreement making standby forces available. After the Gulf war, U.S. Ambassador to the United Nations Thomas Pickering proposed in several speeches reconsidering Article 43 provisions: before the Veterans of Foreign Wars, Washington, D.C., March 4, 1991; and before the American Bar Association, Washington, D.C., April 26, 1991.

31. French absence from the unified command and U.S. control over nuclear weapons complicate matters further.

32. Keohane, "Multilateralism," p. 732.

33. Michael Doyle, *Empires* (Ithaca, N.Y.: Cornell University Press, 1986), ch. 1. Some of the more predatory expressions of the Nazi arrangements came very close to, if they did not actually constitute, the imperial form.

34. Obviously, such technical factors as the existence of nuclear weapons or economic interdependence and externalities can and probably do affect the social constructions states choose. I am not imputing causality here but simply clarifying a concept.

35. Robert O. Keohane, "Reciprocity in International Relations," *International Organization* (Winter 1985), vol. 40.

36. Bilateral balancing need not imply equality; it simply means establishing a mutually acceptable balance between the parties, however that is determined in practice. For an extended discussion of this difference, see Karl Polanyi, "The Economy as Instituted Process," in Karl Polanyi, Conrad M. Arensberg, and Harry W. Pearson, *Trade & Market in the Early Empires* (Glencoe, Ill.: Free Press, 1957).

37. Keohane, "International Institutions."

38. Krasner, *International Regimes*.

39. Steve Weber predicted the emergence of a superpower security regime in

"Realism, Detente, and Nuclear Weapons," *International Organization* (Winter 1990), vol. 44; Robert Jervis discussed the possibility in "Security Regimes," in Krasner, ed., *International Regimes,* and Jervis, "From Balance to Concert: A Study of International Security Cooperation," *World Politics* (October 1985), vol. 38.

40. Franz Borkenau, *World Communism: A History of the Communist International,* new introduction by Raymond Aron (Ann Arbor: University of Michigan Press, 1962).

41. Gerard Holden, "The End of an Alliance: Soviet Policy and the Warsaw Pact, 1989–90," Peace Research Institute, Frankfurt, *PRIF Reports* (December 1990), no. 16.

42. The coordination/collaboration distinction is due to Arthur Stein, "Coordination and Collaboration: Regimes in an Anarchic World," in Krasner, ed., *International Regimes.* See also Duncan Snidal, "IGO's, Regimes, and Cooperation: Challenges for International Relations Theory," in Margaret P. Karns and Karen A. Mingst, eds, *The United States and Multilateral Institutions* (Boston: Unwin Hyman, 1990); and Lisa Martin, "The Rational State Choice of Multilateralism," in this volume. The international property rights of states are invariably, however, taken for granted, even though their stable definition is logically and temporally prior to the other two collective-action problems. I have therefore added this dimension.

43. For a brief review, and an interesting discussion of how these practices may become affected by rising sea levels due to global warming, see David D. Caron, "When Law Makes Climate Change Worse: Rethinking the Law of Baselines in Light of a Rising Sea Level," *Ecology Law Quarterly* (1990), vol. 17, no. 4.

44. It took until the early eighteenth century before piracy, frequently state sponsored, came to be generally defined as being inherently damaging to the legitimate interests of states. Robert C. Ritchie, *Captain Kidd and the War Against the Pirates* (Cambridge, Mass.: Harvard University Press, 1986).

45. Garrett Mattingly, *Renaissance Diplomacy* (Baltimore: Penguin Books, 1964), p. 244.

46. On the emergence of the perception that extraterritoriality played a systemic role, see Adda B. Bozeman, *Politics and Culture in International History* (Princeton: Princeton University Press, 1960), esp. pp. 479–480.

47. Note in this connection that U.N. Security Council Resolution 667 "*strongly* condemns" Iraq for "*aggressive* acts *perpetrated* . . . against diplomatic premises and personnel in Kuwait," whereas Resolution 660, passed in response to Iraq's invasion of Kuwait, merely "condemns" the invasion, without embellishment. The full texts are contained in, respectively, United Nations, Security Council, S/RES/667, September 16, 1990, and S/RES/660, August 2, 1990; emphasis added.

48. Stein, "Coordination and Collaboration."

49. International Telecommunications Unions, *From Semaphore to Satellite* (Geneva: ITU, 1965), p. 45.

50. J. P. Chamberlain, *The Regime of International Rivers* (New York: Carnegie Endowment for International Peace, 1923).

51. Ernst B. Haas, *Beyond the Nation State* (Stanford: Stanford University Press, 1964), pp. 14–17.

52. Kupchan and Kupchan, "Concerts, Collective Security, and the Future of Europe," p. 120. Also note the analysis of the Treaty of Paris (1815) by historian Richard Langhorne: "there appeared at clause 6, in what was certainly Castlereagh's drafting, [a shift in] emphasis from a specific guarantee to a scheme for the continuous management of the international system by the great powers." Langhorne, "Reflections on the Significance of the Congress of Vienna," *Review of International Studies* (October 1986), 12:317.

53. Henry A. Kissinger, *A World Restored* (New York: Universal Library, 1964), p. 5. Kissinger concentrates on the *Congress* system, a subset of the Concert, which ended by about 1823, but my commentary holds for the entire Concert system.

54. Robert Jervis, "Security Regimes"; Jervis, "From Balance to Concert;" and Richard B. Elrod, "The Concert of Europe: A Fresh Look at an International System," *World Politics* (January 1976), vol. 28.

55. Kal Holsti, "Governance Without Government: Modes of Coordinating, Managing and Controlling International Politics in Nineteenth-Century Europe," paper presented at the annual meeting of the International Studies Association, Vancouver, Canada, March 1991.

56. The term is used by Gordon A. Craig and Alexander L. George, *Force and Statecraft* (New York: Oxford University Press, 1983), p. 31.

57. Rene Albrecht-Carrie, *The Concert of Europe* (New York: Walker, 1968), p. 22.

58. Holsti, "Governance Without Government," p. 4.

59. Cited in F. H. Hinsley, *Power and the Pursuit of Peace* (Cambridge, England: Cambridge University Press, 1963), p. 243.

60. *Parliamentary Debates,* House of Commons, London, June 29, 1846, as cited in Jagdish N. Bhagwati and Douglas A. Irwin, "The Return of the Reciprocitarians," *The World Economy* (June 1987), 10:114.

61. For an excellent heterodox treatment of these developments, see Stein, "The Hegemon's Dilemma."

62. Jacob Viner, "The Most-Favored-Nation Clause," in Viner, *International Economics* (Glencoe, Ill.: The Free Press, 1951). The United States continued to reject unconditional most-favored-nations provisions in its trade treaties until 1923.

63. Barry Eichengreen, "Conducting the International Orchestra: Bank of England Leadership under the Classical Gold Standard," *Journal of International Money and Finance* (1987), vol. 6, no. 1.

64.

The key equations of multilateralism were that the United Kingdom itself had a credit balance in its dealings with the primary producing countries, and that they settled their balance of indebtedness by an export surplus to the continental countries and to the United States. The continental countries in their turn financed import surpluses with the primary producing countries and with the United States by export surpluses to the United Kingdom.

Asa Briggs, "The World Economy: Interdependence and Planning," *The New Cambridge Modern History,* 2nd ed., vol. 12 (Cambridge, England: Cambridge University Press, 1968), p. 42.

65. Stein, "The Hegemon's Dilemma."

66. Arthur I. Bloomfield, *Monetary Policy Under the International Gold Standard* (New York: Federal Reserve Bank of New York, 1959), p. 23.

67. Peter Gourevitch, *Politics in Hard Times* (Ithaca, N.Y.: Cornell University Press, 1986), ch. 3.

68. Keohane, "Reciprocity in International Relations."

69. Jervis, "Security Regimes," p. 180.

70. David Kennedy, "The Move to Institutions," *Cardozo Law Review* (April 1987), vol. 8.

71. For a brief though excellent review, see Volker Rittberger, "Global Conference Diplomacy and International Policy-Making," *European Journal of Political Research* (1983), vol. 11, no. 2.

72. Rittberger, pp. 167–168.

73. The counter to my argument would, of course, be that "systemic factors" determine or at least shape the preferences and behavior of hegemons. That too is plausible as a hypothesis. As it concerns this particular instance, however, I attach greater credibility to the actual postwar plans of the Third Reich and to what, since 1917, we knew Leninist world order designs to be than I do to the explanatory/predictive value of systemic theory. For general methodological discussions of counterfactuals, see Philip Nash, "The Use of Counterfactuals in History: A Look at the Literature," The Society for Historians of American Foreign Relations, *Newsletter* (March 1991), vol. 22, and James D. Fearon, "Counterfactuals and Hypothesis Testing in Political Science," *World Politics* (January 1991), vol. 43.

74. The consensus on the basic contours of a desirable postwar monetary order was quite strong and widespread beyond the Axis powers and the Soviet Union; see League of Nations [Ragnar Nurkse], *International Currency Experience: Lessons of the Inter-War Period* (Geneva: League of Nations, Economic, Financial, and Transit Department, 1944), esp. ch. 4.

75. Gardner, *Sterling-Dollar Diplomacy,* chs. 5–8.

76. This is quite clear from the provisions of the Anglo–American Atlantic Charter, promulgated in August 1941.

77. Cited in Pollard, *Economic Security,* p. 2.

78. Gardner, *Sterling-Dollar Diplomacy*, part I.

79. For a depiction of the subsequent economic regimes along these lines, see John Gerard Ruggie, "International Regimes, Transactions, and Change: Embedded Liberalism in the Postwar Economic Order," in Krasner, ed., *International Regimes;* and, for additional documentation, G. John Ikenberry, "A World Economy Restored: Expert Consensus and the Anglo-American Postwar Settlement," *International Organization* (Winter 1992), vol. 46. The historian of the Marshall Plan, Michael J. Hogan, similarly has argued that U.S. postwar planners "married Hull's free-trade dictums to the new theories of economic regulation and countercyclical stabilization." Hogan, "One World Into Two: American Diplomacy from Bretton Woods to the Marshall Plan," Ohio State University, unpublished paper, n.d., p. 7.

80. Dallek, *Franklin D. Roosevelt*, ch. 14. Woodrow Wilson had confronted a similar dilemma at the end of World War I—though, unlike Roosevelt, Wilson sought to transcend what he termed "the evil machinations" of balance-of-power politics in the process of resolving it. "We still read Washington's immortal warnings against 'entangling alliances' with full comprehension and an answering purpose," he proclaimed in a 1918 speech.

> But only special and limited alliances entangle; and we recognize and accept the duty of a new day in which we are permitted to hope for a general alliance which will avoid entanglements and clear the air of the world for common understandings and the maintenance of common rights.

Cited in Ambrosius, *Woodrow Wilson and the American Diplomatic Tradition*, p. 46.

81. John Lewis Gaddis, *Strategies of Containment* (New York: Oxford University Press, 1982), p. 9. According to Dallek, for Roosevelt "a United Nations would not only provide a vehicle for drawing Russia into extended cooperation with the West, but would also assure initial American involvement in postwar foreign affairs." *Franklin D. Roosevelt*, p. 508.

82. For a good discussion of this compromise, see Dallek, ch. 15. On the Kupchans' continuum ("Concerts, Collective Security, and the Future of Europe"), the U.N. design may be described as a collective-security organization grafted onto a concert of powers.

83. The United Nations with U.S. support acquired a more modest collective-security role in the form of peacekeeping in the 1950s and a nuclear nonproliferation role via International Atomic Energy Agency safeguards and the Nonproliferation Treaty in the 1960s.

84. Pollard, *Economic Security*.

85. The requirement that the Europeans cooperate in reconstruction on a multilateral basis produced the Organization for European Economic Cooperation in 1948; it eventually became the Organization for Economic Cooperation and Development (OECD)—the chief mechanism through which economic bureaucrats of all the advanced capitalist countries coordinate the conduct of day-

to-day policies. As for European integration, by 1947 the idea had gained strong support in U.S. media and political circles. Senator Fulbright and Representative Boggs went so far as to introduce identical resolutions into the Congress that year, asking it to endorse "the creation of a United States of Europe within the framework of the United Nations." The bills were passed overwhelmingly. European integration was seen as a more promising idea for European economic recovery than individual national efforts alone, and it offered safeguards for the reindustrialization of Germany, which in turn was increasingly seen as being necessary for European recovery and for the success of the newly articulated U.S. policy of containing the Soviet Union. Michael J. Hogan, *The Marshall Plan: America, Britain, and the Reconstruction of Europe* (New York: Cambridge University Press, 1987).

86. Michael Howard, "Introduction," in Olav Riste, ed., *Western Security: The Formative Years* (Oslo: Universitetsforlaget, 1985), p. 14.

87. John Lewis Gaddis, "The United States and the Question of a Sphere of Influence in Europe, 1945–1949," in Riste, ed., *Western Security.*

88. Martin H. Folly, "Breaking the Vicious Circle: Britain, the United States, and the Genesis of the North Atlantic Treaty," *Diplomatic History* (Winter 1988), vol. 12.

89. Alan K. Henrikson, "The Map as an 'Idea': The Role of Cartographic Imagery During the Second World War," *The American Cartographer* (April 1975), vol. 2.

90. Howard, in Riste, ed., *Western Security,* p. 16.

91. On Article 51, see J. Tillapaugh, "Closed Hemisphere and Open World? The Dispute Over Regional Security at the U.N. Conference, 1945," *Diplomatic History* (Winter 1978), vol. 2. On the Vandenberg resolution, which paved the domestic political way for the eventual negotiations of the North Atlantic Treaty, and its explicit link to article 51, see Daryl J. Hudson, "Vandenberg Reconsidered: Senate Resolution 239 and American Foreign Policy" *Diplomatic History* (Winter 1977), vol. 1.

92. Those who assume that Vandenberg's expressed concerns amounted to nothing more than window dressing have not made a case for why a Republican Senator, who had only recently been converted from isolationism, should have thought it necessary to expend so much energy for so puny a purpose.

93. Marc S. Gallicchio, *The Cold War Begins in Asia* (New York: Columbia University Press, 1988); Gaddis, *The Long Peace,* ch. 4; Pollard, *Economic Security,* ch. 8.

94. For example, the *New York Times* described the April 1943 Hot Springs conference on food and agriculture—which led eventually to the creation of the Food and Agriculture Organization of the United Nations—as "a prologue—a kind of dress rehearsal—preparatory to the world organization [Washington] hoped to set up after the war." Cited in Craig Alan Wilson, "Rehearsal for a

United Nations: The Hot Springs Conference," *Diplomatic History* (Summer 1980), 4:264.

95. The work of Robert Gilpin exemplifies the first, that of Kenneth Waltz the second.

96. Joanne Gowa, "Bipolarity, Multipolarity, and Free Trade," *American Political Science Review* (December 1989), vol. 83.

97. William T. R. Fox, *The Super-Powers: The United States, Britain, and the Soviet Union* (New York: Harcourt, Brace, 1944).

98. Dallek, *Franklin D. Roosevelt*, chs. 14, 15.

99. Gaddis, *Strategies of Containment*, ch. 2.

100. See Viner, "Conflicts of Principle," and Feis, "The Conflict Over Trade Ideologies."

101. Jean Edward Smith, *Lucius D. Clay: An American Life* (New York: Henry Holt, 1990), especially ch. 24. Smith's overall assessment of U.S.–Soviet relations as seen on the ground in Germany is this: "The question of erecting a counterpoise to the Soviet Union did not enter Clay's thinking until late 1947, and until then his relations with the Russians were warm and cordial" (p. 7).

102. Robert Jervis has pointed out that the decisive event in instituting the peculiar form of bipolarity known as the cold war was the Korean War. High U.S. defense budgets, a large U.S. armed presence in Europe to back the North Atlantic Treaty security guarantees, and anti-Communist commitments all across the globe took hold only after that war. What is more, Jervis argues, "there were no events on the horizon which could have been functional substitutes for the war"—and which, therefore, would have been capable of producing those features of the international security environment. Jervis, "The Impact of the Korean War on the Cold War," *Journal of Conflict Resolution* (December 1980), 24:563.

103. The so-called "Gang of Four" (Chalmers Johnson, Clyde Prestowitz, Karel van Wolferen, and James Fallows) has insisted that Japan is different in this regard: "Beyond Japan-bashing: The 'Gang of Four' Defends the Revisionist Line," *U.S. News & World Report* (May 7, 1990). For a dispassionate empirical analysis, which does not reach radically different conclusions, see Edward J. Lincoln, *Japan's Unequal Trade* (Washington, D.C.: The Brookings Institution, 1990).

104. See Michael J. Hogan, "Revival and Reform: America's Twentieth-Century Search for a New Economic Order Abroad," *Diplomatic History* (Fall 1984), vol. 8, stressing the economic/interest group dimension; Anne-Marie Burley, "Regulating the World: Multilateralism, International Law, and the Projection of the New Deal Regulatory State," in this volume, focusing on the administrative and legal revolution that attended the New Deal; and Judith Goldstein, "Creating the GATT Rules: Politics, Institutions, and American Policy," in this volume, showing how the short-term interplay of interests and ideas can result in a longer term stickiness of institutions.

105. Dallek, *Franklin D. Roosevelt.*

106. Thomas G. Paterson, *Meeting the Communist Threat: Truman to Reagan* (New York: Oxford University Press, 1988), chs. 1–8.

107. The debate was triggered by Charles Kindleberger's book, *The World in Depression, 1929–1939* (Berkeley: University of California Press, 1973), which also made popular the analogy between the 1930s and 1970s—and then the 1980s; and now?

108. For example, Mearsheimer, "Back to the Future."

109. Krasner, ed., *International Regimes;* and Keohane, *After Hegemony.*

110. Herbert Feis, *1933: Characters in Crisis* (Boston: Little, Brown, 1966).

111. Arthur M. Schlesinger, *The Age of Roosevelt,* vol. 2: *The Coming of the New Deal* (Boston: Houghton, Mifflin, 1958), p. 229. For a game-theoretic rendering of this case, which not only supports Schlesinger's conclusion but also sheds considerable light on the broader debate, see Kenneth A. Oye, "The Sterling-Dollar-Franc Triangle: Monetary Diplomacy 1929–1937," *World Politics* (October 1985), vol. 38, and Oye, "On the Benefits of Bilateralism: Lessons from the 1930s," paper prepared for the Workshop on Change in the International System, University of Southern California, Los Angeles, May 5–6, 1989.

112. Robert Gilpin raises this, correctly in my judgment, as one potential factor that could undermine the embedded liberalism compromise on which the postwar economic regimes have rested, in *The Political Economy of International Relations* (Princeton: Princeton University Press, 1987).

113. Snidal, "The limits of Hegemonic Stability Theory," and Russell Hardin, *Collective Action* (Baltimore: The Johns Hopkins University Press, 1982).

114. Barry Buzan, "Negotiating By Consensus: Developments in Technique at the U.N. Conference on the Law of the Sea," *American Journal of International Law* (April 1981), vol. 75.

115. See, respectively, "Western Europe Moves to Expand Free-Trade Links," *New York Times* (December 8, 1989), and "Inner Space," *The Economist* (May 18, 1991); and "All Europe's a Stage," *The Economist* (March 16, 1991).

116. Peter M. Haas, *Saving the Mediterranean* (New York: Columbia University Press, 1990).

117. Peter M. Haas, "Epistemic Communities and International Environmental Protection," *International Organization* (Winter 1992), vol.46; James K. Sebenius, "Crafting a Winning Coalition: Negotiating a Regime to Control Global Warming," in Richard Elliot Benedick et al., *Greenhouse Warming: Negotiating a Global Regime* (Washington, D.C.: World Resources Institute, 1991).

118. This has been Waltz's standard refrain; see, for example, "Reflections on Theory of International Politics: A Response to My Critics," in Robert O. Keohane, ed., *Neorealism and Its Critics* (New York: Columbia University Press, 1986).

Part 2

❖

THEORETICAL

DEBATES

❖

2. International Relations Theory and Multilateralism: The Search for Foundations

❖

James A. Caporaso

W HY has the concept of multilateralism not played a more prominent role in theories of international relations? The prima facie
case for the importance of multilateral activity in the international realm
would seem great. The world, we constantly tell ourselves, is increasingly
drawn together. The Swedish economist Assar Lindbeck argues that most
external effects of production and consumption are external not only to
the household but also to the country in which they occur. [1] According to
many different indicators, interdependence is on the increase in nearly all
parts of the world. International political economists talk about global
indivisibilities, ranging from peace to pollution. Most important international problems—including pollution, energy, managing airline traffic,
and maintaining rules for trade and investment—intrinsically involve
many countries simultaneously. What makes a problem international is
that often it cannot be dealt with effectively within the national arena.
Costs and benefits spill into the external arena. These external effects are
frequently so great that domestic goals cannot be accomplished without
coordinated multilateral action.

Multilateralism: Ignored by the World or by International Relations Theory?

The puzzling question motivating this chapter is "Why is multilateralism neglected in international relations theory?" The question contains

I am grateful to the Ford Foundation for financial support of the project. I also acknowledge the
support of the Virginia and Prentice Bloedel Chair at the University of Washington as well as the
Department of International Relations, Research School of Pacific Studies, Australian National
University, Canberra. For their comments on earlier drafts of my chapter, I thank William Drake,
Jeffry Frieden, Ronald Jepperson, Robert Keohane, Edgar Kiser, Stephen Krasner, Lisa Martin,
George Modelski, Richard Sherman, Janice Thomson, Alexander Wendt and several anonymous
reviewers for *International Organization* and Columbia University Press.

an assumption—namely, that the treatment of multilateralism in the scholarly international relations literature is less than would be expected on the basis of its observed importance in the world.

Perhaps this assumption should be questioned. One possible reason for the paucity of theory concerning multilateralism is that there may be so little multilateralism in practice. Advocates of this view might cite the declining importance of the United Nations (UN), at least before 1990, the disaffections with the General Agreement on Tariffs and Trade (GATT), the rise of bilateralism in U.S. trade policy, and the numerous selective arrangements drawn up by the European Community (EC), such as the multifiber arrangements.

One scholar laments that "too many people in both countries [the United States and the Soviet Union] see the problems, and their solutions, as bilateral, overlooking the need for the additional cooperation of Europe in the multilateral world of the late twentieth century."[2] Another, a former member of the U.S. Council of Economic Advisers, argues that the United States has become "the bully of the world trading system" and that it has done so by "unilaterally redefining 'unfair' trade."[3] Finally, Inis Claude, Jr., reflecting on almost thirty years since the publication of *Power and International Relations* (1962), today accords much more weight and effectiveness to the balance of power, which he earlier contrasted with collective security and world government, the latter two options being inherently more multilateral.[4] The balance-of-power system is a decentralized system of relations among powers. It acknowledges little if any debt (in its non-Bullian form) to world order or multilateral commitments.

Claude's assessment is provocative and has at least some validity. He argues that during the last quarter-century, the stock of balance of power (presumably also in its bipolar form) has improved. Decisionmakers no longer believe that universal solutions are invariably best, that peace is indivisible (Europe has been far more peaceful than the Middle East and Southeast Asia), that local clashes should be met with worldwide responses, or that regional alliances are a bad thing.

Another explanation for inattention to multilateralism lies at the ideational level. In what ways, if any, does contemporary international relations theory invite or discourage attention to multilateralism? It would be difficult (but not impossible) for liberal economic theory to explain wars but incoherent to ask about state interests, unequal exchange (in Emmanuel's sense),[5] and theories of development resting on absolute immiseration. It would be difficult for a realist to explain extended cooperation not tied to specific, identifiable gains, but it would not be impossible.[6] But motivating a realist argument about goodwill, community spirit, or a state's desire to minimize its power would be impossible. What theories make impossible to explain their practitioners of necessity avoid. What they make merely difficult to explain often preoccupies most of their practitioners' time. Between that which is conceptually impossible and that which is natural (ergo obvious), there lies the region of what is problematic. For realists, the problem of cooperation is particularly salient. For liberals, why there is ever war, protection, autarky, and Pareto-inferior behavior is often a puzzle so exotic as to discourage inquiry.

Since I anticipate misunderstanding on this point, let me clarify my claim. I am not arguing that multilateral activities and organizations have been ignored. Indeed, multilateralism as a subject matter has been the grist for volumes. The UN itself has spawned a large literature. Complex multilateral negotiations, such as those concerning GATT and the Law of the sea, have been studied. And many processes that do not go under the name of multilateralism, such as regional integration and coordination of economic policies, have occupied our attention. My point is that multilateralism is not extensively employed as a theoretical category and that it is rarely used as an explanatory concept. Indeed, even in cases in which multilateralism provides the central conceptual focus, cooperation or institutions usually turn out to serve as the explanandum.

Multilateralism: Definition and Conceptualization

The terms "multilateralism" and "multilateral" suggest some linguistic considerations. The noun comes in the form of an "ism," suggesting a belief or ideology rather than a straightforward state of affairs. Underlying John Ruggie's conception of multilateralism is the idea of "an architectural form," a deep organizing principle of international life.[7] As an organizing principle, the institution of multilateralism is distinguished from other forms by three properties: indivisibility, generalized principles of conduct, and diffuse reciprocity. These three properties should be treated as a coherent ensemble which is itself indivisible, rather than as additive, detachable indicators of multilateralism. Indivisibility can be thought of as the scope (both geographic and functional) over which costs and benefits are spread, given an action initiated in or among component units. If Germany experiences recession, are there consequences for Germans alone, the French, the members of the EC, or nationals in every corner of the earth? Generalized principles of conduct usually come in the form of norms exhorting general if not universal modes of relating to other states, rather than differentiating relations case-by-case on the basis of individual preferences, situational exigencies, or a priori particularistic grounds.[8] Diffuse reciprocity adjusts the utilitarian lenses for the long view, emphasizing that actors expect to benefit in the long run and over many issues, rather than every time on every issue.[9]

The distinction between multilateral institutions and the institution of multilateralism is cognizant of two levels of related international activity. Multilateral institutions focus attention on the formal organizational elements of international life and are characterized by permanent locations and postal addresses, distinct headquarters, and ongoing staffs and secretariats. The institution of multilateralism may manifest itself in concrete organizations, but its significance cuts more deeply. The institution of multilateralism is grounded in and appeals to the less formal, less codified habits, practices, ideas, and norms of international society. Bilateralism, imperial hierarchy, and multilateralism are alternative conceptions of how the world might be organized; they are not just different types of concrete organization.

There are at least two reasons for maintaining the distinction. The first, as Lisa Martin argues, is that multilateral institutions and the institution of multilateralism do not always mirror one another within a given issue-area. Depending on the structure of interests, one may be strong and the other weak.[10] The second reason is that the two types of multilateralism may be related in complex cause-and-effect ways. Multilateral organizations may provide arenas within which actors learn to alter perceptions of interests and beliefs.[11] The institution of multilateralism may in turn spawn, maintain, alter, and undermine specific organizations. Ernst Haas's study of learning within numerous international organizations, including the International Labour Organization and the World Bank, illustrates the first effect.[12] Jean Monnet's insistence that there be a *unité des faits* among numerous actors in international society before concrete regional organizations can take hold illustrates the second.[13]

The term "multilateral" can refer to an organizing principle,[14] an organization, or simply an activity. Any of the above can be considered multilateral when it involves cooperative activity among many countries.

"Multilateralism," as opposed to "multilateral," is a belief that activities ought to be organized on a universal basis at least for a "relevant" group (for example, democracies). It may be a belief both in the existential sense of a claim about how the world works and in the normative sense that things should be done in a particular way. As such, multilateralism is an ideology "designed" to promote multilateral activity. It combines normative principles with advocacy and existential beliefs.

Definitions have implications for the broader conceptual framework and for theory. First, the term "multilateral" does not analytically pre-suppose any particular number of countries in the way that unilateral, bilateral, trilateral, and universal do. These terms now describe specific points on an underlying continuum from everyone going it alone to everyone participating. Multilateral suggests "many" actors, but it is unspecific as to what number constitutes many. "Many" could refer to anything from a minimum of three to a maximum of all. Multilateral refers to a region, rather than a point, on the continuum and thus can be analyzed in terms of gradations. When conceptualized in this manner, multilateral action is compatible with theories concerning thresholds in groups of less than universal membership.

Second, the definition of the term "multilateral" presumes coopera-tion. Not all cooperation is multilateral, but all multilateral activities include cooperation. In a Hobbesian war of each against all, we do not say that states behave in a multilateral fashion even though they are interacting in highly interdependent ways. However, it is consistent to think of some states as carrying out multilateral activities against others, such as under the auspices of a military alliance.

The question arises as to whether multilateralism is a means or an end, an instrument or an expression, or both. States or their agents are conceptualized as conscious, goal-seeking actors. As such, it is easy to see how multilateralism is one means among many to be used or ignored according to the instrumental calculus. In instrumental theories—that is, theories stressing given preferences and conscious choice—cooperation has been used to mean a process by which states actively adjust their policies to take into account the preferences of others. In game theory, a cooperative choice (which may be part of an overall strategy) generally represents an effort to take account of the other players' interests, even if the dominant interest is to defect. This makes cooperation a "move," an instrumental action that takes place within the overall context of a social dilemma.

While instrumental approaches to multilateralism are important, they do not exhaust the possibilities. Multilateral activities may also be an end, or consumption good, according to which states prefer to do things multilaterally. Stated in this way, the noninstrumental version may be hard to defend. How, for example, can one account for the vastly different forms of organization across different sectors by the same states? But there is something in between the ideal types of means and ends. In uncertain environments, states may be forced to make strong presumptions in favor of one or another approach. In this way, multilateralism may not always be thought out and chosen on the basis of exacting calculations of costs and benefits. To the extent that presumptions in favor of multilateralism exist, it becomes part of our ongoing, taken-for-granted understanding of international life.

As Ruggie argues, multilateralism is a demanding organizational form.[15] It requires its participants to renounce temporary advantages and the temptation to define their interests narrowly in terms of national interests, and it also requires them to forgo ad hoc coalitions and to avoid policies based on situational exigencies and momentary constellations of interests. Yet it is by no means a rare organizational form in the world. This prompts the question, "What coherent theories do we have to account for multilateralism?" Since my approach to answering this question is unconventional, a word of explanation may be in order. My argument is that international relations theory, with few exceptions, does not offer "off-the-shelf" theories to explain multilateralism.[16] This complicates the task and prompts me to look in part outside of the international relations literature. In what follows, I draw from numerous areas, including sociology, experimental psychology, organizational theory, and game theory in an attempt to identify alternative foundations for theories of multilateralism. I identify the elements of three paradigms, pointing out the similarities with and implications for international relations theory.

Three Routes to Multilateralism

In this section, I explore three theoretical routes to understanding multilateral activities. The first route is provided by an individualist paradigm in which states "enter into" contractual relations with other states in a rational, self-interested way. The bare bones equipment of this approach includes states and state interests (both unproblematically given), capabilities, and strategies by which to interact with others. The second route to be explored is found in a loosely connected assemblage of writings labeled the social-communicative approach. The focus of this approach is still on the identities and powers of individual states, but the "interaction repertoires" of states include communication, persuasion, deliberation, and self-reflection. Ontologically, the state is separately constituted, but a bit more sociality is brought into its self-definition.

The exact cutoff point between the first and second approaches is not my concern here. As part of their project, radical individualists may seek to trace the second conception of states from the first and to explain even minimal elements of sociality among states as outgrowths of a model based on nothing more than autonomous, self-interested actors. Similarly, proponents of the second approach may argue that the first works only as long as it imports elements of their model as unexamined premises. They make ask, for example, how self-interested states could contract without some common understandings, rules, and practices. Rather than trying to solve this demarcation issue in the abstract, I pursue the implications of the distinction below.

The third perspective is provided by an institutional approach. Since there are numerous competing "new" institutional approaches, I will try to stake out the ground for the approach dealt with here. Institutionalism has ties to the second approach in its insistence on the importance of communication, reflection, discussion, learning, and interpretation. However, it departs from it in a number of ways. It is not necessarily methodologically individualist, does not treat preferences as exogenous, and does not understand social relations—including multilateral relations—solely as products of individual self-interested calculations. This is a negative way of describing the institutional approach. What the approach stands for in a positive sense will be outlined later.

THE INDIVIDUALIST PARADIGM

The individualist label is meant as a shorthand for a collection of theories that attempt to explain social behavior by appealing to characteristics of individual actors, particularly preferences and capabilities, and their strategic environments. The analogues in international relations theory are realism, neorealism, and game theory. Even some theories of international cooperation, institutions, and organization could be included insofar as they theorize these phenomena as lying outside the defining properties of states. This diverse collection is unified by its focus on states as conscious goal-seeking agents pursuing their interests within an external environment characterized by anarchy and the powers of other states. The paradigmatic question is how states pursue their goals given the constraints under which they operate. When goals are interdependent, the question assumes a strategic form: How can one state achieve what it wants, given the preferences and options of others?

Within this paradigm, the road to multilateralism logically involves two steps not necessarily temporally sequenced. First, there must be an explanation of cooperation. Second, the theory must provide the conditions under which cooperation becomes multilateral. The explanation of one is not reducible to the other. The problem of cooperation is a problem precisely because state interests are independently given, often in conflict with one another, and pursued within an environment of anarchy. Furthermore, most of what we take as social (including rules, shared understandings, and collective beliefs) is not part of the representation of the problem of cooperation in either its verbal or game-theoretic form. In the standard version of noncooperative game theory,[17] agents, preferences, and strategies are represented. Some rules are assumed (for example, if you are a prisoner, you should not grab the warden, thus changing the payoff matrix, or threaten to have your partner killed if he or she defects, thus changing the incentives for cooperation), but this amounts to very little in playing the game. Absent are norms, morality, and the ability to communicate, to promise, and to make binding commitments. To explain why states cooperate in the bilateral case seems difficult enough. To establish cooperation multilaterally is a problem compounded.

I mention these difficulties not to criticize at this point but simply to remind that the individualist approach does not make things easy for itself.[18] Some approaches assume much of what they want to prove. Outcomes to be explained are then progressively revealed by uncovering the assumptions of the theory. Empirical research gives way to deductive elaborations. That is close to the opposite of what the individualist approach has done. Very little sociality is built into its central premises. If this approach works, it is more powerful in that it explains a complex social activity such as multilateralism without access by assumption to much of that sociality. It is as if, from a world of isolated, self-seeking individuals, complex social structure results. Below, I explore how several specific individualist models help explain multilateral actions.

The k Group.   Of the three standard solutions to the problem of cooperation—the *k* group, side-payments, and repetition of the game—the first seems to provide the safest footing for multilateralism. Repetition of the game (Kenneth Oye's "shadow of the future"[19]) may enhance the value of reputation and make it more attractive for participants to think about net benefits in the long run, but it provides little guidance as to how the time frame should affect the comprehensiveness of cooperative actions. Side-payments may help to bring potential defectors in line, but even these incentives would seem to presuppose an already existing pattern of cooperation.

The logic of the k group, however, holds some promise. Given an n-person social dilemma, we know that the dominant individual strategies, if played, yield a deficient equilibrium. In the international environment, which arguably models the n-person social dilemma, the defect option is better regardless of what the others do. But if all defect, as the familiar story goes, the outcomes are next to last in the preference schedules of the players. Now suppose, to counter this result, that among the n players there exists some subset (called k) whose cooperation would ensure resolution of the dilemma, no matter what the others $(n - k)$ did. This still would not ensure multilateral cooperation, since defect would still be the dominant strategy, unless individuals could be convinced that each contribution was crucial to resolving the dilemma. Deciding on the members of the subset would be difficult but critical, and some assurance would have to be given that others do not contribute or, more exactly, that k group members did not think that others would contribute.

While k groups do provide some basis for multilateral cooperation, this approach needs a mechanism to identify or designate who the members of the group are so as to ensure that no one else is perceived as a possible contributor and to establish arrangements for enforcing these conditions. There is another, more important complication, however. The smaller the k group, the easier it is to cooperate but the less multilateral the arrangement will be. The larger the k group, the more multilateral the cooperative arrangement might be but the more difficult it is to pull off cooperation. Solutions may be available to get around the problem, but such solutions make assumptions and introduce variables that take us to the other side of my classificatory divide—from individualist, interest-oriented to social-communicative theories.

Repetition of the Game. A second approach to multilateral cooperation is to relax the assumption that the game is played only once and to allow for an indefinitely large number of plays, more or less as in real life. If the game is played only once or is played a finite, known number of times, the incentive to defect is dominant. If the game is repeated an unknown number of times or if uncertainty is present in other ways, the possibility of benefits from long-term cooperation must be weighed against the possible gains of a defect move in the short term.[20]

Lengthening the time frame over which individuals interact has several effects. One is that it opens the door to concepts such as "dynamic cooperation," in which a comprehensive strategy—that is, a series of related moves or a plan for choosing moves over the entire game—rather than a single move is the object of equilibrium thinking. Another is that it allows for variability in the value of reputation and trustworthiness, as well as conditional if implicit promising and reciprocity. Clearly, the introduction of these concepts allows for a much richer analysis than the one-play games do.

In addition to their increased complexity, iterated games are more supportive of cooperative outcomes. Both Russell Hardin and Michael Taylor demonstrate "the possibility of cooperation," as the title of Taylor's book cautiously puts it.[21] As Robert Keohane argues, "The essential reason for this difference [between single-play and iterated games] is that, in multiple-play Prisoners' Dilemma, defection is in the long run unrewarding, since the short-run gains thereby obtained will normally be outweighed by the mutual punishment that will ensue over the long run."[22]

Robert Axelrod has shown that a mixed strategy of selective cooperation and defection can be a winning strategy.[23] He also demonstrated with considerable success that conditional cooperation is a winning strategy and one that is collectively stable—that is, resistant to any invasion by a different strategy. Axelrod's experiments were carried out in a setting in which one could single out a partner, identify defections and cooperative moves, and bring sanctions or rewards to the appropriate party. The results depended, probably to a considerable extent, on the memory of particular dyads and on the reputations of their constituent members.

Rudolph Schuessler developed a different form of the game, an iterated prisoners' dilemma with an exit option after each play of the game.[24] By constructing the game in this fashion, he was able to explore the conditions of cooperation where there were no memory or reputational effects and where defectors could not be identified, traced, and punished. Instead, if one were exploited, he or she could simply exit. Even under these spare conditions, closer to an anonymous *Gesellschaft* rather than *Gemeinschaft,* Schuessler was able to demonstrate considerable cooperation.

The problems begin when we ask how this cooperative behavior of dyads generalizes to become multilateral. Both Axelrod's and Schuessler's analyses are of dyadic interactions within a large population. Many individuals are involved and they are all playing a PD game, but this is not the same thing as an n-person prisoners' dilemma game. In the language of this article, it is aggregate bilateralism rather than multilateralism. Axelrod's and Schuessler's players are cooperating with specific relevant others—not with the group.

By contrast, in *The Possibility of Cooperation*, Michael Taylor did focus on n-person games, particularly prisoners' dilemma. He developed a supergame consisting of "a countably infinite number of iterations of a single constituent game" in which a player's payoffs were a function of his or her strategy (cooperate or defect) in the constituent game and of the number of other players who cooperate in that game.[25] Here, the incentives to cooperate or defect were in part (perhaps in large part) determined by an unspecified number of other players with whom a given player may or may not be in direct contact. Taylor's conclusion was that "Cooperation amongst a relatively large number of players is 'less likely' to occur than Cooperation amongst a small number."[26] Part of the reason has to do with the obvious fact that since more actors exist, more interests are involved and have to be taken into account. But the main reason, according to Taylor, is that "Cooperation can be sustained only if conditional Cooperators are present and conditional Cooperators must be able to monitor the behavior of others."[27] The difficulties and costs of monitoring, which I discuss below, go up as the number of actors goes up.

Transaction Costs, Multilateralism, and Regimes. Transaction costs are all the costs incurred in exchange, including the costs of acquiring information, bargaining, and enforcement, as well as the opportunity cost of the time allocated to these activities.[28] In a sense, the idea of transaction costs takes us beyond noncooperative games. In the standard version of these games, agents, payoffs, and rules are given by assumption. These parameters are not problematized and do not function as costs of setting up the game. In addition, the idea of enforcement costs is specifically excluded in noncooperative games. Nevertheless, we can think of transaction costs in a thinner sense as the costs of discovering relevant agents and their preferences, of negotiating, of identifying defection or cooperation, and of bringing rewards and penalties to bear on the relevant parties.[29]

What is the relationship between the number of actors involved in a potential multilateral scheme and the costs of transacting? The costs of transacting almost certainly increase with an increase in actors. The costs of identifying the relevant others, of discovering their preferences and strategies, and of devising policies that are capable of discriminating among defectors and cooperators all go up. Just how or by what function this increase takes place is difficult to say. A linear relation suggests that complications are directly proportional to the number of actors involved. An exponential relation suggests that costs rise in reaction to the number of pairs or n-tuples involved. Another possibility is that while costs rise, there are dampening factors as n increases. Taylor suggests that a critical concept for cooperation in large groups is "conditional cooperation," defined as the strategy of cooperating on the condition that others cooperate.[30] Conditional cooperators have to monitor the moves of others; otherwise, their own moves cannot be conditional. However, as Taylor points out, conditional cooperators need to know only that a certain fraction of others cooperated in a prior move, not which ones in particular cooperated.[31] While this may decrease information costs, it does not eliminate them.

What relationship might we expect between multilateral organizations and transaction costs? Ruggie points out that sometimes institutions are multilateral because to organize them differently would be more costly.[32] If the costs are large for each pair of states and if the activities generating these costs are essentially the same (that is, repetitive), large gains may be expected through multilateral organization. Some of these gains may be Smithian, deriving from the same advantages that make factory production more efficient than individual production, advantages such as decreasing the amount of time and resources wasted in moving between different points of production. Keohane refers to political economies of scale.[33] The marginal costs of handling an additional agreement (that is, another bilateral agreement) within a multilateral organization will be lower than the average cost.

But multilateral activity without an organization to facilitate and enforce agreements brings up all the problems that haunt international political cooperation in the first place: absence of trust, weak and unreliable information, incentives to defect, and reneging on agreements when it is convenient. Transaction costs may be lower for multilateral than for bilateral agreements, the arrangements in this case may still be bilateral. Such nonoptimal outcomes are not rare in international politics.

One proposed way around this problem is provided by the literature on international regimes. In *After Hegemony,* Keohane makes the case for regimes lowering transaction costs. At the simplest level, they make it cheaper for governments to negotiate agreements.[34] They provide administrative help, an ongoing forum in which representatives of different states can meet, and a set of rules and procedures for dealing with problems. In addition, regimes provide valuable informational services that facilitate multilateral contact. They collect information, standardize conceptual categories (defining the characteristics of a nontariff barrier, for example), codify rules and practices, and attempt to increase the transparency of both cooperative and defecting moves. Although GATT is a relatively small international organization, it is hard to imagine how individual states would manage their global trade relations bilaterally. Finally, since regimes provide a framework of rules, a continuing organization in which states come back for more every day, they facilitate sanctioning. Even if the actual rewards and penalties are carried out by the states themselves, regimes make the whole idea of a "violation of rules" intelligible and meaningful in some intersubjective sense.

The idea of transaction costs provides a bridge of sorts between the individualist approach and the social-communicative approach. As noted above transaction costs are all the costs associated with pulling off exchanges, costs that are usually assumed to be zero in the perfectly competitive ideal. The concept of transaction costs contains within it much material that is anterior to and outside of exchange and strategic interaction per se. Insofar as this material has to do with the making and implementation of binding contracts, the transaction costs approach overlaps with other approaches.

In a world of zero transactions costs, there would be no need for international institutions, multilateral or otherwise. It is the recognition of positive transaction costs that leads us to inquire about the role of institutions in solving problems of exchange. In this regard, Lisa Martin asks a straightforward but productive question: "What is the instrumental value of multilateral norms under different configurations of state interest?"[35] Taking only the interests of states as primary data, she explores what implications these strategic considerations have for multilateral institutions and the institution of multilateralism.

While Martin focuses on several types of strategic structures, the contrast between coordination and collaboration games is instructive. In coordination games, actors have a strong incentive to reach an agreement and do not have an incentive to depart from it once it has been reached. The constellation of interests given by coordination games does not require a strong, centralized, multilateral institution to enforce solutions, since the temptation for opportunistic behavior is small to nonexistent. By contrast, in collaboration games such as a prisoners' dilemma, there is a strong incentive to defect and a consequent need for monitoring and enforcement mechanisms to prevent unilateral defection. But as Martin argues, multilateral norms are likely to be dysfunctional for collaboration problems. This is because the norms of diffuse reciprocity and indivisibility require unconditional cooperation and may discourage the specific detection and selective punishment required by tit-for-tat strategies.[36] For this reason, opportunistic behavior and free riding can be more effectively dealt with through bilateral arrangements than through multilateral ones.

In broad terms, then, Martin argues that there is a tension between the highly generalized norms of multilateralism on the one hand and the specific knowledge and actions required to enforce complex agreements on the other. Beth Yarbrough and Robert Yarbrough also exploit this tension by arguing that bilateralism can be seen as an enforcement mechanism for dealing with the relentless opportunistic pressures inherent in prisoners' dilemma structures.[37] Bilateralism implies that individual countries bear responsibility for detecting violations of agreements and for imposing sanctions. Imposing sanctions, in turn, requires some capacity to inflict costs for noncooperation. Yarbrough and Yarbrough suggest that the exchange of economic hostages may provide the basis for imposing penalties. "Economic hostages" are defined as binding precommitments to invest in assets that are specific to a transaction and to a partner. Japanese automobiles fitted with pollution devices required by U.S. regulations are one example.

While the theoretical point here is well taken, I am skeptical about generalizing the conditions of economic exchange to multilateral settings. First, we should not underestimate the difficulty of hostage exchange in political terms. A great deal of intragovernmental coordination and power would be required to tailor regulatory policy to the specifications of foreign trade. This suggests a world in which "domestic" regulatory policy is driven by the desire to set up sanctioning mechanisms in the event of the breakdown of foreign exchange. Second, we can question the hostage argument on its own terms. To discourage opportunism, the link between countries must show high asset specificity, since this condition indicates high opportunity costs. But if this condition exists, by definition it works against multilateral generalization. A country cannot have a different regulatory environment in the same issue-area for each partner. By contrast, if assets are standardized (the condition suggested by policy convergence), the costs of shifting to another partner will be low.

A way out of this dilemma might be to tailor regulations to each partner in specific (different) issue-areas. This procedure faces numerous hurdles. Surely regulatory policies will overlap and interfere with one another, limiting the degrees of freedom for policymakers. Moreover, specific assets are sunk costs, which slow adjustment to ever-shifting comparative advantage.

In this section, I have examined the path to multilateral cooperation provided by approaches based on individualist, state-centered theory. Since these approaches build very little sociality into their premises, they are of limited value in explaining multilateral cooperation. In noncooperative games, the rules, the agents, and the preferences, beliefs, and choices of agents are established by assumption. In the one-shot dilemma game, defection is a dominant strategy. By selectively relaxing the assumptions, complexity and realism can be introduced. The game can be repeated so as to allow signaling (a form of communication), interdependent strategies (such as tit-for-tat), and various values for reputation. Cooperative results can be and are produced. Indeed, some argue that they are robust.[38]

Nevertheless, extensive multilateral cooperation is fragile and compounded by increasing the numbers of players. Iterated games imply cooperation but not necessarily multilateral cooperation. As the number of actors increases and power diffuses, the size of the solution set can change.[39] Further, as John Orbell and his colleagues show, cooperative solutions are *behaviorally* dependent on a consensus far in excess of the level of agreement *rationally* needed to produce optimal results.[40] While results could be produced by a *k* group (a subset of *n*), how does a *k* group know that it is one and who should be a member of it? The existence of a minimal contributing set (a small group capable of providing a public good) is not a mechanical question relating to the distribution of capabilities. It requires consciousness about the common situation and shared interests as well as positive actions regarding sharing information and forming coalitions. Moreover, as Taylor emphasizes, even if a *k* group exists it is likely to be the case that it is in the interest of some members to get others to join in place of themselves: "In those cases where *subsets* of the players find it collectively worthwhile to provide the public good, there arises a quite different strategic problem, which results from some players having an incentive to ensure that the subset which provides the public good does not include themselves."[41] Thus, problems of free riding and strategic preferences do not disappear just because a privileged group exists.

The idea of transaction costs, applied in conjunction with regimes, perhaps takes us further toward understanding multilateral institutions. However, it also takes us further away from approaches based purely on interest and strategic choice and closer to those based on communication and making binding commitments.

SOCIAL-COMMUNICATIVE APPROACHES

In making the transition from individualist to social-communicative approaches, we move from representation of autonomous agents engaged in strategic interaction to a view that progressively incorporates social structure and communication. The change is not qualitative but one of degree.

The social approach does not throw out individual rationality; it situates it and broadens it. Individual intentionality is embedded in social relations in which communication, shared beliefs, norms, and identity commitments are present. Thus, the focus is not only on individual choice but on how the choosing agent reflects, discusses, trusts and distrusts, tries to build consensus, alters others' perceptions of the world, and, in general, uses his or her capacities as a social being to identify problems, solve them, and shape the environment. With respect to Jon Elster's metaphors of market and forum, this approach is closer to the forum.[42] With respect to Anatol Rapoport's distinction between games and debates, it is closer to debates.[43] Within game theory proper, it draws more on cooperative than noncooperative game theory. In the remainder of this section, I explore several routes to multilateralism that rely on the social-communicative approach.

Discussion and Persuasion. In noncooperative game theory, whether a Nash equilibrium is reached can depend to a considerable extent on the ability to coordinate policies. One way for this coordination to come about is through preplay communication. Often it is the case that an actor wants the opponent to play his or her best move in response to the actor's own move.[44]

In experimental social psychology, studies concerning how actors deal with social dilemmas have demonstrated that group discussion greatly increases the incidence of cooperation. It does so without any help from a leviathan or central enforcement agency, iteration of the game, side-payments, or other narrowly self-interested reasons. Indeed, some scholars argue, discussion will have an effect on cooperation despite the fact that the cooperative choice is strictly dominated by the defect choice.[45]

The exact mechanism by which discussion works is not clear. By itself it is no panacea. Many discussions and negotiations in international relations produce no agreements at all, and sometimes it is not even possible to get to the negotiating table. If the structure of interests is "deadlock," no amount of discussion alone will produce cooperation; one side must effectively persuade the other to see interests differently. Theoretically, discussion may work to alter preferences, to create a feeling of shared identity, to encourage norms, or to facilitate promising behavior.

How important is discussion in international relations theory? According to the predominant model of strategic interaction in noncooperative games, states act on their interests given the interests and strategy choices of others. The emphasis is on arriving at the best outcomes, possibly one from which there will be no rational incentive to depart. Since not all outcomes have this property, attention is paid to devising mechanisms of monitoring and verification to prevent "cheating" or "shirking." This orientation suggests little role for discussion.

In the descriptive world of international relations, a plausible case can be made for the importance of discussion. For example, Jeffrey Frankel and Katherine Rockett suggest that the ability of discussion to improve cooperative outcomes among decision makers depends on its ability to produce consensus on the "true" model of economic reality.[46] However, they emphasize that the "assumption that policy makers agree on the true model has little, if any, empirical basis."[47] Still others, such as Robert Putnam and C. Randall Henning, see discussion as quite central.[48]

In their case study of the 1978 Bonn summit meeting, Putnam and Henning analyzed the economic policy preferences and interests of seven advanced capitalist countries (Britain, Canada, France, Germany, Italy, Japan, and the United States) and found that the policies adopted were different as a result of negotiations.[49] The core of the Bonn accord involved an agreement on the part of Germany and Japan to reflate their domestic economies in return for the U.S. commitment to raise domestic oil prices to world levels.[50] As the authors pointed out, the interests of the states differed, with each having its own target levels regarding outputs, employment, fiscal policy, interest rates, and energy policy. Moreover, the decision makers' beliefs about which kinds of policies were likely to lead to targeted goals differed markedly. Sometimes these differences had to do with variations in the results of forecasting models. A West German model, for example, predicted growth for 1977 in the 4.5 to 5.5 percent range, a much stronger performance than that forecasted by the Organization for Economic Cooperation and Development (OECD). Sometimes these differences stemmed from theoretical disputes about important parameters in macroeconomic models. How much growth would result from a tax cut of quantity x or a money supply increase of size y? How much unemployment would result from decreasing inflation by a given amount?

The extensive case material provided by Putnam and Henning documents in detail the importance of deliberation, negotiation, and attempts to change the beliefs of others about the macroeconomic environment. Interests, power, and strategic interaction were not irrelevant, but the ability to change perceptions of interest using technical knowledge was important as well: "In practice, negotiation (especially internationally) is more than mere bargaining over a fixed, known payoff matrix. Much of what actually happens is attempted persuasion. Behaviorally at least, our account of the events of 1977–78 suggests that it is highly misleading to disregard the degree to which policy makers, negotiating internationally, actually try to convince one another that their respective models of the world and even their respective preferences are mistaken. Under uncertainty, international communications and persuasion can change minds, move the undecided, and hearten those in the minority, domestically speaking."[51]

Minimal Contributing Sets. A minimal contributing set (MCS) is defined as the smallest number of actors who together could provide a public good if they were willing to do so. As the earlier discussion of k groups indicated, for some subset of n (all actors), total benefits exceed total costs, regardless of what the others do. While the MCS is formally identical to the k group, the literature suggests that there are somewhat different mechanisms to bring these minimal groups into existence.

Within the international relations literature, much attention has been directed toward identifying the conditions that make k groups possible. The investigations have pointed scholars in the direction of structural properties of the international system, properties such as the number of important actors and the concentration either of aggregate power or sectoral power. Thus, shares of world trade, investment, monetary reserves, and energy supplies have functioned as indicators of hegemony or of the concentration of power in the hands of a few states.

Proponents of hegemonic stability theory do not claim that the concentration of power automatically translates into the provision of public goods by the hegemon. The existence of a hegemon may not even be necessary, let alone sufficient.[52] At most, they claim that hegemonic distributions of power are conducive to the provision of international public goods. The stability of the Bretton Woods system from 1945 to 1971 was facilitated by the overwhelming economic power of the United States, just as the dominance of the gold standard was associated with Britain's hegemony during the second half of the nineteenth century.[53]

It is in this context that the experimental literature on MCSs is relevant. It attempts to provide some of the missing links between aggregate structural facts such as the international distribution of power and process-level phenomena. Among other things, the literature focuses on discussion, the dissemination of information (for example, about the identity of members of the MCS), and optimal levels of provision. For public goods with specific threshold provision points, it is important to identify the relevant actors and the required amount of contribution. It may also be important to convince MCS members that each of their contributions is essential; otherwise, there would be a temptation to free ride.

In the experiments set up by Alphonse van de Kragt and his associates,[54] subjects were placed in a social dilemma and given a choice between cooperating (contributing) and defecting (free riding). If they cooperated, the group would be awarded a bonus to be shared by all (a public good). If they did not cooperate, there was no guarantee of a bonus. If the bonus were given, however, they would share in the benefits at no cost. Subjects were divided into twenty-four groups, half of which allowed discussion and half of which did not. In all twelve discussion groups, the members contributed to the public good; and in ten of these discussion groups, they contributed the optimal amount.[55]

According to the designers of this experiment, the most important factor is "criticalness." Each member of the group is motivated to contribute when the contribution of each is seen as a sine qua non for provision of the public good. Individuals are placed in the same relation to goods as they are in private markets: either pay and receive or else pay nothing and receive nothing. If members can be convinced that some others (less than MCS) will not contribute, they are in effect in an equilibrium position from which there is no rational incentive to depart.[56]

While the structural problem addressed by MCS is the same as that addressed by the *k* group, the resolution for the latter is considerably different. Emphasis is placed on discussion and explicit coordination of interests. The ability to designate explicitly who is and is not a member of the *k* group is critical. The logic of the solution is limited to public goods with explicit provision points where participants can be brought into contact with one another, discuss, and designate contributors.

Norms, Promising, and Group Identity. In exploring the effect of norms, promising behavior, and group identity on cooperation in social dilemmas, I discuss the results of laboratory experiments constructed to show the social dimensions of decision making in *n*-person dilemmas. The general form of the experiments is that of a social dilemma in which the set of individually rational moves not to cooperate (not to contribute to the public good) is dominant and therefore produces a deficient equilibrium. I should add that the decision situations are anonymous and limited to one time frame (no iteration); therefore, tit-for-tat strategies are not permitted, and the value of reputation is zero. Although the processes leading up to decisions are social, the actual decisions are completely private.[57]

The first experiment was designed by Robyn Dawes, Alphonse van de Kragt, and John Orbell to determine whether group identity independently affects cooperation, apart from self-interest, reputation, mutual altruism, or even conscience.[58] The subjects were divided into various discussion groups and were told that they could make a contribution to their own group if they wished but not to other groups. The researchers found that individuals gave to their group even when it was not in their self-interest to do so, but they adopted no generalized norm about giving: "Our experiments have led us to conclude that cooperation rates can be radically affected by one factor in particular that is independent of the consequences for the choosing individual. That factor is group identity. Such identity—or solidarity—can be established and consequently enhance cooperation responding in the absence of any expectation of future reciprocity, or current reward or punishment, or even reputational consequences among other group members; moreover, this identity operates independently of the dictates of conscience."[59]

In another experiment, the same researchers attempted to extend their analysis of cooperation by exploring the psychological and group dynamics involved in promise-making and promise-keeping behavior. Starting from a baseline of bilateral promising, they attempted to generalize the logic to multilateral promising in groups of up to fourteen subjects. It turned out that the generalization was not at all straightforward. What they found was that promises in large groups were kept when all group members made them but were much less binding when only some members made them.[60]

The central question is how to make sense of the fact that the investigators found no evidence that promising increases cooperation in cases in which promises were not made universally. A commonsense approach to promising and group identity is to think of the two phenomena as continuously related to cooperative behavior. A little promising or group identity is better than none; a lot is better than a little; and so on. But this commonsense approach does not square with the step-level function observed in the experimental results. Why is unanimity so important, even when the supply of public goods is continuous or when the provision threshold is short of unanimity?

A number of hypotheses come to mind. First, it may be that individuals believe that cooperation will only occur when everyone promises. The hypothesis leaves this belief itself unexplained, but it is suggestive. The fear of an agreement unraveling might highlight the importance of unanimity ("one for all, all for one"; "united we stand, divided we fall"). In addition, unanimity provides a prominent solution in Thomas Schelling's sense—that is, a point which can be singled out and around which expectations can converge.[61] Second, group identity may somehow be triggered by unanimous consent. If everyone agrees, feelings of solidarity among group members are likely to be high. Still, it is hard to accept that a few noncooperative individuals could have so disproportionate an effect. Third, and this is not completely distinguishable from the first hypothesis, universality in promising may simply describe the condition under which individuals perceive their own promises as binding. This amounts to saying that a promise is an offer of cooperation contingent on everyone else also cooperating.

While these interpretations are currently unresolved, let us explore some of the differences between bilateral and multilateral promises. In the bilateral case, the payoffs present clear information about the benefits/costs of different choices. For one of two actors to say "I promise" when the other does not would yield an outcome of "both defect."[62] In the multilateral case, however, there will be levels of cooperation almost always that are less than universal but where the payoff is better than at the point at which all defect.

This point is illustrated in Figure 2.1, which is adapted from the work of Orbell, Dawes, and van de Kragt. There are many points along the *x* axis (number of cooperators) where the gains from cooperation (*y* axis) equal and then exceed the gains from all defecting. This is true even if cooperation is dominated by defection at the individual level (the defect line has the same slope but a higher intercept than the cooperate line). Any point to the right of *k* is socially superior to any point to the left of it. Yet the entire region between *k* and *n* − 1 on the horizontal axis describes a span where cooperation is not forthcoming as a result of promising.[63]

Orbell and his colleagues tentatively conclude that perhaps the answer lies within the realm of uncertainty, cognitive limitations, and the

Figure 2.1. The Structure of Incentives in Multilateral Exchange

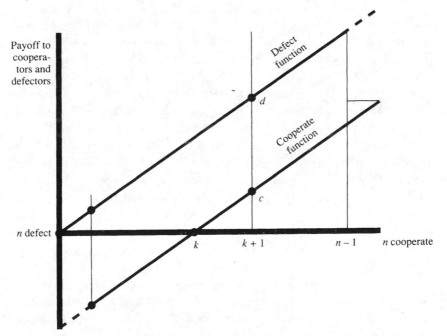

Source: John Orbell, Robyn Dawes, and Alphons van de Kragt, "The Limits of Multilateral Promising," *Ethics* 100 (April 1991), p. 624. Modified and reproduced, with permission, from the authors, *Ethics,* and the University of Chicago Press.

difficulty of specifying a prominent rule, one that is "simple enough to be generally recognized, and general enough to apply to the many *n*–prisoners' dilemma game parameters that are possible."[64] The economically attractive rule "Your promise is ethically binding when any number more than *k* (including yourself) have also promised"[65] would do nicely, but it may be beyond the cognitive competence of the actors. If so, we can see why members of the group might push *toward* universality: it eliminates free riding, diminishes the obstacles that envy and relative deprivation might throw up, and is equitable. However, a multilateral cooperative arrangement that has no mechanisms for dealing with local defections would be extremely fragile.

INSTITUTIONAL APPROACHES

To use the term "institutional" today is to evoke a host of competing conceptions about what institutions are and how they function.[66] First, there is the old (but still alive) institutional economics of John Commons, Clarence Ayers, and Thorstein Veblen.[67] Second, there is the much more recent "new institutionalism" of neoclassical economics, sometimes called "the new economics of organization." This approach, which highlights principal-agent problems and focuses on transaction costs, is discussed in the writings of Douglass North and Oliver Williamson.[68] Third, there is the "new institutionalism" of political science described by James March and Johan Olsen.[69] Proponents of this third approach argue for the relative autonomy of political institutions and the importance of beliefs and norms.

The three institutional approaches are not carbon copies or modified versions of one another. They often differ in philosophical assumptions, core theoretical concerns, research programs, and method. The institutionalism of Commons, Ayers, and Veblen looks to Charles Pearce for his theory of semiotics and to German historicists such as Dilthey.[70] The new economics of organization, tracing its roots to Ronald Coase's 1937 article entitled "The Nature of the Firm," interprets economic institutions as reducing transaction costs involved in certain types of market exchange.[71] The institutionalism of March and Olsen reclaims parts of a much older political science tradition while enriching it theoretically through insights drawn from organization theory and the work of recent social scientists such as Theda Skocpol, Stephen Krasner, and Peter Katzenstein.[72]

I will first describe the major components of the institutional approach employed here and then try to draw out some implications for multilateralism. What I describe borrows selectively from the three approaches discussed above, but the final version is not reducible to any one of them.

The starting point for wanting to develop an institutional paradigm is a dissatisfaction with rational choice, pluralist, and international systemic approaches to international relations theory.[73] Individualistic rational choice approaches focus on individuals attempting to maximize their utility functions. Pluralist approaches view policies and behavior as results of the pulling and hauling of pressure groups, and international systemic approaches explain the range of state options in terms of variations in international structure. All of these approaches are valuable in their own right yet are inadequate for understanding multilateral cooperation. Most choice-theoretic approaches take preferences and rules as given, neglecting the ways in which institutions shape preferences. International systemic approaches help us understand how states overcome collective action problems. They tell us, given a particular constellation of interests,[74] whether a cooperative solution is likely. But they tell us little about the content of that solution.[75] Pluralism, in its traditional versions at least, provides a good account of the social forces underlying decision making, but it treats political institutions as transmission belts conveying demands through the policy process rather than as independent variables in their own right.

These dissatisfactions set the stage for the institutional approach outlined here. I argue that there are three crucial components of the approach. The first is ontological and relates to the status of entities, particularly individual agents and institutions. The second is theoretical and is concerned with the specification of the proper relations among preferences, institutions, norms, and ideas. The third is interpretive and has to do with how we are to understand cooperation.

Ontologically, the institutional approach accepts elements of methodological holism.[76] While the debate regarding whether groups (or individuals) are "real" is singularly unproductive, the issue of which levels of organized complexity "count" is not unimportant. The institutional approach assumes that enduring structures and patterns of rule are important. It seeks to explain individual behavior by reference to "institutional facts" rather than to characteristics of individuals per se. This statement often prompts confusion, since it suggests to some that institutional explanations involve an overriding of rational choice (or intentional) explanations by anonymous institutional forces. I argue that this is not the proper way to understand the relationship between "micro" and "macro" in institutional theory. Institutional theory is not primarily about nonrational, habit-driven, unthinking behavior. It is mostly about quite purposeful, goal-oriented behavior in which the identities, preferences, beliefs, and behavior of microunits are given a structural determination.

The institutional approach attaches primacy to institutions, norms, and roles that shape and constrain, as well as facilitate, certain kinds of activity.[77] While the individual enters the world with numerous options, the structure of choice and certain persistent configurations of choice are part of the "given" environment. The individual may provide the micro-component of institutional theory, but social relations and institutions are not seen as products of freely choosing individuals; instead, agency is given a structural determination.

The strong version of this structural determination argument is that individual actions merely "instantiate" the reproduction of structure.[78] The subjects of structural analysis are particular roles and locations that are "executed" and "occupied" by agents. Structures are deemed to be the appropriate focus because they are more durable than individuals and because they preserve consistent properties in the face of greater variety among their occupants. A less extreme version of the structural determination argument is that structures "loosely determine," "condition," or "establish boundaries" within which actions transpire. Individual agents have some room to maneuver, some space within which to exercise choice, but the boundaries are controlled by underlying structures. This less extreme version allows for a compromise between the view that institutions are by-products of individual utilitarian calculations and the opposite view that normatively oriented individual agents mindlessly reproduce structures. Institutions are treated as a level of organized complexity: they are distinct from the sum of individuals composing them, yet they rest on a basis of human actions that are continually contested, are only partly propelled by norms and role expectations, and always reflect a tension between the desires of individuals and the needs of institutions.[79] An institution is no more unproblematic than an autonomous individual. As Ruggie argues, the "collective situation" must continually be "negotiated by the parties concerned."[80]

The second major claim of institutionalism concerns the relationships among preferences, norms, and beliefs. The approach requires us to rethink the conventional relationships. We can begin by viewing the question or relationships as a type of causal question: Which variable is most important? The basic conceptual issues are then resolved. What remains is to estimate the parameters and determine the share of the variance attributable to each factor. It is important to recognize that both preferences and norms can function as motives, with beliefs supplying information about how to relate means to ends. Both neoclassical economics and realist international relations theory approach their explanatory questions in similar ways. Agents (individuals, states) have preferences (or national interests) and act on them with resources (endowments, national capabilities) at hand. The economic equation is more complete, since it deals with technology (which concerns ideas about combining factor inputs) and offers some insight into decision making in the face of risk and uncertainty. Realist international relations theory provides almost nothing in terms of rigorous theory and research about beliefs.[81] However, international relations scholars outside the realist school are contributing to our knowledge of how ideas and beliefs affect outcomes.[82]

For the kind of institutionalism proposed here, the relative importance of norms, preferences, and beliefs is of less concern than the question of which of these factors are taken as exogenous and which are taken as endogenous. Conventional rational choice models in neoclassical economics start with exogenous preferences, a given distribution of endowments, and a given technology. The behavior of agents is explained by showing that they are responsive to changes in costs and benefits at the margin. In the institutional approach, however, norms, beliefs, and rules occupy a more central position. Individuals come to politics not only with preferences for particular outcomes but also with shared and divisive values and variously developed beliefs about the political process. In addition, politics and individual preferences undergo change: not only do individuals "act out" their preferences politically, but as March and Olsen point out, the political process is a forum within which their preferences and beliefs change "as in the rest of life, through a combination of education, indoctrination, and experiences."[83]

Institutions are thought to be important with respect to preferences, beliefs, and norms in numerous ways. They help shape preferences by changing the payoff matrix (for example, making it easier to punish free riders and defectors within an institutional context) and by offering an environment in which socialization and learning can occur. The continuous contact, exchange of information, and education about various cognitive styles that take place within multilateral institutions serve to alter perceptions about both the content and the means to achieve private interests. In addition to altering preferences, institutions provide information, increase trust, and reduce uncertainty about the actions of others.

By so doing, they increase the capacity of separate agents to achieve interdependent goals by easing coordination problems. Finally, institutions promote the adherence to norms. In the institutional approach norms are not treated as utilities (or as second-order utilities) but as prescriptions lying outside of preference structures. The content of norms has less to do with what agents want concretely than with how they ought to behave in certain situations and what goals they ought to pursue. The UN prohibition on the use of force to acquire territory, people, or resources is a norm. It proscribes the use of force for these ends, even though such ends are represented in the preference schedules of some decision makers.

The third major component of the institutional approach has to do with the proper way to understand cooperation. According to individualist theories, such as neorealism, cooperation is as an outgrowth of individual desires, capacities, and choices. Cooperation is instrumental. While the social atoms of neoclassical economics are individuals, the primitive social units of realism and neorealism are states. These states and their identities and ends are instrumentally defined as separate from the institutions of international society. As Alexander Wendt and Raymond Duvall point out, this has important consequences: "The predominance of neorealism in contemporary international relations theory, with its focus on the conscious choices of self-interested actors, has meant that the story of international institutions and order is currently being told overwhelmingly in terms of the strategic problem of constructing 'cooperation under anarchy' rather than in terms of an international society, albeit an essentially anarchical one." [84]

Institutional theorists see complex patterns of cooperation already embedded within states and the interstate system. There are shared elements of international society (such as common language and norms), diplomatic rules prescribing how states should represent themselves, and rules implied by the very concept of sovereignty. Yet sovereignty, as several have pointed out, is a concept that is laden with social meaning and rests on rules about mutual reconciliation, noninterference in domestic affairs, and rights of foreign diplomats. [85]

The social conception of the interstate system implies a different understanding of cooperation. The fundamental starting point is not atomistic interaction within anarchy. The basic question is not how to cooperate and to derive rules, norms, and sociality from a rule-free, normless state of nature. Rather, the starting point is a social conception of the actors, and the basic questions have to do with how the system of states can reproduce itself, what tensions it incorporates, and what capacity it has for altering its structures and rules to deal with changing environmental pressures.

To summarize the above discussion, proponents of the institutional approach do not view rules, norms, and habits of cooperation exclusively as something external to agents (states), something that agents "bump into" or "run up against" as they interact with one another. Instead, they recognize that these practices are often constitutive of the identities and power of agents in the first place. They also recognize that institutions are not necessarily chosen on a rational basis but instead are the products (residual products) of unconscious trial-and-error activity, coupled with selective pressures in the environment. Whether this unconscious activity is at the cultural level of developing shared symbols and meaning or is hard-wired into states themselves is beyond the scope of this article. However, both conceptions of rules have their advocates.[86]

I have proposed three core principles of institutionalism, the first one ontological, the second theoretical, and the third interpretive. These principles have important implications for how institutionalists identify questions concerning multilateralism, the method of analysis, and the substantive core of their research program.

The core question is decidedly not the state of nature problématique. The "problem of cooperation" is not representable primarily as a game of strategic interaction, although this dimension of interstate behavior surely exists. The emphasis shifts from strategic interaction with given (and fixed) utilities to a model of debate, communication, persuasion, argument, and discursive legitimation. Indeed, as Friedrich Kratochwil notes, "Most of our arguments concerning policy or rights are not so much about the determination of the likely result, given a certain distribution of 'preferences,' as they are debates over which preferences deserve priority over others, which ones ought to be changed, and which judgements deserve our assent. Here the overall persuasive 'weight' of claims rather than their logical necessity or aggregation is at issue."[87]

The international system, then, is not just a collection of independent states in interaction. Sovereignty is not a concept that is sensibly applied to a single state or to numerous states in isolation from one another. It is inherently a relational concept. Multilateralism as an organizing principle would have to focus on the constitutive principles of the state system and to draw out its implicit and sometimes hidden sociality. With respect to multilateral activity, institutionalists heavily emphasize the discursive, deliberative, and persuasive aspects of communication and argument.

The interstate system is a forum as well as a chessboard, and its actors debate, argue, and justify as well as signal moves.

Another implication of institutionalism runs along methodological lines. This implication is clarified by contrasting the institutional approach presented here with economic theories of institutions in the Coase-Williamson tradition. The analytic starting point of the institutional approach requires, in addition to data about power and interests, some extant institutional data, including data about rules, social structures, values, and common understandings that are "historically given." Economic theories of institutions stress the overall fit of institutions to the environment. The emergence of and changes in organizations are efficient responses to environmental challenges.[88] Institutional arguments often stress the contingent, path-dependent nature of institutional change. These arguments generally assume a narrative form in which timing and sequences matter.

These two different approaches suggest two different views of history.[89] The economic orientation relies on efficiency and has an equifinal structure. Institutions may offer some frictional resistance, but in the end they can be incorporated into the general equilibrium model of allocative efficiency.[90] In addition, the model suggests similar (if not uniform) institutional outcomes. Given the starting point described in terms of preferences, endowments, technology, and transaction costs, analysts can predict outcomes, including institutional outcomes. Since the environment in which economic institutions operate is competitive, there are strong selective pressures toward institutional homogeneity. Thus, it does not matter much where the analyst starts and what sequences occur. Institutions respond to changes in the major independent variables independently of the sequences in which they occur. The method of comparative statics drives out narrative. By contrast, the institutional approach is more attuned to variations in initial conditions and to the sequences in which particular events and processes occur. It speaks the language of eras, conjunctures, and historically produced choices. At the microlevel, individuals may still be described in instrumental terms, but their future choices, their perceptions of what is possible, and their beliefs and standard operating procedures are products of past historical choices.

The paradigms of the first, or functional, approach are modernization theory and economic theories of history in which efficiency considerations determine outcomes. An example of the second, or path-dependence, approach is Alexander Gerschenkron's theory, which emphasizes how important the timing of entry into the international market is for development, particularly as it relates to the role of the state in the economy.[91] The stress on historical contingency and path-dependent behavior suggests that many different institutional worlds are possible. What we observe at any point in time is not necessarily efficient (compared with what might have been chosen had other historical contingencies intervened). There is even less reason for believing that uniformity of institutional outcomes is likely, since the model producing these outcomes is highly sensitive to minor variations in its parameters and thus does not have robust properties.

These two views of history have implications for our understanding of the multilateral organization of our contemporary world. Although social scientists do not like to engage explicitly in counterfactuals, it is necessary to do so. To say that something occurred the way it did because of x implies that things would have been different in the absence of x. To pose the issue in this way prompts us to ask several questions: Is multilateralism an inevitable organizational form of the modern state system? Is it the institution that would be recreated if we could replay history with a number of different initial conditions, choice points, and historical trajectories? For example, what would have happened, Ruggie asks, if Germany had prevailed in World War II?[92] Would Schactian bilateralism have been discarded in favor of multilateralism? The apparent differences among the ideas of prewar Germany, postwar Japan, the Soviet Union, and the United States with respect to organizing the world political economy should at least give pause. There is a research program implied by the institutional approach. It is reflected in the numerous puzzles and theoretical challenges suggested by the approach, in the unanswered questions regarding the importance of norms and beliefs, in the tough transition from assumption to theory regarding the independent importance of the institutional level of analysis, and in the task of developing rigorous methodologies to explore theoretical issues historically, as I have used that term in this chapter.

In this research program, norms, ideas, and social purposes will occupy a central location. Mainstream international relations theory relies heavily on power, interest, and anarchy for its explanatory foundation. Indeed, since interest (national interest) is partly determined by the structure of the international system (anarchy and the distribution of power), only two factors can independently vary. Scholars such as John Ruggie, Hayward Alker, and Richard Ashley want to question this paradigm.[93] Ruggie does not accept accounts of regimes that rest on power distribution explanations only. The concentration of power may make it easier to solve collective action problems, but it tells us nothing about the content of the regime. For this, we must introduce ideas, norms, and social purposes.

The institutionalist research program is already being carried out, although not all scholars would subscribe to the label, nor would they necessarily comply with all of the components of the program elaborated here. Ernst Haas's work on the importance of consensual knowledge, common beliefs, learning, and perceptual change in international organizational environments is exemplary.[94] Working within a domestic context, Judith Goldstein has tried to demonstrate how key norms and ideas about free trade have been incorporated into national laws and institutions.[95] The transfer of responsibility for commercial policy from the legislative to the executive branch, the evolution of the International Trade Commission, and the distancing of trade policy from public opinion have all served to preserve free trade, despite periods of high protectionist demands. Goldstein's work shows that multilateralism is not just an international affair; it has crucial domestic components as well. Finally, Alexander Wendt's work focuses on the ways in which power politics, generally taken as an unproblematic given of the modern world, is a construction owing much to processes of socialization, learning, and cognitive change.[96] Our present international system is not eternal; it has a history, and it has a future that we are ill-equipped to theorize, given the static nature of many of our theories.

Conclusion

The basic argument of this chapter builds on the premise that multilateralism has been relatively neglected in international relations theory. While multilateral organizations and practices have been examined empirically, their sources have not been the subject of much concern in realist and neorealist theory. Part of the neglect stems from an implicit ontology that takes states as the social atoms of international society and explores how their interaction might support large-member organizational forms.

An important debate in international relations is taking place between proponents of rationalist theory, which is exemplified by neorealism, and proponents of reflectivism, which is closer to institutionalism as described in this chapter.[97] Both groups are interested in explaining the sociality of states—that is, the manner in which states acknowledge membership in and contribute to international society. However, each addresses the sociality of states in a different way.

The theoretical project launched by the neorealists involves the demonstration that cooperative behavior among many players can emerge as a result of self-interested strategic interactions and can do so within a class of games that is itself noncooperative in its paucity of communications, trust, and third-party enforcement. This is not a project that is doomed to failure. Some significant advances have been made.[98] In addition, there are some research programs broadly related to neorealism that have not been explored here. Theories of public goods could be examined to see if the scope of externalities might provide insight into the question of the generality of cooperation. The economic theory of clubs, which deals with impure public goods and congestion effects, could be examined with the same question in mind.[99] And the bodies of literature on tactical and party linkages have not been explored for the returns they might offer.

There are limitations to neorealist approaches, however. Neorealism underestimates the extent to which cooperation depends on a prior set of unacknowledged claims about the embeddedness of cooperative habits, shared values, and taken-for-granted rules. Further, its assumption that preferences are exogenously given reduces multilateralism to a question of strategic interaction, making it difficult to comprehend multilateralism propelled by collective beliefs, presumptive habits, and shared values. Finally, the absence of a historical (narrative) approach discourages the exploration of counterfactuals and lends support to the view that arrangements including institutional arrangements, are what they are either because they represent functional responses to environmental challenges or because they reflect the prevailing power distribution.

Reflectivists reject the state of nature as the appropriate starting point even for heuristic purposes. If states are characterized only by interests and strategies, cooperative outcomes will not occur. Shared understandings regarding the rules of the game, the nature of permissible plays, the linkages between choices and outcomes, and the nature of agents involved in the game are important preconditions. To say this is to acknowledge that shared understandings and communicative rationality are as important as instrumental rationality.[100]

Instead of deriving sociality from the state of nature, the task of reflectionists is to show how socially defined states, operating within given institutional sites, engage in behavior that is both competitive and cooperative. The problem is how to explain institutions and sociality given some data on extant and prior institutions and sociality. Thus, in trying to deal with the problem of the distribution of wealth internationally, Naeem Inayatullah starts from a conception of state sovereignty that is highly social in its mutual recognition and ongoing practices.[101] The work of Robert Jackson is also exemplary of the tradition in which the social aspects of state sovereignty are taken seriously.[102]

In summary, I have premised this chapter on a broad correspondence between individualist, instrumental approaches and neorealism on the one hand and between institutional approaches and reflectivism on the other. Without rejecting individualist, instrumental approaches, I have tried to identify the limits of their usefulness and to open up a theoretical space for institutional analysis. While an institutional approach to multilateralism should not banish individuals, intentional behavior, and strategic interaction, it highlights different things. It departs from the preference-action paradigm by introducing structure and behavior that draw on habitual, preconscious, taken-for-granted understandings. As such, the institutional approach "defocalizes interest."[103] It might try to understand the emergence of multilateralism as a product of the power, resources, and beliefs of important actors and the reproduction of multilateral institutions in terms of organizational inertia, socialization to system norms, and adaptation to the "needs of the institution."

All three approaches examined here—the individualist, social-communicative, and institutional approaches—are only partly worked out, particularly in their relation to multilateralism. None by itself is a panacea. The questions addressed are big ones, sometimes even daunting. But the promise is considerable, too. Hopefully, this chapter has identified some of the tasks and pointed to the challenges and difficulties on the way ahead.

NOTES

1. Assar Lindbeck, "Economic Dependence and Interdependence in the Industrialized World," *From Marshall Plan to Global Interdependence* (Paris: Organization for Economic Cooperation and Development, 1978), pp. 59–86.

2. Thorold Masefield, "Co-prosperity and Co-security: Managing the Developed World," *International Affairs* (Winter 1988–89) 65:11–14.

3. William A. Niskanen, "The Bully of World Trade," *Orbis* (Fall 1989) 33:531–38.

4. Inis L. Claude, Jr., "The Balance of Power Revisited," *Review of International Studies* (April 1989) 15:77–86.

5. A. Emmanuel, *Unequal Exchange: A Study in the Imperialism of Trade* (New York: Monthly Review Press, 1972).

6. Indeed, this is precisely what Robert O. Keohane does in *After Hegemony: Cooperation and Discord in the World Political Economy* (Princeton, N.J.: Princeton University Press, 1984).

7. See the following works of John Gerard Ruggie: "Unravelling the World Order: The United States and the Future of Multilateralism," mimeograph, University of California, San Diego, 1989; and "Multilateralism: The Anatomy of an Institution," *International Organization* (Summer 1992) 46(3).

8. See Ruggie, "Multilateralism."

9. For a discussion of diffuse reciprocity, see Robert O. Keohane, "Reciprocity in International Relations," *International Organization* (Winter 1986): 1–27.

10. Lisa L. Martin, "Interests, Power, and Multilateralism," this volume, and *International Organization, 46*, forthcoming.

11. See the following works of Ernst B. Haas: *Beyond the Nation-State* (Stanford: Stanford University Press, 1964); *When Knowledge is Power: Three Models of Change in International Relations* (Berkeley: University of California Press, 1990).

12. Ibid.

13. For a discussion of this aspect of Monnet's philosophy of transnational cooperation, see Jean Monnet, *Memoirs,* trans. Richard Mayne (London: Collins, 1978).

14. See Ruggie, "Multilateralism."

15. Ibid.

16. For creative theoretical suggestions along these lines see Martin, "Interests, Power, and Multilateralism"; and Robert O. Keohane, "Multilateralism: An Agenda for Research," *International Journal* (Fall 1990) 45:731–64.

17. See Joseph E. Harrington, Jr., "Noncooperative Games," In John Eatwell, Murray Milgate, and Peter Newman, eds., *Game Theory* (New York: Norton, 1989), pp. 178–84.

18. I understand that the assumptions I have used to characterize the individualist approach can be, and have been, relaxed in both international relations theory proper and game theory. My approach here is a device used to see how far this simplified model can take us.

19. Kenneth A. Oye, "Explaining Cooperation Under Anarchy: Hypotheses and Strategies," *World Politics* (1985) 38:1–24.

20. For the logic behind this approach, see David Kreps and Robert Wilson, "Reputation and Imperfect Information," *Journal of Economic Theory* (August 1982) 26:253–79; and David Kreps, Paul Milgrom, and Robert Wilson, "Rational Cooperation in the Finitely Repeated Prisoners' Dilemma," *Journal of Economic Theory* (August 1982) 27:245–52.

21. See Russell Hardin, *Collective Action* (Baltimore, Md.: Johns Hopkins

University Press, 1982); and Michael Taylor, *The Possibility of Cooperation* (Cambridge: Cambridge University Press, 1987).

22. Keohane, *After Hegemony,* p. 75.

23. Robert Axelrod, "The Emergence of Cooperation Among Egoists," *American Political Science Review* (June 1981), 75:306–18.

24. Rudolph Schuessler, "Exit Threats and Cooperation Under Anonymity," *Journal of Conflict Resolution* (1989) 33(4):728–49.

25. Taylor, *The Possibility of Cooperation,* p. 83.

26. Ibid., p. 105.

27. Ibid.

28. Douglass C. North, "Transaction Costs, Institutions, and Economic History," *Journal of Institutional and Theoretical Economics* (1984) 140:7–17.

29. Here, I am speaking of rewards and penalties resulting from different moves within the game, not from resources outside the game. The latter would amount to an enforcement mechanism.

30. Taylor, *The Possibility of Cooperation,* p. 105.

31. Ibid.

32. Ruggie, "Unravelling the World Order," pp. 26–27.

33. Keohane, *After Hegemony,* p. 90.

34. Ibid.

35. Martin, "Interests, Power, and Multilateralism."

36. Ibid.

37. Beth V. Yarbrough and Robert M. Yarbrough, "Reciprocity, Bilateralism, and Economic 'Hostages': Self-enforcing Agreements in International Trade." *International Studies Quarterly* (March 1986)30:7–8.

38. See, for example, Schuessler, "Exit Threats and Cooperation Under Anonymity."

39. James K. Sebenius, "Negotiation Arithmetic: Adding and Subtracting Issues and Parties," *International Organization* (Spring 1983) 37:281–316.

40. John M. Orbell, Robyn M. Dawes, and Alphonse van de Kragt, "The Limits of Multilateral Promising," *Ethics* (April 1991) 100:616–27.

41. Taylor, *The Possibility of Cooperation,* p. 82.

42. Jon Elster, "The Market and the Forum: Three Varieties of Poiltical Theory," in Jon Elster and Aamund Hylland, eds., *Foundations of Social Choice Theory* (Cambridge: Cambridge University Press, 1986), pp. 103–32.

43. Anatol Rapoport, *Fights, Games, and Debates* (Ann Arbor: University of Michigan Press, 1960).

44. See Joseph Farrell, "Communication, Coordination and Nash Equilibrium," *Economic Letters* (1988) 27:209. If there is only one Nash equilibrium, the equilibrium outcome might result without communication. I am indebted to Richard Sherman for this point.

45. John M. Orbell, Alphons van de Kragt, and Robyn M. Dawes, "Explaining Discussion-Induced Behavior," *Journal of Personality* (May 1988) 54(5):811.

46. Jeffrey A. Frankel and Katherine E. Rockett, "International Macroeconomic Policy Coordination When Policymakers Do Not Agree on the True Model," *American Economic Review* (June 1988) 78:318–40.

47. Ibid., p. 318.

48. Robert D. Putnam and C. Randall Henning, "The Bonn Summit of 1978: A Case Study in Coordination," in Richard N. Cooper et al., eds., *Can Nations Agree? Issues in International Economic Cooperation* (Washington, D.C.: Brookings Institution, 1989), pp. 12–140.

49. Ibid., p. 13.

50. Ibid., pp. 18–19.

51. Ibid., p. 110.

52. Keohane, *After Hegemony,* p. 31.

53. Barry Eichengreen, "Hegemonic Stability Theories of the International Monetary System," in Cooper et al., *Can Nations Agree?* pp. 255–98.

54. Alphonse van de Kragt, John M. Orbell, and Robyn M. Dawes, "The Minimal Contributing Set as a Solution to Public Goods Problems," *American Political Science Review* (March 1983), (77):112–22.

55. Ibid., p. 114.

56. Ibid., p. 116.

57. See Orbell, et al., "The Limits of Multilateral Promising."

58. Robyn M. Dawes, Alphons van de Kragt, and John M. Orbell, "Not Me or Thee But We: The Importance of Group Identity in Eliciting Cooperation in Dilemma Situations: Experimental Manipulations," *Acta Psychologica* (September 1988) 68:83–97.

59. Ibid., p. 86.

60. Orbell, Dawes, and van de Kragt, "The Limits of Multilateral Promising."

61. Thomas C. Schelling, *The Strategy of Conflict* (New York: Oxford University Press, 1963), pp. 57–58.

62. Orbell, Dawes, and van de Kragt, "The Limits of Multilateral Promising."

63. This does not mean that cooperation does not occur in this region. It just means that there are no significant differences in cooperation across groups that promise (short of universal promising) and groups that do not.

64. Orbell, Dawes, and van de Kragt, "The Limits of Multilateral Promising." p. 265.

65. Ibid., p. 265.

66. The contemporary literature on institutions is voluminous and growing rapidly. For an overview of one kind of "new institutionalism," see James G. March and Johan P. Olsen, "The New Institutionalism: Organizational Factors in Political Life," *American Political Science Review* 78 (September 1984), pp. 734–49. For an overview of recent work in international relations, see Robert O. Keohane, "International Institutions: Two Approaches," *International Studies Quarterly* (December 1988) 32:379–96. My use of the term "institutional" does

not exactly replicate the usage of any single approach. Yet it draws heavily on John Ruggie for his emphasis on ideas and norms, on Stephen Krasner for his notions of path-dependence, and on Robert Keohane for his arguments about the ways in which institutions shape incentives.

67. For a description of this approach, see the special issue of *Journal of Economic Issues,* vol. 21, no. 3, September 1987.

68. See Douglass C. North, *Structure and Change in Economic History* (New York: Norton, 1981); North, "Transaction Costs, Institutions, and Economic History"; Oliver Williamson, *Markets and Hierarchies: Analysis and Antitrust Implications* (New York: Free Press, 1975); and Oliver Williamson, *The Economic Institutions of Capitalism* (New York: Free Press, 1985).

69. See March and Olsen, "The New Institutionalism."

70. See Philip Mirowski, "The Philosophical Bases of Institutionalist Economics," *Journal of Economic Issues* (September 1987) 21:1001–37.

71. See Ronald H. Coase, "The Nature of the Firm," *Economica,* vol. 4, 1937; reprinted in Ronald H. Coase, *The Firm, the Market, and the Law* (Chicago: University of Chicago Press, 1988), pp. 33–55.

72. See Theda Skocpol, *States and Social Revolutions* (Cambridge: Cambridge University Press, 1979); Stephen D. Krasner, *Defending the National Interest: Raw Materials Investment and U.S. Foreign Policy* (Princeton, N.J.: Princeton University Press, 1978); and Peter J. Katzenstein, "Introduction: Domestic and International Forces and Strategies of Foreign Economic Policy," in Peter J. Katzenstein, ed., *Between Power and Plenty* (Madison: University of Wisconsin Press, 1978), pp. 3–22.

73. For a similar, but not identical, motivation, see G. John Ikenberry, David A. Lake, and Michael Mastanduno, "Introduction: Approaches to Explaining Foreign Economic Policy," *International Organization* (Winter 1988) 42(1):1–14.

74. This is not a trivial point. It is one that is passed over too quickly in the collective action literature. This literature, of which hegemonic stability theory is one expression, generally assumes some form of mixed-motive game in which outcomes (payoffs) can be improved through coordination of behavior. That is, it assumes the existence of some contingent pairs of strategies which, if played, will yield better outcomes than the noncoordinated solution would provide. If the structure of interests is zero-sum, a hegemonic distribution of power would have markedly different consequences.

75. Ruggie has made this point numerous times. See John Gerard Ruggie, "International Regimes, Transactions, and Change: Embedded Liberalism in the Postwar Economic Order," *International Organization* (Spring 1982) 36:379–415; and Ruggie, "Multilateralism."

76. Institutional approaches need not be methodologically holist, however. They may be committed to the view that individuals are the ultimate units of society and still treat complex social structures and institutions as describing

important emergent effects. In this sense, the ontological argument is a bit misguided in that it is easy to glide from the ontological position that individuals are the ultimate units to the theoretical position that all causation has an individual locus. I am indebted to discussions with Ronald Jepperson for this point; see his article entitled "Institutions, Institutional Effects, and Institutionalism," in Walter W. Powell and Paul J. DiMaggio, eds., *The New Institutionalism in Organizational Analysis* (Chicago: University of Chicago Press, 1991), pp. 143–63.

77. In "International Institutions," p. 384, Keohane stresses that institutions constrain activity, shape expectations, and prescribe roles.

78. For this viewpoint, see Anthony Giddens, *Central Problems in Social Theory* (Berkeley: University of California Press, 1979), pp. 49–95.

79. The phrase "the needs of institutions" may raise some eyebrows, especially for methodological individualists. What I have in mind here is not some reified entity with motives similar to individuals. What I am thinking of is simply types of organized complexity that may be quite important for a collectivity even though they are unimportant or perhaps damaging for the individual. Complex divisions of labor may be alienating for the individual but crucial for societal survival. Hierarchy may be undesirable for everyone in the firm yet necessary for competitive profit levels. The theoretical source supporting this viewpoint is evolutionary theory where the forces operating on institutions are selective pressures in the environment. Thus, institutional decline, survival, and change can be seen as results of a blind trial-and-error model with selective winnowing by environmental forces.

80. John Gerard Ruggie, "International Responses to Technology: Concepts and Trends," *International Organization* (Summer 1975) 36(2):567.

81. In referring to realist international relations theory here, I am not including the literature on psychological images, cognitive structures and perception, and perceptual distortion in crisis decision making. Without devaluing this literature, it strikes me that its purpose is more to identify the sources of perceptual distortion than to argue how better means-ends knowledge or alternative interpretive models can facilitate cooperative outcomes.

82. See, for example, Peter M. Haas, "Do Regimes Matter? Epistemic Communities and Mediterranean Pollution Control," *International Organization* (Summer 1989) 43:377–403; Judith Goldstein, "The Impact of Ideas on Trade Policy: The Origins of U.S. Agricultural and Manufacturing Policies," *International Organization* (Winter 1989) 43:31–71; and Emmanuel Adler, *The Power of Ideology* (Berkeley: University of California Press, 1987).

83. March and Olsen, "The New Institutionalism," p. 739.

84. Alexander Wendt and Raymond Duvall, "Institutions and International Order," in Ernst-Otto Czempiel and James N. Rosenau, eds., *Global Changes and Theoretical Challenges* (Lexington, Mass.: D. C. Heath, 1989), p. 59.

85. See Keohane, "International Institutions"; Friedrich V. Kratochwil, *Rules,*

Norms and Decisions (Cambridge: Cambridge University Press, 1989); and Robert H. Jackson, "Quasi-States, Dual Regimes, and Neoclassical Theory: International Jurisprudence and the Third World," *International Organization* (Autumn 1987) 41:519–49.

86. The work of Richard Ashley and Friedrich Kratochwil seems to be grounded in culturally acquired norms and practices. According to Hayek's conception of rules, however, our rule-based behavior has its origins in evolutionary processes and is the result of blind trial and error and selective retention. Consequently, rules are arrived at unconsciously and are "hard-wired" in the biological organism, at least in part. For a discussion of Hayek's theory of rules, see Anna Elizabeth Galeotti, "Individualism, Social Rules, Tradition: The Case of Friedrich A. Hayek," *Political Theory* (May 1987) 15:163–81.

87. Kratochwil, *Rules, Norms and Decisions,* p. 12.

88. See Charles Perrow, "Economic Theories of Organization," in Sharon Zukin and Paul DiMaggio, eds., *Structures of Capital: The Social Organizaiton of the Economy* (Cambridge: Cambridge University Press, 1990), p. 128.

89. See James A. Caporaso, "Introduction: The State in Comparative and International Perspective," in James A. Caporaso, ed., *The Elusive State: International and Comparative Perspectives* (Newbury Park, Calif.: Sage, 1989), p. 12.

90. For an important exception, see Douglass C. North, "Institutions and Their Consequences for Economic Performance," in Karen Schweers Cook and Margaret Levi, eds., *The Limits of Rationality* (Chicago: University of Chicago Press, 1990), pp. 383–401. On p. 392 of this chapter, North recognizes that the neoclassical economics literature on institutions focuses primarily on institutions as efficient solutions to problems of economic organization.

91. Alexander Gerschenkron, *Economic Backwardness in Historical Perspective* (Cambridge, Mass.: Belknap, 1962).

92. See Ruggie, "Multilateralism."

93. See Ruggie, "International Regimes, Transactions, and Change;" Hayward R. Alker, Jr., "The Presumption of Anarchy in International Relations," mimeograph, Massachusetts Institute of Technology, Cambridge, MA; and Richard Ashley, "The Poverty of Neorealism," in Robert O. Keohane, ed., *Neorealism and Its Critics* (New York: Columbia University Press, 1986), pp. 255–300.

94. See the following works of Ernst B. Haas: *Beyond the Nation-State; Tangle of Hopes: American Commitments and World Order* (Englewood Cliffs, N.J.: Prentice-Hall, 1969); and *When Knowledge Is Power.*

95. Judith Goldstein, "Ideas, Institutions, and American Trade Policy," *International Organization* (Winter 1988), 42:179–217.

96. Alexander Wendt, "Sovereignty and the Social Construction of Power Politics," paper presented at the annual meeting of the International Studies Association, Washington, D.C., 1990.

97. See Keohane, "International Institutions."

98. See Taylor, *The Possibility of Cooperation;* and Schuessler, "Exit Threats and Cooperation Under Anonymity."

99. See Todd Sandler and John T. Tschirhart, "The Economic Theory of Clubs: An Evaluative Survey," *Journal of Economic Literature* (December 1980) 18:1481–1521.

100. See Hayward R. Alker, Jr., "Rescuing 'Reason' from the 'Rationalists': Reading Vico, Marx, and Weber as Reflective Institutionalists," mimeograph, Massachusetts Institute of Technology, Cambridge, 1990, p. 10.

101. Naeem Inayatullah, "Redefining Sovereignty," paper presented at the annual meeting of the American Political Science Association, San Francisco, 1990.

102. See the following works of Robert H. Jackson: "Quasi-States, Dual Regimes, and Neoclassical Theory"; and "Negative Sovereignty in Sub-Saharan Africa," *Review of International Studies* (October 1986) 12:247–64.

103. Paul DiMaggio, "Interest and Agency in Institutional Theory," in Lynne G. Zucker, ed., *Institutional Patterns and Organizations: Culture and Environment* (Cambridge, Mass.: Ballinger, 1988), p. 3.

3. The Rational State Choice of Multilateralism

Lisa L. Martin

S TATES can choose from a wide array of organizing forms, including multilateralism, as patterns by which to organize interactions among themselves. The papers in this volume explore situations in which states have used varying degrees of multilateralism to structure their relations. Some of these studies argue that functional theories cannot explain when governments adopt multilateral norms and organizations.[1] At some level of empirical detail this is surely correct, if for no other reason than the high levels of uncertainty that surround the construction of new institutions. However, the argument of this paper is that studies of state choice can achieve high payoffs by giving serious consideration to functional-contractual arguments that see institutions as a solution to dilemmas of strategic interaction.[2]

Without such consideration, the inadequacy of functional arguments remains an assumption rather than an empirical conclusion. Explanations based on the role of ideas, domestic politics, or any other set of factors cannot establish their analytic superiority over structural explanations until the constraints and incentives arising from strategic interaction are taken into account. I argue here that consideration of the power and interests of state actors in different situations leads to hypotheses about the "form of successful cooperation,"[3] or modal tendencies in the types of norms and organizations that states create to facilitate pursuit of their interests.

I refer to the "institution of multilateralism" as defined by John Ruggie in the introduction to this volume. According to this definition, the institution of multilateralism consists of the three principles of indivisibility, generalized organizing principles (nondiscrimination), and diffuse reciprocity. In this paper, I ask about the instrumental value of

My thanks to Robert Keohane as well as the participants in this project for their valuable comments on this research.

multilateral norms under different configurations of state interests, i.e., in different types of "cooperation problems." The cases examined in this volume demonstrate that state officials believed multilateralism was a valuable means of reaching goals such as liberalization of the international trading system, the security of Western Europe, and economic growth. By treating multilateralism as a means rather than a goal, we open the possibility that alternative organizing devices will be equal or superior in their utility for reaching higher level ends such as liberalization. The choice of tools depends, at least in part, on the configuration of state power and interests in particular issue areas. Thus, I assume that states are self-interested and turn to multilateralism only if it serves their purposes, whatever these may be.

A belief in the utility of multilateralism was expressed after World War II in a drive to create issue-specific organizations as well as a general-purpose organization, the United Nations. In general, multilateral organizations make decisions on a multilateral basis; no small group of members is privileged to make decisions for the others. However, we see a great deal of variation in the degree to which actual organizations conform to the norms of multilateralism. This paper attempts to explain variation in their organizing principles and strength on the basis of the strategic problems facing states. In addition, it suggests hypotheses about relationships among norms, formal organizations, and behavioral outcomes.

The first section of this paper discusses a typology of cooperation problems and the potential role of the institution of multilateralism (IM) and multilateral organizations (MO) in helping states overcome these problems. Each of four ideal types of cooperation problems—collaboration, coordination, suasion, and assurance—presents states with unique challenges. In some, the functions performed by formal organizations, such as monitoring and enforcement, will be essential to the achievement of cooperation. In others, multilateral norms such as nondiscrimination will be more efficient. This consideration illuminates the functional considerations behind alternative institutional solutions for different types of games.

However, at this abstract level of analysis the outcomes remain indeterminate. Multiple feasible solutions exist for each problem. For example, states can achieve coordination in a game of common aversions through either multilateral discussion and notification of intentions or the establishment of a focal point by a dominant player. Therefore, the second section of this paper attempts to decrease the level of uncertainty by taking into consideration two elements of international structure in the postwar era: U.S. hegemony within the Western subsystem and the bipolar distribution of power in the international system as a whole. These factors lead us to consider the strengths and weaknesses of multilateralism from the hegemon's point of view and the impact of a bipolar security structure on relations embedded within this structure.

The first two sections of this paper adopt the approach of comparative statics to develop expectations about the role of norms and organizations. The third introduces a dynamic element to the analysis by asking about changes in institutions in the face of changing distributions of power and other exogenous changes. Some solutions to cooperation problems are preferable to others because certain structures can adapt to changes in relative power; this feature is one of the key advantages of a multilateral architecture. Other forms of cooperation, such as those based on tactical issue linkages forged by a hegemon, will be brittle and susceptible to challenge as the hegemon declines relative to other members. Changes in the distribution of power can lead to shifts in the kind of game being played, in addition to affecting the outcome within specified games. For example, suasion games will tend to give way to collaboration problems as the distribution of power becomes less asymmetric, with predictable changes in the form of successful cooperation.

In this analysis, I find it useful to differentiate among the role of multilateralism at three separate points in the cooperation process. First is the stage of arriving at decisions. States can reach decisions through genuinely multilateral discussions, a series of bilateral agreements, or the imposition of decisions on a unilateral basis. Second, we need to specify the scope of state decisions. Decisions may apply only to those directly involved in their negotiation or may be extended to a broader range of actors. Finally, norms of multilateralism may apply at the stage of implementation. Central problems at this stage involve the monitoring and enforcement of agreements, and states may utilize mechanisms ranging from highly centralized to completely decentralized to solve them. Multilateral norms may, for example, apply to the scope of agreements but not to their negotiation or enforcement. The questions I address in this paper are about the utility of multilateral norms and organizations at each stage and thus about expectations for the multilateral character of the forums within which specific instances of cooperation are embedded. The conclusions I draw should be seen as hypotheses for purposes of future empirical examination.

Strategic Interaction and Multilateralism

As Ruggie notes in the introduction to this volume, multilateralism is a "highly demanding form." It requires that states sacrifice substantial levels of flexibility in decisionmaking and resist the temptations of short-term gain in the interest of long-term benefits. Therefore, it is unrealistic to expect state behavior to conform to pure multilateralism. Instead, we need to ask about the role IM and MO can play under specified conditions. Here, I suggest that focusing on the fundamental problem of strategic interaction within an issue area provides some answers to questions about the likelihood of successful use of IM and MO.

Drawing on the work of Duncan Snidal, Arthur Stein, and others, I present a simple four-category typology of cooperation problems. Each of these problems—collaboration, coordination, suasion, and assurance—presents unique challenges to states considering cooperation. Thus, they lead to different expectations about the role of norms and organizations. Consideration of the strategic dilemmas underlying particular issue areas in their simplest form suggests particular relationships between IM and MO. In addition, each situation leads to different relations between IM or MO and behavioral outcomes. To some extent, these games represent alternative paradigms in international relations theory. Liberals have often implicitly assumed coordination or assurance games between states. Realism, with its emphasis on power asymmetries, has often assumed something close to a suasion game, while neoliberals have explicitly focused on collaboration problems.

Snidal and Stein differentiate between two prototypical cooperation problems.[4] Snidal refers to these as coordination and Prisoners' Dilemma, while Stein discusses coordination and collaboration. In this paper, I use Stein's terminology, for it is more general than Snidal's. I also argue that two additional game types require consideration. Coordination and collaboration both assume symmetrical interests. In a suasion game, defined below, states have asymmetrical interests, so that the equilibrium outcome leaves one of them dissatisfied. Although analysis have downplayed the significance of regimes or institutions in such asymmetrical situations, I argue that the postwar distribution of power often created precisely this kind of problem and that institutions could, nevertheless, facilitate cooperation. In assurance games, institutions have little to contribute to cooperation under conditions of complete information. However, given the structural uncertainty of international relations, states may find some modest level of institutionalization in these situations conducive to their ability to achieve mutual gains.

COLLABORATION PROBLEMS

Collaboration games are characterized by situations where equilibrium outcomes are suboptimal. These games, and the nature of potential solutions to them, have been the subject of extensive discussion among economists and political scientists, who often consider them "the" collective action problem.[5] Prisoners' Dilemma, as shown in figure 3.1, is the most thoroughly studied collaboration game in the international relations literature.[6]

Figure 3.1. A Collaboration Game (Prisoners' Dilemma)

		B	
		0	1
A	0	3, 3	1, 4
	1	4, 1	2, 2

Resolving the dilemma of collaboration games is a matter of mutual policy adjustment, for both players must agree to move away from the suboptimal equilibrium, rejecting their dominant strategy. Many authors have identified factors that allow states to overcome collaboration problems, which focus on using the proper strategy, extending the shadow of the future, and relying on centralized mechanisms such as formal international organizations. Multilateral organizations can play a role in facilitating cooperation in these types of problems. However, the norms of multilateralism do not meet the demands of collaboration games, leading us to expect divergence between the institution of multilateralism and multilateral organizations in these cases. In the rest of this section, I identify these demands and the ways in which multilateral norms fail to resolve, or may even exacerbate, collaboration dilemmas.

Collaboration problems contain strong incentives to defect from established cooperative patterns of behavior. As discussed below, in coordination games no state has an immediate incentive to defect unilaterally from an established equilibrium. In collaboration, on the other hand, states have strong temptations to defect from a cooperative outcome, since defection results in immediate payoffs. Therefore, mechanisms to promote cooperation must focus on *maintenance* of agreements rather than facilitation of bargaining prior to agreement. As Snidal argues, the need for maintenance mechanisms suggests that solutions to collaboration problems will be centralized, creating a significant role for formal organizations.

Two factors in particular promote cooperation in collaboration games. First, states will demand extensive information on others' behavior, since undetected defection will be costly for those who continue to cooperate and will complicate attempts at retaliation. Thus, we should expect extensive monitoring and assessment of compliance questions in successfully resolved collaboration problems. Such activity contrasts with that in coordination games, where exchange of information should take the form of notification of intentions in order to avoid a mutually disliked outcome. According to the logic of strategic interaction, in collaboration, states will exchange information retrospectively; in coordination, prospectively.

Second, in collaboration, states should search for mechanisms to increase the shadow of the future, in order to ensure that the immediate costs associated with cooperation will be offset by long-run benefits of mutual assistance.[7] Formal organizations can perform such functions.[8] Conventions alone, without monitoring or enforcement, cannot ensure cooperation as they can in coordination cases. The solution to collaboration problems in the absence of a state acting as an entrepreneur and in the presence of large numbers of players requires centralization, leading to expectations of relatively strong formal organizations.

Research on current problems of international cooperation supports the plausibility of this argument. Analyses have suggested that the completion of the internal market in the European Community (EC) can be understood in these terms.[9] The removal of internal trade barriers presents a typical collaboration problem, and the members of the European Community have responded by replacing their previous pattern of bilateral, self-enforcing trade arrangements with third-party enforcement mechanisms on an increasingly large range of issues. As expected, the liberalizing process involves a higher degree of centralization and surrender of individual states' decision-making power than commonly found on coordination issues such as transborder data flows. In fact, the necessary surrender of sovereignty by EC member states has been a significant impediment to rapid movement toward a unified economic region.[9]

This finding about the important role of MO does not, however, extend to the norms of multilateralism. In collaboration problems multilateral norms may complicate attempts to cooperate. The norms of diffuse reciprocity and indivisibility, in particular, are not conducive to the solution of collaboration problems. Theoretical and experimental studies of the repeated Prisoners' Dilemma show the value of strategies of specific reciprocity, such as tit-for-tat and trigger strategies, for maintaining cooperation. Diffuse reciprocity, with its lack of direct retaliation for defections, is unlikely to maintain cooperation effectively in demanding collaboration problems, although it may be efficient in less demanding situations.[10] Under diffuse reciprocity, members rely on generalized norms of obligation to promote cooperation. For states that lack a high level of interdependence with other regime members, obligation may not outweigh the temptation to free ride. In a multilateral organization with a large number of members having diverse interests, the problem of temptations to free ride will become especially acute. Although ongoing mutual cooperation provides long-term benefits, without the threat of specific retaliations, the temptation to cheat in order to maximize immediate payoffs rises substantially. Strict adherence to the norm of diffuse reciprocity, particularly at the enforcement stage, would encourage free riding in collaboration situations. Therefore, beyond mechanisms to increase the sense of obligation among states caught in such a dilemma, we might expect to find some compromise of diffuse reciprocity to allow issue-specific sanctioning of egregious free riders. The General Agreement on Tariffs and Trade (GATT), for example, provides for direct retaliation for unfair trading practices, a clear example of specific reciprocity at the enforcement stage.

Similarly, the multilateral norm of indivisibility is antithetical to the solution of collaboration dilemmas. Indivisibility, when combined with diffuse reciprocity, implies nonexclusion and creates publicness. If all threats and decisions apply equally to all members of the regime, and all members must be treated equally, the regime will create public goods where private goods existed previously. Multilateral security arrangements, for example, make exclusion from protection extremely difficult, for states view a threat to one as a threat to all. Numerous authors have discussed dilemmas of collective choice that arise when dealing with public goods. Strict adherence to multilateral principles, rather than solve such dilemmas, would create public goods from private ones. Regime members, under a strict interpretation of such norms, could not be excluded from benefits created by the regime without compromising the indivisibility and diffuse reciprocity principles. Thus, multilateralism creates huge incentives to free ride.

One way around the dilemma of public goods would involve sacrificing some indivisibility and diffuse reciprocity, making regime benefits excludable. Organizations could sanction states that free ride by denying them "entitlements" according to the norms of the regime. One example of such a compromise occurred during the Tokyo Round in the GATT, when states that refused to sign the government procurement and other protocols were denied the benefits they provided signatories.[11] The previous GATT practice of multilateralism in the scope of agreements was modified, making some regime benefits excludable and contingent on policy commitments. In general, we should expect formal organizations to reflect compromises of the indivisibility and diffuse reciprocity norms to allow privatization of benefits and sanctioning of free riders in collaboration games. As Snidal argues, "The possibility of exclusion will be especially important in mitigating the adverse effects of increased numbers of states on the prospects for international cooperation."[12] Thus, regimes in issue areas characterized by collaboration will likely depart significantly from these two multilateral norms at the scope and implementation stages, allowing for specific reciprocity and exclusion. In a mirror image of the coordination case discussed below, the institution of multilateralism will appear weak in collaboration cases, while multilateral organizations should be strong.

Thus far, the logic of collaboration has suggested a limited role for multilateralism at the scope and implementation stages. I turn now to the decision-making stage. Making decisions on a multilateral basis may save transaction costs during periods of "normal politics," when a group of states is faced with only routine decisions. However, open, egalitarian processes will become cumbersome when a group confronts major decisions. For example, multilateral decision making will create problems for an organization attempting to determine members' budget contributions or to respond quickly to some exogenous crisis. In a distributive or crisis situation, multilateral decision making will entail higher transaction costs than centralized mechanisms will. In addition, the collective-choice literature points to the problem of cycling. When confronted with a set of choices, majoritarian voting procedures may not lead to a conclusive outcome, for each new option receives majority approval.[13] An organization may find itself unable to settle on any specific proposal unless some form of agenda control is imposed, again suggesting a role for centralized or hierarchical decision making.

Groups can overcome the difficulties of multilateral decision making by delegating urgent issues to a smaller group of actors or allowing such a subset to exercise agenda control under certain conditions. The U.N.'s Security Council is an example of a compromise of pure multilateralism that fulfills these functions and helps account for the U.N.'s ability to act quickly and decisively in recent crises such as the Iraqi invasion of Kuwait. Without such delegation, it is difficult to imagine swift, successful cooperation in crises. By delegating difficult decisions and agenda control to smaller groups of states, organizations can avoid some of the transaction cost problems caused by multilateral decision making. The logic of delegation in international organizations mirrors that in legislatures, which develop systems such as committees to overcome the problems of multilateralism. [14]

Multilateral organizations typically have a large number of members. As many authors have pointed out, large numbers create problems for states attempting to cooperate. [15] Having many players can increase the conflicts of interest among them, uncertainty about others' preferences, and opportunities for undetected free riding. A multilateral organization could deal with some of these difficulties by devoting substantial resources to surveillance and sanctioning of free riders, as discussed above. However, a cheaper tactic might be to sacrifice some degree of multilateralism by decomposing conflictual issues. For example, the GATT has adopted strategies of allowing major trading powers to negotiate agreements rather than mandate negotiations with the entire membership. [16] By focusing on just a few important actors for specific issues, members avoid some of the problems of numerous participants. Negotiations on arms control have followed a similar pattern of decomposition and de facto delegation to those with the most at stake. [17]

This discussion has stressed the role that MOs can play in solving collaboration problems, although these MOs will be weak on IM; i.e., they will not strictly reflect the principles of multilateralism. However, analysts have noted that at least two other solutions to collaboration problems exist: hegemony and self-enforcing agreements among smaller numbers of players. The argument about the possibility for a single dominant state to provide public goods and thus enforce a solution to collaboration problems has been thoroughly explored under the rubric of hegemonic stability theory. [18] The logical and empirical weaknesses of this theory have also been subject to extensive discussion.[19] For the purposes of this paper, I will simply note that if a hegemon has incentives to provide a public good and/or undertake the costs of enforcement, the strategic situation has changed from collaboration to a suasion game. The hegemon's size creates the incentives to provide public goods, thus changing this player's preference ordering and creating a new type of cooperation problem, one that is discussed below. Also, the hegemonic solution to collaboration problems is available only when a specific configuration of state power obtains. Thus, insofar as no single state is dominant or makes up a "uniquely privileged group," the hegemonic solution is not available.

Another potential response to collaboration problems involves the use of bilateralism at the stage of decision making but multilateralism in the scope of these decisions. In other words, states reach bilateral agreements and then, through application of the norm of nondiscrimination, extend these agreements to other members of the system. This solution has been used in international trade, in both the nineteenth and twentieth centuries, through the application of unconditional most-favored-nation (MFN) treatment.[20]

However, the temptation to cheat on these agreements still exists, suggesting that multilateral norms will not extend to implementation. States could perhaps make such agreements self-enforcing, for example, through an "exchange of hostages" in the form of asset-specific investments.[21] If this solution is to work, the calculation that continued cooperation is more profitable than cheating must hold for *every* state to which MFN treatment is extended, creating complications when large numbers of states are involved. Another numbers problem arises simply through the high transaction costs of negotiating a series of bilateral treaties, as suggested by this model for collaboration.[22] Thus, if the MFN type of solution is to lead to stable cooperation without the use of international organizations with enforcement power, we should expect to find it on only a regional or subregional basis. This leads to the pattern of "minilateralism" discussed by Miles Kahler in this volume.[23] In fact, this pattern of no centralized enforcement has existed throughout the GATT's history. The GATT remains weak in terms of formal organization, illustrating the multiplicity of solutions to collaboration problems.[24] However, as GATT membership and the complexity of issues with which it deals grow, we find increasing use of centralized dispute resolution mechanisms and specific reciprocity. Thus, the ghost of collaboration dilemmas increasingly haunts the multilateral trading regime.

COORDINATION PROBLEMS

Figure 3.2 shows a typical coordination problem, the Battle of the Sexes.

Figure 3.2. A Coordination Game with Divergent Interests
(Battle of the Sexes)

This game has two equilibrium outcomes, one of which is preferred by each of the players. Neither has a dominant strategy, so that the best course of action is dependent on how the other player behaves. The central dilemma in this situation is deciding which of the two equilibria will prevail. The two players disagree on this, and bargaining over the outcome might be quite intense, especially if players expect the result to hold far into the future. Coordination games can have major distributional implications, which sometimes make cooperative solutions difficult to achieve.[25] However, once an equilibrium has been established either by convention or by agreement, neither player has an incentive to defect from it.

Thus, coordination games do not require institutions with strong mechanisms for surveillance and enforcement. Since no state would gain by deviating from the established outcome, they need to devote little attention to the prevention of cheating. However, structures that facilitate bargaining and allow states to identify a focal point will contribute to cooperative outcomes.[26] General multilateral principles—the institution of multilateralism—may play a central role in allowing states to settle on a particular outcome. In such cases, the benefits of multilateralism in reducing the costs of arriving at an agreement suggest that this institution will contribute to cooperative outcomes if used at the negotiation stage. The logic of coordination suggests that a series of bilateral negotiations would be highly inefficient. Thus, in coordination situations, the institution of multilateralism may be quite strong.

However, there is no reason to expect that the strength of these norms will be reflected in strong formal organizations. The roles that such organizations can play—such as providing information about others' actions and sanctioning free riders—are not essential to the maintenance of cooperation in coordination games. We have little reason to expect that states will choose to devote scarce resources to formal organizations that will be superfluous. Thus, while the institution of multilateralism may be most efficacious in coordination games, multilateral organizations will not have strong enforcement powers.

Why might states create formal organizations at all under these conditions? The answer lies in transaction cost savings on the prospective collection of information about state intentions. Consider a case where players are choosing frequencies for radio transmissions. As long as a sufficient number of frequencies exists to satisfy everyone, this is a pure coordination problem. To avoid confusion and the mutually disliked outcome of two players attempting to use the same frequency, they will likely set up a centralized system of notification, to let one another know how they plan to behave. However, this system will only be an efficient means of distributing information, and states will not delegate to it unnecessary monitoring powers since no player has an incentive to cheat by deviating from the announced intention.[27] Information is important to the solution of coordination games, but it is signaling information about future plans rather than retrospective information about compliance that states need. In coordination problems, no incentive exists for surreptitious cheating. Since the point of diverging from an established equilibrium is to force joint movement to a new one, defection must be public. Under these conditions, secret defection makes as little sense as undertaking terrorist operations while attempting to prevent publicity about them. In both cases, the point is to impose high costs on others in order to force them to change their policies in a specified manner, which requires publicity about the reasons for and nature of defection.

In coordination games, the primary instrumental value of multilateral norms appears during the negotiation stage, when states are attempting to reach agreements and set conventions. As in collaboration cases, however, alternative solutions exist. A primary one is action by a dominant player to establish a focal point. If a single powerful state can commit itself to a particular equilibrium, others will find it in their interest to simply go along with this decision. This solution obviates the need for extensive discussions. It may have occurred, for example, during the transition from an allocative to market-based regime in telecommunications, as the United States forced others to move to a new equilibrium.[28] American actions in the establishment of the postwar monetary order could be interpreted in a similar manner.[29]

In problems of standardization, such as transborder data flows, state preferences approach the ideal type of coordination. Although each actor has a preferred standard, each has a strong common interest in avoiding the use of conflicting standards. In these cases, the major analytical puzzle is the establishment of a convention, which typically follows extensive multilateral discussions. Negotiations focus on the creation of new standards rather than arguments about whether members are violating old ones, since nothing is to be gained from concealed deviation from the focal point. States will find it easier to maintain cooperation, once established, in coordination games than in collaboration or suasion games, although some actors will inevitably have preferred a different outcome. Thus, in issues that reflect coordination preferences, the institution of multilateralism will contribute more to cooperative outcomes than formal multilateral organizations will.

SUASION PROBLEMS

Both coordination and collaboration problems embody a symmetry of interests among states. However, the establishment of many multilateral institutions took place under conditions of significant asymmetry. Because the United States far exceeded others in power and wealth, it frequently formed a "privileged group" of one, willing unilaterally to supply public goods. The control of technology sales to the Soviet bloc through the Coordinating Committee on Export Controls (COCOM) illustrates this situation, where the United States often had a dominant strategy to control technology regardless of the policies of other states.[30] In this situation, smaller states have a strong incentive to free ride, knowing that public goods such as control of significant technologies will nevertheless be provided. In the COCOM case, while the United States controlled most production of high-technology goods, the Europeans could reap the benefits of exports while being assured that these sales were insufficient in quantity and quality to change the overall balance of power. This presents the United States, or any hegemon, with a dilemma. The hegemon would prefer others' cooperation and is dissatisfied with the equilibrium outcome of unilateral action. I call this kind of asymmetric situation a "suasion" game, since the dilemma facing the hegemon is to persuade or coerce others to cooperate. Figure 3.3 shows a typical suasion game.

Figure 3.3. A Suasion Game

		B	
		0	1
A	0	4, 3	3, 4
	1	2, 2	1, 1

Suasion problems have equilibrium outcomes that leave one actor dissatisfied. In the situation shown in figure 3, player A (assume this is the United States) has a dominant strategy to cooperate. Knowing this, state B can achieve its most favored outcome by defecting. Faced with this situation, the United States has, in the abstract, two ways to convince the other to cooperate, both of which go beyond the confines of the game illustrated here. First, it could threaten to act irrationally in the short term, defecting if player B does. This would lead to player B's least favored outcome and, if credible, convince B to cooperate. The problem with such a strategy is, of course, establishing credibility. The United States would have to be willing to bear high short-term costs if player B does not respond to this threat. To make the threat credible, the United States would need to find a mechanism to make its defection automatic. This would involve a significant surrender of control over decision making and seems an unlikely course of action.

More frequently, the aggrieved actor will choose the second path—tactical issue linkage.[31] This linkage could take the form of either threats or promises (i.e., side payments). By linking issues, the hegemon can either decrease B's payoff associated with unilateral defection (threats) or increase the payoff for mutual cooperation (side payments). In either case, understanding the emergence of cooperation requires that we look beyond the single issue supposedly at stake. In the nuclear nonproliferation regime, for example, the goal of nonproliferation has been pursued by offering various forms of technical assistance to those complying with regime rules.[32] Private, linked benefits contribute to the supply of a public good (nonproliferation) in suasion games.[33]

What role can multilateralism play? For the smaller states—those being either bribed or threatened into submission—maintaining the appearance of multilateralism may be quite important. Governments that give in to U.S. pressure, for example, may need to conceal this behind a veil of "multilateral agreement," for domestic purposes. Thus, we should expect that actual decision-making processes in these situations are obscured, not transparent to the public. In fact, COCOM was the most secretive of international organizations, its very existence kept secret in many countries. At least before the Korean War, and during some periods thereafter, U.S.–European efforts to control technology exports fit this pattern.

While smaller states may benefit from a "velvet glove" of multilateralism in these situations, there is little reason to expect that multilateral norms play a significant role in constraining state behavior. Actual control over the agenda and decisions will likely be maintained by the hegemonic state, with face-saving arrangements to isolate others from domestic pressure. Strong asymmetries of interests and power may lead to widespread disregard of the nondiscrimination norm, for the functions performed by the hegemonic state will differ significantly from those of the smaller members. In addition, the threats or promises that lead to mutual cooperation will need to be implemented on a basis of specific reciprocity. For example, threats to retaliate against all due to the defection of individuals will be costly and lack credibility. Thus, the institution of multilateralism—the embodiment of multilateral principles—suffers in suasion situations.

Even if the dominant state adopts a linkage strategy, it faces a credibility problem. Carrying out either threats or promises is costly. Thus, the hegemonic actor needs to establish a credible commitment to linkage. For the United States, making tactical linkages credible presents the major challenge in suasion situations. In the COCOM case, for example, a linkage between control of technology and Marshall Plan aid was established by Congress, thus improving the administration's bargaining position within the regime. Peter Cowhey's work on domestic strategies to establish credibility, such as his paper in this volume, captures one dimension of this problem. In addition to domestic strategies, the United States looked to multilateral organizations to make its threats or promises credible. From this perspective, one role of multilateral organizations in suasion games is to tie together issues that have no substantive rationale for linkage.[34] In addition to their role in tactical linkage, organizations can provide the hegemon with information on others' behavior, allowing it to respond quickly to defections.

A useful typology of cooperation problems must include suasion games because the conditions of the early postwar period made this asymmetric type of strategic interaction common. The asymmetry of suasion games suggests that the institution of multilateralism may provide cover for smaller states but will have little impact on actual decision making. Formal organizations, on the other hand, may facilitate the dominant state's attempts at issue linkage. There is no reason to expect, however, that these organizations will operate on the basis of multilateral principles.

ASSURANCE PROBLEMS

For the sake of completeness, I include a fourth type of cooperation problem in this typology. This is the assurance game, as shown in figure 3.4.

Figure 3.4. An Assurance Game (Stag Hunt)

		B	
		0	1
A	0	4, 4	1, 3
	1	3, 1	2, 2

In an assurance game, all players' preferred outcome is mutual cooperation. Thus, in equilibrium, rational states with complete information will cooperate within the confines of this single issue-area, single-shot game. As long as all others cooperate, no gains are to be derived from cheating and so no incentives to defect exist. Although mutual defection is also an equilibrium in this game, mutual cooperation is Pareto-superior and so should quite easily become a focal point, differentiating assurance from the coordination problem discussed above. On this basis, studies of regimes have concluded that institutions have little role to play in assurance games, so that states will not waste resources constructing them.[35]

This conclusion is, however, sensitive to changes in assumptions about the information available to states and about the ability of states to act as unitary actors. Although mutual cooperation makes all players happy, unilateral cooperation is disastrous in assurance games. Thus, two kinds of problems could cause states to fail to reach their preferred outcome: uncertainty about others' payoffs and suspicion that others may not actually be rational unitary actors.

If country A has assurance preferences but believes that some probability exists that B has collaboration preferences, for example, A will be reluctant to take the risk of cooperation. If B did in fact see benefits from unilateral defection, A may need to protect herself by preemptive defection. Similar concerns by B could lead to mutual defection in spite of the fact that mutual cooperation is a Pareto-superior equilibrium. This is Robert Jervis' analysis of the security dilemma, suggesting why defensive rational states in a world of uncertainty may behave in a manner that appears quite irrational.[36]

A second problem involves the question of whether the other player is in fact acting as a rational unitary actor. Although the story underlying this concern differs from the previous scenario, its formal expression is equivalent: a probability distribution over the type of game being played. Here, state A's concern is that B is not in control of her actions. One explanation may simply be a lack of rationality on B's part, leading to some probability that B will defect regardless of her preferences.[37] A second, perhaps more plausible, rendering is that B's policies are the result of a domestic game being played out between factions with different preference orderings. Perhaps the chief executive has assurance preferences, for example, while the legislative branch sees immediate benefits from cheating. In this case, if the outcome of the domestic struggle is unclear, A will want to protect herself against the possibility that the legislature will prevail in the domestic game. The outcome is the same as in the case of uncertainty about preferences. Suboptimal mutual defection can result and will be an equilibrium, for neither state has an incentive to change strategies unilaterally.

Admitting uncertainty into the assurance problem may have, at first glance, created a situation analogous to that of a collaboration game, where rational, self-interested behavior leads to a suboptimal outcome. However, the solution to the problem of suboptimal mutual defection is much less demanding in the assurance than in the collaboration case. In collaboration, stringent systems of monitoring and enforcement are required to prevent cheating. In assurance games, the problem is simply one of assuring all players that each sees no benefits from unilateral defection and is in control of domestic policymaking processes. An efficient solution in this case is provided by transparency in domestic arrangements, so that open democratic governments will see little need for complex international arrangements to solve assurance problems.

However, democracies may also be especially subject to the problem of divided control over policymaking. Analysts often explain U.S. problems with foreign policy, for instance, by reference to the weaknesses of divided government. Thus, governments may choose to bolster their commitment to cooperation through the use of international arrangements. The primary function of these arrangements under assurance conditions would be exchange of information about the preferences of various domestic groups with access to the decision-making process. Multilateral norms, with their emphasis on collective decision making and extensive consultation and their transaction costs savings, will enhance governments' knowledge about one anothers' preferences. States may even centralize information exchange to further economize on transaction costs, as in coordination cases. However, the logic of the assurance situation does not suggest a need for centralized enforcement mechanisms. Although we should expect to see extensive cooperation in assurance games when information is not scarce, it would be a mistake to credit strong organizations or regimes with this success.

In sum, different types of cooperation problems lead us to expect the emergence of different kinds of solutions. While no unique solution to any problem exists, a functional analysis does suggest that certain norms or types of formal organizations will be either dysfunctional or inefficient under specific conditions. In collaboration games, high incentives to engage in undetected cheating lead us to expect the emergence of strong organizations unless enforcement and monitoring are taken over by a hegemon. In this case, multilateral norms cannot promote cooperation except under the restricted circumstances of self-enforcing agreements among a small number of states (minilateralism). Coordination problems, on the other hand, do present room for the use of multilateral norms, since states see no advantages in concealed defection from established conventions. In suasion games, cooperation is achieved through issue linkages. MOs can play some role in this process through committing the dominant power and making agreements easier to sell domestically for smaller states; however, these MOs are unlikely to embody IM to any extensive degree. Finally, assurance games, like coordination games, lead us to expect that IM will be high to encourage transparency. However, also as in coordination cases, the role of formal organizations will be limited to exchange of information.

The Effects of Hegemony and Bipolarity

Thus far, this paper has adopted a functional approach, asking about potential solutions to a variety of cooperation problems. The analysis has adopted a systemic perspective, asking about the "correct" solutions to problems on a macro level. However, more than one solution exists for each type of problem. In addition to the problem of multiple equilibria, we have yet to address the microlevel foundations of various solutions, to ask why individual states would choose to adopt them. To address these concerns, in this section I look at cooperation problems from the perspective of a hegemon, relying on a fundamental characteristic of the period in which postwar institutions were established. Bipolarity in the security realm also distinguished this period. The benefits of various solutions from the perspective of a hegemon in a bipolar system provide further insight into the types of solutions states prefer to adopt.

HEGEMONIC INTERESTS

As Ruggie points out, the United States played a leading role in establishing multilateral institutions after World War II.[38] For this reason, the potential benefits of this organizational form for a dominant state such as the United States deserve attention. These benefits fall primarily into three categories: lower transaction costs, the deflection of challenges to the institution from its weaker members, and increased stability under conditions of changes in relative power. These are benefits from the perspective of any type of hegemon, liberal or illiberal, although different types of regimes may put different weights on these benefits relative to the costs associated with various forms of cooperation. Any type of state gains from reducing its costs of interacting with other countries or preventing challenges to the regimes it establishes.

Multilateralism can lower the transaction costs of interaction among states, particularly when they are attempting to overcome coordination problems. Ruggie uses the example of the International Telegraph Union to illustrate this dynamic.[39] When the distributional implications of agreements are minimal and the major problem is standardization, the transaction cost savings of multilateral institutions may be sufficient to explain why a hegemon would choose the multilateral form. Because a hegemonic power would face higher costs in negotiating a series of bilateral agreements than in negotiating a single multilateral agreement, it should prefer multilateralism. However, the hegemon may be able to establish a focal point in coordination games simply through unilateral action.[40] If so, few short-term gains arise from multilateralism. Only a long-term, risk-averse perspective, anticipating future challenges to unilateral action, could explain hegemonic reliance on multilateralism in such a situation. These incentives are discussed below.

Multilateralism may also have advantages when greater conflicts of interest arise. From the hegemon's perspective, the maintenance costs of a multilateral organization will be lower than those of an organizational form with more concentrated decision-making power. As long as patterns of state interests and power do not change abruptly, a hegemon can expect fewer challenges to an institution in which smaller states have a say in joint decisions than to a unilaterally imposed arrangement. As Miles Kahler has argued regarding the early years of the International Monetary Fund, "Even in these years of American predominance, the United States found it valuable to veil its power through conventions that convinced other countries that the rules of the game were reasonably fair or at least better than no rules at all."[41]

We could consider the establishment of a multilateral organization as a transfer of resources in the form of decision-making power from the hegemon to other actors.[42] This transfer legitimates the organization's decisions in the eyes of weaker states, thus reducing the chance that they will continually challenge the regime.[43] As Margaret Levi has argued in a domestic context, institutionalized bargaining under conditions of asymmetry of power is less costly and risky for the dominant actor than constant expenditure of resources to quell rebellions.[44] Careful institutional design can create "quasi-voluntary compliance," reducing the transaction costs embodied in bargaining, monitoring, and enforcing.

Uncertainty about the actual distribution of benefits will also help make a multilateral institution resistant to challenges from below. All else being equal, we should expect multilateral decision making to result in a more egalitarian distribution of benefits than a regime dominated by one or a few powers. Thus, smaller states should more willingly comply with multilateral decisions than commands from above, reducing the need for the hegemon to expend resources policing behavior and enforcing rules. By investing in multilateral organizations, the United States could expect fewer challenges to their activities and thus lower maintenance costs. As discussed above, a multilateral institution does create incentives to free ride in some situations. However, from the perspective of smaller states, taking advantage of these opportunities might threaten the institution as a whole, leading to the creation of one more detrimental to their interests. When asymmetry of interests and power allows for the possibility of decision making dominated by a hegemon, others may rationally comply with a more egalitarian though demanding arrangement.

On a related note, multilateral organizations may be more resistant to shifts in the balance of power than forums with concentrated decision making are. Because the major power is not overtly privileged in multilateral structures, diffusion of power will not necessarily lead to a challenge to the organization's structure. Crises resulting from changes in the distribution of power that might destroy other types of institutions can be weathered by multilateral arrangements. In this sense, multilateralism makes sense from the perspective of a farsighted hegemon. It requires short-term sacrifices of control over decision making but can result in more stable arrangements over the long term.

As studies of U.S. foreign policy in the 1940s have shown, many key officials adopted a long-term perspective. They saw themselves engaged in the construction of a world order that they wanted to last for more than a few years and were willing to bear short-term costs in pursuit of long-run goals.[45] In addition, as Steve Weber's paper in this volume shows, there was a widespread belief that the situation of American hegemony was ephemeral, and efforts took place to speed up the inevitable diffusion of power. Under these conditions, when a multilateral solution was a feasible option, the United States could rationally prefer it to more brittle solutions such as overt coercion. For a farsighted actor, attempts to exploit its power in the short run could be more costly than the design of a durable decision-making structure.[46] Overall, multilateralism provides a relatively cheap, stable organizational form. In exchange for a loss of some power over decision making and probably some decrease in distributional benefits, the hegemon gains a stable decision-making forum. The choice between unilateral action—a feasible solution—and multilateralism depends heavily on the hegemon's discount rate. The longer the time horizon, the more attractive multilateralism.

THE EFFECTS OF BIPOLARITY

While the United States was the dominant economic and security power within the Western subsystem in the 1950s, this grouping was nested in a larger bipolar security structure. Examination of the effects of bipolarity gives further insight into the kinds of choices a rational hegemon might make when confronted with a range of feasible solutions to cooperation problems.

Realist and neorealist analyses of the effects of bipolarity agree on one central point: a bipolar distribution of power makes exit from cooperative arrangements a less credible threat than it is in multipolar systems.[47] Given the power and threat of the Soviet Union, neither the United States nor Western Europe could credibly threaten to realign, destroying the Western alliance. Although within the bipolar alliance structure numerous conflicts of interest arose, the fundamental stability of alignment was guaranteed by bipolarity. In fact, the very publicity of policy differences among alliance members likely resulted from the understanding that such differences could not lead to defections to the other side.[48]

The central question, in both security and economics issue areas, is why the United States did not take advantage of its unique position to exploit the other members of these regimes. Above, I argued that the more farsighted the hegemon, the less attractive this option becomes. One of the most important impacts of bipolarity is to encourage farsighted behavior on the hegemon's part. Joanne Gowa argues that in a bipolar system the security externalities of exploitation decrease its utility from the hegemon's perspective.

> The discount factors of allies in a bipolar system, in contrast [to a multipolar system], are not subject to the same downward bias: the greater stability of bipolar coalitions allows the value of future to approximate present benefits more closely.[49]

Thus, within both international economic regimes and NATO, the United States was unlikely to prefer solutions such as a series of discrim inatory bilateral agreements that sacrificed long-run aggregate benefits for short-term relative gains at the expense of its allies. This trade-off is the heart of the hegemon's dilemma: whether to pursue its own immediate gains at the expense of its allies or to accept a smaller share of the benefits in exchange for long-run growth and stability. A bipolar system creates incentives to pursue the latter solution, pushing a hegemon toward a multilateral rather than discriminatory solution to cooperation problems.

Although exit is a less attractive option in bipolar than in multipolar systems, significant variations in the credibility of the exit option remain even within bipolar systems. Within the bipolar structure of the Cold War, in particular, exit from the Soviet bloc was a credible threat. While West European states had no credible exit option, creating U.S. incentives as just described, East European countries could credibly threaten to leave the sphere of Soviet dominance. This variation within the bipolar structure can be explained only by domestic differences between the United States and the Soviet Union, not by power differentials. Bipolarity thus creates the possibility of multilateralism but does not require it.

In the aggregate, structural approaches lead us to expect observable differences between the behavior of hegemons in bipolar and multipolar systems; bipolarity may be a necessary condition for multilateralist policies on the part of a hegemon. However, it is not a sufficient condition. If allies have a credible exit option, as East European states did, the hegemon will rationally avoid the sharing of decision-making power and benefits implied by multilateralism. The credibility of threats to exit determine the long-term costs and benefits of multilateralism. Credibility depends in the first instance on structural considerations, for threats to exit are typically quite credible in multipolarity. Bipolarity creates the possibility that such threats will become incredible but does not ensure it.[50]

Overall, consideration of the incentives and constraints created by hegemony and bipolarity gives greater precision to the functional analysis, suggesting how a hegemonic state might choose from among a set of feasible solutions. From a hegemon's perspective, a primary choice is among discriminatory bilateralism, unilateral dominance, and the use of institutions that cede greater decision-making power to other states.[51] Multilateralism provides benefits of transaction cost savings and greater stability. However, these advantages are offset by the loss of short-term direct benefits, for a greater share of the immediate gains of cooperation will accrue to states other than the hegemon. The discount rate of the hegemon, therefore, determines the choice among these options, for a farsighted state will value the benefits of multilateralism more highly than a shortsighted one. As other authors have argued, bipolarity creates stability and thus encourages farsighted behavior. Thus, the U.S. preference for multilateral over discriminatory bilateral solutions can be seen as a result of structural considerations.

Institutional Change

The previous sections of this paper have adopted a comparative statics approach to institutional choice, asking about the likelihood of finding different patterns of norms and organizations under different configurations of interests and power. This section turns to the question of change. I do not attempt to develop a fully dynamic theory of change, which would require endogenizing the factors that lead to observable changes in institutions. Instead, I treat the causes of change as exogenous. Thus, this discussion does not address the possibility discussed elsewhere in this volume that participation in a multilateral regime may itself change states' conceptions of their interests. The explanatory puzzle involves the most likely causes of change in each type of cooperation problem discussed above. Assuming that a pattern of cooperation has been established in an issue area, what factors are likely to upset it?

In collaboration situations, crises will result from constant temptations to defect in order to reap short-term benefits. Two factors in particular can lead to crises in collaboration: developments that decrease the shadow of the future for individual states and changes that decrease states' ability to remain informed about the behavior of others. Numerous factors— impending change of government, threats to national security, domestic strife, increasing multipolarity—can lead to a shrinking of states' relevant time horizon. Any could increase states' temptation to defect sufficiently to lead to crisis within an issue area. Similarly, if institutions' ability to provide information is threatened—for example, by technical innovations that make verification of agreements more difficult—the likelihood of defection will increase. Compared with coordination cases, crises are likely to occur more frequently in collaboration situations.

In coordination cases, crises will arise when one state whose actions matter to other participants develops a particularly strong interest in changing the established equilibrium. This may occur for a number of reasons, such as domestic political change or a change in technology that makes maintenance of the existing equilibrium more costly. Changes that give rise to a *longer* time horizon will likely lead to attempts to change the regime. As states value the future more highly, the short-term costs of forcing movement to a new equilibrium may be outweighed by the long-run benefits of the new outcome. Thus, in contrast to collaboration cases, cooperation is threatened rather than enhanced by a larger shadow of the future.

The state desiring change, if it believes its participation is vital enough to other actors that they can be influenced by its actions, may challenge the existing equilibrium. If this state is a major player, the challenge could eventually succeed in spite of the short-term costs in deviating from the established standard. U.S. actions in challenging the telecommunications regime could be interpreted this way, for changes in technology and domestic politics led the U.S. government to challenge the existing regime, looking for an outcome more conductive to its interests in the long run.[52] Because the United States was an important player in this regime, its defection was costly to other states, and it eventually forced them to a new equilibrium, one based more on market principles.

In sum, crises arise in coordination games when some exogenous force leads an important state to challenge the existing conventions, even though this challenge will be costly in the short term. An important difference from collaboration cases lies in the fact that such challenges to the established pattern will be public. Since nothing is to be gained from unilaterally moving to a different standard, any challenge will be a public attempt to force others to accommodate. Thus, technological developments that threaten cooperation in coordination problems are not those that decrease transparency but those that change the costs and benefits of specific outcomes for key members of the regime.

Regimes that rely on tactical issue linkage to foster cooperation in suasion games will face crises as the power of the hegemon declines. In this situation, the threats and promises that maintain cooperation will become less credible, increasing others' temptation to defect. This effect may be offset, however, by changing patterns of interests that result directly from changes in power relationships. A declining hegemon may no longer find it worthwhile to provide any public goods unilaterally, thus changing the cooperation problem from suasion to collaboration.[53] We should expect a fundamental shift in the nature of the regime under these conditions, though we might not see a significant decline in overall cooperation. As asymmetries of power and interest decline, the de facto monopoly of decision making by the hegemon should give way to more genuinely multilateral behavior. Organizations that merely collected information may gain monitoring and enforcement powers. The International Atomic Energy Agency seems to illustrate this pattern, for it has continued to function as U.S. power has declined.[54] Overall, crises in suasion situations will typically arise from changes in the distribution of power.

Assurance problems, in spite of their high degree of common interest, are not immune from crises. Changes in the domestic political arrangements of key actors, or technological innovations that create uncertainty about preference orderings, will create a desire to protect oneself from others' defection. Thus, the kinds of factors that threaten collaboration also challenge cooperation in assurance games. These threats to stable cooperation will, however, be moderated by the existence of viable multilateral institutions. If states have created international arrangements for the exchange of information, whether formal or informal, they will ease the adjustment process to exogenous changes in assurance games.

Conclusions

This paper has outlined a rational-choice approach to the relationships among the institution of multilateralism, multilateral organizations, and international cooperation. The first section developed expectations about institutions and state behavior by focusing on four types of cooperation problems and considering functional constraints. Previous work has shown that the solutions to coordination problems will differ from those to collaboration problems. Putting this work in the context of multilateralism, I argue that the relationships among principles, organizations, and behavior depend on the nature of strategic interaction in particular issue areas. This paper develops hypotheses about these relations, offering anecdotal evidence to establish plausibility. The next step in this research program should involve similar development of hypotheses from competing perspectives and systematic collection of empirical evidence that will allow us to evaluate their respective explanatory power.

Collaboration should lead to relatively strong organizations but disregard of multilateral principles, particularly diffuse reciprocity and indivisibility. In coordination situations, on the other hand, the institution of multilateralism may be strong, but formal organizations are hardly necessary and will be quite weak. The institution of multilateralism will be weak in suasion situations. In suasion, formal organizations will probably play a larger role than in coordination, but less so than in collaboration games. The potential role of IM and MO in assurance games is similar to that in coordination. The central problem in both is provision of information about preferences and intentions, and multilateral norms provide an efficient means of information exchange. However, there is no reason to expect strong organizations with enforcement power, and unilateral action by a hegemon may constitute a functional substitute for multilateralism.

As seen, one weakness of a purely functional approach is indeterminacy. Although we can rule out certain kinds of solutions for each type of cooperation problem, more than one potential solution usually remains. Analysis can further narrow the range of feasible solutions, however, by considering the structural characteristics of the international system. The institutions studied in this volume were, for the most part, created under conditions of American hegemony and a bipolar distribution of power. The second section of this paper thus examined preferred solutions from the perspective of a hegemon, asking why multilateralism might ever be preferred to an architecture where the hegemon could more directly exercise dominance. The security externalities of different kinds of arrangements and the possibilities for exit make some solutions more attractive than others. In particular, the stability of the Western alliance under conditions of bipolarity led the United States to behave as a farsighted hegemon, willing to bypass exploitative solutions in favor of long-term benefits and stability.[55]

In the third section I argued that any "crisis of multilateralism" will result from different factors in each of the four situations. Changes in the distribution of power will be most threatening to cooperation in suasion games. Factors that reduce transparency will challenge both assurance and collaboration games, while increasing discount rates will be most troubling for collaboration. Coordination games are most likely to be upset by technological innovations that alter the cost–benefit calculus of existing conventions for key players.

Looking at a highly simplified characterization of the cooperation problem in various cases, therefore, helps explain the variations we find in multilateral organizations and the strength of the institution of multilateralism. While this type of analysis cannot explain all details of institutional solutions to various problems, it does represent an important element of such explanations by providing rational-choice baseline expectations about behavior.

NOTES

1. For examples, see the papers in this volume by Judith Goldstein, James Caporaso, Anne-Marie Burley, and Steve Weber.

2. Robert O. Keohane, "Multilateralism: An Agenda for Research," *International Journal* 45 (Autumn 1990) 1:731–64.

3. Beth V. Yarbrough and Robert M. Yarbrough, "Cooperation in the Liberalization of International Trade: After Hegemony, What?" *International Organization* (Winter 1987), 41(1):4.

4. Duncan Snidal, "Coordination Versus Prisoner's Dilemma: Implications for International Cooperation and Regimes," *American Political Science Review* (1985), 79:923–42; Arthur A. Stein, "Coordination and Collaboration: Regimes in an Anarchic World," in Stephen D. Krasner, ed., *International Regimes* (Ithaca, N.Y.: Cornell University Press, 1983), pp. 115–40.

5. Michael Laver, "Political Solutions to the Collective Action Problem," *Political Studies* (June 1980), 28(2):195–209.

6. I illustrate only two-person games here. Obviously, situations of multilateralism involve more players. However, many of the fundamental dilemmas of cooperation appear in these simple two-person illustrations.

7. The Folk Theorem specifies that cooperation can be maintained as an equilibrium in repeated Prisoners' Dilemmas, conditional on a low discount rate (i.e., the future is valued highly). See Dilip Abreu, "On the Theory of Infinitely Repeated Games with Discounting," *Econometrica* (1988), 56:383–96; James Friedman, "A Noncooperative Equilibrium for Supergames," in *Review of Economic Studies* (1971), 38:1–12; Robert Axelrod, *The Evolution of Cooperation* (New York: Basic Books, 1984).

8. For an example, see Paul Milgrom, Douglass North, and Barry Weingast, "The Role of Institutions in the Revival of Trade: The Medieval Law Merchant, Private Judges, and the Champagne Fairs," *Economics and Politics* (1989), 1:1–23.

9. Beth V. Yarbrough and Robert M. Yarbrough, "International Institutions and the New Economics of Organization," paper delivered to the University of California, Berkeley Institutional Analysis Workshop, May 1990; Geoffrey Garrett, "International Cooperation and Institutional Choice: The European Community's Internal Market," *International Organization* 46, no. 2 (Spring 1992), 46(2)533–60.

10. Robert O. Keohane, "Reciprocity in International Relations," *International Organization* (Winter 1986), 40(1):1–27.

11. John H. Jackson, "GATT Machinery and the Tokyo Round Agreements," in William R. Cline, ed., *Trade Policy in the 1980s* (Washington, D.C.: Institute for International Economics, 1983), pp. 159–87.

12. Snidal, "Coordination Versus Prisoner's Dilemma," pp. 929–30.

13. Kenneth J. Arrow, *Social Choice and Individual Values,* 2d ed. (New Haven, Conn.: Yale University Press, 1963), pp. 2–3; Richard P. McKelvey, "Intransitivities in Multidimensional Voting: Models and Some Implications for Agenda Control," *Journal of Economic Theory* (June 1976), 12:472–82.

14. Barry R. Weingast and William J. Marshall, "The Industrial Organization of Congress; or, Why Legislatures, Like Firms, Are Not Organized as Markets," *Journal of Political Economy* (1988), 96(1):132–63.

15. For example, see Kenneth A. Oye, "Explaining Cooperation Under Anarchy: Hypotheses and Strategies," in Oye, ed., *Cooperation Under Anarchy* (Princeton: Princeton University Press, 1986), pp. 18–22.

16. Jock A. Finlayson and Mark W. Zacher, "The GATT and the Regulations of Trade Barriers: Regime Dynamics and Functions," in *International Regimes,* pp. 273–314.

17. My thanks to Patrick Morgan for suggesting this example.

18. Charles P. Kindleberger, *The World in Depression* (Berkeley: University of California Press, 1973); Steven D. Krasner, "State Power and the Structure of International Trade," *World Politics* (April 1976), 38:317–43; Robert O. Keohane, "The Theory of Hegemonic Stability and Changes in International Regimes, 1967–1977," in Ole Holsti, ed., *Change in the International System* (Boulder, Colo.: Westview Press, 1980), pp. 131–62.

19. For example, see John A. C. Conybeare, *Trade Wars: The Theory and Practice of International Commercial Rivalry* (New York: Columbia University Press, 1987), pp. 55–72.

20. Arthur A. Stein, "The Hegemon's Dilemma: Great Britain, the United States, and the International Economic Order," *International Organization* (Spring 1984), 38(2):355–86.

21. Beth V. Yarbrough and Robert M. Yarbrough, "Reciprocity, Bilateralism, and Economic 'Hostages': Self-enforcing Agreements in International Trade," *International Studies Quarterly* (1986), 30:7–21.

22. Conybeare, *Trade Wars,* p. 278.

23. See also Yarbrough and Yarbrough, "Cooperation in the Liberalization of International Trade."

24. The strategic problems states confront in international monetary affairs differ substantially from those in commercial activities. Under the Bretton Woods regime, for example, the central role of the United States prevented the cooperation problem from being one of collaboration. Indeed, we saw a significant asymmetry of interests, creating perhaps a suasion game as discussed below.

25. See Stephen D. Krasner, "Global Communications and National Power: Life on the Pareto Frontier," *World Politics* (April 1991), 43:336–66.

26. See Geoffrey Garrett and Barry Weingast, "Ideas, Interests, and Institutions: Constructing the EC's Internal Market," prepared for the Annual Meeting of the American Political Science Association, Washington, D.C., August 28–September 1, 1991.

27. For another perspective on the functions regimes can perform in coordination games under conditions of imperfect information, see James D. Morrow, "Modeling International Regimes," paper presented to the Annual Meeting of the American Political Science Association, San Francisco, California, September 1990.

28. See Peter F. Cowhey, "The International Telecommunications Regime:

The Political Roots of Regimes for High Technology," *International Organization* (Spring 1990), 44(2):169--99.

29. Barry Eichengreen, "Hegemonic Stability Theories of the International Monetary System," in Richard N. Cooper, et. al., *Can Nations Agree? Issues in International Economic Cooperation* (Washington, D.C.: The Brookings Institution, 1989), pp. 255–98.

30. Michael Mastanduno, "Trade as a Strategic Weapon: American and Alliance Export Control Policy in the Early Postwar Period," *International Organization* (Winter 1988), 42(1):121–50; Lisa L. Martin, *Coercive Cooperation: Explaining Multilateral Economic Sanctions* (Princeton: Princeton University Press, 1992).

31. For discussions of this strategy, see James K. Sebenius, "Negotiation Arithmetic: Adding and Subtracting Issues and Parties," *International Organization* (Spring 1983), 37(2):281–316; Arthur A. Stein, "The Politics of Linkage," *World Politics* (1980), 33:62–81; Michael D. McGinnis, "Issue Linkage and the Evolution of Cooperation," *Journal of Conflict Resolution* (March 1986), 30(1):141–70.

32. Benjamin N. Schiff, "Dominance Without Hegemony: U.S. Relations with the International Atomic Energy Agency," in Margaret P. Karns and Karen A. Mingst, eds., *The United States and Multilateral Institutions: Patterns of Changing Instrumentality and Influence,* Mershon Center Series on International Security and Foreign Policy, vol. 5 (Boston: Unwin Hyman, 1990), pp. 57–89.

33. Mancur Olson, *The Logic of Collective Action* (Cambridge, Mass.: Harvard University Press, 1965).

34. See Robert O. Keohane, *After Hegemony: Cooperation and Discord in the World Political Economy* (Princeton: Princeton University Press, 1984), pp. 91–92, for a general discussion of the role of institutions in issue-linkage.

35. Stein, "Coordination and Collaboration," p. 119.

36. Robert Jervis, "Cooperation Under the Security Dilemma," *World Politics* (January 1978), 30:58–79.

37. The impact of small deviations from intended strategies has led to the concept of trembling-hand equilibria. See Reinhard Selten, "Re-examination of the Perfectness Concept for Equilibrium Points in Extensive Games," *International Journal of Game Theory* (1975), 4:25–55.

38. John Gerard Ruggie, "Unraveling World Order: The United States and the Future of Multilateralism" (mimeo, University of California, San Diego, 1989), ch. 1, p. 2.

39. Ibid., ch. 2, pp. 26–28.

40. See Krasner, "Global Communications and National Power."

41. Miles Kahler, "The United States and the International Monetary Fund: Declining Influence or Declining Interest?" in Karns and Mingst, eds., *The United States and Multilateral Institutions,* p. 97.

42. Giulio M. Gallarotti, "Revisions in Realism: The Political Economy of

Domination," paper presented at the Annual Meeting of the American Political Science Association, Atlanta, Georgia, September 1989.

43. Stephen D. Krasner, *Structural Conflict: The Third World Against Global Liberalism* (Berkeley: University of California Press, 1985), p. 62.

44. Margaret Levi, *Of Rule and Revenue* (Berkeley: University of California Press, 1988), p. 28.

45. Robert A. Pollard, *Economic Security and the Origins of the Cold War, 1945–1950* (New York: Columbia University Press, 1985).

46. Joanne Gowa, "Rational Hegemons, Excludable Goods, and Small Groups: An Epitaph for Hegemonic Stability Theory?" *World Politics* (April 1989), 41(3):307–24. Gowa also emphasizes the point made earlier in this paper that the excludability of free trade is an essential element of its maintenance.

47. Glenn H. Snyder, "The Security Dilemma in Alliance Politics," *World Politics* (July 1984), 36(4):461–95; Joanne Gowa, "Bipolarity, Multipolarity, and Free Trade," *American Political Science Review* (December 1989), 83(4):1245–56; Kenneth N. Waltz, *Theory of International Politics* (Reading, Mass.: Addison-Wesley, 1979).

48. Snyder, "The Security Dilemma," p. 473. The question of burden sharing within the alliance is, however, an entirely different issue. Here, the asymmetry of power within the alliance put the United States into a suasion game where it contributed a disproportionately high level of resources to the alliance.

49 Gowa, "Bipolarity, Multipolarity," p. 1250.

50. Current changes in the structure of security arrangements in Europe bear out this logic. East European states are turning to NATO for security. However, NATO, wary of the reliability and stability of the new East European regimes, is insisting on a series of bilateral arrangements rather than formal incorporation into the multilateral framework. See statement of Manfred Woerner reported by the Associated Press, October 17, 1990.

51. As discussed above, we have good reasons to expect these MOs to diverge in significant ways from the norms of IM.

52. Cowhey, "The International Telecommunications Regime."

53. Duncan Snidal, "The Limits of Hegemonic Stability Theory," *International Organization* (Autumn 1985), 39(4):579–614.

54. Schiff, "Dominance Without Hegemony," p. 78.

55. According to this logic, the current movement toward multipolarity should tend to favor solutions other than multilateralism. For example, we might expect to see greater use of self-enforcing agreements among smaller numbers of players, as those who see a move toward regionalism in the global economy argue is happening. Note, however, that this does not imply that the goal of liberalization will disappear but simply that solutions other than multilateralism will become increasingly important for its realization.

Part 3

❖

DOMESTIC

CONTENT

❖

4. Regulating the World: Multilateralism, International Law, and the Projection of the New Deal Regulatory State

Anne-Marie Burley

T HE multilateralism that characterizes postwar international regimes
is a fundamental characteristic of a *liberal* world order. In particular,
it is characteristic of international institutions designed by the United
States—the liberal state most inclined and most able to project its
domestic political and economic arrangements onto the world. The distinctive features of multilateralism—the emphasis on general organizing
principles, with the corollary characteristics of indivisibility and diffuse
reciprocity—are also the organizing principles of the liberal conception
of a polity.[1] The United States sought to project these principles onto
the world as a macrocosm of the New Deal regulatory state.

To understand the role of legal analogy in postwar planning, I turn
first to a distinctive characterization of the postwar international order in
the international law literature—the identification of "the international
law of cooperation." The international law of cooperation has been understood to differ fundamentally in substance, scope, and nature from the
pre-1945 "law of coexistence." International lawyers have traced the
sources of this shift directly to changes in *domestic* law, specifically the
emergence of welfare liberalism. The Great Depression taught American
policymakers two enduring lessons: (1) the existence of an inextricable
link between economic prosperity and political stability and (2) the
affirmative responsibility of governments to assure the minimum welfare
of their citizens. After the chaos of the war, coupled with the widespread
perception that laissez-faire economics and laissez-faire politics had had

*I am indebted to Abram Chayes, Stephen Gilles, Robert Keohane, Larry Kramer, Andrew Mo-
ravcsik, Cass Sunstein, Alan Sykes, John Ruggie, Bill Drake, and all the other contributors to this
volume for excellent comments. I also benefited much from the suggestions of three anonymous
reviewers. David Christie and Jeffrey Seitzer were invaluable researchers. Research was supported by
the Ford Foundation and the Russell Baker Fund at the University of Chicago Law School.

equally pernicious effects abroad, these tenets were readily translatable to the international sphere.

With an eye to uncovering the more precise origins of specific postwar institutions, I examine U.S. plans for the postwar order—formulated from 1939 through 1945, largely prior to any actual negotiation with other states but during a period when U.S. leaders increasingly understood that they must take responsibility for shaping the postwar world. The identity of the participants and the results of this planning process confirm that policy planners not only sought to project the scope and substance of domestic law onto the world, but also that they recapitulated the legal and administrative forms of the New Deal regulatory revolution. In virtually every issue area, ranging from the Food and Agricultural Organization to the projected International Trade Organization to the International Civil Aviation Organization, U.S. policymakers sought to establish autonomous, centralized, and relatively depoliticized regulatory organizations. This institutional design had been the domestic solution of choice in the New Deal, when U.S. domestic policymakers found themselves confronted with similar problems. Private problems required institutionalized public intervention, at home and abroad.

I conclude that the form of the postwar order was strongly influenced by the U.S. conceptualization of international problems and their solutions in domestic legal terms. The distinctive features of the international law of cooperation—the regulation of the physical, economic, and social welfare of individual citizens by affirmative governmental measures—reflect the role of law in a domestic liberal polity. The history of the postwar planning process recapitulates this dynamic on a more specific level. The formal characteristics of multilateralism are the byproduct of a distinctively American effort to regulate the world.

The first part of this article sketches the principal themes and postulated origins of the international law of cooperation. The second part examines the similarities between the New Deal regulatory state and the postwar multilateral order as envisioned by the State Department planning teams charged with designing the postwar world. The third part explores the larger connections between the international projection of a liberal legal order and multilateralism as a generic institutional form.

The International Law of Cooperation

International lawyers have not addressed the phenomenon of multilateralism per se other than in the nominal sense of institutions involving three or more parties.[2] However, an important strand of postwar international legal scholarship long ago identified a sea change in the nature and function of international law beginning in the early part of this century and gathering speed after 1945. In 1964 Wolfgang Friedmann pioneered a distinction between the "international law of co-existence," the traditional body of customary and conventional rules governing diplomatic interstate relations, and a new phenomenon he dubbed the "international law of cooperation."[3]

The international law of cooperation differs from traditional public international law in its scope, subjects, and function. First, on the question of scope, it is a body of law seeking to regulate far more widely than the traditional issue areas of interstate relations. It encompasses substantive domains historically thought to be of purely domestic concern, such as human rights, health care, economic conditions, and environmental protection.

Second, the subjects of the international law of cooperation are individuals as well as, and sometimes instead of, states. The purpose of twentieth-century international institutions is not merely to coordinate state action but also "to develop an international organization of *mankind* for purposes of cooperation."[4] Friedmann drew on the work of Wilfred Jenks, who described the evolution of international law from "rules governing the mutual relations of states" into a "common law of mankind."[5] The picture is not of an emerging world government but of an emergent world citizenry.

Third, the distinction between the international law of coexistence and the international law of cooperation rests on an evolving conception of the nature and function of law. The international law of the nineteenth century had a primarily negative function: to restrain and coordinate state action to allow each state maximum freedom to pursue its national interests with minimum interference from and imposition on others. According to a leading international law casebook, the U.N. system "marked the transition of international law from the traditional system of formal rules of mutual respect and abstention to an incipient system of organized, cooperative efforts."[6] The international law of cooperation is thus the instrument of collaborative ends, a system of positive inducements facilitating and structuring cooperative action.[7]

According to a major report issued by the International Law Commission, similar characteristics emerged in the law of multilateral treaties. Traditional multilateral "treaties of settlement" reconciled opposing interests, the subjects of war and hence of peace, that were the exclusive preserve of states in their external relations with one another. Twentieth-century multilateral "law-making treaties," by contrast, "extended beyond the strictly narrow traditional subjects of international law to regulate certain efforts at international cooperation in the humanitarian and social fields such as the suppression of the slave trade."[8] The "common interests" that gave rise to these treaties are interests historically the province of national governments only in their domestic relations—matters not between state and state, but between state and citizen.[9]

The international law of cooperation is itself distinctively multilateral. The formal organizations and treaty regimes that instantiate this law—in areas ranging from security to environmental protection—all incorporate general organizing principles applicable equally to all their members or specific classes of members. Further, the international law of cooperation assumes that the basis of these regimes and organizations is the identification of common threats and common interests. Finally, the duration of the affirmative duties of cooperation imposed in accordance with the general organizing principles is open-ended, thereby implicitly accepting that the distribution of costs and benefits associated with compliance may be unequal at any given point.

SOURCES OF THE INTERNATIONAL LAW OF COOPERATION

The classic scholarly accounts of the creation and growth of concrete international organizations focus primarily on technological advances permitting increases in the frequency and speed of diplomatic relations, as well as technical innovations such as the multilateral treaty.[10] The progenitors of the international law of cooperation, however, point to a very different source. Friedmann attributed the structural change resulting from "the intrusion of social and economic matters into international relations" to a new domestic philosophy of government embodied in the social welfare state.[11] The growing concern of domestic governments with the "supervision, regulation, and active shaping of . . . economic and social conditions" simply carried over into the international realm.[12]

Political scientists of Friedmann's vintage shared this perception. Inis Claude published the first edition of his classic college text on international organization, *Swords into Plowshares,* in 1956. For him the connection was clear. Contrasting the United Nations system with the League of Nations, he argued that both systems were grounded in liberalism. "But," he continued, "if the liberalism which inspired the League was essentially a nineteenth-century phenomenon, the doctrinal foundation of the night-watchman state, the liberalism which underlay the new system was the twentieth-century version, the theoretical support of the welfare state."[13] This new liberalism

> supported the assumption by governments of vastly expanded functional responsibilities and a capacity for regulatory intervention in many areas formerly considered outside the range of their appropriate concerns. Correspondingly, the Charter reflected a newly enlarged conception of the necessary and proper role of international organization in world affairs; it envisaged for the United Nations and Specialized Agencies a functional sphere and an agenda of activity far more ambitious than that mapped out for the League in 1919.[14]

Unlike arguments—Ruggie's "embedded liberalism," for example—about the ways in which international institutions have had to *accommodate* domestic interventionism,[15] the chroniclers of the international law of cooperation offer a domestic explanation for the very existence of those institutions. Their claim is not that states could no longer create international regimes without regard for their domestic impact. It is rather that international regimes grew out of the same transformation in the philosophy of government that spawned new domestic regimes.

I propose to take this logic a step further and seek a more specific domestic referent, one that can explain not only the substantive scope of postwar international regimes but also their generic multilateral form and to some extent their specific organizational design. The origins of welfare liberalism may be traced back to the Industrial Revolution, but the domestic origins of the specific contours of the postwar international order lie in the historical experience of one liberal state: the United States during the New Deal. By 1941, having finally accepted that the United States could not effectively isolate itself from the world, U.S. policymakers determined instead to remake the world in the American image. They did not fully succeed, of course, given that the order that finally emerged necessarily required negotiation and compromise with other nations. But their plans reveal an underlying conception of the world that made unilateralism or bilateralism virtually unthinkable.

Projecting the U.S. Regulatory State

The Great Depression was midwife to the U.S. regulatory state, which had been developing in embryo over the previous two decades. It taught U.S. policymakers two unforgettable lessons: the inseverable link between economic prosperity and political security and the responsibility of government to exercise its power affirmatively to promote the welfare of its citizens.[16] Historian Carl Degler formulates these teachings in terms of a newfound domestic perception of indivisibility—the Depression as "a threat to all"—and the necessity of "a collective defense."[17]

The original blueprint for the postwar international order was drawn up by American policymakers who projected the philosophy, substance, and form of the New Deal regulatory state onto the world. Many of the same people who had taken responsibility for reshaping American domestic government now took responsibility for the world. They adopted the same generic solution for the world's problems as for the nation's: government intervention through specialized administrative organizations. The specific types of organization proposed to solve different specific regulatory problems varied over the same range, both domestically and internationally. Finally, the plan for linking these specific organizations together in a larger centralized scheme matched a widely discussed plan for a reform of the domestic New Deal government.

PLANNING THE WORLD

The most comprehensive designs for the postwar order were drawn up in Washington. The best general guide to this planning process is the State Department account of postwar foreign policy preparation. Other U.S. government departments engaged in their own planning for how to order international regulation of their substantive issue areas, and, as in the case of Harry Dexter White's Treasury Plan for an international monetary organization, the State Department planners did not always win.[18] But it was the State Department that was charged with preparing a coherent foreign policy blueprint "in regard to every aspect of international relations, in all areas of the world, under the circumstances probable or possible at the end of the war." As the Department's subsequent account of this process, begun in 1939 and completed only with the convening of the United Nations in 1945, explains:

> This work as a whole required consideration of the political, territorial, military, economic, and social conditions essential to enduring peace and to human progress in an era when the philosophies and desires of peoples, the relationships and power positions of states, and the scope of United States concern in international cooperation had all become subject to profound change.[19]

The first phase of postwar planning was carried out by the Advisory Committee on Problems of Foreign Relations from 1939 to 1941. This

Committee, composed primarily of State Department officials, was charged with determining U.S. interests in the establishment of a postwar "world order" and designing policies to promote those interests "both as a basis of our own action and of our attempts to influence other nations."[20] By 1941, as the war spread and the outlook for the anti-Hitler forces dimmed, both the President and Congress began to perceive that "the fields that would present postwar problems continued to expand."[21] Two weeks after Pearl Harbor the President authorized the creation of a new committee to conduct "preparatory work on all phases of postwar foreign policy."

The new committee, first convened in February 1942 and dubbed the Advisory Committee on Post-War Foreign Policy, was chaired by the Secretary of State and composed of a much broader membership of senior officials from the State Department and other government departments and agencies, members of Congress, and a few prominent individuals from private life.[22] Its charter, as envisioned in Hull's recommendation to the President, was to "continue and expand [the Department of State's] work of preparation for this country's effective participation in the solution of the vast and complicated problems of international relations which will confront us and the world after the final defeat of the forces of aggression."[23] In practice, the Committee immediately divided into six subcommittees,[24] many of which subdivided further. These various entities set about identifying policy problems, analyzing U.S. interests, and developing the broad outlines of possible solutions.

The period from July 1943 to November 1944, when formal preparations for the United Nations Conference began, was a phase of "extraordinary" preparation.[25] The planning focus was no longer exploration and analysis of policy problems but rather the generation of major policy alternatives and preparation of negotiating positions for a host of international conferences in the fall of 1943 and the spring of 1944.[26] By July 1944 the Post-War Programs Committee had formulated tentative policy options in twenty-six fields in preparation for the Dumbarton Oaks Conversations on general international organization. By November 1944 the State Department's "planning" was virtually completed, as matters in virtually all areas had moved into the "operational" phase.[27]

TAKING RESPONSIBILITY FOR THE WORLD

Just as the New Deal government increasingly took active responsibility for the welfare of the nation, U.S. foreign policy planners took increasing responsibility for the welfare of the world. It was widely believed that they had little choice. The United States was going to be a world power by default. It could not insulate itself from the world's problems. As at home, moreover, it could not neatly pick and choose among those problems, distinguishing politics from economics, security from prosperity, defense from welfare. In the lexicon of the New Deal, taking responsibility meant government intervention on a grand scale.[28]

In the early days of the war, the public posture and private planning of U.S. officials had a detached, almost abstract quality. In 1940 President Roosevelt urged U.S. citizens to "work out for themselves the several alternatives which lie before world civilization."[29] Cordell Hull spoke only of "throwing the weight of our country's moral and material influence in the direction of creating a stable and enduring world order under law."[30] From the perspective of the planners themselves, the original Advisory Committee constituted in 1939 understood its mandate largely in terms of addressing concrete "problems of peace and reconstruction," particularly economic problems such as the impact on the United States of the warring powers' necessary readjustment to peacetime production."[31]

Pearl Harbor, naturally enough, was the catalyst for a more activist approach. When the Advisory Committee on Post-War Foreign Policy first met in February 1942, "[T]he chief certainties were merely the anticipated fact of victory and the consequent fact that this country— emerging from the victory with tremendous power—would have profound new responsibilities in connection with practically all vital problems of world affairs and would have to state a policy or at least express an attitude on such problems."[32]

By April 1944 Secretary of State Hull gave a foreign policy address in which he described U.S. foreign policy as "the task of focusing and giving effect in the world outside our borders to the will of 135 million people through the constitutional processes which govern our democracy."[33] And in March 1945 Roosevelt exhorted the U.S. Senate to prepare themselves for the ratification of whatever document would be drafted at San Francisco in the following terms:

> There can be no middle ground here. We shall have to take the responsibility for world collaboration, or we shall have to bear the responsibility for another world conflict.[34]

Here the responsibilities for domestic welfare and for international welfare had become one and the same. The ratifiers of Roosevelt's plans for reshaping domestic government were being asked to take on the world.

ORGANIZING THE WORLD

In practice, taking responsibility for the world meant organizing it according to the same general institutional design as the U.S. government. Once again, while not all the postwar organizations were finally implemented according to U.S. design, to the extent they were, their inspiration was the U.S. domestic regulatory system. The evidence for this proposition falls into three categories. First, a large number of the same people who had been involved in domestic policymaking in the New Deal moved into the foreign policy sphere. This was true even of the State Department planning teams, even more so the separate planning staffs run by other U.S. bureaucracies such as the Treasury. Second, the wide range of international organizations proposed by these planners corresponded to the range of domestic regulatory agencies established during the New Deal. Third, the larger U.S. organizational scheme mirrored a plan favored by Franklin Roosevelt for reform of the U.S. regulatory system but never implemented domestically.

The Organizers

Many of the individuals involved in the postwar planning process were the actual planners and beneficiaries of these domestic solutions. As the planning tasks expanded, the ranks of the planners themselves swelled far beyond the State Department. Every division of a committee into a clutch of subcommittees meant the inclusion of members of Congress, officials from other government departments, a few private citizens, and heads and subheads of the newly established administrative agencies.

The membership of the Twelve Special Economic Committees of the Committee on Post-War Foreign Economic Policy is telling. The Special Committee on International Aviation included the chairman of the Civil Aeronautics Board. The Special Committee on Labor Standards and Social Security was chaired by the Secretary of Labor and included the presidents of all the major U.S. labor unions and the chairman of the Social Security Board. The Special Committees on Private Monopolies and Cartels, Relaxation of Trade Barriers, and Commodity Agreements and Methods of Trade were liberally sprinkled with members from the domestic Tariff Commission, together with assorted members from the Securities and Exchange Commission, the Office of Price Administration, and domestic divisions of the Departments of Commerce and Agriculture. Similarly, of the twenty members of the Special Committee on Communications, the chairman of the Subcommittee on Global Communications was the member from the recently created Federal Communications Commission.[35] Finally, Adolf Berle, a key member of Roosevelt's original brain trust, was head of no fewer than three of the Special Committees—communications, aviation, and shipping—and a member of a fourth.

The Institutional Solution

The Domestic Institutional Solution. For political philosophers, and students of American government more generally, the New Deal is about a redefinition of the responsibilities of power—the abandonment of limited government. For political economists, it is about a new understanding of the American economy—coordinated monopoly versus regulated competition.[36] But for lawyers it is above all about a proliferation of institutions—administrative agencies combining traditionally separated legislative and executive functions to create new forms of government to regulate vast areas of American life.[37]

The New Deal was an *institutional* revolution. Eighteen administrative agencies were created from 1900 from 1929; seventeen more were created from 1930 to 1940 alone.[38] These included such fixtures of modern American life as the Social Security Administration, the Federal Communications Commission, the Securities and Exchange Commission, the Federal Deposit Insurance Corporation, the Federal Housing Administration, and the National Labor Relations Board. Other agencies such as the Food and Drug Administration and the Federal Trade Commission were significantly expanded. And yet others, such as the Civil Works Administration, the Works Progress Administration, and the Civilian Conservation Corps made a major mark on the regulatory landscape of the time.

These diverse agencies were the product of similarly diverse regulatory strategies, from the corporatism of the "First New Deal," from 1933 to 1935,[39] to the spending and social welfare programs of the "Second New Deal," from 1935 to 1937,[40] to the creation of more traditional technical regulatory agencies and monitoring institutions throughout.[41] This profusion of regulatory forms and functions suggests that the New Deal was "moving in many directions simultaneously"[42]—a dynamism and goal orientation entirely in keeping with the pragmatism of the President.

There was, however, a lowest common denominator. Regardless of the specific substantive approach selected to solve a particular policy problem, it was implemented—"administered"—via a specialized institution. Some of the resulting "administrative agencies" emphasized independent expertise; others were quasi-judicial; others provided a negotiating forum for normally conflicting parties. All assumed that long-term political, economic, and social problems required long-term, institutionalized regulation by some form of central authority.

The International Institutional Solution. U.S. policymakers involved in the international planning process did not set about building a multilateral world order out of idealism. The task facing the planners had less to do with ends than means. The researchers for the Advisory Committee on Postwar Foreign Policy approached every issue with the following questions: "What does the United States want? What do other states want? How do we obtain what we want?"[43] As in the domestic context, the emphasis was on pragmatic solutions to concrete problems rather than on implementing any grand theoretical design.

The official members of the innumerable planning committees and subcommittees generated a wide variety of answers as to the substance of U.S. desires in different issue areas. But their invariable answer to the question of "how do we obtain what we want?" was to create a specialized regulatory institution. When the planning process, in all its complexity and detail, was finally complete, the result was "negotiations among the major powers, and exchanges of view with other United Nations members looking toward the establishment of international agencies of both a transitional and permanent character in various specialized fields."[44]

The faster substantive consensus could be achieved in a given issue area, the faster the process of negotiating the creation of an international agency could begin. Food and agriculture was the perhaps easiest area in which to secure such agreement. Roosevelt deliberately chose it as a "relatively noncontroversial subject on which to proceed for the first full United Nations conference"—a conference intended to establish "international machinery dealing with standards of nutrition and more rational development of food resources."[45] Substantive agreement on economic foreign policy was fairly advanced even at the beginning of the war, moving to the organizational stage in several key areas with the Bretton Woods Conference in 1944.[46] Similarly in the area of postwar cultural relations: the Special Subcommittee on International Organization had recognized the potential need for "an international agency in this field" as early as 1942. By June 1943 the General Advisory Committee on Cultural Relations recommended that the Department of State "actively" explore creation of such an agency as soon as possible.[47]

In the political arena, by contrast, the substantive agenda was less clear. The Political Subcommittee had to begin its work by "clarify[ing] for its own guidance the fundamental concepts of American policy that should underlie its approach to the problems and uncertainties of the future,"[48] a process subject to "shifts and alternations of . . . major proportions."[49] Nevertheless, by late 1944 the State Department account took satisfaction in noting movement toward the creation of international organizations on all fronts:

> It was equally apparent, from the progress of the Post-War Programs Committee . . . from the outcome of the Dumbarton Oaks Conversations, and from the advances toward the establishment of specialized international economic and social organizations, that the bulk of essential preparatory work was done and the remainder, with only certain exceptions, was becoming an adjunct to operations.[50]

These "exceptions" constituted the "unfinished business"[51] remaining for State Department planners between winter 1944 and spring 1945. Here too, the proliferation of institutions continued. Most of the remaining work fell under the mandate of the Executive Committee on Economic Foreign Policy, which promptly established a new Subcomittee on Specialized International Economic Organizations in November 1944. The charter of the new Subcommittee was explicitly to formulate recommendations concerning "the organizations of such agency or agencies as may be required to carry out the economic programs, as approved by the Executive Committee, of the Committees on Private Monopolies and Cartels, Commodity Agreements, and Trade Barriers."[52] And indeed, the upshot was recommendations for an international trade organization, and international commodity organization, and an International Office of Business Practices, all with accompanying multilateral conventions for implementation.[53] Other remaining business concerned "specialized international organizations for economic and social cooperation."[54]

Yet other specialized agencies planned for during this period included the International Civil Aviation Organization, an international shipping organization, the reorganization and strengthening of the International Telecommunications Union or else the establishment of a new international telecommunications organization, a European inland transport organization, a world health organization, and an international refugee organization.

Further parallels can be identified at a more specific level as well—in terms of the design and modes of governance of individual institutions. Additional research is necessary to explore the details of how U.S. planners actually envisioned each of these specific organizations and to establish the extent to which they explicitly relied on domestic models.[55] Even a general overview, however, reveals the following similarities.

- The purpose of an "intergovernmental commodity organization," for instance, was to "facilitate cooperation in the solution of world commodity problems," to "participate in and supervise international commodity arrangements," and to "review the operations of such arrangements in the light of the general code of principles."[56] These functions correspond to early New Deal efforts to institutionalize corporatist strategies designed to regulate excess supply and demand.

- The planned "international commercial policy organization" was to fulfill the following purposes: "(1) provide information to member countries; (2) afford a source of consistent interpretation of the convention, (3) carry out investigative and fact-finding functions, (4) adjust differences among members, and (5) recommend amendments to the convention."[57] This much more "judicial" model, with an emphasis on policing and enforcement, was analogous to the domestic Securities and Exchange Commission.

- The "International Office for Business Practices" was to "facilitate the development and administration" of "a coordinated program by which each nation undertakes to prohibit the most restrictive cartel practices which burden international trade."[58] Similarly, the grand International Trade Organization was to supply "permanent machinery for international collaboration in matters affecting international commerce, with a view to continuous consultation, the provision of expert advice, the formulation of agreed policies, procedures and plans, and to the development of agreed rules of conduct in regard to matters affecting international trade."[59] These were institutions analogous to the domestic risk-spreading institutions that forged a "partnership" with business and management to reduce economic disruptions.

- The more technical international institutions in areas ranging from telecommunications to air traffic had domestic counterparts in essentially the same fields. Here the emphasis was on independence and specialized expertise.

Thus far we have established a striking institutional correlation between the domestic and the international policy solutions adopted by U.S. policymakers to address a wide range of problems. The generic answer was centralized intervention by a government or governmental facsimile, administered and implemented through concrete organizations charged with specific regulatory tasks. The specific institutional designs of these organizations corresponded to the various domestic models developed during the New Deal to implement a specific regulatory mandate.

Centralizing Global Authority

An additional category of evidence for the projection of the New Deal regulatory state onto the international system comprises the plans made for linking the proposed international regulatory organizations to one another. The argument here is that the President's advisers gradually adopted a scheme on the international level that had been proposed and approved by the White House as part of a comprehensive domestic reform program but never implemented.

Although the precise definition of an "administrative agency" varies considerably, many of the most important qualify as "independent" regulatory commissions. Their activities are authorized and loosely "supervised" by Congress; their members are appointed by the executive, but they are directly controlled by neither. The proliferation and expanded authority of such entities during the New Deal, often with overlapping jurisdiction and responsibilities, did not make for efficient administration. In 1936 Roosevelt appointed an independent commission, chaired by administrative theorist Louis Brownlow, to recommend reforms in the process of administrative management.

In a radical and wide-ranging report, the Commission recommended subsuming the independent regulatory commissions under the jurisdiction of existing cabinet departments and establishing a permanent planning board in the White House that would control regional planning boards and executive offices throughout the country.[60] Although Roosevelt strongly supported these recommendations, all the major proposals were defeated in Congress. Historian Barry Karl ties Roosevelt's personal support for this reorganization plan, together with his contemporaneous assault on the Supreme Court, to "the degree to which planning had begun to govern his approach to his second term in office," and his concomitant attempt to secure "the managerial authority he needed."[61]

Roosevelt's charge to the Brownlow Commission to formulate a reorganization plan arose from his recognition that his substantive domestic policy goals were "being jeopardized by a lack of coordination among the new agencies he created."[62] The "new administrative strategy" developed by the Commission was designed to centralize control over the fast-growing regulatory bureaucracy.[63] Although Roosevelt ultimately failed in this endeavor at home, his planners eventually adopted a very similar scheme abroad.

In 1943, Roosevelt envisioned conferences such as the Food and Agriculture Conference as prototypes for a series of permanent international agencies in social and economic fields. According to Russell and Muther, "The President's thought at this time was to have these separate organizations established on a decentralized basis, without references to any kind of over-all coordinating body."[64] A year later his thinking had decidedly changed. The "Possible Plan for the Establishment of an International Organization for the Maintenance of International Peace and Security," drawn up by the Informal Political Agenda Group from December 1943 to July 1944 in preparation for the Dumbarton Oaks Conversations, envisaged that the international organizations for specialized economic or other functions, known as the "functional organizations," "should be related to the general international organization in the sense that the latter would be an over-all organization with power to coordinate international activities in these functional fields."[65]

By January 6, 1945, Roosevelt was referring to a "democratic and fully integrated world-security system."[66] And by 1945 the State Department had developed a detailed chart of what looked very much like a formal world government. It is noteworthy, however, that even this plan did not resemble a world government as might have been conceived by U.S. planners prior to the New Deal, designed from the top down with most regulatory functions encompassed within the international analogue to the executive branch. Here, by contrast, all the different specialized agencies and organizations being folded into the U.N. system had independent identities and decision-making procedures to carry out a variety of functions.

The Problem of Motives

Such a striking correlation of form should also be accompanied by a correlation of motive. Why did the architects of the New Deal believe that discrete administrative agencies were so well suited to achieve specific regulatory tasks? And did they employ the same strategy for the same purposes on the international level?

Several connections stand out. First, the creation of independent administrative agencies domestically and discrete organizations internationally can be understood as part of an effort to depoliticize normally charged political issues and render them amenable to rational resolution. Charles Maier has argued, for instance, that the U.S. vision of the postwar international economic order was fundamentally shaped by the New Deal strategy of recasting political conflicts as "neutral" problems of efficiency and productivity.[67] Taken as a whole, the New Deal administrative agencies represented a new, "depoliticized" arm of the federal government, centralizing power and delegating it to "technically sophisticated officials promoting the public interest."[68]

David Mitrany elevated this focus on pragmatic problem solving to an entire theory of international government. Mitrany cited his observation of the workings of the Tennessee Valley Authority as the "clearest evidence" of his theory of functionalism, according to which a durable international peace order could be built piecemeal by creating functional organizations dedicated to the performance of specific and necessary tasks.[69] He understood the "lesson of the New Deal" as the achievement of a "constitutional revolution through pragmatic action."[70] Roosevelt tackled each problem solely "as a practical issue in itself," without any effort "to relate it to a general theory or system of government," yet at the end of the day "the new functions and the new organs, taken together, have revolutionized the American political system."[71]

Mitrany explicitly held up the New Deal as a model for the postwar world.

> In many of its essential aspects—the urgency of the material needs, the inadequacy of the old arrangements, the bewilderment in outlook—the situation at the end of this war will resemble that in America in 1933, though on a wider and deeper scale. And for the same reasons the path pursued by Mr Roosevelt in 1933 offers the best, perhaps the only, chance for getting a new international life going.[72]

In some aspects, at least, the postwar planners did seem to rely on something akin to Mitrany's functionalist logic. As noted above, for instance, Roosevelt deliberately chose a "noncontroversial" subject like food and agriculture to launch his first organizational initiative.[73]

Other evidence exists, however, that international organizations were also seen as a means of harnessing a particular set of political attitudes—a strategy more akin to the corporatist approach of the early New Deal. Mitrany wrote his impassioned appeal for a functionalist world government in 1943. By 1946, however, with the issuance of the fourth edition of his celebrated pamphlet, he noted the opposition to his theory from various quarters and commented sadly, referring to the "grandeur" of the U.N. system: "Since then [1943] we have moved fast but not well."[74] His disappointment arose from the effort to organize directly in the political sphere, the antithesis of the functional emphasis on building cooperation via nonpolitical "functional" channels. Scholars of the postwar order have largely confirmed his verdict, crediting his theory, and its New Deal origins, as the inspiration for the U.N. "specialized agencies" but regarding the U.N. system as a whole largely as a defeat for his ideas.[75]

Roosevelt himself argued for international organization to capture and fix the wartime spirit of cooperation. In a letter to the opening session of the Food and Agriculture Conference, he explained:

> In this and other United Nations conferences we shall be extending our collaboration from war problems into important new fields. Only by working together can we learn to work together, and work together we must and will.[76]

Conversely, the State Department regarded evidence of increasing fissures in the United Nations coalition in 1943 as a reason to move as quickly as possible to "negotiations to convert the wartime United Nations coalition into an international organization for cooperation to preserve peace after the war."[77]

Although statements such as these do not specify precisely *how* international organization was going to bring about multilateral cooperation, U.S. planners clearly saw a general connection between the two. Here the State Department account of the planning process is quite straightforward. As the discussion of the "unfinished business" of 1944–1945 explains:

> The preparation in the economic and social fields had resulted not so much in development of wholly new policy as it had in elaboration and modification of existing policies and in extension of their scope to meet anticipated postwar conditions. Special effort had been made toward the development of worldwide specialized international organizations, in order to obtain multilateral cooperation in the major fields of economic and social advancement.[78]

Liberalism and Multilateralism

Consider the evidence. The postwar international order is a generally multilateral order, in the sense of being architecturally "open" and collective.[79] It is composed of various types of multilateral regimes and formal multilateral organizations. Although the final structure and details of all these entities required extensive multilateral negotiation, with results that often departed significantly from the proposals developed by U.S. planners, the U.S. plans remained the basic blueprint for a system of global economic, political, social, and cultural regulation.

The U.S. blueprint can be plausibly understood as the projection of a domestic regulatory revolution onto the rest of the world. The New Deal represented a revolution not only in the substance and scope of government regulation but also in its form. The same people who designed a wide range of domestic agencies to administer this regulatory revolution adapted the same generic institutional solution to tackle the world's problems. Their larger organizational scheme for relating these organizations to one another bore a strong resemblance to a domestic plan for organizational reform.

Yet even if the hypotheses above could be definitively proven, even if all the memoirs of individual policymakers and minutes of specific meetings devoted to the design of particular international institutions confirmed that U.S. planners self-consciously sought to regulate the world along U.S. lines, we would still have to confront the larger question posed in this volume. If the postwar international order reflects the American domestic order, at least in principle, and the distinctive characteristic of the postwar order is that it is multilateral, *what is it about the projection of the U.S. legal and political system onto the world that would produce multilateral institutions, in the Ruggie sense, rather than the unilateral hierarchy of Leninism or the bilateral preference system of National Socialism?*

A realist answer would assume that U.S. policymakers, who did, after all, seek to calculate U.S. interests in the international realm and how best to achieve them,[80] believed that the United States would be able to dominate whatever international organizations it created and thus that they would foster, not cooperation per se, but rather cooperation as a means to specifically U.S. ends. They sought to establish regimes on the basis of general organizing principles, in other words, but only as long as the United States could dictate the content of those principles.

In this view, domestic political and legal ideology explains the policy goals, while realism explains the means used to attain them. The generality of the solutions proposed by the United States, the USSR, and Germany, as opposed to the flexible bilateral arrangements supported by various Western European nations, reflected their relative power to impose rules on the world.[81] Yet this account overlooks a number of points. First, it seems odd that U.S. policymakers could not have foreseen the situation that in fact emerged in many of these organizations decades later—that general principles coupled with common decision-making procedures could produce a situation in which other members of these multilateral organizations would seek to make the rules for the United States. Second, without gainsaying the element of U.S. self-interest in the postwar proposals, the distinction between the juridically general American proposals and the asymmetrical proposals of Hitler and Stalin remains.

I propose instead a liberal explanation.[82] The concept of "projecting the U.S. domestic regulatory system onto the world" logically redefines the world as a liberal polity. To students of international relations— scholars, policymakers, and diplomats alike—such a notion may seem hopelessly naive. But many of the U.S. architects of the postwar order were *not* students of the international realm. They were domestic policy- makers who had reshaped the American domestic political, economic, and social system and were now setting out to reorganize the world. Further, even the diplomats and foreign policy experts among them appeared to treat the world as an extension of the U.S. polity, economy, and society. In interpreting its mandate from the President, the Advisory Committee on Post-War Foreign Policy "agreed that its work should be approached from the general standpoint of the kind of world that the United States desired after the war."[83] And, as noted above, U.S. poli- cymakers were increasingly willing to take responsibility for shaping that world.

Substantively, the U.S. President wanted the same world he wanted at home. Addressing Congress on the State of the Union on January 6, 1941, as Hitler's shadow loomed considerably larger, Franklin Roosevelt called for a world "founded upon four essential human freedoms." These included freedom of speech, freedom of religion, "freedom from want," and "freedom from fear." The first two are traditional U.S. constitutional rights. The third and fourth he "translated into world terms" as: "eco- nomic understandings which will secure to every nation a healthy peace- time life for its inhabitants," and "a world-wide reduction of armaments" such that "no nation will be in a position to commit an act of physical aggression against any neighbor."[84] Two years later he was to incorporate these freedoms, along with the other social and economic commitments of the New Deal, into a second American Bill of Rights.[85] However distant that charter may seem from the perspective of contemporary American politics, it played a role at least as part of America's historical vision at a crucial time in its global history.

At the most fundamental level, an image of the world as a projection of the United States means that international order, like domestic order, requires the rule of law. From this perspective, multilateralism is nothing more that the internationalization of the liberal conception of the rule of law. Look again at the definition of multilateralism distilled here: "an institutional form which coordinates relations among three or more states on the basis of generalized principles of conduct: that is to say, principles that specify appropriate conduct for a class of actions, without regard to the particularistic interests of the parties or the strategic exigencies that may exist in any specific occurrence." To an American lawyer, this looks like a definition of *law*. Law operates on the premise that general rules can be applied equally to all. Differences are recognized, of course, but only for the purpose of classifying a particular legal subject or a given set of facts within the domain of another generalizable rule.[86] Ad hoc individual arrangements with specific individuals tailored to specific circumstances is a world governed, not by law, but by the fortuitous distribution of power. Room can be created for such arrangements within a legal system—witness the domestic enforcement of individual contracts and the bargaining mechanism of the GATT—but only subject to more general rules of interpretation and parameters specifying legitimate scope.

Without embarking on a long jurisprudential journey, we can accept the consensus of liberal philosophers since Kant that the liberal rule of law rests on the faith that rules *can* be developed and applied "without regard to the particularistic interests of the parties or . . . strategic exigencies . . . in any specific occurrence." Stephen Holmes has recently identified the "self-exemption taboo" as the first core norm of liberal thought: "the injunction to play by rules which apply equally to all."[87] From this perspective, communist hierarchy or fascist bilateralism equally reflect violations of that taboo. In the final analysis, the meaningful alternatives to multilateralism in the twentieth century can all be reduced to efforts to establish an asymmetrical set of rules favoring the dominant power. These efforts were equally reflective of the domestic ideology of their sponsor states; the ideology in question simply demanded the arrogation of ever more power or the consolidation of hierarchy for revolutionary purpose.

The distinction between the multilateralism of the United States and the bilateralism of other—equally liberal—Western European nations poses a harder question.[88] Here again, however, the difference in policy approaches can be explained by the distinctive national experiences of the countries involved. The United States, geopolitically isolated and relatively inexperienced in foreign affairs, was more inclined to argue from a domestic analogy. The planners at Roosevelt's disposal, like the planners in Berlin and Moscow, drew directly on their experience of shaping a new domestic order.[89] In states like France and Britain, by contrast, centuries of diplomatic interaction impelled leaders to view the international world as distinct and separate from the domestic one. Thus although they shared the liberal understanding of law as a set of general principles, they remained skeptical of the possibilities of establishing such principles beyond national borders. Clemenceau and Lloyd George struggled with Woodrow Wilson at Versailles on precisely this theme.

In the end, of course, U.S. leaders had their own Wilsonian ghosts to contend with and were quite prepared to recognize some very real differences between Washington and the wider world. They did also ultimately have to reach agreement with their allies. Thus as the documents from San Francisco amply attest, all nations were *not* to be treated equally. One set of rules would be recognized for great powers and another for lesser states. Similarly, the new guardians of the world economy, the IMF and the World Bank, had weighted voting systems for the largest contributors. The domestic analogy could only run so far but, nevertheless, far enough to stamp the American postwar order as distinctively multilateral.

Multilateralism is thus the form to be expected from a set of international regimes established by a liberal state with a strong tradition of seeing the world in its own image and a missionary drive to make it so. Liberal domestic polities can have a profoundly realist understanding of international relations; 1945 was the heyday of American realists. Nevertheless, taking responsibility for the world meant regulating abroad as at home, in form as well as substance; more importantly, however, a mindset that could transfer the American administrative revolution to the world by formulating every problem in terms of a need for centralized intervention and every solution in terms of a regulatory institution was a mindset that itself was shaped by a liberal conception of the rule of law.

Earlier multilateral regimes can also be distinguished in terms of the relative strength of the domestic analogy. Not surprisingly, they originally flourished in the regulation of the global commons—an area in which international property rights could be analogized to domestic property rights. Similarly, Holsti's description of the Concert of Europe emphasizes that the participants understood that "force could be used individually or collectively for enforcing certain decisions and for coercing those who threatened the foundations of the order or the system of governance."[90] This is the common understanding of the legitimate use of force under domestic law. The prevalence of multilateralism after 1945 does indeed reflect an *American* hegemony, rather than an American *hegemony*—the hegemony of a liberal state that had relatively little experience or tradition of differentiating between the international and the domestic spheres.

Conclusion

The domestic analogy waxes and wanes among policymakers and scholars alike.[91] I have argued that a widespread realization of the need for steadily increasing domestic regulation among the major industrialized powers fed a desire to regulate the world. The broad phenomenon identified by international legal scholars as the international law of cooperation highlights this causal sequence. The principal characteristics of this body of law—its affirmative nature and the breadth of its substantive scope—correspond closely to the evolution of domestic law in the United States, Canada, and Europe in the 1930s. Laissez-faire was left behind, supplanted by a growing belief in the value, and indeed the necessity of, government regulation.

The similarity in substance and scope between the domestic law of the liberal welfare state and the international law of cooperation in the postwar world has long been recognized. By taking a closer look and examining the ways in which the American plans for the postwar order also reflected the specific institutional *forms* of the New Deal, projected onto the world by many of the domestic architects of the New Deal, I have suggested that the roots of contemporary multilateralism lie in one particular liberal state's vision of the world as a domestic polity, economy, or society writ large. It is thus no accident that the distinctive features of the international law of cooperation correspond to domestic law: "domestic" concerns like health and welfare, citizens rather than states as subjects, the imposition of affirmative rather than negative duties. They are the hallmark of a new and distinctively liberal conception of a world under law. A fundamental premise of that conception is that although law can regulate different groups or classes of subjects differently, its principles must be generalizable within each class or group. The form of multilateralism is thus ultimately a byproduct of the substance of liberalism.

What does this approach say about the future of multilateralism? Several distinctive predictions emerge. First, the shape, strength, and task of particular multilateral organizations can be expected to wax and wane roughly in line with the swings of domestic attitudes toward governmental regulation in the most powerful member states. The domestic regulatory state has grown apace since 1940. To sketch the U.S. experience, thirty-four additional administrative agencies were created since 1960.[92] According to Thomas McCraw, however, the 1960s witnessed the beginnings of "a curious two-pronged reform movement: pointing, on the one hand, toward deregulation and, on the other, toward a new wave of large-scale social and environmental regulation."[93] The pressures for domestic deregulation in countries like Britain and the United States in the late 1970s and 1980s offer an interesting correlation with increasing doubt about the wisdom or effectiveness of various international institutions. On the other hand, the domestic phenomenon that Cass Sunstein has labeled a "rights revolution"—a profession of regulatory statutes and agencies focused on antidiscrimination, general management of social risks, and emerging environmental rights—would be expected to generate an international analogue in the social and environmental areas.

The larger lesson of my analysis, however, is that the rise and fall of specific multilateral organizations has relatively little bearing on the strength and endurance of multilateralism in the generic sense. That phenomenon depends much more fundamentally on the ability of national governments to conceive of law operating in the international realm. The decline of the domestic analogy and the corresponding vision of the international sphere as essentially lawless lead to unilateralism—making up specific rules to suit specific interests in specific circumstances. Ronald Reagan saw the world as a place radically unlike home, a place where the effort to apply general rules could only handicap some nations—the good nations—at the expense of others.[94] This was a challenge to the very core of multilateralism. Conversely, however, the current proliferation of at least would-be liberal democracies should resurrect and recreate a host of multilateral institutions.

In sum, the meaning of multilateralism has much to do with the meaning of law. John Maynard Keynes once had occasion to praise the role of lawyers in building an important part of the postwar multilateral order. In moving the final act of the Bretton Woods conference, he offered the following toast:

> And for my own part, I should like to pay a particular tribute to our lawyers. All the more so because I have to confess that, generally speaking, I do not like lawyers. I have been known to complain that, to judge from results in this lawyer-ridden land, the *Mayflower,* when she sailed from Plymouth, must have been entirely filled with lawyers. . . . Too often lawyers busy themselves to make common sense illegal. Too often lawyers are men who turn poetry into prose and prose into jargon. Not so our lawyers here in Bretton Woods. On the contrary they have turned our jargon into prose and our prose into poetry. And only too often they have had to do our thinking for us. We owe a great debt to Dean Acheson, Oscar Cox, Luxfor, Brenner, Collado, Arnold, Chang, Broches, and our own Beckett of the British Delegation. I have only one complaint against them which I ventured to voice yesterday in Commission II. I wish that they had not covered so large a part of our birth certificate with such very detailed provisions for our burial service, hymns, and lessons, and all.[95]

May lawyers prove equally adept at recovering the deeper meaning of the institution of law.

NOTES

1. All references to multilateralism in this article refer to the generic institutional form defined by Ruggie in the introduction to this volume: "an institutional form which coordinates relations among three or more states on the basis of generalized principles of conduct: that is to say, principles that specify appropriate conduct for a class of actions, without regard to the particularistic interests of the parties or the strategic exigencies that may exist in any specific occurrence."

2. The best overview of important legal scholarship on international organization in the 1950s and early 1960s is contained in an International Law Commission report commissioned by the General Assembly on the relations between states and intergovernmental organizations. The report was commissioned in 1958, issued in 1963, and revised in 1967. Abdullah El-Erian, a leading international legal scholar, was the special rapporteur. El-Erian, "Relations Between States and Inter-Governmental Organizations," *Yearbook of the International Law Commission* (1963), 2:159 (hereafter referred to as ILC Report). For a comprehensive multilingual bibliography of international law "treatises, textbooks, and primers" on this subject prior to 1950, see L. Sohn, *Cases and Other Materials on World Law* (Brooklyn: Foundation Press, 1950), p. 1. More

recent bibliographies can be found in J. P. Baratta, *Strengthening the United Nations: A Bibliography on U.N. Reform and World Federalism* (New York: Greenwood Press, 1987) and Michael Haas, *International Organization: An Inter-Disciplinary Bibliography* (Stanford, Calif.: Hoover Institution Press, 1971).

Legal analyses of the *form* of multilateral institutions have generally produced typologies distinguishing between types of institutions on the basis of type of membership (universal versus closed), specific function (judicial, governmental, administrative, and legislative), and so forth, depending largely on the classificatory imagination of the author. See, e.g., Georg Schwarzenberger, *A Manual of International Law,* 5th ed. (New York: Praeger, 1967).

3. Wolfgang Friedmann, *The Changing Structure of International Law* (New York: Columbia University Press, 1964).

4. Ibid., p. xli (emphasis added). Recognition of the link between the growth of international organizations and the emergence of individuals as subjects of international law in their own right is widespread. See, e.g., Higgins, "Conceptual Thinking about the Individual in International Law," *New York Law School Law Review* (1978), vol. 24; Janis, "Individuals as Subjects of International Law," *Cornell International Law Journal* (1984), vol. 17; L. Sohn, "The New International Law: Protection of the Rights of Individuals Rather Than States," *American University Law Review* (1982), vol. 32; L. Henkin, "International Human Rights as 'Rights,' " *Cardozo Law Review* (1979), vol. 1.

5. W. Jenks, *The Common Law of Mankind* (New York: Praeger, 1958), pp. 8, 17.

6. L. Henkin et al., *International Law, Cases and Materials,* 2d ed. (St. Paul, Minn.: West Publishing Co., 1987), p. xli.

7. See Friedmann, *The Changing Structure of International Law,* p. 60.

8. *ILC Report,* p. 163.

9. See Lord McNair, "The Functions and Differing Legal Character of Treaties," British Year Book of International Law 11 (1930), reprinted in McNair, *The Law of Treaties* (Oxford, England: The Clarendon Press, 1961), p. 740; Manfred Lachs, "Le Developpement et les Fonctions des Traites Multilateraux," *Recueil De Cours* 92 (1957).

10. Derek Bowett, for instance, attributes the development of international organization prior to World War II to increasing international intercourse, a development that he in turn describes as "a constant feature of maturing civilisations," a combination of "advances in the mechanics of communications . . . [and] the desire for trade," producing "a degree of intercourse which ultimately called for regulation by institutional means." *The Law of International Institutions* (London: Praeger, 1963), p. 1. A more recent account by a leading Dutch scholar concurs, relating the devolution of power to the international level to technological change. Henry G. Schermers, *International Institutional Law,* 2d ed., (Amsterdam: Sijthhoff & Noorhoff, 1981), p. 8. Other factors include three important technical innovations that are said to have supported a new institu-

tional superstructure: multilateral treaties, the regularization of international intercourse through the institutionalization of periodic international meetings, and the creation of permanent secretariats. On the emergence of the multilateral treaty as an instrument of diplomacy in the Congress of Vienna, see Lord McNair, "The Functions and Differing Legal Character of Treaties"; Manfred Lachs, "Le Developpmement et les Fonctions des Traites Multilateraux," p. 238 n. 5.; Harold Nicolson, *The Congress of Vienna: A Study in Allied Unity: 1812– 1822* (New York: The Viking Press, 1961), pp. 240–243; and Sir Charles Webster, *The Congress of Vienna: 1814–1815* (New York: Barnes & Noble, Inc., 1969), pp. 98–102.

11. Friedmann, *The Changing Structure of International Law,* p. 8.

12. Ibid.

13. I. Claude, *Swords Into Plowshares* (New York: Random House, 1956), pp. 87–88.

14. Ibid., p. 88. Later legal scholars have often reversed this causal sequence, assuming that the transformation of international law was a secular trend, which then affected domestic politics. For instance, Professor Louis Henkin and his co-authors describe the postwar multilateral order as responsive to the "needs of an international society." Global communication and interdependence combined with the rise of global security, population, and environmental problems "no longer permit an international attitude of laissez-faire." Henkin et al., *International Law,* p. xlii. This society apparently evolves according to its own logic and momentum, focusing less on "interstate diplomatic norms" and instead "deeply penetrat[ing] the economic and social fabrics of national life." Ibid., p. xlii. See also Lachs, "Le Developpement et les Fonctions des Traites Multilateraux," p. 240; Schermers, *International Institutional Law,* p. 4; J. G. Starke, *An Introduction to International Law,* 8th ed. (London: Butterworths, 1977), pp. 10– 15. These scholars have apparently lost access to the original story told by Friedmann and others and thus treat the international law of cooperation as self-generating.

15. John Gerard Ruggie, "International Regimes, Transactions, and Change: Embedded Liberalism in the Postwar Economic Order," *International Organization* (Spring 1982), 36:379, 388. Albert Hirschman has similarly documented the "export" of the Keynesian Revolution from the United States around the world. Hirschman, "How the Keynesian Revolution Was Exported from the United States, and Other Comments," in Hall, ed., *The Political Power of Economic Ideas: Keynesianism Across Nations* (Princeton: Princeton University Press, 1989), pp. 347–359. Hirschman, however, is chronicling the export of a substantive U.S. policy to other nations for adoption as domestic policy.

16. See Asa Briggs, "The World Economy: Interdependence and Planning," in C. L. Mowat, ed., *The New Cambridge Modern History,* vol. 12 (Cambridge, England: Cambridge University Press, 1968); William E. Leuchtenburg, *Franklin D. Roosevelt and the New Deal: 1932–1940* (New York: Harper Torchbooks,

1963), pp. 326–348; Richard Hofstadter, "The New Deal and the New Opportunism," in Alonzo L. Hambly, ed., *The New Deal, Analysis and Interpretation* (New York: Weybright and Talley, 1969), pp. 185–209, especially p. 191.

17. "The Third American Revolution," reprinted in Hambly, *The New Deal, Analysis and Interpretation,* p. 179.

18. Richard Gardner, *Sterling-Dollar Diplomacy in Current Perspective: The Origins and Prospects of International Economic Order,* rev. ed. (New York: Columbia University Press, 1980), pp. 71–77.

19. *Postwar Foreign Policy Preparation, 1939–1945,* Department of State Publication 1 (Washington, D.C.: 1949). This is virtually a step-by-step account of every initiative, committee meeting, report, or speech by U.S. government officials relating to all questions concerning the postwar international order.

20. Ibid., p. 20.

21. Ibid., p. 58. On May 5, 1941, Senator Elmer Thomas of Utah introduced a Senate resolution to authorize the Committee on Foreign Relations to make a fully study of all matters pertaining to the establishment of a lasting peace throughout the world. S. Res. 110, 77th Cong., 1st sess., *Congressional Record,* (May 5, 1941), 87:3551. This initiative occasioned correspondence between the Foreign Relations Committee and the State Department concerning the postwar planning process. See *Postwar Foreign Policy Preparation,* pp. 46–47.

22. The full Committee eventually included eleven members from the Department of State, three members from the War and Navy Departments and the Joint Chiefs of Staff, four members from other government Departments, three members from the White House staff, one from the Library of Congress, four from the wartime agencies, one from the continuing agencies of the Government, five Senators and three Representatives, and ten members from private life. Ibid., p. 72.

23. Ibid., p. 63.

24. These were the Subcommittee on Economic Reconstruction, the Subcommittee on Economic Policy, the Subcommittee on Political Problems, the Subcommittee on Territorial Problems, the Subcommittee on Security Problems, and the Subcommittee on Coordination.

25. The Advisory Committee never resumed operation as originally constituted but splintered into a variety of subsidiary structures in response to the emergence of specific and immediate problems. The two economic subcommittees had already been reconstituted as the Committee on Post-War Foreign Economic Policy, which had been in turn subdivided into twelve subcommittees on a wide range of economic issues. For a detailed list, including committee and subcommittee membership, see *Postwar Foreign Policy Preparation,* appendix 25. On the political side, a group known as the Informal Agenda Group took over policy coordination directly under the aegis of the Secretary.

26. To facilitate more detailed preparations along these lines, the State Department reshuffled again in January 1944 and created two superior commit-

tees directly under the Secretary: the Policy Committee to consider immediate policy questions and the Post-War Programs Committee to aid the Secretary "in formulating post-war policies and making the appropriate international arrangements for their execution." Ibid., p. 208.

27. See Ibid., p. 167.

28. According to Robert Rabin, New Deal regulatory efforts were premised on the belief that "comprehensive government intervention was not only a useful corrective but an essential ingredient for maintaining a general state of equilibrium in the economy." Rabin, *Federal Regulation in Historical Perspective*, Stanford Law Review (1986), 38:1248. The translation of this precept into actual programs soon began to condition public expectations of and reliance on the government as a "guarantor" of a certain minimum standard of living. Ibid., p. 1253.

29. Address to Congress, January 3, 1940, H. Doc. 528, 76th Cong., 3d sess., serial vol. 10501.

30. Statement, January 1, 1940, *Department of State Bulletin*, II, 11.

31. *Postwar Foreign Policy Preparation*, pp. 20–21.

32. Ibid., p. 151.

33. *Department of State Bulletin*, X, 335–342.

34. Ibid., XII, 321–326 and 361.

35. For a complete listing of all the members of these committees and subcommittees, see *Postwar Foreign Policy Preparation*, appendix 25.

36. See A. Schlesinger, *The Age of Roosevelt* (Boston, 1960). R. Moley, *After Seven Years* (New York: Harper & Brothers, 1939), pp. 365–376 (detailing the incoherence of New Deal economic policies due to the contradiction between the philosophy of "Concentration and Control" versus that premised on the "curse of bigness.")

37. Much of the legal debate about these institutions then and now turns on the constitutionality of combining constitutionally separated powers in an independent regulatory agency and of both usurping and shirking the powers granted the coordinate branches of government in the process. See, e.g., Cass Sunstein, "Constitutionalism After the New Deal," *Harvard Law Review* (1987), 101:491–500; Aranson, Gellhorn, and Robinson, "A Theory of Legislative Delegation," *Cornell Law Review* (1982), 68:63–67; Schoenbrod, "The Delegation Doctrine: Could the Court Give It Substance?" *Michigan Law Review* (1985), 83:1249–1274; Miller, "Independent Agencies," *Supreme Court Review* (1986), pp. 96–97.

38. For a complete list, see "Administrative Procedure in Government Agencies," Report of the Committee on Administrative Procedure, Senate, 77th Cong., Doc. No. 8, (Washington, D.C.: U.S. Government Printing Office, 1941), p. 10. See also Sunstein, "Constitutionalism After the New Deal," 424 n. 9; ibid., *After the Rights Revolution: Reconceiving the Regulatory State* (Cambridge, Mass.: Harvard University Press 1990), pp. 23–25; appendix C.

39. The National Recovery Act is the premier example of the corporatist approach during this period—an "ambitious attempt to fashion a social peace treaty between business and labor." D. Brand, *Corporatism and the Rule of Law* (Ithaca, N.Y.: Cornell University Press, 1988), p. 21. Competition had to be replaced by cooperation; the national economy was to be governed, not by the dictates of the market, but by "affirmative national planning" by business, labor, and government. Schlesinger, *The Age of Roosevelt,* p. 389. See also Ellis W. Hawley, *The New Deal and the Problem of Monopoly* (Princeton: Princeton University Press, 1966), p. 13; Barry D. Karl, "Constitution and Central Planning: The Third New Deal Revisited," *Supreme Court Review* (1988), p. 163. For a discussion of the peculiar failure of American-style corporatism, see Margaret Weir, Ann Shola Orloff, and Theda Skocpol, eds., *The Politics of Social Policy in the United States* (Princeton: Princeton University Press, 1988).

40. The hallmarks of this period are programs like the Works Progress Administration (WPA) and social security. From an economic perspective the emphasis shifted from control of supply to stimulation of demand. From a social-political perspective, the government became relatively less concerned with restoring business confidence and more with guaranteeing minimum individual protections. At the same time, on the business side, the Second New Deal also heralded what Schlesinger describes as a transition from a "managed to a mixed economy: the one tried to convert business through new institutions, the other tried to discipline it through new laws." Schlesinger, *The Age of Roosevelt,* p. 392.

41. The SEC, established in 1934, or the Public Utility Holding Company Act of 1935 fall into this category. More technical regulatory agencies such as the Marine Administration, the Civil Aeronautics Authority, and the Federal Communications Commission also flourished.

42. Rabin, *Federal Regulation in Historical Perspective,* p. 1252. For a general discussion of how all these strategies overlapped, see ibid., pp. 1243–1253.

43. *Postwar Foreign Policy Preparation,* p. 151.

44. Ibid., p. 208.

45. Ibid., pp. 143, 208.

46. Ibid., p. 133.

47. Ibid., pp. 235–236.

48. Ibid., p. 101.

49. Ibid., p. 133.

50. Ibid., p. 342.

51. Ibid., p. 339.

52. Ibid., p. 354.

53. Ibid., p. 358. For an expanded discussion of the purposes such organizations were intended to serve, see the memorandum titled "Bases of Our Program for International Economic Cooperation," submitted by Secretary Hull at the Moscow Conference on October 20, 1943. *Postwar Foreign Policy Pre-*

paration, appendix 30; see also "Statement of the Problem and Summary of the Issues and Recommendations on International Commodity Preparation" (April 4, 1944), ibid., appendix 44; "Summary of the Interim Report of the Special Committee on Relaxation of Trade Barriers" (December 8, 1943), ibid., appendix 45; "Summary: Tentative Program for Dealing with International Cartels" (May 29, 1944), ibid., appendix 46; "Proposals for Consideration by an International Conference on Trade and Employment" (November 1945), ibid., appendix 47.

54. Ibid., p. 354–355.

55. The full record of the substance of all the discussions merely described in *Postwar Foreign Policy Preparation* is newly available from the National Archives. These documents have recently been made available as a collection of more than 5,000 microfiche under the title *Post World War II Foreign Policy Planning.* The collection reproduces Record Group 59 at the National Archives and is available from University Press of America.

56. *Postwar Foreign Policy Preparation,* appendix 44, p. 621.

57. Ibid., appendix 45, p. 624.

58. Ibid., appendix 46, p. 625.

59. Ibid., appendix 47, p. 627.

60. See Barry Karl, *The Uneasy State* (Chicago: Chicago University Press, 1983), pp. 155–164.

61. Ibid., p. 163.

62. Brand, *Corporatism and the Rule of Law,* 313.

63. Ibid. See also Barry Karl, *Executive Reorganization and Reform in the New Deal* (Chicago: Chicago University Press, 1963).

64. Ruth B. Russell and Jeannette E. Muther, *A History of the United Nations Charter: The Role of the United States 1940–1945* (Washington, D.C.: The Brookings Institution, 1958), p. 66. See also *Postwar Foreign Policy Cooperation,* p. 143 (In 1943 Roosevelt "favored . . . the establishment of entirely separate functional agencies in the economic field.").

65. Ibid., p. 271.

66. State of the Union Address, January 6, 1945, *Department of State Bulletin,* XII: 27.

67. Charles S. Maier, "The Politics of Productivity: Foundations of American International Economic Policy after World War II," *International Organization* (1977), 31:607.

68. Sunstein sees the New Deal "reformation" as having a substantive as well as an institutional component, involving an assault on the common law as a *reflection* of the laissez-faire status quo. Sunstein, "Constitutionalism after the New Deal," pp. 508–509.

69. Mitrany, "The Prospect of Integration: Federal or Function," in Paul Taylor and A. J. R. Groom, eds., *Functionalism: Theory and Practice in International Relations* (New York: Crane, Russak & Co., 1975), p. 67.

70. David Mitrany, *A Working Peace System,* 4th ed. (London: National Peace Council, 1946), p. 3.

71. Ibid., pp. 29–30.

72. Ibid., p. 30.

73. It is also possible that U.S. policymakers envisioned that international organizations could be used to circumvent the problems of sovereignty just as domestic administrative organizations had succeeded in circumventing the checks on effective action imposed by the constitutionally mandated separation of powers. Within the American constitutional framework, the new regulatory institutions were all designed to liberate the policymaking process from many of the checks and balances so carefully inserted by the Framers. The premise for such a departure was that the problems facing the nation could be solved only within a "system of centralized and unified powers," elevating the national government over the states and the Presidency over the courts and Congress. Sunstein, *After the Rights Revolution,* p. 23.

A similar conclusion could have been drawn in the face of the checks and balances of the sovereign state system. It is arguably a sign of the thinking of the time that the celebrated realist Hans Morgenthau drew precisely this analogy, comparing the checks and balances written into the U.S. Constitution and with those automatically operating by virtue of the balance of power among independent sovereigns in the international system. Hans J. Morganthau, *Politics Among Nations* (New York: Knopf, 1948), pp. 126–129. Morgenthau, of course, saw great merit in these constraints in both contexts, as a safeguard both of the stability of the systems and the "autonomy of their constituent elements." New Deal policymakers and postwar planners would have been less conscious of these virtues.

74. Mitrany, *A Working Peace System,* p. 5.

75. Mark F. Imber, *The USA, ILO, UNESCO and IAEA* (New York: St. Martin's Press, 1989), pp. 15–16; Douglas Williams, *The Specialized Agencies and the United Nations* (New York: St. Martin's Press, 1987), p. 2; Hidemi Suganami, *The Domestic Analogy and World Order Proposals* (Cambridge, England: Cambridge University Press, 1989), p. 120.

76. *Department of State Bulletin,* (May 22, 1943), 8:455–456.

77. *Postwar Foreign Policy Preparation,* p. 163.

78. Ibid., p. 356.

79. John Gerard Ruggie, "Multilateralism: The Anatomy of an Institution," in this volume.

80. See the account of the questions posed by U.S. planners discussed above.

81. See Ruggie, "International Regimes, Transactions, and Change," p. 382, on the ability of power to dictate "the *form* of the international order, but not its *content.*" In this view, content instead flows from fusion of power with social purpose.

82. For a systematic elaboration of the "liberal paradigm" in international

relations theory, isolating and explaining the differences in substantive assumptions and methodological approaches between realists and liberals, see Andrew Moravcsik, "Liberal Internationalism and International Relations Theory" (working paper presented at the University of Chicago Program on International Politics, Economics, and Security, January 1992).

83. *Postwar Foreign Policy Preparation,* p. 79.

84. State of the Union Address, January 6, 1941, H. Doc. 1, 77th Cong., 1st sess., serial vol. 10598. The Atlantic Charter, signed in August 1941, proclaimed these principles to the world, explicitly incorporating "freedom from fear" and "freedom from want," and according to Roosevelt, implicitly including freedom of speech and of religion. See *Postwar Foreign Policy Preparation,* pp. 50–51.

85. F. D. Roosevelt, "Economic Bill of Rights" (1944), reprinted in Walter Laqueur and Barry Rubin, eds., *The Human Rights Reader* (New York: New American Library, 1979), p. 269.

86. For the classic explication of this process, see Edward Levi, *An Introduction to Legal Reasoning* (Chicago: University of Chicago Press, 1949), particularly pp. 1–8.

87. Holmes, "The Liberal Idea," *The American Prospect* (Fall 1992), p. 89.

88. For a description of early Western European proposals for a series of bilateral trade and defense agreements, see the accounts by Ruggie, "Multilateralism: The Anatomy of an Institution" and Steve Weber, in this volume.

89. Steve Walt has shown that revolutionary regimes are far more likely to see the world through the lens of their domestic experience. Walt, "Revolution and War," *World Politics* (April 1992), vol. 44, no. 2.

90. Holsti, "Governance without Government," cited in Ruggie, this volume, note 55.

91. For an excellent recent study of the role of the domestic analogy in major international reform efforts from Napoleon to the present, see Hidemi Suganami, *The Domestic Analogy and World Order Proposals.* Suganami advances very similar arguments about the importance of the post-New Deal domestic analogy. See pp. 118–120.

92. Charles Schultze, *The Public Use of Private Interest* (Washington, D.C.: Brookings Institution, 1977), pp. 7–12; see also Sunstein, *After the Rights Revolution,* pp. 24–30.

93. Thomas K. McCraw, *Prophets of Regulation* (Cambridge, Mass.: Harvard University Press, 1984), p. 303.

94. For the most concise and pungent exposition of this view, see Robert Bork, "The Limits of 'International Law,' " *The National Interest,* (Winter 1989/90), no. 18, p. 3.

95. I *Proceedings and Documents of the United Nations Monetary and Financial Conference,* Bretton Woods, N.J., July 1–22, 1944, 1109 (1944).

5. Elect Locally—Order Globally: Domestic Politics and Multilateral Cooperation

❖

Peter F. Cowhey

W HY does multilateralism work? Multilateralism is a demanding form of international cooperation because it embraces commonly applicable rules for all countries, which in turn imply a greater degree of nondiscrimination and diffuse reciprocity, in the provision of linked international agreements (e.g., money, trade, and security).[1] These stiff requirements should ring alarm bells for an optimistic neo-Grotian, much less a neorealist.

Multilateralism is not an absolute. It can strongly shape the operation of an era's regimes without excluding all other organizing principles. While countries have not slavishly adhered to multilateralism in practice, by historical standards a remarkable degree of multilateralism has dominated the global scene for the past forty-five years. The unusual prominence of multilateralism since 1945 reinforces three perennial questions about international cooperation. First, how do the parties of a regime work out its subsequent interpretation and adaptation? When a contract (such as a regime) leaves open important questions about implementation and adjustment, the original agreement hinges on expectations about how these will be worked out. This question is closely linked to a second. Given the vital role of the dominant powers within a·regime for its implementation and adaptation, and given their relatively numerous options for foreign policy (relative to lesser powers), how can other countries trust the good faith of the dominant powers?[2] This is particularly worrisome because multilateralism provides even fewer external checks on dominant powers than purely bilateral or minilateral orders do. Third, why should other countries agree to support multilateralism ac-

I thank Jonathan Aronson, Deborah Avant, Jeff Frieden, Gary Jacobson, Robert Keohane, Sam Kernell, John Odell, Paul Papayoanou, John Ruggie, Rip Smith, and Steve Weber for their comments. Gary Cox, Mathew McCubbins, and Frances Rosenbluth made several important suggestions while I was formulating my initial ideas.

tively, rather than some other form of internationalism?[3] Second-tier powers certainly have to be more flexible about the international order, but they have little reason to support a noxious or fickle one. If the hegemon can freely rewrite the rules, for example, a smart "follower strategy" (that is, betting resources on playing for advantages within the rules) can be easily ruined.

Thus, the dominant power has latitude in formulating the international order, but limits exist on the set of acceptable alternatives. Others will not become fully committed to working within the multilateral order unless they believe the dominant powers intend to stay with it. And it is in the interest of great powers to reduce their burdens by winning voluntary compliance.[4]

The balance of this paper examines when the promises of dominant powers are credible in a multilateral order. The first part further specifies the problems pertaining to credibility by showing that multilateral orders realistically require some form of hierarchic contracting. The second part sets out a model of the conditions concerning domestic politics that enhance the credibility of promises about multilateral regimes. This paper examines two cases in more depth. The third part shows that the electoral and governance system of the United States was far more propitious for credible American commitments in 1945 than has been recognized. New institutional designs for the governance of foreign policy further strengthened these commitments by adroitly reconciling diverse political incentives of the President and Congress. At the same time, many specific features of the current multilateral order grew out of the demands of domestic U.S. politics. These features include items that deviate from the ideal type of multilateralism and those that lend a special American twist to multilateralism. The fourth part examines how the current institutional structure of Japanese politics severely limits the credibility of its promises. Two routes are possible for altering Japanese credibility—redesign of its internal political economy in response to global negotiations or changes in its electoral system.

Multilateralism and Contracting

Multilateralism reduces some forms of transaction costs (such as those incurred by numerous bilateral deal), but a broad social contract covering many issues for an indefinite period of time may also create its own variety of transaction costs. In particular, no state joining a multilateral order can foresee all possible contingencies. All nations recognize that much of the practical meaning of the norms, principles, and rules of a multilateral regime depend on how the great power(s) interprets and adapts to them. This feature of multilateral regimes is in fact a common response to this type of collective-action problem.[5] *Hierarchic contracts* are those whereby two or more parties enter into a contract with several unspecified important terms and within broad limits grant one party (or perhaps a few parties) much more authority over how to adapt to unforeseen contingencies. Recognizing the dependence of a multilateral regime on hierarchic contracting is similar to Hedley Bull's argument that great powers have different obligations in international society because of common needs of international society.[6]

Multilateral regimes succeed if, like a successful corporate culture, they convey the practical meaning of the regime's organizing principles (especially about implementation and adaptation), provide focal points for behavior (such as rules of thumb for action), and communicate this common understanding to stronger and weaker powers alike.[7] These expectations will help all states to understand how the strong are bound by the regime and how to assess compliance by all parties. The constancy of great powers and the ability of others to judge the good faith of great powers are vital to the regime. Obviously, the dominant power has an interest in building a solid reputation for reliability because it will lower the transaction costs of leadership. So, to this extent, the regime itself is a valuable source of stability because dominant powers find it more worthwhile to invest in their own reputation by supporting the regime. But good reason exists to doubt that prudent regard for one's own reputation is enough to convince other players of reliability.[8]

The problem is no different in principle than the one faced by lenders to a sovereign government. The "new monarchs" in Europe's eighteenth century tried to increase borrowing for waging war. But the monarchs were legally untouchable. There was nothing to stop them from unrealistic spending and borrowing. This made private capital wary of doing business with them except at premium rates. However, the rise of power of the English Parliament created a new check on the spending policies of the king. This institutional control lowered the cost of borrowing for the British and abetted their war effort. In short, proper checks and balances on political leaders can reduce transaction costs by making their promises believable.[9]

Checks were vital even if it was in the interest of the king to act faithfully. First, the king may have a long-term interest to follow the strategy, but short-term difficulties may call his resolve into question.[10] Second, imagine that the question is not paying the monthly interest on a loan but enforcing the law subject to the restrictions of the Magna Carta. Substantial variance is likely to exist around the mean level of performance. This makes it hard for others to judge performance and grant discretion in the absence of other checks on the king's performance. Third, the "monarchy" (or royal family) may have a concern over its reputation, but this king in particular may have other private incentives that are overriding.

This logic shows why it is not enough to argue that a change in the international interests of dominant powers assures their credibility.[11] This is particularly true as multilateralism grows in importance because the specific international checks on the great powers are less binding.

Analogous experiences with the types of collective-action problems common to multilateralism point not only to the importance of hierarchic contracts but also to the conditions that bolster chances for success.[12] In general, these contracts work better if the private incentives and institutional checks on such leaders as company presidents are consistent with their mission as defined by the corporate culture.[13] If incentives are inconsistent and checks are weak, cooperation will break down because others will discount promises by executives.

To illustrate, the firm's leadership should have an incentive to follow the rules of the corporate culture even if short-term costs are involved simply because it is too costly to her reputation if she defects. But this logical self-interest is likely to prove insufficient assurance to others. Hence, specialized institutional rewards and checks reinforce reputational motivations. If executive leadership of the firm has a monetary stake in it, then the executive has fewer incentives for seizing short-term opportunistic gains that come at the long-term interest. (Hence, the common practice of equity holdings as compensation for executives.) Firms also try to define specific ways in which executives can build their reputations to further their careers (e.g., short-term cuts in costs or improved employee morale).[14] Internal controls in large firms also typically include extensive auditing.

How then do the leading powers make their commitment credible in a multilateral order? This paper argues that domestic politics are critical for the credibility of a dominant power. Multilateral orders are more credible if countries believe the political leadership of the major power(s) is subject to significant domestic constraints on defecting from the rules of the multilateral order. Once this credibility is established it makes sense for second-tier powers to cooperate within a multilateral framework.[15] While other devices may also enhance credibility, domestic political factors are virtually indispensable.[16]

The efficacy of multilateralism, then, is contingent in part on the credibility of great-power promises. These promises are more credible if domestic political incentives are favorable to the multilateral commitment. In particular, multilateralism will be more credible if: (1) the structure of political competition in the country (e.g., type of voting system and voter preferences) provides incentives for leaders to advocate the provision of international collective goods[17]; (2) the structure of political competition makes it difficult for an individual party or leader to reverse major foreign policy commitments quickly; (3) conflicts between domestic political incentives and multilateral commitments can be eased by adaptation of domestic and international institutions; and (4) domestic political and economic decisions are transparent to interested third parties.

How should we think about the structure of domestic political incentives? My analysis pays special attention to the electoral system. Some electoral systems make it far easier to produce collective goods (such as the fruits of multilateralism) than others do. Parties in these systems have incentives to produce collective goods favored by the "median voter" despite the normal collective-action problems posed by the narrow electoral interests of individual legislators. The United Kingdom is a classic example.[18] Other electoral systems disproportionately reward the supply of private goods, as the discussion of Japan will show. When electoral systems of leading powers make it extremely hard for political leaderships to innovate concerning the supply of collective goods, then special "institutional" fixes may be necessary to handle foreign policy commitments.

Domestic Politics and Credibility

Domestic politics play four important roles in making multilateral commitments credible. First, the current agent holding power in the dominant power (and her counterparts in second-tier powers who also have to follow the rational strategy of long-term gains by contributing) needs private incentives consistent with the long-term interests of the country. Thus, a leading power should have an electoral system that rewards leaders for proposing and delivering broad collective goods, such as multilateralism. To the extent that the system is disproportionately geared to private goods, it is less likely to reward political leaders for multilateral commitments.[19]

Second, the benefits for leadership of defecting have to be limited. Thus, the great power is more credible if the electorate's position on multilateralism is basically favorable. This means that the defection by any current political leaders from multilateralism is less likely to be permanent simply because the policy space for any winning coalition is likely to stay attached to multilateralism over time. The domestic opposition will punish the defector. For example, the Social Democratic Party's willingness to attack Helmut Kohl over his public reluctance to promise respect for the Polish boundary in 1990 was one spur for a reversal of his position. Once he did so in public it enhanced the credibility of his diplomatic pledges.[20]

A corollary to the argument about the costs of defection is that the multilateral order is more stable if it has more than a minimum base of support in the domestic politics of the dominant power. Creating a multilateral design in the 1940s that won bipartisan support in the United States made the order more secure and credible. It also meant that the leading power's culture and society were pumping out support for the multilateral order full bore to the rest of the world. The United States was not just the workshop of the world for many years, it was the idea shop for the world culturally and intellectually. A multilateral order resonant with the United States benefited from the enormous flow of socialization of world elites flowing out of the United States.[21]

Third, political leadership may create secondary political institutions to reinforce multilateralism by making the forms of multilateral commitment more consistent with the electoral imperative. Commitments are more credible to the extent that institutional adaptation by the leading power resolves political dilemmas posed by multilateralism.[22]

Fourth, because focal points are ambiguous, compliance to them is never unambiguous. Other countries have more faith in the order if they can independently judge intent and compliance.[23] Political orders that are not easily transparent to other countries are less credible. For example, consider the problems for establishing the Soviet Union's credibility on arms control and detente commitments prior to perestroika or Japan's current problems when pledging open markets.[24]

Furthermore, a central problem for the hegemon is how to make the workings of its domestic economic institutions credible to other countries. So much of the power and performance of the dominant power and the multilateral order is economic that the domestic market of a leading power sets a critical term for public order. If other countries consider the market to be discriminatory and secretive in its workings, it is hard to have faith in the multilateral order. Jeff Frieden summarizes the challenge nicely in his description of what it took for the United States to establish the Bretton Woods system:

> The ability of the United States to construct a stable and lasting international investment position depended on the reliability of a number of American commitments. First, U.S. goods markets were generally open to the country's real or potential debtors. Second, the market for U.S. dollars was open and predictable, so that savers and investors at home and abroad would be willing to engage in foreign currency operations; this also required some form of international monetary cooperation. Third, U.S. capital markets were free enough from major government manipulation to overcome investors' and borrowers' fears of political risk.[25]

In sum, the multilateral order can define an acceptable form of relationship between leading and secondary powers that enhances the productivity of the multilateral order. The order helps to define the prerogatives and obligations of the leading powers and secondary powers. But the burden of leading adaptation to change is in the hands of the dominant powers. Therefore, their incentive structure is crucial. While international incentives are important (the United States got to be the military head of NATO), no account would be persuasive in the absence of an examination of the impact of domestic politics. The next two sections explore the variables defining the impact of domestic politics through reflection on the U.S. and Japanese involvement in multilateralism.

U.S. Politics

The conventional wisdom about the U.S. pledge to the multilateral order is that the U.S. system of governance was either irrelevant or a hindrance to our credibility. The best justifications for this view are twofold. First, Congress is inclined to worry about local constituencies more than foreign policy, and the United States has a much weaker executive branch than many countries (a weak state). Second, there was a long powerful strain of isolationism in American politics, especially in the Republican party, that made multilateralism a precarious product of bipartisanship largely through the courting of Senator Vandenberg.[26]

I shall make five arguments about why American political institutions contributed to the credibility of U.S. promises about internationalism in general and an American version of multilateralism in particular. First, the U.S. electoral system encourages parties to take stands on issues involving the public good and makes it risky for a party to reverse positions if they are close to the position of the median voter. Second, substantial electoral incentives existed to support multilateralism. Third, the division of control over the U.S. government makes reversal by one branch of government of a major commitment difficult to achieve. Fourth, the division of power also permits fine-tuning through new institutional arrangements to resolve political problems in promulgating multilateralism. Fifth, the political economy of the United States made its internal market and its regulation relatively transparent and credible to other countries.

A Model of U.S. Politics

Institutional analysts have pointed out that the structure of the electoral system and the division of power among the branches of government shape the patterns of politics. It has become commonplace among analysts of American foreign policy to argue that U.S. institutions erode a strong foreign policy because Congress is fickle and particularistic about foreign policy (owing to members' search for votes and the inability of congressional leadership to control the nomination process for congressional seats) and the executive branch is relatively weak.[27] In contrast, this section argues that institutional structure in the United States was relatively conducive to credible commitments.

The structure of the U.S. electoral system influences the ability to make foreign policy commitments. On one hand, the concern over party identity provides incentives for parties to take consistent stands on major issues of foreign policy. On the other, the differences in electoral incentives for the President, Senate, and House also lead to diverging approaches to foreign policy.

The single-member district (with victory for the highest vote count) for Congress has two broad consequences. The first is the well-known tendency to pursue the median voter through a two-party system in order to build a majority. The second is to make party positions on matters of broad public policy far more salient than, say, in the Japanese electoral system. Simply put, a two-party majoritarian system gives elected federal officials an interest in building the reputation of their party for successful conduct of policies designed to build the public good. It also gives politicians an incentive to find and organize new constituencies who may represent substantial chunks of votes in many districts even if they are currently diffuse interests. (Consider the congressional aid given to Nader's early consumer efforts.) Party identification is still an important determinant of electoral fortunes.[28]

The more vital point is whether foreign policy matters much to voters. A widespread view in the literature on voting and U.S. foreign policy has held that the low level of information on international affairs possessed by voters means that foreign policy is not important. This equation between information and importance, and between information and rationality, is now under strong attack in the voting literature. Studies suggest that voters do make judgments on issues where they have little information (including many pocketbook domestic issues) and do so in ways that make sense given limited information.[29] Foreign policy may matter less consistently to voters, but foreign policy issues always have the potential of igniting retrospective punishment by voters.[30] While congressional members may often be relatively ignorant about specifics of foreign policy, they delegate power to members who are willing to pay attention and accommodate the political dictates of the party.[31]

The implication of brand name identities for parties is more than a willingness, and necessity, to address major issues. It also suggests that parties have a tough time reversing positions once they have made a major public commitment. Unless the position of the median voter has changed radically, a major shift in party position is likely to leave significant openings for the opposition. Thus, shifts in the ideological position of particular incumbents in office are less likely to produce major changes because the party as a whole has few incentives to move dramatically. If it does, it will strengthen the opposition. In the postwar era the rejection of the presumed causes of the Depression (autarky and isolationism) and the opposition to communism kept the electorate extremely focused for at least twenty-five years.

To be sure, institutional affiliation also shapes incentives. House members tend to be the most parochial and have the shortest time horizons for judging programs, Senate members less so, and the President has to be the most cosmopolitan simply because he is most directly identified with certain swings in national well-being. Accordingly, the House should most strongly view foreign policy through the lens of local distributional impacts and the concerns of specialized voter groups in districts (e.g., German Americans in Milwaukee or the Nissan plant in his district).

The differences in electoral incentives should lead to institutional innovations for major new commitments in order to reconcile different time horizons and size of constituencies.[32] Many of these innovations will create: (1) new bureaucracies to advocate and safeguard the policy innovation over time in return for advocates getting less than they want now; (2) institutional "fire alarms" (devices making it easy for the disgruntled to get information and complain); (3) "trip wires" (requirements for explicit authorization of certain uses of a general authority) to satisfy critics about contingent dangers of an innovation; (4) "time limits" on authority to force executors of the policy to constantly pay attention to critics; (5) "stacking the decision process" to make sure that all key interests get represented.[33]

Moreover, all elected officials choose policies that disproportionately favor their supporters and emphasize particularistic benefits in the design of collective goods. We have had a potent national defense for forty odd years and a bloated budget to do so. Oil resources for the postwar world were developed quickly but at the cost of a price formula decreed by the Marshall Plan that protected U.S. domestic oil production and legitimated significant rents for the international oil companies.[34]

In summary, we should expect that political parties will invest in creating collective goods concerning foreign policy because these create political reputations for the party, because these commitments are hard to reverse absent a massive shift in voter preferences (in part because of the counterstrategies available to the opposition), because differences in electoral incentives should force institutional innovation to reconcile new foreign policy commitments with electoral considerations, and because all political leaders will tend to favor collective goods offering particularistic benefits.

The United States and the Creation of Multilateralism

How closely did U.S. politics fit the expectations just set forth? Did party leadership think that they would do well in elections by supporting multilateralism? I argue that support for internationalism was strong, and multilateralism was a politically attractive version of internationalism, especially after it was given an American twist.

Good evidence shows that internationalism was good politics. The restructuring of Europe and Japan to avoid another war was a critical U.S. mission consistent with voter preferences. As Michael Barone trenchantly notes, the consensus on foreign policy was already established by 1944. Although isolationists had run well in some congressional districts in 1942 (when the news on the war was bad), by 1944 both potential candidates of the Republican party, Willkie and Dewey, strongly supported an "internationalist" platform. Moreover, in a race where Franklin Roosevelt's electoral victory was far from sweeping (despite the electoral college vote), both Fish of New York and Nye of North Dakota lost on isolationist platforms. Taft only squeaked by in Ohio. And in 1946, a major Republican year, the two leading isolationists of the party lost their Senate seats in Montana and Massachusetts. Moreover, the Dewey wing of the party seized control in 1944 of the presidential wing of the party for the next twenty years.[35] When Dewey faced Truman in 1948, standard accounts of the campaign show foreign policy played either a minor role or a moderately positive one for the Democrats because the Democrats had created a policy with generally broad public support.[36]

Perhaps most tellingly, when the Republicans controlled Congress in 1946, they chose Vandenberg as chair of the Foreign Relations Committee even though he had already clearly shown himself to be committed to an internationalist order. Given what we now know about party caucus control over chairmanships, this is a clear indication that the Republican congressional membership did not want to fight over internationalism.[37] The glue that bound the two parties was, of course, the willingness of the Truman White House to identify internationalism with anticommunism, the one horror that even Midwest conservatives could not stomach.[38]

A bedrock message from the electorate drove both parties—government was not to repeat mistakes that led to the Depression, and the United States would intervene when necessary to avoid a threat to peace and security. American political leaders had concluded that protectionism, autarky, and trading blocs were deep threats to macroeconomic prosperity and a major source of conflict.[39] Moreover, neither congressional party challenged the fundamental premise that government should play an active role in guiding macroeconomic trends with some concern for social welfare. With widespread fears of a possible depression, not even conservatives wanted to press for a reaffirmation of Hoover.[40]

The broader battle was over general economic philosophy and the precise terms of internationalism. The 1946 electoral resurgence of Republicans led to a cap on the growing power of labor unions (which were widely blamed for inflation), less spending, and rejection of detailed micromanagement of the economy (by wage and price controls, for example).[41] The election also reinforced the middle-of-the-road wing of the Democratic party in Congress that was more skeptical of government planning. The Democrats did not become laissez-faire, but they also rejected any version of industrial policy or corporatism built around a troika of much-strengthened unions, big business, and big government.

Thus, one might expect that U.S. foreign economic policy would permit measures to stimulate general global recovery and open markets but that this would lead to sharp debate over any plans to have the government administer markets. Ironically, this skepticism of planning enhanced the credibility of the United States in its commitment to open world markets.

The quick passage of the huge (2+% of government spending) Marshall Plan was a testimony to the potency of anticommunism and the fears of rising protectionism in a dollar-starved Europe.[42] While there were protests about the potential of bleeding the United States for Europe and creeping socialism through foreign aid, the Marshall Plan was a wonderful tonic for grassroots political and economic interests. It represented a dramatic yet nonmilitary response to communism just when American voters were thoroughly wary of Russia. More crucially, it was an enormous economic boost for all potential U.S. exporters. Republican farmers sold wheat to Europe, and Democratic union workers got job security from manufactured exports.[43]

But why did internationalism become multilateralism, and why did multilateralism endure? In part, as Ruggie argues, it represented the influence of ideas on American leadership.[44] But significant disagreement also arose about many of these ideas, and some institutional designs flopped. Multilateralism succeeded in part because it avoided certain types of political problems that would have plagued other internationalist solutions.

The practical politics of multilateralism meant that it bore the strong imprint of an order tailored to the preferences of America's political leadership, as opposed simply to dreams of the executive branch's planners. These political roots show up in four ways. First, multilateralism had deep political roots in the practical politics of ethnicity in the United States. This made it Eurocentric. Second, the insistence on public economic institutions reflected long-standing suspicions of delegating power to Wall Street, especially among Democrats. Third, the degree of national control over the International Monetary Fund (IMF) was also a legacy of traditional fears in U.S. politics of foreigners "bleeding the United States dry." The counterpart in security affairs was the strong insistence on concrete force commitments by allies to NATO, coupled with insistence on "trip wires" and "stacking the decision process" on any use of force. Fourth, the Keynesian synthesis for embedded liberalism largely bore the conservative stamp of the 1946 U.S. election. It was reinforced by the numerous exceptions to multilateralism that Congress insisted upon for such arenas as commodities and service markets. Altogether, these controls, conditions, and Eurocentric globalism made the world order less than fully multilateral, although the United States did insist on frameworks that allowed it to define links between its Atlantic and Pacific spheres of interest.

Multilateralism in Europe solved a fundamental political dilemma for both parties because it included the homelands of key ethnic minorities. Therefore, it avoided the crossfire created by the politics of continuing ethnic ties to European homelands by American voters. For example, Irish Americans always resented relying primarily on Britain, and German Americans had been isolationist because internationalism traditionally had been defined as anti-German until the Marshall Plan and NATO. Dean Acheson ordered the end of all internal State Department studies organized around a special relationship with Britain.[45] The United States explicitly rejected the United Kingdom's effort to structure the defense of Europe along a dumbbell structure—the United Kingdom–France–Benelux pact on one side and a United Kingdom–Canada–United States pact on the other with the United Kingdom as the special link. The United States wanted to negotiate only about a multilateral North Atlantic pact.[46] Multilateralism favored everybody's homeland, unless the Soviets forbade it.

Indeed, one might argue that the global order after 1945 was, as a practical "corporate culture," really a Eurocentric order. American voters in 1945 were largely European, and so was the practical thrust of the multilateral innovations.[47] The United States was the pivot that then imposed a link between its multilateral arrangements for Europe and its largely bilateral, ad hoc commitments to Asia (where there was less intensive common ground to bind together allies and far less voter sensitivity to bilateralism favoring any one power).[48]

Moreover, the practice of multilateralism also addressed many of the concerns over internationalism possibly bleeding America while other countries shirked. Collective public institutions (e.g., NATO or the World Bank)[49] with conditions on access to their benefits provided standardized criteria for resolving the endless possibilities for disputes on burden sharing posed by bilateralism. In short, from the viewpoint of reducing domestic political quarrels over the issue of fairness in burden sharing, multilateral standards and institutions had many advantages.

So far, I have argued that the electoral system rewards the support of collective goods, and the electorate broadly favored U.S. internationalism. Other political considerations reinforced multilateral versions of internationalism. Now I suggest that the division of power in government influenced the continuity of foreign policy and the specific content of the multilateral order in two ways.

Once multilateralism was established, it takes a shift in both the presidential party and the majority congressional party in order to get a major reordering of foreign policy. For example, that bastion of the "state" in foreign policy, the State Department, often cared less about American commitments to multilateralism under Reagan than the Democratic Congress did (with significant Republican help). For another, many critical commitments to multilateralism are the product of law and treaties. While treaties may become attenuated in practice (as with some regional security treaties), this can happen only because of de facto congressional acquiescence.[50] Thus, the division of power can increase continuity and credibility.

Still, the division of powers does pose problems for all international commitments. The electoral incentives of the President and Congress differ, as do their institutional interests concerning power in the government. These differences can, and did, shape the blueprints of multilateralists. In general, Congress and the White House each constitutes a veto point over policy. We should expect that it is harder to shift policy when control over the White House and Congress is divided between the two parties. Even if one party controls both branches, foreign policy will still reflect an anticipation that Congress is even more sensitive than the White House about: (1) creating such visible burdens for constituents as the draft, taxes due to higher government budgets, and import competition for weak industries; (2) ensuring regional (and multidistrict) distribution of benefits by formulating measures to stabilize international monetary markets and economic assistance to foreign governments that would not would favor Wall Street banks (long unpopular in the heartland) or promote socialist competitors to American enterprises; (3) protecting various clumps of ethnic voters' personal interests about foreign policy by creating a military policy that also protected foreign countries dear to important constituents' hearts.

Did foreign policy reflect these dynamics? The scope of the multilateral trading order was shaped by the internal battle over the International Trade Organization. In essence, the struggle between the executive branch and Congress produced a commitment to free trade in manufactured goods and processed commodities but not raw commodities or services.[51] It also excluded multilateral management of commodity markets except in very specialized cases.[52]

The story of tinkering with how the United States formulated foreign trade policy is well known, and it illustrates how Congress can delegate power to the executive branch in order to resolve collective goods problems. Congress retained oversight by enfranchising selected interest groups in the trade advisory process ("stacking the decision process"), requiring the executive to issue regular reports on its plans, putting short time limits on each authorization for trade talks, and retaining veto rights over agreements. In addition, trade agreements had to have an escape clause for dealing with temporary surges in imports. These measures ensured that Congress could keep trade policy responsive to electoral interests without degenerating into a lowest common denominator policy.[53]

The agreements concerning money and aid also reflect institutional tinkering. First, the emphasis on public international institutions (the IMF and the World Bank) in the new multilateralism was itself a logical outgrowth of an incentives problem within U.S. politics.[54] The alternative was to streamline the delegation of power to the private sector, much as the Bank of England had been private or the Morgan Bank had once served many of these functions. But no way was available to delegate these powers in a politically acceptable manner. Not only did objective problems arise with the compatibility of incentives of private institutions and public programs (as witnessed by the windfall profits for J. P. Morgan from one of his stabilization efforts), but also political problems were present because suspicion of Wall Street's power remained substantial in America.[55] Moreover, unlike the oil industry, the Democrats had at best mixed ties with the leading Wall Street banks. Public institutions were the only viable political solution.

Another feature of the monetary and aid order was the insistence of much more explicit national control over the multilateral institutions than the executive branch envisioned. The voting system organized around national executive directors of the IMF was a direct outgrowth of congressional intervention to ensure accountability (and stop Europe from upsetting U.S. interests on monetary policy). Just as critically, congressional authorization "stacked the decision process" by insisting that the U.S. executive director get prior authority on key concerns of the Congress from a cabinet-level committee set up by Congress.[56] The International Bank for Reconstruction and Development (IBRD) received U.S. funding only by agreeing to keep its role targeted initially on Europe (which was much more popular in a European-descended U.S. voting population) and strictly tied to business-like investments in infrastructure of the type long supported in the United States. Moreover, these projects yielded large sales to U.S. engineering firms in the West and manufacturing firms in the East and Midwest. Throughout this process the U.S. Congress made receptiveness to flows of private U.S. capital a benchmark for judging the acceptability of multilateral or bilateral aid to countries, and it insisted that the U.S. participation in the IMF be based on clear movement to convertible exchange rates.[57]

The evolution of multilateral security policy also had to accommodate domestic incentives questions. The early emphasis on economic recovery and the psychological shoring up of European military security (via a NATO that entailed no troop commitments), and the later emphasis on building regional military groupings, reflected both strategic thinking and the dickering between the executive branch and Congress over how to formulate multilateralism. It was not a battle over whether to be multilateral. Congress wanted to avoid the draft if possible, keep tight fire alarms on any executive branch thinking that might threaten war, and hold down spending (especially if it threatened the domestic economy). These concerns were strongly reinforced at first by fears in Congress that Truman was not to be trusted fully on foreign policy.

A few specifics show how institutional tinkering and the movement in voter opinions responded to these problems. Some controls came through controlling the means of providing defense. Despite repeated requests by Truman, Congress consistently refused the draft until the Korean War provided a basis for moving public opinion about conscription. Other controls involved approval procedures for military actions. The NATO accord explicitly included the right of each member to follow its constitutional processes in determining how to fulfill its commitment to mutual defense.[58] The emphasis on regional security efforts also allayed fears about the budget and the possibility that foreign allies would entrap the United States without risking their own forces.[59]

Another set of checks involved a reconstruction of the executive branch process of decision making. Congress literally changed the laws governing how foreign security policy got made in order to increase the fire alarms and restack the decision process. The National Security Council (NSC) was created in part as an effort to hem in Truman by a set of senior officials representing diverse constituencies (and also raising the chances of disclosure of plans upsetting those constituencies).[60] One legal scholar has shrewdly noted the act followed the approach of the Administrative

Procedures Act of the previous year. It regularized the process of decision making in order to make it accountable to Congress. The act also extended these procedures to intelligence operations for the first time, a choice of very great consequence at a time when the State Department was forecasting that the covert action struggle was the key to success in Europe.[61] Moreover, in the reorganization of the Pentagon, Congress gave the head of the Joint Chiefs of Staff authority to bypass the administration entirely and report directly to Congress. Finally, the congressional budget process not only forced disclosure of information by fostering interservice rivalry but also largely rewarded only those initiatives designed to fight large-scale battles in Europe. Congress largely denied the President other tools (including control over personnel) that might have let the executive redefine the mission and strategy of the U.S. military.[62]

In short, beyond the incentives of public opinion and the electoral system, the division of powers was not inconsistent with institutional tinkering produced by differing incentives for the legislature and executive. These controls took two forms. One was the design of decision making to enhance accountability to the legislative branch and improve the chances for disgruntled constituents to complain. The other was the design of the program mandate so as to preclude (or discourage) projects that ran afoul of the priorities of Congress. The design of these controls moved the policies closer to the median position of voter support, and by so doing it made commitments in the name of these policies more credible. If one party had abandoned them, the other would have reason to turn it into an electoral issue.[63]

Even if the intricate maneuvering of U.S. politics was compatible with credible promises, other countries still had to understand it. This is one reason for the importance of transnational society and the peculiar staying power of foreign policy establishments (such as the Council on Foreign Relations). If transparency helps credibility (and assists foreign countries in pursuing their interests), then they and we had strong incentives to make their elites smart about U.S. domestic affairs. The enormous education of foreign elites (through Fulbright exchange programs, etc.) about the United States makes the U.S. society more transparent, and it is easier for them to judge our likely compliance with the multilateral order over time. The easier it is to judge American direction, the easier it is to get their cooperation.

Most importantly, American politics are in themselves relatively transparent to motivated foreign observers. Political debate, regulatory policies, and executive decision making are open and accessible to almost anyone. This means that it is fairly easy for foreign political and economic interests to figure out where policy is going and how to influence it. The multilateral regime also got an important boost because foreign economic interests largely had equal economic standing in law and practice in the United States. While foreign lobbying in Washington was small change in 1950, foreign economic operations in the United States were also not subject to much attack. Most fundamentally, no mysteries existed about the U.S. market. For example, U.S. technology was relatively open and accessible. Whatever the faults of U.S. policy, it was hard to believe that its marketplace was shrouded in economic or political mystery.

In summary, the political terrain for multilateralism was better in the 1940s than often supposed, and parties had an incentive to respond. Commitments once made are hard to reverse in American politics. So private electoral incentives and checks on changing American commitment to multilateralism were present. Still, multilateralism cut different ways for the politics of the White House and the Congress. Therefore, one would expect both a tailoring of the substance of multilateralism and new institutional innovations designed to reconcile these political incentives. This is what happened. At the same time, the broader political economy of the domestic U.S. market stabilized around a consensus that enhanced U.S. transparency and credibility.

Japan—Private Goods and Multilateral Credibility

Writing about Japan as a leading power assumes that patterns of economic growth and military power work out in a way consistent with further increases in Japanese influence. I make this assumption because it simplifies how to think about the challenges facing multilateralism.

Suppose that Japan emerges as a major enough international power that it challenges the United States for leadership. For present purposes we need to think, not about military equality, but simply about a narrowing economic gap between the two economies and the continued growth of Japan as a coequal financial center for the world economy. While this situation would also be sensitive to the fate of a united Europe and a reformed Soviet Union, let us simply ask whether or not multilateralism would thrive if Japan is solidified as a leading power. My answer is that Japanese pledges to support multilateralism are less credible than those of the United States after World War II. This would change only if both the structure of domestic political incentives in Japan and if the procedures of Japanese policymaking changed. This section examines two possible routes to change—political economic restructuring in response to international negotiations or reform of the electoral system.

Whether Japan's mixture of a "developmental state" and porkbarrel politics explained Japanese economic success is less important than the way it defined the political landscape.[64] As Japan grew in international importance, the pressures on it to conform to the existing multilateral order escalated. Also fair to say is that confidence in Japanese good faith is not high in other countries even though Japan has, for example, fewer formal trade barriers than most industrial countries. Either Japanese bureaucracies are not powerful (because they cannot easily deliver on promises to meet multilateral obligations) or they do not want to fulfill these promises.

The debate over Japan has two issues. One is over which features in its political system have produced so many programs to restructure and shelter its economy by a combination of active warring bureaucracies and very cautious political leaders. The other is the debate about how much of Japan's economic success can be attributed to industrial policies.

For the sake of simplicity I sketch a model of Japanese politics with analytics similar to the last section. Other analytic alternatives could also be worked out. They would suggest different paths toward domestic reforms necessary for international credibility. But my purpose is to show how the logic of this paper applies, not to resolve the deep disputes among Japan experts about the proper model of its politics.[65] My point is that *Japanese commitments are not credible absent adaptation of its domestic institutions*.

Resolving the debate over the efficacy of industrial policy is also not necessary for present purposes. For example, the Liberal Democratic Party and the bureaucracy may have served as the guardians of real growth in some (or many) sections, rather than simply dispense protection to stagnant producers à la Latin America. But strong evidence shows that such a virtuous role was not necessary for overall Japanese success.[66] Comparative studies indicate the sheer scale of the Japanese domestic market allowed protectionism to generate economies of scale and learning curve experience that later generated export growth.[67] Moreover, the structure of large Japanese firms themselves gave them intersectoral perspectives so that the idea of moving up the scale of industrial sophistication yielded fewer clashes between less and more sophisticated industries than in the United States. Thus, a policy largely driven by narrow demands for protection could have yielded virtuous outcomes given Japanese industrial structure.[68] It could have also produced what may be the most disruptive feature of Japanese economic practices for the multilateral economic order, a type of preemptive assault on all niches in an industry.[69]

A Model of Japanese Politics

This section assumes the primacy of power of the political leadership. It hypothesizes that the parliamentary system permits broad delegations of power to bureaucracies, while the electoral system leads to exceedingly particularistic politics in Japan and an absence of any meaningful party competition on broad issues concerning the collective good.

The Japanese system is parliamentary. As a rule, parliamentary systems are more capable of delegating extensive authority to bureaucracies than U.S.-style ones. The unified control of the executive and legislature means that no rivalry exists in control of the bureaucracy by the legislature and executive to inspire limits on what powers are awarded the bureaucracy. This means that designing quiet but effective controls over the bureaucracy is easier. This is especially true when one party holds power continuously because the bureaucracy has learned what is expected.[70] The purpose of delegation is to get the benefits of a committed and expert actor, but delegation does not mean the end of political control. If important constituents complain, political leadership acts. Political leaders also settle ministerial feuds over turf precisely because the choice of the lead ministry is the implied resolution of which types of policy preferences (and constituents) will prevail.

What is that the bureaucracy is told to do? The cues should be in the electoral system.[71] The Japanese Diet is elected through multimember (two to six seats) districts with each voter having a single vote. The only way for a party to win a majority is to run several candidates in each district. The implication of this particular voting system is that no candidate has any incentive to run on broad policy issues because members of the LDP (Liberal Democratic Party) could undercut each other in the same district. (Imagine that they all ran on similar issues and one of them was the best at explaining the issues. This candidate might attract most LDP voters and lead to losses by all other LDP candidates to candidates of other parties.) Instead, candidates win by building a dedicated minority bloc of voters cultivated largely by extensive campaign spending and lavish patronage politics.[72] Personal favors, not policies, catered to the household. This in turn leads to the notorious money politics of Japan.

Perhaps most critically for multilateralism, the incentives for the political leadership of the LDP were hopelessly skewed toward particularism of a special type until recently. Members have no pressing concern to run issue-oriented campaigns, so the party leadership had few incentives to make issues an identifiable part of their bids for influence, nor did incentives exist for the LDP members as a whole to organize leadership to represent positions on broad policies unless absolutely necessary. (I discuss this shortly.) This system largely converged around policies that support concentrated interest groups in the strongest form of the capture theory of government more commonly associated with the United States.[73]

Capture in Japan leads to the creation of policy catering to well-organized corporate interests, small businesses with single interests that are numerous through many LDP members districts (e.g., mom-and-pop stores were the backbone of Japanese distribution, and their owners were virtually a single-issue constituency), and the notoriously sheltered agricultural sector.[74] Japanese industrial policy, then, catered to the specialized demands of these industries for increased economic rents or public investment in collective goods narrowly tailored to the needs of industrial groups. While the bureaucracy may itself have helped to broker and enforce a consensus among firms in these industries, the coherence and effectiveness of industrial policy proved sensitive to the industrial organization of the industry. Less concentrated industries with more specialized clashing niche strategies had weaker industrial policies.[75]

No political party is totally without an electoral identity, but the LDP makes the GOP look like a philosopher's club. Still, the LDP is the party of economic growth and global competitive success.[76] Thus, the party's general message of growth and international economic prestige reinforces the propensity to give key industries what they want.

What does Japan do when tough choices are to be made, such as when deficit spending may force tax increases or the United States threatens the export strategy in a trade dispute? The senior party leadership has two types of control over the rank and file. It controls nominations for Diet seats. It also controls large pots of money for campaigning. Indeed, the LDP is divided into factions led by a senior politician that are almost wholly organized around money and campaigns, not policy.

Fortunately, the factions recruit members from all the policy *zoku* in the party because each faction leader wants to build membership size in order to claim party leadership, and the *zoku* are important for building up favors in the ministries. (The *zoku* are specialized study groups that provide LDP Diet members with their closest counterpart to the policy expertise of congressional subcommittees). Therefore, the factions are relatively cosmopolitan and representative of the party as a whole. More vitally, the rise to the top of a faction is on the basis of money and the ability to bargain and broker across issues. The senior leadership has a vested interest in the survival of the party as the majority ruler of Japan because it enhances the value of their own posts.[77] Hence, when critical questions arise on the issues that can crimp the LDP, the faction leaders are the ones who pull together a collective policy response that goes beyond the normal rote of particularism.

Two sets of issues apparently worry the leadership most. The first is how to protect Japanese industry now that its strategy of exporting and foreign investment is under attack overseas. Large Japanese multinationals, and the smaller suppliers who follow them overseas, support selective changes in economic protection and industrial policies at home to buy peace abroad. Also, as these firms globalize, they do not always like some of the rigidities imposed by industrial policies at home. The demands for adjustment of international and industrial economic policies naturally clash with the demands of smaller firms, import-competing large firms, and agriculture. The second set of issues pertains to the younger urban voters who are the dominant demographic wave. These voters are less susceptible to the politics of personal favors because they want second bedrooms, not an extra tatami mat. As the costs of direct favors to voters rise, the LDP has to find a way to woo these voters with such substitutes as consumer policies.

While the leadership can act, it is at best an imperfect campaign from the viewpoint of multilateral commitments. Its control over rank and file is quite imperfect because Diet members can woo local voters with small favors that are not under the restrictive control of leadership. Moreover, the vital tool of campaign finance support is double-edged. The senior leadership is necessarily closely tied to the large corporations of Japan because they are (like Willie Sutton's banks) where the money is, and money is indispensable to leadership. This imparts a special twist to Japanese high politics. Even when it intervenes to reduce barriers to foreign competition, the leadership also has an incentive, as Calder notes, to favor continued administrative regulation of markets in order to collect political rents from all market participants.[78]

The interests of LDP leadership do not, therefore, permit us to conclude that the growing internationalization of Japanese business will surely lead to a matching commitment to the obligations of the multilateral economic order. To be sure, the most likely cases for policy commitment occur when specific sectors of large businesses are in accord on the need to liberalize at home to protect their foreign market access. When large industry is both highly organized and antagonistic to multilateral cooperation, the political leadership is at best cautious even if general diplomatic strategy strongly suggests the need to remove barriers to foreign entry.[79] But most fundamentally, even when business is largely in favor of increased competition, Japanese political leaders have a strong interest in keeping markets subject to controls in order to collect political rents from arbitrating terms of market competition. Hence, the LDP favors measures that significantly reduce the market's transparency and increase the nontariff obstacles to foreign entry.

The upshot of this system was a predilection for the protection of industry in the name of controlling excess capacity and assisting smaller firms. There is also little reason to voluntarily seek broader roles as a leader in the multilateral system with the attendant burdens that brings. Indeed, so low profile is Japanese leadership globally that it was news when Japan at the 1990 summit asserted its right to help China irrespective of what other nations did. This move to shore up the Japanese position in China was primarily an exercise in bilateralism. Meanwhile, Japan has played a scant role in world trade talks.

Right now Japanese politicians have few immediate incentives to improve Japanese performance on multilateralism. The resulting dynamic is largely one where various crises (often provoked by the United States over trade) force choices between staying pat or reforming.[80] At this point, the senior LDP leadership has to invest politically in overcoming the dissent of its membership over giving international concessions. It does so in order to avoid confrontations that could damage Japanese export or military goals severely. But this function is as narrowly defined as possible because no incentive exists to rework policy on behalf of foreign policy, consumers, or any other diffuse interest that cuts across election districts. Indeed, Japanese analysts often argue that the only opposition party in Japan is the American diplomatic establishment, and progress on many needed reforms depends on this opposition.[81] Certainly, turning indirectly to the Americans for help is a favorite tactic of Japanese firms wishing to enter domestic markets where regulations have curtailed competition.[82]

Institutional Innovations

Is there any prospect for a change in the basis of political incentives for adherence to multilateralism? Or is bilateralism the only alternative? This section examines two alternatives—U.S. pressure and electoral reform. These are not mutually exclusive paths, as I shall discuss, but understanding the implied dynamics of each approach is useful.

Let us begin by looking at the possibility of establishing credibility by tinkering with specific policies. The reform mongering may cumulatively establish enough transparency and predictability for foreign firms to make their parent governments confident of Japanese intentions. But this could happen only if foreign governments figured that Japanese politics itself had moved to a new equilibrium position about protectionism and multilateral commitments. How could this happen?

If the political system is particularistic and tied especially to the interests of large firms, then a transformation in the interests of these firms to favor a more open and cosmopolitan home economy may lead to a more genuine commitment to multilateralism. These companies may fear foreign retaliation or simply find domestic controls less attractive as they move closer to the frontiers of technology and genuinely global production strategies.[83] For example, the upward revaluation of the yen did change import patterns into Japan, and the process appears to be self-reinforcing even after the change in exchange rates is no longer driving adaptation.[84] The political logic is akin to that offered by Helen Milner about why protectionism is tough to bring back when U.S. and French firms have internationalized.[85] Therefore, it is possible that ad hoc fixes of specific features of the Japanese economy could indirectly catalyze a shift in the political agenda of a particularistic political leadership. But the form of liberalization would still have to reconcile the other elements of the LDP coalition. This reconciliation means that the simple liberalization in response to shifting business interests is not in the cards.

We would expect liberalization to advance only when a high level of harmony exists within a specific industry. Dissent-ridden industries would not be easily overridden. The formula will also give special attention to compensating small firms and rural regions through such initiatives as pump priming for high-tech infrastructure in less populated areas. Finally, one would expect a preference for approaches to liberalization that introduce the costs of adjustment indirectly (as in exchange rates) rather than directly while reaffirming the retention of administrative controls even in liberalized markets in order to earn political rents for the LDP. It is precisely such administrative oversight that raises questions about Japanese credibility.

If one is to find signs of institutional and policy tinkering in response to cues from international pressures, it ought to come in the United States–Japan trade negotiations. And signs of this process are evident.

The continuing U.S–Japanese trade impasse has taken a remarkable turn over the past five years. It has transformed the trade dialogue from an analysis of tariff and quota barriers to a debate over how countries regulate their domestic markets. This internationalization of domestic regulations is not being done for the traditional rationale of improving technical efficiency or for the real rationale (but usually denied) of mutually reinforcing national monopolies. Rather, it is an attempt to define the legitimate power of governments over markets.

While pursuing greater exports to Japan the United States has adopted the position that effective market access requires a tranformation of how Japan structures its markets. The first demand was to limit Japanese "export offenses" in key markets. This has typically led to a number of voluntary export restraint agreements administered by MITI (Ministry of International Trade and Industry) after negotiation with the United States. These cover such industries as automobiles and machine tools.

Why would Japan accept the VERs (Voluntary Export Restraint)? The two obvious reasons are that they are better than trade retaliation and they offer economic rents to Japanese producers in return for limits on exports. These rents can finance product upgrading. But the third basis for their acceptability is political. VERs reinforce the political position of the Japanese government by getting MITI into the business of organizing export cartels. This in turn means that the Japanese export industry is dependent on the government for its allocation of the quotas.[86] The possibilities for political profit are endless both for the ministry and the LDP as a whole.

The more innovative and challenging test of Japanese politics starts with the second cluster of demands. These are requests for transparency in the Japanese administrative process. So far, this has focused on a sector-by-sector attack on the prevalence of unwritten regulations, insufficient periods to meet government administrative deadlines, and inaccessibility of key administrative organs to foreign participation. Access to advisory councils of ministries and commissions that set technical standards received special attention. U.S. negotiators pressed Japan with some success to adopt a uniform code of administrative procedures because its absence justifies closed and idiosyncratic procedures at each ministry.[87]

Almost all these trade crises on transparency have required intervention by the LDP. Support from Japanese business for the U.S. position has largely (but not always) come from MITI and MOFA (Ministry of Foreign Affairs) in their role of representing the interests of Japanese industry in moderating trade disputes. Japanese industry has not been all that keen in these changes except in one sense. As Japanese firms move into new markets, such as going from computing into telecommunications, they are often less favored players in the traditional bureaucratic network for the new market.[88] Therefore, they may favor relaxation of bureaucratic authority in general although they may not care overly about the normal benchmarks of transparency because they are experienced players in the Japanese administrative process.

A third focus for internationalization has been on the organization of capital markets and the firm. In addition to seeking greater opportunities for U.S. firms to do business in financial markets, the United States has pressed steadily to make Japan's capital freely available to world markets in order to bid up interest rates in Japan to world levels. It has also nudged Japan to move its banks to capital reserve levels comparable to other nations in order to reduce any financial leverage and advantage given to business as a result of Japanese practices.[89]

Perhaps the most remarkable example of the process attended the Plaza accord of 1985, which reset currency rates among the leading industrial nations. The upward revaluation of the yen caused slight hardship to large firms and moderate difficulties for small firms that exported on their own or were not in the trade sector. But it was necessary if major trade imbalances (and conflict) with the United States were to be stemmed. Hence, the LDP overruled the Ministry of Finance and decided to move the value of the yen. Significantly, the LDP explicitly preferred a more valuable yen to reducing trade restrictions that caused immediate attributable pain for import-competing industries or bolstering public spending (that drives up imports and also taxes, the latter much to the annoyance of big firms). It then introduced some measures to compensate smaller businesses financially for the revaluation of the yen, although these only partly offset the adverse impact of the restructuring. Frances Rosenbluth described the process as one step forward and half a step back.[90]

Yet another U.S. goal has to been to stiffen the antitrust laws so as to limit the *keiretsu* system. This feature of the Structural Impediments

Initiative (SII) yielded a pledge from Japan to increase the powers of its FTC and revise antitrust laws. Many analysts question whether this agreement will get much practical adherence, but it has already touched off discussions in Japan about the "open *keiretsu*."[91] Japan could opt to push its *keiretsu* to include American companies rather than break up the *keiretsu*. Some speculate that this could be one eventual outcome of the United States–Japan diplomacy over semiconductor markets.

The logic of Japanese politics suggests that the open *keiretsu* policy is possible only if it generated strong support from large business or small business. The latter has little incentive to do so. The former would do so only to avoid trade disputes and only to the degree that it could be done consistently with global production programming. Thus, if the United States wants any meaningful enforcement, it would have to accept some Japanese guidelines about how to incorporate American firms into the Japanese model of production.[92]

A fourth bundle of U.S. initiatives tries to rework the infrastructure necessary to support open markets in Japan and to make the infrastructure itself more competitive. The initiatives on infrastructure in support of open markets included negotiations about the way that Japan ran its research and development (R & D) system, reform of the distribution system, reform of pricing mechanisms, and changes in the physical infrastructure. Reforms in the infrastructure itself include opening up competition for government procurement spending and liberalizing classic infrastructure markets, like telecommunications.

Although the Japanese government spends far less than the United States on R & D, its coordination of industry initiatives has consistently alarmed the United States. Both Europe and the United States have experimented with Japanese-style formulas, and now international negotiations are trying to establish rules to govern these efforts. R & D policies are largely exempt from GATT jurisdiction, but, to cite one case, the United States has pushed hard to distinguish between R & D policies and commercial development efforts disguised as R & D. Thus, the United States opposed Japanese communications satellite projects restricted only to Japanese firms on the basis that significant participation and financing by NTT (which would use the experimental satellite) made it a de facto commercial project. Other negotiations have worked on ways to share R & D in new ways. One feature of these efforts is to allow private intercorporate deals stand as a surrogate for formal intergovernmental arrangements.[93]

The satellite case nicely illustrates the political logic of change. The first U.S. campaign for procurement of U.S. satellites (in 1985) won the backing of several major Japanese firms that wanted entry into the telecommunications network market eased by sharing risk and expertise with American satellite manufacturers. Thus, the LDP solved the problem by overruling the ministry and approving the purchase of U.S. systems. At the same time, it backed continuation of the NTT (Nippon Telephone and Telegraph) effort. The 1989 negotiation was tougher because no Japanese domestic constituent for the change existed other than a general desire to avoid fights with the United States. Thus, a principle that U.S. firms thought had been established in 1985 proved no more than a single administrative decision, and the entire political struggle had to be duplicated in 1989.[94]

Critics rightly note that individual measures mean little as long as all incentives for the Japanese government run toward cautious protectionism as a rule and every piece of liberalization has to be carved out and maintained on a case-by-case basis. As Adam Smith always taught, the desire for protection is not a cultural attribute; it is sound business practice for any individual business. But the cumulative impact of the trade talks and the continuing globalization of all Japanese companies could have an impact on the political profile of Japan.

Yet even the LDP leadership wonders if this is possible. It is not an accident that the mounting pressures to increase agricultural imports, reform distribution, and bolster access for foreign products have also led to an LDP debate about a need to reform the Japanese electoral system. Rogowski has argued that deepening exposure to the international economy can cause a crisis in governance that will force electoral reforms.[95] This is the most extreme form of institutional innovation to reconcile domestic political incentives with multilateral commitments. But Japan has already done this in one form and is openly discussing doing it in a second.

As the prior analysis showed, money is critical to Japanese leadership. Its priorities must be sensitive to its funding; to the degree that funding is dependent on money that is protectionist, the problems of managing multilateral commitments to open economic orders grow. Thus, it was a major reform in the political incentive system for multilateralism when the Diet changed electoral laws in such a way as to limit contributions by the patriarch of Japanese industrial federations, *Keidenran,* and increase spending by individual Japanese firms. The effect of weakening the federation was important because it was strongly influenced by large import-competing firms such as the steel industry. Indeed, many analysts thought that one reason for the vigor of prosecution of the Recruit scandal was precisely because it was a counterattack against the new sources of money offered by high-technology entrepreneurial firms.[96]

As even more dramatic possibility is under discussion. The Kaifu government backed a proposal to reduce seats in the Diet from 512 to 501, switch 301 of the seats to single-member districts, and undertake significant reapportionment. The redistricting would drop the value of rural votes from 3.18 times to twice the value of urban votes.[97]

Restructuring the political system would increase the importance of urban interests in infrastructure, more competitive pricing, and other consumer interests. More fundamentally, the single-member district would change incentives about how to run for office because positions on issues would become gradually more important.[98] Perhaps the strongest effort in recent years to articulate a new multilateral vision of the world came from Nakasone, a man committed to an unusually activist form of leadership. But the basic incentives for leadership (money and factions, not popular support) undercut him.[99]

Knowing what vision of multilateralism might emerge (if any) from either path to reform is difficult. But surely it will force some changes in the organization of the multilateral order because multilateralism must accommodate some features of the domestic political order of leading powers. The problem of maintaining a multilateral regime becomes harder if power dissolves from a single dominant power to a small group of leading powers. Although the new great powers may have been partly "socialized" to the values of the existing regime, they almost certainly will require accommodation. This is as likely to force a revision in some of the existing ways of doing business of the United States as in Japan, as I argued above in regard to antitrust and government regulation. It may also lead to more functional specialization in leadership by issue area.

One might guess that one feature to cater to Japan would be more emphasis on commercial than military arrangements for settling some security disputes. This seems to be the model for Japanese initiatives being discussed for building political reconciliation of the Koreas and China in East Asia. As became widely known during the Iraq war, Japan largely viewed military action as an inappropriate response to what was largely a commercial issue in the view of Japanese bureaucrats and (evidently) the general population. Japan has also shied away from new Asian security organization and still largely stresses U.S. leadership in this area.[100] A second would be the restructuring of industries globally to allow for more horizontal or vertical keiretsu relationships across borders. A third would be agreement to much more openness to foreign competition combined with a greater retained right for oversight of individual market performance. Put differently, the United States would get its wish for entry and transparency, and the Japanese would get their desire to let bureaucracies constantly negotiate with the market.

Summary

This paper has three points. Multilateralism contains many obligations and opportunities that cannot be spelled out in advance and cannot be easily constrained by forms of specific reciprocity without destroying much of the efficiency of multilateralism. Hierarchic contracting allowing leadership by the major powers is critical for resolving this problem. Second, hierarchic contracting in multilateral regimes poses serious questions about the credibility of the promises of dominant powers. The credibility of the promises of the strong are strongly influenced by the degree to which their external obligations make sense in light of their domestic political preferences and institutions. For democracies the nature of the electoral system, the distribution of preferences of voters, the structure of governing institutions (including the fine-tuning of institutions to make multilateralism easier), and the transparency of the political system are important determinants of the credibility of foreign policy promises by the strong. Third, multilateral orders are strengthened if they fit more closely with the domestic political profiles of the dominant powers. As the mix of dominant powers changes, some features of the multilateral regimes should shift in order to improve the fit with domestic political imperatives among the new leaders.

The analysis showed that U.S. political institutions helped to sustain the credibility of the multilateral order after 1945. But it raised doubts about the credibility of Japanese commitments as it assumes a leading role in the 1990s. Analysis often expend enormous energy judging the degree of Japanese trade and financial concessions or the size of its military effort. This paper argues that our attention should focus on the reform of its domestic political institutions. While international economic negotiations may be one route leading to change, the most significant innovations would target the fundamental structure of Japanese political representation.

NOTES

1. In my view a multilateral order must cover a variety of important economic and security issues, not just one or two in isolation. It does not have to cover every issue. The definition is from John Gerard Ruggie, "Multilateralism: The Anatomy of an Institution," in this volume.

2. This paper discusses dominant powers because it wishes to explore both a case of hegemony (the United States for most of the past forty-five years) and a nonhegemonic world (the role of Japan in the future). While the debate over theories of hegemonic leadership provided useful insights into why the strong ought to support collective goods disproportionately, it shed little light on problems posed by multilateralism. Depending on how theorists depicted the degree of publicness of the goods of world order and the precise motives of hegemons, the fragility and desirability of hegemonic orders differ. Robert O. Keohane, *After Hegemony: Cooperation and Discord in the World Political Economy* (Princeton: Princeton University Press, 1984). Duncan Snidal, "The Limits of Hegemonic Stability Theory," *International Organization* (Autumn 1985), 39:579–614.

3. Selective incentives and coercion by the hegemon in themselves are unlikely to induce more than half-hearted support by second-tier powers.

4. Glenn Palmer, "Corralling the Free Rider: Deterrence and the Western Alliance," *International Studies Quarterly* (June 1990), 34:147–164.

5. Ruggie argues that collective security schemes necessarily commit against unknown enemies and for unknown victims. "Multilateralism." In reality, figuring out how to apply this principle raises precisely those enormous issues of judgment that Kreps argues are common to certain collective-action arrangements:

> Transactions can be characterized by the adjudication processes that meet unforseen contingencies. In particular, some transactions will be hierarchical in that one party will have much more authority in saying what adaptation will take place.

Common examples include students enrolling in universities, most people going to their doctor, or many firms hiring specialized contractors for technically difficult challenges. So, too, does congressional rank and file with congressional leadership accept a hierarchic contract in order to improve their welfare. David Kreps, "Corporate Culture and Economic Theory," in James Alt and Kenneth Shepsle, eds., *Rational Perspectives on Positive Political Economy* (Cambridge, England: Cambridge University Press, 1990), pp. 90–143 (quotation from page 92).

6. While the conclusion is the same, hierarchic contracting emphasizes rational choice calculations of consent rather than the sociological model suggested by Bull. This paper also gives a greater weight to domestic politics. Hedley Bull, *The Anarchical Society* (New York: Columbia University Press, 1977).

7. Much more authority is not equivalent to unlimited authority. Workers grant management broad, not unlimited, discretion. Kreps, "Corporate Culture." Oliver Hart and Bengt Holmstrom, "The Theory of Contracts," Working Paper #418, Department of Economics, Massachusetts Institute of Technology (March 1986).

Although I use the tools of rational choice to make this argument, the intuition goes back to the classic work by Chester Barnard and Herbert Simon on why the central problem of all management is to win the consent of workers and shareholders to their exercise of authority. Chester Barnard, *The Functions of an Executive* (Cambridge, Mass.: Harvard University Press, 1938). Herbert Simon, *Administrative Behavior,* 2nd ed. (New York: McMillan, 1957).

8. While such devices as minilateralism may help, they cannot achieve "self-enforcing" contracts.

9. Concerns over reputation were not in themselves sufficient. Douglas C. North and Barry R. Weingast, "Constitution and Commitment: The Evaluation of Institutions Governing Public Choice in Seventeenth-Century England", the *Journal of Economic History* (December 1989), 49:803–832.

10. Bargaining theory, such as "the folk theorem" of noncooperative games, has established that formal organizations and contracts are not required to resolve all cases of transaction costs. The theorem says that cooperation will occur as long as each party can judge the other's good faith *ex post* and refuse to cooperate after a defection. Unfortunately, the folk theorem is often little better than folk medicine. There are multiple equilibria to this game, and many include frequent defection because it is hard to define defection. For a more general analysis, see Kreps, "Corporate Culture."

11. A good example of an interest-based theory is: Richard Rosencrance and Jennifer Taw, "Japan and the Theory of International Leadership," *World Politics* (January 1990), 42:184–209. Scott C. James and David A. Lake, "The Second Face of Hegemony," *International Organization* (Winter 1989), 43:1–29, model how the actions of the leading power of the day may influence the domestic politics of a future dominant power. But their model cannot show how changing economic incentives become translated into binding switches in public policy. If we know anything about politics it is that translation is not automatic.

12. The following reasoning relies on the common practice in international relations theorizing of looking for broader classes of strategic behavior problems in the theory of the firm.

13. A corporation's culture provides focal points that permit all parties to accept *ex ante* a contract that cannot anticipate all contingencies and to grant one specialized party the latitude to guide adaptation. So long as the "subordinates" can assess performance post hoc in light of the focal points of the culture and have the power to retaliate and defect, then the "subordinates" can rationally count on the consistency of the hierarchical "superior." Defection may not include exiting the contract. It may simply lead to shirking duties.

14. For example, sales of equity holdings by senior corporate officers must be fully disclosed in order to discourage short-term manipulation of profits. The same question of how to match the private incentives of leaders with institutional tasks is present in politics. For example, congressional party leadership is almost entirely drawn from individuals whose reelection is from districts with voters close to the median position of party supporters. Gary W. Cox and Mathew D. McCubbins, *Parties and Committees in the U.S. House of Representatives* (Berkeley: University of California Press, 1991).

15. Two important conceptual issues remain. First, how similar must the core countries in a multilateral order be in their domestic political institutions? G. John Ikenberry and Charles A. Kupchan, "Socialization and Hegemonic Power," *International Organization* (Summer 1990), vol. 44, nicely pull together the evidence on this issue. Second, how would accommodation to the domestic political demands of dominant powers show up in the negotiating process? Probably, all parties would *ex ante* anticipate the broad constraints and factor them in their positions. Thus, the negotiations could be marked by an unending series of demands by secondary powers for concessions to their needs, yet the equilibrium position would include prime deference to the implicit position of the leading power.

16. For example, the United States largely built its defense posture around Europe. These specialized capabilities could be shifted to other uses only with great difficulty. Such costs in specialized assets made U.S. defense pledges to Europe more credible. But a great power by definition has greater latitude to reverse defense postures, so this constraint is limited.

17. W. Edward Deming, the efficiency expert revered in Japan, prescribed a cohesive "corporate culture" for reviving U.S. auto makers. Point four included: "Move toward a single supplier for any one item, on a long-term relationship of loyalty and trust." In short, a view of external relations was inseparable from the terms for granting trust and authority internally. Deming is quoted on p. 35 of Maryann Keller, *Rude Awakening—The Rise, Fall and Struggle for Recovery of General Motors* (New York: Morrow Press, 1989).

18. Rein Taagepeta and Matthew Shugart, *Seats and Votes: The Effects and Determinants of Electoral Systems* (New Haven, Conn.: Yale University Press, 1989).

19. Collective goods associated with multilateralism can also yield private goods, a benefit for political leaders that can ease the problem of supplying collective goods, as the discussion of the United States will show. Nonetheless, private incentives cannot reliably be counted upon to solve the full measure of the collective-goods problem.

20. A more powerful Germany raised sensitive lingering questions about existing borders, especially the Polish boundary (the Oder–Neisse line). Although Chancellor Kohl offered many diplomatic assurances to Poland, he refused to commit himself in public inside West Germany. Countries discounted

his promises until he showed that he was willing to stand up to regional interests in his party that favored boundary revisions. The Social Democratic opposition already favored pledges to respect boundaries. Kohl reassured Poland only when he delivered public speeches endorsing existing boundaries. Standing up to some members of his own party enhanced his credibility. It also possibly meant that Kohl accepted that the median voter in Germany was closer to the Social Democrat position. (Obviously, this promise did not involve multilaterialism.) Thomas L. Friedman, "Two Germanys Vow to Accept Border with the Poles," p. 1; Craig R. Whitney, "Kohl Outlines a Vision: A Neighborly Germany," p. 4: both *New York Times* (July 18, 1990).

More generally, Zeev Maoz and Dan S. Felsenthal have argued that self-binding commitments ("a unilateral credible commitment to act in a certain way regardless of what other players would do") (p. 187) are often the best way to achieve Pareto-optimal solutions to multilateral bargaining. They note that Sadat's pledge to peace in Jerusalem was credible because it involved "tremendous personal and political risks" (p. 191). "Self-Binding Commitments, the Inducement of Trust, Social Choice, and the Theory of International Cooperation," *International Studies Quarterly* (June 1987), 31:177–200. The flip side of this logic is that the limits on domestic support for multilateralism shape the way in which multilateral strategies must be formulated. For a suggestive treatment, see Bruce Bueno de Mesquita and David Lalman, "Domestic Opposition and Foreign War," *American Political Science Review* (September 1990), 84:747–766.

21. The logic follows from Bruce Russett, "The Mysterious Cost of Vanishing Hegemony: Or, Is Mark Twain Really Dead?" *International Organization* (Spring 1985), vol. 39.

22. Analysts in the statist tradition often point to the State Department as a guardian of state interests. In my view the Marshall Plan was more credible because it was removed from the State Department, put in an office with a temporary life cycle, and led by someone who was appointed solely to deliver a viable program subject to the demands of Congress not to harm the industrial Midwest via foreign aid.

23. Lisa Martin makes the important point that cases involving the most multilateral tensions, collaboration games, are most sensitive to conditions about transparency and the shadow of the future: "Interests, Power, and Multilateralism," in this volume. Domestic political arrangements in the leading powers significantly influence these variables. Keohane developed the issue of transparency in *After Hegemony*.

24. For example, the comparative closure of Soviet politics posed a consistent problem. What were the Soviets thinking? How did they view their costs of defection from an agreement? Who was in favor and who was opposed? The ability to believe in any cooperative relationship was eroded by these problems.

25. Jeffrey A. Frieden, "Capital Politics: Creditors and the International Political Economy," *Journal of Public Policy* (July–December 1988), 8 (3–4):274.

26. James M. Jones, *The Fifteen Weeks* (New York: Viking Press, 1955). A third argument is that U.S. allies, like Great Britain, did not trust U.S. domestic politics but saw no other option than to cooperate. This asymmetry in power certainly mattered, but it does not explain the degree of postwar commitment by the lesser powers or their support for a multilateral order. The fears of London of 1942 about the U.S. domestic scene gave way to the recognition by 1943 or 1944 that the United States would lead but that the multilateral order was going to fit special U.S. political needs. Britain then tried to whittle down the idiosyncrasies of the order and tilt it toward its own special needs, often by seizing the initiative on proposing new plans. On British fears in 1942, see: David Reynolds, "Roosevelt, Churchill, and the Wartime Anglo–American Alliance, 1939–1945: Towards a New Synthesis," pp. 17–41, in William Roger Louis and Hedley Bull, eds., *The 'Special Relationship': Anglo–American Relations Since 1945* (Oxford, England: Clarendon Press, 1986).

27. Stephen Krasner, *Defending the National Interest* (Princeton: Princeton University Press, 1978).

28. Analysts debate whether party reputation for congressional candidates as actively built by members of Congress is reminiscent of a quasi-parliamentary party or whether the President largely defines party reputation. (For Democrats in a Republican administration it would do so by the President's defining the range of targets against which the Democrats seek to find the best mix of opposition stands—we care more about middle-class tax burdens—and for congressional Republicans the President largely defines an agenda because the party would lose credibility if he was consistently rejected.) Both approaches suggest positions matter for electoral success, and parties act on policy agendas for this reason. Samuel Kernell, "The Primacy of Politics in Economic Policy," pp. 325–378, in Samuel Kernell, ed., *Parallel Politics—Economic Policymaking in Japan and the United States* (Washington, D.C.: Brookings Institution, 1991).

Ronald Rogowski, "Trade and the Variety of Democratic Institutions," *International Organization* (Spring 1987), 41:203–224, argues that McKelvey showed multidimensional politics in a U.S.-style system is more prone to cycling and undisciplined parties than proportional representation is. Subsequent work on cycling shows that cycling is possible, but it is likely to be within a well-defined policy space. This limits the problems discussed by Rogowski. Gary W. Cox, "The Uncovered Set and the Core," *American Journal of Political Science* (1987), 31:408–423.

29. Popkin argues that voters are rational to invest few resources in gathering information about a public good (a better informed vote). But they reason rationally in ways consistent with limited resources. Attributable benefits (or persuasive denial of blame) are the key to a politician's success. Presidents like foreign policy especially because they have clear claims to control. Nonetheless,

party identification is an important "default" value on issues that voters care about but lack other information. This is especially true in congressional races. Party identification in turn is based on retrospective assessment of performance, and voters will change their assessment of party competence on major issues fairly rapidly. Samuel Popkin (*The Reasoning Voter* Chicago: University of Chicago Press, 1991).

30. John H. Aldrich, John L. Sullivan, and Eugene Borgida, "Foreign Affairs and Issue Voting: Do Presidential Candidates 'Waltz Before a Blind Audience?' " *American Political Science Review* (1990), make a powerful case for retrospective accountability on foreign policy. Nincic's model of swings in U.S.– Soviet relations based on presidential election cycles is very useful, but it ignores the ways in which political parties and Congress constrain policies. Miroslav Nincic, "The United States, The Soviet Union, and the Politics of Opposites," *World Politics* (July 1988), vol. 40. Microslav Nincic, "U.S.–Soviet Policy and The Electoral Connection," *World Politics* (April 1990), 42:370–396). Elite opinion as studied, for example, by Holsti and Rosenau, matters mainly as cues for public attention. Once an issue is publicized, elite control over terms for its resolution may decline. Ole R. Holsti and James N. Rosenau, *American Leadership in World Affairs* (Boston: Allen and Unwin, 1984).

31. Foreign policy officials can regale listeners with tales of woeful congressional ignorance. Walter Isaacson and Evan Thomas, *The Wise Men: Six Friends and the World They Made* (New York: Simon and Schuster, 1986). But the same is true about the mechanics of social security, welfare reform, tax legislation, and the legalities of federal funding for abortion. No one thinks that Congress fails to shape these domestic policies. Moreover, when foreign economic policy was central to voters (silver versus gold in the nineteenth century), it was a central defining feature of politics. A potent issue with less day-to-day connections with the voter is likely to lead to delegation of authority to committee chairmen, for example, who represent the views of the party caucus.

32. Further complicating the problem is that the party does not control nomination to congressional seats. Therefore, party discipline weakens when local issues arise.

33. This list reflects the dynamics analyzed in Sharyn O'Halloran, "Politics, Process, and American Trade Policy: Congress and the Regulation of Foreign Commerce" (Ph.D. dissertation, University of California, San Diego, 1990).

34. Peter F. Cowhey, *The Problems of Plenty: Energy Policy and International Politics* (Berkeley: University of California Press, 1985), ch. 4.

35. The Eastern states were critical for winning the nomination, and their leadership largely aligned with the Dewey wing. Michael Barone, *Our Country: The Shaping of America from Roosevelt to Reason* (New York: Free Press, 1990), pp. 167–181.

36. The Donovan account suggests that it was small. Robert J. Donovan, *Conflict and Crisis, The Presidency of Harry S. Truman* (New York: W. W. Norton,

1977). Barone, ibid., cites the bipartisan tone that benefited Truman but does not consider it the big issue. The key to Truman's victory was his swing toward liberal policies (civil rights, national health insurance, strong prolabor) that carried the New Deal constituency forward in presidential voting.

37. Vandenberg was as important for his role in defining the internal consensus within the Republican party as for bipartisanship. He defined the terms for the Midwestern wing of the Republican party to join the Eastern wing in accepting multilateralism championed by Democrats. Truman's later choice of a Republican industrial executive from Indiana to head the Marshall Plan further recognized this key issue. Cox and McCubbins' study of party caucus control over committees *(Parties and Committees)* found that the House Foreign Affairs has some Northern domination because of lower electoral externalities of most of its fare, but the median position of committee member reflects the party as a whole.

38. When Marshall and Acheson first tried to rely on the humanitarian basis for money for the reconstruction of Europe, congressional leaders replied that Americans were sick of being bled dry for charity. Truman and Acheson then said that the aid was for fighting communism, and the Republicans turned positive. Truman decided that this was how to cast the program to the nation. Daniel Yergin, *Shattered Peace—The Origins of the Cold War and the National Security State* (Boston: Houghton Mifflin, 1977). Harry S. Truman, *Years of Decision* (Garden City, N.Y., Doubleday, 1955). Timothy P. Ireland, *Creating the Entangling Alliance—The Origins of the North Atlantic Treaty Organization* (Westport, Conn: Greenwood Press, 1981).

39. Stephen Haggard: "The Institutional Foundations of Hegemony: Explaining the Reciprocal Trade Agreements Act of 1934, *"International Organization* (Winter 1988), 42:91–120, admirably shows how this worked for trade. A broader question is whether a rejection of autarky necessarily implied multilateralism. Multilateralism was not the only possible solution, but it was certainly the best known alternative, and, as John Odell notes, much is to be said for an alternative that is well known and that apparently predicted the failure of past policy. John S. Odell, "From London to Bretton Woods: Sources of Change in Bargaining Strategies and Outcomes," *Journal of Public Policy* (July–December 1988), 8:287–316.

40. Even Robert Taft, a representative of urban Ohio, was a major booster of public housing programs.

41. Barone, *Our Country,* argues that the Taft–Hartley bill was the most important consequence of the Congress elected in 1946 because it brought union expansion to a virtual halt while not reversing prior gains by labor. This set the stage for twenty years of politics geared to fiddling around the margins in the balance of programs desired by big business and large unions. Henry Nau, *The Myth of America's Decline* (New York: Oxford University Press, 1990), notes the conservative overtones to American commitments.

42. Robert Pollard, *Economic Security and the Origins of the Cold War, 1945–1950* (New York: Columbia University Press, 1985). Even Taft voted for the Greece–Turkey assistance act. James Jones, *The Fifteen Weeks*, p. 19, reported that it took one day of consultation with Congressional leaders to get their backing. After Taft called a draft of the Marshall Plan "a TVA for Europe" the heightened fears of Soviet gains in Europe led isolationists in Congress to back its adoption. Isaacson and Thomas, *The Wise Men*, pp. 401, 434, and 441.

43. Harriman cautioned that the United States should not emphasize its interests in European export markets lest this give Europeans any bargaining leverage. In short, voices were low key on the topic, but everyone saw the distributional benefits of the Marshall Plan. Michael Hogan, "European Integration and the Marshall Plan," in Stanley Hoffman and Charles Maier, eds., *The Marshall Plan: A Retrospective* (Boulder, Colo.: Westview Press, 1984).

44. Ruggie, "Multilateralism."

45. Henry Ryan, p. 31, reports that Britain tracked U.S. opinion polls in 1944 that showed 71% approval in the Midwest for the United Nations, and pp. 34–36 suggest that anti-United Kingdom feeling in Irish and German voters may have bolstered the U.S. position on decolonization. Ryan, p. 41, also points out that China's role in the United Nations and postwar planning was an important tool used by Roosevelt to build support for globalism—this would play to conservative Republicans—and Churchill agreed as a bone to U.S. opinion. Henry Butterfield Ryan, *The Vision of Anglo–America—The U.S.–U.K. Alliance and the Emerging Cold War, 1943–1946* (New York: Cambridge University Press). Dean Acheson, *Present at the Creation* (New York: W. W. Norton, 1969), p. 387, on his actions.

46. Bradford Perkins, "Unequal Partners: The Truman Administration and Great Britain," pp. 57–58, in Louis and Bull, eds., *The 'Special Relationship.'* Ireland, *Creating the Entangling Alliance*, shows the diplomatic bargaining logic preferring multilateralism.

47. Reynolds, "Roosevelt, Churchill," p. 26, notes that 20–30 percent of all Americans favored a negotiated peace with Germany in 1942 while the same polls showed no sympathy to Japan. My thanks to Rip Smith for this hypothesis.

48. Republican conservatives favored limiting commitments to Europe (as witnessed by its opposition to U.S. troops going to Europe to serve in NATO in 1950) in order to redeem America's destiny in Asia, a position popular with the missionary wings of the Protestant and Catholic churches. Reichard further points out that, in 1948, thirteen of the fifty-one Republican Senators were "hard-core" opponents of Truman policies, and eight (including Taft) were unreliable. But much of this came from Truman's calculus that he would bear the blame for foreign policy so he should also seize aggressive command over foreign policy initiatives. Republicans chose to bargain over the form of multilateralism and its geopolitical priorities. Gary W. Reichard, "The Domestic Politics of National Security," in Norman Graebner, ed., *The National Security,*

Its Theory and Practice, 1945–1960 (New York: Oxford University Press, 1986), pp. 243–274. The Korean War's stalemate provided the political opportunity to make the case for an anticommunist campaign in Asia, and Taft was viewed as sympathetic to this priority. But Taft had to moderate his views as the 1952 nomination campaign became heated. Still, the Dewey wing of the party blocked Taft by turning to Eisenhower, who was an adamant multilateralist and Europe-first candidate. Barone, *Our Country.*

49. Ireland, *Creating the Entangling Alliance,* p. 89, argues that Vandenberg was responsible for casting NATO as an organization stressing "mutual aid and self-help" precisely to assure Congress that NATO was not a one-sided bargain.

50. Glenn Palmer, "Corralling the Free Rider," notes that treaties also raise external credibility by making the commitment a bigger political issue if abandoned.

51. Specialized regulation of domestic U.S. markets meant that policymakers had to worry over how global market arrangements would reinforce or undermine markets subject to intense political oversight at home. U.S. administrative law had also evolved many of the devices of congressional oversight noted earlier. From the viewpoint of Congress, global counterparts to the domestic institutions were generally attractive.

52. Control over commodity policies was in committees that came closer to iron-triangle models than most of Congress. These committees in turn greatly strengthened the hands of the cabinet agencies most sympathetic to the commodity producers. Cox and McCubbins, *Parties and Committees,* 1991.

53. Sharyn O'Halloran has shown how standard techniques for overseeing delegated authority allowed Congress to obtain co-equal power while improving collective welfare: "Politics, Process, and American Trade Policy."

54. The executive branch successfully framed Bretton Woods as a referendum on the rejection of the causes of the war. At the time, Democrats controlled Congress, so this was a less difficult task than it might have been. Republican opponents largely had to rely on arguing the technical merits of the gold standard and fears of bleeding American treasure to the world. Alfred E. Eckes, *A Search for Solvency* (Austin: University of Texas Press, 1975).

55. Henry Morgenthau told one audience that Bretton Woods would "drive the usurious money lenders from the temple of international finance." Richard N. Gardner, "Sterling-Dollar Diplomacy in Current Perspective," p. 192, in Louis and Bull, eds., *The 'Special Relationship.'* Ron Chernow, *The House of Morgan* (New York: Atlantic Monthly Press, 1990). In addition, delegation of power to private parties would be easier in a parliamentary system than in one based on the division of powers.

56. Richard Gardner, *Sterling Dollar Diplomacy* (New York: Oxford University Press, 1969), pp. 129–143, points out that the negotiators explicitly watered down the power of the IMF to supervise domestic economic policies in

order to please Congress. The majority of Republicans supported Bretton Woods in Congress.

57. Pollard, *Economic Security,* pp. 15–17, makes the point about controls over Bretton Woods institutions. Obviously, aid in itself was unpopular because it required spending to help someone other than U.S. voters, but the massive procurement of U.S. goods for the Marshall Plan offset this problem.

58. The executive also delayed pushing for ratification until after the 1948 election and the approval of the Marshall Plan. Perkins, "Unequal Partners," pp. 58–59.

59. John Lewis Gaddis, *The Long Peace: Inquiries Into the History of the Cold War* (New York: Oxford University Press, 1987) pp. 93–94, relates the building of a consensus about military Keynesian policies.

60. Truman understood the magnitude of the challenge, and he accordingly refused to attend early NSC meetings in order to reassert his independence. I. M. Destler, Leslie H. Gelb, and Anthony Lake, *Our Own Worst Enemy—The Unmaking of American Foreign Policy* (New York: Simon and Schuster, 1984).

61. Harold Jongju Koh, *The National Security Constitution* (New Haven, Conn.: Yale University Press, 1990), 84–99. The State Department saw covert action as part of the political battle for Europe, of which NATO was one part. Perkins, "Unequal Partners," p. 58.

62. Deborah Avant, "The Institutional Sources of Military Doctrine: The United States in Vietnam and Britain in the Boer War and Malaya," Ph.D. dissertation, Department of Political Science, University of California, San Diego, 1991.

63. Steve Weber has pointed out that the credibility of Soviet commitments may have been lower on many fronts because highly concentrated power made it easier to reverse policy. Private communication.

64. Japanese public policy consistently favored the development of industry bolstered by an export-led strategy, the protection of agriculture, and the protection of small businesses (especially in the distribution sector) until recently. The Japanese bureaucracy churned out initiatives to restrict foreign competitors in Japan, emphasize savings, and channel these to industry, target selected industries for growth, and favor business at the expense of the consumer. Chalmers Johnson, *MITI and the Japanese Miracle* (Stanford, Calif.: Stanford University Press, 1982).

65. For example, one could emphasize how late development empowered the Japanese bureaucracy (with the support of big business) and reduced the importance of the political leadership. This line would question whether significant change in the economic structure of Japan is possible at all and certainly would deny the possibility unless other countries imposed stiffer sanctions.

66. If the bureaucracy performed well according to the developmental state textbook, it still may have only gilded the lily. Alternatively, even if it erred, it may not have stopped growth.

67. See Motoshige Itoh and Kazuhara Kiyono, "Foreign Trade and Direct Investment," pp. 155–1823, in Ryuturo Kumiyo, Masahiro Okuno, and Kotaro Suzumura, eds., *Industry Policy of Japan* (Tokyo: Academic Press, 1988), who do not differ all that much in this conclusion from Johnson's observation on protection as the key to domestic growth before exporting. They also note that all Japanese firms had to wrestle with a shortage of foreign exchange until the early 1960s and the implications of continuing large import bills for commodities. This would have led manufacturers to look for ways to make claims on foreign exchange through exporting.

68. Masahiko Aoki, *Information, Incentives and Bargaining in the Japanese Economy* (Cambridge, England: Cambridge University Press, 1988).

69. Edward Lincoln, *Japan's Unequal Trade* (Washington, D.C.: Brookings Institution, 1990).

70. This is not an argument that the political leadership hands the bureaucracy detailed guidelines; often guidance is in implied preferences about the outer limits of the substance of policies and a series of detailed expectations about who will be rewarded by any policy. In contrast, Edward B. Keehn argues (much like observers of U.S. bureaucracies) that asymmetries of information between the bureaucracy and political leaders so favor the former as to negate oversight: "Managing Interests in the Japanese Bureaucracy—Informality and Discretion," *Asian Survey* (November 1990), 30:1021–1037.

71. Kent E. Calder, *Crisis and Compensation—Public Policy and Political Stability in Japan* (Princeton: Princeton University Press, 1988), esp. pp. 63–70. The following analysis of Japan draws heavily on: Frances Rosenbluth, "Japan's Response to the Strong Yen: Party Leadership and the Market for Political Favors" (December 1990).

72. The electoral system has other fundamental consequences. For one, the opposition is not compelled to seek majority status. The Japan Socialist Party (JSP) normally fields only one candidate per constituency. This strategy enhances the chance of one candidate's finding a targeted minority in the district to support his/her election. Current office holders have no incentive to encourage a second candidate because strong job security exists with the present strategy (assuming the candidate courts local constituents). The consequence of this strategy is, however, that the JSP stands no chance of challenging for a majority status in the Diet. Gerald Curtis, *Election Campaigning Japanese Style* (New York: Columbia University Press, 1971). Samuel Kernell, "The Primary of Politics in Economic Policy."

73. For a discussion of the comparison, see: John Creighton Campbell, "Democracy and Bureaucracy in Japan," pp. 113–137, in Takeshi Ishida and Ellis S. Krauss, eds., *Democracy in Japan* (Pittsburgh: University of Pittsburgh Press, 1989).

74. The long-standing control of the LDP has further slanted the system because it permitted the continuation of massive imbalances in apportionment

that favored conservative rural voters. Shifts in public policy concerning distributive goods that are associated with rising power of urban districts (e.g., a reduction in subsidies to rural infrastructure that leads to more competition in many economic sectors) were largely muted.

75. This is the implication of Richard Samuels, *The Business of The Japanese State: Energy Markets in Comparative and Historical Perspective* (Ithaca, N.Y.: Cornell University Press, 1987).

76. Takashi Inoguchi, "The Political Economy of Conservative Resurgence Under Recession: Public Policies and Political Support in Japan, 1977–1983," pp. 189–255, in T. J. Pempel, ed., *Uncommon Democracies: The One-Party Dominant Regimes* (Ithaca, N.Y.: Cornell University Press, 1990).

77. Yasuhiro Tase noted that the five factional leaders would likely downplay fights over leadership if the economy took a downturn in 1990. Otherwise, he predicted an intense struggle. This is the logic I am describing. "Abe's Illness May Force Basic Realignment in LDP," *Japan Economic Journal* (October 13, 1990), p. 9.

78. See Kent Calder, "International Pressure and Domestic Policy Response: Japanese Informatics Policy in the 1980s" (Research Monograph no. 51, Center of International Studies, Princeton University, 1989) on telecommunications and software.

79. See Dennis J. Encarnation and Mark Mason, "Neither MITI nor America: The Political Economy of Capital Liberalization in Japan," *International Organization* (Winter 1990), 44(1):25–54, on the key role of Japanese international business in liberalizing selectively.

80. Karel van Wolferen notes that foreign policy and defense are among the worst specialities for electoral security or advancement in the party simply because they do not generate large flows of campaign monies: *The Enigma of Japanese Power: People and Politics in a Stateless Nation* (New York: Knopf, 1989).

81. Kent E. Calder, "Japanese Foreign Economic Policy Formation: Explaining the Reactive State," *World Politics* (July 1988), 40:517–541. Polling data revealed that Japanese voters supported some of the U.S. initiatives to open competition in consumer markets. *Japan Economic Journal* (April 7, 1990), p. 6.

82. These firms typically support increased U.S. entry and the opening of domestic competition. Often these firms pledge to work with American firms as part of their strategy to show why their entry will serve the Japanese public interest in responding to the trade problem with the United States. (Interviews, Tokyo, 1989.)

83. David C. Mowery and Nathan Rosenberg, *Technology and the Pursuit of Economic Growth* (New York: Cambridge University Press, 1990) make these points.

84. Robert Lawrence analyzed only a five-year trend, and one could hardly call the change sufficient to alter all the problems. Moreover, while MITI's ability to coordinate numerous export cartels to reduce trade fictions indicate

that export interests do understand the problem confronting Japan overseas, these tasks have also sapped MITI of some of its political support: "How Open Is Japan?" Paper prepared for NBER Conference on "The United States and Japan: Trade and Investment" (October 1989). The MITI campaign to encourage foreign purchasing by large firms through sliding-scale tax credits for imports is an example of political compensation for inconvenience that is found universally in politics. *Japan Economic Journal* (January 20, 1990), p. 5.

85. Helen Milner, "Trading Places: Industries for Free Trade," *World Politics* (April 1988), 40:350–376.

86. Kenneth Flamm, "Managing New Rules: High-Tech Trade Friction and the Semiconductor Industry," *The Brookings Review* (Spring 1991), pp. 22, 29.

87. The absence of a uniform code fits a system based on particularistic favors for well-organized clients. Codes assist newcomers and consumers unless they are explicitly designed to retard them. *Japan Economic Journal* (December 2, 1989), p. 1. *Nikkei Weekly* (October 5, 1991), p. 3.

88. Kent Calder, "International Pressure."

89. One vehicle for this effort is the BIS guidelines on reserve requirements, which also serve the broader purpose of assuring solvency of global banks. Ethan B. Kapstein, "Resolving the Regulator's Dilemma: International Coordination of Banking Regulations," *International Organization* (Spring 1989), 43:323–347.

90. Frances Rosenbluth, "Japan's Response."

91. Iwo Nakatani, "Opening 'Keiretsu' System to Scrutiny Is Crucial Task for Japan's Prosperity," *Japan Economic Journal* (May 26, 1990), p. 8.

92. This development implies the introduction of "reverse restructuring" of the global economy as elements of the Japanese political economy set ground rules for restructuring multilateral markets. In this case, antitrust policy would become part of the global agenda but influenced by models of Japanese industrial organization. This is precisely how multilateral orders have to accommodate the domestic political orders of leading powers if promises are to be credible.

93. See Peter F. Cowhey and Jonathan David Aronson, *Managing the World Economy: The Consequences of Corporate Alliances* (New York: The Council on Foreign Relations, 1992).

94. Michael Mastanduno, "Do Relative Gains Matter? America's Response to Japanese Industrial Policy," *International Security* (Summer 1991), 16:73–113. *Japan Economic Journal* (June 3, 1989), p. 2; (February 17, 1990), p. 3.

95. Ronald Rogowski, "Trade and the Variety of Democratic Institutions," *International Organization* (Spring 1987), 41:203–224.

96. This point was made abundantly clear to me in interviews with leaders from some of the high-technology startup companies with an internationalist strategy (Tokyo, 1989). On the complaints of service firms, see: *The Nikkei Weekly* (November 2, 1991), p. 1. The LDP has also tried to centralize fund raising as one way to bring more internal discipline to the party in the midst of scandal. *Japan Economic Journal* (February 3, 1990), p. 3.

97. Sam Nakagama, "In Japan, Farm Supports Prop Up More Than Farms," *New York Times* (August 13, 1990). Roughly two hundred LDP Diet Members are active supporters of the farm lobby, and about sixty of those seats are from agricultural districts. Prime Minister Miyazawa indicated that he would keep reform on the agenda. *Nikkei Weekly* (October 19, 1991), p. 2.

98. It also might make it possible for a consolidated opposition to take the LDP on successfully. This may be the reason why the Miyazawa cabinet appeared ready to abandon the reform in winter of 1992.

99. Kernell, "The Primacy of Politics," notes that the Prime Minister has neither the staff nor a sufficient time in office to do much more than shore up his faction and fight polity fires.

100. On the regional proposals, see: "Security Plan Fails to Impress," *Japan Times Weekly* (August 13–19, 1990), p. 3. Akihiko Tanaka stresses U.S. military leadership while Japan serves as a "facilitator": "International Security and Japan's Contribution in the 1990s," *Japan Review of International Affairs* (Fall/Winter 1990), pp. 187–208.

6. Creating the GATT Rules: Politics, Institutions, and American Policy

Judith Goldstein

Introduction

THE General Agreement on Tariffs and Trade (GATT) is among the most successful of the group of multilateral organizations built at the close of World War II. Created in 1947 as a temporary skeleton—its obsolescence was planned to coincide with the inauguration of the International Trade Organization (ITO)—the GATT subsequently orchestrated a radical reduction in international barriers to trade. In the past decade, the explanation for the success of this and other international organizations has focused on the role institutions can play in supporting cooperation. The virtues of reciprocity norms, of precise monitoring procedures, and of the dissemination of information have been cited as central elements in efficient international organization.[1]

This focus on organizational rules and norms reflects the current intellectual weight of "Prisoners' Dilemma" explanations for international cooperation. With this metaphor in hand, analysts have turned their attention to how nations with common interests—such as the potential welfare gains from trade liberalization—can overcome collective-action problems only if some mechanism is found to forestall cheating. According to such logic, GATT rules were appropriate because they assuaged the fears of potential regime participants that they would receive the "Sucker's Payoff" if they lowered tariff barriers. Interpreting the breakdown of the trading system in the interwar period as a market failure—mutual defection reflected the decline of rules, not of common interests, in international trade—the credit for the resurgence of trade

I would like to thank Jeffry Frieden, Geoff Garrett, Robert Keohane, John Ruggie, Steven Weber, and the other participants in this project for excellent comments on previous drafts. Georgia Markou, Ourania Markou, and Scott Wilson provided valuable research assistance.

under GATT is given to the institutionalization of efficient monitoring and enforcement procedures.

The problem is, however, that this analysis assumes far more common interest among the potential signatories of GATT than in fact existed. Although it may be true that the subsequent success of the GATT can be attributed to the inclusion of a clear set of procedures for punishing offenders, these were not the central issues of debate over regime rules. At the close of the war, significant differences existed in the trade preferences of the Western nations. While countries could agree on the general need to forestall a return to interwar trade competition, no common support was in place for a particular alternative. Rather, in GATT talks each nation defended the rules that they perceived as maximizing their particularlistic economic interests.

Since distributional issues were in the forefront of debate, the game-theoretical metaphor that better captures GATT negotiations is a "Battle of the Sexes." Here, the issue is not getting to the "Pareto frontier," but rather where participants will settle along it.[2] Solutions to this problem have been many, ranging from focal points to the naked exercise of power.[3] In the case of the GATT, the asymmetry in capabilities suggests that the United States could have imposed the policy of its choosing.[4] Still, the observation derived from this metaphor—that the United States was powerful and could thus choose the rules of the game—merely begs the key question of why one set of rules for the new trade regime was preferred by American policymakers over others.

Seeking an explanation for America's preferences is especially important since with the benefits of hindsight, it is clear that GATT rules did not serve America's long-term economic interests. Most significantly, GATT rules facilitated the exclusion of agricultural trade from liberalization efforts. While this may have been consistent with American interests in the 1940s, the GATT's sanctioning of agricultural protectionism thereafter closed off foreign markets to America's most competitive products.[5]

How do we explain American trade policy preferences in the 1940s? Explanations that derive preferences from America's place in the international system have difficulty accounting for both the timing and the sectoral variation in American policies. For example, in the period between 1929 and 1947, America's commercial policy moved from nonnegotiable tariffs, to support for bilateral trade reductions, to advocacy for a multilateral trade regime. These considerable changes in economic policy in a relatively short time span dwarf changes in American power. Similarly, American reticence at the height of her power over support for a more open world economy suggests that theories that derive trading interests from the distribution of power do not explain this case.[6]

American indifference to higher levels of trade liberalization in the 1940s can be explained by the same variables that explain the inability of GATT to open up markets today. Policies, once adopted by governments and institutionalized in rules and procedures, spawn interests that make change difficult—even after the policy itself is recognized to be functionally deficient. In the United States, policies created in the 1930s subsidizing agricultural production created powerful domestic interests that foreclosed American support in the 1940s and 1950s for agreements that would reduce quantitative barriers to agricultural trade. Thereafter, GATT's agricultural exceptions legitimated antifree-trade constituencies in nations with uncompetitive agricultural sectors—in Europe and Asia—that subsequently made it hard for policymakers to trade off agricultural protections for other benefits from trade liberalization.

The explanation for American behavior suggested below relies on the conventional variables of international relations analysis, that is, power and interest. But as well, careful attention is paid to a third factor: the strategy chosen by political entrepreneurs to translate power resources into valued outcomes. Policies are chosen based on beliefs about their efficiency in a given environment. Objective "preferences" rarely translate into a singular method of reaching the desired goals. Political actors do not merely have preferences over "outcomes," they have preferences over "actions." Thus politics entails a fight not only over whose interests will be maximized *but also* over the method to be used to maximize those interests. Considerations of strategy are investigations into the beliefs—causal and normative—of political entrepreneurs who make decisions in an uncertain environment on how best to maximize their, their constituents, and the nation's interests.[7]

America entered GATT negotiations with specific preferences on the form and scope of the new trade regime. The most concise explanation for why the United States did not push for more "liberal" rules—as would have been predicted from America's relative economic position in world trade—was that domestic groups feared increased agricultural imports. These groups were efficacious not only because of their ability to organize effectively but also because institutional resources—the organization of Congress and existing legislation—biased policy in their direction.[8] The United States did not get what was in her objective best "interest," not because of a lack of power but because of domestic institutional, ideational, and social constraints.

To show how these domestic dynamics translated into GATT rules, this essay proceeds as follows. First, I examine the domestic determinants of America's trade preferences at the end of World War II. Second, I turn to the negotiations themselves and the translation of American preferences into international practice. Finally, I explore the deleterious consequences of this initial choice of rules—in light of changes in American preferences over time and in the legitimation of antifree-trade coalitions abroad.

American Trade Policy Preferences

When Roosevelt came into office—after years of Republican party hegemony—"New Deal" policies were still on the drawing boards. In the early days of his administration, Roosevelt's advisors—Cordell Hull, Rexford Tugwell, and George Peek—devised radically different trade strategies to combat growing economic malaise. On one hand, the administration unilaterally devalued the dollar (the equivalent of a 50 percent increase in tariffs), abstained from international attempts to stabilize currencies, and initiated programs that forestalled trade liberalization. Legislation indicative of this "nationalist" policy strategy included the Agriculture Adjustment Act and the National Industrial Recovery Act, both of which explicitly argued for higher, not lower, levels of import restrictions.[9] Simultaneously, however, the administration pursued programs that were potentially trade expansionist. Following on the President's first-year promise that a new trade program was imminent, for example, a trade reform act was passed in 1934.

Although not appreciated at the time, this 1934 legislation fundamentally altered American trade policy. Although members of the economic community had urged the liberalization of the U.S. export–import mix consistently after 1890, government officials knew little and cared less about their advice. And while America's status as a creditor nation after World War I further necessitated a change in import policy, Woodrow Wilson's attempt to lower tariffs had been short-lived. Once Congress confronted economic problems in the 1920s, they turned to their usual panacea: a high tariff policy. The 1934 act was critical because it generated a change in authority; once legislated, free traders were able to implement their particular vision of economic policy. Thus in mid-decade—after the National Recovery Administration (NRA) was ruled unconstitutional—Hull and others turned to the administrative structures legislated in 1934 to pursue trade liberalization.[10] Their efforts met with success for manufacturing products but were stymied in agricultural trade because preexisting legislation mandated explicit market controls.

Thus, a decade before the GATT was negotiated, agricultural and manufacturing trade policies had bifurcated in the United States. In the area of manufacturing trade, Congress repeatedly relegislated negotiating authority to the executive office, which facilitated, by the start of the war, the conclusion of trade agreements with twenty countries.[11] Agricultural subsidy programs forced trade polity in a second direction. Agricultural groups—well entrenched in Congress—made it impossible for American negotiators to gain congressional assent for any international agreement that undermined the ability of the United States to use import restraints to protect farm incomes. Farm incomes had risen substantially under price support programs. Between 1938 and 1948, wholesale prices for farm products increased 50 percent more than prices for nonagricultural goods did. Although this was due more to the war than to government programs, farm groups associated increased farm incomes with American subsidy programs.

Why did such different policies develop? Neither variations in interests nor the power of each sector explains these policy outcomes; neither bilateral tariff reductions nor agricultural protectionism was a functionally "optimal" economic policy. Policy preferences reflected different strategic choices by each sector on how to maximize economic growth. Whereas the policy on manufacturing trade was characterized by attention to the twin ideas of reciprocity and most-favored-nation (MFN) status, agricultural trade was guided foremost by the notion of parity, mandating overt government intervention to maintain high prices. The choice over strategy—the belief in one policy practice rather than another—became incorporated in legislation and split America's foreign economic policy by sector.

RECIPROCITY AND MFN STATUS

Until 1934, reciprocity was an idea closely associated with Republican high-tariff policy. Reciprocity legislation in the nineteenth century had given the executive authority to punish other nations that did not give American exporters "fair" access to their markets. As early as in 1883,

President Arthur asked Congress whether it would be "advisable to provide some measure of equitable retaliation in our relations with governments which discriminate against our own."[12] Again in 1890, the idea appeared in section 3 of the trade act, which provided penalty duties on items imported from countries whose duties on American products were, in the opinion of the President, "unequal and unreasonable." Thus, reciprocity was seen as a way to penalize other countries—not a carrot to liberalize world trade, but a stick to be used if foreign nations discriminated against American products.[13]

Just as reciprocity could be used either to encourage or to discourage trade, the MFN principle was also potentially two-sided. By accepting an unconditional MFN principle, a country promised that it would give all importing nations the lowest tariff barrier it had negotiated with any one of them. Such a principle did not exist in the United States before the 1920s. Until that time, the United States negotiated agreements based on conditionality or on the provision that tariff concessions would be extended only to countries that gave the United States the same concessions. Such a proviso of conditionality led to discriminatory agreements among parties. If all nations could not benefit from a tariff reduction, then the agreement, by definition, would be discriminatory.

Thus, from February 1778—when the United States concluded a trade treaty with France—until the 1920s, all American treaties retained this qualification:[14]

> The most Christian King and the United States engage mutually not to grant any particular favor to other nations, in respect of commerce and navigation, which shall not immediately become common to the other party, who shall enjoy the same favor *freely if the concession was freely made, or on allowing the same compensation if the concession was conditional.*

The *italicized* phrase guaranteed that third parties did not get the same treatment as the signor of the agreement unless a specific concession was made to the United States. Such disregard of the unconditional wording in MFN agreements was relatively unusual, even in the eighteenth century.[15]

The United States formally adopted the principle of unconditional MFN status in 1923. Acceptance of the principle was celebrated with little fanfare, and there was minimal understanding of the impact this small procedural change would have on future trade relations.[16] Perhaps because no mandate to lower tariffs existed in the 1920s, the issue of unconditionality was of little concern to those in Congress. Only when tariffs became negotiable in 1934 did this decision take on meaning. By then, however, the United States had a decade of these type of treaties.[17] Did Congress intend to liberalize trade in the 1920s when they adopted a change in MFN status? Some scholars have argued this was the case.[18] Such a position is, however, hard to defend since this same Republican Congress had previously endorsed high levels of trade protection! But whether knowingly or not, the United States had agreed to the policy that became the operational backbone of the postwar trading regime.[19]

Not only did a new form for trade treaties emerge in this period, but even more importantly, a fundamental change occurred in the interpretation and use of the term *reciprocity*. Before the 1930s, reciprocity was understood much as it had been in the 1840s when Congress first considered reciprocal treaties. Then, reciprocity referred to substantive bilateralism.[20] Agreements were exclusive. The United States negotiated to give and to gain equal concessions. At a time when the United States granted only conditional MFN status, such negotiations were discriminatory by definition and were difficult to expand multilaterally.

Such an approach was challenged by the supporters of liberalization, who spoke of reciprocity in terms of formal bilateralism, that is, bilateral action with multilateral implications.[21] Put more simply, negotiations, they suggested, should be conducted between countries whose import–export mix gave them an incentive to grant one another a trade concession (presumably with the low-cost producer). Once a concession was granted to the principal supplier, other nations were also to be granted that new tariff. In the United States, those who argued for formal bilateralism were, in effect, arguing for negotiations based on unconditional MFN principles. As long as the United States maintained a single-column tariff system (until 1934) a change in a tariff resulting from a bilateral agreement would benefit any importer of that product.

The change in thinking on reciprocity was gradual. In 1919, the Tariff Commission issued a report on the history of American reciprocity. The report concluded that the "policy of special arrangements, such as the United States has followed in recent decades, leads to troublesome complications."[22] But with the election of a Republican government came a return to isolation and little interest in using international bargains to maximize America's economic interests. Then, in 1931, in response to the failing economy, the Democrats promoted a bill at the start of the 72nd Congress that included, among other features, a call for reciprocal trade agreements "under a policy of mutual concessions." Although this bill was vetoed by Hoover, its reciprocity proposal appeared in the tariff plank of the Democratic national platform and was endorsed by then governor Roosevelt, as well as by exporting interests and key academics.[23] Because of this change in sentiment, the 1934 act was unlike previous legislation supported by the Democrats. The Act gave the executive authority to negotiate with other nations reciprocally to lower tariffs—it was not a unilateral decree to lower tariffs.

Ambiguity remained, however, in both the Democratic party's position on trade negotiations and in the implications for trade of the 1934 endorsement of reciprocity and unconditional MFN treaties. Most members of the party still advocated the contradictory visions of reciprocity as retaliation *and* the idea of unconditional MFN agreements. Even the State Department's interpretation of the Trade Agreements Act of 1934 failed to absorb the new meaning of reciprocity, contending that the act "provides that the duties . . . shall be extended to all countries but provided that they may be confined to such countries as do not discriminate against American commerce.[24] The State Department's press release argued that such ability to punish was, in fact, "wholly in accord with the unconditional MFN principle."[25]

Different members of the administration voiced similar misunderstandings. Hull, who viewed the 1934 act as a doorway to liberalization, saw no contradiction between the 1922 and 1930 acts, which legislated retaliatory provisions through the maximum and minimum provision, and the 1923 decision to conclude only unconditional MFN agreements. He argued that if the United States signed with the principal low-cost producer, no industry would be hurt by secondary importers. This view was not universally shared. The more common view was represented by George Peek, the Special Advisor for Foreign Trade, who argued that the ideas of reciprocity and unconditional MFN principles were not compatible.[26] He continued to advocate barter and negotiations only on a country-by-country basis. In the short term, Peek's exit from government allowed Hull to orchestrate multilateral trade agreements. In the longer term, the successful culmination of trade agreements and the ensuing rapid recovery are what assured a multilateral meaning for reciprocity.

THE 1934 ACT

In all respects the 1934 trade act differed markedly from prior legislation. Politically, whereas the 1930 Smoot–Hawley Act had elicited 11,000 pages of testimony in forty-three days in the House, testimony on the proposed 1934 act was given by fourteen witnesses, six of whom were from the administration.[27] For the first time in years, the minority was permitted to help formulate the bill and to amend the act on the floor.[28] The week-long Senate committee hearings were brief, but considerably more discussion took place on the floor.[29] The chief controversy surrounded the delegation of authority to the executive.[30] In the end, the act passed as an amendment to the 1930 act in a nearly perfect partisan vote. The bill enabled the President to reduce rates up to 50 percent from Smoot–Hawley levels. Henceforth, he was also able to conclude trade agreements without further congressional action. Commenting on the loss of this traditional congressional power, the minority report stated that the bill "places in the hands of the President and those to whom he may delegate authority the absolute power of life and death over every industry dependent on tariff protection."[31]

Fundamentally, the 1934 law legislated into force new ideas on tariff administration and bargaining. No longer would the United States have a single-column tariff system. New trade agreements brought lower rates for all countries with MFN status while others would receive the higher Smoot–Hawley rates. Private parties, once so influential in setting their own rates, could still have their hearing, but now in an arena tangential to tariff setting. If interest groups were the big losers, the big winner was the President, who gained power over tariff classification and reclassification, control of valuation procedures, the statutory right to reduce rates, and the ability to prevent unfair competitive practices and discrimination against American exports.

As important as the creation of new organizational structures was the appointment of people whose professional and personal interests lay in tariff reductions. Within the Department of State, three committees focused exclusively on the foreign policy aspects of trade. These committees were America's first organizational advocates of multilateral trade. The Executive Commercial Policy Committee was created in November 1933 to coordinate American policy "with a view to centralizing in the hands of one agency supervision of all government action affecting our imports and export trade."[32] Members were high officials from various government departments. The Trade Agreements Committee, created after the 1934 act, included representatives from the Departments of State, Agriculture, Treasury, and Commerce. Finally, the Committee for Reciprocity Information was formed to ensure Roosevelt's promise that "no sound and important American interest (would) be injuriously disturbed" by the trade agreements program.[33] Its chief activity was to hold public hearings. Over the ensuing few years, members of all three committees became convinced of the value of trade liberalization. Functionally, they diverted attention from Congress; professionally, they saw their jobs as assuring the continuation of the liberalization program.[34]

In sum, the 1934 trade act ushered in a new political era. In 1934, Congress abdicated direct tariff-making responsibility and adopted a new role for itself in the making of policy. Henceforth, Congress would act as a "balancer" and a broker; it would ensure the passage of "fair" trade bills and act as a watchdog for America's interests at home and abroad.[35] These changes allowed the United States to create a liberal trade regime a decade and a half later. But as will be shown below, a liberal trade policy was in no way guaranteed by America's ascendence to hegemony.

AGRICULTURAL TRADE POLICY AND THE IDEA OF PARITY

The path to trade liberalization—from the 1923 decision on MFN agreements, to the 1934 act, and ultimately to the creation of a multilateral trade organization—was only one side of American trade policy. On the other side were events that occurred simultaneously in the area of agricultural trade.

If the 1934 trade act set the United States down a path of reducing barriers to manufacturing trade, the 1933 Agricultural Adjustment Act accomplished just the opposite. While liberalization in nonagricultural goods was guided by the twin assumptions of reciprocity and MFN agreements, agriculture policy was far more influenced by the idea of parity. Whereas the former concepts granted a place for international markets to regulate the demand and price of American products, the latter idea forced government to regulate just about all aspects of production.

The notion of a parity price developed in the 1920s. In essence, it implied that the agricultural sector should garner prices and profits akin to those found in industrial production, or at minimum, at a time when the agricultural sector was relatively prosperous. Legislative guarantees of a parity price were to be unrelated to economic factors, such as the world price for a particular commodity. Once established as the backbone of agricultural policy, competing notions that prices should be set by world supply-and-demand conditions were ignored.[36] The policy implication of guaranteed parity was problematic from the perspective of those who advocated open trade borders: the parity price maintained farm prices in the United States above those found on world markets, which created incentives for producers in other nations to export farm products to the

United States. Without some controls, government-set prices would be undermined.

FARM LEGISLATION

Legislators well understood that increased competition in the home market held the potential of undermining agricultural supports. The response was to enact trade restrictions. Thus Congress included in the original and subsequent authorizations on farm subsidies the right both to set import quotas and to give export subsidies, if necessary to maintain prices. The ideological underpinning of the trade liberalization—that is, that government should rely on markets to set price and quantity—was never accepted as a tenet of agricultural policy.

The 1933 act, which revolutionized American farm policy, was the last of a series of attempts to deal with an agricultural depression that began at the end of World War I.[37] Created by the 1933 act, the Agricultural Adjustment Administration (AAA) in the Department of Agriculture was given the authority to reduce production and to increase prices for seven basic crops—wheat, cotton, corn, hogs, rice, tobacco, and milk and its products. In subsequent acts, other commodities were added and other means were given to the administration to elevate farm prices. The focus of government activity was an attempt to reduce supply; ultimately, direct cash payments were used as an incentive for farmers to stop production. Between 1934 and the outbreak of the war, the government paid about $4.4 billion to producers in return for their not bringing crops to market.[38]

From the start, farm groups had little interest in and much apprehension about the reciprocal trade agreements program. In testimony, the Grange—one of the best organized of the farm groups—opposed all forms of trade liberalization, and the Farm Bureau argued that only industrial tariffs should be lowered. Their attempt to exclude agriculture from the program lost by a relatively small margin (54–33) in the Senate in 1934. Farm opposition did not, however, disappear with the passage of the 1934 act. As late as the 1945 extension of the Reciprocal Trade Agreements Act, wool, cattle, sugar, and dairy interests, among others, opposed the extension in testimony before the House.

In retrospect, these groups had little to fear. The Roosevelt administration showed itself willing to protect agricultural products if necessary to maintain farm incomes. On the heals of the 1934 trade act, Congress passed, and Roosevelt signed, the Jones–Costigan Act, explicitly mandating sugar import quotes. Further, under section 22 of the AAA, the administration authorized import quotas on wheat and wheat products, butter, milk products, cheese, oats, barley, rye, rye flour, peanuts, wheat, wheat flour, cotton, and cotton waste. The administration also limited imports of filberts, almonds, flax seed, linseed oil, and peanut oil through import fees. Import licenses were deemed necessary for other products, including butter and apples. Wheat, wheat flour, cotton, and cotton waste imports were allocated by country, in direct conflict with the equal-treatment concept that was to become a central GATT norm.

But it was more than the use of import quotas that revealed fundamental conflict between free-trade ideas and American policy. Under section 32 of the AAA, the U.S. government was authorized to use export subsidies for agricultural exports. Under the 1935 version of the law, the Secretary of Agriculture was granted the right to use up to 30 percent of gross custom receipts to increase farm exports "by the payment of benefits . . . or of indemnities for losses incurred in connection with such exportation." In his January 1936 budget message to Congress, Roosevelt publicly acknowledged the contradictions in his legislative proposals. His public response was explicit support for liberalization. Roosevelt requested that export subsidy provisions be repealed. But indicative of sentiment at the time, he was ignored by Congress. Thus in 1944, just as Roosevelt's State Department declared America's intention to ensure a multilateral and liberal future for world trade, the Agricultural Department allocated $118 million to subsidize exports of wheat, cotton, corn, tobacco, fruits, tree nuts, and dairy and meat products.[39]

In general, the increased domestic and foreign demand for American farm products during World War II had made prewar agricultural programs inoperative. After the Lend-Lease Act passed Congress in 1941, agricultural products were shipped abroad in ever-increasing amounts. By the end of 1944, 5 billion dollars worth of agricultural products had been exported under the program's provisions. Cotton export subsidies were stopped in 1942; wheat export subsidies ended in 1943.[40] Although price supports were in effect for 166 different agricultural goods in 1945, the policy was cheap; the war kept market prices at about their price-support level. The result was that at the close of the war, the agricultural sector had expanded by 20 percent.[41] Prices paid to farmers were about 200 percent above their prewar levels.[42]

To encourage war production and assuage the fear of drastic price declines at the close of the war, the Steagall Amendment to the extension of the Commodity Credit Corporation in July 1941 increased government supports not only for the original group of protected products but also for expanded supports to other agricultural goods. Few forgot what increased output in WWI had done; government officials assumed and promised that at the end of the current war, price and production controls would be used to avert a second agricultural depression. Yet counter to these predictions, the war's end did not herald a slump in prices. The demand for American products actually rose, leading to even higher farm prices. Output reached unprecedented levels. By 1947, the average prices received by farmers were 25 percent above that received the year before! This meant that the provisions established by the Steagall Amendment remained dormant. Only in a few products—potatoes, eggs, butter, dried milk, wool, and turkey—did the government employ price support programs.

Even so, as American negotiators moved ahead on the trade regime, they found that agricultural supports and farm protections were difficult—if not impossible—to overturn. In the 1945 renewal of the trade act, Congressman Pace of Georgia had offered an amendment to safeguard further the farm program from trade treaties. Though not passed, it was clear that Congress' commitment to liberalization did not extend to the removal of protections to agriculture. When in 1948 the demand for agricultural goods finally fell, price support programs went immediately into force. The Steagall Amendment—which was set to expire—was replaced by similar and more permanent protections in the Agricultural Act of 1948.[43] And in 1951, the extension of the trade act formally stated that trade agreements could not be concluded in violation of existing agricultural programs.

In sum, as the United States embarked upon the creation of a new trade regime, its own domestic policy was mired with inconsistencies. Although the State Department was unequivocal on the benefits of multilateral trade liberalization for the American economy, the Department of Agriculture declared simultaneously that under no conditions could the United States delegate control over import protections for farm products. It was not that the intrinsic interests of the agricultural sector were orthogonal to trade liberalization. By the late 1940s, the prosperity of American agriculture was clearly associated with exports: the United States was supplying 39 percent of the world's wheat, 41 percent of the world's tobacco, and 49 percent of the world's cotton. Few could ignore the importance of agriculture to America's export economy (see table 1). Yet, both farm groups and elected officials were politically wedded— because of organized private interest, congressional committees and exist-

Table 6.1 The Importance of Agricultural Trade
1945–58

Year	%Total U.S. Exports	Index of Export Importance*
1945	34	41
1946	28	51
1947	25	51
1948	30	51
1949	30	40
1950	27	47
1951	26	54
1952	19	36
1953	19	37
1954	21	40
1955	21	43
1956	23	58
1957	21	50
1958	22	43

*Index is a measure of the changing importance of foreign trade to agriculture. Computed as total domestic exports of agricultural commodities divided by index of total farm output. 1967 = 100.

Sources: U.S. Bureau of the Census, *Historical Statistics of the United States* (1975), Series K 414-429; U.S. Department of Agriculture, *Agricultural Statistics* (1960), table 813.

ing legislation—to government controls on price and supply. It would take twenty years for producers and political leaders to realize the costs of this strategy.

Constructing the Trade Regime

During World War I, Cordell Hull proposed in a resolution to the House of Representatives that the United States establish a multilateral trade organization. Although dismissed at the time, the idea reappeared in State Department discussions as early as 1939. Post war planning, suggests Richard Gardner, was infused by a common interest in ensuring that unlike after the last great war, there would not be "inadequate handling of economic problems. Consequently, [planners] placed great emphasis on economics in drawing blue-prints for a better world."[44]

Early in the war State Department officials began formal and informal meetings with British and Canadian officials on postwar trade issues. In these talks and from ensuing policies, America's support for applying multilateral principles to commercial policy became increasingly apparent. In the Atlantic Charter in August 1941, in article VII of the Master Lend-Lease agreement in 1942, at Bretton Woods in 1944, and at the San Francisco conference to establish the United Nations, there were declarations of a causal relationship between commercial policies and peaceful relations among states. Then two documents—the *Proposals for Expansion of World Trade And Employment,* completed by State Department officials in December 1945 and the *Suggested Charter for an International Trade Organization of the United Nations* released in September of the following year—revealed specific plans for a trade regime that was both multilateral and nondiscriminatory. Both the GATT, which came into formal existence on January 1, 1948, and the ITO Charter, ratified in the fall of 1947 in Havana, have their intellectual origins in these American documents.

In moving from these blueprints, State Department officials confronted numerous problems. Perhaps most fundamental was that nations agreed only abstractly to a new multilateral trade regime. They disagreed, however, on just what the regime should do. The variation in national objectives was most visible in talks between the two key negotiating nations: Britain and the United States. The British argued that the goal of trade policy was full employment; trade liberalization was an acceptable strategy only to the extent that it met this goal. State Department negotiators, however, agreed only that changes in trade policy should not be at the cost of the economic vitality of particular sectors or producers. They—as opposed to America's own Department of Agriculture—never agreed that the trade regime should be created to meet domestic political goals. Indicatively, ITO negotiations were "a head-on collision between those who were wedded to the idea of a free multilateral trading system . . . and those who placed the whole emphasis on full employment policies on a national basis."[45]

In the original American *Proposal,* a general position was outlined:

> What is needed is a broad and yet detailed agreement among many nations, dealing at one time with many different sorts of government restrictions upon trade, reducing all of them at once on a balanced and equitable basis, and stating rules and principles within which the restrictions permitted to remain should be administered.[46]

Later, in 1946, the American policy was further clarified by Clair Wilcox, the head of the American delegation in London negotiating with the British on the ITO:[47]

> Every nation stands to gain from the widest possible movement of goods and services. . . . That international trade should be abundant, that it should be multilateral, that it should be non-discriminatory, that stabilization policies and trade policies should be consistent—these are propositions on which all nations, whatever their forms of economic organization, can agree.[48]

Whereas American negotiators argued that the primary principle of a trade organization was to reduce barriers to trade, Stafford Cripps, representing the British, suggested that the prime object was to "achieve an agreement as to the manner in which the nations can co-operate for the promotion of the highest level of employment and the maintenance of demand and can bring some degree of regulation into world trade and commerce."[49] Such a position made little sense to American negotiators. The Americans doubted that nations could or should ask others to participate in domestic policies to maintain full employment. Employment, it was argued, could not be "as absolute as in the case of other matters which lie entirely within the volition and control of nations."[50] But it was not only the right of a multilateral organization to set domestic employment goals that sat poorly with the American delegation. As well, they differed on what should be the national employment objective. In 1945, the Full Employment Act had been rejected by Congress; its alternative in 1946 was far closer to the American conception of the responsibility of government, that is, ambiguity on both what constituted full employment and executive discretion over the use of economic tools to meet employment goals. The Americans would only concede that nations should not use "measures likely to create unemployment in other countries."[51]

The British were, however, adamant on this point. Unlike the United States, their commitment to a Keynesian demand policy led to a fear that domestic expansion could be undermined by exports undercutting British production. Thus, the British proposed for the ITO Charter an unambiguous statement that full employment be "the main condition for the maintenance of satisfactory levels of living" and thus its maintenance on "a reasonably assured basis was essential . . . to the expansion of international trade."[52] And at minimum, the British wanted the ITO to allow them to resort to trade protections to defend employment goals.

The outcome on the ITO was a series of compromises. The heart of the settlement was the exceptions to rules under specific conditions relating to balance of payments adjustments. In London, the British got the assurance that

> in case of a fundamental disequilibrium in their balance of payments involving other countries in persistent balance of payments difficulties, which handicap them in maintaining employment, [nations] will make their full contribution to action designed to correct the maladjustment.[53]

Among actions to be taken, countries could, when necessary, resort to quantitative restrictions.

In many respects, quantitative restrictions were the fundamental issue of the times. When the Gold Standard collapsed in 1931, competitive devaluations made tariffs an insufficient mechanism for the protection of the economy. Nations then moved to explicit quantitative controls as a means of sheltering domestic industry. From the perspective of the State Department, quotas—unlike tariffs—not only were inherently discriminatory but also were associated with the economic nationalism of the interwar period. As early as 1933, the State Department pointed to quotas as the more onerous form of trade restriction, explaining that at least tariffs were potentially open to reciprocal bargaining.[54]

Although the trade regime ultimately allowed quotas, both British and American negotiators shared a general distaste for quantitative restrictions. Thus, they agreed that the trade regime should prohibit quantitative restrictions. But confronted with domestic political pressures, both agreed that special circumstances must occur when that principle could be ignored. To accommodate both parties, these exceptions grew to include a range of situations, from postwar transition, to balance of payment disequilibrium and domestic support programs.

This last category was introduced specifically by the American delegation. Before the war ended, American negotiators had informally indicated that they could sign no agreement that did not award special consideration to American agriculture. In response, American negotiators argued that quantitative restrictions to protect either an international commodity agreement or a domestic commodity program were legitimate extensions of previous principles. Then in line with its own needs, the United States proposed that restrictions be allowed only for domestic programs that controlled output. And when used, quotas and other restrictions would operate in such a way "as would reduce imports relatively to domestic production as compared with the proportion prevailing in a previous representative period."[55]

In the spring of 1947, the United States further clarified its position to the fifty-six participating nations at the Geneva United Nations Conference on Trade and Employment. Now, American acceptance of a trade regime was contingent upon four exceptions being written into both the ITO charter and the General Agreement. First, in 1946 the United States had included a new safeguard in its trade treaty with Mexico that allowed for portions of that agreement to be rescinded under specific conditions. Now the United States asked that such an escape clause—allowing suspension or withdrawal of tariff agreements if serious injury occurred to a domestic producer—be included in all its future agreements. Second, although GATT and the ITO were to forbid quantitative restrictions, such restrictions were to be allowed for the protection of agricultural commodities under specified conditions. Third, agricultural exports were to be an exception to any general pledge against export subsidization.[56] And fourth, if necessary to protect essential security interests, any obligation specified in the charter could be abrogated.[57] These exceptions were not negotiable. Thus, the United States vetoed a motion by China to extend the exceptions to include manufactured goods; likewise, they refused a motion by China, India, and the Netherlands to allow quantitative restrictions to apply to all domestic price stabilization measures.[58]

But the inclusion of these exceptions was still insufficient to garner domestic approval.[59] By the time Congress considered the final ITO Charter, almost every important group was lined up against ratification. Some groups argued with the National Foreign Trade Council that the employment provisions, "would operate inexorably to transform the free enterprise system of this country into a . . . planned economy . . . and threat[en] the free institutions and liberties of the American people."[60] Others suggested that the ITO would allow countries to pursue inflationary policies and still maintain quantitative restrictions against American exports. The sanctioning of restrictions for balance-of-payments reasons and rules on foreign direct investment, argued business groups, were inconsistent with their interpretation of the purpose of the multilateral trade regime.[61]

The administration made an additional mistake that made passage difficult. Throughout the negotiation process, the State Department had insinuated that the price of American involvement in a trade regime was the demise of British imperial preferences. When it became clear in 1950 that negotiators had not procured the elimination of British tariff preferences, many in Congress failed to see how the ITO Charter served American interests in any way. Commenting on the failure of the ITO, Richard Gardner argues that the two major sponsors . . . sought to incorporate in the Charter a detailed statement of their favorite economic doctrines. . . . The result was an elaborate set of rules and counter-rules that offered imperfect standards for national policy. These rule and counter-rules satisfied nobody and alienated nearly everybody.[62]

The demise of the ITO was not the end of the multilateral trade regime. The heart of what America wanted in a trade regime, that is, the commercial policy provisions of chapter V, were incorporated into part II of the GATT. This new document now codified America's preferences on trading relations as stated at the start of the negotiating process. Like the ITO, the GATT was multilateral. Fundamental control of the organization was shared by all members; all agreed to give others MFN status, and nondiscrimination was a central norm. But in operation, the GATT was a network of simultaneous bilateral reciprocal agreements. Unlike the ITO, the GATT did not aspire to be a multilateral mechanism for the formal control of all aspects of trade.[63] In this way, the United States finessed demands by other nations to specify policy guidelines for the new regime. But this limited purpose was an asset; even while the ITO Charter was being discussed in national capitals, the GATT initiated its first round of trade talks. These talks, called in 1947, were the first of eight major bargaining sessions that GATT would sponsor.[64]

GATT's success was not due to its being a better multilateral organization. As with the ITO, the document was riddled with exceptions. Article 11 contained the attempt to eliminate quantitative restrictions, except for restrictions on agricultural or fisheries products, and article 19 included the escape clause. The only item that may be construed as bowing to British demands was inclusion of article 12, providing the general safeguard for restrictions, if necessary, for balance of payments reasons. This general safeguard was, however, consistent with international monetary policies simultaneously being pursued in Washington.

The GATT Regime:
Multilateralism with Exceptions

By the late 1960s America's vision of the GATT had changed. Congress began to place pressure on GATT negotiators to get results on agricultural as well as manufacturing trade liberalization. But, as opposed to the 1950s when other countries were willing to entertain agreements in all trade arenas, American negotiators now found America's trading partners unable or unwilling to ignore farm constituencies that stood to lose from any liberalizing agreement. American policies of the 1940s and 1950s were coming "home to roost."

Finally, in 1948, on the eve of the first GATT talks, the demand for American farm products plummeted. As had been feared, the United States now had an oversupply of agricultural products, much as in the post-WWI years. But farm product price increases in the previous decade now exacerbated the problem. By 1948 the index of farm prices had reached 307, compared with an index of industrial prices that stood at 265. The parity price in 1948—116—was the highest level reached since 1918. From an index of 76 in the period 1935–39, farm output advanced to 104 in 1948. Further, between 1938 and 1948, wholesale prices of farm products had increased 50 percent more than the prices of nonfarm products did.

To maintain incomes, policymakers eschewed trade liberalization as a policy option and turned instead to existing regulatory policies. But a program of substantial government intervention to control production, prices, and imports now meant that the United States would need a further waiver by the GATT.[65] Thus, in 1954, the United States went to GATT where it requested, and received, approval for a further change in GATT rules. To maintain prices the United States now needed GATT to allow it to halt imports **even if** there was no domestic program restricting output. This exception would become the legal basis for European claims that the Common Agricultural Policy (CAP) did not defy GATT rules.

Further, in this ninth GATT session, American negotiators made clear that the United States would condone no commodity agreement and would invoke the GATT principle if one was passed that any new activity by GATT would not automatically obligate existing members.[66] The formal American position as stated in these talks was that "the United States feels that the further venture into the commodity field . . . is unwise and unnecessary . . . because we believe that enough machinery already exists for dealing with commodity problems."[67]

Not only did the United States halt early talks on commodity trade, but also these actions encouraged others to increase barriers to American products. This is most clear in the case of European policy on agriculture.

THE CAP

At the time of the writing of the Treaty of Rome in 1957, the six signatories operated different types of agricultural support programs.

Germany and Belgium, dependent on agricultural imports, used both trade restrictions and price supports to provide an income supplement to farmers. In contrast, France and Italy were self-sufficient in agricultural products, suffering instead from periodic surpluses. These countries not only restricted imports but also subsidized exports. The Netherlands and Luxembourg maintained relatively more liberal agricultural trade policy.

The Common Policy for Agriculture, adopted in January 1962, integrated these policies. Under the new rules, all national policies affecting prices, such as trading restrictions, local usage regulations, and subsidies were replaced by regulations for the Community as a whole. The marketing conditions for most agricultural products were fully controlled through direct market intervention. Target prices for individual products were set for the market as a whole. To ensure that these prices were not undermined by world market conditions, a system of variable import levies was created. These levies were calculated so as to offset any price advantage for imports, completely insulating producers from world price developments. To ensure that surpluses would not undermine target prices, the CAP provided for disposal of excess production through subsidized exports and subsidized consumption.

In practice, the target prices in the 1960s were not a weighted average of the previously ruling national prices but rather were a figure that exceeded that figure. In Brussels, it was far easier to agree to higher prices than to lower individual price levels. Thus the Community maintained higher levels of protection for agricultural products after the CAP than had previously been in force by any individual states.[68]

The Europeans offered two legal defenses of the CAP to GATT members. First, they argued that the restrictions that had previously affected agricultural production and trade in each state were simply being substituted for a comprehensive program that was not ruled out by any provision of the GATT. Second, and more important, the Europeans relied on American precedent. The variable levy was compared with the American system of price supports. Both, it was suggested, maintained a domestic price unrelated to the world price; both called for use of import restrictions and export subsidies. Europeans suggested that article 11, which provided that imports be restricted only if domestic production or marketing was also curtailed, was no longer pertinent. The United States itself, in 1951, had legislated an amendment to the Defense Production Act requiring the Secretary of Agriculture to impose restrictions on imports of a number of products, including dairy, for which no domestic production controls existed. Further, in 1955 GATT had granted a general waiver for these quotas and others imposed under the 1951 extension of section 22 provisions. Given the U.S. example, GATT had no legal grounds to constrain the Community from enacting barriers to agricultural trade.[69]

In sum, the United States constrained GATT's efforts to deal with agricultural protectionism in two ways. First, in the 1950s, the United States refused to participate in any new agreements on commodity trade. The United States vetoed all proposals to have agricultural trade covered in separate commodity agreements, and in the GATT—as in the ITO charter—agriculture products were included in the general framework.[70] Thus, attempts by other GATT members to create separate agreements that would cover agricultural products were stymied by a lack of American participation.

Second, the United States undermined article 11 as a means of ending reliance on quantitative restrictions. While other primary commodity exporters waited for the time when countries would no longer rely on the exceptions to the use of quantitative restrictions for reasons of balance-of-payment disequilibrium, the United States itself actively used its waiver to impose such restrictions on agricultural products. The United States provided neither leadership nor support for the expansion of GATT into commodity trade. With agricultural trade restrictions off the agenda, nations recovering from the war were free to grant trade protection to inefficient agricultural producers for domestic political purposes. Before the late 1950s, no country on the continent made the argument that their participation in GATT was contingent on the exclusion of agricultural products. In the 1940s, Italy and France, the two countries with the least efficient farm sectors, were far more interested in an uninterrupted supply of agricultural supplies from the United States than in the needs of their nascent agricultural sectors. While dependent upon American food, there was no defiance to America's interests in reducing existing quantitative and nonquantitative restrictions. Agricultural protectionism returned to Europe and elsewhere with the tacit support of the United States.

Conclusions

Three general points may be drawn from this essay. First, GATT's creation stemmed from American power. It was the United States that envisioned a multilateral postwar world. That vision motivated individuals in the State Department to embark upon multilateral discussions that led to both the ITO Charter and the GATT. The specific rules written into both documents reflected American ideas on trade policy. Yet, American power did not ensure that the document constructed would adhere to the functional needs of the United States. Although negotiators might have thought that the agreement served the long-term interests of the American economy, neither the original GATT document nor the stickiness of these rules over time has proved optimal from the American perspective. In short, it may be true—but uninteresting—that regimes are created by the powerful. Power alone can explain neither the choice of rules nor the distributional implications of a particular regime.

How do we explain the choice of rules for a multilateral organization? Some suggest that GATT rules reflect an international "logroll." The United States agreed to exceptions in order to gain approval from other nations. There is little evidence to support this hypothesis. Only for the British—and only minimally—did the United States agree to deviate from the original American proposals. GATT rules and the structure of trade liberalization were absolutely consistent with America's original design for a trade regime. Whereas the ITO charter included compromise, especially to British interests, the GATT did not. In short, America had sufficient power and influence in 1947 to ensure that GATT rules reflected American demands.

Even so, the American delegation neither demanded nor obtained an unadulterated liberal trade order. Although the United States espoused multilateral principles, the American position on specific policy issues was a hybrid. In the 1940s, liberal trade ideas were relatively new; their worth was still an open question. Especially in the field of agricultural trade, no policymaker was willing to give up control to market forces when the alternative was a politically salient system of rules and procedures that had proved capable of ensuring agricultural growth. In short, no consensus existed in 1947 that liberalizing trade would be sufficient to ensure economic stability. Instead, a fear arose that the return to normalcy would bring on the agricultural depression akin to the one that followed World War I. Thus, the United States limited its delegation of authority to the ITO and GATT through a series of escape clauses and exceptions.

By the 1960s, American opinion had changed.[71] But GATT rules had not. Thus, the problem for the United States thereafter was to attempt, through diplomacy, to establish new operating procedures by which to liberalize agricultural trade. As evidenced by the Uruguay

Round, Americans have had only limited success. Where in the 1940s the United States could use either of two strategies to ensure compliance from her trading partners, that is, the United States could threaten to "exit" from negotiations or offer lucrative side payments, the decline of American power makes both of these strategies costly. In short, although America's commitment to liberal trade increased over the century, GATT's rules continued to allow other nations to pursue particularistic trade policies.

This suggests a second point. Policies once institutionalized are difficult to uproot. This is true in both domestic and international organizations, essentially for the same reason. Once in force, policies create interests who benefit from that particular constellation of rules and procedures. These interests—within and outside government—become a formidable political force, making change difficult. Thus, once agricultural subsidies became American policy, even groups who once scorned such government intervention found themselves aligned together defending the distributional aspects of the policy. This group made it impossible for American negotiators to delegate any authority to the GATT that would undermine the subsidy program. Similarly, once GATT allowed quantitative exceptions for agricultural products, it encouraged the creation of agricultural protections abroad. Europe could construct the CAP, which in principle deviated from the liberal trade regime, and still be in compliance with GATT. And once protected, European agricultural groups made it politically impossible for governments to withdraw aid.

On both the domestic and international level organizations codify a particular set of ideas. But although the organization may be the creation of the powerful and represent the strategy of the "winning coalition," the distributional aspects of the new regime may deviate markedly from that predicted by its creators. Not only may the strategy selected be suboptimal in the short term, but also in the long term, unintended consequences may follow from the creation of a set of rules and procedures that ultimately counter the interests of the organization's creators.

This is no more evident than in the case of agricultural trade. American negotiators wanted agricultural markets opened to American products. Thus they were adamant about not separating agricultural negotiations from talks on manufactures. But simultaneously, the American Congress demanded the writing of an exception into the rules for agricultural subsidies. Once the rule existed, it created the incentive for both Europe and Japan to protect inefficient agricultural producers. The political coalitions that developed from such protections left the United States at a disadvantage, with little it could either offer or threaten in order to gain concessions from these governments.

This suggests a last point. From the American perspective, the GATT has serious flaws. Central among these problems is the continued inability of GATT to liberalize trade for America's key export items. Although true, such a perspective may be shortsighted. While these exceptions undermined the creation of a truly liberal trade regime, they may have been the regime's great strength. By allowing governments to pursue domestic interventionist policies—by supporting "embedded" and not orthodox liberalism—the regime retained the support of members and succeeded, with minimal resources, in fundamentally changing postwar commercial relations.[72] This compromise between free-trade ideas and domestic autonomy was never formally decided in multilateral negotiations. Rather, it was the unintended consequence of a series of compromises to ensure British and, more important, American involvement in the regime.

NOTES

1. See, for instance, Robert Keohane, *After Hegemony,* (Princeton: Princeton University Press, 1984); Kenneth Oye, *Cooperation Under Anarchy* (Princeton: Princeton University Press, 1986); Stephen Krasner *International Regimes* (Ithaca: Cornell University Press, 1983).

2. Stephen Krasner, "Global Communications and National Power: Life on the Pareto Frontier" *World Politics,* (July 1991) vol. 43.

3. Focal points were first considered by Thomas Schelling *Strategy of Conflict* (Cambridge: Harvard University Press, 1960). For a more recent application see: Geoffrey Garret and Barry Weingast, "Ideas, Interests and Institutions: Constructing the EC's Internal Market," MS. 1991. On the ability of the powerful to get its desired outcome see: Stephen Krasner, "State Power and the Structure of International Trade," *World Politics,* (April 1976) vol 28, and Duncan Snidal, "The limits of hegemonic stability theory" *International Organization* (Autumn 1985.) vol. 39(4).

4. On American power after the war and the creation of regimes see: Krasner, "State Power" *and International Regimes;* Robert Keohane, "The Theory of Hegemonic Stability and Changes in International Economic Regimes," in O. Holsti, R. Siverson, and A. George, eds. *Change in the International System* (Boulder: Westview, 1980); Snidal, "Limits of Hegemonic Stability Theory."

5. It is interesting to speculate about what would be the condition of America's trade deficit if farm products were traded as freely as are nonfarm

products. One cannot ignore the radical shifts in American trade account in years in which some exogenous variable caused an increase in demand for American farm products, for example, famines or world-wide bad weather. By one estimate, access to European and Japanese markets would bring in more than 25 billion dollars to the trade account and balance the American budget.

6. On why hegemons would favor liberal trading regime see: Krasner, "State Power"; Keohane, "Hegemonic Stability."

7. See Judith Goldstein and Robert Keohane, "Introduction," *Ideas and Foreign Policy*, MS, 1991

8. This does not suggest that a policy of price supports did not meet the needs of the agricultural producers. The more autarchic policies promoted by agricultural groups was "functional" in the 1940s. However, worldwide trade liberation was a superior policy choice since it would have met both the short term and long-term interests of the farming sector.

9. Section 3(e) of the NIRA gave the president broad powers over imports so that the United States would not "render ineffective or seriously . . . endanger the maintenance of any code or agreement." In section 22 of the AAA it is stated that imports ought not to "render ineffective, tend to render ineffective or materially interfere with" AAA programs; Section 32 authorized the secretary of agriculture to set aside 30 percent of annual customs revenues to subsidize exports.

10. Although a counterfactual, we can imagine that if liberals had not been able to influence trade policy, the executive's enlarged power could well have been used for many other purposes. For example, if influenced by the existing German model, a much more mercantile or hierarchical system could have been inaugurated under American hegemony. What is apparent from congressional votes is that it was not until the 1950s that the liberalization of trade policy had bipartisan support. On the 1930s and trade liberalization see: Judith Goldstein, *Ideas, Interests and American Trade Policy,* (Ithaca: Cornell University Press, forthcoming).

11. By 1938 the U.S. was claiming concessions on more than half its exports and declared a 45 percent reduction in tariffs. Curzon notes, however, that half of the agreements concluded before World War II were with Latin America and on noncompetitive products. Only the agreements with Canada, Europe, and Great Britain covered products in which American producers lost their price advantage. In general, these agreements did little to increase world trade since American tariffs remained very high and most-favored nation status was extended to few countries. Gerard Curzon, *Multilateral Commercial Diplomacy* (London: Michael Joseph, 1965), p. 27.

12. Quoted in John Day Larkin, *The President's Control of the Tariff* (Cambridge: Harvard University Press) 1936. p. 48.

13. It was not until 1940 that both political parties agreed to any notion of reciprocity. Indicative of the slow change in preferences, the 1936 Republican

platform still advocated repeal of the Reciprocal Trade Agreements legislation. The 1940 platform however, undertook to distinguish between "genuine reciprocity and "so called reciprocal trade agreements." Thus, for the first time, both parties ran simultaneously on a platform of reciprocity. Thereafter, the Republican criticism moved to executive control of tariff treaties and multilateralism. In 1944 the party platform argued that, "We will always bear in mind that the domestic market is America's greatest market and that tariffs which protect it against foreign competition should be modified only by reciprocal bilateral trade agreements approved by Congress." Porter and Johnson, *National Party Platforms* (Urbana: University of Illinois Press, 1961).

14. Richard Carlton Snyder, *The Most-Favored-Nation Clause* (N.Y.: Kings Crown Press, 1948), p. 29.

15. In 1933, even as countries were increasing protections against their trade partners, the vast majority of agreements included an unconditional MFN statement. Out of the 625 most-favored-nation agreements in force, only 48 were conditional. Snyder, *Most-Favored-Nation Clause,* p. 211.

16. The move to unconditionality developed out of a controversy over differing interpretations of the powers granted in the flexible tariff provision of the Tariff Act of 1922. As understood at time of passage, flexibility was supposed to stop discrimination against U.S. exports in the tradition of earlier reciprocity clauses. Its inclusion was championed by Senator Reed Smoot (of Smoot-Hawley fame). Congress gave no hint in its discussion that it interpreted this section to mean that, in the future, the United States should avoid discriminatory agreements. However, one member of the Tariff Commission, a proponent of unconditionality, understood the legal implications of the wording of the section. After passage, William Culbertson wrote to Secretary of State Hughes explaining that if the intent of Congress were to be followed, all discriminatory agreements had to be eliminated. According to Culbertson, Congress had mandated that the United States increase duties in all cases in which a nation did not give U.S. exports the same preferential treatment given to those of another country. This meant that the President must increase the tariff on the goods of all nations that were party to a tariff agreement without the United States. Culbertson went on to argue that Congress could not have intended Section 317 to be used in this fashion So, to fulfill the will of Congress, the United States would need to render all treaties unconditional. Secretary Hughes communicated this to President Harding, who with little thought, approved this new policy. In August, it was announced that all future treaties would contain an unconditional MFN clause. See: William J. Culbertson, *Reciprocity* (New York: McGraw-Hill, 1937), pp. 244–58.

17. At the time of passage of the 1934 Act, the US had negotiated unconditional form treaties with 10 countries representing 12 percent of total American exports. In addition, there were executive agreements with 17 other countries representing 10 percent of total exports. Still in force were 13 conditional

treaties and conditional executive agreements covering 34 percent of exports. Previous to the change in policy in 1923, the U.S. had signed only 3 unconditional treaties in 1850, 1871 and 1881, and these were recognized as exceptions to policy. Percy W. Bidwell, *Tariff Policy of the United States: A Study of Recent Experience: Report to the Second International Studies Conference on The State and Economic Life* (New York: Council on Foreign Relations, 1933), pp. 4, 5, 8.

18. Culbertson, *Reciprocity*, p. 69; and Henry J. Tasca, *The Reciprocal Trade Policy of the United States* (Philadelphia: University of Pennsylvania Press, 1938), pp. 116–21.

19. There were sound, functional reasons for a shift from conditional to unconditional MFN policies after World War I. In William B. Kelly, Jr., ed. *Studies in United States Commercial Policy* (Chapel Hill: University of North Carolina Press, 1963), pp. 44–98, Kelly argues that the United States enjoyed relative immunity from discrimination before the war because 1) few U.S. actions before 1890 might have inspired foreign retaliation; 2) the United States benefited from the unconditional treaties of other nations (particularly European treaties); and 3) noncompetitive agricultural goods dominated American exports. However, increasingly hostile trade, the necessity of new treaties, growing reliance on manufactured goods, and the shift from debtor to creditor made the United States vulnerable to discrimination after World War I.

20. Tasca, *Reciprocal Trade Policy* p. 6. On the history of reciprocity see: Robert O. Kohane, "Reciprocity in International Relations" *International Organization* (Winter 1986) 40:1–28.

21 Tasca, *Reciprocal Trade Policy* p. 6.

22. Bidwell, *Tariff Policy of the United States,* p. 52.

23. Ibid. pp. 57–59.

24. Cited in Larkin, *President's Control,* p. 54.

25. Ibid., 1936, p. 54.

26. Ibid., 1936, p. 55.

27. Lawrence Chamberlain, *President, Congress and Legislation* (New York: Columbia University Press, 1946), p. 133. All but two of the nonadministration witnesses opposed the bill, although all supported the general objective of increasing trade. For a more thorough study of the 1934 Act see: Stephen Haggard, "The Institutional Foundations of Hegemony: Explaining the Reciprocal Trade Agreement Act of 1934," *International Organization* (Winter 1988), vol. 42.

28. The act came to the floor without a closed rule but with a large enough majority to ensure that all opposition amendments were rejected. One of the more telling points made by the minority was that the position now advocated by the Democrats on the issue of Presidential control was contradictory: in 1929, eight democratic members of the Senate Finance Committee had publicly declared themselves unalterably opposed to the principle of permitting the President to control tariff rates.

29. Hearings ran from April 26 through May 1. Sixty-five witnesses either appeared or filed briefs. Chamberlain, *President, Congress and Legislation,* p. 135.

30. One significant addition to the administration's act was a Finance Committee amendment to require "public notice of the intention to negotiate an agreement." Widespread sentiment in both houses had favored integrating public hearings into the process. In keeping with this provision, the interdepartmental Trade Agreements Committee and the Committee for Reciprocity Information were later formed. These became the progenitor of the interbranch committees that characterized the American trade program throughout the century.

31. Cited in E. E. Schattschneider, *Politics, Pressures and the Tariff: A Study of Free Enterprise in Pressure Politics* (New York: Prentice-Hall, 1935), p. 145.

32. Tasca, *Reciprocal Trade Policy,* p. 29.

33. John Day Larkin, *Trade Agreements: A Study in Democratic Methods* (New York: Columbia University Press, 1940), p. 69.

34. For a thorough explanation of the initial state groups charged with trade liberalization, see Tasca, *Reciprocal Trade Policy,* pp. 45–73. The Trade Agreements Committee continued to exist until 1962 when it was replaced by the Cabinet-level Trade Information Committee, chaired by the Special Trade Representative.

35. On the post-1934 role of congress see: Robert A. Pastor, *Congress and the Politics of U.S. Foreign Economic Policy, 1929–76* (Berkeley: University of California Press, 1980) and I. M. Destler, *American Trade Politics: System Under Stress* (Washington, D.C.: Institute for International Economics, 1986).

36. In the Agricultural Adjustment Act of 1933, prices were to be set so as "to reestablish prices to farmers at a level that will give agricultural commodities a purchasing power with respect to articles that farmers buy, equivalent to the purchasing power of agricultural commodities in the basic period [i.e., 19909–1914]." In the Soil Conservation and Domestic Allotment Act of 1936, the parity goal shifted from price equality of agricultural commodities and the prices of things farmers purchased to income equality between farm and nonfarm populations. In 1938, the Act moved back to an emphasis on agricultural incomes and the products farmers consume by providing for direct parity payments to producers of the basic crops equal to the difference between the market price and the fair exchange value. As one commentator noted in 1938, "The congressmen did not want to hear any more nonsense about equalizing incomes-what they wanted was a proper price for their cotton and corn. If they got that, income would take care of itself. John Black, *Parity, Parity, Parity* (Cambridge: The Harvard Committee on Research in the Social Sciences, 1942), p. 57.

37. See Judith Goldstein, "The Impact of Ideas on Trade Policy: The Origins of U.S. Agricultural and Manufacturing Policies" *International Organization* (Winter 1989), vol. 43, no. 1.

38. Allan Rau *Agricultural Policy and Trade Liberalization in the United States, 1934–1956* (Geneva: E. Droz 1957), p. 66.

39. Roosevelt's response to the lack of congressional action was to use his control of the Agricultural Department to limit use of supports. This led to some success in keeping export subsidies down. The 118 million dollar figure is relatively small considering that in 1935 alone, congress had allocated $90 million for export subsidization. Rau, *Agricultural Policy*, p. 80.

40. Under the Surplus Property Act of 1940, export subsidies for cotton were begun again in 1944.

41. Compared with WWI, the agricultural sector produced 50 percent more during WWII with only five percent more land and 10 percent fewer employees. Rau, *Agricultural Policy*, p. 88.

42. Rau, p. 88.

43. Even in the face of GATT rules, the 1948 Act endorsed export subsidies, budgeting $300 million for such supports. In addition, Section 22 authority was expanded to allow the imposition of import fees or quotas whenever unrestricted imports interfered with "any loan, purchase or other program or operation undertaken by the Department of Agriculture or any agency operation under its jurisdiction." Any product could now be protected under the provision.

44. Richard N. Gardner, *Sterling-Dollar Diplomacy*, (New York: McGraw-Hill 1969), p. 4.

45. Cited from an address by Eric Wyndham While, Executive Secretary of the GATT, at the Fletcher School, April, 1949. In Curzon, *Multilateral Commercial Diplomacy*, p. 31.

46. Cited in Edna Wilgress, *A New Attempt at Internationalism*, (Paris:Societe D'edition D'enseignmement Superieur, 1949) p. 12.

47. Cited in Gardner, *Sterling-Dollar Diplomacy*, p. 270.

48. In a speech during the London conference, Wilcox clarified what multilateral trade meant:

"International trade should be multilateral rather than bilateral. Particular transactions, of course, are always bilateral. One seller deals with one buyer. But under multilateralism, the pattern of trade is, in general, many-sided. Sellers are not compelled to confine their sales to buyers who will deliver them equivalent values in other goods. Buyers are not required to find sellers who will accept payment in goods that buyers have produced. Traders sell where they please, exchanging goods for money, and buy where they please, exchanging goods for money, and buy where they please, exchanging money for goods. Bilateralism, by contrast, is akin to barter. Under this system, you may sell for money but you cannot use your money where you please. . . . Imports are directly tied to exports and each country must balance its accounts, not only with the world as a whole but separately, with every other country with whom it deals." Wilgress, *New Attempt at Internationalism*, p. 37–38.

49. Gardner, *Sterling-Dollar Diplomacy*, p. 271.

50. Ibid.

51. Ibid., p. 272.

52. Ibid., p. 274.

53. Ibid., p. 276.

54. At the London Conference of 1933 a draft annotated agenda stressed the necessity of doing away with import quotas "whether they take the form of prohibitions or of quotas or licence, have in recent years become exceptionally widespread and are so numerous that they now constitute an almost insurmountable barrier to international exchanges." Curzon, *Multilateral Commercial Diplomacy*, p. 128.

55. Gardner, *Sterling-Dollar Diplomacy* p. 150.

56. The proposal specified that members who were paying export subsidies on agricultural commodities cooperate in negotiations of commodity agreements. But if no agreement was reached, export subsidies would be allowed provided they did not increase the products share of the world market relative to a past representative period.

57. The elasticity of this proposal was quickly recognized when the United States used the security release to justify import restrictions on cheese and on wool.

58. Rau, *Agricultural Policy* pp. 111–12.

59. See Gardner, *Sterling-Dollar Diplomacy*, pp. 348–81.

60. Ibid., p. 376.

61. The condemnation by the International Chamber of Commerce was sweeping. "It [ITO charter] is a dangerous document because it accepts practically all of the policies of economic nationalism; because it jeopardizes the free enterprise system by giving priority to centralized national governmental planning of foreign trade; because it leaves a wide scope to discrimination, accepts the principle of economic insulation and in effect commits all members of the ITO to state planning for full employment." Ibid., p. 377.

62. Ibid., p. 379.

63. Because of its more minimalist task, the GATT was authorized through presidential decree under rights given by the trade agreements program instead of through congressional assent. In practice, this meant that its legal basis was somewhat unclear. It was not until 1968 that the President asked Congress for and received permanent authorization for contributions to the running of the organization. Previously, American contributions were buried in a State Department line item entitled "international conferences and contingencies". *Ibid.*, p. xxxiv.

64. The other talks were the Annecy in 1949, Torquay In 1951, Geneva in 1956, the Dillon Round in 1960–61, Kennedy Round in 1964–67, the Tokyo Round concluded in 1979, and the ongoing Uruguay round.

65. In the mid-1950s, policymakers began to see the costs associated with

American actions. At the sixth session of GATT in 1951, Denmark, the Netherlands, Canada, Australia, New Zealand, Italy, Norway, and France lodged a formal protest against restriction under section 104 of the 1950 Defense Production Act, stating it was a violation of the agreement. The following year these countries demanded compensation, which they received.

66. The leader of the United States delegation stated that the "real reason for standing aside was that the extension of the scope of activities into the commodity field, beyond the trade aspects which were already within the scope of the General Agreement, would endanger the full and firm participation of the United States in the new organization, under explicit congressional approval, which the U.S. government hoped to see accomplished." Curzon, *Multilateral Commercial Diplomacy*, p. 169.

67. Ibid., p. 169.

68. For example, Hill gives figures for pre-and post-CAP levels of protection for the following items. Live animals, 14.4 to 48.5 percent; meat, 19.0 to 52.1 percent; dairy products, 18.6 to 137.3 percent; cereals, 13.5 to 72.4 percent. See: Brian Hill, *The Common Agricultural Policy: Past, Present and Future* (London: Methuen), 1984.

69. John Evans *The Kennedy Round in American Trade Policy: The Twilight of the GATT?* (Cambridge: Harvard University Press, 1971) pp. 70–86.

70. Here, the United States had sided with the other agricultural exporting nations, including some of the European nations—such as Denmark and Holland—whose interests in the trading organization were tied to agricultural trade liberalization.

71. If we look at section 22 petitions as a measure of interest in agricultural quotas, we see petition activity declining from seven a year in the 1950s to less than two a year in the early 1960s, a little more than one a year in the late 1960s and less than one a year by the mid-1970s. Similarly, acceptance rates go down 50 percent in this period. Goldstein, *Ideas, Interests*, p. 70.

72. On the idea of embedded liberalism see: John Ruggie, "International Regimes, Transactions, and Change: Embedded Liberalism in the Postwar Economic Order" in Stephen Krasner, *International Regimes* (Ithaca: Cornell University Press, 1983).

7. Shaping the Postwar Balance of Power: Multilateralism in NATO

Steve Weber

AT the end of the 1940s, the United States and several states of Western Europe allied to defend themselves against invasion by the Soviet Union. Balance-of-power theory predicts the recurrent formation of such balances among states. But that argument says little about the precise nature of the balance, the principles on which it will be constructed, or its institutional manifestations.[1] The North Atlantic Treaty Organization (NATO) has been a peculiar mix. As a formal institution, NATO has through most of its history been distinctly non-multilateral, the United States commanding most decision making power and responsibility. At the same time, NATO provided security to its member states in a way that strongly reflects multilateral principles.[2] Within NATO, security was indivisible. It was based on a general organizing principle, that the external boundaries of alliance territory were completely inviolable and that an attack on any border was an attack on all. Diffuse reciprocity was the norm. In the terms set out by Ruggie, NATO has generally scored low on "MI" but high on "IM".[3]

The capabilities of the Red Army meant that the United States faced greater constraints in setting up institutions for security than it faced in money, trade, and the like. But those constraints did not determine either the principles or the institutional form of NATO. This paper argues that two sets of ideas governed the way in which the United States shaped the postwar balance of power through NATO.

The first set of ideas was *political*. It was derived from fundamental beliefs about the relationship between the number of powerful actors in the international system ("polarity") and stability, as well as peace. The second set of ideas was driven by *military* considerations, having to do with the deterrence of invasion and nuclear strategy.

Under the influence of the first set of ideas, U.S. foreign policymakers sought a security system that would do more than simply prevent Soviet aggression. They strove to construct institutions for peace management, cooperation, and progress that would promote long-term stability in international politics. The best way to do that, according to American foreign policy beliefs, was to foster the development of an autonomous European "pole" as the first step toward a multipolar international system. In politics, multilateralism was a means of promoting evolution toward multipolarity. But the twin concepts of multilateralism and multipolarity were frequently at odds with a second set of ideas about the military requirements for deterrence of invasion. These ideas were directly connected with the challenge of preventing Soviet aggression through the use or the threat of force. Multipolar systems present opportunities for risk-acceptant states committed to a quick and decisive military challenge against the status quo. When that scenario came to dominate American views of European security, ideas about deterrence took immediate precedence over the longer term purposes of multipolarity.

The "deterrence scenario" overcame the "multipolarity scenario" first during NATO's birthing process at the end of the 1940s, but its victory was only partial and temporary. The multipolarity scenario proved over the 1950s to be stronger and more deeply engrained. From about 1956 to early in 1961, the Eisenhower administration spearheaded a direct move toward multilateralism in NATO, through the sharing of nuclear weapons within the alliance. The rationale behind this effort had little to do with the credibility of extended deterrence or other strategic arguments. It was first and foremost a political move, designed to speed the transformation of Europe into an integrated defense community with an independent nuclear force that would recast the nature of the balance of power between East and West.

This effort was blocked when the deterrence scenario came back to the fore under the Kennedy administration. That scenario was now bolstered with a new set of arguments about nuclear strategy that overcame politics and pushed the multipolarity scenario into the background. As the distribution of power between the United States and Europe evened out gradually over the succeeding decades, NATO barely evolved in response.

None of this holds much interest in the stark neorealist image of the security problem facing states. In that vision, security should be a strong case for explaining institutions on a rationalist basis with utilitarian or functional logic and without recourse to ideas. In any case, the institutional form and principles of an alliance hardly matter for what the alliance does and for its impact on the basic character of international politics.

These blind spots need to be filled in. The balance between two sets of ideas and the resulting history of multilateralism within NATO had important consequences for international politics during the cold war, and some of these will be perpetuated as Europe develops a new security system in the 1990s. I argue thus that multilateralism as a set of principles for an alliance is a dependent variable that begs explanation, because it is also an independent variable with autonomous causal impact on outcomes. Some of those outcomes may challenge realism's basic premises about power.

Security, Alliances, and Multilateralism

Assume that states balance power to provide security and that they prefer to do so in ways that maximize their prospects for autonomy.[4] Is multilateralism an obvious institutional form for these purposes? If the institution is nearly determined by a nexus between this basic deduced preference and objective features of the environment (such as the good to be supplied, the number of actors, etc.), no need would arise to go further in explaining NATO.

A priori, at least one alternative is available for an alliance system made up of one very powerful state and several smaller states. That is for the large state to cut a series of bilateral deals with each of the subordinates. In the abstract, bilateralism has several advantages from the perspective of the great power. Security becomes an excludable good, which makes it also a bargaining resource. The great power can threaten to abandon a smaller state from the alliance; because such a threat would not challenge the basis of other agreements, it can be relatively credible. It also becomes possible for the great power to demand differential terms of alliance with each of the small powers, depending upon its strategic, economic, or political value. Small states may not benefit particularly by these arrangements, but faced with a direct threat to their existence from an opposing alliance, they would have little choice but to take the price that the market offers.

This is not just a theoretical alternative. To the East, the Soviet Union between 1945 and 1948 imposed a set of bilateral security arrangements on each of its Eastern European neighbors. The organizing principle for this alliance system was "divide and conquer," and the purpose was to maximize Soviet influence over the subordinate states. Certainly some costs to Moscow were involved in choosing this institutional form. Stalin sacrificed some military efficiency and a good deal of legitimacy and in consequence any serious prospect that his alliance system would serve as a basis for broader cooperation among a "socialist community" or as a means of spreading communism throughout the world. But he was willing and able to do this to extract payment for the provision of security and to prevent the development of any East European federation that might challenge exclusive Soviet control.[5]

This institutional form was not just a theoretical alternative in the West either. Proposals that the United States should provide security guarantees to selected European states on a strictly bilateral basis were championed in Washington by Senator Robert Taft through much of 1947. In March 1947, France and Great Britain signed a bilateral treaty of "alliance and mutual assistance," the Dunkirk Treaty, which pledged them to unite in case of renewed German aggression. In January 1948, British Foreign Secretary Ernest Bevin recommended that the West develop a "defense union" by extending the Dunkirk model into a network of bilateral agreements that would include the United States. The structural position of the United States vis-à-vis Western Europe was different certainly from that of the Soviet Union vis-à-vis Eastern Europe, which means that an American version of bilateralism would have looked necessarily more balanced than Stalin's. But that structural position did not produce NATO. The United States could have interpreted bipolarity and the Soviet threat as a license to develop a more coercive and extractive subsystem for security that the Western European states would have been nearly obliged to accept.[6]

Multilateralism was an alternative institutional form with a different array of potential benefits.[7] For the United States, multilateralism could reduce some transaction costs within the alliance by enhancing its legitimacy in the eyes of West Europeans. Because the United States would not be overtly privileged at the outset, changes in the relative capabilities of the member states over time would be less likely to inspire direct challenges to the organization's structure. This would allow Washington to make long-term "investments" in its allies' defense capabilities as well as facilitate cooperation between the secondary states, leading probably to an overall increase in efficiency for supplying security.[8] But the price of multilateralism also promised to be high. Multilateral institutions may substantially increase the costs of making decisions, particularly when an alliance must negotiate contributions to its budget or the collective provision of scarce resources like manpower. Even the institution of multilateralism, which NATO did adopt, could be costly. If security is treated as indivisible and an attack on one is an attack on all, the large state sacrifices the ability to differentiate among its allies. In NATO, the United States made a commitment to the security of Belgium that was equal to its commitment to the security of West Germany, despite the greater importance of the latter state. And by adopting a general strategic principle of forward defense against the Soviet Union, the United States sacrificed any claim on its allies' assistance in "out of area" operations that it might feel the need to pursue, even in the service of NATO interests.[9]

Multilateralism tends to make security a nonexcludable good. This minimizes the hegemon's coercive power and its ability to extract payment for protection. It makes the sanctioning of free riders difficult and threats of abandonment almost impossible. From a choice-theoretic perspective, multilateralism does not seem a convincing bargain or a determinate solution.

These factors represented real trade-offs for the United States at the end of the 1940s. On abstract logic the outcome looks indeterminate, but to the extent that utilitarian or functional analysis points in any direction it points *away* from multilateralism as an institutional form for solving the West's security problem. Consider first the constraints. With the Red Army firmly in place in the East, pressure was present to gain as much security as possible for the West as quickly as possible, and the incentives to minimize immediate transaction costs among the allies were strong. Add to this weight of recent history, particularly the poignant lesson of the Nazi state capitalizing on its opponents' tendency to free ride or shirk alliance guarantees. The postwar relationship between West Germany and France was a further challenge. A multilateral alliance would need both states as equal participants, but Paris (and London for that matter) was resistant. The British also had many other reasons to try to hold on to their special relationship with Washington and not submerge it within a multilateral alliance

Finally, the new factor of nuclear weapons emerged. Nuclear weapons would have made it relatively easy and inexpensive for the United States to conclude a series of bilateral deals with specific partners, because the same arsenal of bombs could be used to offer extended deterrence to more than one state. Strategic nuclear deterrence for Western Europe was nearly a nonrival good, in the sense that the United States could extend the umbrella to additional states without detracting from the security of any. But nothing about nuclear deterrence per se makes it nonexcludable—indeed, states outside the Soviet orbit that did not join NATO, such as Sweden and Switzerland, were excluded. Nuclear deterrence became a public good (nonrival *and* nonexcludable) within NATO because of institutional choices that do not follow directly from objective features of the environment.[10]

The general point is that the nature of the good did not determine the institutional form through which it would be provided: there were alternatives to multilateralism in NATO. Indeed, the constraints and incentives facing the United States should have pushed the outcome to lean away from multilateralism. Why did NATO turn out differently?

The Immediate Postwar World

Franklin Roosevelt's familiar vision of a postwar balance of power did not rest on naive faith that the interests of the "Four Policemen"—China, Britain, and most importantly the United States and the Soviet Union—would coincide neatly. What Roosevelt did presume was that each of these states could be induced to behave in foreign policy matters mainly according to pragmatic calculations, through what contemporaries might have called the "geopolitical" consequences of multipolarity. In Roosevelt's view the large states would themselves be constrained immediately to practice prudence and caution in their foreign policies as a result of their cross-cutting interests that would line up differently on separate issues and in different regions of the world.[11]

In the somewhat longer term the same pressures would reduce the troubling tendency of these states to indulge in extreme ideologies, particularly American versions of unilateralism and Soviet proletarian internationalism.[12] Roosevelt's reasoning here slipped beyond power politics per se. He believed that the process of politics, the coordinating and the compromising between great powers' interests, would do good things over time to the *internal* characteristics of these states that would in turn make them act in more peaceable and cooperative ways. For that reason, it was critical to integrate Moscow directly into the postwar order and not create even the appearance of a rigid anti-Soviet alliance. Roosevelt hoped to reinforce thereby the pragmatic elements within Soviet domestic politics that would support a more substantial foundation for broader U.S.-Soviet cooperation over time.[13]

While Roosevelt's arguments about the Soviet Union were not shared widely by American elites in 1944, his strategic vision of a multipolar balance of power was, albeit for different reasons. If Roosevelt were wrong and the Soviet Union was going to be a determined adversary, then the principal danger was American isolationism and the challenge to keep the United States engaged substantively in European and world affairs for the long term. This would require an intellectual rationale that fit the material realities of power and could be sustained within American public opinion. The arguments of Nicholas John Spykman, further developed and popularized by Walter Lippmann in his influential *U.S. Foreign Policy: Shield of the Republic,* were adapted to fill that niche. Both authors based their arguments on an attack on isolationism as a doctrine that neglected power. But alternatives to isolationism existed apart from a messianic universalism that would drive a state to seek tight control over events all over the world. On their logic it was neither necessary nor desirable that the United States try to extend its hegemony over very much of the world.[14] Instead, U.S. security and Washington's broader interests in world politics were best promoted by aiming to ensure as a minimum necessary goal that no single state would came to control the territory and resources of the Eurasian landmass. This was a doctrine of balance of power by "denial" extended to a global context, which rendered in effect its geopolitical requirements easier to fulfill. As for the U.S. public, sustaining the needed level of commitment would be easier if American foreign policy could be presented as favoring diversity and flexibility in a realistic way while encouraging progressive change on a worldwide basis. Rather than confront the Soviet Union openly in a bipolar contest, the United States would look to be "on the side of history," supporting the development of other centers of power and continually readjusting to changing interests instead of trying to prevent change from occurring.

Truman, like many others in Washington, did not share Roosevelt's confidence in Stalin as a willing collaborator. He soon ran up even more directly than Roosevelt at the end of his life had against the practical complications of the four-policeman scheme. But at the start of his administration, the new President held to his predecessor's view that a managed multipolar balance between what was now the "big three" was possible and would promote peace in the postwar world. Following the counsel of his advisors and particularly Averell Harriman, Truman took a more forceful approach with Stalin but still sought until the end of 1945 at least to coopt the Soviet Union into a broad collaboration along with the United States and Britain.[15]

The State Department was generally less optimistic that Moscow could be made a part of this scheme. George Kennan in particular doubted that

American leverage could do much to influence Soviet cooperativeness, at least in the short term. According to the logic of the Long Telegram, the balance of power in the postwar world was not going to be a cooperative one because the Soviet Union, with its potent blend of communism and totalitarianism, was simply not ready to play by those rules.[16] Soviet expansionism might have been driven in substantial measure by insecurity and an almost paranoid tendency to view the outside world as hostile, but the United States could do little quickly to ameliorate those causes. If peace was going to be sustained expansionism would have to be "contained" actively, which demanded a more competitive balance of power. But for Kennan and others around him, equally important for the long term was that the balance be, not bipolar, but multipolar. The consensus at and around the State Department was that the United States could not and should not try to balance Soviet power more or less on its own.[17]

Why not? After all, a "realist" power calculation (and Kennan certainly saw himself as a paramount realist) led inexorably to the conclusion that only the United States was in a position to balance Soviet power and that the states of West Europe could at best play a supporting role. Indeed, a 1945 Office of Strategic Services (OSS) analysis predicted that the Soviet Union would likely place Eastern Europe in precisely this kind of subordinate role and extract as many resources from those states as possible, in an attempt to maximize its own power vis-à-vis the United States.[18]

Kennan did not, however, believe that the United States could sustain a bipolar balance of power with the Soviets over time, and he was convinced that if we tried, the result could very well be war. The logic behind this position began with the fear, common to both Roosevelt and Truman, that a stark bipolar confrontation between two very powerful states would encourage ideological extremism that could take the form not only of an ambitious internationalism but also of isolationism on the part of Americans. Kennan argued further that the constraints of a world with more than two centers of power would be favorable because the presence of other "poles" in the system would restrain both the Soviets and the Americans from taking too many foreign policy risks and from indulging in crusades to reshape the world in their own image.[19] Kennan recognized that to put this argument into practice meant countenancing a powerful Germany, since without a revitalized German center the states of Western Europe could not be expected together to play a substantial independent role in the balance of power. He also recognized the deep anxiety of the British and the French regarding Germany, but he was resolved to work toward overcoming their reluctance as the necessary price for peace. In his mind, the bipolar alternative was worse, because it meant a divided Europe locked into the front lines of a face-to-face U.S.– Soviet confrontation, with World War III a nearly inevitable result.[20]

Kennan, like Roosevelt, also went beyond geopolitics in his belief that a multipolar international system would safeguard the domestic character of the American state and polity. He worried that an attempt by the United States to balance Soviet power on its own would lead to the establishment of spheres of domination made up of dependent states, to whom each superpower would dictate its vision of how to organize a society. For Kennan, attempts to impose American political institutions abroad forcibly would eventually threaten the character of those institutions at home, since democracy rested precisely on a willingness to tolerate diversity.[21] The multipolar alternative offered a unique convergence between the demands of realpolitik and the peculiarities of American democracy—the United States could best serve its interests in both spheres by encouraging, as Gaddis describes it, the evolution of a "world order based not on superpower hegemony but on the natural balance only diverse concentrations of authority, *operating independently of one another*, could provide."[22]

Kennan's policy recommendations for "containment" followed closely on this logic. The United States was to play a facilitative role in constructing a balance of power and then a key suppporting role once other centers of power were in place—but in no sense did the containment strategy prescribe that America should attempt on its own to balance Soviet power. In fact, Kennan's policy arguments through most of 1948 were aimed precisely at avoiding that outcome. Kennan stressed economic and political instruments as a way of restoring European confidence that the continent could take care of itself in large part for this reason. He also stood firmly against formal American military commitments in the interim and did not give up that position until quite late in the game.[23] The general ends of this balance-of-power design were quite clear. The principal goal was to prevent a division of the world into Soviet and American spheres, to avoid bipolarity. Instead, the United States would encourage the evolution of a "limited" multipolar international system—a small numbers system that is not two—by promoting the emergence of independent centers of power in Europe (and in Asia as well). This was not just a new kind of isolationism; Kennan and those around him did not argue that the United States could leave the balance of power in the hands of others. Nor was it an attempt to promote a world of free-wheeling alliances that would operate more like the Europe of the nineteenth century. The flexibility that was sought in the new multipolarity was partial, enough to insure the presumed benefits of restraint and to avoid the excesses of a bipolar world.[24] The critical thing was that the United States not make the mistake of sacrificing long-term advantages and objectives in this multipolarity for the sake of "quick" fixes to security and other problems, made alluring by the possibilities of American dominance and the constraints of Soviet power.

Implementing the Plan

As those constraints and the apparent Soviet threat loomed larger through 1947, the Truman administration was compelled to involve the United States more directly in the European balance of power. Yet it was careful to do so in ways that were calculated to preserve as much as possible the multipolarity scenario. Central to that vision was the idea that policies that might encourage the dependency of European states on the United States for security would be systematically avoided. This remained a guiding principle for American foreign policy in Europe so long as two assumptions held sway in Washington. The first was that the "real" Soviet threat in Europe was not the prospect of a Red Army blitzkrieg but was instead long term and political. The second was that alliances in the postwar world would in fact be at least moderately flexible, that the inevitable spheres of influence would be loosely held "areas of association," not tightly dominated and controlled "regions of subservience."[25]

Two important policy innovations in early 1947 reflect this conception. The first was the Truman Doctrine, announced to Congress on March 12. The President's powerful rhetoric, "that it must be the policy of the United States to support free peoples who are resisting attempted subjugation by armed minorities or by outside pressures," camouflaged crucial limitations of that "support." It was to be carried out with dollars and with advisors but not with American military forces, and no explicit commitment was made to preserve governments or territory, despite the deep sense of gravity with which most of official Washington viewed the threat of a communist takeover in Greece.[26] Subsequent clarifications made it evident that the doctrine did not establish a precedent for similar action elsewhere.[27] The objectives of the policy were limited: to deny

Greece and Turkey to communist revolution and by implication to the Soviet Union but not to establish American control—because the latter, while offering the most assurance that additional territory would not fall to Moscow, would have compromised the multipolarity scenario. As one of the committees in charge of drafting the March 12 speech reported, "the present power relationships of the great states preclude the domination of the world by any one of them. Those power relationships cannot be substantially altered by the unilateral action of any one great state." [28]

The second policy innovation, the Program for European Recovery or "Marshall Plan" of June 1947, reflected similar designs for the rest of Western Europe. The threat here was not seen as a "matter of days," but it was no less serious for that: as Under Secretary of State William Clayton put it, there was a near-term risk that "economic, social, and political disintegration will overwhelm Europe." [29] Clayton himself believed that this situation left the United States no choice but to step into a power vacuum and take up the challenge of a bipolar world: in a series of imploring memos, he wrote that "The United States must take world leadership and quickly, to avert world disaster" and that when it came to Western Europe's future, "the United States must run this show." [30]

U.S. policy did not follow Clayton's prescription. In the June 5 speech, Marshall explicitly stated that the initiative for recovery had to come from Europe, and he suggested that the European states join together to examine their needs and draft proposals. [31] This was a consequence of a growing concern at State that "the extension of U.S. economic aid was becoming a substitute for European efforts." [32] Kennan was keen on this point. When he finally overcame his ambivalence about the Marshall Plan in the autumn it was with the caveat that "it should be a cardinal point of policy to see to it that other elements of *independent power* are developed on the Eurasian land mass as rapidly as possible, in order to take off our shoulders some of the burdens of bipolarity." [33] Congressional hearings on the Marshall Plan in January 1948 showed that Kennan's views were widely shared. From Washington's perspective, the ERP (European Recovery Program) was supposed to reconstitute a European community that could play an independent role in a multipolar balance of power without a security guarantee from Washington. [34] These were not just pious statements. If the United States had sought to maximize its influence over the states of Western Europe or encourage their dependency, Washington could have unilaterally set the terms for recovery aid in a series of bilateral deals with each individual state.

Instead, the terms were essentially set by the Europeans, via the newly formed Organization for European Economic Cooperation that included sixteen participant states.[35]

Washington's design in fact ran against the preferences of many European elites. The British in particular wanted an explicit American security guarantee and were willing to pay a substantial price, in terms of accepting a subordinate role to U.S. power, for it.[36] In January 1948, Bevin proposed that the United States join a "Western Defense Union" to be constructed through a network of bilateral alliances along the lines of the Dunkirk Treaty. In February, he scaled down his ambitions and floated the idea of a simple bilateral security pact between Britain and the United States. Truman and the State Department in particular balked at both propositions.[37] France, for its part, was generally more direct about the fear of a revitalized Germany.[38] When it became clear after the London Conference of November–December 1947 that three zones of Germany would be rehabilitated as a part of the West, Paris redoubled its efforts to engage the United States in a formal security plan. Truman turned back these demands as well.[39] As late as early 1948, the United States would accept only minimal compromise to the vision of a multipolar balance of power with an independent Europe, which now clearly entailed forcing recalcitrant allies to accept a central role for a powerful German state.

Assumptions Undermined

One of the two key assumptions behind the American vision was that alliances in the postwar world would be flexible and that spheres of influence would be relatively loose. After the dramatic Czechoslovak coup in February 1948, that assumption no longer seemed tenable. Stalin looked intent on creating a tight sphere of influence in which the Soviet Union could dominate the domestic politics as well as the foreign policy alignments of its East European "allies." The arguments of Kennan and others at State, that the Communist sphere could not maintain itself as a monolith over time, were greatly weakened by these developments.[40]

The Czechoslovak coup was also a critical turning point in the perceptions of Secretary of State Marshall, who for the first time conceded that the United States might have to formally associate itself with a European security organization.[41] Belgium, France, Luxembourg, the Netherlands, and Britain were already moving forward with precisely such a plan. On

March 17, 1948, these states concluded negotiations on the Brussels Pact, which carried with it a barely implicit message to Washington—Europe was ready to organize for defense, but it needed the United States to play the central role in holding a balance of power against the Soviet threat.

Kennan's staff and allies at the National Security Council were unconvinced. In several reports examining options for linking Washington with the Brussels Pact, both groups argued strongly that the United States should offer an "informal association" based on a unilateral declaration of support for the treaty by the President and nothing more.[42] The British called this insufficient and continued to push for a formal U.S. commitment, claiming that only a legal treaty approved by the Senate would still lingering fears of American isolationism on the Continent.[43]

Washington demurred. On April 27, the administration offered only to declare its support for the principle of "effective self-help and mutual aid" by associating itself informally with the Brussels Pact.[44] The very next day, Canada's Foreign Minister Louis St. Laurent raised the stakes by proposing a single mutual defense system that would supersede the Pact by binding the United States and Canada to it. This plan was welcomed in London but not in Washington. Bevin continued to push the United States through the end of May. In a fervent letter to Marshall, he reminded the Secretary of the immediacy and magnitude of the Soviet threat and pleaded that a simple declaration of support for the Brussels Pact without more specific and explicit commitments from Washington *might* not deter the Soviets and *would* not inspire adequate confidence in Europe.[45] But the United States continued to resist on principle anything more than an informal association, and when the Vandenberg Resolution passed the Senate on June 11, the road was paved for this "solution" to be put into place.

Less than two weeks later, the Soviets closed all routes of supply except air traffic to West Berlin. The first U.S.–Soviet cold war crisis in Europe brought the other assumption underlying Washington's multipolarity scenario under severe pressure. For the moment at least, it seemed as if the Soviet threat might in fact be imminent and military, not long term and political. With both assumptions weakened, the "deterrence scenario," the need to prevent a victory for the Soviets that was achieved by force in Western Europe, took immediate precedence over a continuing commitment to avoiding European dependency.

But while moving to fill the emergency gap in military capabilities,

Washington still went as far as it could to preserve its longer term vision. In July, Robert Lovett informed the Brussels Pact nations that the United States was now prepared to move ahead on a "loose" association agreement more explicit than that envisioned several months before but would still decline any formal commitment or an obligation for an "automatic" response to attack.[46] Through a series of intricate negotiations over the summer, the United States continued to resist pressure from Britain and particularly from France for a "more precise and definite mutual obligation."[47] The talks produced a compromise working paper in early September 1948, but the precise terms of U.S. commitment were still vague.[48] The working paper used the words "formal treaty," but the United States held to its position that any military commitment would depend on American constitutional processes and would not be automatic in case of attack. Washington stressed that it saw itself only as a marginal supporter of what had to be primarily a European effort. Instead of a formal guarantee it offered "continuous and effective self-help and mutual aid, to strengthen . . . the capacity of the parties to resist aggression."[49] The United States did not take charge of the military affairs of the evolving alliance (which it could have readily done at this juncture) or even promise a continuing American military presence on the Continent. When the Western Union at the end of September set up a formal military body to coordinate defense activities, it did not include an American.

Still dissatisfied with Washington's response, the powers of the Western Union formally requested at the end of October negotiations with the United States on a North Atlantic Treaty. Kennan lent his support reluctantly to this in November, with the strong caveat that tight ties between the United States and the defense of Europe should be seen as a short-term exigency driven by the immediate Soviet threat. In his view, Washington's long-term interests lay still in promoting the military and political cohesion of a European "third force" that would facilitate the withdrawal of the superpowers' troops from the continent "and absorb and take over the territory between the two." The U.S. government's position paralleled the substance of Kennan's logic on what became the central point of principle in the treaty negotiations.[50] Over vehement British and French protest, Washington rejected a December 1948 draft treaty that seemed to imply a formal obligation to commit troops in response to attack. When the final version of the North Atlantic Treaty was completed in February 1949, it included an important caveat about domestic constitutional processes that explicitly left each signatory free to take whatever action its own government deemed appropriate in case of war. The treaty also described armed force as a "possible" response to aggression, not a necessary one.[51]

The United States bound itself into the European balance of power when it signed the North Atlantic Treaty on April 4, 1949, but it did so in ways calculated to maintain as much of the multipolarity scenario as was possible at the time. Nothing in the Treaty gave the United States a privileged position within the military or political structures of the alliance. For political governance, the treaty established a North Atlantic Council made up of the Foreign Ministers of member states, where decisions would be taken on the principle of one-country, one-vote. When it met for the first time in September 1949, the Council established a number of subordinate political bodies with the same voting rule. It also set up several permanent military bodies including a "Defense Committee" made up of the Defense Minister of each member country. This Committee was supported by a permanent "Military Committee" composed of the chiefs-of-staff of each state, which absorbed the functions of the Western Union Defense Organization. The decision-making structure of both committees was also one-to-one. The first four-year defense plan for NATO, which came into force in April 1950, preserved the principle of national command for military forces and had no special privileges, command or otherwise, for Washington.[52] The notion of an integrated force under a centralized or supreme commander would come later, under different circumstances. For the moment, the alliance scored high as both an "institution of Multilateralism" and a "multilateral institution."

The Korean War

It was not until the invasion of South Korea in June 1950 that the predominance of the deterrence scenario was confirmed in Washington, prompting moves toward a reorganization of NATO institutions away from the principle of multilateralism, which the United States had before fought tenaciously to maintain.[53] Events now moved quickly. In late July, the administration announced that it would ask Congress to appropriate an additional $10 billion for defense, about half of which would be earmarked for the alliance. A few days later, the NATO Council Deputies elected Charles M. Spofford, an American, to be their permanent chairman.[54] In early September, Truman made public his plans to send additional American troops to Europe.[55] A few days later, the North Atlantic Council adopted the principle of forward defense for Europe.

This was a critical decision. The axiom of forward defense, that alliance territory would be defended along a line as far to the east as practicable, demanded a reorganization of NATO, simply because of the level of forces and the kind of coordination between them necessary to carry it out militarily. Recognizing this, the Council instructed the Defense Committee to develop plans for "the establishment at the earliest possible date of an integrated force under centralized command and control."[56] This was a crucial step away from multilateralism, which was consummated in December when the Council approved formally the establishment of an integrated military force under central command. SACEUR would be an American, General Dwight D. Eisenhower, and the United States would immediately pledge to a substantial increase in the number of American ground forces stationed in Europe.[57] Further reorganizations over the next year brought the merger of the Western Union Defense Organization into NATO's unified command, the establishment of SHAPE, agreements on the status of forces and civilians of one member country stationed under NATO auspices in another, and the final recognition of NATO as a permanent organization, in February 1952.[58]

The new institutional structure of NATO met several immediate needs. It provided a framework for a substantial expansion of forces-in-being and promised greater efficiency in their use by placing them under integrated command.[59] It also provided means to keep the French and the Germans together in a security institution. This was no mean feat. Until the summer of 1950, the United States hoped to mollify over time French fears about incorporating the Germans as partners in European defense. But after Korea, the demands of the deterrence scenario meant that the United States could no longer wait for the French (and the British, to a lesser degree) to grow strong and confident enough to join together with a revitalized Germany, as the multipolarity scenario had foreseen. Instead, the United States had to commit itself as a predominant actor in the European balance of power and in so doing reassure the government in Paris that it would not face a Faustian choice between subservience to Russia and subservience to Germany.

Arguments about promoting multipolarity and avoiding the dependency of Europe took second place, for the moment. Yet alternative institutional forms were available that could have been adopted at this juncture and that would have been even more damaging to the multipolarity scenario. The United States did not have to force the rearmament of Germany on France or accept the concessions it did in order to keep these two countries together under its terms. Washington could have sided with the French on the question of German military status and relied on Paris' plan for partially integrating the Federal Republic into Europe through economic and political means.[60] But the United States still viewed security and specifically NATO as a formula for promoting the integration of Europe. NATO's new institutional structure was in part a means of accelerating Germany's return to semisovereign status. German resources would in the short run minimize the defense burden on the United States, but in the longer run, a NATO that contained both Germany and France still held out the promise of an integrated independent Europe taking care of its own defense without direct American involvement. In effect, the United States acted to meet the exigencies of power and threat in Europe, but it did so in ways calculated to preserve as much of the multipolarity scenario as was possible at the time.

The partial "victory" of the deterrence scenario in any case proved short-lived. Once the fear that the Korean War was a prelude to an invasion of Europe dissipated during 1951, the U.S. Congress sliced $4.3 billion (about 9%) from Truman's FY 53 military budget. The British raised a call to scale down the ambitious Lisbon force goals for NATO's conventional armies, and these were essentially rescinded by the Council in December 1952 less than a year after they had been agreed upon. When Eisenhower took office the next month, his administration quickly picked up the momentum.

Eisenhower's Vision

The new administration's designs for Europe were driven at one level by economics and by the President's fervent interest in cutting American expenditures for defense.[61] This had two important consequences for NATO. The first was a determined effort to incorporate West Germany fully into the alliance and make efficient use of its resources for NATO's military posture. That issue was settled with the Paris Agreements in October 1954, which recognized the status of the Federal Republic as a sovereign state and paved its way for NATO membership. The second was a decision to increase massively United States and, by implication, NATO reliance on nuclear weapons. In October 1953, NSC 162/2 (the basis of the "New Look") in principle called for the use of nuclear weapons in any future conflict where their use might be deemed advantageous. In December 1954, the NATO Council agreed to bring "NATO strategy into line with American strategy and authorized SHAPE to base its military planning on the assumption that nuclear weapons would be used in future conflicts."[62]

Assimilating the Federal Republic was a clear prerequisite to the multipolarity scenario. But the New Look *seemed* to cut in the opposite direction. A priori, the decision to rely on nuclear weapons for the defense of Europe might have sealed the fate of NATO, putting both multilateralism and the vision of multipolarity to rest—so long as the alliance's critical weapons were owned and controlled by just one member. The United States would now own a privileged position within the alliance. And if the Europeans could rely on Washington and its nuclear weapons to maintain the balance of power and ensure their security, they would have even less incentive to take on burdens for their own defense or to make the difficult choices on integration. Yet none of these suppositions was correct.

There was a second level to Eisenhower's designs, a deeper political vision that recapitulated the multipolarity scenario of previous administrations. The new President shared Truman and Roosevelt's fear of a continuing bipolar face-off between the United States and the Soviet Union, and like Kennan he worried that America's democratic institutions would suffer severely under the pressure of prolonged and inconclusive cold war.[63] Eisenhower's preferred scenario looked much like Kennan's vision of a stable multipolar international system, where the balance of power would rest on the principle of denial. For Eisenhower as for Kennan, this would do more than just effectively contain the Soviet Union and "world communism." By encouraging the development of independent forces in the world capable of resisting and determined to resist the threat on their own, the United States would bolster its own domestic character and set the stage for broader progress beyond the stark necessities of cold war competition.

Europe was the central focus for these aspirations. First as NATO SACEUR and later as President, Eisenhower consistently portrayed the U.S. role in defending Europe as but a temporary compromise, to "bridge the crisis period during which European forces were building up."[64] The sentiment was built not just on economics. Like many of his generation, Eisenhower held strong views about the traditional place of Britain, France, and even Germany as great powers in world politics. The current position of these states as secondary actors caught in the middle of a U.S.–Soviet struggle was simply unnatural and did not make sense from a political perspective.[65]

This had important implications for NATO. In a general sense, Eisenhower did not believe that the United States should go on "treating its trusted allies as junior members."[66] He was troubled by what he saw as a growing dependency where the Europeans had come to rely with relative comfort on the United States to maintain the balance of power.[67] Over and over again, Eisenhower stressed the point that the Western alliance was held together by trust, confidence, faith, and most importantly, a shared sense of purpose among peers. Formal institutions that had been set up to meet an emergency were no excuse for free riding.

Was this not a paradox? After all, these political ideas would have been hard to reconcile with the place that nuclear weapons had come to hold in the military plans of the alliance. In effect, the Europeans' junior partner status followed from the fact that Washington had been asking its "trusted" allies to supply and pay for infrastructure and conventional forces, when security in the end rested on strategic nuclear weapons that only the United States would control.

But this was precisely the "paradox" that Eisenhower was anxious to resolve. Answering a reporter's query about NATO's arrangements for ownership and control of nuclear weapons and how these fit with the President's view of the alliance overall, Eisenhower stated simply that "from the very beginning . . . I have always been of the belief that we should not deny to our allies what the enemies, what your potential enemy already has."[68] John McCone, chairman of the Atomic Energy Commission, offered a similar assessment, to which Eisenhower heartily agreed: "we would not be able to have vitality on the part of our European partners as long as we refuse to give them the weapons."[69] Because he was convinced that "our allies were not going to be willing to fight with bows and arrows while we have guns," Eisenhower agreed that the United States should "be prepared to provide what the NATO nations truly need for their defenses." This was barely disguised code for the President's interest in sharing nuclear weapons within the alliance.[70] As his secretary reported of a discussion on the problems of intraalliance cooperation in 1957 "He [the President] does not believe that this can be accomplished if we deny control over the missiles, with their warheads, to the recipient nations. Denying such control, in his opinion, will result in rejection of the U.S. program."[71]

Eisenhower's view of nuclear weapons and the NATO alliance began with a simple political logic: nuclear weapons were thought to be of sufficient importance in world politics that great power states would want to have their own. The British and the French of course gave the U.S. President good reason to think so. In London, Prime Minister Harold Macmillan spoke of the bomb as the ultimate guarantor of self-reliance and as the "ticket of admission" to great-power status.[72] The French were even more explicit about their view of nuclear weapons as the critical "currency of power" in the modern world. In 1955, Prime Minister Pierre Mendes-France declared his support for the French nuclear weapons program with the comment "one is nothing without the bomb in international negotiations."[73] Charles de Gaulle had a more ambitious world role for the French in mind, and it was the force de frappe that would make it possible. In his words, "France is not really herself except in the front rank. France cannot be France without greatness" and it was clear that nuclear weapons were a necessary source of that "greatness."[74] Eisenhower was for the most part sympathetic to these arguments. Although he often found de Gaulle's nationalist rhetoric unsettling, he frequently expressed "considerable sympathy" for the substance of the French leader's position on nuclear weapons.[75] More than once, the U.S. President expressed his conviction that "we would react very much as de Gaulle does if the shoe were on the other foot."[76]

This political logic pointed in a single direction—the United States should share nuclear weapons with its allies. What is central for understanding Eisenhower's initiatives is that for Eisenhower, the political logic meshed comfortably with his beliefs about the weapons themselves and the conditions for stable nuclear deterrence. It is important in this not to project backward in time strategic reasoning and doctrines that were developed later and for different reasons.

The New Look and the doctrine of massive retaliation for Eisenhower did not rest on delusions about Strategic Air Command's (SAC's) ability to carry out a disarming first strike against Soviet forces or on notions of fighting "limited" or "protracted" nuclear wars in Europe. Quite the contrary: the President knew from the day he entered office that Soviet nuclear strikes would bring intolerable destruction to the American homeland.[77] But he was quietly certain that this war would never be fought. The New Look depended upon Eisenhower's nearly absolute confidence in the efficacy of nuclear deterrence for Europe. For Eisenhower, massive capabilities and the possibility however small that the weapons might be used were sufficient to deter Soviet moves against the NATO alliance. Credibility would not be a major problem, because the punishment for misjudgment would be so severe.[78] Nuclear weapons, at least for interests as vital as NATO, came close to providing an existential deterrent.

The nuclear sharing issue among the European allies was thus not fundamentally about strategic stability, the credibility of extended deterrence, or other military/doctrinal matters. The abstract arguments of the strategic thinkers who would set out demanding criteria for fulfilling these conditions were not a major consideration for the President. Nuclear deterrence was credible. And it would be no more and no less credible if our allies had their own nuclear weapons, provided only that they were able to control them responsibly. The issue did not really belong in the military realm. It was first and foremost a political question, and for political reasons, the United States should not deny its allies' legitimate aspirations to possess nuclear weapons.[79] To do that would be to try to block a natural evolution in the status of states destined to be great powers and thereby confound a deeper logic of politics and history.

There was an alternative. If the United States were willing instead to act courageously and get out in front of the trend, it now had a singular and alluring opportunity to reshape the postwar balance of power in a desirable way. Eisenhower believed that nuclear aspirations, properly channeled, could be the crucial spur to European integration that would place Washington's multipolarity scenario back on track.[80] By nurturing schemes for the Europeans to cooperate in a nuclear force, the United States could foster the process of European integration, avert tensions that might arise from further proliferation of independent national nuclear forces, and solve the problem of Germany's special status. This could reassert the principles of multilateralism that had been diluted with NATO's formal structure after 1950. Most importantly, an integrated nuclear force would take Europe one critical step closer to unification as a "third force" and thus toward the fulfillment of the multipolarity scenario.[81]

Nuclear Sharing Under Eisenhower Before 1960

The North Atlantic Council's December 1954 decision to substitute tactical nuclear weapons for large conventional forces in Europe brought NATO doctrine into line with America's New Look. According to SACEUR Lauris Norstad, the main task of NATO shield forces now was to act as a "tripwire" for U.S. strategic nuclear forces, to "hold an attack until the total weight of the retaliatory power could be brought to bear."[82] Eisenhower's confidence in this doctrine was not universally shared. As early as 1954, U.S. civilian and military strategists were engaged in open and sometimes rancorous debate about the credibility of massive retaliation as a military strategy.[83] But the political implications came to the fore first, during the Suez Crisis of fall 1956. Faced with the uglier side of their dependence on the United States, the British and the French each drew lessons about how the current arrangements in NATO complicated their aspirations to pursue independent foreign policies in areas of vital interest. Leaders in both capitals also expressed new doubts about the credibility of the American guarantee to retaliate for Soviet aggression in Europe.[84] At the December 1956 meeting of the North Atlantic Council, the British (with support from Germany, Holland, and Turkey) called for more extensive sharing of short-range nuclear weapons within the alliance, in order to reinforce that guarantee. The French went further, asking the United States to give up its exclusive control over atomic warheads and transfer them to national forces.[85]

Eisenhower, sensitive to the political rationale behind these requests, was neither surprised nor dismayed. Even before Suez, he had given enthusiastic support to a Norstad proposal for the United States to offer delivery systems to the allies and create a stockpile of warheads under SACEUR authority that could be released to NATO armies on the command of the North Atlantic Council. Dulles called this an "act of confidence which would strengthen the fellowship of the North Atlantic Community."[86] In fact, the administration had already considered going further, toward a full transfer of nuclear weapons control to the allies.[87]

Eisenhower's expressed interests in moving in that direction were viewed nervously from several different places in his own administration.[88] The strongest opposition came, however, from the Joint Committee on Atomic Energy (JCAE), which under the McMahon Act of 1946 and subsequent revisions was entrusted with a de facto veto on transfers of nuclear technology. This committee had historically been a reservoir of sentiment against the sharing of nuclear weapons technology, dating from its origins in the "Atom Spies" scandal of February 1946. In part because the suspected Soviet spy ring was operating in Canada and because British scientists were implicated as key figures, the committee's resolve to inhibit dissemination of nuclear know-how came to include the countries of the developing Western alliance as well as the Eastern Bloc.[89] After Suez, the committee warned the President that it would continue to oppose efforts to go very far toward the sharing of nuclear weapons with the NATO allies.[90] The administration put together a compromise acceptable to the committee, in what became known as the "dual-key" stockpile concept. This meant that the Europeans would purchase delivery systems and station them with their NATO forces, while the United States would retain physical custody over nuclear warheads and the right to veto firing.

The United States and Britain moved quickly toward implementing the stockpile plan. At the Bermuda summit in March 1957, Macmillan agreed to purchase sixty Thor IRBMs and station them with the Royal Air Force under the dual-key arrangement. In April, Eisenhower offered to discuss similar deals for short-range ballistic missiles, cruise missiles, and air defense systems (all under dual key) and to extend the arrangement to other allies.[91] But the launch of *Sputnik* in October 1957 dramatically changed the context of the discussions.

In December, Adenauer told Dulles of widespread fear in Europe that "there might be a change of U.S. sentiment due to the fact that [U.S. territory] would come under fire from Soviet ICBMs" and that "this might even lead to the United States exercising its right to withdraw from NATO." These fears were taken seriously in Washington.[92] Dulles reassured Adenauer and others that the coming of Soviet intercontinental ballistic missiles (ICBMs) would not really change the *military* situation very much (because the United States "had already assumed that Soviet bombers with megaton weapons would be able to inflict massive destruction on the United States"). At the same time, the Secretaries of State and Defense and the National Security advisor acknowledged that from a *political* perspective the "European doubt was rational" and that the crisis in the alliance was real. Eisenhower's faith was not going to inspire sufficient confidence in Europe. The allies were "demanding a surer strategic concept." If the United States did not provide it, the consequence would probably be a move to "try to develop their own nuclear stocks so as to create nuclear war, if they wish, without the United States." The other possibility was a turn to neutralism and a withdrawal from NATO to cut separate deals for peace with Moscow.[93]

One option for the United States at this point would have been to sacrifice notions of multilateralism within the alliance and contract instead to protect the most important and powerful of the European states through selective bilateral deals. This was never considered seriously by the President. Instead, Eisenhower called an unprecedented meeting of the North Atlantic Council at the level of heads of government, in Paris during December 1957, wherein he aimed to reaffirm the multilateral principles of the alliance. The United States offered two concrete initiatives in that direction. The first was a formal resolution to establish a nuclear stockpile throughout the alliance.[94] The second was an offer to extend the Bermuda summit deal to any other ally that wished to accept American intermediate-range ballistic missiles (IRBMs). The United States, however, found so little interest in the nearly obsolete Thor system that Dulles had to reassure the allies that the United States would not "press these missiles in the hands or on the territory of any country that doesn't want them."[95] At Paris, the heads of government tiptoed over the issue by agreeing to a lukewarm endorsement of further "Bermuda deals" in principle and directing SACEUR to explore the possibilities.

Norstad had already raised the ante. By the middle of 1957, Supreme Headquarters Allied Powers Europe (SHAPE) was arguing that the stockpile and the Thor even together were inadequate for European defense. SACEUR instead wanted a new force of mobile, medium-range ballistic missiles (MRBMs) under NATO command. This was a significant step, because the MRBMs would have been the first nuclear weapons of strategic range based in Europe and explicitly given over to NATO.[96] In February 1958, SHAPE responded to the NATO council's directive with a comprehensive plan that went even further. Under the new proposals, American-supplied Thor and Jupiter IRBMs under dual key would be replaced as soon as possible by a new MRBM to be built by a consortium of NATO countries using U.S. blueprints. The next step would be for the NATO consortium to design and build its own follow-on systems with more advanced technology. According to Steinbrunner, "the proposal was understood as a first step toward giving the allies a nuclear capability by arming not the individual countries but the NATO military apparatus."[97] It was clearly consistent with Eisenhower's determination to use the crisis in the alliance as a means of advancing the larger vision of an integrated Europe independent of the United States for its nuclear defense.

In fact, Eisenhower had already tried to take a number of steps in that direction through other channels. In January 1958, the administration launched an initiative to amend the McMahon Act so as to permit greater sharing of information on weapons design and nuclear propulsion. Following the President's logic, administration officials justified this venture before the Congress on political grounds—Dulles argued that the proposal was designed specifically to restore the allies' confidence in a way that would promote European integration at a critical juncture in that process.[98] The JCAE balked predictably, but not because it was opposed to the administration's larger political goals. The committee simply stuck to its long-standing fixation with stopping the dissemination of U.S. nuclear technology. As a result, the McMahon Act was revised only marginally in 1958. The JCAE lent provisional approval to the stockpile arrangement, but with severe regulations designed to insure tight American control of warheads.[99]

When it came to putting that arrangement into practice, the administration would interpret these provisions quite loosely. A JCAE team visiting NATO bases in Europe during 1960 found that dual key operationally meant "fighter aircraft loaded with nuclear bombs sitting on the edge of runways with German pilots inside the cockpits and starter plugs inserted. The embodiment of control was an American officer somewhere in the vicinity with a revolver."[100] In effect, the stockpile served as a way to provide the NATO allies and particularly the Germans with a large number of tactical-range nuclear systems under tenuous American control.

This was by no means the administration's ultimate goal. As the nuclear stockpile plan went into place, SHAPE was continuing its negotiations with the allies over Norstad's more ambitious mobile missile plan. By summer 1959, the discussions had come to focus on a compromise plan by which the United States would provide a British–French–West German consortium with blueprints and technical data to produce a mobile missile that would be deployed under SACEUR's command and supplied with American warheads under dual key.[101] For Eisenhower, the dual-key caveat was an interim arrangement. The President endorsed the plan because he saw it as an important step toward an integrated European nuclear force that would soon graduate to full independent status. In the meantime, the President told Norstad, "we are willing to give, to all intents and purposes, control of the weapons. We retain titular possession only."[102] Norstad agreed, declaring in a public speech of December 1959 that going forward with the consortium plan would be the critical step in making NATO "a fourth nuclear power" of the first rank.[103]

By January 1960, the question of nuclear sharing within the alliance had jelled around two specific initiatives. The first was the nuclear stockpile, where the United States maintained some control over tactical systems through the dual key. The second was the consortium plan under which the Europeans would produce the most advanced American strategic missiles for SACEUR's command. While the details of control over this force were never fully spelled out, it was understood that NATO's ability to fire these missiles would rest to some extent on the U.S. President's authorization so long as the warheads were provided by the United States. Eisenhower would soon, however, make it even more obvious than he already had that this was only a form of window dressing and a temporary one at that. He intended that the consortium evolve into an integrated and independent nuclear force for the European NATO allies.

Nuclear Sharing Under Eisenhower, 1960

The JCAE was not blind to these intentions. Early in February 1960, the committee challenged the administration on the current state of nuclear sharing within the alliance.[104] Eisenhower responded sharply at a press conference the following day. Asked directly if it was his intention to give nuclear weapons over to the allies' control, the President said that he felt the United States should arm its allies with what they needed to defend themselves. Pressed further, he said that the McMahon Act currently blocked him from transferring weapons but that he strongly favored a change in the law.[105] Over the next few days, Eisenhower fleshed out these statements in a series of conversations with Goodpaster and Herter, leaving little doubt about his designs. He even informed Khrushchev.[106]

The JCAE reaction was equally sharp. The chairman of the committee, Senator Clinton P. Anderson, warned that he would oppose any revision of the McMahon Act while other members promised "massive and obstructive opposition" to Eisenhower's plan.[107] In fact, the JCAE in June did propose a change in the McMahon Act that would have *tightened* U.S. control over stockpiled warheads, replacing what the Committee referred to as "fictional custody arrangements." Eisenhower responded in kind. He proclaimed that The McMahon Act, a "terrible and defective law," should be rescinded and the JCAE dissolved so that it could no longer obstruct the President's most important foreign policy initiatives in Europe.[108]

In public, administration official backed off just slightly, but the President continued to push his plan forward.[109] In April, Secretary of Defense Thomas Gates presented Norstad's MRBM plan to the NATO Defense Ministers for immediate consideration. The allies were interested, particularly when it was made clear to them that Washington intended this scheme as a prelude to an even larger and more independent nuclear role.[110]

With the Secretaries of State and Defense behind Eisenhower's initiative and with serious expressions of interest from Europe, the inertia behind the MRBM plan intensified. This created a new current of worry in the State Department and particularly at the Policy Planning Staff, headed now by Gerard Smith.[111] Smith largely shared Eisenhower's convictions about European integration and agreed that the nuclear sharing issue was a critical one, but he doubted Eisenhower's strategy for bringing it about. The stakes were being set too high. If Eisenhower's bold initiatives should fail, Smith worried in particular that the Germans would be sharply humiliated and frustrated by their treatment in NATO and that this would be a tremendous setback for Europe.[112] In the spring of 1960, he called in his predecessor Robert Bowie to head a comprehensive study of the defense needs of the alliance aimed at finessing this problem.

The Bowie Report reaffirmed the argument that NATO's minimum task of preventing Soviet aggression should be met in a way that would promote a continuing process of European integration, so that Europe would assume the leadership role of a great power on a scale nearly equal to that of the United States. The report also agreed that NATO's current nuclear posture was an impediment to that end.[113] The major proposal on this score envisaged a two-step move toward a NATO strategic nuclear force of Polaris submarines. At first, the United States would simply assign five submarines to SACEUR. Later, additional Polaris subs would be launched with multinational crews made up of sailors from at least three NATO countries.[114]

This was a more gradual approach toward creating a multilateral nuclear force for Europe than Eisenhower's MRBM consortium was. The Bowie proposal looked as though it would sidestep early and excessive liberalization of weapons control and in so doing reduce the possibility that such control would ever rest solely in German hands. The President recognized the domestic political value of these modifications and seized on Bowie's plan as a practical alternative that he thought would be more saleable to Congress. In a set of meetings with Bowie and others, Eisenhower repeatedly diverted discussion away from the practical military rationale for the multilateral force (MLF) and from the details of warhead control and launching authority.[115] He reassured his advisors that London and Bonn would be interested in the plan, and he was even confident of his ability to convince de Gaulle. The major concern in his mind was still how to get it past the JCAE, but he was convinced that if he could do so the MLF might turn out to be the critical event in the drive to unify Europe.[116]

The mood in the White House during the fall of 1960 on the nuclear sharing issue was approaching one of urgency. An NSC policy paper of early September set the tone, arguing that a crisis in NATO was imminent and that the nuclear question would be the central factor determining how it was resolved.[117] Eisenhower seemed bent on closing a deal with the Europeans before he left office in the new year. The President told the chairman of the Atomic Energy Commission that "interallied cooperation with respect to atomic weapons" was the most important issue on his agenda and that he fully agreed with Norstad's approach to "collective security, including the collective handling of atomic weapons."[118] Meanwhile, Norstad had been sent to lobby Adenauer and NATO Secretary General Paul Henri Spaak on the nuclear sharing plan, with the promise again being that the United States would make NATO "the fourth atomic power."[119]

The pace of events picked up further in October. In two meetings on October 3, Eisenhower approved a slightly modified version of the Bowie Report's MLF proposal and informed both State and Defense that he would push forward with this plan on "an urgent basis." When reminded of likely JCAE opposition, Eisenhower responded in frustration that "we must get it understood in the Congress that we must have faith and confidence between allies if we wished our alliances to work."[120] At a breakfast with Spaak the next morning, the President seconded the Secretary General's argument that the European allies must in case of a threat to their vital interests "be able to respond with atomic weapons, if need be without the concordance of the United States." Eisenhower proposed an "integrated nuclear strike force" as a "kind of foreign legion under exclusive NATO control."[121] Spaak was enthusiastic, and he agreed with Eisenhower's assessment that Adenauer would accept the plan and that de Gaulle could be convinced. In the President's mind, the only serious impediment left was the JCAE. Eisenhower left Spaak with the clear impression that if it were not for this so-called intrusion on the President's power (which he told Spaak he considered "nonconstitutional" in any event) he would have acted to bring a multilateral nuclear force for NATO into being on his own initiative and without any delay.[122]

The President backed off only slightly after John F. Kennedy's victory in November.[123] On November 17, Eisenhower told the NSC that the United States would formally propose the MLF plan to its NATO allies in December. Two weeks later, he sent Under Secretary of Defense Dillon to London, Paris, and Bonn to brief European leaders on the plan.[124] In early December, he approved a draft statement of policy on the NATO MRBM force that Secretary of State Herter would carry to the North Atlantic Council summit in Paris.[125] On December 17, Herter made the formal offer: five Polaris submarines for a NATO MLF force that would later be supplemented with additional submarines to be purchased from the United States by the European allies. The United States would promise to "commit" the warheads to NATO—implying that launch authority would rest with SACEUR and not be contingent on the American President.[126] In case any doubts remained about Washington's larger objectives, Herter stressed that the U.S. decision to share its most sophisticated strategic systems should be seen as just "the first step towards broader sharing in the control of nuclear weapons." The goal was to create a nuclear force "truly multilateral, with multilateral ownership, financing, and control . . . that would have immense political significance for the cohesion of the NATO alliance."[127]

U.S. goals were consistent—to lay the groundwork for transition to a multilateral alliance where the European states as an integrated unit would be fully responsible for their own defense. Ironically, it was nuclear weapons combined with a set of ideas that at the end of the 1950s seemed to put within Eisenhower's grasp what had evaded Kennan, Truman, and others at the end of the 1940s. Eisenhower discounted military arguments about credibility, but he was deeply sensitive to the political sources and implications of the Europeans' lack of confidence. He saw it as natural that the former great powers of Europe would want to reclaim that status when their recovery from World War II permitted. But to be a great power now was also to have nuclear weapons, and the United States could damage its longer term interests by denying those trappings to its allies. The crisis in the alliance presented a unique opportunity for Washington to seize the initiative and channel nuclear ambitions into institutions that would facilitate European integration. The crisis, if seized, could be used to reinstate multilateralism in NATO. This was instrumental to a larger goal, the multipolarity scenario that had been a basic principle behind American thinking about the alliance since its inception.

Could Eisenhower have succeeded in this quest? The allies reacted cautiously to the December 1960 proposal, but this was in large part a result of the U.S. administration's lame-duck status.[128] The MLF became much less attractive to them later on when the Kennedy administration reconfigured the plan to add strict American veto power on launch authorization. But it was never Eisenhower's intention to dupe the Europeans into paying for an American-dominated nuclear force, as the later MLF plan would appear. At each point in the story I have recounted, the President went as far as he could to share nuclear weapons with the European allies and transfer control of those weapons to them.

Eisenhower ultimately failed in his quest, but not because of any constraints that follow from structural theories of international politics. He failed because of historical accidents that were disconnected from the major stream of events. The most important was strong opposition from a congressional committee that a decade earlier had been endowed with power over nuclear transfers and had adopted a set position against the sharing of nuclear technology. That position came about originally in 1946 as part of an effort to stem the flow of basic nuclear know-how to the Soviet Union, but by the late 1950s that issue was moot. In the interim, the JCAE held to its doctrinaire position against nuclear sharing even among the NATO states for reasons that had little to do with American power vis-à-vis its allies and were thus separate from what Eisenhower was trying to accomplish in Europe. If these highly contingent conditions had been different, the issue of nuclear sharing would have been "solved" by the President long before December 1960. And the evolution of the NATO alliance past that point would also have been radically different.

Kennedy and the Triumph of the Deterrence Scenario

John F. Kennedy entered office with his own rhetoric about a "grand design" for European integration and a revitalized Atlantic partnership. But rhetoric aside, the new President held a more restrained and "pragmatic" view than Eisenhower did of European states as presumptive great powers either separately or otherwise.[129] Kennedy was also more concerned than Eisenhower had been with military strategy when it came to the credibility of extended deterrence.[130] Kennedy's top advisors and particularly Secretary of State Dean Rusk shared his concern, and Rusk argued that something had to be done on this score forthwith.[131] Within two weeks of his inauguration the new President asked former Secretary of State Dean Acheson to chair a small committee that would reevaluate the basis of U.S. military strategy with special attention to NATO.

Acheson brought in Robert Bowie to work with him on this project.

But he also brought in Albert Wohlstetter, the RAND strategic analyst who had recently published his influential critique of massive retaliation, "The Delicate Balance of Terror." [132] Wohlstetter represented a developing school of strategic analysts who were using game theory and other tools to explore new doctrines for nuclear weapons and nuclear deterrence in an era of mutual vulnerability. [133] Unlike Eisenhower, these strategists took seriously the idea that the United States might actually have to fight a war in Europe and use or at least threaten to use nuclear weapons. They also reasoned that no American President would set out down that road if by doing so he was necessarily choosing Armageddon. Since the Soviet leaders could reason as well, Washington needed more than just a capability for massive retaliation. In order to deter the Soviet Union effectively, the United States would have to have a strategy and the necessary capabilities to make limited use of nuclear weapons for tactical purposes and for bargaining, which meant a closely controlled process of raising the risks of escalation. These arguments about the military and doctrinal requirements of deterrence had profound implications for Washington's defense posture in Europe.

The Acheson committee's recommendations were presented to Kennedy in March 1961 and approved with a small number of changes as official U.S. policy in National Security Action Memorandum 40 (NSAM-40) on April 21. [134] Under its new doctrine of flexible response, NATO strategy was to be reoriented away from the emphasis on general war and toward "preparing for the more likely contingencies" short of nuclear or massive nonnuclear attack. The first priority was, of course, to strengthen and modernize the alliance's conventional forces.

On nuclear forces, the directive was much more of a watershed. NSAM-40 argued that Washington should control all potential uses of nuclear weapons in Europe *on its own,* including (if possible) the national forces of Britain and France! [135] This demanded an immediate revision of Herter's December proposal to the North Atlantic Council. The United States would now offer to commit five and eventually several more Polaris submarines to NATO for the life of the alliance subject to a new provision, that all missiles would remain under the exclusive launch authority of the U.S. President with the North Atlantic Council having only an "advisory and consultative" input. The directive was quite severe in setting conditions for moving past this stage:

> If the European NATO countries wish to expand the NATO seaborne missile force, *after* completion of the 1962–66 non-nuclear buildup, the U.S. should then be willing to discuss the possibility of some multilateral contribution by them. The U.S. should insist, in any such discussion, on the need to avoid

(i) national ownership or control of MRBM forces; (ii) any weakening of centralized command and control over these forces; (iii) any diversion of required resources from nonnuclear programs. The United States should not facilitate European production of MRBMs or procurement of MRBSs for European national forces, whether or not these forces are committed to SACEUR.

This represented a fundamental shift in U.S. policy on the control of nuclear weapons by the European allies.[136]

What caused this shift? It was driven most directly by a new set of ideas about nuclear strategy and requirements for maintaining deterrence or fighting a limited nuclear war. Flexible response meant more than just an increase in the number and variety of conventional forces. It also meant planning to use nuclear weapons in a limited and precisely controlled manner, in "strategic games" of signaling, bargaining, intrawar deterrence, and raising the level of shared risk. Each move in these strategic games would require exact and thus *centralized* control over the targeting and use of any weapons. One decision maker would have to govern the carefully plotted nuclear bargaining game, and that decision maker would be the U.S. President. For the moment, as Richard Betts puts it, strategy—particularly nuclear strategy—seemed to overwhelm politics.

The Berlin Crisis brought these new ideas to the fore in a dramatic way and confirmed their ascendence in U.S. policy for NATO. Convinced that Khrushchev's June ultimatum was a test of Washington's broader commitment to Europe, Kennedy found himself stuck with few desirable military options.[137] The President quickly called for a rapid buildup of NATO conventional forces to expand his range of choices. But he also had to consider strategies for the use of nuclear weapons if hostilities should break out.

The nuclear strategists now had a chance to make their arguments at the highest levels. Thomas Schelling, for example, prepared a memo in July arguing that if nuclear weapons were to be used in Berlin, "their purpose should not be 'tactical'. . . . We should plan for a war of nerve, of demonstration, and of bargaining. . . . Success in the use of nuclears will be measured not by the targets destroyed but by how well we manage the level of risk." Schelling was quite direct about what this meant for control of the weapons: "Control over nuclear weapons in Europe must be tight and centralized . . . and designed to permit deliberate, discriminating, selective use for dangerous nuclear bargaining . . . *particular* weapons will be fired from *particular* locations to *particular* targets at *particular* times."[138]

This was the language of a nuclear strategist and not of a political decision maker. Yet the implications of this kind of thinking were evident in Kennedy's planning both during and after the crisis. Apart from underscoring the gaps in NATO conventional capabilities, consultations with allied leaders during the crisis showed how difficult it was for NATO decision makers to agree on nuclear options even as contingency plans. Washington responded by setting a course first to gain more and modern conventional forces with greater contributions from the European allies.[139] When it came to nuclear weapons, the administration moved to pull the reins of control ever tighter to Washington.

The United States formally presented its new strategic perspective to the allies the following spring at a NATO ministerial in Athens.[140] Secretary of Defense McNamara here assured his colleagues that the United States was now close to attaining a secure second-strike force but that this, according to the new perspective, would not in itself suffice to deter war in Europe. Flexible response also demanded the ability to use nuclear weapons selectively, in limited attacks, for signaling (as in Schelling's memo) *and* for tactical strikes against Soviet military targets. In either case, it was essential to the strategy that the selective use of nuclear weapons *not* escalate more or less automatically to general war. Intrawar deterrence, as it was called, rested in turn on tight and precise control over every decision to use a nuclear weapon. The strategy demanded an "individual" targeting plan for the alliance that would assure "unity of planning, concentration of executive authority, and central direction" for the nuclear bargaining game.[141]

National nuclear forces in Europe were anathema to that reasoning, and a multilateral force under NATO was not much better. The argument was simply that any proliferation of "decision centers" would complicate the problem of implementing a precise nuclear strategy and thus undermine the logic of flexible response. Tight control was the sina qua non, and that control belonged to Washington. This was not just a change in declaratory policy. The Kennedy administration moved first to tighten U.S. control over tactical nuclear systems under the dual key by installing permissive action links (PALs) on many of these weapons.[142] It then moved to undermine the MLF.

In June, U.S. Ambassador to NATO Thomas Finletter told the NATO council that Washington no longer saw any need for a NATO MRBM force.[143] The logical move would have been for the United States to withdraw the MLF proposal entirely, but what Eisenhower had already done to advance the plan could not be immediately or easily undone. The allies' and particularly the Germans' expectations had been raised more than a little. At the same time, influential voices at the State Department continued to argue the political "imperatives" of going ahead with some scheme for nuclear sharing.[144]

Kennedy and his close advisors understood the trade-offs. The political stakes riding on the MLF were high. But at each important decision point *after* 1961 nuclear strategy won out over politics. At the end of 1962 the MLF proposal was revised formally to include the conditions that Kennedy had raised in May 1961 as well as new conditions attached to the issue of launch authority. The MLF would now fall under the command, not of SACEUR, but of SACLANT, an American admiral with headquarters in Virginia, and the United States would retain effective veto over launch decisions for the indefinite future.[145] In essense, the MLF was recast as an American proposal to get the Europeans to pay the lion's share for some variant of an MRBM force that they had been told they did not need and that in any case would remain under American control. That little enthusiasm for the plan existed in most of the capitals of Europe was not surprising.[146]

John Steinbruner's *Cybernetic Theory of Decision* chronicles the fate of the MLF over the next several years. The plan underwent manipulation at the hands of American bureaucracies with rival and sometimes inconsistent goals, but one thing stayed constant: the U.S. President would not relinquish control.[147] The MLF proposal was finally and formally dropped by the Johnson administration in 1965. It was, in effect, the last substantial effort to address the relationship between nuclear strategy within NATO and the prospects for European integration.

The deterrence scenario won out in 1961. This, time, however, its victory was sustained by a new set of ideas about nuclear deterrence and the requirements for fighting nuclear war. Aspects of those ideas would change, sometimes dramatically, over the next thirty years. But there were certain constants in American strategic thought, the most important being the argument for centralized control over any decision to use nuclear weapons. That control would stay in the hands of the Americans. And so long as the defense of the alliance depended on those weapons and on the decision to launch them, the United States would have a privileged position within NATO. Eisenhower had hoped that nuclear weapons could be used to promote European integration and to advance and channel the transition to a multipolar world. Instead, nuclear weapons ended up as an impediment to both. Multilateralism and the multipolarity scenario to which it was instrumental became victims to nuclear strategy.

They did so not because of any objective or concrete characteristics of the weapons themselves. The victory of the deterrence scenario under Kennedy did not reflect any enduring realities of power or of structural theory, any more than the predominance of the multipolarity scenario had under Eisenhower. Both were the products of sets of ideas about politics and about nuclear weapons that were complementary in the earlier case and conflictual in the later. To explain the character of NATO requires an understanding of the consequences of those ideas for the decisions that the leaders of powerful states took at critical junctures in the evolution of the alliance. Events that were traveling in different streams and were separate from the ideas at play set the context of those junctures and affected the degree to which these ideas made their mark on the alliance. But the ideas themselves did make a mark.

Conclusion

States ally to increase their security against potential adversaries. But the principles on which an alliance is constructed and its institutional form are blind spots for neorealism. The history of multilateralism in NATO, both as a dependent and an independent variable, challenges that stark version of the security problem facing states.

MULTILATERALISM AS A DEPENDENT VARIABLE

If the choice of institutional form were determined by objective features of the environment no need would arise to go further in explaining it. That was not true of NATO, even at the end of the 1940s. A choice-theoretic analysis of possible institutional forms for an alliance leads to indeterminate predictions, and that indeterminacy is reflected in history. To the extent that functional or utilitarian logic points in any direction at all, it points *away* from multilateralism as an institutional form for managing the West's security problem at the end of World War II.

But the institutions that emerge end up toward the opposite side of the range of possibilities, much closer to the multilateral form. Generally, U.S. policymakers did what they could to foster multilateralism within the alliance. Specifically, at critical points of decision, they took steps that were either most consistent with those principles or least damaging to them, given the exigencies of deterrence.

The explanation for this behavior lies in a set of ideas held by decision makers in a powerful state. Those ideas rested on beliefs about multipolarity with historical roots in American foreign policy thought. The ideas were political in the traditional sense instead of microeconomic, and they relied heavily on "second-image" reasoning. They also inverted neorealism's arguments about the conditions for stability in international systems. Most American policymakers believed that bipolarity would pit the United States and the Soviet Union against each other in an ideologically charged, competitive struggle that would be at best a temporary interlude to war. In contrast, multipolarity would induce caution and restraint in states' external behavior, and this would cause stability in the international system. Living with diversity at the international level would also do good things to states domestically, making them more tolerant and cooperative at home and with each other.[148] This was a world in which the United States could and would flourish.

Naturally, the strength of these ideas varied across individuals within the decision-making elite. That meant that when the multipolarity scenario came under pressure from the exigencies of deterrence, policymakers disagreed about how much compromise away from multilateralism was necessary. Yet it would be wrong to conclude from that controversy that multilateralism was only an institutional form for "low politics" or that the ideas supporting multilateralism came into play only under conditions of low threat.[149] The Eisenhower decade cuts strongly against that argument. The 1950s were not generally a time of low threat perception in Washington. And Eisenhower's commitments to multilateralism within the alliance were not noticeably weakened by periods of increased threat, including the many U.S.–Soviet crises, the Suez debacle, or the *Sputnik* launch. If anything, these events reinforced the President's determination to transform NATO through the sharing of nuclear weapons with the allies. Because Eisenhower's determination was driven by ideas about politics and not by military considerations or abstract strategic arguments about the credibility of extended deterrence, multilateralism could do more than just survive high threat and high politics under Eisenhower; it was positively aided by it.

The Kennedy administration reversed Eisenhower's policy on nuclear sharing. But the reasons for this were not that new threats pushed the issue of multilateralism in NATO from low politics into high. Instead, multilateralism was overwhelmed by a new set of ideas about nuclear weapons that set fresh requirements for maintaining deterrence and planning for nuclear war. This set of ideas maintained itself, in different manifestations and again with varying levels of strength, for the better part of thirty years while threat perceptions underwent several cycles.

Multilateralism neither came in with low politics nor went out with high. Its movements are better explained by the movements of sets of ideas that were disconnected from any objective exigencies of security.

MULTILATERALISM AS AN INDEPENDENT VARIABLE

In the world of neorealist theory, states do not normally make conscious efforts to disperse vital resources of power among other states or coalitions.[150] Yet that is precisely what the Eisenhower administration hoped to do vis-à-vis the Europeans at the end of the 1950s. This impulse was based on long-standing and widely held beliefs about the advantages of living in a multipolar international system. It was also based on a set of ideas about nuclear weapons that were held by the President, ideas that were shared with less conviction by some elites and that were totally rejected by others.

Yet acting on his own ideas, Eisenhower came very close to transferring full control of nuclear weapons to the NATO allies. If he had succeeded, there would certainly have been a major transformation of NATO with important implications for U.S.–European and East–West relations during the 1960s and beyond. Other, more dramatic outcomes are possible. If Eisenhower's plan had led to an integrated European security organization with an independent nuclear deterrent in the 1960s, that probably would have accelerated greatly the change from a bipolar international system to a multipolar one. This, I think, challenges some basic neorealist premises about power. How can a "unit-level" actor or even a single decision maker transform the structure of the international system by choice, influenced by a set of particular ideas? The answer to this question goes back to a blind spot in neorealist balance-of-power theory: it neglects the role of alliance principles and institutions that "shape" the balance of power and affect its evolution over time.

My challenge rests on a counterfactual, because Eisenhower did not in the end succeed in his quest. Does that conspicuous fact rescue realism's austere perspective? Important to keep in mind is *why* Eisenhower failed.[151] His initiative was frustrated principally by a congressional committee that had acted as a repository of simple antiproliferation sentiment since its founding in the late 1940s. This committee barely responded to the realities imposed by the demonstrated independent ability of the British and later the French to acquire the bomb. Its effort to block Eisenhower came from an alternative set of ideas: that proliferation of nuclear knowledge was undesirable under any circumstances. But those ideas were no more logically grounded in or linked to the causal arguments of neorealist theory than Eisenhowers' were, nor did they respond more directly to changes in the environment.

Kennedy's reversal of Eisenhower's policy was similarly driven by a new set of ideas derived from something other than objective or structural factors. What if the logic of the new strategic theories had not been thought through and available to decision makers, so that McNamara could adopt it as his own in 1962? It is quite possible that the Kennedy administration might instead have followed through in Eisenhower's footsteps. JCAE restrictions would likely have been overcome or designed around, in time.[152] It is important to acknowledge that none of these things happened. But *the way in which they did not happen* should not give much comfort to the stark neorealist perspective on power.

The case for multilateralism as an independent variable does not rest entirely on counterfactuals. As history actually turned out, the character of the balance of power in Europe has been and will, I think, continue to be substantially different than it would have been in the absence of an American commitment to multilateralism. This is because multilateralism in NATO created a new set of possibilities for the provision of security in Europe, possibilities that the actors did not previously envision.

The most important of these came out of the way in which NATO dealt with the Franco–German relationship. If U.S. leaders had chosen the bilateral alternative and "split" the security of Germany and France, all sorts of configurations that we now take for granted would have been heavily disfavored, most importantly the European Community. NATO also caused security to become linked with the domestic characteristics of states according to a set of additional propositions that go far beyond security per se. In this conception, security institutions have a broad mandate for peace management, economic and social progress, and other kinds of positive cooperation between states. Within NATO, security became tied to political standards of multiparty democracy, human rights, and economic freedom.[153]

That linkage was more than just a reflection of American power, and it is being propagated into the next generation of security institutions in Europe. That is not overdetermined. The world may no longer be bipolar, but multilateralism is not a necessary outgrowth of multipolarity. In 1993, even more so than in 1949, alternative institutional forms for providing security are available in Europe. In the abstract, European security could become a game played by "clubs" of several states, bilateral alliances, or by individual states protecting their borders with small arsenals of nuclear weapons. Again on abstract logic, the bilateral alter-

reformulate domestic politics within their subordinate states, or they can join with other states regardless of their internal characteristics.

2. From Ruggie, "Multilateralism: The Anatomy of an Institution", in this volume, I abstract three features that distinguish multilateralism from other patterns of relations between states: indivisibility, generalized organizing principles, and diffuse reciprocity.

3. See "Multilateralism: The Anatomy of an Institution," in this volume. Ruggie discusses "collective security," which is *one* possible manifestation of multilateralism in security. It is not the only one, although a full collective-security system would be the modal case.

4. This is consistent with the standard neorealist arguments about alliances. See Kenneth Waltz, *Theory of International Politics* (Reading, Mass.: Addison Wesley, 1979); Stephen M. Walt, *The Origins of Alliances* (Ithaca, N.Y.: Cornell University Press), 1987.

5. By early 1948, the Soviet Union had concluded bilateral "Treaties of Friendship and Mutual Assistance" with Poland, Czechoslovakia, Romania, Hungary, and Bulgaria. The treaties bound each country to Moscow and prevented them from dealing directly with each other on security issues. The Red Army was given a free hand to modernize and reorganize the East European armed forces. See A. Ross Johnson, "The Warsaw Pact: Soviet Military Policy in Eastern Europe," in Sarah Meiklejohn Terry, ed., *Soviet Policy in Eastern Europe* (New Haven, Conn.: Yale University Press, 1984) p. 259. Until the Warsaw Pact was signed in 1955, Moscow did not even offer the facade of an integrated defense organization to its allies, as it had done earlier in the economic field through the Council for Mutual Economic Assistance. See Robert L. Hutchings, *Soviet–East European Relation: Consolidation and Conflict* (Madison: University of Wisconsin Press, 1983); Thomas Wolfe, *Soviet Power and Europe*, (Baltimore: The Johns Hopkins University Press, 1970).

6. Indeed, the British and the French in particular might have been more content to the extent that bilateralism would have saved them from having to countenance and deal directly with a revitalized state and military force in Germany.

7. See Lisa Martin, "The Rational State Choice of Multilateralism," in this volume for a generalized discussion.

8. The analogy is to transaction costs economic analysis. See Oliver Williamson, ed., *Industrial Organization* (London: Edward Elgar, 1990).

9. The United States also sacrificed legitimate claims to greater recompense for providing security to relatively exposed states like Turkey than to well-protected states like Great Britain. In effect, the promise was to make an equal sacrifice for highly unequal causes.

10. I differ here in emphasis with Olson and Zeckhauser's classic model, which assumes that strategic nuclear deterrence is a public good and uses that assumption to analyze burden-sharing problems within NATO. Mancur Olson

and Richard Zeckhauser, "An Economic theory of Alliances," *Review of Economics and Statistics* (August 1966), 48:266–279. My point is that the publicness of nuclear deterrence within NATO was a *result* of voluntary institutional choices that themselves need to be explained.

11. See John Lewis Gaddis, *Strategies of Containment* (New York: Oxford, 1982), p. 10; John Morton Blum ed., *The Price of Vision: The Diary of Henry A. Wallace, 1942–46* (Boston: 1973), p. 146; Michael Schaller, *The U.S. Crusade in China 1938–1945* (New York: Columbia University Press, 1979) pp. 98–99, 176–178.

12. Warren F. Kimball includes both isolationism and messianic internationalism as manifestations of unilateralism, "the American urge to go it alone in the event that others did not accept American demands." *The Juggler: Franklin Roosevelt as Wartime Statesman* (Princeton: Princeton University Press, 1991), p. 84.

13. On these points, see Gaddis, *Strategies of Containment,* ch. 1; Robert Dallek, *Franklin Delano Roosevelt and American Foreign Policy 1932–1945* (New York: Oxford University Press, 1979), esp. pp. 390–391; Deborah Larson, *Origins of Containment: A Psychological Explanation,* (Princeton: Princeton University Press, 1985), ch. 2. An important exception was Roosevelt's summer 1943 decision *not* to share voluntarily information about the atomic weapons program with Moscow, but the U.S. President resisted consistently Churchill's efforts to expand the scope of this subpartnership to the exclusion of the Soviet Union. Kimball, correctly in my view, interprets Roosevelt's decision on the atomic issue as a way to hedge his bets on Stalin. (*The Juggler,* ch. 5).

14. Nicholas John Spykman, *America's Strategy in World Politics: The United States and the Balance of Power* (New York: Harcourt, Brace, and World, 1942); Walter Lippmann, *U.S. Foreign Policy: Shield of Republic* (Boston: Little, Brown, 1943). This argument had intellectual roots in British foreign policy thought as well; see, for example, Sir Halford Mackinder, "The Geographical Pivot of History," *Geographical Journal* (April 1904), 23:421–444.

15. Gaddis, *Strategies of Containment,* pp. 14–19. In a major foreign policy address of June 1945, Truman pronounced that "unless there is complete understanding between [the] three great powers there will be no peace" and that the alternative, competition between two great powers, would end up "a truce-armistice, which will be just like the one we had in 1920." Press Conference, the Association of Radio News Analysts, June 16, 1945, quoted by Larson, *Origins of Containment,* p. 141.

16. The original "long telegram" is in *Foreign Relations of the United States (FRUS)* (1946), 6:696–709; Kennan later offered his own retrospective clarifications in his *Memoirs: 1925–1950,* Boston: Little, Brown, 1967), pp. 292–295, 354–367. Truman resisted similar conclusions for some time. Consider, for example, his reaction to Churchill's iron curtain speech, discussed by Larson, *Origins of Containment,* pp. 264–265.

17. See, for example, Secretary of State George Marshall's speech at Chicago, November 18, 1947, in *Department of State Bulletin* (Nov. 23, 1947), 27:1026, where he argued vehemently against a bipolar spheres of influence "solution" for Europe. The views of Charles Bohlen and former ambassador to Moscow William Bullit, two extremely hard-line critics of Soviet behavior who retained substantial influence in Washington, are discussed in Will Brownell and Richard Billings, *So Close to Greatness: A Biography of William C. Bullit* (New York: MacMillan, 1988).

18. Office of Strategic Services, "American Security Interests in the European Settlement," research and analysis report no. 2284 (June 29, 1944), Washington, D.C.: Modern Military Records Branch, National Archives.

19. Of course, Kennan did not believe that the United States was as vulnerable to this was the Soviet Union was, but he did not view the United States as immune. See, for example, Kennan to Cecil B. Lyon, October 13, 1947, Department of State Policy Planning Staff Records, Box 33, "Chronological— 1947," Diplomatic Branch, National Archives; where Kennan argues that the "first and primary element of 'containment' . . . is the "encouragement and development of other forces resistant to communism" and that "it should be a cardinal point of our policy to see to it that other elements of *independent* power are developed on the Eurasian land mass as rapidly as possible" (my emphasis). John D. Hickerson, director of State Department Office of European Affairs, would later write that the notion was to foster a European "third force . . .; a real European organization strong enough to say no both to the Soviet Union and to the United States." Hickerson Memorandum, January 21, 1948, *FRUS* (1948), 3:11.

20. Kennan's memos show that he had few illusions about the resistance his ideas about the restoration of German power would encounter, but he viewed the alternative of a bipolar world as certainly more dangerous. In that vein Kennan would later write somewhat sardonically that "the only thing wrong with Hitler's new order was that it was Hitler's." Kennan to Acheson, Policy Planning Staff Minutes, October 18, 1949, Policy Planning Staff Records Box 32, Diplomatic Branch, National Archives. Kennan thought that Washington could successfully combine reassurance, persuasion, and gentle coercion to convince others to accept German power in the context of a united Europe.

21. This was a key theme in Kennan's fundamental optimism about the United States and the strategy of containment: he argued repeatedly that Moscow's inability to tolerate diversity would turn out to be the "weakest and most vulnerable point in the Kremlin armor." From a speech by Kennan to the Naval War College in October 1948; quoted in Gaddis, *Strategies of Containment*, pp. 43–44.

22. Gaddis, *Strategies of Containment,* p. 42. My emphasis.

23. See John Lewis Gaddis, *The Long Peace: Inquiries Into the History of the Cold War* (New York: Oxford University Press, 1987), pp. 43, 57–58, 64. I

discuss the State Department's evolving position on military guarantees in the next section.

24. Kennan fully expected that an "independent" Europe on most important issues would find its interests coincident with Washington's. The vision was of a U.S.–West European partnership of sorts that would be robust enough to withstand the Soviet threat but still sufficiently contingent to restrain the United States. For a different view that emphasizes more strongly the importance of lingering American isolationism, see Michael Howard, "Introduction," in Olav Riste, ed., *Western Security: The Formative Years* (New York: Columbia University Press, 1985), pp. 11–22.

25. Both of these assumptions underlay Kennan's argument in the long telegram. They were also consistent with the U.S. military's assessments of Red Army capabilities following the war. See Walter S. Poole, "From Conciliation to Containment: The JCS and the Coming of the Cold War 1945–46", *Military Affairs* (February 1978), 42:12–15.

26. In late February, Acheson told his journalist friend Louis Fischer that he was convinced that "the thing is not so urgent in Turkey but in Greece it is a matter of days." Quoted in Larson, *Origins of Containment*, p. 303. On February 26, Marshall gave to Truman a memo reporting a similar consensus among the Departments of State, War and Navy—that the situation was critical and that "we should take immediate steps to extend all possible aid to Greece." *FRUS* (1947), 5:58–59. It was also agreed that the fall of Greece to the communists would probably not be an isolated event: Marshall, for example, warned congressional leaders in late February that "we are faced with the first crisis *of a series* which might extend Soviet domination to Europe, the Middle East, and Asia." Quoted in Larson, *Origins of Containment*, p. 306.

27. See, in particular, Acheson's executive session testimony in U.S. Congress, Senate Foreign Relations Committee, *Legislative Origins of the Truman Doctrine*, 80th Congress, 1st Session, 1973, pp. 17, 21–22.

28. "Informational Objectives and Main Themes," *FRUS* (1947) 5:77–78.

29. Clayton memorandum, "The European Crisis," May 27, 1947, *FRUS* (1947), 3:231. See also the testimony of General George A. Lincoln of the War Department General Staff on April 2, 1947, *Legislative Origins of the Truman Doctrine*, p. 160. For the military assessment of U.S. power vis-à-vis the Soviet Union at this time, see JCS 1769/1, April 29, 1947, *FRUS* (1947), 1:734–741.

30. The first memo (dated March 5) is quoted and discussed in Ellen C. Garwood, *Will Clayton: A Short Biography* (Austin: University of Texas Press, 1958), pp. 115–118. The second (prepared in late May as input for Marshall in drafting his June 5 Harvard speech) is abstracted in Kennan to Acheson, *FRUS* (1947), 3:231–232.

31. It is notable that Marshall bypassed Clayton, who as Under Secretary of State for Economic Affairs had at least equal claim to the assignment, and instead called on Kennan and the Policy Planning Staff to head the central study

on the ERP. Policy Planning argued that the European countries should themselves author the plan. John Gimbel, *The Origins of the Marshall Plan* (Stanford, Calif.: Stanford Press, 1976), pp. 199–203.

32. "Report of the Policy Planning Staff," *FRUS* (1947), 1:772.

33. Kennan to Cecil B. Lyon, October 13, 1947, State Policy Planning Staff Records, Chronological File, Box 33, Diplomatic Branch, National Archives. My emphases.

34. U.S. Congress, Senate Committee on Foreign Relations, *European Recovery Program,* 80th Congress, 2nd Session, January 1948. Very few objections to this scenario arose during the hearings. For an isolated example, see the comments of Senator Bourke Hickenlooper, who doubted that the Europeans could sustain the requisite military capabilities under any circumstances (p. 490).

35. Many of the factors favoring bilateralism that I discussed in the previous section would have applied to Marshall Plan aid as well. Apart from the gain to the United States of being able to differentiate among aid recipients, the bilateral alternative would have significantly reduced transaction costs, since the multilateral solution required getting sixteen states to agree on a comprehensive plan. As it turned out, an agreement to establish the new organization (OEEC—the forerunner to the Organization for Economic Cooperation and Development or OECD) was not completed until April 1948. For a different view, see A. W. DePorte, *Europe Between the Superpowers* (New Haven, Conn.: Yale University Press, 1979), ch. 7.

36. Gaddis quotes Bevin telling his cabinet that "the closest association with the United States is essential" for defense, despite the fact "that such a policy might well require the subordination of British and European interests to those of the United States." *The Long Peace,* p. 69.

37. "Inverchapel to Marshall," January 13, 1948, *FRUS* (1948), 3:4–5; also "Memorandum of Conversation by Lovett," p. 13; "Inverchapel to Lovett," pp. 14–15; and "Lovett to Inverchapel," p. 17.

38. Timothy Ireland, *Creating the Entangling Alliance: The Origins of the North Atlantic Treaty Organization* (Westport Conn.: Greenwood Press, 1981), pp. 48–58, describes the French concern expressed at the July 1947 meeting on Marshall Plan aid.

39. The United States made only minor concessions in the interest of bolstering a fragile government in Paris. Ibid., pp. 50 and 60–63.

40. In less than a year, Soviet-backed communist parties had gained nearly exclusive control over governments in Budapest, Sofia, Bucharest, Warsaw, and Prague. While substantial influence over foreign policy might have been consistent with the American view of "loose spheres," the infiltration and exclusive control of domestic politics by forceful subversion, secret police activity, and the reorganization of the military under the Red Army was not.

41. In an emergency telegram sent right after the coup, Marshall said that he now envisioned a long-term and direct U.S. involvement in Europe, includ-

ing "protracted security guarantees." "Marshall to Douglas," February 28, 1948, *FRUS* (1948), 2:101. Marshall was supported by Under Secretary of State Robert Lovett and by Hickerson, both of whom now agreed that the time had come for the United States to take on formal security treaty obligations in Europe. Ireland, *Creating the Entangling Alliance*, p. 80.

42. One paper recommended that the United States should make even its informal support contingent on the willingness of the Brussels Treaty States to expand their organization to include, among other Western European nations, Germany. "Butler Memorandum," March 19, 1948, *FRUS* (1948), 3:58–59; "Report of the Policy Planning Staff," March 23, 1948, *FRUS* (1948), 3:62–63.

43. And, most importantly, calm the French about eventual German involvement. Ireland, *Creating the Entangling Alliance*, pp. 83–85.

44. This language was a compromise outcome of discussions among Marshall, Lovett, John Foster Dulles, and Senators Arthur H. Vandenberg and Tom Connally. Vandenberg worried that even this much would encourage European dependence on the United States, but he nevertheless came close to accepting the administration's preferences, as put forward in NSC-9 of April 13. "Souers to the NSC," *FRUS* (1948), 3:86–87. The Vandenberg Resolution, which passed the Senate on June 11, 1948, incorporates similar language.

45. See Gaddis, *Strategies of Containment*, p. 72. The French government took a similar position on May 20, after the Senate Foreign Relations Committee informed the French of the precise language specifying the nature of the U.S. commitment that it was putting together for the Vandenberg Resolution. "Douglas to Marshall," *FRUS* (1948), 2:266–268.

46. Even this was qualified: Lovett, following policy recommendations set out in a June 28 NSC paper, told the British that the United States would not offer even an informal commitment until the Western Union (the defense organ of the Brussels Pact) moved to organize itself more effectively. See Ireland, *Creating the Entangling Alliance*, pp. 100–103; George Kennan, *Memoirs 1925–1950*, p. 407.

47. "Memorandum of Conversation by Bohlen," *FRUS* (1948), 3:206.

48. "Memorandum by the Participants in the Washington Security Talks, July 6 to Sept 9, Submitted to Their Respective Governments for Study and Comment," *FRUS* (1948), 3:239.

49. The compromise draft reflected the American position almost entirely on these important points. For a comparison between the preferred wording of the European nations, the Americans, and the eventual compromise, see Ireland, *Creating the Entangling Alliance*, p. 106.

50. "Considerations Affecting the Conclusion of a North Atlantic Treaty" *FRUS* (1948), 3:284–288. Kennan continued to argue this line until he left Policy Planning at the end of 1949. As late as April 1949 he initiated a new study aimed at determining "whether the emergence of a unified Western

Europe postulates the formation of a third world power of approximately equal strength to the United States and the Soviet Union." Quoted in Gaddis, *The Long Peace,* p. 67; see also "Bruce to Acheson," October 22, 1949, *FRUS* (1949),. 4:343.

51. See, in particular, articles 3 and 5 of the North Atlantic Treaty, reproduced in *The North Atlantic Treaty Organization: Facts and Figures* (Brussels: NATO Information Service, 1989), pp. 376–378.

52. The United States even rejected pleas from Paris to participate in regional defense-planning groups for Western Europe, Northern Europe, and Southern Europe–Western Mediterranean, limiting its activities to the groups that would draw up defense plans for the North Atlantic Ocean and Canada–United States. "Report of the Working Group on Organization to the North Atlantic Council," *FRUS* (1949), 4:322–336.

53. The invasion lent some credibility to the argument that the West might anticipate a surprise attack in Europe once Red Army capabilities had been adequately expanded. See on this point "NSC-68, United States Objectives and Programs for National Security," April 14, 1950, *FRUS* (1950), 1:251, 267. For at least a short time in June and early July, the notion that Korea might be a "feint" devised to lure American forces and tie them down in the periphery in preparation for an attack on Europe was taken seriously in Washington and elsewhere. Gaddis, Strategies of Containment, p. 110.

54. The Council Deputies, made up of deputies to the Foreign Ministers of each of the NATO countries, was established in May 1950 to meet in continuous session and act essentially as a secretariat for the North Atlantic Council.

55. *New York Times* September 10, 1950, p. 1.

56. North Atlantic Council Resolution of September 26, 1950, in "Acheson to Webb," *FRUS* (1950), 3:350.

57. SACEUR is Supreme Allied Commander Europe. "Report by the North Atlantic Military Committee to the North Atlantic Defense Committee," *FRUS* (1950), 3:557; "U.S. Delegation Minutes of Second Meeting of Sixth Session of North Atlantic Treaty Council with Defense Ministers," *FRUS* (1950), 3:595–596. Acheson informed the Congress in February that the United States would send four additional divisions, to add to the two already on occupation duty in Germany.

58. In December 1950, April 1951, June 1951, and February 1952, respectively. SHAPE is Supreme Headquarters Allied Powers Europe.

59. NATO forces grew from about 15 divisions and less than 1000 aircraft in early 1951 to about 35 divisions and about 3000 aircraft by December. Lord Ismay, *NATO: The First Five Years 1949–1954* (Paris: North Atlantic Treaty Organization, 1954), pp. 40, 101–102.

60. The French preferred to use the European Coal and Steel Community, rather than NATO, as a way of incorporating West Germany into Europe. Another alternative at this juncture would have been for the United States to cut

bilateral deals with Germany and with France on separate terms, as I suggested earlier. See Robert McGeehan, *The German Re-armament Question* (Urbana: University of Illinois Press, 1971), p. 161.

61. It is well known that Eisenhower feared that inappropriately large defense expenditures threatened to cripple the U.S. economy. At the same time, the new President desired strongly to regain a level of positive initiative in American foreign policy, which he felt had deteriorated under Truman. See, for example, Samuel Huntington, *The Common Defense* (New York: Columbia University Press, 1961), pp. 64–88; Gaddis, *Strategies of Containment,* pp. 146–147.

62. The Council later set a goal of thirty nuclear armed active-duty divisions to defend the European central region. Gaddis, *Strategies of Containment,* pp. 148–150; Huntington, *The Common Defense,* pp. 80–81; see also Alain C. Enthoven and K. Wayne Smith, *How Much Is Enough? Shaping the Defense Program 1961–1969* (New York: Harper & Row, 1971) pp. 120–121.

63. Eisenhower used phrases like *general mobilization, regimentation,* and *garrison state* to capture his concerns about the possible impact on U.S. democratic institutions of a prolonged bipolar cold war; he worried that "all that we are striving to defend would be weakened and . . . could disappear" under the unmitigated pressure of this kind of confrontation. Quoted by Gaddis, in a summary discussion in *Strategies of Containment,* pp. 133–135.

64. "Memorandum of Conference with the President," Andrew Goodpaster, October 2, 1956, White House Office (WHO), Office of the Staff Secretary (OSS), International Trips and Meetings (ITM), Box 3, Eisenhower Presidential Library (EPL), Abilene, Kansas.

65. As Steinbrunner put it, Eisenhower firmly believed that a situation in which "nations which had long dominated world politics had been eased into subordinate relationships and no longer controlled the forces upon which the defense of their people and sovereign territory rested . . . did not square with the tradition of Europe and its historical sense of identity." John D. Steinbruner, *The Cybernetic Theory of Decision* (Princeton: Princeton University Press), p. 171.

66. Press Conference of February 3, 1960, reported in *New York Times* February 4, 1960, p. 1.

67. In the President's view, the Europeans' ability to free ride on the American security commitment had in fact led to some of the consequences that Kennan had predicted and feared. Eisenhower saw the French rejection of the EDC, which he had "swore, prayed, almost wept for," as a critical turning point in this story. "Memorandum of Conversation Between the President and Paul Henri-Spaak," November 1959, WHO, OSS, ITM, Box 5, EPL.

68. Transcript of Press Conference, February 3, 1960, Ann Whitman File (AWF), Press Conference Series, Box 3, EPL.

69. "Memorandum of Conference with the President," September 13, 1960, WHO, OSS, Subject series, Alphabetical Subseries, Box 4, EPL. Goodpaster added that Eisenhower stood firm for "the collective handling of nuclear weap-

ons" within the alliance, because he "thought it clear that we must carry out cooperation of political significance with the others if we wish the alliance to be healthy."

70. President's Communication to the House Committee on Foreign Affairs, *Report on Foreign Policy and Mutual Security,* 85th Congress, 1st Session, June 11, 1957; Committee Report in WHO, Office of the Special Assistant for National Security Affairs (OSANSA), Special Assistant Subseries, Subject Subseries, Box 7, EPL.

71. "Memorandum for Goodpaster of Meeting with Congressman Carl Durham, Chairman of the JCAE," December 7, 1957, WHO, OSS, Subject Series, Alphabetical Subseries, Box 4, EPL.

72. Macmillan, in a television interview of February 1958, quoted in Lawrence Freedman, *The Evolution of Nuclear Strategy* (New York: St. Martin's, 1981), p. 311. For Clement Atlee, joint possession of the bomb also symbolized the Anglo–American special relationship. See David N. Schwartz, *NATO's Nuclear Dilemmas,* (Washington, D.C.: Brookings, 1983), pp. 59–61.

73. See John Newhouse, *War and Peace in the Nuclear Age* (New York: Knopf, 1989), p. 131.

74. See Charles de Gaulle, *Memoirs of Hope,* Terence Kilmartin trans. (London: Weidenfeld and Nicolson, 1971), pp. 208–209; also Robert E. Osgood, *NATO: The Entangling Alliance* (Chicago: University of Chicago Press, 1962), pp. 276–296.

75. "Memorandum of Conference with the President," August 8, 1960, WHO, OSS, ITM, Box 5, EPL. Eisenhower went on to remind NATO SACEUR Lauris Norstad that the nuclear weapons issue was not in his mind different from any other in alliance relations and that "we should be as generous with our allies in this matter as we think they should be in other questions regarding the alliance."

76. "Memorandum of Conference with the President," December 12, 1958, WHO, OSS, Subject Series, State Department Subseries, Box 2, EPL.

77. In January 1953 (seven months *before* the Soviets tested an H-bomb), NSC 141 informed the President that Moscow would have between 300 and 600 bombs by 1955 and "that the net capability of the Soviet Union to injure the United States must already be measured in terms of many millions of casualties." See Richard Betts, *Nuclear Blackmail and Nuclear Balance* (Washington, D.C.: Brookings, 1987), p. 150. Eisenhower never showed much confidence in the ability of a preemptive strike to reduce American casualties. See Betts, pp. 164–169. In any event, he severely doubted that he or any other American President would ever be willing to launch a first strike: "this would not only be against our traditions but it would appear to be impossible that any such thing would occur." Private diary entry on January 23, 1956, p. 2, Ann Whitman File, Dwight David Eisenhower (DDE) Diaries, Box 12, EPL.

78. Betts, *Nuclear Blackmail and Nuclear Balance,* gives a balanced assessment

of the doctrine of massive retaliation without cartooning it. In public, Eisenhower sometimes claimed that limited nuclear war was in fact possible. But in his private diaries and in the notes of his meetings he consistently argues that any use of nuclear weapons would escalate to general war. He was particularly adamant on this point when it came to Europe. See the comments of George B. Kistiakowsky, *A Scientist at the White House: The Private Diary of President Eisenhower's Special Assistant for Science and Technology* (Cambridge, Mass.: Harvard University Press, 1976), p. 400; notes on a private conversation with James Hagerty, cited in Gaddis, *Strategies of Containment,* p. 175; John Duffield, *The Evolution of NATO's Conventional Force Posture,* Ph.D. dissertation, Princeton University, 1989, ch. 5; and notes from a discussion with NATO Secretary General Paul Henri-Spaak in October 1960, where the President waved off questions about nonnuclear or limited conflicts in Europe as "academic." "Memorandum of Conference with the President," October 3, 1960, WHO, OSS, ITM, Box 5, NATO 1959–60, EPL.

79. Consider, for example, Dulles' argument that while European security and safety were assured by American nuclear weapons, "psychological and morale factors" demanded something more. The political value of "countries which themselves are subject to . . . intermediate missiles having their own intermediate missiles with which to hit back is an element that has to be weighed in the scales." "Dulles Background Briefing for American News Correspondents," December 15, 1957, WHO, OSS, ITM, Box 4, EPL.

80. The President saw "Atoms for Peace" as an important part of this blueprint, but Euratom (The European Atomic Energy Agency, founded in February 1957) was only a first step: "if the six countries set up an integrated institution possessing effective control . . . in the field of peaceful uses of atomic energy, control over military uses of atomic energy by these six countries would be simplified." See "Memo of Lewis L. Strauss (Chairman of Atomic Energy Commission) to the President," January 25, 1956, WHO, OSS, Subject Series, Alpha Subseries, Box 5, EPL; also Dulles to Eisenhower, "European Integration and Atomic Energy," January 1956, WHO, OSS, Alpha Series, Atomic Energy Commission, Box 3, EPL.

81. Eisenhower was supported in this vision most deeply by the State Department, although sometimes for different reasons and with different emphases. Dulles shared generally the President's view that a European nuclear force was the best alternative to either independent national arsenals or "neutralism" on the part of the allies. See, for example, Secretary Dulles's Statement before the Joint Committee on Atomic Energy, April 17, 1958, *Department of State Bulletin* (May 5, 1958), 38:741–742. Europeanists at State were particularly worried about Germany, and they took seriously Adenauer's protestations that his country was being singled out as less than equal. The possibility that a frustrated Germany might seek an independent nuclear force and then repudiate the West in favor of a separate peace with Moscow was viewed seriously. European

integration was the most promising way to solve the German problem, and the sharing of nuclear weapons in a multilateral force was one way to bring that about. See the "Bowie Report," officially "The North Atlantic Nations: Tasks for the 1960's" August 1960, WHO, Office of the Special Assistant for Disarmament, Box 9, EPL; NSC 5727, "Draft Statement of U.S. Policy on Germany," 1959, WHO, NSC Series, Box 23, EPL; NSC 6017, "NATO in the 1960s," November 8, 1960, WHO, NSC Series, Box 11, EPL; and Catherine McArdle Kelleher, *Germany and the Politics of Nuclear Weapons* (New York: Columbia University Press, 1975), pp. 21–29, 90–94.

82. Testimony in U.S. Congress, Senate Committee on Foreign Relations, *Mutual Security Act of 1958*, 82d Congress, 2d session, 1958, pp. 187.

83. See Dulles' speech "The Evolution of Foreign Policy," *Department of State Bulletin* January 25, 1954, 30:107–110. Academics such as William Kaufman, Bernard Brodie, and Henry Kissinger responded with critiques of massive retaliation that were later reprinted in William W. Kaufmann, ed., *Military Policy and National Security* (Princeton: Princeton University Press, 1956). Generals Maxwell Taylor and Curtis LeMay were key players in the military debate. See, for example, Taylor, *The Uncertain Trumpet* (New York: Harper & Row, 1979), pp. 178–180. For a summary of the arguments, see Robert E. Osgood, *NATO: The Entangling Alliance,* pp. 145–146.

84. Particularly troubling was Washington's lukewarm response to Krushchev's rather overt nuclear threats against the allies. See, for example, Hans Spier, "Soviet Atomic Blackmail and the North Atlantic Alliance," *World Politics* (April 1957), 9:307–328.

85. Steinbrunner, *The Cybernetic Theory of Decision,* p. 174.

86. See Stephen E. Ambrose, *Eisenhower* (New York: Simon & Schuster, 1983), p. 405. Dulles later justified the stockpile plan with the argument that the allies should not be left "in a position of suppliants . . . for the use of atomic weapons. . . . We do not ourselves want to be in a position where our allies are wholly dependent upon us. We don't think this is a healthy relationship." *New York Times* (July 17, 1957), p. 6. Eisenhower quickly defended Dulles on this point, saying that the Europeans "ought to have the right, the opportunity, and the capability of responding in kind" to a nuclear strike. *Public Papers of Dwight D. Eisenhower 1957* (Washington, D.C.: GPO, 1958), p. 550.

87. Steinbrunner notes that "military planners had seriously considered directly providing the allies with both missiles *and warheads* as a logical extension of liberalization of weapons control in the United States." *Cybernetic Theory,* p. 175, my emphasis.

88. See Marc Trachtenburg's summary discussion in *History and Strategy,* (Princeton: Princeton University Press, 1991), pp. 184–186.

89. See Gregg Herkin, *The Winning Weapon: The Atomic Bomb in the Cold War* (New York: Vintage, 1982) pp. 114–136. Originally drafted to secure civilian control over atomic technology that would promote peaceful applications

and international cooperation, the MacMahon act was later amended as a result of the spy scandal and increasing concern about Soviet–American relations in the summer of 1946. Herkin notes, indicative of the change in mood surrounding the bill, that a section earlier titled "Dissemination of Information" was changed to "Control of Information" and the military was left with greater responsibility for the stockpile of fissionable materials than had been originally planned.

90. See *New York Times* (February 16, 1957), p. 1; Jeffrey D. Boutwell, Paul Doty, and Gregory F. Treverton, eds., *The Nuclear Confrontation in Europe* (London: Croon Helm, 1985), pp. 12–13.

91. Michael H. Armacost, *The Politics of Weapons Innovation: The Thor–Jupiter Controversy* (New York: Columbia University Press, 1969); *New York Times* (April 13, 1957), pp. 1, 6.

92. Dulles seems to have believed that Adenauer's feelings were on the whole representative of the mood in other European capitals. "Memorandum of Conversation with Chancellor Adenauer, Paris," December 14, 1957, Dulles Papers, General Correspondence and Memos, Box 1, EPL. Trachtenburg discusses German nuclear aspirations and American responses in *History and Strategy*, pp. 180–185.

93. "Memorandum of Conversation with Chancellor Adenauer, Paris," December 14, 1957, Dulles Papers, General Correspondence and Memos, Box 1, EPL; "Memorandum of Conference with Secretary of Defense, Service Secretaries, Joint Chiefs, and Special Assistant for National Security Affairs," June 17, 1958, WHO, OSANSA, Special Assistant Series, 1578 Limited War, EPL.

94. The resolution was vague on operational details, leaving it to NATO military authorities to "prepare a general plan for the posture of these weapons to be decided upon by the council later." "Chronology," Heads of Government Meeting in Paris, December 18, 1957, WHO, OSS, ITM, Box 5, EPL. After a heated domestic debate, the Federal Republic agreed in the summer of 1958 to take a large number of tactical nuclear systems under the dual-key arrangement. Mark Cioc, *Pax Atomica: The Nuclear Defense Debate in West Germany During The Adenauer Era* (New York: Columbia University Press, 1988), ch. 4.

95. Armacost, *The Politics of Weapons Innovation*, p. 188. With limited range (about 1500 miles), liquid fuel, and above-ground basing, the Thor had all the disadvantages of being a vulnerable and tempting target for preemption by Soviet missiles.

96. The set requirement was for between 300 and 700 such missiles. Steinbrunner, *Cybernetic Theory*, p. 176–177.

97. Steinbrunner, *Cybernetic Theory*, p. 184.

98. Dulles argued also that if the United States did not act soon, additional European states would almost certainly develop national nuclear forces on their own and that this would signal the end of both NATO and the emerging EEC. Testimony reported in *U.S. Department of State Bulletin*, May 5, 1958, p. 741. Also see the testimony of Robert Murphy in U.S. Congress Joint Committee on

Atomic Energy, *Hearings Amending the Atomic Energy Act of 1954,* 85th Congress, 2d session, 1958.

99. The JCAE authorized the administration to transfer only enough information that allied troops would be ready to fit warheads to missiles and fire them under dual-key control in the event of war. It approved minimal substantive sharing of weapons design information, and then only with Great Britain. Of course, the cat was already out of this bag, since London had just tested its own H-bomb in 1957. See Steinbrunner, *Cybernetic Theory,* p. 181; Comments by Senator John Pastore, Chairman of the JCAE, in *Congressional Record,* Senate, 1958, p. 11927.

100. Steinbrunner, *Cybernetic Theory,* p. 182. In a briefing immediately following the December 1957 NATO meeting, Dulles had foreshadowed the administration's intentions with regard to the stockpile when he commented that the United States would retain control over the warheads for legal purposes and the right to withhold consent but that in "certain unspecified contingencies consent is automatically given." "Dulles Background Briefing," December 20, 1957, WHO, OSS, ITM, Box 5, EPL.

101. The negotiations were stuck over two issues: whether the consortium would have a mandate to produce additional missiles for national forces once SACEUR's requirements had been met and whether the United States would be committed to supplying warheads for any such missiles. David N. Schwartz, *NATO's Nuclear Dilemmas,* pp. 76–77; Steinbrunner, *Cybernetic Theory,* pp. 184–185.

102. "Memorandum of Conference with the President," June 9, 1959, WHO, OSS, ITM, Box 5, EPL. The National Security Council endorsed the plan in August, despite some expressed concerns about proliferation. The argument was that the allies were quite likely to attain nuclear weapons in any event and that the best outcome from Washington's perspective was for this to happen in the context of "NATO arrangements . . . for holding custody of and controlling the use of nuclear weapons." "Status of Mutual Security Programs as of June 30, 1958," NSC 5819, WHO, OSS, NSC Series, Status of Projects Subseries, Box 8, EPL; "Basic National Security Policy," NSC 5906/1, August 5, 1959, WHO, OSANSA, NSC Series, Policy Papers Subseries, Box 27, EPL.

103. "Pasadena Speech," December 11, 1959, Papers of General Lauris Norstad, Policy Papers, Box 1, EPL. In the summer of 1959, the Draper Committee (President's Committee to Study the United States Military Assistance Program, under the chairmanship of U.S. ambassador to NATO William Draper) argued that SACEUR's requirement for a NATO IRBM would be best met by Polaris, the United States' long-range, solid-fueled, submarine-launched ballistic missile, which could readily be adapted to land-mobile launching platforms. SHAPE agreed, and by the end of 1959 the plan was for the European consortium to produce Polaris missiles from American blueprints and deploy the

missile on trucks and railroad cars. Polaris could easily strike targets deep within the Soviet Union from deployment sites in the Federal Republic.

104. *New York Times* (February 3, 1960), p. 1.

105. "Transcript of Press Conference of February 3, 1960," Anne Whitman File (AWF), Press Conference Series, Box 9, EPL.

106. To Krushchev, Eisenhower wrote "states with major industrial capabilities cannot be expected to be satisfied indefinitely with a situation in which nuclear weapons were uncontrolled and they themselves do not have such weapons for their defense." "Telegram from Herter to U.S. Mission to NATO," summarizing Eisenhower's letter of March 12, March 16, 1960, Norstad Papers, Atomic–Nuclear Policy, Box 85, EPL. The President told Goodpaster that "he had simply said in the press conference what he believed and what he said before." "Memorandum of Conference with the President," February 10, 1960, WHO, OSS, Presidential Subseries, Box 4, EPL. When Herter reminded him of the need for "new legislation to authorize transfer of atomic weapons to our allies," the President responded with the "fixed idea that we should treat our allies properly" and that the JCAE's opposition was a source of "great trouble" in this. "Memorandum of Conference with the President," February 5, 1960, WHO, OSS, Subject Series, State Department Subseries, Box 4, EPL.

107. *New York Times* (February 5, 1960), pp. 1, 12; and (February 10, 1960), p. 4. Representative Chet Hollifield, the senior Democrat, warned the President that he was facing "the greatest debate of our generation."

108. "Memorandum of Conference with the President," September 12, 1960, AWF, DDE Diary Series, Box 53, EPL.

109. Herter said that the White House had not finalized "concrete intentions" for sharing weapons with the allies, and Norstad, while admitting that the MRBM plan was designed to transform NATO into "a multilateral fourth nuclear power," portrayed it as an "idea for discussion rather than a firm proposal." *New York Times* (March 11, 1960), p. 1.

110. "Talking Paper for Secretary Gates: MRBM's for NATO," April 1, 1960, WHO, OSS, Subject File, Department of Defense, Box 2, EPL. According to Herter, the United States here "made a specific offer in fulfillment of the 1957 offer to aid in a second generation IRBM Program for NATO." "Telegram from Department of State to Embassies in London, Paris, Bonn," June 4, 1960, WHO, OSS, ITM, Box 5, EPL. Eisenhower intended for launch authority to rest with SACEUR, but in "discussing the possibility that Congress might seek to stipulate that the post of Supreme Allied Commander be reserved to an American as a condition for providing nuclear weapons, the President said such a condition could not be justified and should not be contemplated." "Memorandum of Conference with the President—NATO Atomic Force," October 4, 1960, WHO, OSS, Subject Series, Department of State, Box 4, EPL.

111. At the Department of Defense, there was early concern over the details of military arrangements for the MRBM force, such as its possible vulnerability

to preemptive strike or to seizure. Later, Defense would press for greater precision on the questions of control, ownership, and authorization to fire the missiles.

112. Steinbruner, *Cybernetic Theory*, p. 188. Others in the State Department also worried that this might be just enough to push Germany toward a national nuclear effort, imitating the French. On Smith's logic, a Germany that was "forced" to acquire its own nuclear weapons in opposition to U.S. and NATO policy might go further than de Gaulle and actually turn away from the West to make a separate deal with the Soviet Union.

113. "The North Atlantic Nations: Tasks for the 1960s," August 1960, WHO, Office of the Special Assistant for Disarmament, Box 9, EPL. A more thoroughly declassified version of the Bowie Report is at the National Archives, although much of the detail on nuclear strategy and nuclear sharing has been removed.

114. Several ambiguous conditions were attached for moving on to the second stage, including the notion that the participating states would have to agree on a precise formula for authorizing launch that would make the weapons invulnerable to being commandeered by any one country. In later discussion, Bowie added the phrase "should the Europeans desire it" as an important condition. "Memorandum of Conference with the President," October 3, 1960, WHO, OSS, ITM, Box 5, EPL. The report itself suggested that fulfillment of new goals on conventional forces should also be a rerequisite.

115. Where Eisenhower was consistently specific was in his rejection of any bilateral alternatives for nuclear sharing. He told Norstad in no uncertain terms that "Germany, France and Britain would all want such weapons. They should be handled as NATO weapons." "Memorandum of Conference with the President," August 3, 1960, WHO, OSS, Subject Series, Department of State, Box 4, EPL; see also "Memorandum of Conference with the President," August 18, 1960, WHO, OSS, Subject Series, Department of State, Box 4, EPL.

116. The President told Bowie that he could "easily convert Adenauer" and that he could sell the plan to the British "in terms that they would be going back to the balance of power, contributing their wisdom, experience, and sturdiness to European affairs." De Gaulle would be more difficult, but with an "intensive effort" he too might be brought on board. "Memorandum of Conference with the President," August 3, 1960, WHO, OSS, Subject Series, Department of State, Box 4, EPL; "Dillon to American Embassy in Paris," August 19, 1960, WHO, OSS, ITM, Box 5, EPL.

117. See "NATO in the 1960s: U.S. Policy Considerations, September 9, 1960, Draft, European Region, WHO, OSS, ITM, Box 5, EPL. This paper favored the MRBM plan as a political gesture and a "symbol of NATO unity" to "assure that nations gain the self-respect and stamina to withstand Soviet bloc threats."

118. "Memorandum of Conference with the President," September 12, 1960,

AWF, DDE Diary Series, Staff Notes, Box 53, EPL. Chairman McCone agreed with Eisenhower "that we would not be able to have vitality on the part of our European partners as long as we refuse to give them weapons." He also told the President that a carefully designed multilateral scheme might be acceptable to the JCAE. Eisenhower complained in response about the JCAE's power to intervene, saying "if the President had in the field of nuclear affairs the same authority the Commander in Chief has in other security affairs, the problem could be readily resolved."

119. "Telegram 1024 from Paris," September 10, 1960, WHO, OSS, ITM, Box 5, EPL. Adenauer told Norstad directly that "Europe must have something in the atomic field." Norstad responded that the "U.S. people are not going to turn over atomic weapons to any country for *independent* use" but offered the MRBM consortium plan as the obvious alternative. Adenauer "demonstrated great enthusiasm for the scheme." When Spaak questioned Norstad about operational details of control over the MRBMs, Norstad reminded him that this was unimportant since the plan was primarily a political, not a military, initiative. He "pointed out that NATO had made much progress without answering unanswerable questions of exactly how the alliance goes to war and thought still further progress could be achieved without doing so."

120. "Memorandum of Conference with the President, NATO MRBM Force," October 3, 1960, WHO, OSS, Subject Series, Department of State, Box 4, EPL; "Memorandum of Conference with the President," October 3, 1960, WHO, OSS, ITM, Box 5, EPL. On Eisenhower's continuing frustration with the JCAE, see "Memorandum of Conference with the President," November 8, 1960, WHO, OSS, Subject Series, Alphabetical Subseries, Box 4, EPL.

121. "Memorandum of Conference with the President, NATO Atomic Force," October 4, 1960, WHO, OSS, Subject Series, Department of State, Box 4, EPL. Eisenhower brushed off Spaak's queries about operational issues for the force. These were unimportant since "the obligation for the United States to act under NATO provisions specifying that an attack on one was an attack on all was clear and there was no doubt it would be observed by the United States." His focus remained squarely on the "psychological benefit to more specifically reassuring arrangements" and on how this would "raise the morale of the NATO members." Also see "Memorandum of Conference with the President, NATO MRBM Force," October 3, 1960, WHO, OSS, Subject Series, Department of State, Box 4, EPL.

122. As it was, Eisenhower told Spaak that he would work to get Congress' approval for the plan, although he again remarked in frustration that this was necessary only because "Congress had reserved for itself as far back as 1947 certain prerogatives which should belong in the executive branch." "Memorandum of Conference with the President, NATO Atomic Force," October 4, 1960, WHO, OSS, Subject Series, Department of State, Box 4, EPL.

123. While he professed reluctance to paint his successor into a corner on the issue, Eisenhower did make a concerted effort to set the terms of the debate for Kennedy in a way that would force the new President to confront early the question of nuclear sharing.

124. "Record of Action, NSC Meeting 467, Action no. 2334," November 17, 1960, WHO, NSC Files, Meetings with the President, Box 5, EPL. The President also sent a personal note to Adenauer on the subject. "President Eisenhower to Chancellor Adenauer," Cable to American Embassy Bonn no. 961, November 26, 1960, WHO, OSS, ITM, Box 6, EPL.

125. "Memo by Herter for Upcoming Ministerial Meeting," WHO, OSS, ITM, Box 5, EPL.

126. The only caveat was that "a suitable formula to govern decision on use would have to be developed to maximize the effectiveness of this force as a deterrent and to establish its multilateral character." "Secretary's Statement at NATO Ministerial Meeting Under Long Range Planning," December 7, 1960, WHO, OSS, ITM, Box 5, EPL.

127. Ibid.: also *New York Times* (December 17 and 19, 1960).

128. Boutwell, Doty, and Treverton, eds., *The Nuclear Confrontation in Europe,* p. 34.

129. See, for example, Kennedy's speech reported in *New York Times* (February 9, 1961), pp. 1, 5. Theodore Sorensen labeled Kennedy's attitude as "pragmatic," which meant that the President "did not look upon either the alliance or atlantic harmony as an end in itself . . . [Europe was] a necessary but not always welcome partner whose cooperation he could not always obtain, whose opinions he could not always accept, and with whom an uneasy relationship seemed inevitable." Theodore C. Sorensen, *Kennedy* (New York: Harper & Row, 1965), pp. 562–563.

130. By 1960, there was a broad consensus among the national security community inside and outside official Washington that something had to be done to revamp massive retaliation and add "flexibility of response" to U.S. strategy. Eisenhower, through his last days in office, was a holdout. See "Memorandum of Conference with the President," November 29, 1960, WHO, OSANSA, Special Assistant Series, Presidential Subseries, Box 5, EPL. Kennedy had long been a critic of massive retaliation—as presidential candidate in 1960 he labeled it a dangerous and incredible doctrine that put the United States "into a corner where the only choice is between all or nothing at all, world devastation or submission." Kennedy, *The Strategy of Peace,* Allan Nevins, ed. (New York: Harper & Row, 1960), p. 84.

131. See memo by Rusk, "Foreign Policy Considerations Bearing on U.S. Defense Posture," February 4, 1961, National Security Files, Departments and Agencies, Box 273, John F. Kennedy Presidential Library (JFKL).

132. *Foreign Affairs* (January 1959), 37:211–235. Wohlstetter roundly crit-

icized Eisenhower's position and argued that the United States had to think seriously about and act on the requirements for fighting a nuclear war in order to maintain deterrence.

133. See my "Interactive Learning in U.S.–Soviet Arms Control," in George W. Breslauer and Philip E. Tetlock, eds., *Learning in U.S. and Soviet Foreign Policy* (Boulder, Colo.: Westview, 1991), pp. 784–824.

134. "A Review of North Atlantic Problems for the Future," March 1, 1961, National Security Files, Regional Security, NATO, General, Box 221, JFKL. The citations in the text are from "NATO and the Atlantic Nations, NSAM-40," April 21, 1961, National Security Files, National Security Action Memoranda, Box 329, JFKL.

135. The directive labeled it "most important to the United States that use of nuclear weapons by the forces of other powers in Europe should be subject to U.S. veto and control." It continued "the United States should urge the United Kingdom to commit its strategic forces to NATO . . . and over the long run, it would be desirable if the British decided to phase out of the nuclear deterrent business. . . . The United States should not assist the French to attain a nuclear weapons capability, but should seek to respond to the French interest in matters nuclear in the other ways indicated above [commit to NATO]."

136. Accordingly, Kennedy began quickly to back off from Eisenhower's MLF proposal. Speaking at the Canadian Parliament in May, the President offered to commit five Polaris subs to NATO at once but only to "look to the possibility of eventually establishing a NATO seaborne force which would be truly multilateral in ownership and control, if this should be desired and found feasible by the allies, once NATO's non-nuclear goals have been achieved." *New York Times* (May 18, 1961), p. 12.

137. Arthur M. Schlesinger, *A Thousand Days: John F. Kennedy in the White House* (Boston: Houghton Mifflin, 1965), pp. 370–388; Sorenson, *Kennedy*, pp. 584–586. Existing contingency plans for defending Berlin were built on the assumption, from massive retaliation, that nuclear weapons would come into play early. McNamara had thought about this problem before the crisis started and had warned the President in May that a defense of Berlin meant almost immediate resort to nuclear war.

138. Schelling argued that any use of nuclear weapons outside the "master plan" would constitute "noise that might drown the message" and thus could not be tolerated. "Nuclear Strategy in the Berlin Crisis," July 5, 1961, provided to me by the author, emphasis in original.

139. Jane E. Stromseth, *Origins of Flexible Response: NATO's Debate Over Strategy in the 1960's* (New York: St. Martin's Press, 1988), p. 38.

140. See "Remarks by Secretary McNamara, NATO Ministerial Meeting, May 5, 1962, Restricted Session," pp. 18–19; Released August 17, 1979 under the Freedom of Information Act. In June 1962, McNamara presented publicly a version of this argument at the University of Michigan, Ann Arbor.

141. From McNamara's speech at the University of Michigan, quoted in *New York Times* (June 7, 1962).

142. Kelleher, *Germany and the Politics of Nuclear Weapons,* p. 161. PALs are basically "electronic combination locks" that inhibit the arming of warheads without proper authorization.

143. Finletter tried to reassure the allies that U.S. strategic forces would meet the requirements for nuclear deterrence. To deploy MRBMs in Europe would be expensive and at best redundant; the force was said to be unnecessary if it did not devolve control and positively dangerous if it did. Steinbruner, *Cybernetic Theory,* p. 207.

144. Deputy Director of Policy Planning Staff Henry Owen became a central voice in this debate when he prepared an April 1962 paper arguing that Kennedy's speech before the Canadian Parliament the previous year could provide a basis for a new MLF proposal.

145. The administration continued to offer a vague promise, to relinquish American control over the force at some point in the future if the Europeans should achieve an unspecified degree of unity. For example, see the statements by Secretaries Rusk and McNamara before the December 1962 NATO meeting, in *New York Times* (December 15, 1962), p. 1.

146. See, for example, Schlesinger, *A Thousand Days,* p. 855; for an alternative view, see two articles by Alastair Buchan, "The Reform of NATO," *Foreign Affairs* (January 1962), 40:165–182; "The MLF: A Study in Alliance Politics," *International Affairs* (London) (October 1964), 40:619–637.

147. See Steinbruner, *Cybernetic Theory,* especially p. 256.

148. This reflects, I think, a standing tradition (frequently associated with John Stuart Mill among Americans) in liberal thought about the inherent virtues of diversity, more than a direct transplant from what we now call economic liberalism.

149. Looking only at the case of the late 1940s, that conclusion might seem tempting. The interpretation would go something like this: once U.S. policymakers recognized that the Soviets were creating an inflexible alliance structure and that the threat to the West might be immediate and military, even Washington with its vast power resources had little freedom to pursue multilateral ideals in its relations with the Western European allies. Multilateralism was an easy victim to the imperative of providing the most security quickly and in the most efficient way possible.

150. For an interesting argument specifying conditions under which hegemons are likely to make more limited investments of power resources in allies, see Joanne Gowa, "Rational Hegemons, Excludable Goods, and Small Groups," *World Politics* (April 1989), 61:307–324.

151. To be explicit about my criteria: structural theories do not accumulate confirmation simply by correlation with historical outcomes. To claim that a historical event is explained by a theory or that a case supports a theory's claims,

the process or causal chain that takes independent variables to dependent variables in the theory should be demonstrably reproduced in the empirical case. Otherwise, the most one can possibly say is that the evidence does not disconfirm the theory, and that is an extremely weak claim when a theory permits a very wide range of outcomes. I discuss this in more detail in my *Cooperation and Discord in U.S.–Soviet Arms Control* (Princeton: Princeton University Press, 1991), chs. 1, 3, and 7. For a different position, see Christopher Achen and Duncan Snidal, "Rational Deterrence Theory and Comparative Case Studies," *World Politics* (January 1989), 61:143–169.

152. Much as Nixon and Kissinger would later do with regard to sharing of nuclear information between the United States and France: see Richard H. Ullman, "The Covert French Connection," *Foreign Policy* (Summer 1989), 75:3–33.

153. By "positive cooperation" I mean cooperation that is more than simply avoidance of shared aversion. See my "Realism, Detente, and Nuclear Weapons," *International Organization* (Winter 1990), 44:55–82. There were always some compromises, most obviously in the case of Turkey.

154. That is, the United States is powerful and ideologically compatible, yet relatively far away and lacking in imperial pretensions. It has nuclear weapons. Finally, it has over the course of the Cold War established a firm reputation for a willingness to make sacrifices for allies when necessary. I discuss further the desirability of the United States as a bilateral ally in "The United States, the Soviet Union, and Regional Conflicts After the Cold War," in George W. Breslauer, Harry Kriesler, and Benjamin Ward, eds., *Beyond the Cold War: Conflict and Cooperation in the Third World* (Berkeley: Institute of International Studies), pp. 382–408.

155. "London Declaration on a Transformed North Atlantic Alliance," issued by Heads of State and Government participating in the meeting of the North Atlantic Council in London on July 5, 6, 1990. I discuss NATO's reformulated strategy and evolving institutional structures in "Does NATO Have a Future," in Beverly Crawford, ed., *The Future of European Security*, forthcoming 1992.

156. I combine here arguments from institutions about Robert Keohane, "International Institutions: Two Approaches," *International Studies Quarterly* (December 1988), 32:379–396; and Joseph M. Grieco, "Anarchy and the Limits of Cooperation: A Realist Critique of the Newest Liberal Institutionalism," *International Organization* (Summer 1988), 42:382–408.

Part 4

❖

INTERNATIONAL CHANGE

❖

8. Multilateralism with Small and Large Numbers

❖

Miles Kahler

MULTILATERALISM, international governance of the "many," was defined by the United States after 1945 in terms of certain principles, particularly opposition to bilateral and discriminatory arrangements that were believed to enhance the leverage of the powerful over the weak and to increase international conflict.[1] Postwar multilateralism also expressed an impulse to universality (John Ruggie's "generalized organizing principles"[2]) that implied relatively low barriers to participation in these arrangements. A ticket of admission was always required, whether a state was acceding to the General Agreement on Tariffs and Trade (GATT) or joining the International Monetary Fund (IMF) and the World Bank. Nevertheless, the price of that ticket was not set so high that less powerful or less wealthy states could not hope to participate.

Closely linked to multilateralism's aspiration to universality and welcoming of large numbers of participants, was a strong leveling impulse. Open admission and nondiscrimination implied that participation did not require the patronage of a great power. Multilateralism was thus associated with another principle that became entrenched as decolonization proceeded after 1945: the sovereign equality of states. Smaller, weaker states were believed to be disadvantaged by bilateralism, nondiscrimination awarded them advantages that had been denied them in the world of the 1930s. In their formal institutional designs at least, most postwar multilateral institutions incorporated a larger role in decision making for states that were not great powers and could not aspire to be.

International institutions embodying these multilateral principles and modes of governance stimulated two critiques. The first, offered by

I gratefully acknowledge the Ford Foundation's financial support for this project. I also thank Stephen Krasner, John McMillan, and two anonymous reviewers of *International Organization* for their comments on an earlier version of this article and Stephen Saideman for his research assistance.

realists, argues that multilateralism will fail because great powers wish to exploit their advantages and pursue their national interests in bilateral bargaining, immune from the scrutiny of other states. The leveling impulse of multilateralism simply does not fit the hierarchical power configuration of the international system. Should they agree to engage in collaborative ventures, great powers will not choose to do so in institutions that risk domination by the many.

The second critique, offered by neoliberals, addresses the univeralist impulse of multilateralism, its preference for global rather than regional or other more limited organizations. The memberships of most global multilateral organizations, less than fifty immediately after World War II, had grown to one hundred or more by 1990. Neoliberal skepticism about multilateralism emphasizes the obstacles to cooperation in groups with large memberships. Any advantages of multilateralism pale when compared with the apparent inefficiencies of such a cumbersome system of rule creation and governance. The formal, conventional agreements on which most multilateral institutions are founded also heighten obstacles to cooperation when compared with the customary accretions that provide a decentralized source for much of international law.

Each of these criticisms of multilateralism confronts anomalies of its own. Realist skepticism must deal with the fact that the most powerful nation in the postwar system, the United States, was also the most fervent and consistent supporter of multilateral norms and procedures. Since others have addressed the question of American motivations in supporting multilateralism,[3] I will not offer an explanation for the anomalous opposition of the United States to bilateralism.

The following section of my article addresses neoliberal arguments that cooperation with large numbers faces significant, perhaps insurmountable, obstacles. Although certain costs do rise with increasing numbers, neoliberal pessimism has been overdrawn. The next section reexamines the history of multilateralism in the postwar decades and discovers that realist and neoliberal arguments find some supporting evidence in state practice: both minilateral "great power" collaboration within multilateral institutions (to reduce the barriers to cooperation raised by large numbers) and bilateral and regional derogations from multilateralism (as the great powers exerted their bargaining power) were commonplace. The weakening or "crisis" of multilateralism in the 1980s, however, has often been attributed exclusively to the regional, bilateral, or other clublike practices that have become increasingly popular over the decade. Equally significant, and more often overlooked, is a need, for the first time since World War II, for "genuine" multilateralism—regimes that incorporate very large numbers of players. More powerful countries in several key issue-areas are no longer willing to accept free riding on minilateral bargains by their weaker counterparts.

The subsequent section describes three separate efforts at regime creation or extension within "large number" multilateralism: the Third United Nations Conference on the Law of the Sea (UNCLOS III); the Uruguay Round of trade negotiations under GATT; and the new negotiations and agreements on the global environment, which include the Vienna Convention on the Protection of the Ozone Layer (1985), the Montreal Protocol on Substances That Deplete the Ozone Layer (1987), and prospective negotiations on global warming. In each of these cases, the principal barriers to cooperation appear to be great power defection rather than any inherent inability to organize cooperation among large numbers of states.

Each of these cases has also produced institutional experimentation to solve the problem of large-number cooperation and has enjoyed a different measure of success. In the final section, these solutions will be examined in light of "new institutionalist" arguments drawn from domestic politics. Without attempting to construct direct analogies from domestic experience, one can discover parallel solutions to the problem of large-number cooperation in the international examples described. Those solutions in turn offer some suggestion of more efficient institutional designs for a world in which large-number multilateral solutions are likely to become more, rather than less, essential.

Cooperation with Large Numbers: The Misplaced Pessimism of the Neoliberals

In neoliberal analyses, large numbers are often portrayed as a nearly insuperable obstacle to cooperation. The neoliberal arguments and the support that they have seemed to offer hegemonic stability theory are based in large measure on a reading of Mancur Olson's *The Logic of Collective Action*. Olson's well-known treatment of the provision of collective goods argues that *"the larger the group, the further it will fall short of providing an optimal amount of a collective good."*[4] Olson provides three reasons for his conflation of size and the likelihood that a group will be latent (unable to provide a collective good): the fraction of the group benefit received by any one individual declines as group size increases; and organization costs increase with an increase in group size.[5]

Both Michael Taylor and Russell Hardin have called into question the intuitive relationship that Olson attempts to establish between group size and the possibility of collective action.[6] As Hardin notes, the second and third assertions by Olson are matters for empirical verification and are not inherent in the logic of his argument. In the case of organization costs, the negative effects of increasing size may be offset by economies of scale in the production of a collective good, an effect that is confirmed by the "piggybacking" of new collective ventures on existing organizations.[7]

Olson's first reason for pessimism is the most interesting and ambiguous, particularly for the large-number instances of cooperation discussed below. Although his argument that individual benefit declines with increasing group size clearly holds for goods characterized by crowding (individual benefit declines as more consume the good), the collective goods provided by many international regimes, including those discussed below, were not of this type. Unlike a private club whose benefits may decline for individual members as the membership grows, the benefits for individual members (nations) in these instances *grew* as more joined the collective arrangement. This effect was particularly striking in the case of the Law of the Sea, where participation approaching universality (or at least very large-number acceptance) was a far superior outcome to any minilateral arrangement. This perception of an increasing cost to free riding has also become characteristic of certain trade agreements under GATT and of recent environmental agreements.[8] Although this characteristic of the collective good may not wholly erase the barriers to large-number collective action, it does suggest a greater likelihood that larger powers will exercise leadership or, in some cases, make side-payments to encourage acceptance of the agreement by other nations.

Dynamic analysis of collective action, particularly the iterated prisoners' dilemma game, emphasizes a different set of obstacles to collective action by large groups. The chief drawback, according to Taylor, is "the *increased difficulty of conditional cooperation* in larger groups."[9] This drawback has been subdivided by Kenneth Oye into a number of specific hindrances to cooperation: declining feasibility of sanctioning, "recognition and control problems" (declining transparency regarding the action of other players), and a declining ability to identify common interests.[10] The principal devices suggested by neoliberals to compensate for these costs of increasing group size for international action are decomposition through subdividing the large-group collective action problem into a series of small-group interactions and institutionalization through the creation of international regimes.[11] Unfortunately, as Oye admits, reducing the size of the group—the minilateral solution—will "generally diminish the gains from cooperation, while [increasing] the likelihood and robustness of cooperation."[12] In other words, the static analysis of incentives to participate would suggest a declining individual payoff that could offset the gains from smaller group size. This declining efficacy of minilateral solutions became characteristic of some of the issue-areas considered below after the 1960s.

Institutionalization through regime creation permits the construction of a thick "network of mutual interactions" that Hardin identifies as a crucial difference between small and large groups.[13] Unfortunately, this solution is bedeviled by the same problem that undermines Olson's argument for the use of selective incentives to encourage collective action: collective action in large groups may be enhanced by regimes *if they exist,* but the regimes must themselves be explained. A convincing explanation for the formation of large-group multilateral arrangements at the international level is still required.

Minilateral leadership by great powers, whether military or economic, will go some distance in explaining the creation and extension of regimes since the 1950s, but that leadership was of diminishing value over time in many issue-areas, as discussed below. Instead, institutional mechanisms for creating and extending regimes to incorporate larger numbers of active participants were required. That this innovation was embedded in an existing network of international institutions was clearly important. Nevertheless, large-number cooperation eventually required new institutional devices that combined the hierarchical structure of many issue-areas with the need for wider participation.

Multilateralism, Minilateralism, and Bilateralism After 1945

Through inflation of the barriers to cooperation among large numbers of nations, hegemonic power has often been portrayed as the only solution to multilateral collective action dilemmas after 1945: collaboration was attributable to the ability of the United States to provide collective goods (while others were free riders) or to sanction those who attempted to free ride on the multilateral bargain. The supposed end of this tale of postwar collaboration has been challenged by Duncan Snidal, who has extended the findings of Hardin to undermine the assumption that international collective goods will only be provided under configurations of hegemonic power. Snidal argues instead that the "major Western economic powers" may continue to engage in collective action, sustaining an existing international economic order in the face of hegemonic decline.[14] Minilateral cooperation may successfully supplant hegemonic power.

Such arguments are given even more force by a different, nonhegemonic story of the postwar years. The obstacles to multilateral institution building were often dealt with not by American hegemony but by creating a core of minilateral cooperation among the economic powers. Even in the early years of the postwar era when the power of the United States in most issue-areas was at its peak, the United States sought collaborators, particularly in Western Europe. Where multilateral institutions flourished, they were typically supported by a minilateral cooperation among the Atlantic powers, a "disguised" minilateralism that provided the essential frame for a multilateral order.

This revision of the hegemonic narrative must go further. Not only did minilateral cooperation lay at the core of postwar multilateralism, but multilateral principles were violated far more often than allowed in conventional accounts. Although minilateral cooperation supported multilateral norms in most cases, multilateralism was also circumscribed by a large number of persistent derogations from its injunctions: its rivals, discriminatory and bilateral forms of organization, were far from vanquished in the decades following World War II.

In a number of issue-areas, disguised minilateralism and lingering bilateralism were significant during the years of apparent American hegemony. Although American military predominance made security relations the least likely arena in which to find these deviations, leadership by the United States was far from unquestioned even in alliance relations. Michael Mastanduno's account of the early years of CoCOM, a system of export controls that the United States engineered as the cold war deepened, indicates that the European allies were able to skirt the controls and expand their trade with the East while lobbying for a relaxation of the regime's rules.[15] Although Steve Weber's account of the North Atlantic Treaty Organization (NATO) places that institution within the multilateral paradigm,[16] NATO was the exception in security relations. As the collective security mechanisms of the United Nations (UN) atrophied, the U.S.-backed security system outside of Europe came to resemble the spokes on a wheel: a series of bilateral treaties with a host of much weaker and dependent allies. This was particularly the case in the Pacific, a second arena of cold war competition where multilateral options, such as the Southeast Asian Treaty Organization, failed to overcome regional divisions and America's overwhelming presence.

The organization of international economic relations frequently demonstrated the same mixture of a multilateralism supported by great power collaboration and diluted by bilateralism. Even the leverage of the Marshall Plan did not permit the United States to impose its version of multilateralism on recalcitrant Europeans. As Alan Milward describes, the United States attempted to use the Organization for European Economic Cooperation (OEEC) as a means to further the integration of Europe according to American design. Despite the preferences and the economic influence of the United States, the "OEEC ended by being no such thing. . . . It marked the defeat of American ambitions for the one, common, unregulated market with an uncontrolled flow of factors which the ECA [Economic Cooperation Agency] wanted to see as the first step toward the United States of Europe." [17]

In global economic organizations, the outlines of minilateralism took longer to emerge. The formula of weighted voting in the Bretton Woods organizations—the IMF and the World Bank—appeared to be a clear indicator of predominant American influence in those organizations. Special majorities (greater than a simple majority) also ensured a continuing American veto over many changes, even as the formal voting weight of the United States declined. As Europe and Japan rebuilt, the same structure of rules also guaranteed them growing power within the organization on the same basis of economic and financial weight. Nevertheless, even in the years of its maximum influence, the United States had to bargain to a greater extent than its predominance may have predicted. [18]

Indeed, Barry Eichengreen's historical survey of international monetary regimes since the nineteenth century finds the same pattern of collaboration among the great powers at the core of most stable regimes: "Despite the usefulness of hegemonic stability theory when applied to short periods and well-defined aspects of international monetary relations, the international monetary system has always been 'after hegemony' in the sense that more than a dominant economic power was required to ensure the provision and maintenance of international monetary stability." [19] The United States also evinced little interest in an all-out campaign against the many remaining discriminatory exchange relationships during the first decade after 1945. Only after the mid-1950s did the IMF launch a "major assault" on the over four hundred bilateral exchange agreements that littered the international landscape.[20]

Ironically, in the trade regime that emerged (by historical accident) under the multilateral principles stipulated in the charter of GATT, one could perceive most clearly by the 1960s the minilateral core of a regime that embodied both multilateral principles and limitations on those principles. The careful hedges in the GATT system also reflected a world in which the great powers still preferred bilateralism for at least some of their trading relationships. The Kennedy Round, characterized by Gilbert Winham as "the first significant negotiation in GATT after the initial negotiation," was also the first in which the United States and the European Community (EC) negotiated as rough equals.[21] That successful round of tariff negotiations also demonstrated the difficulty of translating multilateral, most-favored-nation principles into bargaining practice.

The only practicable mode of negotiation soon became bilateral or minilateral negotiations between the principal supplier and its major importing nations for a particular product; the negotiating group of key countries during the Kennedy Round was aptly named the "bridge club." Concessions negotiated among the dominant traders were then extended to other participants on the basis of most-favored-nation treatment. As a result, Winham argues, "what was a multilateral negotiation in name became a large, complicated series of bilateral (or plurilateral) negotiations in fact. The main action of the negotiation often occurred away from the multilateral chambers."[22] The great power hierarchy that was already apparent in the Kennedy Round became entrenched during the Tokyo Round. As Winham describes, a "pyramidal" structure emerged "where agreements were initiated by the major powers at the top and then gradually multilateralized through the inclusion of other parties in the discussions."[23] In these negotiations, the role for smaller trading countries and particularly the developing countries was small to nonexistent.

Equally significant (and alarming to multilateralists) were the lingering bilateralism of imperial or quasi-imperial relationships and the resurgence of new forms of regional and discriminatory trading relationships. Gardner Patterson's description of the first two decades of the GATT regime could be entitled "embedded bilateralism." No serious effort was made to dismantle existing preferential systems, such as those based in the British Commonwealth or the French Union.[24] Indeed, those systems would ultimately be "multilateralized" into such postcolonial discriminatory arrangements as the Yaoundé and Lomé Conventions, relationships that shared the burdens of development assistance with other European states but did little to constrain the bilateral exercise of influence on the part of ex-colonial powers.[25]

Nevertheless, by the mid-1950s, the international pressure to multilateralize these discriminatory agreements and the fading economic importance of the agreements led some to believe that multilateral norms and institutions would be strengthened in the trade regime. Instead, the decade from 1955 witnessed resurgent interest in two new forms of discriminatory trading relations: regional blocs, for which the model was the new European common market, and bilateral nontariff protectionism, directed primarily at the East Asian industrializers. In addition, the developing countries succeeded in winning agreement to the principle of discrimination in the interests of development. As Patterson indicates, the European initiative was the beginning of a "worldwide movement that was to have reached [by the mid-1960s] such dimensions that just over half of the contracting parties to the GATT would be linked to a regional economic bloc in some stage of development."[26]

The industrialized countries also experimented during these years with bilateral, discriminatory trading arrangements that were ultimately sheltered under the GATT umbrella: the norm of nondiscrimination was given up in order to retain the principle of multilateralism. The most extended and important example of this kind was the successive agreements to manage first one portion and then others of the textile sector. Over time, however, bilateralism inherent in the hybrid textile trade regime grew, and the degree of multilateral oversight declined.[27] By the mid-1960s, often regarded as the apogee of American influence and a high point of multilateralism," discrimination according to source was a widely used and in most policy-formulating circles a thoroughly respectable policy instrument," Patterson notes. "Unconditional-most-favored-nation treatment was under attack from all sides."[28]

Limitations on multilateral principles and practice in the trade regime and in other issue-areas did not mean that multilateralism had no impact. American attachment to multilateral norms did make a difference. The concern of the United States over the proliferation of bilateral restrictions in the textile sector led it to campaign for placing textile agreements under GATT and its multilateral surveillance.[29] As Sidney Weintraub argues, American policy demonstrated an adherence to multilateralism and nondiscrimination, but only in the context of a clear ranking of policy goals: "politics over economics; world leadership over national economic interests; anticommunism over U.S. trading interests; Western

Europe over developing countries."[30] Even a pessimist such as Patterson admitted the value of a multilateral framework in forcing new discriminatory grouping to avoid harm to others and in guaranteeing that those injured by discrimination could have their complaints heard.[31] Nevertheless, the principles of multilateralism in the trade regime were constantly questioned, and the multilateral regime itself was governed by a minilateral structure of the largest trading powers.

Minilateralism was a chosen means of governance for the United States in those issue-areas in which free riding by the other principal economic powers was unacceptable (often for domestic political reasons), additional legitimation was required, and exclusion or threat of exclusion from the regimes was undesirable (often for reasons of international security). The price paid for minilateral collaboration was an institutional structure that placed some curbs on the unilateral exercise of American influence. Derogations from multilateral norms were sometimes an additional price paid for European collaboration. In other instances, bilateralism reflected American preferences in settings where multilateral alternatives seemed unworkable (Pacific security relations) or bilateralism offered the United States increased influence (Latin America).

The minilateral system of governance through great power collaboration that developed in international economic affairs after 1945 came under increasing attack as the number of independent developing countries grew during the 1960s. In the 1970s, a developing country "bloc" view of governance was proposed. This view had found its expression first in the UN Conference on Trade and Development (UNCTAD), which was formalized in 1764, and later in other institutions, existing and proposed. The attempt by developing countries to bring the weight of their numbers and the leverage of their commodity power to bear on governance was subsequently expressed in demands for a new international economic order (NIEO), demands that foundered on worsening economic conditions in the 1980s and heightened ideological resistance by the industrialized countries.

Collapse of the NIEO program could not conceal the need for a new multilateralism in certain issue-areas, however. The major powers could not construct or extend regimes in some cases without the consent and participation of countries outside the club of industrialized countries. If minilateralism was inadequate and a two-bloc model had been ruled out, bilateral efforts were highly inefficient or impossible in many of these cases. The predicament of the industrialized countries had historical precedent. After World War I, the International Commission for Air

Navigation began as an effort at collaboration among countries most successful at exploiting the new aviation technology. The members of this proto-regime soon discovered that the price for greater legitimacy and wider compliance with new rules was a change in the governance of the regime. In giving up some of their governing power, however, the core members defined the commission's competence very narrowly and continued to combat efforts to extend majority principles of voting—a perfect precursor of one strategy that was followed decades later by the industrialized countries.[32]

If the great powers rediscovered a need for resurrected multilateralism in the 1980s, the developing countries also redefined their interests in ways that made them likelier allies of the smaller industrialized countries in sustaining a multilateral structure. Although the North–South divide had hardly disappeared, the interest of the developing countries in preserving multilateral checks on the bargaining power of the biggest players—an argument for multilateralism that had always been powerful among the smaller industrialized states—grew as they opened their economies in the 1980s. As the heterogeneity of the developing world increased, the appeals of bloc action in the interests of the NIEO declined as well.

Recognition of a need for new collaborative bargains that moved from great power minilateralism to more multilateral modes of governance does not produce such bargains, however. Bargaining was made more complicated by the rapid expansion of membership in the UN, GATT, and IMF since 1960, illustrated in figure 8.1. Although sheer membership numbers had always merited these institutions the label "multilateral," new issues forced their memberships and governance to confront a need for large-number collective action. In the most recent efforts at regime construction or innovation, one begins to detect institutional devices that may permit successful completion of bargains within a large-number multilateral framework.

Multilateralism with Large Numbers: An Examination of Three Cases

The cases of UNCLOS III, the Uruguay Round, and global environmental agreements illustrate the declining efficacy of minilateralism as a basis for multilateral regimes. In each instance the industrialized countries found the free riding of key developing countries increasingly costly, yet

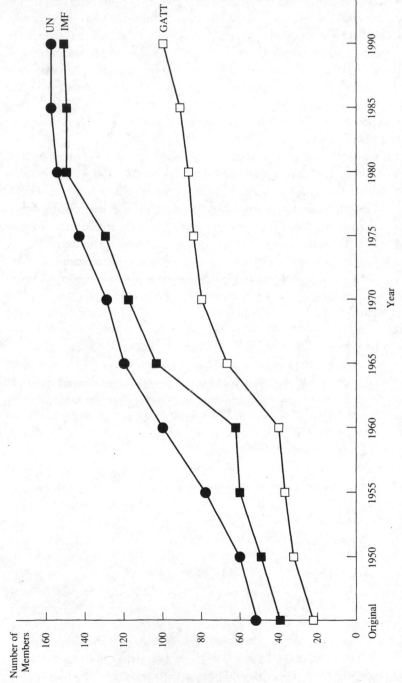

Figure 8.1. Membership in International Organizations Since Founding

Sources: United Nations (UN), *Yearbook of the United Nations* (New York: UN, various years); International Monetary Fund (IMF), *Annual Report* (Washington, D.C.: IMF, various years); and General Agreement on Tariffs and Trade (GATT), *Focus Newsletter* (Geneva: GATT, various years).

an alternative mode of collaboration and governance—a minilateral club (with the possibility of exclusion) or bilateralism—was also unattractive. A major part of the institutional innovation that took place stemmed from the search by industrialized countries for an institutional forum and decision-making rules that would retain the hierarchy of their interests and influence in each issue-area. Any innovation also had to meet the demands for wider influence and participation on the part of smaller countries. Governance became a pressing issue as members searched for new devices to ease collaboration among large numbers of countries.

The three cases also illustrate the shift in developing country preferences from a bloc model of governance (most apparent in negotiations over the Law of the Sea) toward an acceptance of decision-making formulas that reflect both the heterogeneity of the developing countries and their principal bargaining asset—numbers. Finally, these cases suggest that the line between bargaining to create or extend a regime on the one hand and efforts to maintain a regime on the other has become increasingly blurred: bargaining and rule making in the new environmental regimes seem likely to occur with little break.

THE THIRD UNITED NATIONS CONFERENCE ON THE LAW OF THE SEA

UNCLOS III was the most ambitious effort to modify a multilateral regime using multilateral negotiations since 1945. Refusal by the American government to accept the final bargain, negotiated over a period of six years, has obscured much of the meaning of these negotiations. They have been cast as the last of failed efforts to construct a NIEO rather than the first negotiations in a new multilateralism that, despite its slow pace and cumbersome procedures, managed to produce a set of complex bargains among a very large number of states. The negotiations achieved that end without ceding principal negotiating responsibility to the great powers (whose representatives often seemed to have little power in these negotiations) and without limiting bargaining to a purely North-South arena.

The global negotiations represented by UNCLOS III had been preceded by efforts on the part of major maritime powers to construct minilateral or regional arrangements that would confirm new rules governing national control over the oceans and their resources.[33] Several features of the oceans regime eroded the hierarchy that would have permitted a stable pattern of great power collaboration. As the issue of territorial limits rose in prominence, the distribution of resources favored the industrialized and maritime states less. Any developing (or communist) state with a lengthy coastline could thwart the achievement of a coherent set of rules. Moreover, the imbalance of coercive means (and the willingness to use those means) between the major powers and smaller, coastal states had diminished. But the threat of minilateral clubs was not limited to the maritime powers. The Latin American coastal states, leaders in the extension of national control over the continental shelf, formed a relatively coherent group that could plausibly constitute a regional regime if global negotiations failed.[34]

By 1970, minilateral and regional options appeared as distinctly second-best solutions, however. Relentless extension of national claims over maritime resources and activities pushed the maritime and industrialized countries toward global negotiations in a UN framework, one that offered them few institutional advantages. In addition, developing country members of the UN General Assembly has in 1969 voted a moratorium on any efforts to exploit the resources of the seabed outside national jurisdiction. By this nonbinding instrument, they had called into question the legal framework for any seabed mining attempted by the industrialized countries or their corporations.[35] In doing so, they created additional pressure for negotiations and a new regime.

For their part, the maritime and industrialized powers could threaten unilateral action under existing international law if their interests were overridden, a credible option given their technological and economic advantages.[36] Both the maritime and the developing countries had a strong interest in a legitimate global regime that was widely ratified. The conference was mandated to achieve one "package deal," not a series of separate treaties, and this linkage increased the leverage of the developing countries. Achieving such an institutional bargain with a large number of participants and a complicated agenda required a series of institutional innovations.

The voting rules of UNCLOS III contributed to the breadth of a final agreement but clearly reduced the efficiency of negotiation. In a preparatory session for the conference, the developing countries had conceded the majority voting rules that typically governed the UN General Assembly. Instead, the conference would be governed by consensus; the search for consensus could be determined to have failed only by a two-thirds vote of those present and voting, provided that the two-thirds majority included at least a majority of the states participating in the session. Although the formula on which the states finally agreed was believed to protect the interests of the developed and maritime powers, it also protected any minority interests, including those of the landlocked and geographically disadvantaged states, which possessed little leverage apart from their votes in the conference.[37]

The consensus rules adopted by the conference guarded against an exit by any influential group of participants (and some not so influential). Unfortunately, it took considerable time for the conference committees to devise institutions that would enhance the efficiency of decisions made cumbersome by the search for consensus. Although the major maritime powers were able to guarantee that no agreement would be reached over their objections, they were not able to control the proceedings through their normal conference roles in the general and drafting committees.[38] Given the large number of participants, one device that might have been employed in UNCLOS III was representation. Unfortunately, the formal structure of groups that emerged during the conference did not fully capture the interests of states: the predominant groupings were regional (including both coastal and landlocked states) and the Group of 77 (G-77). In such circumstances, creating a representative structure based on the existing groups was unlikely to be successful.[39] Other, more fluid and issue-specific groups, which cut across preexisting cleavages (such as the coastal states), lacked institutionalization and, because of their size, had difficulty agreeing on a common policy stance.[40]

Finally, however, ad hoc measures produced reasonably representative groups on a scale appropriate to negotiation. In Committee I, which was charged with the legal regime of the deep sea bed, the formula that succeeded in reducing group size without generating resentment over exclusivity was one that rotated representation among members of the committee. In addition, the G-77 organized a "contact group" as a channel for the views of those who were not part of this negotiating group. In this way, as Mohamed El Baradi and Cloe Gavin argue, Committee I "found a way to negotiate which both reduced the number of negotiators to a functional level and concurrently gave the rest of the delegates a sense of indirect but effective participation."[41] In other instances, the interested parties simply made bargains that created "strong focal points for wider agreement" without the need for formal rules of representation.[42] Perhaps the most important of these groups was the Juridical Experts Group, commonly referred to as the Evensen Group, which began meeting in 1973. Despite its effort to appear representative, it tended to mirror the views of coastal states. Moreover, it was criticized for its "elitist approach to the negotiations" by those who were not members of the group, a further indication of the ideological obstacles to constructing representative negotiating for UMS at the conference.[43]

UNCLOS III was unusual in its wariness of another familiar device that facilitates collective action: delegation. In earlier conferences of this size, a first draft was typically produced by a committee of experts delegated the task by conference participants. That was not the case with UNCLOS III. It was only during the 1975 Geneva session that the participants "out of desperation" delegated the preparation of an informal single negotiation text to the heads of the three main committees, a decision born of the failure to reach agreement on formulas for representation. That decision to delegate in turn increased the effective power of developing country views and created tensions with the United States.[44] In negotiations over the financial aspects of a seabed authority, Chairman Tommy Koh invited a group of "financial experts" to work with the group; even here, however, formal delegation was avoided.[45]

UNCLOS III, which seemed to its critics to epitomize the weaknesses of collective action at the global level, did nevertheless construct a complex bargain that appeared to satisfy most participants. The structure of that bargain was not minilateral great power leadership later extended to other participants—an option that had been ruled out as impracticable throughout the negotiations. Nor did the strong element of North–South bloc bargaining that many had feared survive the complexities and conflicting interests of the lengthy negotiations. Instead, through a messy and often ad hoc process of institutional innovation, the participants negotiated rules that both satisfied the major powers and won the necessary consent of the developing countries.

That bargain failed, ironically, because of shifting ideological winds in the United States. During the Carter presidency, the United States began to toy with minilateral possibilities once again, as an expression of American displeasure with the sixth session of the conference. At that time, the U.S. government decided to persevere in the global negotiations.[46] The Reagan administration, however, found the agreement on seabed mining too costly. In deciding to free ride on the global agreement that had been reached, it argued that the consensus of those negotiating was not new, conventional law but was instead a reflection of customary law that supported U.S. claims as a maritime power. As James Sebenius notes, the Reagan administration also relied on bilateral ties to key straits states and on the implicit threat of unilateral military action if U.S. claims were challenged.[47] The U.S. government's unwillingness to accept the new multilateral bargain and its efforts to reassert both hierarchy and selective bilateralism as part of its strategy point to a weakness in efforts to extend multilateral governance. In a reversal of the benevolent image of hegemonic power, the strong exploit the weak and their desire for rules that will constrain the more powerful. The failure of UNCLOS III in its final stage, however, could not be attributed to the impossibility of large-number multilateral governance in an issue-area of considerable complexity.

THE URUGUAY ROUND

Although the structure of GATT and the negotiations it oversees differ from those of the Law of the Sea, the current Uruguay Round demonstrates many of the same dilemmas of large-number multilateralism.[48] While the impetus for a new round of trade negotiations came primarily from the United States, smaller trading powers played a major role in the launching of the round at Punta del Este in September 1986. They have also played an active role in certain of the issue-areas being considered in the negotiations, although the limitations of small-group coalitional activity have become apparent as the negotiations have become more specific.

The logic of greater involvement by smaller trading countries coincided with movement away from the purely minilateral or bipolar logic of the Tokyo Round and closely resembled the changing interests represented in UNCLOS III. The United States sought not only a new round of trade negotiations but also a controversial extension of GATT into services and other new areas as well as a strengthening of GATT institutions. In addition, the industrialized countries were no longer willing to accept the free riding of developing countries on such issues as intellectual property rights. The desire for inclusion of key developing countries in these negotiations and the need for a consensus in extending the GATT regime gave the developing countries and smaller industrialized countries more leverage than they had possessed in earlier rounds.[49]

Some of the larger developing countries opposed the attempt to launch a new trade round, since a backlog of trade issues of much greater interest to them—issues such as safeguards and textile trade restrictions—still remained on the old agenda. Winham's account of the launching of the Uruguay Round portrays this opposition by the Group of 10 (G-10), led by Brazil and India, as the principal developing country effort to influence the new round. According to Winham, the G-10 effort was predictably overwhelmed by the hierarchical (American- and European-dominated) structure of power in the trading system: "In the end the main surprise was that the resistance had been as effective and as long-lasting as it turned out to be."[50]

The story told by Colleen Hamilton and John Whalley, which is a far more interesting one, indicates that coalitional activity on the part of developing countries took two paths.[51] The G-10 effort to organize resistance to the inclusion of services in the new negotiations was only the first. Other developing countries instead supported a second draft declaration proposed by a group of smaller industrialized countries, which consisted of Australia, Canada, New Zealand, and five members of the European Free Trade Association. Developing countries supporting the draft declaration of this group grew to nearly fifty in number and included such significant players as Colombia (cosponsor with Switzerland of the text), Indonesia, Thailand, and Venezuela. In endorsing this text, a large group of developing countries had defined their interests as defending the multilateral trading system through support for a new round of trade negotiations.[52]

These two declarations, with a third from Argentina, were put before the ministerial meeting that was to launch the new round at Punta del Este. In this case, much like that of UNCLOS III, divisions among the participants were too deep to allow for delegation of the task of constructing a draft for consideration by all voting parties. At the ministerial meeting, initiation of a new round was placed in doubt not only because of G-10 opposition to the new agenda but also because of European, and particularly French, resistance to efforts to place agriculture on the agenda.[53] At this point, institutional devices were critical in reinforcing coalition building in support of the round described above. The chairman tried to reduce the unmanageable size of the negotiation group first by establishing a "little plenary," next by forming a "consultation committee" consisting of invited members representing the major interests at the meeting, and ultimately by supplementing these groups with two parallel groups dealing with services and agriculture.[54]

These mechanisms, however, did not break the negotiating deadlock. Instead, waning support for the positions of the G-10 members and the French was finally overcome by the consensual decision-making rules of GATT. According to Winham, the United States threatened to force a formal vote, which might have overturned the progress already made. Face-saving gestures offered to the most recalcitrant, coupled with fear of isolation in the context of a consensual institution, brought the hold-outs around. The successful conclusion of the ministerial meeting demonstrated that "the will of a large majority is ultimately persuasive in a consensual organization even in the face of a powerful and determined minority."[55]

What Hamilton and Whalley call the agenda-moving role of the lesser powers in GATT was not the only effective course of action by these powers in the Uruguay Round.[56] The Cairns Group of Fair Trading Nations, which was formed in 1986, demonstrated the same coalitional behavior across the North–South divide in favor of a particular agenda item: agriculture. As characterized by Richard Higgott and Andrew Cooper, the Cairns Group is "a heterogeneous group of states bound together in the pursuit of a specific single interest."[57] Other informal groups that organized around particular interests (such as the De la Paix Group, concerned with strengthening the GATT system) proliferated during the negotiations, but the Cairns Group, led by Australia, has played the most prominent role in making proposals during the negotiating process.[58] Whether its interventions in the round merited it the title of a "third force" in agricultural negotiations between the United States and Europe and whether the group has provided focal points for agreement that might eventually bridge the gap which led to breakdown in December 1990 are two matters of debate.[59] The Cairns Group's North–South composition and its ability to maintain coherence despite strains on its unity do mark it as a different sort of player in the multilateral arena, one that might permit the representation of interests in a setting of large numbers.

As Hamilton and Whalley argue, however, a move from joint proposals to actual negotiations is a large step, and it is in detailed discussions within the Uruguay Round negotiating groups (fourteen for goods and another for services) that the final bargains must be struck.[60] The formation of negotiating coalitions is a formidable task: broad coalitions representing a variety of trading interests, such as the EC, face complicated internal negotiations that simply replicate the cumbersome character of the multilateral forum. Single-issue coalitions, such as the Cairns Group, face strains because their members assign to that issue differing degrees of importance when weighed against other issues.

The Uruguay Round's successful conclusion will be determined, as past multilateral trade negotiations have been determined, by agreement among the major trading powers, particularly the United States and the EC. Nevertheless, from the start of the Uruguay Round, a purely minilateral structure of negotiation was regarded as unacceptable to the industrialized countries. Their desire for wider compliance with an extended

GATT structure of rules required changes not only in the substance but also in the procedures and governance of the negotiations. Whether the expanded number of active participants in the Uruguay Round can reach agreement is the stiffest test since 1947 of GATT multilateralism. A failure of the negotiations would, however, more likely result from an inability of the major trading powers to reach agreement than from the inability of a revived framework of multilateralism to accommodate expanded participation.

GLOBAL ENVIRONMENTAL REGIMES

The record of the "new" multilateralism in GATT is not yet clear; global negotiations on the environment provide even less hard evidence on the adaptability of multilateralism. These new exercises in regime creation share with those described above the need for adhesion on the part of many, if not all, developing countries: great power agreement and small-economy free riding will not be enough.[61] A need for large-number participation in any regime to deal with chlorofluorocarbons (CFCs) or greenhouse gases places these negotiations squarely within the dilemmas of the new multilateralism. In addition, like the Law of the Sea and GATT negotiations, these efforts at regime construction remained colored by North–South divisions at the same time that new mechanisms were created for collaboration across the North–South divide. In the case of CFCs, however, since the contribution of the developing countries to the problem of ozone depletion lay primarily in the future, reaching a cooperative outcome was somewhat less complicated—at least on the question of numbers—than in the other examples.

Negotiations for the Vienna Convention on Protection of the Ozone Layer (1985) and the Montreal Protocol on Substances That Deplete the Ozone Layer (1987) initially took a minilateral form, since the major producers and consumers of CFCs are industrialized countries. But as Richard Benedick points out, from the start "the major CFC-producing and -consuming countries had recognized that their actions alone would be insufficient to protect the ozone layer."[62] During negotiations for the Montreal protocol, Mostafa Tolba, the executive director of the UN Environment Programme (UNEP), functioned as an active broker for agreement and served as a proxy for or representative of parties (primarily developing countries) that were not present in the minilateral discussions. In addition, however, the developing countries that participated in the negotiations, including Argentina, Mexico, and Venezuela, also voiced the interests of the nonparticipants and exercised leadership in pressing for more stringent controls on CFCs.[63] The number of developing countries taking part in the negotiations grew from only six in December 1986 to over thirty at Montreal in September 1987.[64]

Despite developing country participation, the crucial negotiations on control measures were essentially minilateral and involved countries with a substantial presence in the current CFC market. Nevertheless, the Montreal protocol did contain some incentives to encourage the developing countries to avoid large-scale production of CFCs. For example, it offered a grace period of ten years during which they could continue to increase their consumption. A number of major developing countries, including Brazil, China, and India, declined to join the protocol, however, until clear undertakings regarding technology transfer and financial incentives were made in June 1990.[65]

It was in the negotiations following agreement on the Montreal protocol that developing countries played a central role, negotiations in which the key industrialized participants in the new regime bargained to win accession from at least those developing countries whose absence would eventually fatally weaken the regime.[66] The new negotiations centered not on the grace period of CFC usage that had been incorporated in the Montreal agreement but instead on assistance to enable the developing countries to move rapidly to alternative technologies designed to substitute for CFC use. Negotiations in London in June 1990 on revision of the protocol centered on governance of the new multilateral regime as well as on provisions for both financial assistance and technology. The familiar North–South lines seemed to be drawn: industrialized countries opposed the creation of new institutions, while developing countries demanded more control over governance and greater guarantees for financial assistance and expeditious technology transfer.

The final compromise owed a great deal to an ingenious voting formula that governed not only future changes in CFC reduction schedules (of concern to the developing countries) but also oversight of the new fund. The United States preferred weighted voting, which would have awarded control to the industrialized countries. The developing countries on the other hand, argued for a two-thirds majority rule. The compromise solution established a two-thirds majority rule, but one that had to subsume simple majorities from both North and South. Thus, both the industrialized countries and the developing countries had the capability to block decisions. This rule, applied to votes of the parties as a whole, also provided a means for China, India, and other key developing countries to accept assurances on technology transfer and accede to the protocol. The leverage awarded the developing countries under this formula permitted any future dissatisfaction on their part to threaten the further development of the regime.[67]

The construction of a regime to reduce the emission of gases that produce global warming is likely to be much more difficult than the creation of the CFC control regime was, since the scientific data on global warming are more uncertain and the range of economic activities affected is potentially far greater.[68] James Sebenius, however, offers a plausible model for a global warming regime that parallels the two-track, minilateral template of negotiations followed in Vienna and Montreal. The major contributors to greenhouse gases, the industrialized countries, would negotiate a framework regime of emission controls that would begin a reduction in levels before the regime was "globalized." The design of any new institutions would need to take developing country interests into account and to provide attractive incentives for eventual accession.[69]

Several issues will need to be addressed for this approach to succeed. Since the developing countries will need to be involved in the negotiations in some fashion to encourage future participation, many of the large-number issues thus reappear, albeit in less critical form. If the price that the developing countries demand for accession is too high, the members of the convention might be forced to apply selective sanctions to induce compliance. The question remains whether the parties to such a convention could serve collectively to bring about compliance. And, of course, this model assumes greater ease of agreement among the largest economic powers than between the industrialized and the developing economies, an assumption that recent American policy places in doubt.[70]

Institutional Solutions for the New Multilateralism

In the issue-areas described, a need for regime creation or extension involving large numbers of states became apparent. On the one hand, from the point of view of the major industrialized countries, great power collaboration with continued free riding on the part of smaller countries became less desirable. On the other hand, the smaller industrialized countries and growing numbers of developing countries came to see multilateral institutions, however imperfect, as preferable to a world of resurgent bilateralism. Larger numbers have begun to play a more active role in supporting these institutions in the face of threatened defection or conflict among the great powers. This new multilateralism, however, requires changes in governance that entail significant departures from small-group minilateralism. In each of the cases described—UNCLOS III, the Uruguay Round, and the creation of a regime to control CFCs—the participants, using a combination of past experience and trial and error, devised institutions that permitted large-group collaboration to succeed.

The study of domestic political institutions should be applied with care to the international realm. Nevertheless, solutions to collective action problems in domestic political institutions with large numbers of actors, such as legislatures, demonstrate certain parallels to the solutions devised in the international realm. The realist distinction between an anarchic international sphere and domestic politics may be overdrawn in any case. As Kenneth Shepsle has observed, in a legislature, there is no "exogenous enforcement mechanism, like an umpire or a court of law" to enforce agreements among members.[71] In the cases described above, one can often detect a groping toward devices that will permit collective decision making when leadership is unclear and influence is more widely diffused.

In both domestic politics and in international relations, institutions help resolve the tension between efficiency in decision making and the legitimacy conveyed by wider participation. Several institutional devices familiar from domestic politics have served as a means of adaptation to large-number multilateralism. These include voting systems, representation, delegation, and reduction in numbers, each of which is described in further detail below.

Voting systems, once central in the study of international organizations, have been regarded as superfluous in most recent analyses of international institutions. Neorealist arguments have convinced many that, whatever the formal voting in these organizations, the weight of the great powers and their threat of exit will find expression in policy. The fact that governments bitterly contest voting rules suggests that these institutional devices are more important than current scholarly opinion allows.[72] In the three cases described above, the system of voting (or not voting) was central to the ability to achieve a cooperative outcome.

Voting systems in international institutions, however, display important differences from those in domestic models. Domestic parallels with voting systems in multilateral regimes must be modified to take into account the threat that nations, particularly large ones, may exercise the exit option and leave the negotiated bargain. Simple majority voting rules are therefore less common in international politics. The appropriate analogies on this dimension would appear to be highly divided or faction-alized political systems that require elaborate means of protecting the rights of minorities who might take the exit option of secession or civil war. In addition, equality in voting power (one nation, one vote) is less common than it is in domestic politics: voting systems reflect the hier-archy of capabilities in the international system. The only domestic parallel would be systems that awarded multiple votes to particular classes of the population, a phenomenon that had faded in most political systems by the twentieth century.

Historically, states have sought to protect their interests by instituting a unanimity rule for many international institutions. The costs for effi-ciency in decision making have been so high, however, that even under the League of Nations unanimity was increasingly disregarded in prac-tice.[73] Multilateralism after 1945 seemed to mark a turn toward majority voting on the basis of the equality of states. But the minilateral core of many postwar economic organizations was supported by important devia-tions from these voting rules. Two voting devices in particular supported great power collaboration within multilateral regimes: weighted voting and special or super majorities (majorities greater than a simple majority), which have been combined in such organizations as the IMF and the World Bank.[74] By allowing the key actors to exercise blocking power on questions that affect their core interests (thereby ensuring a consensus of the most influential as the basis for a winning coalition) and by granting those actors as a group a majority or substantial plurality of the votes, such voting systems permit majority voting or action by consensus much of the time. Although such systems may add efficiency, particularly when compared to unanimity rules, their critics argue that agreement on appropriate criteria for weights and periodic decisions to readjust those weights can be contentious. In addition, if the minilateral coalition is too dominant and undivided, smaller states may simply exit the institution or free ride on its decisions.

In many cases, including institutions with elaborate formal systems of weighted or majority voting, such as the IMF, prevailing practice favors consensus decision making.[75] Consensus in itself is a convention worthy, of further investigation, however. Its core is the search for a substantial positive majority without the divisive consequences of a vote or the barriers to efficiency posed by a formal unanimity rule. (The ability of states to abstain permits the unanimity principle to be preserved.) Under the opaque exterior of consensus undoubtedly lie rules of thumb not only concerning the degree of consensus that must be achieved but also concerning which of the parties must be included—rules of thumb often based on the formal voting rules. One suspects that most institutions have a tip point at which a large majority becomes a consensus, a rough marker at which the bandwagon begins to roll. Consensus as a decision rule also implies a high degree of delegation to the consensus builder, whether it be the head of a committee or a permanent member of the secretariat.

Each of the instances of multilateralism with large numbers described above was shaped by the voting and decision rules applied. A broad agreement, involving more than the most powerful actors, was ensured by consensus decision making at UNCLOS III (with a two-thirds majority rule underpinning it) and at the start of the GATT Uruguay Round. The bandwagon effect that a consensus rule could have in the face of a die-hard minority was clearly observable in the Uruguay Round case: successive rounds of negotiations and face-saving gestures rendered the position of the die-hards more and more untenable. In the crafting of the Montreal protocol and during successive negotiations on CFC emissions, a multilateral bargain was obtained by an innovative voting formula borrowed from commodity organizations: distributed majority voting, in which concurrent majorities from distinct sets of participants are required. This mechanism has bridged the North–South divide in a number of instances by permitting either of two "parties" to block an unwanted action. In many respects, the mechanism is reminiscent of "vote pooling" to encourage the building of consensus in ethnically divided societies.

Representation is a another plausible institutional device for improving the chances for collective action by reducing decision-making numbers. In the cases described above, however, representation seemed to be difficult to engineer on more than an ad hoc basis. The Bretton Woods organizations have elaborate systems of constituencies, organized largely on geographical bases; the UN elects members to the Security Council. Given these precedents and the familiar pattern in international organizations of a plenary body electing an executive body, it is striking that participants in UNCLOS III, the Uruguay Round, and the environmental negotiations were unable to agree on simple systems of representation. In the Law of the Sea negotiations, two barriers were apparent. First, established representative entities, such as the G-77, did not capture the central interests of states in the negotiations. Also, governments disliked exclusion from the negotiations, an obstacle resolved by the institution of a "contact group" to ensure communication between representatives and those represented. The shape of any decision to strengthen the GATT system of governance should indicate whether more attention will be paid to representative formulas as an aid to large-number collaboration.

More widely used than representation in these cases is delegation. This device, which can take many organizational forms, has received much attention from students of domestic politics.[76] Although considerable resistance to delegation is apparent in the examples of large-number multilateralism presented here, delegation was often a crucial part of successful collective action. Responsibility was delegated on the basis of position (to the committee heads in UNCLOS III and to the executive director of UNEP) or on the basis of expertise. Delegation to experts has been at the core of the functionalist view of international institutions; but in these recent cases, it is striking how seldom such delegation took place, although experts were frequently consulted. The lack of institutionalized delegation suggests that the new multilateralism may be more political and less technocratic than the old. The cases described here, however, also suggest that the role of a broker in achieving consensus becomes increasingly important as numbers grow. Mostafa Tolba, executive director of UNEP, played this role in the Vienna and Montreal convention negotiations. The variation in and limits to delegation in large-number cases is an important issue for further investigation.

Finally, these cases demonstrate the value of a reduction in numbers, with minilateral decision making and negotiation occurring within the multilateral framework. Traditionally, small-number collaboration has been hierarchical, with great power agreements later extended to those outside the club. More recently, two significant new forms of small-group collaboration, both of which are horizontal rather than hierarchical, have emerged. First, the small group can serve as a "broker," creating a focal point for a negotiating equilibrium. The Cairns Group (or at least Australia) seems to have cast itself in this role in negotiations over agriculture in the Uruguay Round. Moreover, Sebenius has argued, informally constituted small negotiating groups played a similar role in UNCLOS III.[77] Second, horizontal minilateralism can take the form of a two-track model of extending a regime. The role of a "progressive club within a club" is apparent in recent environmental negotiations and has been used as a means of reaching an agreement more ambitious than the lowest common denominator.[78] Recent free trade agreements, such as those between the United States and Canada and between Australia and

New Zealand, could be regarded in this way. Other examples are the EC's exchange rate arrangements and the Vienna and Montreal model of environmental regime building. As Cromwell Riches noted regarding interwar international institutions, two-track differentiation offers a safety valve for organizations that would otherwise face exit by those wishing to forge ahead or by minorities that cannot accept an accelerated pace.[79] Such minilateralism needs to be embedded in the larger multilateral institution, however, to prevent free riding by those who are not participants and to prevent deviation from institutional norms by those who are.

Conclusion: The Future of Multilateral Governance

The collective action problems posed by multilateral governance were addressed for much of the postwar era by minilateral great power collaboration disguised by multilateral institutions and by derogations from multilateral principles in the form of persistent bilateralism and regionalism. In certain issue-areas, such as international monetary affairs and economic policy coordination, it is likely that great power minilateralism will continue to dominate, since the collaboration of lesser economic powers is neither necessary nor desirable from the point of view of the United States, Japan, and the EC. In several other issue-areas, however, the ability of minilateralism to produce satisfactory cooperative outcomes had eroded by the 1980s. To obtain the cooperation of less powerful states, it was necessary to negotiate not only the substance of a new bargain but also new modes of governance, incorporating large numbers of participants and their interests.

In this respect, certain issue-areas are developing multilateral governance for the first time. Some have despaired of the possibility of reaching cooperative bargains in a world of large numbers. The accounts here of several early experiments in large-number collaboration give grounds for greater optimism. The achievements should not be overstated: the results of UNCLOS III were ultimately rejected by the United States; the Uruguay Round of trade negotiations may yet fail; and negotiations on global warming will be far more difficult than those that produced the Vienna and Montreal agreements on CFCs. Nevertheless, in these narratives two features are prominent. First, failure or the threat of failure did not result from the inefficiencies of large-number collaboration but, rather, from the inability of the great powers to reach agreement. (The negotiations to revise the Montreal protocol in 1989–90 are partial exceptions to this observation.) Second, through an uncertain process of experimentation, institutional mechanisms that eased at least some of the burden which numbers placed on cooperation were discovered.

Although institutional devices have received the most attention here, their role should not be overstated. In the cases examined, the fact that the collective goods at issue permitted exclusion, particularly in the trade regime, served to discourage free riding; and side-payments were employed in the Montreal protocol revisions. In addition, the substance of the bargains struck was not evaluated: the content of cooperation, not simply its existence, needs evaluation. In the new world of multilateral governance that is making its halting appearance, however, the institutions of collective action will become increasingly important. Careful institutional design will be required to achieve the difficult balancing of decision-making efficiency and legitimacy (compliance) that is necessary for successful multilateralism with large numbers.

NOTES

1. This aspect of multilateralism is described by Richard Gardner in *Sterling-Dollar Diplomacy* (New York: Columbia University Press, 1980), pp. 42–47 and 56–62.

2. See John Gerard Ruggie, "Multilateralism: The Anatomy of an Institution, chapter 1 of this volume.

3. See Steve Weber, "Shaping the Postwar Balance of Power: Multilateralism in NATO," chapter 7 of this volume.

4. Mancur Olson, *The Logic of Collective Action* (New York: Schocken, 1968), p. 35; emphasis in the original text.

5. Ibid., p. 48.

6. Michael Taylor, *The Possibility of Cooperation* (Cambridge: Cambridge University Press, 1987); and Russell Hardin, *Collective Action* (Baltimore: Johns Hopkins University Press, 1982), chap. 3.

7. Hardin, *Collective Action*, p. 43.

8. This aspect of certain collective goods is a key assumption in Chamberlin's critique of Olson. See John Chamberlin, "Provision of Collective Goods as a Function of Group Size," in Brian Barry and Russell Hardin, eds., *Rational Man and Irrational Society?* (Beverly Hills, Calif.: Sage, 1982), pp. 197–212, and the comments by Barry and Hardin, p., 196. Some of these collective goods also resemble the lumpy goods described by Taylor in *The Possibility of Cooperation*, pp. 51–53.

9. Taylor *The Possibility of Cooperation*, p. 12; emphasis in the original text.

10. Kenneth Oye, "Explaining Cooperation Under Anarchy," in Kenneth Oye, ed. *Cooperation Under Anarchy* (Princeton: Princeton University Press, 1986), p. 19.

11. Ibid., pp. 20–21.

12. Ibid., p. 21.

13. Hardin, *Collective Action,* p. 228.

14. Duncan Snidal, "The Limits of Hegemonic Stability Theory," *International Organization* 39 (Autumn 1985), p. 612.

15. Michael Mastanduno, "Trade as a Strategic Weapon: American and Alliance Export Control Policy in the Early Postwar Period," *International Organization* 42 (Winter 1988), pp. 121–50.

16. Weber, "Shaping the Postwar Balance of Power."

17. Alan S. Milward, *The Reconstruction of Western Europe, 1945–51.* (Berkeley: University of California Press, 1984), p. 169.

18. For an account of these years, see Miles Kahler, "The United States and the International Monetary Fund: Declining Influence or Declining Interest?" in Margaret P. Karns and Karen A. Mingst, eds., *The United States and Multilateral Institutions* (Boston: Unwin Hyman, 1990), pp. 94–97.

19. Barry Eichengreen, "Hegemonic Stability Theories of the International Monetary System," in Richard N. Cooper et al., eds., *Can Nations Agree?* (Washington, D.C.: Brookings Institution, 1987), p. 287.

20. See Gardner Patterson, *Discrimination in International Trade: the Policy Issues, 1945–1965* (Princeton, N.J.: Princeton University Press, 1966), pp. 54–60. These agreements concerned not only East-West trade but also a substantial part of the trade within Western Europe and Latin America. By 1963, they had been whittled down to agreements that concerned state trading countries.

21. Gilbert R. Winham, *International Trade and the Tokyo Round* (Princeton, N.J.: Princeton University Press, 1986), p. 34.

22. Ibid., p. 65.

23. Ibid., p. 376.

24. Patterson, *Discrimination in International Trade,* pp. 14–15.

25. On the Lomé Convention, John Ravenhill, *Collective Clientelism: The Lomé Conventions and North–South Relations* (New York: Columbia University Press, 1985).

26. Patterson, *Discrimination in International Trade,* pp. 140–141.

27. On the evolution of the textile trade regime, Vinod K. Aggarwal, *Liberal Protectionism: The International Politics of Organized Textile Trade* (Berkeley: University of California Press, 1985).

28. Patterson, *Discrimination in International Trade,* p. 388.

29. Aggarwal, *Liberal Protectionism,* pp. 78–80.

30. Sidney Weintraub, "Selective Trade Liberalization and Restriction," in Ernest H. Preeg, ed., *Hard Bargaining Ahead: U.S. Trade Policy and De-*

veloping Countries (New Brunswick, N.J.: Transaction Books [ODC], 1985), p. 170.

31. Patterson, *Discrimination in International Trade,* p. 390.

32. This interesting history is recounted in Cromwell A. Riches, *Majority Rule in International Organization* (Baltimore: The Johns Hopkins University Press, 1940), pp. 267–272.

33. Ann L. Hollick, *U.S. Foreign Policy and the Law of the Sea* (Princeton: Princeton University Press, 1981).

34. Barry Buzan, *Seabed Politics* (New York: Praeger, 1976), p. 134.

35. Ibid., pp. 99–100.

36. Mohamed El Baradi and Cloe Gavin, *Crowded Agendas, Crowded Rooms, Institutional Arrangements at UNCLOS III* (New York: UNITAR, 1981), pp. 4–6.

37. See Hollick, *U.S. Foreign Policy and the Law of the Sea,* p. 282; Buzan, *Seabed Politics,* pp. 216–218; Edward Miles, "The Structure and Effects of the Decision Process in the Seabed Committee and the Third United Nations Conference on the Law of the Sea," *International Organization* (Spring 1977), 31:180–185; James K. Sebenius, *Negotiating the Law of the Sea* (Cambridge, Mass.: Harvard University Press, 1984), p. 13.

38. Hollick, *U.S. Foreign Policy and the Law of the Sea,* pp. 378–379.

39. Miles, "Structure and Effects of the Decision Process," p. 232.

40. Buzan, *Seabed Politics,* pp. 138–139.

41. El Baradi and Gavin, *Crowded Agendas, Crowded Rooms,* p. 19.

42. Sebenius, *Negotiating the Law of the Sea,* p. 209.

43. Hollick, *U.S. Foreign Policy and the Law of the Sea,* p. 304; Buzan, *Seabed Politics,* p. 264.

44. Hollick, *U.S. Foreign Policy and the Law of the Sea,* pp. 299–300, 378.

45. Sebenius, *Negotiating the Law of the Sea,* p. 26.

46. Hollick, *U.S. Foreign Policy and the Law of the Sea,* p. 363.

47. Sebenius, *Negotiating the Law of the Sea,* p. 91.

48. For an account and documentation of the issues in the Uruguay Round and the early phases of the negotiations, see Sidney Golt, *The GATT Negotiations, 1986–90: Origins, Issues and Prospects* (London: British–North American Committee, 1988).

49. For an excellent account of the negotiations leading to the Uruguay Round, see Colleen Hamilton and John Whalley, "Coalitions in the Uruguay Round," working paper no. 2751, National Bureau of Economic Research, Cambridge, Mass., 1988.

50. Gilbert R. Winham, "The Prenegotiation Phase of the Uruguay Round," in Janice Gross Stein, ed. *Getting to the Table: The Processes of International Prenegotiation* (Baltimore: Johns Hopkins University Press, 1989), p. 54.

51. See Hamilton and Whalley, "Coalitions in the Uruguay Round," pp. 17–18.

52. Ibid.

53. See ibid., p. 18; and Winham, "The Prenegotiation Phase of the Uruguay Round," p. 59.

54. Winham, "Prenegotiation Phase," pp. 60–61.

55. Ibid., p. 65.

56. Hamilton and Whalley, "Coalitions in the Uruguay Round."

57. See Richard A. Higgott and Andrew Fenton Cooper, "Middle Power Leadership and Coalition Building: Australia, the Cairns Group, and the Uruguay Round of Trade Negotiations." *International Organization* (Autumn 1990) 44:601. This source provides a detailed account of the history and activities of the Cairns Group.

58. On other groups, see ibid., p. 591; and Hamilton and Whalley, "Coalitions in the Uruguay Round," pp. 32–36.

59. In "Middle Power Leadership and Coalition Building," Higgott and Fenton argue that the Cairns Group has played such a role. In The Prenegotiation Phase of the Uruguay Round," however, Winham argues that the great powers have continued to be predominant in the bargaining.

60. Hamilton and Whalley, "Coalitions in the Uruguay Round."

61. See James K. Sebenius, "Crafting a Winning Coalition: Negotiating a Regime to Control Global Warming," in Richard Elliot Benedick et al., eds. *Greenhouse Warming: Negotiating a Global Regime* (Washington, D.C.: World Resources Institute, 1991), p. 79; and Eugene B. Skolnikoff, "The Policy Gridlock on Global Warming," *Foreign Policy* (Summer 1990) 17:84–85.

62. Richard Elliot Benedick, *Ozone Diplomacy: New Directions in Safeguarding the Planet*. (Cambridge: Harvard University Press, 1991), p. 99.

63. Ibid., pp. 6, 69, and 101–2.

64. Ibid., pp. 69 and 74.

65. See Richard Elliot Benedick, "Ozone Diplomacy," *Issues in Science and Technology* (Fall 1989) 6:49–50; and Sebenius, "Crafting a Winning Coalition," pp. 80 and 91.

66. As Benedick notes in *Ozone Diplomacy*, p. 150, the threat posed to the Montreal regime was real. By 1989, three of the prospective largest consumers of CFCs had ratified the Montreal protocol, but only fourteen developing countries had become parties.

67. This account is drawn from the excellent narratives presented by Benedick in *Ozone Diplomacy*, pp. 178–89.

68. For one pessimistic view of the possibilities for negotiating a regime of global limits on greenhouse gases, see Michael Grubb, "The Greenhouse Effect: Negotiating Targets," *International Affairs* (January 1990) 66:67–89.

69. Sebenius, 'Crafting a Winning Coalition," pp. 90–91.

70. See William K. Stevens, "At Meeting, U.S. Is Alone on Global Warming," *The New York Times*, September 10, 1991, pp. B1 and B8.

71. Kenneth Shepsle, cited by Mathew D. McCubbins and Terry Sullivan in

Congress: Structure and Policy (New York: Cambridge University Press, 1987), p. 315.

72. On some of the controversies concerning voting during the 1970s, see Stephen Zamora, "Voting in International Economic Organizations," *American Journal of International Law* (July 1980) 74:583–88.

73. See C. Wilfred Jenks, "Unanimity, the Veto, Weighted Voting, Special and Sample Majorities and Consensus as Modes of Decision in International Organisations," in *Cambridge Essays in International Law* (London: Stevens & Sons, 1965).

74. On the Bretton Woods organizations, see Frederick K. Lister, *Decision-Making Strategies for International Organizations: The IMF Model* (Denver, Colo.: University of Denver, 1984); Zamora, "Voting in International Economic Organizations," pp. 576–78; and Joseph Gold, "Weighted Voting Power: Some Limits and Some Problems," *American Journal of International Law* (October 1974), pp. 687–708.

75. On consensus decision making see John Kaufman, *Conference Diplomacy: An Introductory Analysis* (Dordrecht: Martinus Nijhoff, 1988), pp. 24–25; and Jenks, "Unanimity, the Veto, Weighted Voting, Special and Simple Majorities and Consensus," pp. 55–62.

76. See, for example, D. Roderick Kiewiet and Mathew D. McCubbins, *the Logic of Delegation: Congressional Parties and the Appropriations Process* (Chicago: University of Chicago Press, 1991).

77. Sebenius, *Negotiating the Law of the Sea,* p. 209.

78. Peter H. Sand, "Preserving the Global Environment: The Challenge of Shared Leadership," background paper prepared for the American Assembly, Arden House, Harriman, N.Y., 1990, p. 19.

79. Riches, *Majority Rule in International Organization,* p. 106.

9. Multilateralism and Security: Prospects in Europe

Patrick M. Morgan

> The most important and indeed most neglected question in contemporary international relations scholarship is: what will the West do, when and if the Soviets decline? How we answer that question will perhaps determine whether there will be war or peace in our time.
>
> *Raymond Aron*[1]

AMID the satisfactions that recent developments in international politics afford practitioners and analysts is one they have been denied. Few can claim they foresaw these events and said so. Analysts who have emphasized that the field has difficulty coping with change have now been borne out.[2] Revolution in the Soviet Union, its foreign policy transformation, the obliteration of the East–West dispute, the reorganization of Europe—none were anticipated.

Envisioning profound change in the Soviet system was crippled by neglect of the steam of reformist thinking that percolated through Soviet political history, neglect that bred a skepticism that lasted well into the Gorbachev era and reinforced the reservations displayed in its first year by the Bush administration.[3] The best advice available on Eastern Europe was to "settle in for a long haul of evolutionary change" and recognize the absence of "any genuine prospect of German reunification." Even a volume devoted to the theme that "the time might now be right for dramatic and lasting changes in the Eastern Bloc's domestic as well as foreign policies" stopped well short of predicting the collapse of the old order.[4]

For some time James Rosenau has been insisting that "global politics is, at all levels, undergoing enormous change. New economic, social, and political structures are emerging and old ones are being transformed."[5] However, analysts tended to approach the notion of fundamental change, particularly on cooperation to enhance security, with all the skepticism of shoppers for used cars. The most compelling goal of security cooperation would be to forestall systemwide warfare, but influential analyses suggested that systemwide war was linked to the predictable decline of a hegemonic state, something that seemed to characterize the present era.[6] Equally pessimistic was the view that systemic war is "the principal mechanism of change throughout history" for a system in serious disequilibrium, offering dim prospects for less apocalyptic methods of adjustment.[7]

Analyses focused precisely on the U.S.–Soviet rivalry, including explorations of past cases of rapprochement, have been extremely tentative about the chances for a major breakthrough and certainly did not describe as the critical first step the ideological/political reorientation of one contestant.[8]

Security has been seen as a particularly difficult area for cooperative arrangements and practices. The literature on alliances suggests they are of uncertain duration and value.[9] High hopes for arms control eventually yielded in the 1970s to a consensus on the serious obstacles to effective and durable agreements.[10] With anarchy as the starting point, analysts contend that states have no choice but to view cooperation with suspicion and rely heavily on their own efforts. Thus one reaction to recent developments is the prediction that they will diminish cooperation and return Europe to a multipolar system under which "the prospects for major crises and war in Europe are likely to increase markedly."[11]

The Opportunity

Recent developments in East–West relations are certainly striking in view of all this. An epidemic of cooperative inclinations and activities has broken out. They are now pursued to deal with formerly severe political issues and security problems, from U.S.–Soviet relations to the Persian Gulf, on an unprecedented scale. This is occurring in advance of or alongside many other kinds of interchanges we have long believed would have to precede and lay the groundwork for fundamental political and security cooperation. We would seem to have an improbable cart running before an underdeveloped horse.

The emergence of a significant opportunity for refashioning great-power relationships, possibly for enhancing order and security, has usually been seen as closely associated with either great-power warfare or its near outbreak. For some analysts, a systemwide war supplies the opportunity by creating a new distribution of power, rights, and responsibilities that is, for the time being, beyond challenge. In another version it is not (or not just) these results of the war but its terrible consequences—and thus a fervent desire to avoid another one—that drives great powers to attempt cooperative management of their affairs. [12] Short of war, it has been proposed that an exceedingly serious crisis can be the catalyst, inducing steps to ease the political conflict that brought it about and opening the door to cooperation. [13]

Thus recent developments were a surprise. They arrived after a long great-power peace and were not provoked by a grave international crisis. Some suggest that the East–West dispute was the functional equivalent of a great war, provoking a similar interest in cooperative management. However, the long peace has also regularly been cited as evidence that nuclear deterrence, hardly the ultimate in cooperative management, is a quite satisfactory way of coping instead. Thus it is hard to see why great powers have now responded to the long peace in one way, enhanced cooperation, rather than the other—stable nuclear deterrence amid serious political competition.

Preoccupation in the field with system-level analyses and processes meant undervaluing domestic sources of state behavior—in this case of Soviet foreign policy. Added was an understandable insensitivity to the implications of domestic difficulties in Soviet-bloc nations. That those governments lacked ideological appeal, were bureaucratically stultified, and faced serious economic problems and ethnic tensions was the standard Western view. But prior hopes that fundamental changes were brewing had been followed by disappointing reforms and no fundamental shift in Soviet (and bloc) approaches to security. Soviet interest in cooperative management seemed confined to something like a superpower duopoly placed to supervise a continued global conflict between East and West.

The opportunity today arose, therefore, from a fundamental reordering of Soviet perspectives and priorities under Gorbachev. ("The most far-reaching changes in international politics involve changes in national goals and values." [14]) Although a sharp shift in a great power's foreign policy goals can readily emerge from a domestic political crisis, past examples—the French Revolution, the Russian Revolution, the rise of Hitler—are hardly reassuring about the implications for great-power cooperation. What is distinctive about the present case is that the domestic changes are (thus far) not, and not intended to be, of a sort that set the Russians apart from and at odds with other major states. Thus it need not have the disruptive consequences of the earlier examples. (Of course, we have to keep our fingers crossed!)

Its benign impact is readily apparent in Europe. The critical conflict in the East–West dispute was always over Europe, especially Germany. The Cold War and the division of Europe were artifacts of the division of Germany, which was, in turn, an awkward but effective solution to the German problem. It is probably correct that a more cooperative approach to the ordering of Europe after the war was handicapped by the availability of this one.[15]

The shift in the former Soviet foreign policy reopened the entire matter, and the postwar structure for maintaining a modicum of security in Europe has now dissolved. The division of Germany has ended. Soviet military power in Central and Eastern Europe is evaporating. The old order in Eastern Europe is gone, and with it the division of Europe. The superpower status and capabilities of the former Soviet Union have disappeared as the national community unravels. Another bulwark of the old structure—an ample American military presence and political leadership—is also fading as its rationale, or at least the only rationale capable of commanding domestic political support, slips away.

No one was prepared for all this, and uncertainty is inevitable when the piers on which analysis and policy have rested are being washed away. Hence it is understandable that a new European security structure is not ready for unwrapping and trouble-free installation. What is striking is the rapid emergence of efforts at a multilateral approach and a fair degree of consensus about what it should look like. The devil may yet be in the details, but the early steps have proceeded with minimal difficulty. The goal is to seize the "opportunity for the incorporation of the Soviet Union into an international system based on the notions of interdependence and restraint"[16] and in so doing to settle old issues and construct arrangements that will repress the emergence of new ones. The following are key components of the consensus.[17]

1. A Unified Germany
   While unification can be ascribed to fading fears about Germany due to its good behavior, it is also a reflection of confidence in multilateralism as the way to preclude both an uncontained Germany and the reemergence of a Europe of separate, competing nations within which Germany was so dangerous.
2. Erasing the Division of Europe

Alongside elimination of the hostile alliances, an end to the political division is expected via emergence of comparable political cal systems, particularly in the major nations. Democracy is expected to eliminate ideological cleavages, contain pursuit of destabilizing foreign policies, and facilitate a high level of cooperation that tempers fears and suspicions. There is a parallel belief in the salutary effects of comparable economic systems, accompanied by a high level of economic interaction and, ultimately, integration. This means a high level of Western trade, aid, and investment vis-à-vis the East. Everyone agrees that it is appropriate to anticipate the eventual expansion of the European Community into, among other places, Eastern Europe. Moreover, emphasis is placed on eliminating the division in intellectual and cultural realms via the collapse of the previous barriers to flows of people and information.

3. Substantial Arms Reductions

    Large cuts in forces, especially offense-configured units and weapons systems, are underway, along with the removal of all Soviet and most U.S. forces from Central Europe, cuts in German forces, and reductions in or removal of the other forces stationed in Germany. Nearly every nation has instituted defense budget cuts of some magnitude. American and the former Soviet tactical land-based nuclear weapons are now being eliminated, and major reductions in strategic nuclear forces are now under way. While these measures further reduce security concerns and enhance mutual confidence, their most important objective is to embody and reinforce *the principle that war is unacceptable in Europe.*

4. Reaffirmation of Existing Borders

    No government now sees challenges to borders as compatible with security in Europe. However, popular consensus does not extend to the sanctity of existing national communities. Thus the real threat of loss of territory facing various governments comes from separatist ethnic groups, which other governments have therefore been quite reluctant to endorse or encourage.

5. U.S. Participation

    The United States has been so intimately associated with the security structure now being dismantled that its participation and support are taken as vital for the design and implementation of a new one, not least in Washington. There is also the necessary American role in negotiating reductions in forces in Europe.

6. Institutionalization

Strong interest exists in new agreements and in either creating new institutions or refurbishing existing ones. The agreements, actual or intended, cover arms reductions, general norms of behavior, new economic relationships, and regular processes of political consultation that could eventually encompass provisions for the management and resolution of disputes. As for the institutions, a variety of plans and proposals have appeared, including [18]:

> adapting NATO into an all-European security framework
> expanding the European Community
> enlarging and strengthening the Council of Europe
> mounting a new version of the Marshall Plan
> establishing a new all-European parliamentary assembly

While these have not yet been adopted, several others are now being implemented, including the East European Development Bank. The Paris Agreements envision discussions on establishment of a Conference on Security and Cooperation in Europe (CSCE) parliamentary assembly of Europe, perhaps based on the meeting of parliamentarians under the Council of Europe. The agreements also provide for [19]:

> a biannual meeting of CSCE heads of state or government
> a Council of Ministers for Foreign Affairs, to meet annually
> a Committee of Senior Officials to prepare Council meetings,
>   implement decisions, and possibly deal with emergencies
> a CSCE follow-up meeting every two years
> a CSCE Secretariat (in Prague)
> a Conflict Prevention Center, with a Consultative Committee
>   of the chief negotiators from the Confidence and Security
>   Building Measures (CSBM) talks
> an Office for Free Elections (in Warsaw)
> an annual CSBM meeting at the Conflict Prevention Center
> a new communication system for priority messages on CSBM
>   matters

Multilateralism

To understand what is going on in Europe we need to refine our conceptual equipment. Virtually nothing that has happened in these matters, and the way it has happened, can be explained by reference to standard theoretical perspectives in the field, and they may well be of limited value for anticipating the future. This applies in particular to fundamental cooperation on peace and security.

The project of which this paper is a product has been an effort to update and significantly refashion our concept and understanding of multilateralism. Leading governments reacted to the astonishing developments of 1989–1991 by declaring their readiness to undertake unprecedented adventures in multilateralism to enhance regional (European) and global security. The term is now clearly out front and the phenomenon is getting top billing. We need a coherent conception to match.

A detailed discussion of multilateralism opens this volume, and only limited comments are needed here. Multilateralism is elaborate and demanding compared with many other cooperative endeavors among states. It involves recurring interaction among a set of states (at least three) on the basis of some generalized principles of conduct, rather than by considerations linked to specific situations or particular conditions and concerns. This is not, in itself, distinctive, because norms are a regular feature of international politics, and norm-driven interaction in the form of regimes is common.[20] Hence what distinguishes multilateralism is not the existence and application of norms per se but rather the fact that the states involved seek to use them to push cooperation among themselves to an unusual level, by precluding behavior commonly displayed or mandating behavior that is relatively uncommon, which includes extending cooperation into realms of interaction where it is usually absent.

Following from this is that the collection of states to which multilateralism applies agree to treat themselves, on the relevant matters, as indivisible. All subscribe to principles that apply to each, and expectations of this guide their decisions and behavior. Accompanying such an arrangement, and an important contribution to it, are expectations of diffuse reciprocity so that participants can anticipate benefits of their association over an extended time frame rather than look for them only in a quid-pro-quo fashion in approaching each interaction.

Distinguishing here between the institution of multilateralism and multilateral organizations is important. The former can exist without being given expression through elaborate organizations, and the existence of an organization with several member states is no guarantee that the members are actually pursuing multilateralism.

Finally, multilateralism is an approach to *international politics* and not an escape from it, a way of achieving quite a large measure of cooperation among what remain separate and sovereign states. Thus many steps that carry a set of states toward integration are multilateral, but once it arrives, then the relationship is no longer multilateral.

With respect to multilateralism in security, the original conception of the League of Nations is a good illustration.[21] Members were to constitute a community for safety. Principles of conduct included not using force unless authorized by the League to combat aggression and ready participation in any such league-sponsored endeavor. Benefits were available to a member threatened with aggression or attacked, within the expectation of reciprocal treatment for the other members in the future. The League also turned out to be a good example of the gap that may exist between multilateralism and the operation of a multilateral institution.

To describe contemporary multilateralism in Europe a brief comparison with the Concert of Europe may be helpful. Although the nineteenth-century Concert was not a well-developed exercise in multilateralism, some of the latter's salient features were already present.[22] More was involved than is encompassed by describing it as a "regime" or a collectively operated balance-of power-system.[23] It originated in the strong desire to avoid great-power wars in the wake of the Napoleonic struggles. Elements of the Concert included[24]:

- great-power assumption of responsibility for "the peace of Europe"
- great-power acceptance of certain norms and attitudes: respect for treaties; noninterference in each other's internal affairs; no unilateral action or aggrandizement, particularly on territorial questions (at least in Europe); participation (under a unanimity rule) in all major decisions
- equal status for great powers and no humiliation of any of them
- limitations imposed on internal instability and revolution

As a result of these principles, the great powers: "did not seek to maximize their individual power positions, they did not always take advantage of other's temporary weaknesses and vulnerabilities, they made more concessions than they needed to, and they did not prepare for war or quickly threaten to use force when others were recalcitrant."[25]

The best description of what resulted is provided by Paul Schroeder, who refers to it as a "political equilibrium." It included the enjoyment of stability and peace, freedom from threats and isolation, and recognition by the great powers of each other's legitimate interests and status. "In objective terms, political equilibrium required that (1) the rights, influence, and vital interests claimed by individual states in the international system be somehow balanced against the rights, influence, and vital interests claimed by other states and the general community and (2) that a balance or harmony exist between the goals pursued by individual states, the requirements of the system, and the means used to promote one's interests. Oversimplified, political equilibrium meant a balance of satisfactions, a balance of rights and obligations and a balance of performance and payoffs, rather than a balance of power." [26]

Parallels between the Concert and multilateralism are clear. The participants accepted the view that they were lodged within a system, that their actions had to be conditioned by concern for peace on the continent. They embraced, imperfectly it is true, generalized principles that envisioned common enjoyment of certain rights and responsibilities. A well-developed expectation of diffuse reciprocity existed. Also relevant is the fact that rules applied without elaborate international organizations, very much in keeping with the distinction in this volume between multilateralism and multimember organizations.

Then what are the differences between the Concert and multilateralism in Europe today? The essence of the matter is as follows. The Concert was an adjunct to anarchy; the participants agreed to coordinate their behavior to moderately manage what clearly remained a system of separate states and societies. Their cooperation was limited to security matters and negatively motivated by a fear of war and revolution. They retained the right to use force, agreeing only to suspend its implementation. Today's multilateralism arises from a broader, deeper conception of Europe (and North America) as a community. It is an attempt to have an association of states for security grow out of a shared civilization and be one expression of it. Forgoing the use of force is not just derived from fear but is an essential component of the community. Respect for the rights and interests of the members of a limited association (the Concert) is turned into respect for a broader membership's more elaborate necessities for health and welfare, so that security is much more an instrumental value than the end product of their cooperation.

Like the Concert, member difficulties are not an opening for exploitation and securing unilateral advantage and can become grounds instead for the extension of assistance. But the assistance now being undertaken goes beyond stabilizing regimes to helping to create and sustain healthier societies. The denial of exploitation has meant that the crumbling of the East's military position is accompanied by important reductions in Western forces and the offer of new security arrangements meant to be of equal benefit to all participants. It has also meant consistent support for the survival of central governments, especially in the Soviet Union, and strong reluctance to recognize breakaway republics.

As in the Concert, concern arises today that the major members not experience outright humiliation, which has taken some doing. None of the major shifts—German reunification, in Eastern Europe, in troop cuts—has been allowed to appear as direct exploitation of Western superiority.[27] Extensive consultation with Moscow, often leaving it the initiative, was accompanied by immense praise for the Soviet leadership, subsidies for Soviet expenses, and concessions to the Soviet Union's great-power status. Hence an elaborate effort was made to cater to Soviet views and concerns on the Persian Gulf war and the Middle East negotiations, ignoring the incapacity of that government to claim a major role on the basis of its current capabilities.

For institutionalization, the Concert used periodic high-level conferences to confront problems and resolve issues—the relevant institution was directly related to the goal of security and order. Now much discussion takes place about what comparable institutions of the new multilateralism should be like—a redesigned NATO, adjusted CSCE, strengthened WEU (Western European Union), etc. This tends to obscure the fact that, since security is to grow out of burgeoning interactions of an elaborate community, the crucial institutions for security are, in large part, not security oriented. The EC is expected to play the main role in providing security by containing Germany, not by acquiring an official security function but by deepening Germany's interdependence with its neighbors.[28] In the same way, the relationships deemed vital for security often have little to do with it overtly—they concern flows of people, ideas, and goods within a context of shared views about how best to organize the participants' economies, societies, and political systems.

Explanations

Two questions naturally arise. Where does this pronounced inclination toward multilateralism come from? And is a multilateral approach along these lines to be considered a reasonable possibility—can it be fully established and is it likely to be effective for the foreseeable future?

To tackle the first we need to give some attention to the fact that security has not been considered a highly promising target for cooperative endeavors. This is not for lack of proposals.

After the conclusion of every great war, in 1648, 1713–1714, 1763, 1783, 1801, 1807, and 1809, there had been statesmen who desperately yearned for peace, wanting not just peace treaties but durable peace settlement.[29]

The nineteenth century brought the Concert of Europe, the twentieth saw the League of Nations, arms control efforts, and the United Nations. The great powers have been more interested in cooperation to avoid really serious warfare than they are traditionally given credit for. As the failures nonetheless piled up, one result was an emphasis on the nature of international politics itself as the source of the difficulty.

The culprit is normally said to be anarchy. On the international system, "its organizing principle . . . is anarchy in the literal sense of the term, meaning the absence of formal organs of government. . . . It is anarchy that creates the insecurity that is the fate of every country."[30] This anarchy is somehow connected with conflict and is thus harmful to cooperation.

Conflict is common among states because the international system creates powerful incentives for aggression. The root cause of the problem is the anarchic nature of the international system. "Each state living under anarchy faces the ever-present possibility that another state will use force to harm or conquer it. Offensive military action is always a threat to all states in the system."[31]

If anarchy is indeed responsible we still must explain why. Otherwise we are simply treating anarchy as equivalent to insecurity, which seems unwise since many states do not seem to behave as if being attacked is an "ever-present possibility." The literature on strategic surprise emphasizes that decision makers often have difficulty in taking the possibility of an attack seriously, even from a hostile state.[32]

One possible explanation is that states may be aggrandizers in an environment of scarcity, so much so that they are quite willing to resort to force. The contribution of anarchy is the absence of authoritative restraint. Thus anarchy is *facilitative*—the root cause is the existence of potentially lethal conflicts among states, which, as anarchy leaves states on their own, makes each open to attack and therefore insecure. If this is the case, then a resolution of political conflicts between two states or a set of states would reduce their insecurity—anarchy would not stand in the way of cooperation. This is one implication of Rock's recent study of great-power rapprochement and is what the Kupchans suggest in stating that a security dilemma can be greatly eased "when the major powers hold compatible views of an acceptable international order and share a minimum sense of political community."[33]

Another possibility is that anarchy itself incites mistrust. The most notable variant of this is the security dilemma, under which unilateral steps for protection produce collective insecurity. In another variant anarchy *creates* political conflicts, as in the following:

> States seek to survive under anarchy by maximizing their power relative to other states, in order to maintain the means for self defense. . . . Thus, states seek opportunities to weaken potential adversaries and improve their relative power position.[34]

Thus anarchy forces states into competitive behavior that generates political conflicts.

This powerful and attractive analysis is, nonetheless insufficient. The obvious answer to the insecurity fostered by anarchy is cooperation, and it is necessary to explain why cooperation is impractical or impossible. States cooperate for many purposes, sometimes quite effectively. With respect to preventing great-power warfare, states once cooperated to good effect over an extended period of time in the nineteenth century. Cooperation is evidently not impossible. If achieving security unilaterally is a grave concern, a considerable burden, and beyond the resources of most states most of the time, and if the costs of suffering an attack and the warfare that would result are extremely severe, then cooperation to achieve security ought to be very appealing. Of course, states can respond to this by cooperating in alliances. But an alliance is really a way of spreading the costs and achieving better management of a continuing insecurity arising from the possibility of being attacked. It is not the security that eliminating that possibility would provide. The latter is of particular interest in the treatment of multilateralism here.

One reason cooperation may be impractical is that states are selfish. Caring only about their own security, each readily finds the cost of sustaining cooperative security arrangements unacceptable if its own security is not at stake—and cooperation collapses. Selfishness also means that resorting to force for the state's own purposes (abandoning cooperation) is at times appealing. Thus it is difficult to get the necessary cooperation initially and to sustain it over time. States cannot take the risk of relying on cooperation to keep safe because the defection of others is plausible. This is reinforced by the stakes involved.

> Not only is security the most highly valued goal because it is a prerequisite for so many things, but the security area is unforgiving. Small errors can have big consequences, . . . Temporarily falling behind others can produce permanent harm.[35]

This is a powerful argument. Politics is often licensed selfishness, and tension between the general welfare and a self-interested desire for gain that contravenes the general welfare is ubiquitous. Nevertheless, it should be expected to give way if the burden of insecurity, the costs of pursuing security unilaterally, and the costs of warfare are sufficiently large, i.e., prohibitive. Under these circumstances *self-interest dictates cooperation,* and expectations of cooperation should emerge that override the perceived risk.[36]

A glaring possibility is that the costs of warfare are not "sufficiently large" to a potential attacker. If so, then the risks of cooperation cannot be overridden and cooperation is far more difficult. In this connection much has been made of defensive versus offensive weapons and postures; when the former are naturally dominant, then vulnerability to attack is low, the costs of attacking are high, and thus the impact of the security dilemma is eased.[37] But when available technology favors the offense, then the temptation to resort to force and the fear that others will do so is greater, damaging the chances of cooperation. It may be that available technology is less important than what strategists and leaders think can be done with it, so that a "cult of the offensive" makes warfare seem affordable.[38] Another route to the same point is the suggestion that in coping with the problem of great-power warfare in this century the greatest difficulty has been the persistent reappearance of strategies promising quick, or in other ways relatively painless, victory—such as the "short war illusion" prior to 1914 and preemptive nuclear war or blanket defense conceptions in our time.[39]

If this is, in fact, the difficulty, it is not clear that it precludes cooperation. The initial response in this century to the need to make war so sufficiently unprofitable as to prevent it was a proposal for cooperation, Wilsonian collective security, to provide collective deterrence. Cooperation in the form of arms control/disarmament to curb or eliminate offensive military capabilities is a recurring idea that is again getting very serious attention. Even nuclear deterrence, the dominant solution over the past forty-five years, involves a form of cooperation—albeit a strange one. Given a sufficient commitment by great powers to the need to put an end to great-power wars, cooperation to make attacks very improbable in these ways, by negating offensive capabilities and quick victory strategies, ought to be quite plausible, not impossible. If the political conflicts among these states are so severe that the necessary cooperation cannot be installed, then we are back to blaming the conflicts, not anarchy.

Perhaps something else keeps the burdens of insecurity and costs of war from being intolerable. The best candidate is love of the autonomy that accompanies anarchy. States would rather be free than safe. As Mandelbaum says of the aftermath of World War I:

> The war did demonstrate that anarchy could have terrible consequences, but it did not demonstrate that it was unbearable. The powers had suffered great losses, but not so great as to make independence, and the insecurity that comes with it, intolerable.[40]

This argument can be sharpened by considering what states mean by autonomy. What they have always included as the core or essence of autonomy is the freedom to use force themselves for purposes of their own choosing. Cooperative arrangements that would cancel the use of force would therefore strip them of a vital component of their freedom as they have traditionally defined it.

To look at things this way requires a refinement of the concept of a security dilemma. If states agreed to renounce the use of force against each other and could do so in a highly convincing fashion, then the security dilemma as traditionally conceived could be resolved. But being safe from attack is not all there is to security. It presumably also involves safeguarding one's supreme values. If autonomy is exceedingly valued, and freedom to use force is a preeminent component of that autonomy as states define it, then to compromise that aspect of autonomy is to suffer a serious loss of security in their eyes. The most profound form of the security dilemma is that defining autonomy as they do puts states in the position of setting the security of being safe from attack at odds with the security of sustaining autonomy. It is not anarchy that causes the true security dilemma but what states have wanted to assert they are entitled to do under anarchy that creates it.

From all this, two broad prerequisites would appear to exist for the successful pursuit of security via cooperation among some designated set of states. On the one hand there must be no intense, war-threatening, political conflicts among them—any that exist must be resolved or at least very severely curbed. On the other hand, they must arrive at a general and convincing renunciation of the use of force in their relations, abandoning—at least among themselves—the traditional view of the prerequisites of autonomy. While these broad prerequisites might well facilitate lesser forms of cooperation, they lend themselves well to being expressed in terms of, and further elaborated by, multilateral endeavors. All the other conditions or factors usually cited as facilitating or inhibiting the emergence of cooperation—fear of war, transparency, etc.—can be assessed in terms of their contribution to, or detraction from, the emergence and maintenance of these two master conditions.

With the prerequisites in mind, we can turn directly to multilateralism for security in Europe. The opportunity to vastly expand a cooperative approach to security has been provided by the metamorphosis of the former Soviet foreign policy and the former Soviet political system. That has permitted a *resolution* (so far) *of every major issue* in East—West, and particularly intra-European, relations, thereby providing the first prerequisite. These changes also have important implications for the credible renunciation of force (the second prerequisite), though other steps have been, and will be, needed. What needs exploration is why the states involved are so interested in multilateral endeavors.

To begin developing an answer we must turn to the concerns of the major states involved. They have a problem of grave proportions and long standing—the deadly consequences of immense great-power wars. After each bout of such warfare in the past two centuries the great states involved in Europe have promptly reached for a cooperative, and usually multilateral, arrangement to try to prevent a recurrence the Concert, the League, the United Nations, Western European integration, and the multilateralism in NATO, along with periodic efforts at arms control. This is testimony to the potency of the problem and the durability of the impulse to cooperation.

The cooperation has frequently dissolved either immediately (in the United Nations) or eventually (the Concert). Jervis suggests why. In the wake of the war an intense appreciation of its costs and disruptive effects arises. A fund of experience also exists with close and successful cooperation within the winning coalition, plus fear that if it is terminated, the enemy will soon recover and again pose a threat. But these conditions fade. Memories of war's horrors weaken, habits of cooperation give way to renewed competition, and fear of the former enemy shrinks.[41]

This explanation best fits only the decay of the Concert. The reappearance of serious conflicts is certainly a major factor but at least as important is the perceived availability of *alternative noncooperative solutions* to the problem of great-power wars. The combination of renewed conflict and adoption of one or more of these solutions is what has undermined cooperation.

In the nineteenth century states came upon two of these "solutions." One was a discovery that war among two or three great powers need not turn into a general conflagration, as had been feared since 1815. A series of conflicts from the Crimean to the Franco—Prussian Wars demonstrated that restrained objectives and careful efforts to prevent horizontal escalation could work. Assisting in this was the Prussian development of a formula for a quick victory at modest cost, even against another great power, thereby avoiding what could otherwise have been long and exhausting wars that disrupted the domestic order. This had an immense effect on the military thinking and planning of European states, enabling them to ignore the (more relevant) lessons of the American Civil War and promoting illusions that helped bring on World War I.

After that conflict, President Wilson took the lead in designing a new venture in cooperation. As we know, it was dogged by serious political conflicts from the start, over the Versailles settlement and with the new Bolshevik government. Still, revulsion at the war was so deeply instilled in Britain and France that, upon the failure of the League and the Locarno arrangements, the resulting urge to cooperate led to the appeasement policy that Hitler so deftly exploited. What London and Paris had in mind, of course, was the reestablishment of a great-power concert, another cooperative approach to security. In the meantime, the United States reverted to its traditional solution to the horror of great-power warfare, which was to stay out of Europe's quarrels and any entanglements there. In terms of Wilson's, and later Roosevelt's, preferences, this is an instance of "involuntary defection" in which willingness to cooperate is frustrated by domestic political constraints.[42] As for the Soviet Union, its ideological perspectives were incompatible with cooperation because Lenin had defined great-power wars as inevitable in the last stage of capitalism (thus the true solution was to overthrow that system) and as offering, when they occurred, fertile conditions for just such a revolutionary change.

As the war approached, policies were again dictated not only by the difficulty of cooperation due to serious conflicts but also by misperceptions that alternative solutions were available, misperceptions as deadly as those in 1914. Hitler sought to employ the successful Prussian combination—keeping any war from becoming a general conflict plus a way of fighting that would make war short, triumphant, and limited in cost. Hence his expectation that, given the nonagression pact with Stalin, Britain and France would not go to war or would be amenable to a negotiated settlement once Poland disappeared. Stalin ended up opting for a combination of appeasement and noninvolvement. Britain and France, drawing on the "lessons" of World War I, were determined to remain on the defensive until Germany was exhausted and thereby keep their casualties and other costs to tolerable levels.

Such solutions had in common keeping great-power warfare limited in consequences for oneself either as participant or nonbelligerent. After World War II, and political conflicts that promptly made cooperation impossible, the great states seized on nuclear deterrence as a solution. As it grew in scope and in the magnitude of the arsenals, so did the belief that it was all that stood in the way of another systemwide war. Great-power restraint had to be coerced by holding everyone hostage.

While the prospect of cataclysmic destruction has certainly played an important role in discouraging new great-power wars (numerous analysts believe it is the only reliable solution), its manifest costs and difficulties have helped spur interest in multilateralism once the opportunity arose, not just as a supplement but as a replacement. In the interests of space these costs and difficulties can be summarized as follows. Nuclear deterrence has a serious, inherent credibility problem that has consistently aroused fears that states could, correctly or not, perceive the possibility of again fighting a cheap and successful great-power war. It also has a serious stability problem because nuclear weapons are ideal for short-war, quick-victory strategies, and both the inclinations of military planners and the path of technological change have encouraged recurring fears of vulnerability to strategic surprise attack. Coping with these difficulties has not been cheap and has sometimes been nerve wracking. It does not help that the theory of nuclear deterrence lacks an internally consistent and compelling explanation of why it is certain to work, rather disturbing in view of the stakes.[43] Finally, a serious political liability is the fact that nuclear deterrence is not compatible with what most people mean by "security".—which is that weapons are not stockpiled in vast numbers and the armed forces are not constantly primed because the neighbors are peaceful and arrangements exist that indicate they will stay that way.

Nevertheless, with all these difficulties nuclear deterrence has long seemed both the best that could be expected for preventing another great war and, in any case, reasonably effective. The hostile relationships that created and reinforced it seemed impervious to resolution. Any cooperative approach, other than to make deterrence work better (i.e., Strategic Arms Limitation Talks [SALT]), could be dismissed as unrealistic, and thus deterrence has had a tendency to mask and deflect the underlying pressure for collective management.

By claiming to have solved the problem of nuclear weapons, deterrence dogma dissipated the sudden urgency that this devastating capability had brought to the search for new ways of managing interstate relations. The pressure for a new approach had been building up for fifty years and more, with World War I and II demonstrating the inherent limits of the existing system. But the steam was let out of the movement by the promise of deterrence.[44]

Thus if the first answer to the question of where recent multilateralist inclinations come from is that they are a logical response to a continuing grave problem, the second is disenchantment with the alternatives, including nuclear deterrence. Keeping great-power wars limited seems unpromising given history and nuclear weapons. Nuclear deterrence is just not appealing, and if some more cooperative approach to security in Europe cannot be constructed, then, as Mearsheimer predicts, the logical recourse is apt to be nuclear proliferation there, which no one regards as an appetizing prospect.[45]

The third answer would be that multilateralism has been an important component of European international politics since 1945. With the collapse of wartime cooperation and no prospect of a viable Security Council, states turned to parallel, competitive, (and supposedly) multilateral security arrangements in the belief that security could not be left to the usual ways of sorting out political–military relationships. The American and Soviet governments eventually applied the view that security in Europe required multiplying states that imitated their own nature and character. This was hardly a new idea. The Concert of Europe rested in part on the desire to keep Europe's governments autocratic, while Wilson championed collective security among democratic states demarcated via national self-determination. (Even the classic balance of power was widely taken by statesmen to require a set of homogeneous states.[46]) In postwar Europe, therefore, a standard alliance was deemed insufficient; the allies ought to have similar socioeconomic and political systems, plus a much more elaborate level of peacetime military cooperation. This translated into multilateral endeavors to develop and/or sustain these parallel systems—cooperation had to extend to shared values, extensive economic coordination, and high levels of intellectual/cultural interaction. Multilateralism had to be multilayered.

Another facet of this was that decision makers in Moscow and Washington came to assume only their state had the necessary vision and strength to foster, lead, and sustain the appropriate arrangements. This fit well with each state's ideological perspectives and pretensions, and was in accord with their views on how European governments had helped bring on the last war.

There were, of course, crucial differences in what resulted. One lay in the inherent appeal for Europeans of the two societies offered for imitation. Another was the manner in which the arrangements were installed and maintained—one was, and largely remained, hierarchical and directive, the other emanated from a more invited and facilitative predominance, which put members in a more consensual framework for collaboration. Then there was the fact that the U.S. was not generally seen as part of Europe's seacurity problem, unlike the Soviet Union, so that its way of doing things could not be readily seen (other than in France) as intrinsically threatening. Finally, the U.S. was willing to accept more limitations of its dominance, even willing to contemplate a decline in its leading or hegemonic position; it was willing to accept additional multilateral arrangements of great import among its associates and considerable military strength in the hands of key allies. In contrast, the Soviet Union was unwilling to have its allies develop a weighty military capability of their own and oriented other cooperative endeavors of signifiance around itself. As a result of all this, multilateralism on one side was confronted by a pseudo-multilateralism on the other.

The triumph of the West was not only a victory of democracy or the market system, *it was also a triumph of Western multilateralism.* The traditional great powers are now reflecting the impact of a very extended, and expensive, learning process. To an early appreciation (by 1815) that systemwide warfare could be awful they have gradually added both an understanding that the standard ways of making it tolerable are quite unlikely to work and a wealth of experience with nuclear deterrence that discourages exclusive reliance on that. They have also had an opportunity to practice or observe a still unfolding, and quite unprecedented, exercise in multilateralism under which the participants have flourished and their opponents have not.

The powerful impact of this learning process is reflected in the semiautomatic impulses to simply enlarge the exercise with which governments have responded to recent developments. What Western governments clearly have in mind today is applying the same formula for the same objectives in order to get the same results so as to resolve the same basic security problem. The parallels extend beyond the application of multilateralism to the employment of roughly the same *strategy* for implementing it.

As in the early postwar years, a sense of crisis exists in the dominant participant (the West) about how things are going for the other participants—including fear that the wrong sorts of governments and societies may emerge that pursue unfortunate foreign policies. Once more, the dominant party (now parties), drawing on the inherent appeal of its system and holding out the alluring prospect of closer association with it, is utilizing its political and economic leverage—especially in massive assistance—to try to produce more states and societies in its mode. As in that earlier era, it is extracting concessions for its aid, trade, and security assistance in the form of steps by the recipients to reorder their domestic systems and policies—they are to take the initiative in this regard.[47] Then there is the dominant partner's strong desire, as in the late 1940s, to sustain a centralized, coordinated approach as opposed to fragmentation along national and ethnic lines, based on a strong distaste at the prospect of being drawn into traditional regional and ethnic quarrels. Another parallel is the idea of drawing the new partners into multilayered relationships that build interdependence and could well extend to integration. This is to continue the erosion of old conflicts, prevent the emergence of new ones, and result in a pluralistic security community—making resort to force among the new participants as improbable as it has become among those in the West. The shared benefits enable this multilateralism to serve not only as the vehicle but also as *the source of legitimacy* for the effort, easing fears of dominance and exploitation.

Given the limited repertoires of governments under most circumstances, the accumulated experience with this one, and its past success, it does not seem odd that this is the preferred option today. Whatever else it may be, it is not new. Everything envisioned has been around for some time in Europe, only on a half-continent scale.

Evaluation

Assessing this "new" venture in multilateralism is best approached by examining the steps undertaken in light of the prerequisites for cooperation to eliminate great-power warfare: curbing the political conflicts and credible renunciation by those states of the right to use force in their relations. To do this I find it useful to refer to Lisa Martin's depiction, elsewhere in this volume, of several types of situations characteristic of multilateralism. In a *coordination* situation, actor preferences significantly overlap, but the preferred outcome is not the same for each actor, so some conflict exists over which of several acceptable outcomes to adopt. In a *collaboration* situation, by contrast, actor preferences overlap only in a desire to avoid the worst outcome—otherwise, they are sharply at odds.

For cooperation to be sustained, much more emphasis must be placed on surveillance and enforcement to prevent defection; application of norms such as indivisibility and diffuse reciprocity will have less appeal and less effectiveness.

In a *suasion* situation, a hegemon has good reason to prefer cooperation, but the cooperation it seeks can leave others somewhat dissatisfied or tempted to defect because the benefits will probably be available anyway. Thus the hegemon must find ways to persuade, or coerce, them into cooperation. One way to do this is by issue linkage to raise the costs of defection or the benefits of participating. Multilateralism then becomes a useful rationalization for what is taking place, conveying legitimacy even though its application may be limited initially.

In applying this perspective we begin by noting that the states in Europe have a strong desire to discard the collaborative situation in which they were lodged. This has now been made possible. However, remnants of that situation remain as does fear that it might, soon or someday, return, so various insurance-against-defection measures are needed. These primarily pertain to retention of NATO, elaborate verification of big cuts in military capabilities, or other transparency-boosting measures. Alongside this, however, has been the abrupt emergence of a suasion situation. The West is a hegemon with good reasons to prefer cooperation; it is now engaged in ways to coerce or persuade the states in Eastern Europe to accept its version of that cooperation. It seeks to do this within the framework of multilateralism. This requires contending that the ultimate objective and outcome will be a coordination situation, in keeping with the preferences of those in the East. Thus the coercion and persuasion involved must be legitimized by credibly avoiding the appearance of an exploitative intent and conveying a long-term preference for moving away from them. Multilateralism is the primary avenue for achieving this and is probably the only way it can be achieved.

We can now turn to factors often considered relevant for determining the success or failure of security (and other) cooperation.

EROSION OF THE PERCEIVED UTILITY OF WAR

Many analysts have emphasized that erosion of the perceived utility of war is crucial for cooperation on security.[48] For the great powers the loss of war's utility has long been ascribed to nuclear weapons. Commentaries on the current situation in Europe frequently refer to the widespread view that war would be intolerable, coupled with perceptions that its probability is exceedingly low, as a key contributor to prospects for cooperation.[49]

As noted above, this involves moving away from a collaboration situation, making it necessary to greatly enhance the credibility of participants' renunciation of war. The difficulty lies in finding ways to prevent residual concerns from poisoning the shift to a suasion, and ultimately a coordination, situation because states retain military capabilities "just in case" that could detract from this credibility.

Steps to meet this difficulty have received much attention. Large cutbacks in forces have been undertaken. Credibility on war renunciation is much enhanced when cutbacks are *independent but parallel,* rather than only via carefully crafted agreements—the latter imply continued mistrust. Thus it was extremely important that the Soviet Union unilaterally reduced conventional forces, generally and in Europe, and added agreements to pull forces from Eastern Europe that did not involve the West. Also important was that East European governments announced cutbacks in forces and military spending and that the West had begun moving in that direction even before any comprehensive conventional arms agreement. These steps were the best possible sign, displaying attitudes that strengthened the impact of the eventual agreement on troops in Germany and German forces and the Paris agreement on overall reductions in military forces.

For the same reason, NATO's abandonment of plans for theater nuclear forces modernization enhanced prospects for further cooperation, as did the U.S. and Soviet plans to eliminate most chemical weapons without waiting for a treaty that bans them. Missing until recently was a comparable step on nuclear forces, the superpowers having been preoccupied instead with negotiating elaborate START (Strategic Arms Reduction Costs) or other nuclear arms pacts. Now we have had the astonishing spectacle of the United States offering unilaterally to eliminate its land-based tactical nuclear weapons and withdraw its sea-based ones, followed by the Soviet Union offering the same and throwing in a unilateral cut in its strategic nuclear forces—all without any preceding arrangements agreed upon for verification!

At the conventional level, Soviet advocacy of a strictly defensive posture, coupled with withdrawal of offensive-oriented forces from Germany, added greatly to the credibility of its renouncing the use of force because these steps were unilateral. It has now been reinforced by the conventional forces agreement in Paris, which transformed the military situation in Europe.

Other features of a more general nature have also had a positive impact. The fact that the changes in Eastern Europe could not be ascribed to Western military pressure or threats left little basis for fears or suggestions that the West must inevitably attempt to politically exploit its present military superiority, fears that would challenge the credibility of its renouncing the use of force. The Western willingness to alter the character of NATO also seems to have been taken by Moscow as a favorable sign in this connection.

Also relevant was the experience the two sides had accumulated in trying to cooperate on arms control, nuclear proliferation, and crisis management. The intellectual starting point for all this was the assertion, by Americans and other Western strategists, that nuclear deterrence was ultimately a cooperative endeavor, that it involved interdependent security, a mutual interest in stability, and mutual stakes in facilitating restraint. Not long ago it was fashionable to ridicule the notion that the U.S. (and the West) was "educating" the Soviet government about this. Judged by recent developments, just such an education is what has taken place. A good example was the Soviet retreat from the deeply ingrained tradition of secrecy as a national security asset, which has led to unprecedented arms control verification and confidence-building measures. It signaled a new appreciation of why transparency is important and why the West has been harping on it for years.

In a similar vein, Soviet acceptance of a united Germany is of an importance greater than the reduction of an old political dispute. A customary explanation for the postwar division of Europe has been that an understandable Soviet insistence on containing Germany meant dominating Eastern Europe and projecting power into Germany (with forces designed to fight any war there by means of a rapid offensive and as far from the USSR as possible). This inevitably aroused Western fears, creating a politically and militarily hostile response. What happened to this security dilemma?

It is too facile to conclude that Soviet leaders had no choice but to accept collapse of the German Democratic Republic, the Warsaw Pact, and the Soviet position in Eastern Europe. Western governments were ready to accept more modest steps in this direction and at a slower pace, making allowance for Soviet concerns. Nor was the Soviet leadership too preoccupied with domestic reform—domestic difficulties rarely lead great powers to dismiss vital security concerns. Also unsatisfactory is citing the "new political thinking" that shifted the Soviet focus away from military strength and toward interdependence, arms control, and a defensive military posture. This begs the question of what happened to the old conception.

What now seems plausible is that the salience of classic security consideration in Soviet policies in Europe declined some time ago. Its position in Eastern Europe no longer represented a deeply held fear of attack but reflected other interests and concerns. What has now occurred is not just a redefinition of security but also an end to rationalizing, via the old security concerns, policies driven by other objectives. This would not have happened unless those other objectives and the traditional ways of pursuing them had been reconsidered and found wanting. The redefinition of security was not the critical initial step but an outcome of this reexamination.

In this transformations a two-stage process was probably involved. In the first phase, the strict security considerations must have markedly declined. The main factors were probably the coming of stable strategic nuclear deterrence, appreciation that perceptions of another war in Europe as unthinkable were widespread, and realization that no serious prospect of attack existed from Germany, NATO, and the United States. This would put the first phase at roughly 1970–1975, coinciding with strategic parity, SALT I, Ostpolitik, detente, and the Helsinki accords.

Although onset of the second phase can be located in 1985 with the arrival of the "new thinking," it surely germinated in the prior decade.[50] A realization must have been spreading that upholding Stalin's legacy in Europe was damaging Soviet influence, undermining the health and prestige of socialism, reinforcing Soviet isolation from the West, and costing a pretty penny in subsidies to prop up the Eastern European governments, and all the while it was poisoning detente and serving the bureaucratic interests of the military establishments, both of which would inhibit effective reform at home.

Thus a postwar security dilemma arose, but it and the resulting failures in cooperative security management were not due to anarchy. Certain Soviet perceptions and the associated security policies were responsible.[51] The important point is that the foreign policies of Russia and the other former Soviet republics now reflect great confidence in the peaceful intent of the West. The security dilemma began to fade some years ago, and Russian foreign policy enhances the possibility of eliminating it entirely.

An analysis of the continued credibility of a commitment to forgo war that stretches across Europe would not be complete without reference to two significant elements that are cause for concern. One pertains to the continued participation of the United States in European security, identified earlier as a major feature of the consensus in Europe about objectives for security. With the decline of the threat and the melting away of the American military presence in Europe now underway, the United States is beginning to experience anew an old credibility problem. How is it to allay fears it will eventually detach itself from European security, particularly since its dominant political position is going to disappear?

Similar concerns in the early days of NATO played a major role in the decision to intervene in Korea. It is not too farfetched to suggest that one consideration in the prompt response to the seizure of Kuwait was the desire to reinforce the credibility of assertions that the United States will remain an important player in Europe. The parallel with the Korean War is striking.

However, it is unlikely to work. Quite apart from the fading of the former Soviet threat, a continuing role for the United States in Europe's security is undermined by the absence of a *superpower* in Europe—if there is no superpower to balance, then the complaint that there is no need for the United States to defend a rich and dynamic Europe will mount. Unless a resurgent and threatening Russian state emerges, the new European security order is going to have to stand on its own. Good wishes will be the major American contribution in the long run.

The other, much more serious, matter is the civil war in Yugoslavia. The multilateralist approach to security in Europe was often criticized for lacking any enforcement mechanism, any arrangements for intervention to keep the peace or ganging up on an aggressor. In a successful pluralistic security community, *no need exists for such a capability.* Indeed, if the capability is needed, then the community does not exist. If everyone in Europe understands that war is quite unacceptable there, then a problem like the Yugoslav civil war should not arise. That is one reason others in Europe have been so reluctant to intervene. Quite apart from all the political and military difficulties of doing so is the fact that to intervene means that a flaw may exist in the overall design for European security.

Those who take comfort from the fact that this time trouble in the Balkans has not set off a scramble among major European powers to gain advantage, that Europe has clearly changed for the better in this respect, are being too optimistic. An emerging norm, crucial for the new security structure, has been violated, opening up the possibility that this will not be an isolated instance.

RESTRICTING THE NUMBER OF PARTICIPANTS

Oye asserts that "the prospects for cooperation diminish as the number of players increases."[52] He cites as reasons the concomitant increase in transaction and information costs, the greater likelihood of defections and of recognition and control problems, and the declining feasibility of punishing defectors. Geoff Garrett also concludes that regional cooperation ventures, with a smaller number of players, are more likely to succeed with global ones.[53]

In keeping with this, concern has arisen about the large number of states involved in the new multilateralism in Europe. The chief criticism of CSCE is that it has too many members for comfort. With former Soviet and Yugoslav republics having become independent, the number of eligible states is growing. This could pose a serious problem.

A more sanguine view can be taken. To begin with, a key ingredient of a safer Europe in the eyes of many observers is a gradual enlargement of the European Community. This now seems likely though the difficulties for the European Community of accommodating such a horde of potential applicants must not be understated. This would reduce the numbers problem considerably. That a roughly similar arrangement in what used to be the Soviet Union would be good has often been suggested; that would have virtually eliminated the numbers problem, but it now seems out of the question.

If the problem will not go away, its effects may be contained. If the crucial security problem is great-power warfare, then the great powers are the truly important participants, and they are few in number. Their cooperation could legitimize the reinforce norms on nonrecourse to force, and they could collectively bring great pressure to bear to deter violations. This implies that institutions and agreements that encompass all the North American and European states must be accompanied by a network of specific deals and contracts, bilateral and multilateral, among the major states. Examples include the Four Power Agreement on Berlin, the extensive agreements between Germany and the USSR in connection with German unification, and the American–Soviet START Treaty and ensuing deal on tactical nuclear weapons. Needed will be regularized great-power summits and the development of procedures, and possibly institutional mechanisms, to cope with potential disruptions of the peace.

If the Yugoslav situation is a forerunner of other challenges to the security order, and it turns out to require an intervention and enforcement capability, then great-power cooperation will be crucial to its design and application.

Thus calls for the revival of something like the Concert of Europe are quite appropriate but incomplete. A new great-power concert should exist *within a multilateralist context* that embraces all the states of Europe and in order to uphold that context. In this way the concert can be prevented from turning into an alternative to the kind of security system that nearly everyone now seems to prefer and to be seeking.

Still, optimism about this must not be carried too far. A big winner in the recent developments has been nationalism and ethnic identity. This can readily undermine steps toward democracy, disassemble the consensus on the sanctity of existing borders, and overload emerging multilateral institutions and processes. The pressures on a number of governments and societies are very great. In prospect is a continuing race between community building and nationalism making for fragmentation.

HOMOGENEOUS GOVERNMENTS AND SOCIETIES

That the governments, economies, and societies of the former Soviet bloc must come to resemble those in the West if extensive cooperation is to be successful now seems widely accepted. Most common is an insistence on democratic governments as the ones suitable for true continental security.[54] Fear has been expressed that in Southeastern Europe and the former Soviet Union the West will continue to face alien societies or that tentatively liberalizing states may give way to praetorian politics with domestic interests plying nationalist appeals and exaggerated threat assessments.[55] Renewed interests has arisen in Deutsch's contention that security communities must rest on the politically relevant strata of the participants having compatible values.[56]

This is a sensitive feature of the shift from a collaboration to a suasion situation, because it is primarily here that a mix of persuasion and coercion is necessary. Many analysts and officials now think and talk in precisely these terms: economic assistance has been conditioned on Eastern Europeans revamping their economies; membership in the Council of Europe and the European Community will not be considered for undemocratic governments; and so forth.

On democracy, a renewed interest has arisen in the expectation (descending from Kant) that it can directly diminish the security problem in international politics, a view reinforced by the absence of war among liberal democratic states over what is now quite a long period. Little has been done to explain why this is the case, probably because that would ultimately require thoroughly revising the study of international politics. The Wilsonian view, echoing the nineteenth-century socialists, that the masses who would be the cannon fodder will not support wars has had little appeal for analysts but can still be heard. More interest is now expressed in the norm of nonviolent resolution of disputes and the perception of politics as nonzero sum, elements of democracy held to carry over into the relations of democratic states.[57]

From the perspective of the literature on facilitating cooperation under anarchy, the most valuable contribution of democracy is enhanced transparency, particularly on security matters where states' fear of defection, especially via a surprise attack, can be especially high.[58] Democracy can make European governments' mutual understanding easier. It would also make them more open to penetration by the intercessions of outsiders.

> Governments contemplating international cooperation need to *know* their partners, not merely know *about* them. This . . . suggests that governments that successfully maintain "closure," protecting the autonomy of their decision-making processes from outside penetration, will have more difficulty participating in international regimes than more open, apparently disorganized governments. "Closed" governments will be viewed with more skepticism by potential partners.[59]

While no conclusive evidence exists that democracy *must* have these salutary effects on a permanent basis, what evidence we have does not contradict such conclusions. However, no way is known for one group of states to coerce another group into democracy—indeed, to do so would contradict the meaning of democracy. About all that can be done is to encourage, to persuade by example and enticement, and to threaten to suspend relations and assistance. This is far more promising work if the target societies have already generated considerable momentum in this direction. Evidence of this last condition is plentiful with respect to Eastern Europe and the former Soviet Union but far from convincing, and good reason exists to fear that the momentum toward democracy cannot be maintained.

As for spreading other facets of Western civilization, the key difficulty is envisioning the former Soviet republics' becoming truly European, truly Western, in view of that area's history, geography, cultures, and ethnic composition. Two things can be said. One is that the West now embraces a broad range of societies—it may be that many elements of the former Soviet Union can be similarly encompassed. The other is that as the former Soviet state continues to unravel, the most nonwestern of its peoples, as independent societies, need not be candidates for inclusion in the West.

While a durable peace through multilateralist interactions and inter-dependence sustained by similarity in the societies involved is the long-term objective, it is plausible that a highly satisfying security community could be constructed in the interim among societies still significantly disparate. The latter is something to which foreign policy can make a considerable contribution via firm reinforcement of perceptions that all the significant states have ruled out the use of force. The ultimate object of complex interdependence is thereby facilitated, for "The key character-istic of complex interdependence is the well-founded expectation of the inefficacy of the use or threat of force among states."[60]

SHIFTING PAYOFFS TO FAVOR COOPERATION AND ENHANCE EXPECTATIONS THAT OTHERS WILL COOPERATE

The necessity to provide suitable payoffs and enhanced expectations of cooperation, particularly to "lengthen the shadow of the future," is a salient feature of analyses on how international cooperation is facili-tated.[61] This is a key aspect of multilateralism, with its component of diffuse reciprocity, and is clearly a prime target of the West's strategy.

Steps to eliminate recourse to war are of vital importance in this regard, and thus much of the earlier discussion is also relevant here. However, the strategy has a far more positive orientation toward steadily enlarging participation in a sequence of collaborative endeavors, seeking to induce "a benign circle and a self-fulfilling prophecy of cooperation."[62] The Western states are inviting the rest of Europe to join the distinctive international system they have created and promising important benefits and high levels of cooperation even as they start to do so.

Thus cooperation under anarchy is not a suitable description of what is being envisioned and attempted. The objective is a deliberate, collective, permanent *retreat from anarchy* on an enlarged regional basis as the ulti-mate displacement of the old conflicts and security dilemmas. Freedom from war would be rooted in a further extension of the Western model for interstate relations and of the Western European model for organizing a continent-sized multiethnic community. To quote NATO's Secretary-General:

> We must come to terms with a more diffuse concept of security in which economic integration and assistance and the internal democratization of states become as important as traditional military defence in maintaining security

and preventing the degeneration of instabilities into tensions liable to cause conflicts.[63]

What are the prospects for this when it requires building on the experience and habits of cooperation of one set of states but working with another set that has not shared them? The problems do not seem insurmountable. East European states have been officially in accord for years with the idea that security must be sought collectively, be rooted in the emergence of a large community, and rest on that community's encompassing roughly similar states and societies. They just ended up in the wrong community. Their choice now is to have no community, construct a new one, or link up with the one in the West, and it is clear which they prefer. This does not eliminate the difficulties, but at least the natural inclinations are in the right direction.

The foremost difficulties pertain to the former Soviet Union. The plainly displayed sentiments there, expressed at every level, about the need to enter the West's world are encouraging. The problem is how to provide payoffs of sufficient scale. In security this is possible. Under the new security structure the Russians face no meaningful threat from the West. The trouble is, as noted earlier, this probably ceased to be such an overwhelming concern for the Soviet Union some time ago and has not been a serious concern in Eastern Europe. Hence the really suitable payoffs need to be of another sort, falling in the realm of increased economic progress in particular. These are payoffs that will be very expensive and politically difficult to make.

Nevertheless, if the West is to recapitulate the success of postwar multilateralism, it must not neglect one of its most original and effective components: hegemonic extension of economic assistance on a massive scale along with concessions that facilitated trade. Proposals along these lines have thus far received a paltry reception, despite the determined Western efforts to provide a good deal of stopgap assistance, and this is most unfortunate.

The usual source of resistance is concern about domestic political instability and economic underdevelopment. The Soviet government has collapsed and thus cannot handle aid of major proportions, and the situation in the republics is almost as chaotic. Similar concerns are expressed about portions of Eastern Europe.

Missing from such views is the idea that the new hegemon, like the old, can use a massive intervention to help *provoke the right conditions*. This means intervention to break the descending cycle of dispair and disarray. Missing is the postwar appreciation that the most important dimension in the Eastern part of Europe may be psychological—that confidence is a mainstay of multilateral endeavors, to be induced not only in the target states but also through a firm and costly commitment of the hegemon that displays confidence as well. A new Marshall Plan is just what is needed, the sooner the better. North America, Western Europe, and Japan can collectively meet the costs involved with no great difficulty.

But will they? Here, again, it is hard to be highly optimistic. The difficulty does not seem to be in the principle or in lack of public support for the principle—the idea of giving aid to former enemies to make them into comfortable friends seems to have become widely accepted. The problem is that if it is not clear whether the aid will be effectively used, then selling the aid politically is difficult. Perhaps only a continued deterioration in the situation will provoke the necessary willingness to take the risk.

Conclusion

The Europeans are trying to apply multilateralism to devise a security system based on a web of relationships within which a set of norms, especially on the sanctity of borders and the nonuse of force, constitutes a pluralistic security community. Because of the nature of such a community, these efforts have not included provisions for elaborate enforcement institutions, peacekeeping capabilities, and dispute resolution resources.

The initial design has had to be quickly adjusted several times, German unification, the collapse of the Warsaw Pact, and the looming disintegration of the former Soviet Union led to adding much more aid to the East than originally expected, more arms reductions, an intensification of EC integration (with the German problem in mind), and a consistent effort to resist reform-threatening disintegration in the former Soviet Union and Yugoslavia.

The underlying problem has turned out to be that the security system was meant to cope with threats arising from of state-to-state conflicts, but the real threats come from the internal decay of states and the resurgence of ethnic loyalties and conflicts. Banning alterations in borders, for instance, was meant to keep states from reviving old territorial disputes, but borders all over Eastern Europe are now threatened by the fragmentation of existing states, which could be a backdoor way of getting state-to-state territorial clashes back onto center stage. And ethnic tensions have provoked one outright war with no readily available means of intervention or conflict resolution.

Thus the design is undergoing additional modifications. The Europeans are groping toward collective conflict control and conflict resolution in Yugoslavia via diplomatic intervention backed by economic sanctions. At this writing talk has arisen about peacekeeping forces from the United Nations, and the final communique of the NATO meeting in November 1991 noted the existence of proposals to consider legitimizing intervention in a state *against its wishes* when it clearly violates CSCE norms (something France strongly opposes). These developments (plus the Iraq war) have also increased the pace of steps toward creating a distinctively European (Community) defense capability in and through the WEU, including a common foreign and defense policy.[64]

A modest optimism about the eventual outcome of all this seems to be in order if the analysis offered in this chapter is sound. Cooperation of the sort envisioned is not intrinsically impossible and, given the postwar experience and inclinations of the peoples and governments involved, appears quite feasible. The sorts of prerequisites for cooperation on security that can be derived from the literature are within reach, though clearly problems to be overcome and dangers to be skirted remain. But we are witnessing a remarkable experiment being conducted under highly fluid and dangerous conditions. This makes any prediction quite conditional.

One of the reasons for this is that, as has been apparent throughout this chapter, *domestic* factors have been the most prominent in shaping the prospects for the new multilateralism. Citing the dynamics of the international system does not, therefore, take our understanding very far. A domestic political upheaval in the Soviet Union opened up the opportunity to completely redesign European security. Whether enough changes will occur in the former Soviet Union and Eastern Europe, and of the right sort, to make for a sufficiently homogeneous Europe is largely dependent on domestic developments in those societies. Whether the West will make the maximum effort to influence those developments is almost certainly to be decided by the domestic political and economic difficulties it now faces. This strongly supports theview that the "next major step forward in understanding international cooperation will have to incorporate domestic politics fully into the analysis."[65]

NOTES

1. Cited in Pierre Hassner, "The Priority of Constructing Western Europe," in Gregory F. Treverton, ed., *Europe and America Beyond 2000* (New York: Council on Foreign Relations Press, 1990) p. 21.

2. See various chapters in O. Holsti, R. Siverson, and A. George, eds., *Change in the International System* (Boulder, Colo.: Westview Press, 1980); and Barry Buzan and R. J. Berry Jones, eds., *Change and the Study of International Relations: The Evaded Dimension* (New York: St. Martin's Press, 1981).

3. The best analysis is Stephen Cohen, *Rethinking the Soviet Experience* (New York: Oxford University Press, 1985).

4. See Lincoln Gordon, ed., *Eroding Empire: Western Relations with Eastern Europe* (Washington, D.C.: Brookings, 1987) p. 5; and Nicholas Kittrie "Introduction: The Undoing of a Monolith, Responding to Diversities in the Eastern Bloc," in Kittrie and Ivan Volgyes, eds., *The Uncertain Future: Gorbachev's Eastern Bloc* (New York: Paragon House, 1988) p. 6.

5. James Rosenau, "Global Changes and Theoretical Challenges: Towards a Postindustrial Politics for the 1990s," in Ernst-Otto Czempiel and Rosenau, eds., *Global Changes and Theoretical Challenges: Approaches to World Politics for the 1990s* (Lexington, Mass.: Lexington Books, 1989) pp. 4–5. Also Rosenau, *Turbulence in World Politics: A Theory of Change and Continuity* (Princeton: Princeton University Press, 1990).

6. As in George Modelski, "Long Cycles of World Leadership" in William Thompson, ed., *Contending Approaches to World System Analysis* (Beverly Hills, Calif.: Sage, 1983) pp. 115–39. For analysis of the theory of hegemonic stability and its implications for cooperation, see Robert Keohane, *After Hegemony: Cooperation and Discord in the World Political Economy* (Princeton: Princeton University Press, 1984); Duncan Snidal, "The Limits of Hegemonic Stability Theory" *International Organization* (Autumn 1985), 39:579–614. For the case against declining American hegemony, see Bruce Russett, "The Mysterious Case of Vanishing Hegemony; or, Is Mark Twain Really Dead?" *International Organization* (Spring 1985), 39:207–31.

7. Robert Gilpin, *War and Change in World Politics* (New York: Cambridge University Press, 1981), p. 15.

8. Some examples: Stephen Rock, *Why Peace Breaks Out: Great Power Rapprochement in Historical Perspective* (Chapel Hill: University of North Carolina Press, 1989); Daniel Nelson, "Conclusion: To Change the Course of Soviet–American Relations," in Nelson and Roger Anderson, eds., *Soviet–American Relations: Understanding Differences, Avoiding Conflicts* (Wilmington, Del.: Scholarly Resources, 1988); Nish Jamgotch, Jr., "Security Communications: Risk Reduction and Confidence Building in Superpower Relations" and "Superpower Cooperation: The Way Ahead," in Jamgotch, ed., *U.S.–Soviet Cooperation: A New Future* (New York: Praeger, 1989); Arnold Horelick, ed., *U.S.–Soviet*

Relations: The Next Phase (Ithaca, N.Y.: Cornell University Press, 1986); Alexander George, Philip Farley, and Alexander Dallin, eds., *U.S.–Soviet Security Cooperation: Achievements, Failures, Lessons* (Oxford, England: Oxford University Press, 1988).

9. A summary of findings is in Charles Kegley, Jr. and Gregory Raymond, *When Trust Breaks Down: Alliance Norms and World Politics* (Columbia, S.C.: University of South Carolina Press, 1990), pp. 63–73. Stephen Walt, *The Origins of Alliances* (Ithaca, N.Y.: Cornell University Press, 1987), suggests that the cooperation involved is primarily in reaction to direct, clearly perceived threats, which by implication would downgrade the chances for broad cooperation by states for security "in general."

10. See Patrick M. Morgan, "On Strategic Arms Control," in Edward Kolodziej and Morgan, eds., *Security and Arms Control* (New York: Greenwood Press, 1989), 2:299–318.

11. John Mearsheimer, "Back to the Future: Instability in Europe After the Cold War," *International Security* (Summer 1990), 15:6. See also Jack Snyder, "Averting Anarchy in the New Europe," *International Security* (Spring 1990), 14:5–41.

12. Robert Jervis, "From Balance to Concert: A Study of Security Cooperation," in Kenneth Oye, ed., *Cooperation Under Anarchy* (Princeton: Princeton University Press, 1986), pp. 58–79.

13. Stephen Rock, *Why Peace Breaks Out*, pp. 17–18; Robert Jervis, "Security Regimes," *International Organization* (Spring 1982), 36(2):278. Rock derives his view from Richard Ned Lebow, *Between Peace and War: The Nature of International Crisis* (Baltimore: The Johns Hopkins University Press, 1981), p. 309. Jervis notes the similar suggestion in Herman Kahn, *Thinking About the Unthinkable* (New York: Horizon Press, 1962) pp. 148–49.

14. Robert Jervis, "Realism, Game Theory, and Cooperation," *World Politics* (1988) 40:343.

15. Robert Jervis, "From Balance to Concert," pp. 67–68.

16. Johan Jorgen Holst, "Military Stability and Political Order in Europe," in Gregory Treverton, ed., *Europe and America Beyond 2000* (New York: Council on Foreign Relations Press, 1990), p. 115.

17. Many elements of the consensus were initially set forth in the CSCE Final Act adopted in Helsinki in 1975, with its references to refraining from the threat or use of force, the inviolability of frontiers, respect for human rights, and division-reducing cooperation on matters ranging from science and technology to culture and education. The November 1990 "Joint Declaration of Twenty Two States" and the "Charter of Paris for a New Europe" reaffirm the Helsinki Final Act Principles. What they add, either singly or jointly, is the assertion that the security of all CSCE participants is indivisible, provisions for arms reductions, assertion of the necessity for democracy and market economies, and an endorsement of German unification. The Treaty on Conventional Armed

Forces in Europe, with attached protocols, details the arms reductions to be undertaken. The "Vienna Document 1990" provides for elaborate confidence-building measures with respect to military security.

18. Proposals, or discussions of proposals from nongovernment sources, can be found in, for example, Gregory Flynn and David Scheffer, "Limited Collective Security" *Foreign Policy* (Fall 1990), 80:77–101; Richard Ullman, "Enlarging the Zone of Peace," *Foreign Policy* (Fall 1990), 80:102–20; Jonathan Dean, "Building a Post-Cold War European Security System," *Arms Control Today* (June 1990), 20:8–12.

19. See the "Supplementary Document to Give Effect to Certain Provisions Contained in the Charter of Paris for a New Europe" and the "Vienna Document 1990." An excellent review of proposals prior to the agreements is Adam Rotfeld, "New Security Structures in Europe: Concepts, Proposals, and Prospects" in *SIPRI Yearbook 1991: World Armaments and Disarmament* (Stockholm: SIPRI, 1991) pp. 1–16. Early U.S. official views appeared in Secretary of State Baker's speeches of December 12, 1989, in Berlin and June 7, 1990, in Scotland, which appeared in the State Department's *Current Policy* series numbers 1233 and 1284.

20. Charles Kegley and Gregory Raymond, *When Trust Breaks Down*, pp. 14–27.

21. See Inis Claude, *Power and International Relations* (New York: Random House, 1962) pp. 94–149.

22. It has also been proposed as a model for today's Europe in John Muller, "A New Concert of Europe" *Foreign Policy* (Winter 1989–90), 77:3–16; and Charles and Clifford Kupchan, "Concerts, Collective Security, and the Future of Europe," *International Security* (Summer 1991), 16:114–61.

23. It is treated as a regime in Robert Jervis, "Security Regimes," and as a managed balance of power in Michael Mandelbaum, *The Fate of Nations* (New York: Cambridge University Press, 1988) pp. 11–12.

24. See Richard Elrod, "The Concert of Europe: A Fresh Look at an International System," *World Politics* (January 1976), 28:159–174; Richard Langhorne, *The Collapse of the Concert of Europe: International Politics, 1890–1914* (New York: St. Martin's Press, 1981), pp. 4–28; F. R. Bridge and Roger Bullen *The Great Powers and the European States System 1815–1914* (London: Longman, 1980) pp. 1–40; Paul Schroeder, "The 19th-Century International System: Changes in the Structure," *World Politics* (October 1986), 34:1–25.

25. Robert Jervis, "Security Regimes," pp. 362–63.

26. Paul Schroeder, "The Nineteenth Century System: Balance of Power or Political Equilibrium?" *Review of International Studies* (1989), 15:143.

27. Sergei Karaganov, "The Year of Europe. A Soviet View," *Survival* (March/April 1990), 32:121–28, stresses the curtailing of Western defense efforts even prior to agreements on reductions and the "restrained and civilized approach" of the West on Soviet nationalities problems and the dissolution of the Warsaw

Pact. Another example: the way German reunification was "foisted on the stronger country by the weaker one" according to Joseph Joffe, "Once More: the German Question," *Survival* (March/April 1990), 32:129–140, especially p. 132.

28. Extensive discussion of the relationship between European integration and security can be found in Mathias Jopp, Reinhardt Rummell, and Peter Schmidt, *Integration and Security in Western Europe* (Boulder, Colo.: Westview, 1991).

29. Paul Schroeder, "The 19th-Century International System," p. 4.

30. Mandlebaum, *The Fate of Nations*, p. 1.

31. John Mearsheimer, "Back to the Future," p. 12.

32. See Klaus Knorr and Patrick Morgan, eds., *Strategic Military Surprise* (New Brunswick, N.J.: Transaction, 1983).

33. Rock, *Why Peace Breaks Out;* Charles and Clifford Kupchan, "Concerts, Collective Security," p. 134.

34. John Mearsheimer, "Back to the Future," p. 12. Joseph Grieco expands further on this to assert that anarchy forces states to worry that in cooperative endeavors their partners will make greater relative gains, that this is an additional barrier to cooperation (which presumably applies to security cooperation). See Grieco, *Cooperation Among Nations* (Ithaca, N.Y.: Cornell University Press, 1991).

35. Robert Jervis, "Security Regimes," p. 359.

36. Or, to use the terms employed in a recent analysis, under these circumstances states' interest in relative gains in security through unilateral action—as opposed to absolute gains via cooperation—should be diminished. See Duncan Snidal, "Relative Gains and the Pattern of International Cooperation," *American Political Science Review* (September 1991), 85:701–726. Extended discussion on how a search for relative gain makes cooperation far more difficult is in Arthur Stein, *Why Nations Cooperate* (Ithaca, N.Y.: Cornell University Press), pp. 113–50.

37. Robert Jervis, "Cooperation Under the Security Dilemma" *World Politics* (1978) 30(2):167–213. Also relevant is the treatment of the "cult of the Offensive" in Stephen Van Evera, "Why Cooperation Failed in 1914," in Kenneth Oye, *Cooperation Under Anarchy*, pp. 80–117, which lists other works that stress this factor.

38. Jack Snyder, *The Ideology of the Offensive: Military Decision Making and the Disasters of 1914* (Ithaca, N.Y.: Cornell University Press, 1984).

39. See Patrick Morgan, "Nuclear Deterrence and Strategic Surprise," in Stephen Cimbala, ed., *Challenges to Deterrence* (New York: Praeger, 1987), pp. 85–110.

40. Mandelbaum, *The Fate of Nations*, p. 83.

41. Jervis, "From Balance to Concert," p. 61.

42. See Stephen Haggard and Beth Simmons, "Theories of International Regimes," *International Organization* (Summer 1987), 41:491–517, particularly pp. 514–515.

43. Patrick Morgan, *Deterrence, A Conceptual Analysis,* 2nd ed. (Beverly Hills, Calif.: Sage, 1983).

44. Michael MccGwire, "Deterrence: the Problem, Not the Solution," *SAIS Review* (Summer/Fall 1985), 5:121.

45. Mearsheimer, "Back to the Future," pp. 37–40.

46. See Edward Vose Gulick, *Europe's Classical Balance of Power,* (New York: W. W. Norton, 1955), pp. 19–24.

47. Hence Western aid, trade, etc. have at various times been tied to economic and political reform (in Romania and Bulgaria); adoption of a comprehensive reform program (USSR); no use of force against the Baltics (USSR); an end to fighting (Yugoslavia); and no proliferation of nuclear weapons (Soviet republics).

48. For example, see Robert Jervis "Security Regimes," pp. 361–362, or his "From Balance to Concert," p. 64. April Carter reflects a widespread view that arms control is possible primarily when "there is widespread disillusionment with military strength and great power politics based on military force," in Carter, *Success and Failure in Arms Control Negotiations* (New York: Oxford University Press, 1989) p. 277. Lawrence Freedman finds that general deterrence of long standing can result in expectations that force will not be used in disputes, thereby allowing a deep conflict to dissolve "into an essentially nonantagonistic relationship," in Freedman, "General Deterrence and the Balance of Power," *Review of International Studies* (1989), 15:208.

49. Robert Tucker notes the passing of a "reliance in the last resort on forcible methods for achieving the ends of statecraft" in Europe, "now that the last great representative of these methods has apparently abandoned them," in "1989 And All That," *Foreign Affairs* (Fall 1990), 69:98–99. Richard Ullman sees great promise in building on the fact that "The people of Europe already regard war among the Continent's major powers as an event with a probability of zero." in "Enlarging the Zone of Peace," p. 109.

50. Michael MccGwire traces the shift not only to a decline in the perceived threat of war but also to a growing Soviet sense that the highly offense-oriented Soviet forces in Europe were damaging detente and provoking American missile deployments that would make war more likely. Thus the shift began before Gorbachev came to power. See MccGwire, *Perestroika and Soviet National Security* (Washington, D.C.: The Brookings Institution, 1991), pp. 24–42, 159–69.

51. In "Realism, Game Theory," Jervis suggests that "perhaps the security dilemma and the resulting DD is more a creature of biases and domestic interests than the structure of the international system" (p. 341).

52. Kenneth Oye, *Cooperation Under Anarchy,* p. 18.

53. Memo to project participants. The numbers problem is extensively examined by James Caporaso in this volume.

54. Examples: Gregory Flynn and David Scheffer, "Limited Collective Security"; Richard Ullman, "Enlarging the Zone of Peace"; Josef Joffe, "Once More:

The German Question"; and comments by Rudolph Rummel and Bruce Russett in "Conversations; Speaking About Democracy and Peace," *United States Institute of Peace Journal* (June 1990), 3:1–4.

55. See Michael Howard, "The Remaking of Europe," *Survival* (March/April 1990), 32:99–106; and Jack Snyder, "Averting Anarchy."

56. See Karl Deutsch et al., *Political Community and the North Atlantic Area* (Princeton: Princeton University Press, 1957).

57. See Bruce Russett, "The Politics of an Alternative Security System: Toward a More Democratic and Therefore More Peaceful World," in Burns Weston, ed., *Alternatives to Nuclear Deterrence* (Boulder, Colo.: Westview, 1990). Mearsheimer, in "Back to the Future," reviews the argument that democracies do not make war on each other, citing relevant works by Michael Doyle and others, and rejects the idea that it can guarantee peace in Europe. See pp. 48–51. He also rejects economic liberalism as the solution.

58. On the importance of increased transparency, see Jervis, "From Balance to Concert," pp. 73–76, and Ullman, "Enlarging the Zone of Peace." On the importance of transparency generally, see Robert Keohane, *After Hegemony*, p. 95; and Frederich Kratochwil and John Gerard Ruggie, "International Organization: A State of the Art on the Art of the State" *International Organization* (Autumn 1986), 40:753–75.

59. Robert Keohane, *International Institutions and State Power: Essays in International Relations Theory* (Boulder, Colo.: Westview, 1989), p. 118.

60. Robert Keohane *International Institutions,* p. 9.

61. Example: Robert Jervis, "From Balance to Concert"; Robert Axelrod and Robert Keohane, "Achieving Cooperation Under Anarchy"; and Kenneth Oye, "Explaining Cooperation Under Anarchy," all in Kenneth Oye, ed., *Cooperation Under Anarchy* (Princeton: Princeton University Press, 1986), pp. 58–79, 226–54, and 1–24, respectively.

62. Jervis, "From Balance to Concert," p. 76.

63. Manfred Worner, "The Atlantic Alliance in the New Era," *NATO Review* (February 1991), 39:8.

64. See Jopp, Rummel and Schmidt, *Integration and Security in Western Europe* for opinion and analysis on this.

65. Robert Keohane, *International Institutions,* p. 30.

10. International Cooperation and Institutional Choice: The European Community's Internal Market

❖

Geoffrey Garrett

THE European Communities' (EC) decision to complete their "internal market" by the end of 1992—embodied in the Single European Act 1986 (SEA)—represents arguably the most ambitious instance of multilateral cooperation since the construction of the post-World War II international order. Its economic objective is the removal of a wide array of nontariff barriers to trade (such as border controls, national standards, preferential procurement policies, and industrial subsidies) that elsewhere have proved politically intractable. The institutional structures underpinning the internal market are more constraining on the behavior of sovereign states than has been the case for other international regimes. The SEA replaced unanimity voting (national vetoes) in the primary decision-making body of the European Community, the Council of Ministers, with a system of majority voting over matters pertaining to the internal market. In addition, the internal market is buttressed by an elaborate and powerful legal system. European law is considered to have supremacy over national laws and to have "direct effect" in domestic jurisdictions (that is, irrespective of whether it is explicitly incorporated through legislation).

How can these attributes of the internal market be explained? A large literature exists on cooperation between self-interested states in the anarchic international system.[1] It is commonly assumed that most issues—including the coordinated opening of domestic markets—can be understood as collective-action problems. All states would benefit from cooperation, but powerful incentives for individuals to defect from cooperative arrangements. These problems—usually cast in terms of the familiar Prisoners' Dilemma—may be mitigated when actions are repeated, when the time horizons of states are long, and when the utility of mutual cooperation is high.[2] Moreover, wide agreement exists that political institutions may help overcome the informational problems that frequently beset cooperative solutions by monitoring the behavior of states, by identifying transgressions, and thereby facilitating the operation of the retaliation and reputational mechanisms highlighted in recent studies.[3]

At least two basic weaknesses are, however, present in this literature. First, the assumption is usually implicitly made—in keeping with the basic thrust of transactions costs economics[4]—that the cooperative arrangements that emerge represent uniquely efficient solutions to the problems facing states. But in most of the interesting issues in international relations, and in the social sciences more generally, discriminating between different potential outcomes in terms of their efficiency is often very difficult.[5] Existing studies can show, *ex post,* that the set of arrangements settled on was loosely "efficient." But they tell us little about why this particular set was chosen from the array of viable alternatives.

The literature's concentration on the functional aspects of the evolution of cooperation—arrangements are generated to solve common problems—also downplays distributional conflicts between states and the impact of power asymmetries on their resolution. In a recent critique, Krasner argues that in many cases, "the problem is not how to get to the Pareto frontier but which point along it will be chosen."[6] If contending solutions to collective-action problems cannot be easily differentiated in terms of their impact on aggregate welfare, and if the various outcomes have significant distributional consequences, studies that concentrate solely on the shared interests of states rather than on conflicts between them will be inadequate.[7]

Many interests were common to all members of the European Community in the mid 1980s and provided the stimulus for the completion of the internal market—most generally, a desire to increase the competitiveness of European goods and services in global markets. Equally apparent, however, is that substantial differences also existed in the preferences of the member states. Thatcher's Conservative government in Britain, for example, sought to replicate its sweeping domestic deregulation agenda at the European level. For other countries wedded to more highly regulated domestic regimes, such as France and Germany, the wholesale adoption of Thatcherite principles was unacceptable. Furthermore, the less developed members of the EC argued that the removal of barriers to trade should be accompanied by extensive financial assistance to mitigate the dislocating effects of market adjustments on the less developed economies.

Second, most studies implicitly assume that the institutions associated with international cooperation have little impact on the political structure of the international system (most simply, the sovereignty of nation states is unchallenged). The common understanding of the role of international institutions is that they monitor the behavior of participants in cooperative agreements and paint "scarlet letters" on transgressors. The punishment of violations is carried out by the states themselves; all the international institution does is to provide information that allows states to further their own interests. Thus, no substantive political authority is seen to be delegated to international institutions. These institutions are construed, not as "governing structures," but merely as informational clearing houses.[8]

The post-1992 European Community may still be some distance from "Europe's would-be polity" as envisaged by early analysts of regional integration: an EC federation with sovereign powers.[9] Characterizing the institutions supporting the internal market as just the apolitical providers of information would, however, be wrong. In contrast with the national vetoes that obtain in most international regimes, a qualified majority of states in the Council of Ministers may impose its will on other members. Moreover, the European Community's legal system operates as if the Treaty of Rome 1958 and the SEA comprise something akin to an EC "constitution," rather than just another international agreement—even if formalized through a treaty, in which each signatory determines the extent of its own obligations.[10] The European Free Trade Association (EFTA), for example, has no formal legal structure for resolving disputes between members.

Thus, analysis of the formation and operation of the European Community's internal market requires moving beyond the approaches prevalent in the international-relations literature on cooperation. This paper adapts approaches developed in other areas—such as spatial theories of political competition, analyses of bargaining games, the effects of incomplete information, and the dynamics of incomplete contracting—to explore four central questions about the internal market.[11] These questions pertain directly to the dynamics of bargaining over the internal market, the impact of power politics on them, and the nature of the institutional choices ultimately agreed to by the members of the European Community:

- What led EC members in the mid 1980s to reinvigorate the integration process?
- What explains the basic political and economic reforms enunciated in the Single European Act?
- What are the implications of the introduction of qualified majority voting in the Council of Ministers for the rules that will govern the internal market?
- How does the European Community's legal structure affect the implementation of the internal market?

This chapter is divided into four sections that correspond to these questions. The first develops a simple functionalist argument that by the mid-1980s economic decline and increasing economic interdependence provided strong incentives for European countries to contemplate coordinated responses to their economic problems.

But this functional analysis cannot explain why the specific form of the internal market within the European Community was chosen from the many possible arrangements that would have represented Pareto improvements for the Community. Interstate bargaining over the SEA is analyzed in the second section, which explains why the specific set of political and economic principles was chosen and why these closely reflected the preferences of France and Germany.

The last two sections then speculate about the consequences of the SEA for the emergent European political economy, with respect to the passage and implementation of internal market rules. The third section explores the institutional relationships among the Council of Ministers, the EC Commission, and the European Parliament in the formulation of internal market rules. While the power of individual governments has been lessened vis-à-vis the Parliament—and especially the Commission— the preferences of the most powerful members are still likely to have a substantial impact on outcomes.

The final section then assesses the role of the European Community's legal system in the implementation of internal market rules. The European Court of Justice has considerable power to impose EC law on recalcitrant states. At the same time, however, most legal decisions about the implementation of rules—as with their formulation—can be expected to accord largely with the interests of powerful states, most importantly, Germany.

The Incentives to Complete the Internal Market

The interstate politics of trade may be characterized as a series of Prisoner's Dilemma games between national governments (figure 10.1).[12] The governments recognize that mutual free trade (A) is preferable to mutual protection (D). Short-term political costs (c) are, however, involved for governments (in terms of those sectors and regions adversely affected by market dislocations) associated with pursuing free-trade policies, even if in the economists' "long run," unilateral free trade benefits all segments of society.[13] Each would most prefer, therefore, a situation in which the other opened its market but in which it was free to protect the home market (gaining the benefits of access to the other's market, P, without incurring the costs of opening the home market, c). Conversely, each government is most fearful of a scenario in which it would open the home market but would not gain free access to that of the other economy (incurring costs, c, without gaining P).

The implications of this game are well known. In a single play, governments would choose to protect their home markets. Iteration creates, however, the possibility that free trade may be sustained. Mutual liberalization is more likely the less governments discount the future and the greater the benefits of access to the markets of others relative to the costs of opening the home market.[14]

With respect to the European Community's internal market, it is clear that the ever-growing trade dependence of the European economies—combined with more than a decade of poor and declining economic performance ("Eurosclerosis")—greatly increased the benefits of completing the common market relative to the costs of participation. The linkages between national economies grew rapidly within Europe between the early 1960s and the early 1980s.[15] With increasing openness, the efficacy of economic strategies based on the manipulation of the domestic

Figure 10.1. The Simple Trade Dilemma.

		Other	
		Free Trade	Protect
Government	Free Trade	$P-c, P-c$ (A)	$-c, p$ (B)
	Protect	$P, -c$ (C)	$0,0$ (D)

where: the payoffs for government of different outcomes are expressed first; P: the benefits of open markets in the other country; c: the costs to a country of opening its home market; $P>c>0$

market and protection from external forces was significantly reduced. Instead, all governments were forced to concentrate on improving the competitiveness of national goods and services in world markets and promoting rapid adjustment to changing market conditions.[16] Furthermore, the power of large transnational firms increased significantly during the early 1980s. Given the strong preferences of such companies for free access to other markets and for reducing cross-border transactions costs, the greater influence of transnational business added further to the pressures for trade liberalization in Europe.[17]

Developments in the relationships among European nations, Japan, and the United States were also very important in generating incentives for further regional integration within the EC. The European economies had suffered through more than ten years of industrial unrest and stagflation when the world economy began to recover from the second OPEC shock in the winter of 1982–1983. But while the American and Japanese recoveries were swift and strong, the European economies did not rebound nearly so quickly.[18] Concomitantly, government instability increased dramatically during the latter 1970s and early 1980s as voters punished their leaders for not arresting economic decline. Some governments, in efforts to remain in power, were forced to abandon their traditional strategies and to undertake radical policy U-turns (most notably, Mitterrand in France).[19]

That trade liberalization was appealing to European governments at this time is not surprising, therefore. The economic—and ultimately political—costs of the status quo were very high. The potential payoffs of an EC internal market were large. Such a conclusion need not rest solely on the findings of economic analyses projecting significant improvement in aggregate economic performance accruing from reduced transactions costs and the logic of comparative advantage and scale economies.[20] Rather, developing the European Community was also desirable to member states feeling the pressure of international competition as a device for creating new and ingenious forms of protection (the "Fortress Europe" so feared by American and Japanese firms).

Moreover, institutional reform would likely have been an important element in the mutual liberalization of trade in the European Community. Wide agreement exists that for cooperation to "evolve" in the manner envisaged by Axelrod, all participants must know a great deal about the past behavior of each other. In the simplest case, the playing of "tit-for-tat" strategies is contingent upon actors' knowing how each other played in the last round of the game. While this may be relatively simple in dyadic interactions, the existence of multiple actors greatly increases the probability that players will not know enough about the past behavior of others to make informed strategic choices.[21] Furthermore, in the complex world of the contemporary integrated world economy, the ability of any single actor—whether a firm or government—to know whether another has played fair or cheated in past games must be seriously questioned.[22]

Institutions that monitor the behavior of participants to a cooperative agreement and that identify transgressions of the agreement are likely to be vital to the retaliation and reputational processes that undergird the logic of the iterated Prisoners' Dilemma.[23] In the context of the European Community, therefore, one could have expected that the establishment of institutions for overcoming incomplete information problems would have been an essential component of moves to complete the internal market.

Political Bargaining Over the Single European Act

The analysis presented in the preceding section provides considerable insight into the incentives in the mid-1980s for the European states to coordinate their responses to economic decline and heightened interdependence, why these are likely to involve the liberalization of trade within the European Community, and why institutional reform was likely to have been an integral element in this process. Nonetheless, these arguments betray the weaknesses inherent in all functional analysis. While they shed considerable light on the broad opportunities and constraints facing political actors, they are far less well equipped to explain the specific choices made by these actors.

With respect to the European Community, potential internal market reforms could have taken numerous forms. Member states could have agreed to the pervasive deregulation of national political economies, in accordance with neoclassical economic principles. But they could also have supplemented such national deregulation with new regulatory regimes at the EC level. These could have ranged from attempts to standardize practices across all EC members (referred to as "harmonization") to providing extensive development assistance to countries adversely affected by the dislocations of adjusting to market forces.

Moreover, EC members faced myriad choices with respect to the political institutions to undergird the internal market. The extant system of unanimity voting (national vetoes) in the Council of Ministers could have been maintained. If members wished to quicken the pace of integration (whatever its economic form), they could have adopted a majority voting rule in the Council. With respect to the implementation of the internal market, members could have affirmed the existing system in which the European Court of Justice played a central role. But the European Community could have chosen to increase the power and resources of the Commission (and the Council) to monitor adherence to internal market rules and to punish transgressions.

The choice of economic and political institutions to govern the internal market should clearly be a central element of analyses of European integration. The conventional cooperation literature tends not to concentrate on these issues. Rather, it only suggests that the chosen institutional solutions conform with efficiency criteria. In situations where numerous potential solutions exist to collective-action problems that cannot easily be distinguished in terms of their consequences for aggregate welfare—and the internal market is one—the "new economics of organization" lexicon masks the fundamental political issue of bargaining over institutional design.[24]

The remainder of this article is devoted to explaining the institutional choices made by EC members since the mid-1980s. The analysis begins with the signing of the Single European Act, in which member states decided on the basic economic principles and political institutions that would govern the internal market. Subsequent sections examine how the political institutions translate these basic principles into an elaborate set of detailed rules and how these rules are enforced.

THE ECONOMIC PREFERENCES OF EC MEMBERS OVER THE INTERNAL MARKET

Before examining in detail the preferences of the different member states over the general form of the internal market, brief discussion is warranted of how these preferences have been adduced. The countries' preferences over the internal market are not based in a structural realist framework, where the "national interest" is derived solely from the position of a country in the international system.[25] Rather, they reflect the political interests of the national governments that were in place in the mid-1980s. These were undoubtedly affected by international economic conditions and by the position of national economies in the world division of labor. However, these economic incentives were significantly mediated by domestic political and institutional factors, such as electoral competition, government partisanship, ideology, and the organization of economic interests.[26]

The national preferences presented in this paper are aggregated over the multitude of issue areas pertaining to the internal market. The preferences of EC members are not assumed to be identical across all areas. Rather, the analysis seeks to capture the fundamental orientation of the different national governments with respect to the general type of internal market they preferred. How pervasive should have been the deregulation of national political economies? To what extent should such deregulation have been replaced by new regulations at the EC level?

The European status quo (SQ) of the early 1980s afforded states considerable opportunities for protecting domestic markets (see the top panel of figure 10.2). Tariffs had been reduced with successive rounds of the Generalized Agreement on Tariffs and Trade (GATT), but numerous impediments to free trade remained. Significant physical barriers existed to the movement of goods, services, and people, embodied in customs controls, restrictions on interstate freight transportation, and the like.[27] The existence of elaborate national standards and other regulations significantly curtailed the free flow of goods and services.[28] Public procurement constituted around 15 percent of total EC Gross Domestic Product (GDP), and governments strongly favored national suppliers in the awarding of contracts.[29] Large variations occurred between countries in rates of Value Added Taxation (VAT).[30] Annual industrial subsidies for EC members averaged about US $65 billion in the early 1980s.[31]

For the reasons outlined in the preceding section, all member governments were interested in moving away from this status quo through revision of the Treaty of Rome 1958 (revisions required the unanimous approval of all twelve members). But national preferences over the nature of internal market reforms varied considerably.[32]

Thatcher's Conservative government in the United Kingdom preferred a truly laissez-faire trade regime in Europe: the translation of its domestic reform agenda of the 1980s onto the EC stage. Britain advocated pervasive deregulation of the political economies of member states. In addition to the removal of physical barriers, the Thatcher government supported the "mutual recognition" of national standards (good and services sold in one country should be saleable in all others without restriction), the elimination of preferential public procurement and other industrial policies such as subsidies, and liberalization of the financial sector.[33] Moreover, the Conservatives were staunchly opposed to any reregulation at the

Figure 10.2. Bargaining Over the Single European Act

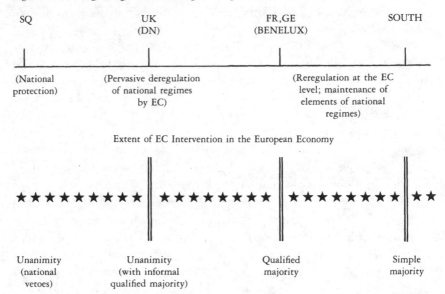

Extent of EC Intervention in the European Economy

Voting in the Council of Ministers

where: SQ = the pre-1986 status quo; UK = the United Kingdom; DN = Denmark; BENE-LUX = Belgium, Luxembourg, and the Netherlands; SOUTH = Greece, Ireland, Italy, Portugal, and Spain.

EC level, particularly with respect to industrial relations issues. To a considerable extent, the views of the Danish Christian Democratic-led government were similar to those of the British government.[34]

The preferences of the other two majors players in the European Community—France and Germany—differed significantly from those of the United Kingdom. The German Christian Democratic–Free Democratic coalition was a strong supporter of the liberalization of trade, but only where this would increase the penetration of highly competitive German exporters into other EC markets. Thus, they too advocated the elimination of physical barriers and mutual recognition. At the same time, however, the government was wary of British attempts to undermine the institutional and regulatory complex that is at the foundation of the German economy. In particular, the Germans would have no truck with efforts to deregulate the financial sector—such as removing the large barriers to hostile takeovers or reducing the stake of banks in the stock market—which allowed firms to adopt the long-term time horizons deemed central to competing in high value-added markets.[35] Furthermore, the German government (and particularly the Foreign Minister and leader of the Free Democratic Party, Genscher) supported the harmonization of the practices of EC members in numerous areas. These included various elements of social policy, from a concern that differences in transfer payments and the like would result in outflows of capital and low-skilled jobs to countries with lower levels of welfare provision (so-called "social dumping").

The failure of Mitterrand's experiment with "socialism in one country" in the early 1980s led his Socialist administration to assume a stance on European integration that was close to that of the German government.[36] The French supported the mutual recognition of national standards and products but were opposed to sweeping deregulation of national political economic regimes within Europe. Their primary concern was to protect the interventionist industrial policies that had long been central elements of France's overall economic strategy. The French were somewhat stronger proponents of regulation at the EC level than the German government was. This is partly explicable in terms of the ideological predilections of leaders of the French Socialist Party (including Delors, who subsequently became President of the EC Commission). Clearly, Mitterrand's desire to be a leading figure on the EC stage was also important.

The Benelux countries closely followed the lead of France and Germany over the internal market. As small, open economies that were competitive in high value-added sectors, these countries shared many structural interests with France and especially with Germany. Moreover, these economies were inextricably entwined with those of their much larger neighbors. Government leaders realized that irrespective of their own behavior, France and Germany could unilaterally agree to change the nature of their economic relationships and that the Benelux countries would have little choice but to acquiesce in these changes. Thus, it was reasonable for them to support the positions taken by the French and German governments from the outset (in the hope that they might have some influence over common positions).

Finally, the poorer, predominantly southern European states favored an even more interventionist internal market than France, Germany and their allies did.[37] For these countries, further integration into the European economy was essential to their development in the long run, but significant dislocation costs were associated with the liberalization of domestic markets in the short term. As a result, these governments—

especially those dominated by Social Democratic parties—were concerned that deregulation of national political economies be attended by significant development assistance, paid for by the wealthier member states, and distributed by the European Community.

BARGAINING OVER INSTITUTIONAL REFORM IN THE SEA

What was the impact of these national preferences on bargaining over the internal market? The Single European Act did not lay out in detail the extent and types of EC interventions that would govern the internal market. Rather, members approved only the general objective of removing all barriers to the movement of capital, goods, persons, and services within the European Community. The SEA posits the goal of harmonizing the practices of member states by the end of 1992 but acknowledges that after that date the principle of mutual recognition should obtain.

The SEA did, however, make institutional reforms with respect to the mechanism by which these general principles would be translated into detailed rules governing the internal market. Unanimity voting in the governing body of the European Community—the Council of Ministers—was replaced by a "qualified" majority rule for most matters pertaining to the internal market.[38] The Council's mandate is to decide whether and how to institutionalize the 279 reforms identified by the EC Commission's 1985 White Paper as essential to the completion of the internal market. Votes in the Council are apportioned as follows: France, Germany, Italy, and the UK each receive 10 votes; Spain, 8; Belgium, Greece, the Netherlands, and Portugal, 5; Denmark and Ireland, 3; and Luxembourg, 2; 54 of the 76 votes constitute a qualified majority.

How can this institutional reform be explained? It is reasonable to assert that national preferences over final economic outcomes—the extent of national deregulation and EC reregulation system—informed the interests of member governments with respect to institutional reform in the Council of Ministers (see the bottom panel of figure 10.2).

The British government's primary objectives with respect to the SEA were to facilitate the deregulation of national regimes and to block any attempts by other member states to impose any EC-level reregulation. Since its entry into the Community, Greece had provided a significant roadblock to efforts to deregulate the European economy. As a result, the British government advocated informal mechanisms by which such opposition could be vitiated.[39] However, Thatcher was deeply opposed to formal changes in Council procedures that would have to be embodied in a treaty revision, which was viewed by many in Britain as tantamount to a derogation of national sovereignty.

The preferences of the French and German governments were different. They were interested in establishing some form of majority voting that would not permit the United Kingdom to exercise a veto over efforts to create an internal market that was more interventionist than that envisaged by Thatcher. At the same time, France and Germany had also to be wary of institutional reforms—such as simple majority voting with each country receiving one vote—that would tilt the balance of power considerably in favor of the less developed member states. Thus, the French and Germany governments preferred a voting system in which supermajorities were required and in which votes were weighted in accordance with economic power.

The interests of the southern countries and Ireland would have been best furthered by the introduction of simple majority voting in the Council. Under such a rule, the support of any two other countries would have been sufficient to allow them to foist their preferences—for example, for extensive development assistance—onto their more wealthy northern neighbors.

Given this array of preferences, the qualified majority system that was ultimately settled on in the Single European Act most closely approximated the preferences of France, Germany, and their Benelux allies. Voting weights in the Council were determined at the moments when community membership was expanded and hence were not deemed negotiable during bargaining over the SEA.[40] Nonetheless, the supermajority (54 76) criterion did satisfy the central concerns of France and Germany. The opposition of these countries and their Benelux neighbors was sufficient to veto measures of which they disapproved. Britain (even with the support of Denmark) could not stop the enactment of interventionist reforms.[41] Moreover, the support of these countries would likely be essential for the passage of any directives.

How can this outcome be explained? Why were France and Germany better able to further their preferences than the other members of the Community were? The decisions of the less developed countries are not problematic. Following Hirschman's classic argument about asymmetric economic dependence, their bargaining position vis-à-vis the northern states was very weak.[42] Put simply, these countries needed access to the markets and resources of the wealthier states much more than these countries required them. In addition, France and Germany further sweetened the SEA for these countries by doubling the funds for structural assistance to less developed regions.[43]

The acquiescence of the United Kingdom (the other major player in the European Community) in qualified majority voting requires closer investigation. At least three factors—which in many ways were similar to those influencing the behavior of the less developed countries—affected the bargaining dynamics between France and Germany, on the one hand, and Britain, on the other.[44]

First, it is clear that the economic power of France and Germany (when combined with the Benelux countries, well over half of total EC output) was very important. Threats by these countries to "go it alone" to create some sort of free-trade area between themselves were highly credible, and Kohl and Mitterrand consistently raised this prospect when negotiations with Britain became bogged down.[45] French and especially German domestic markets were the motor for EC growth; these two economies also dominated export markets in Europe.[46] Thus, the United Kingdom—and the other EC members—had to be fearful of being treated like any other third country (such as Japan or the United States) in trade with France and Germany: subject to national treatment or mutual reciprocity ("you can trade with us only if your goods meet our standards") rather than governed by the principle of mutual recognition.

Second, countries that wished to trade with France and Germany would inevitably have been forced by economic necessity to conform to the rules chosen by these powerful economies regardless of whether they were parties to trade agreements with France and Germany. It was thus in the interests of other countries to join the internal market at the outset—and have some say over what the rules of the market would be—rather than merely later acquiesce in rules over which they had no control. Such a fear was particularly salient for the United Kingdom. It was widely perceived that Britain had suffered considerably from not joining the European Community until the early 1970s, when the Common Agricultural Policy and budgetary practices detrimental to Britain were already entrenched. Furthermore, many criticized the Conservative government for not joining the exchange rate mechanism of the European Monetary System (EMS) until 1989, when Britain's inflation rate was well above the average of countries already disciplined by the strictures of the exchange rate mechanism.

Finally, deep divisions within the Conservative government weakened the bargaining power of the United Kingdom in negotiations over the SEA.[47] Many members of the government were considerably more "pro-European" than Thatcher was, and this was well known among government leaders from other EC states. As a result, those pushing for a more radical internal market than that favored by Thatcher could expect that her ability to continually oppose such initiatives would ultimately be limited by the need to hold together her domestic coalition.[48]

In sum, there were good reasons—ranging from the structure of the European economy to Conservative Party politics—why France and Germany were able to gain the acquiescence of the British government in the qualified majority voting reform of the SEA. In turn, one would expect that the institution of qualified majority voting would have resulted in subsequent internal market legislation that accorded closely with the economic preferences of France and Germany.

The Passage of Internal Market Directives: The Council of Ministers, The Commission, and the European Parliament

The introduction of qualified majority voting in the Council of Ministers on matters pertaining to the internal market was the most important institutional reform in the Single European Act. The previous section suggested that this reform would result in the generation of specific rules that furthered the interests of France and Germany.[49] Before this conclusion can be substantiated, however, it is necessary to delve more deeply into the dynamics of decision making in the European Community after the passage of the SEA. The relationships among the Council, the Commission and the European Parliament are depicted in figure 10.3.[50]

Three salient features of the internal market decision-making procedure should be highlighted:

- The Commission alone may make proposals about the completion of the internal market (drawn from the two hundred seventy-nine directives in the White Paper).
- The Council of Ministers may amend Commission proposals only in the last instance and only by acting unanimously.
- The European Parliament may approve, reject, or amend a Council decision.[51] If it rejects a Council decision, the Council may overturn

Figure 10.3. The Passage of Internal Market Directives

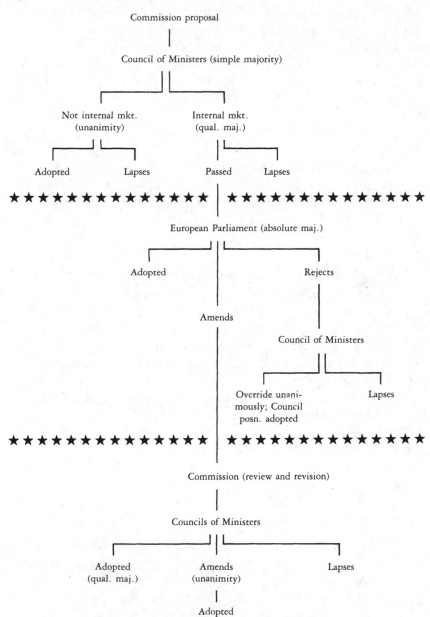

it only by a unanimous vote. If the Parliament amends a decision, the amendments are then considered by the Commission, which may alter them before they are sent back to the Council.

The implications of this complex decision-making procedure for internal market outcomes merit close analysis. The Commission would seem to have considerable power by virtue of its agenda-setting role (that is, to make proposals on which the Council votes). The threshold for invoking qualified majority voting is quite low. The Commission's assertion that a matter pertains to the internal market stands unless challenged by the member of the Council.[52] If a simple majority of members agrees with the Commission, voting is taken by qualified majority.

If the Council then votes by qualified majority, the Commission may effectively choose the proposal closest to its preferred outcome for which there is support from any qualified majority. This can be illustrated simply by adding the preferences of the Commission to those of the member states as previously discussed. Assume that for a given directive, the preferences of member states are as follows: the United Kingdom and Denmark prefer the least interventionist outcome (and command thirteen votes); the less developed countries want the most; and France, Germany, and the Benelux countries occupy an intermediate position (thirty-two votes). Furthermore, also assume that the Commission's preference is for even more regulation at the EC level than is wanted by the less developed countries (see figure 10.4).[53]

The Commission would appear to be able to make a proposal at any point to the right of the preferences of France, Germany, and their allies so long as this proposal was closer to the preferences of these countries than the status quo is (such as the proposal depicted in figure 10.4). Such a proposal would gain at least sixty-three votes in the Council of Ministers.[54] Moreover, the ability of the Council to amend Commission proposals is heavily circumscribed (see below). The Commission could,

Figure 10.4. Qualified Majority Voting and Commission Power

| SQ | UK (DN) | FR,GE (BENELUX) | SOUTH | COMMISSION PROPOSAL |

Commission proposals preferred by
FR, GE to SQ

therefore, select among the viable proposals—those that would be supported by a qualified majority—and choose the one closest to its preferred position.[55]

The new decision-making structure of the Single European Act did not, however, affect only the Council and the Commission. It also increased the influence of the European Parliament (see the middle panel in figure 10.3). The Parliament's role before 1986 was purely advisory and consultative (and as such, very limited). Following the SEA, directives that generate the support of a qualified majority in the Council are then submitted to the Parliament. At this stage, the Parliament may take any of three decisions by absolute majority: to adopt, reject, or amend the legislation.

If the Parliament rejects a directive from the Council, it returns to the Council for further deliberation. Unless the Council chooses unanimously to override the Parliament's rejection, the matter under consideration lapses. Thus, the Parliament has the ability to veto directives of which as many as eleven of the twelve members of the Council approve.

If, however, the Parliament wishes to take a constructive role in the passage of directives, it may choose to amend proposals that receive the support of a qualified majority in the Council. At first blush, this ability to amend directives for reconsideration by the Council appears similar to the agenda power of the Commission analyzed above. If this were the case, the Parliament would be able to exercise even more influence over the passage of directives than the Commission would (by acting after it). In fact, however, this potential power is considerably weakened by the Commission's ability to modify Parliament's amendments before they are again voted on by the Council (the bottom panel of figure 10.3). Thus, Parliament amendments merely allow the Commission again to make its own proposals.

Given this structure, the Commission will likely consult with and pay heed to the preferences of the Parliament before it makes its initial proposals to the Council. It is not in the interests of the Commission to make a proposal (even one receiving support of a qualified majority in the Council) that will be rejected by an absolute majority in the Parliament. Nor should the Commission be expected to make proposals that the Parliament will amend. In addition to adding a further cycle of Council voting, amendments make it possible for the Council itself to amend Commission proposals and to adopt them through a unanimous vote. Even though such an eventuality is unlikely, the Commission nonetheless should be anticipated to prefer the simplest path for the passage of internal market directives (Commission proposal, passed by a qualified majority in the Council and supported by an absolute majority of the Parliament).

In sum, the analysis above suggests that the Commission—acting in concert with the Parliament—should be able to effectively exercise its agenda-setting power to facilitate the passage of internal market directives that accord quite closely with its own preferences.

Little evidence exists, however, that the Commission has exercised this power. Although about two thirds of the White Paper's recommendations for internal market directives were passed by the middle of 1991, the Commission has not pressed ahead with many of the measures it deems most important, such as harmonizing indirect taxation and social policy and creating an EC company statute. Moreover, those passed directives that have significantly decreased the autonomy of national governments—and hence were likely to generate the most opposition in the Council of Ministers—have tended to accord with the preferences of the most powerful member states, especially Germany. Perhaps the most significant directives have pertained to the liberalization of public procurement. These have made it much more difficult for national governments to give preferential treatment to domestic suppliers, to the advantage of countries with more competitive producers of goods and services.[56]

Why has the Commission been unable to impose its preferred legislation on the Council? Senior members of the Commission are political appointees of limited tenure (four years), and hence their governments may choose not to reappoint them if they do not act in their governments' interests.[57] Furthermore, there is an implicit legitimacy constraint on the Commission. The Commission is pursuing a strategy of only slowly pushing forward the bounds of its authority because commissioners are fearful that, if they should act too radically, the members of the Community might significantly curtail their power.

Most importantly, the Commission may be constrained by the prospect that governments in the Council may vote strategically not to support all proposals that are preferable to the status quo. Member governments understand that if a qualified majority should not support a Commission proposal, the proposal would lapse. Now reconsider the voting behavior of France, Germany, and the Benelux countries. It has been assumed that these countries would support all Commission proposals so long as they were marginally closer to the preferences of these countries than the status quo was. But knowing that without their support the Commission's proposal would lapse, these countries might choose strategically not to vote for the proposal—forcing the Commission to make a new proposal. In fact, they might continue so to act until the Commission made a proposal that was quite close to their own preferences.

The structure of this iterated bargaining resembles a "divide the dollar" game between the Commission and France and Germany, in which the side that has the greater interest in achieving a compromise more quickly would have less influence on the outcome.[58] Thus, the Commission's failure to pursue many of its preferred directives may reflect a greater desire on its part to pass internal market directives than is the case for France and Germany. This might result, among other things, from the limited duration and political nature of commissioners' appointments or from the need for the Commission to earn its legitimacy by presiding over the completion of the internal market.

If this is the case, again it seems as if the countries that had the greatest bargaining leverage over the Single European Act generated institutional reforms that would reflect this power in the passage of internal market directives. France and Germany can hold out for proposals that are close to their most preferred outcomes, anticipating that the Commission will ultimately bow to their preferences to generate an agreement.

Implementing Internal Market Directives: The European Court of Justice, Domestic Courts, and National Governments

The formulation of economic rules is not the final step in translating the SEA into a functioning internal market. Rather, these rules have then to be enforced in member states. The basic structure of the implementation procedure is depicted in figure 10.5.[59]

The SEA envisages that the basic mechanism for implementing the internal market is for national governments to legislate into domestic law directives that are duly passed in the manner discussed in the preceding section. If this procedure is followed—and it has been in many instances[60]—there is no puzzle to adherence to internal market rules. These simply become part of national law.

Many other ways exist, however, in which internal market rules can

Figure 10.5. The Implementation of the Internal Market

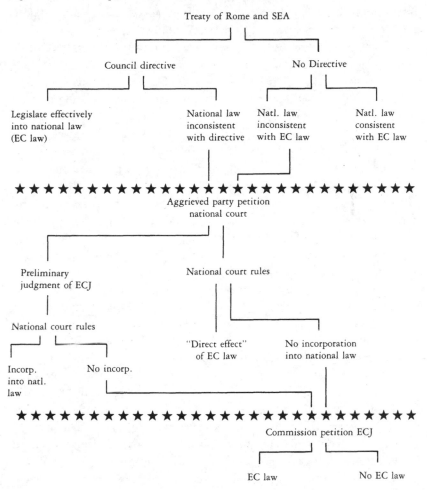

be implemented. Consider the options available to a private party that has suffered from the transgression of an internal market rule. What can the aggrieved party do if it believes that national law is inconsistent with a directive that has been passed by the Council (either because the national government has not legislated the directive into national law or has done so inappropriately) or if no directive exists and the party considers prevailing national law to conflict with Treaty of Rome or the SEA (the first panel of figure 10.5)? In either case, the aggrieved party may petition a domestic court.

A national court hearing such a case has two options. First, it may simply apply what it believes to be EC law: this is the so-called "direct effect" of European law.[61] Second, the domestic court may ask the European Court of Justice for a preliminary ruling as to the status of EC law relating to the case at hand.[62] If by either of these procedures, the national court rules in favor of the plaintiff, EC law may effectively have dominated both the will of the national government and existing national law. This is the so-called "supremacy" of EC law (the middle panel of figure 10.5).[63] If the national court does not rule in favor of the aggrieved party, the party may then request that the EC Commission petition the Court of Justice directly. At this point, the Court may then find in its favor (the bottom panel of figure 10.5).

This system has been quite effective. No systematic difference exists in the extent to which EC laws are followed relative to purely national ones.[64] Furthermore, EC laws have effectively constrained the behavior of members even in areas that impinge directly on the traditional authority of national governments. In the light of the recent EC public procurement directives, some liberalization of public tendering has occurred. In 1990, a German company won the contract to build the Marseilles metro and an Italian corporation was awarded the tender to construct a road bypass around Lyon.

Furthermore, the threat of an action being brought before the Court of Justice significantly affected the behavior of the Danish government with respect to a large contract to build the Great Belt Eastern Bridge between Denmark and Sweden.[65] After receiving bids from both national and foreign firms, the Danish government gave the contract to a domestic company. A British–French consortium believed that its tender was more competitive and took its complaint to the EC Commission. The Commission threatened to prosecute the Danish government in the European Court of Justice (ECJ). Fearing an adverse judgment in the Court, the Danish government ultimately agreed to pay costs and damages to the foreign consortium rather than to proceed with the case.

Cases have also occurred in which the Court of Justice has explicitly declared that national laws contravene existing EC law. Following an appeal to the Commission by an Italian subsidiary of Du Pont, the Court ruled in 1990 that an Italian law requiring 30 percent of contracts to be awarded to firms based in southern Italy violated the public procurement directives.[66] In a second instance, a British court referred to the Court of Justice for preliminary judgment a case in which Spanish fishermen claimed that a 1988 British law restricting the right of foreign boats to be registered in the United Kingdom was inconsistent with the European Community's principle of the freedom of establishment. The Court ruled in favor of the Spaniards and declared that the British law was inconsistent with its EC treaty obligations.[67]

Despite these instances, the powers of the EC legal system should not be overstated. In the British and Italian cases mentioned above, the responses of the national governments are not yet certain, and both governments will likely find ways to subvert at least partially the intent of the Court of Justice. In the Danish bridge case, while the government was willing to pay fines and damages to the aggrieved consortium, it was not prepared to reopen tenders for the very lucrative contract. More generally, the EC legal system is not based on a solid institutional foundation. The operation of the direct-effect doctrine and the referral of cases of the Court of Justice for preliminary judgment are both contingent upon the continued willingness of national courts to acquiesce in the supremacy of EC law. The Court's sanctioning powers are very limited. Its decisions are supposed to be "binding" on national governments, but it cannot enforce such decisions directly.

Nonetheless, the EC system of laws is clearly far more constraining on the behavior of actors within member states—both firms and governments—than other bodies of international treaty law are. This raises two fundamental and closely related questions. Why do sovereign states abide by the dictates of EC law even when these are detrimental to their interests? Why did member governments, when formulating the SEA, decide not to alter the structure of this system so as to lessen the constraints it imposes on national political authority?

Legal scholars argue that the extension of the power of the European Court stems largely from inattention on the part of national governments. According to Stein, "although the issues determined in the judicial process often have significant long-term implications, the political decision makers view them mostly as 'technical,' and thus lawyers are given a more or less free hand."[68] A slightly modified version of this argument would be that the costs and difficulties of changing this system outweighed the benefits. Such explanations may have been plausible prior to the signing of the SEA. They seem much less persuasive given the decision to complete the internal market, which necessarily entailed a significant expansion in the scope of EC law. If the national governments had wished to change the EC legal system, they could have done so in the SEA.

A more powerful explanation for the maintenance of the EC legal system is that it is actually—and seemingly paradoxically, given its consequences for national authority—consistent with the interests of member states. In order to make this argument, one must view the delegation of authority to the European Court of Justice in terms of the monitoring and incomplete contracting problems confronting EC members.

Conventional analyses of cooperation tend to assume both that members of a community will, *ex ante,* agree on an exhaustive set of rules to govern all their future interactions and that compliance with and transgressions of these rules will be transparent. Both assumptions, are often, however, unwarranted.

Let us begin by returning to the basic trade dilemma facing the EC members. All countries would most prefer for EC rules to constrain the behavior of all others, so long as they were free to flout internal market rules when they so desired. Our discussion to this point has assumed that all EC members would know when firms and governments in other countries attempted to free ride. Thus, compliance with the internal market would be promoted through fear of retaliation or losses of reputation.

Given the multitude and complexity of interactions in the European Community, it is a practical impossibility for all governments to know precisely whether actors have transgressed common agreements in the past. Such uncertainty would potentially have significant deleterious consequences for the stability of the internal market. If members could not be sure how and why others behaved previously—and if they believe their own behavior could not be monitored effectively—the incentives to violate internal market rules would be very strong.[69]

Thus, the existence of a legal system that monitored the behavior of participants and identified transgressions of commonly agreed rules would contribute significantly to the efficacy of cooperative agreements. In the context of the internal market, the ability of injured parties to bring potential violations of EC law to the attention of national courts and the Court of Justice substantially strengthens the internal market. If national governments are to ignore judgments brought against them, they must do so in a very public manner—by passing statutes that transparently violate their EC commitments. In extreme cases, governments might be moved to so act—indeed the SEA acknowledges this possibility. But in general it is likely that the ability of the EC legal system to paint scarlet letters on transgressors of internal market rules will significantly reduce such transgressions.

The EC legal system also performs another important role for member states: mitigating the incomplete contracting problems facing them. It is always very costly—if not impossible—for actors to make exhaustive agreements that anticipate every dispute that may arise between them. Rather, parties will inevitably make agreements that only sketch the broad "rules of the game" and then delegate the authority to apply and adapt these rules to specific cases.[70] This is clearly what the members of the European Community had in mind in the SEA with respect to the role of the Council of Ministers in the passage of directives.[71]

However, directives are intended only to provide guidelines for the passage of national laws. Furthermore, even relatively detailed national laws require interpretation in the light of specific cases. This is precisely the role played by the national courts and the Court of Justice in the European Community. The EC legal system provides a mechanism through which the types of general agreements about the rules of the game supplied by the EC treaties and internal market directives can be applied to the myriad interactions that constitute the EC economy.

The EC legal mechanism would be in the interests of the member governments only if national courts and the Court of Justice faithfully implement the collective internal market preferences of members. At a general level, it may be argued that courts wishing to maintain their authority, legitimacy, and independence must strive not to be over-turned.[72] As a consequence, the actions of all courts are fundamentally political, in that they anticipate the possible reactions of other political actors in order to avoid their intervention.

The incentives for the European Court of Justice to act in this manner are strengthened by its institutional weaknesses. Its position is not explicitly supported by a written constitution. Twelve of the thirteen justices of the Court are selected by each member state, and they must be reappointed every six years. It is thus reasonable to expect that the justices of the European Court would choose not to act in ways of which powerful political actors in the Community would disapprove.

The justices know that decisions against individual states may not always be adhered to by the disaffected governments if they deem the Court's rulings to violate fundamental national interests. The oppro-brium of individual states would be ineffective if most members—or at least the powerful members—favored the Court's decision (given the logic of the preceding subsection). The Court must be fearful, however, that a coordinated attack on its behavior and competencies—through systematic noncompliance or at the extreme, a treaty revision—would be disastrous.

As with the other functional arguments addressed in this article, the analysis above of the efficiency of the EC legal system begs the critical question: in whose interests do the courts act? Here again, it seems that the principles governing decisions of the Court of Justice—and hence of national courts following its rulings—are consistent with the preferences of France and, particularly, Germany. Recall that these states have an interest in the mutual recognition of national standards. In order to increase their shares of foreign markets, these countries would like there to be no barriers to the entry into other markets of all goods and services that can be sold domestically. France and Germany are both, however, concerned that the internal market not result in the dismantling of aspects of their domestic political economic regimes (such as stringent financial regulation and active industrial policies) that they deem central to their economic performance.

The Court of Justice was committed to this agenda before the signing of the SEA. Its ruling in the landmark 1979 case, *Cassis de Dijon,* firmly established the principle of "mutual recognition" as the foundation of EC law, and it has been unwavering in its application of this principle since. Moreover, the Court has been unwilling to extend the scope of this essentially deregulating and laissez-faire doctrine to others, including precisely those cherished by the French and German governments.

Thus, the EC legal system serves the purposes of the French and Germans very well. It is true that the system facilitates the monitoring of the behavior of firms and governments and the application of general internal market rules to a wide array of cases not explicitly covered by the SEA or by Council directives. But more important is that the "rules of the game" the Court applies conform closely with the interests of France and Germany.

Conclusion

The European Community's internal market is manifestly very different from the regimes commonly studied in international relations. Its economic objective is to tackle an array of nontariff barriers to trade that have proved highly resilient to change in other international institutions. The political structure underpinning the internal market is elaborate, involving a formalized legislative process (the passage of internal market directives by the Council of Ministers, the Commission, and the European Parliament) and a judicial system (embodying the Court of Justice and national courts that follow its rulings) that exercises considerable authority over the behavior of governments and firms in individual member states.

Conventional theories of international cooperation are not well suited to analyzing the internal market. Most importantly, studies have tended to assume a functional orientation—the agreements and institutions that emerge represent uniquely efficient solutions to common problems. The lexicon of collective-action problems is very helpful in delineating the general environment in which cooperative solutions may emerge and the general institutional forms such solutions may take. This approach downplays, however, the fundamentally political nature of most bargaining over cooperative agreements. Many potential solutions to collective-action problems that conform with Pareto criteria are likely to emerge. However, in most instances these different solutions are likely to have significant distributional consequences, and hence the preferences of participants between these may differ considerably. Thus, the focus on common problems should be supplemented by explicit attention to the dynamics of bargaining over the detailed form that cooperation will take.

This article has undertaken such analysis with respect to the decision of the EC members in the mid-1980s to complete the internal market between them. Both the economic rules and political institutions governing the internal market reflect the preferences of the most powerful countries in the European Community—France and particularly Germany. This is not to suggest that no common problems faced all EC members in the mid-1980s and that the internal market has not helped resolve these. At the same time, however, it is equally apparent that the form of the internal market has been significantly influenced by the preferences of the most powerful countries. It is reasonable to presume that efforts to further integrate the European Community—such as economic and monetary unions, political union, and expansion—will be similarly affected by power politics.

Acknowledgments

This article was prepared for the Ford Foundation workshop on Multilateralism, organized by John Gerard Ruggie. I gratefully acknowledge the Ford Foundation's financial support for this project. Additional financial support was provided by the Center for Advanced Study in the Behavioral Sciences, the Hewlett Fund, and the Institute for International Studies,

Stanford University. James Caparaso, Jeffry Frieden, Judith Goldstein, Lloyd Gruber, Robert Koehane, Stephen Krasner, Peter Lange, Lisa Martin, Andrew Moravcsik, James Morrow, Douglas Rivers, John Ruggie, David Soskice, George Tsebelis, Helen Wallace, Barry Weingast, and Stephen Woolcock gave helpful comments on various aspects of this paper. Gabriella Montinola gave very helpful research assistance.

NOTES

1. For good collections of such research, see Stephen D. Krasner, ed., *International Regimes* (Ithaca, N.Y.: Cornell University Press, 1983); and Kenneth Oye, ed., *Cooperation Under Anarchy* (Princeton: Princeton University Press, 1986).

2. Robert Axelrod, *The Evolution of Cooperation* (New York: Basic Books, 1984); David Kreps et al., "Rational Cooperation in the Finitely Repeated Prisoner's Dilemma," *Journal of Economic Theory* (1982), 27:245–252; and Michael Taylor, *The Possibility of Cooperation* (New York: Cambridge University Press, 1987).

3. Robert O. Keohane, *After Hegemony: Cooperation and Discord in the World Political Economy* (Princeton: Princeton University Press, 1984); and Paul Milgrom, Douglas North, and Barry Weingast, "The Role of Institutions in the Revival of Trade: The Medieval Law Merchant, Private Judges, and the Champagne Fairs," *Economics and Politics* (1989), 1:1–23.

4. Ronald Coase, "The Nature of the Firm," *Economica* (1937), 4:386–405; and Oliver Williamson, *The Economic Institutions of Capitalism* (New York: Free Press, 1985).

5. The most general statement of this perspective is the so-called "folk theorem" in noncooperative game theory. For repeated games with nontrivial information structures, an infinite number of outcomes may be sustained in equilibrium (including many that are not Pareto-optimal). Drew Fudenberg and Eric Maskin, "The Folk Theorem in Repeated Games with Discounting or with Incomplete Information," *Econometrica* (May 1986), 54:533–554.

6. Stephen D. Krasner, "Global Communications and National Power: Life on the Pareto Frontier," *World Politics* (April 1991), 43:336–366.

7. Thus, it is appropriate to supplement analyses based on games such as the Prisoners' Dilemma with those that focus explicitly on distributional conflict along the Pareto frontier, such as the battle of the sexes. Geoffrey Garrett and Barry Weingast, "Ideas, Interests and Institutions: Constructing the EC's Internal Market," presented at the Annual Meetings of the American Political Science Association, Washington, D.C., August 28–September 1, 1991; and Krasner, "Life on the Pareto Frontier."

8. Lloyd Gruber, "From Anarchy to Organization: Towards an Institutional Theory of International Politics," mimeograph, Stanford University, Stanford, California, 1991; and Williamson, *The Economic Institutions of Capitalism.*

9. Leon Lindberg and Andrew Scheingold, *Europe's Would-Be Polity: Patterns of Change in the European Community* (Englewood Cliffs, N.J.: Prentice Hall, 1970).

10. Eric Stein, "Lawyers, Judges and the Making of a Transnational Constitution," *The American Journal of International Law* (1981), 75:1–27.

11. For a recent survey of spatial theories, see Keith Krehbiel, "Spatial Theories of Legislative Choice," *Legislative Studies Quarterly* (1988), 13:259–319. Overviews of bargaining theory include Eric Rasmusen, *Games and Information* (New York, Blackwell, 1989), pp. 227–243; and John Sutton, "Non-Cooperative Bargaining Theory: An Introduction," *Review of Economic Studies* (October 1986), 53:709–724. For an analysis of incomplete information and reputation, see David Kreps and Robert Wilson, "Reputation and Imperfect Information," *Journal of Economic Theory* (1982), 27:253–276. Politically salient studies of incomplete contracting include David Kreps, "Corporate Culture and Economic Theory" and Paul Milgrom and John Roberts, "Bargaining Costs, Influence Costs, and the Organization of Economic Activity," both in James Alt and Kenneth Shepsle, eds., *Perspectives on Positive Political Theory* (New York: Cambridge University Press, 1990).

12. This characterization of trade politics is similar to an n-player game in which the collective good (free trade) is continuous—that is, in which there is no threshold below which the collective good is not produced. For a detailed analysis of the n-player Prisoners' Dilemma, see Taylor, *The Possibility of Cooperation.*

13. For a recent analysis of the politics of protection, see Stephen Magee et al., eds. *Black Hole Tariffs and Endogenous Policy Theory* (New York: Cambridge University Press, 1989).

14. The latter observation accords closely with the common argument that increased economic interdependence creates strong incentives for international cooperation. An early statement of this perspective is that by Richard Cooper, *The Economics of Interdependence* (New York: McGraw-Hill, 1968).

15. The average trade openness of the EC-12 economies (exports + imports/ GDP) rose from less than 40 percent in 1960 to more than 60 percent by the early 1980s. OECD, *Economic Outlook—Historical Statistics, 1960–1985* (Paris: OECD, 1987). Moreover, intra-Community trade as a portion of the total trade of EC members also grew in the same period from around 40 percent to almost 55 percent. Jeffrey Harrop, *The Political Economy of Integration in the European Community* (Aldershot, England: Gower, 1989), p. 169.

16. Geoffrey Garrett and Peter Lange, "Political Responses to Interdependence: What's 'Left' for the Left?," *International Organization* (Autumn 1991),

45:539–564; and Peter Katzenstein, *Small States in World Markets* (Ithaca, N.Y.: Cornell University Press, 1985).

17. John Goodman, "Do All Roads Lead to Brussels?" in Norman J. Ornstein and Mark Perlman, eds., *Political Power and Social Change* (Washington, D.C.: American Enterprise Institute, 1991) and Wayne Sandholtz and John Zysman, "1992: Recasting the European Bargain," *World Politics* (1989), 42:95–128.

18. Japanese performance remained superior to that in Europe throughout. U.S. growth in 1984 was 6.7 percent, compared with −2.5 percent in 1982, whereas growth rates for the EC had changed from significant negative figures in the early 1980s only to 2.4 percent by 1984. More importantly from a political standpoint, the disparity in unemployment performance was even larger. The U.S. rate declined from its zenith of 9.5 percent in 1982 to 7.1 percent in 1985, while EC unemployment continued to rise to over 10 percent by 1985. OECD, *Economic Outlook—Historical Statistics, 1960–1985*.

19. Geoffrey Garrett, "Between Autonomy and Constraint: Government Economic Strategy in the Advanced Industrial Democracies," mimeograph, Stanford University, Stanford, Calif., 1991; and Peter Hall, *Governing the Economy* (London: Polity, 1986).

20. Paulo Cecchini, *The Benefits of a Single Market* (Aldershot, England: Gower, 1988); Michael Emerson, *The Economics of 1992* (New York: Oxford University Press, 1988); and Tomasso Padoa-Schioppa, *Efficiency, Stability and Equity: A Strategy for the Evolution of the Economic System of the European Community* (New York: Oxford University Press, 1987).

21. Milgrom, North, and Weingast, "The Role of Institutions in the Revival of Trade."

22. Garrett and Weingast, "Ideas, Interests and Institutions."

23. For an empirically sensitive treatment of these issues, see Keohane, *After Hegemony*, pp. 85–109.

24. Terry M. Moe, "The New Economics of Organization", *American Journal of Political Science* (November 1984), 28:739–777.

25. Kenneth Waltz, *Theory of International Politics* (New York: McGraw-Hill, 1979).

26. For a detailed analysis of the effects of the international division of labor on domestic political economies, see Jeffry Frieden, "Invested Interests: The Politics of National Economic Policies in a World of Global Finance," *International Organization* (Autumn 1991), 45:425–451. For a view that stresses the mediating effects of domestic institutions, see Garrett and Lange, "Political Responses to Interdependence."

27. There were also significant restrictions on capital flows in many EC states, which the SEA stipulated would be eliminated. The removal of capital controls and its consequences for the Economic and Monetary Union are beyond the scope of this paper.

28. Germany alone had more than 20,000 different standards and Britain—

even after the Thatcher decade—had more than 12,000. "Business in Europe: On the Defensive," *The Economist* (June 8, 1991), p. 10.

29. In the last 1980s, only about 2 percent of public-sector contracts in the EC were awarded to foreign firms. "Business in Europe," *The Economist*, p. 9.

30. Standard VAT rates ranged from 12 percent in Luxembourg and Spain to 23 percent in Ireland. "Business in Europe," *The Economist*, p. 10.

31. "Business in Europe," *The Economist*, p. 12.

32. *The Financial Times* and *The Economist* provided excellent descriptions of the bargaining positions of EC members over the SEA. For more analytic treatments, see David Cameron, "The 1992 Initiative: Causes and Consequences," in Alberta Sbragia, ed., *Europolitics* (Washington, D.C.: the Brookings Institution, 1992); Andrew Moravcsik, "Negotiating the Single European Act: National Interests and Conventional Statecraft in the European Community," *International Organization* (Winter 1991), 45:19–56; and Stephen Woolcock et al., *Britain, Germany and 1992* (London: Pinter, 1991).

33. Mutual recognition was the principle for EC trade enunciated by the European Court of Justice in the 1979 case, *Cassis de Dijon*.

34. In the years since the signing of the SEA, the Danish government has changed its orientation on certain issues and is now often opposed to the positions taken by the United Kingdom.

35. For an analysis of the German financial system and its implications for economic performance, see David Soskice, "The Institutional Infrastructure for International Competitiveness: A Comparative Analysis of the United Kingdom and Germany," in Anthony Barnes Atkinson and Renato Brunetta, eds., *The Economics of the New Europe* (London: Macmillan, forthcoming).

36. Cameron, "The 1992 Initiative: Causes and Consequences"; and Moravcsik, "Negotiating the Single European Act."

37. Ireland is not geographically proximate to these countries, but its level of economic development is closer to those of Greece, Portugal, and Spain than to the German or French. The interests of political actors in Italy cleave between north and south. The northern Italian economy is characterized by firms that are competitive in the world market, whereas the southern part of the country remains far less well developed. The Christian Democrat-dominated government has always, however, been very careful to protect the interests of its political heartland in the south.

38. The Council of Ministers is an umbrella term covering the regular meetings between cabinet ministers from member states for the various jurisdictions of the European Community. The exceptions to the qualified majority voting rule over the internal market are fiscal (primarily tax) issues, the movement of people, and the rights and interests of workers. The roles of the Commission and the European Parliament were also affected by the SEA. Relations between the Council, the Commission, and the Parliament are discussed in the next section.

39. Moravcsik, "Negotiating the Single European Act," p. 32.

40. I am indebted to Helen Wallace for this point. Note also that the larger countries are still underrepresented—in terms either of population or economic output—in the current voting system.

41. Note, however, that the British government did win significant concessions in that both industrial relations and immigration issues were exempted from qualified majority voting.

42. Albert O. Hirschman, *National Power and the Structure of Foreign Trade*, expanded ed. (Berkeley: University of California Press, 1980).

43. By 1993, these funds are projected to represent fully one quarter of the EC budget (U.S. $11 billion): a significant side payment. Gary Marks, "Structural Policy in the European Community," in Alberta Sbragia, ed., *Europolitics* (Washington, D.C.: Brookings Institution, forthcoming).

44. The British government's acceptance of the SEA was also made more likely by German and especially French concessions over the EC budget and the Common Agricultural Policy. Moravcsik, "Negotiating the Single European Act," pp. 34–38.

45. Moravcsik, "Negotiating the Single European Act," p. 38.

46. In the mid 1980s, French and German exports constituted more than 40 percent of all intra-EC exports. Cameron, "The 1992 Initiative."

47. For a more general analysis of the effects of domestic politics on international bargaining, see Robert Putnam, "Diplomacy and Domestic Politics: The Logic of Two-Level Games," *International Organization* (Summer 1988), 42:427–460.

48. In this context, note that EC issues—particularly with respect to the exchange rate mechanism of the EMS—played a significant role in the subsequent defeat of Thatcher and the elevation of John Major to Prime Minister late in 1990.

49. This argument does not depend on votes actually being taken in the Council. In fact, most matters are resolved consensually in the Council, without recourse to qualified majority voting. However, the specter of a vote—and its probable outcome—is sufficient to allow France and Germany to influence significantly the content of the "consensus" position.

50. For details of these institutional procedures, see Renaud Dehousse, "Completing the Internal Market: Institutional Constraints and Challenges," in Ronald Bieber et al., eds., *1992: One Internal Market?* (Baden-Baden: Verlagsgesellschaft, 1988); and Neil Nugent, *The Government and Politics of the European Community* (Durham, N.C.: Duke University Press, 1988), p. 247.

51. This rule pertains to the "second reading" of a Commission proposal (i.e., after it has been passed in the Council). The Parliament also issues opinions on proposals at a "first reading," before they are initially submitted by the Commission to the Council.

52. On the assumption that the matter is not exempted from majority voting in the SEA.

53. The President of the Commission, Delors, has pressed for radical extensions of the scope of internal market regulation by the European Community. Delors' statements betray a more general interest of bureaucrats in the Commission to increase their own roles and power.

54. This holds so long as there are no incentives for governments in the Council to vote strategically—that is, not to support Commission proposals they prefer to the status quo. The implications of strategic voting are analyzed below.

55. Noted also that such an outcome might not represent a Pareto improvement for the European Community, since it could be further from the ideal point of Britain and Denmark than the status quo is.

56. "Business in Europe: On the Defensive," *The Economist*, p. 9.

57. The most important instance of this was Thatcher's decision not to reappoint Lord Cockfield as an EC Commissioner in 1989 because he had been a prime mover behind many internal market initiatives of which the British government disapproved.

58. Ariel Rubinstein, "Perfect Equilibrium in a Bargaining Game," *Econometrica* (1982), 50:97–109; "A Bargaining Model with Incomplete Information About Time Preferences," *Econometrica* (1985), 53:1151–1172. The Commission–Council game is somewhat different from that analyzed by Rubinstein because only the Commission may make proposals.

59. For analyses of the role of EC law in implementing the internal market, see Mauro Capalleti et al., eds., *Integration Through Law*, vol. 1 (New York: De Gruyter, 1986); Renaud Dehousse and Joseph Weiler, "The Legal Dimension," in William Wallace, ed., *The Dynamics of European Integration* (New York: Pinter, 1990); Garrett and Weingast, "Ideas, Interests and Institutions"; Martin Shapiro, "The European Court of Justice," in Alberta Sbragia, ed., *Europolitics* (Washington, D.C.: Brookings Institution, 1992); and Stein, "Lawyers, Judges and the Making of a Transnational Constitution."

60. The United Kingdom and Denmark have the best records for legislation implementing internal market directives. The southern European states have tended to be laggards. This pattern is a result of the fact that most directives have dealt with the elimination of barriers to the free movement of goods and services, rather than the creation of a more interventionist internal market.

61. The doctrine of direct effect was established in the *Van Gend* case (1963). The Court of Justice ruled that in order to protect the rights of individuals and other private actors with respect to the Treaty of Rome, it was necessary for the Treaty to have "direct effect" in national courts (since individuals do not have direct recourse to the Court of Justice). This doctrine was extended in *Van Duyn* (1974) to directives passed by the Council of Ministers but not legislated into national law.

62. Such preliminary judgments—in contrast to cases brought directly before it—constitute the vast majority of decisions made by the Court of Justice. Stein, "Lawyers, Judges and the Making of a Transnational Constitution," p. 6.

63. The supremacy of EC law was first asserted by the Court of Justice in *Costa v. ENEL* (1964).

64. Robert Keohane and Stanley Hoffmann, "Conclusions: Community Politics and Institutional Change," in William Wallace, ed., *The Dynamics of Regional Integration* (New York: Pinter, 1990).

65. *European Report,* No. 1554 (January 13, 1990); No. 1590 (May 30 1990); No. 1597 (June 23, 1990).

66. *The Financial Times* (March 21, 1990), p. 2.

67. "Fishing Boat Registration Rules Contravene EC Law," *The Financial Times* (August 14, 1991), p. 11.

68. Stein, "Lawyers, Judges and the Making of a Transnational Constitution," p. 3.

69. Kreps and Wilson, "Reputation and Imperfect Information"; and Milgrom, North, and Weingast, "The Role of Institutions in the Revival of Trade."

70. Kreps, "Corporate Culture and Economic Theory."

71. For a detailed analysis of incomplete contracting and the construction of the internal market, see Garrett and Weingast, "Ideas, Interests and Institutions."

72. For recent analyses of judicial politics and public law, see John Ferejohn and Charles Shipan, "Congressional Influence on Administrative Agencies: A Case Study of Telecommunications Policy," in Larry Dodd and Bruce Oppenheimer, eds., *Congress Reconsidered,* 4th ed. (Washington, D.C.: Congressional Quarterly Press, 1990); Brian Marks, "A Model of Judicial Influence on Congressional Policy Making," Working Paper, Hoover Institution, Stanford, California, 1990; McNollgast, "Positive and Normative Models of Due Process: An Integrative Approach to Administrative Procedures," *Journal of Law, Economics and Organization* (1990), 6:307–322; and Pablo Spiller and Rafel Gely, "Congressional Control or Judicial Independence: The Determinants of U.S. Supreme Court Labor Decisions, 1949–1987," mimeograph, University of Illinois, Champaign, Illinois, 1991.

11. Multilateral Organizations and the Institution of Multilateralism: The Development of Regimes for Nonterrestrial Spaces

Mark W. Zacher

A RE international organizations and multilateral organizations identical, or do the latter constitute a distinct subset of the former? This question cannot be answered simply since almost all organizations are multilateral to one degree or another and since their multilateralism varies along different dimensions. According to John Ruggie multilateralism is distinguished by three traits: generalized principles of conduct, indivisibility, and diffuse reciprocity.[1] With respect to the organizational component of multilateralism, the key generalized principles of conduct are equal rights of participation and equal voting power,[2] and the most important traits of indivisibility (apart from the existence of the organization itself) are the legal bindingness of decisions and the inability of a small number of states to block decisions. Diffuse reciprocity does not enter explicitly into decision-making arrangements since it relates basically to the long-term mutual advantages that flow from adherence to substantive rules.

It is clear from initial reflection on the two main generalized principles of conduct and the two major traits of political indivisibility that international organizations differ in important ways in the nature and strength of their multilateralism. Some organizations, like most of those associated with the U.N. system, score high in equal participation, equal voting rights, and the inability of a small group of states to block organizational decisions. At the same time they are weak in terms of the bindingness of

The author would like to thank the other contributors to this volume (particularly John Ruggie, Peter Cowhey, and Geoff Garrett), M. J. Peterson, and several anonymous reviewers for their comments. He would also like to thank Tim Carter, Sandra Katalinic, and Deepa Khosla for research assistance and comments.

their decisions. Other organizations such as the International Monetary Fund or the European Community are weak in terms of the inequality of states' voting power and the power of a small group of states to block organizational decisions but are strong with regard to the legal binding-ness of decisions. In other words, the egalitarian bodies generally have recommendatory powers, and the hierarchical bodies usually have at least some significant authoritative powers.[3] Of the more than 300 intergov-ernmental organizations at the present time a large majority of them are probably better classified as egalitarian rather than the hierarchical.[4] While some observers might dismiss the egalitarian organizations as unimportant, they are making an error in judgment. Many are, in fact, important arenas for the development and reform of substantive multilat-eral regimes and important promoters of the operational effectiveness of these regulatory regimes.[5] One reason they produce important multilat-eral regimes is that powerful states press for, and other states accept, a significant degree of "minilateralism" in the diplomatic bargaining pro-cess,[6] but this does not negate the significance and influence of these multilateral organizations in the form and effectiveness of international collaboration.

This paper analyzes three roles that egalitarian multilateral organiza-tions perform in the development of multilateral regulatory regimes, and it does so by examining the evolution of the jurisdictional regimes for nonterrestrial spaces—namely, the oceans, airspace, and outer space. The three roles concern: multilateral organizations' influence on the creation/reform, strength, and nature of the regimes; their influence on the operation or effectiveness of the regimes; and the influence that the organizational components of regime proposals have on the political acceptability of the general proposals.[7] This latter role is, of course, quite different from the first two in that it refers to states' anticipatory judg-ments of how organizations might affect their interests rather than how organizations have actually affected them. The paper also analyzes why certain issue areas (and more particularly those concerning the use of international commons) are particularly susceptible to the involvement of multilateral organizations.

A general assertion of this article is that multilateral organizations have had modest, but important, impacts on the policies of states and the strength, nature, and effectiveness of regimes. However, "proving" this evaluation is difficult since any analysis must conjecture at least implicitly what would probably have occurred if these organizations (or the basic multilateral practice of negotiating regimes in global bodies) had not been used. Such analysis must query: whether certain existing regimes would have lost their legitimacy or certain regime proposals been unable to gain adequate diplomatic backing if it had not been for the deliberations and resolutions of multilateral organizations; whether particular proposals would have been as likely to emerge and gain broad support (especially from the most powerful states) if the diplomatic deliberations had occurred outside multilateral organizations; and whether certain regimes would have been as acceptable without the development and operation of related regimes by multilateral organizations. Good arguments can be mounted to address these questions, but an element of speculation and uncertainty is inevitable in entering the counterfactual realm.

This article also embodies several more specific theses. First, with regard to the impact of organizations on the creation of the regimes for nonterrestrial spaces, the regular meetings of multilateral organizations have certainly facilitated the emergence of consensuses on norms and rules, but the organizations have also given the majority of Third World states the opportunity to extract modest concessions that they probably could not have obtained outside these bodies. Third World victories have significantly been associated with the extension of states' jurisdiction in international spaces and with partial adoption of international resource planning (or common heritage arrangements). Second, multilateral organizations facilitate the operation or effectiveness of regimes for nonterrestrial spaces to a very limited extent by monitoring compliance, settling disputes, and sometimes imposing sanctions. They have a more important (albeit implicit) role in promoting the effectiveness and continued acceptability of the basically free-access regimes by assuring a modicum of order in states' use of the common property resources. Their roles in controlling unintentional damage to commercial participants and third parties and assuring a measure of equity are absolutely crucial in legitimizing the basic practice of free access.

Third, regime proposals that provide for multilateral organizations with binding legal authority over international resources are almost sure to meet rejection. States are willing to contemplate on occasion ad hoc planning for segments of the resources in question, but they are not willing to commit themselves to accept decisions by a majority of their peers with regard to allocation of the entire resources. In other words, strong constraints exist with regard to the development of international organizations' authority over international resources. Fourth, nonterrestrial spaces generally have certain characteristics that attract strong involvements by multilateral organizations and promote strong multilateral regimes, and an important one is that they are common property resources. As John Ruggie notes, "Where the definition and stabilization of at least some international property rights is concerned, there appears to exist an ultimate inevitability to multilateral solutions—though 'ultimate' may mean after all possible alternatives, including war, have been exhausted."[8] He also remarks that "it is exceedingly difficult if not impossible in the long run to vindicate a property right that is not recognized as being valid by the relevant others in a given community."[9] It should, therefore, be kept in mind in evaluating the roles of multilateral organizations that nonterrestrial spaces are very hospitable areas in which such bodies can operate.

The three roles on which this study focuses have certainly been discussed in past studies of international organizations and regimes. The assertion that multilateral organizations influence the *creation, strength,* and *nature* of multilateral regimes is certainly not a unique one although realist writers would see such bodies as epiphenomenal to the emergence of political outcomes. "Institutionalist writers have always stressed that cooperation can be fostered by institutions."[10] International organizations provide vehicles for launching negotiations on issues, reduce the transaction costs of negotiations, generate and disseminate information that is crucial to international policy coordination and agreements, increase trust, and constrain states to work within existing norms and regulatory arrangements.[11] In the words of Alan James the most important contribution of international organizations is that they have "facilitated, encouraged, or enabled something to be said or done which is of some diplomatic import and which would not have occurred but for the institution's existence."[12] It is likewise not unusual to note that the existence of organizations gives the many weaker states in the international system an opportunity to exert influence on the shape or nature of rule systems by coordinating their diplomatic efforts and power. Multilateral organizations are certainly "catalysts for coalition formation" and "arenas for political initiatives and linkage by weak states."[13] In fact, two decades ago Robert Cox and Harold Jacobson wrote that "Over their longer history, the greatest potential for change from international organizations may lie in the opportunity they give the less powerful to influence the climate of opinion and the accepted values according to which action is determined."[14] Quite apart from whether international organizations give one group or another greater leverage than they might have outside the organizations, "The policies of governments cannot help but be influenced by the extent to which their states are enmeshed in webs of networks of international organizations."[15]

The role of international organizations in promoting the *effectiveness* of regulatory regimes is not highlighted in the international relations literature as much as their role in the creation of rule systems, but it is certainly alluded to a great deal in discussions of specific organizations as well as in some of the general literature on international institutions.[16] Organizations generate information on compliance and the development of new problems, and they provide procedures and norms for facilitating decisions to deal with various issues. It is, however, important to make a distinction that is not made in the literature between *explicit* and *implicit* *roles* of multilateral organizations in the operation of regimes. Explicit roles specifically concern the promotion of compliance with regime prescriptions and proscriptions. Implicit roles, on the other hand, are activities that mitigate any shortcomings or negative impacts of the regulatory regime—thus making the central aspects of the regime more acceptable. As will be noted below, these implicit roles have been very important to the operation of jurisdictional regimes especially those based on the free-access principle.

A final role on which this article comments is different from the previous two in that it refers, not to the effects of existing organizations, but to the effects of suggestions for the creation of particular multilateral organizations on the *acceptability* of general regime proposals. Little has been written on the types of organizational structures that are likely to elicit support from a large community of states, but some good analyses exist. A key conclusion is that in the case of organizations that have legally binding powers or distribute significant financial resources, it is important to have all or most states involved in the decision-making process. However, influence must be distributed roughly in proportion to resources or power, and both the most powerful states and the majority of states must have a veto. In fact, multilateral organizations that do not enjoy broad political support can become the enemy of the institution of multilateralism.[17]

Jurisdictional arrangements concerning nonterrestrial spaces are fruitful areas in which to explore the influence of multilateral organizations on regimes because these organizations have been so active in these areas. Jurisdictional issues concern which states have law-making and law-enforcing authority over certain activities in particular geographical areas. The law of the sea is one of the oldest legal regimes in the modern state system in that it began to evolve as early as the seventeenth century. The legal regime for the airwaves can be traced back to the first decade of the twentieth century with the advent of commercial radio communications, the formation of the International Radiotelegraph Union, and the regular convening of International Radio Conferences, and the regime for outer space began to take shape in the United Nations very soon after the first satellite was launched in 1957.

At the heart of all negotiations to formulate international regimes for nonterrestrial spaces is the issue of the relative weights that should be given to three principles in the design of the norms and rules. Two of the principles are: free access and national enclosure. By free access is meant that all states should be able to use or exploit the resources of an area as long as they do not interfere with the activities of other states. Such areas are viewed as common property resources, and their legal status is captured by the Latin concept of *res communis*. Juxtaposed to this traditional legal conception is the principle of national enclosure or jurisdiction. It means simply that states are able to legislate or make laws concerning certain activities in a particular geographical area. Noteworthy, however, is that hybrid arrangements can arise that give different weights to these two principles in a particular area. For example, in the territorial sea, states control all resource exploitation and can legislate for certain limited shipping matters, but they must allow "innocent passage" to foreign vessels that want to pass through it. [18]

The third principle that has emerged in jurisdictional debates for nonterrestrial spaces is the common heritage of mankind. It prescribes that an area should be regarded as a common property resource, but unlike the notion of free access it requires that the use of the area be politically managed by international bodies so as to promote greater equity and more orderly relations among nations. The concept of common heritage did not arise explicitly until 1967 when the Maltese ambassador to the United Nations Arvid Pardo proposed that the exploitation of the seabed be managed by an enterprise under the United Nations and that the proceeds be distributed to promote greater economic equality. [19] As will be noted below, the concept did arise implicitly in the interwar period in the context of the telecommunications regime and was referred to as "a priori planning." With regard to the common-heritage concept as proposed by Pardo, the British legal scholar D. P. O'Connell noted that it had the effect of metamorphosing *res communis* into something akin to *"res condominata."* [20] Pardo and Carl Christol labeled the common-heritage principle as *"res communis humanidatis."* [21]

Most developed countries, realizing that they could not eliminate the term *common heritage* from debates on nonterrestrial spaces, sought to redefine it. They tried either to make it synonymous with free access or to make it imply solely that some efforts should be made in international bodies to assure reasonable benefits for the developing countries. They attempted, in other words, to deprive it of the strict meaning that all use or exploitation requires approval of the international community.[22]

It is to the struggles over the weight to be assigned to these three principles in the three issue areas and the roles of multilateral organizations in shaping these regimes that this study now turns.

The Oceans

The traditional law of the sea evolved between the seventeenth and nineteenth centuries as customary law and as such mirrored international legal processes in most other issue areas. Its main provisos were the existence of a three-mile territorial sea in which coastal states had complete jurisdiction except that they had to allow "innocent passage" to foreign ships passing through the area and the right of free access to the oceans outside this narrow coastal band (that is to say, on the high seas).[23] International organizations did not play any role in the early development of the law of the sea, and in fact it was not until the League of Nations convened a conference on the law of the sea in 1930 (which ended unsuccessfully) that a major intergovernmental conference was called. In retrospect, this conference of forty-four states was a landmark in that it set a precedent for the law of the sea being addressed in universal organizations.[24] Also significant is that the maritime powers led by Britain were stymied by a coalition of smaller states in securing acceptance of a three-mile territorial sea. While the major maritime states were generally able to pressure states to abide by the three-mile limit after the conference, they were concerned that the failure of the League conference to support the traditional limit could undermine its legitimacy in the long run. The absence of an important role for international organizations in the "creation process" of the law of the sea before the post-1945 period can be explained in part by the prevalence of the customary development of international law prior to the early twentieth century, the relatively small number of issues in the law of the sea, and very importantly an acceptance of a rather hierarchical relationship between the great powers and other members of the interstate system. On the other hand, it is important to recall that the seeds of a new order based on a need to secure broad backing in multilateral conferences began to emerge with the 1930 conference sponsored by the League of Nations.

Before World War II international organizations also played a minor role in influencing the operational effectiveness of the law-of-the-sea regime—including the elimination of any related shortcomings in maritime law such as inadequate safety regulations. An important reason is that jurisdictional regimes based on the principles of free access and/or national enclosure do not require a great deal of explicit international management. (However, they may need implicit management—an issue to be taken up below.) The great powers were concerned that all serious violations of the traditional law of the sea be reversed, but they generally acted on their own in assuring compliance by weaker states.[25] Some maritime law making occurred on issues such as vessel safety, and it was in part motivated by a desire of maritime states to discourage unilateral legislation by states for their territorial waters. Although the conferences to develop maritime law were not sponsored by intergovernmental organizations, they did from the early twentieth century onward take on a multilateral character. States, instead of following customary law or British maritime law, gathered at conferences (albeit generally sponsored by Britain or Belgium) in order to adopt multilateral conventions. In the early part of the twentieth century the conditions that affected demands for revision of maritime law did not change so rapidly, and the enforcement problems relating to the law of the sea or maritime law were not so serious that permanent organizations were required to oversee the operation and periodic revision of conventions.

After World War II significant changes took place in the law of the sea and in the process of law making. A growth in international commerce, more frequent changes in ship technology, greater legitimacy of democratic values, and the growth in the number of states encouraged support for law making within permanent multilateral organizations and made the United Nations the logical organization in which to negotiate new public law conventions. In the early 1950s the U.N. General Assembly asked its International Law Commission to codify the law of the sea, and this led to the conclusion of four treaties at the 1958 First United Nations Conference on the Law of the Sea (UNCLOS I), which formulated accords on all main issues apart from the breadth of the territorial sea and a contiguous fishing zone. There was an abortive UNCLOS II in 1960, which failed to resolve the latter two issues,[26] and the main reason was the refusal of a large group of developing countries (concerned to extend their control over fisheries and/or their sovereign territory) to accept the maritime powers' insistence on narrow territorial seas and fishing zones. The leading Third World expansionists were the Latin American countries, many of whom had extended their fisheries jurisdiction or their territorial seas to two hundred miles in the late 1940s and 1950s. The Western maritime states feared that extended jurisdiction (particularly a twelve-mile territorial sea in straits) might impinge eventually on freedom of navigation—according to a dynamic of "creeping jurisdiction." As at the 1930 and 1958 conferences a growing coalition of developing coastal states and the Soviet bloc were able at the 1960 conference to block the maritime states' central goal of achieving a stronger legitimacy for free access to coastal waters—and especially international straits.

Beginning in the late 1960s conflicts over the law of the sea multiplied and intensified as many coastal states (especially the growing number from the developing world) pressed for expanded fisheries jurisdiction and as the issue of mining manganese nodules on the deep seabed emerged on the agenda. The United States and the Soviet Union (now adopting a more maritime orientation than it had at UNCLOS I and II) pressed for a multilateral conference to resolve the issues concerning the breadth of the territorial sea (especially in international straits) and a fisheries zone, but they were stymied by the insistence of Third World countries that they would not address the navigation issue until the developed powers were willing to negotiate all maritime resource questions. This impasse led to a 1970 decision to convene UNCLOS III in 1973. Between 1973 and 1982 UNCLOS III formulated the United Nations Convention on the Law of the Sea, which covered a tremendous range of issues. The number of states participating in UNCLOS III was around 150—as opposed to 88 at UNCLOS II in 1960. The core of the 1982 treaty was a trade-off between the maritime powers and the developing countries. The developed countries accepted an extension of coastal state jurisdiction over fisheries within a two hundred-mile Exclusive Economic Zone (EEZ) and a common-heritage/free-access hybrid arrangement for the deep seabed, and the developing nations acceded to a strong free-access regime for navigation.[27]

Sometimes easy to forget is that the most important outcome of UNCLOS III was the acceptance of the 200-mile EEZ and of coastal state jurisdiction over continental margins that extend beyond 200 miles. And the EEZ would quite possibly have not come into existence if it had not been for the ability of coastal developing states to use the U.N. forum to mobilize support within the Group of 77 and to bargain with the developed countries for acceptance of the EEZ in exchange for the approval of the latter's proposals for freedom of navigation. A large number of small and/or developing states held up acceptance of a navigation regime favored by the maritime powers from 1930 through the 1960s because they did not obtain the extended resource jurisdiction they wanted. And if the negotiation of these issues had not been enmeshed in multilateral negotiating contexts, it is unlikely that the nonmaritime countries would have been nearly so effective in weakening the legitimacy of the traditional jurisdictional provisions and ultimately garnering acceptance of a new regime. Eventually an extended fisheries zone would have been likely to emerge as a result of stock depletions in some areas and unilateral extensions by coastal states, but whether it would have assumed the character it did outside the U.N. negotiating context or would have emerged so soon is doubtful.

The maritime powers, including those such as the United States that stood to gain from extended fisheries jurisdiction per se, stood fast against an extension of coastal state authority over fisheries outside a narrow coastal zone until the mid-1970s. They realized finally at this time that the coalition of coastal states in the United Nations would not retreat and that their accession to the EEZ was a necessary concession in order to achieve guarantees for freedom of navigation. On the other hand, the prolonged and intense bargaining showed the coastal states that they were going to have to give the maritime powers greater certainty of freedom of navigation (in particular, "transit passage" through straits) if they were going to secure acceptance of the EEZ. The kind of learning and working out of specific texts that occurred at UNCLOS would have been exceedingly difficult outside a multilateral context with its pressure for broad consensus and mutual gains and its diplomatic opportunities for bringing major groupings together in sustained negotiations.[28]

Considerable attention must be given at this point to the third major issue (apart from coastal zone resources and navigation) at UNCLOS III— namely, deep seabed mining. The reasons are that the debate over the weight to be assigned to the free-access and common-heritage principles was strongly influenced by the U.N. negotiating context and that in no issue area did proposals for a new international organization have such a major influence on the acceptability of a particular multilateral regime. The issue first arose in 1967 when Ambassador Pardo of Malta announced that a vast store of wealth in the form of manganese nodules resided on the floor of the deep seabed and that the only way the developing countries could hope to benefit from its exploitation was to place the area under the control and management of a U.N. body. As previously noted, for Pardo the common heritage of mankind meant a recognition that a common property resource had to be politically managed by a global organization and that that body had to support Third World economic development through its dispersal of revenues. It was a double-barreled principle (community management and revenue sharing to promote economic equity), and the two facets did not have to go together. The aspect of the common-heritage principle that is crucial for the purpose of this article is that a regime based on it must have a multilateral organization with binding legal powers to manage the area (called the International Seabed Authority in the case of the deep seabed negotiations). For the first time in the law-of-the-sea negotiations the design of an organization was central to negotiations over a jurisdictional regime. In fact, it could not have been otherwise as long as the Third World was committed to the common-heritage principle.[29]

Between 1968 and 1975 the developing and developed countries put forward proposals for an International Seabed Authority (ISA) that reflected their attachment respectively to the principles of common heritage and free access. The developing countries proposed that a U.N. body should control all aspects of mining of the deep seabed and that within this organization the developing countries should have a controlling voice. What they were, in fact, advocating was an international public corporation that would have property rights to the entire deep seabed. The developed states, on the other hand, supported the creation of an international body whose sole function would be the registry of plots that states chose to exploit. The developed states saw the organizational model advocated by the developing countries as reducing them to an impotent role in international decision making concerning the deep seabed. Early in the negotiations in 1969 and 1970 the Third World states were able to secure the passage of two important resolutions in the U.N. General Assembly. One (not supported by the developed states) called for a moratorium on deep seabed mining until the acceptance of a U.N. treaty covering the issue, and the other declared the deep seabed the "common heritage of mankind." These resolutions definitely put constraints on the negotiating process and on seabed mining itself, and their influence is still being felt.[30]

In 1976 the process of compromise began as the Group of 77 and the industrialized countries sought to fashion a compromise agreement or hybrid regime that combined elements of free access and common heritage. The essence of the compromise, which emerged in 1980 and is included in part XI of the 1982 treaty, is a system of parallel development whereby states will be allowed to exploit parts of the ocean, and the International Seabed Authority (or its operational arm called the Enterprise) will be permitted to exploit other areas. The system works such that a state designates two plots that it (or more likely a national corporation) would like to exploit, and the ISA then chooses one that it reserves for future exploitation by the Enterprise. A key provision that the developed states secured is that if the ISA does not choose one of the two plots in a short period of time, the state itself can choose a plot. Other important provisions in the compromise are that the developed states must transfer technology to the Enterprise to give it the capability to mine the seabed and that there be production limits on seabed exploitation to protect land-based producers. There are also, of course, obligations to transfer funds to the ISA to support its activities.[31]

The decision-making arrangements for the deep seabed regime were an issue of considerable debate. The Council of thirty-six states was designated the central decision-making body. It.was given a rather complicated system of representation with most of its key votes requiring either two-thirds or three-quarter majorities. The developed states never, however, received assurance that the system of representation would give them the power to block important decisions in the Council. The fact that the ISA could not block their ability to mine one of the two sites they proposed provided some compensation for their uncertainty about the Council. Another very important aspect of the overall decision-making system relates to the amending of part XI. The convention stipulates that fifteen years after the commencement of mining, a review conference will be convened. It will seek to formulate amendments acceptable by consensus, but if this is not possible after five years, two thirds of the signatories are entitled to pass amendments. What this did was to give the deep seabed regime a stronger element of common heritage in the long run. Certainly strong differences existed within developed-country governments about the procedures for amending the treaty, but in the end they went along with it because they thought that their technological superiority would give them the bargaining leverage required to protect their interests.

The fact that the negotiations to reach agreement on an International Seabed Authority lasted twelve years from 1968 to 1980 indicates how crucial the form of a multilateral organization can be when it is necessary to the implementation of a jurisdictional regime. Also, its importance is indicated by the fact that in 1981 the United States under President Reagan decided to go back on the U.S. commitment to the part XI compromise and then voted against the treaty in April 1982. The U.S. stance has led a number of other developed countries to join it, and most other developed states have voiced various reservations. No developed countries have thus far ratified the 1982 treaty, and the future of the deep seabed regime seems very much in doubt. This indicates how difficult it is to secure agreement on a regime strongly oriented toward common heritage because of the need to agree on provisions for quite a powerful multilateral organization.[32]

In the next decade or two an agreement is likely to be reached to revise the free-access/common-heritage hybrid regime in part XI of the treaty so as to give it a little more weighting toward free access. A hybrid regime is still the one that will probably benefit most states. However, a chance remains that differences over the nature of the International Seabed Authority or eventually tremendous conflict over the operation of the ISA could lead to a different outcome. One possibility is that states could extend their jurisdiction outside the EEZ so as to turn the world's oceans into "national lakes," and the other is that states could simply agree to give a portion of the proceeds from their mining operations to a Third World development fund. While revenue sharing would provide some economic benefits for the Third World, it would, of course, seriously compromise the notion of community political management inherent in the common-heritage principle. A precedent exists for this revenue-sharing option in the provisions of the 1982 treaty concerning the exploitation of those portions of the continental margin that extend beyond the 200-mile EEZ. In this area states are obliged to give 7 percent of the revenues from any mineral exploitation to the International Seabed Authority.[33] It is still quite possible that the ISA in a revised form will be seen as a politically more realistic compromise than carving up the oceans into national lakes or implementing a revenue-sharing scheme that would benefit the Third World. A combination of the 1969 moratorium resolution and the 1982 treaty has made the developed countries reluctant to embark on any seabed mining (even on an experimental basis) without the approval of Third World states for fear of engendering their political hostility, causing them to violate navigation provisions of the 1982 treaty, and/or provoking them to extend national claims beyond the EEZ. Accords developed within the U.N. multilateral framework are still exerting a strong constraining influence on the evolution of the deep seabed regime.

Turning from the impact of multilateral organizations on the creation of regimes to their influence on the operation and effectiveness of jurisdictional regimes, it is first important to note that there is little need for organizations to assume explicit roles with respect to the navigation regime. The reason is that the regime continues to be based on free access and, to a limited extent, on national enclosure. Over the postwar years the only clear role an international organization has had in the operation of the law of the sea for shipping is the rather limited role that the International Court of Justice has played in giving opinions on a few conflicts. In the 1982 convention provisions exist for the establishment of a tribunal that will be involved in dispute settlement, but it is not likely to be a major influence on the acceptability of the navigation provisions. Hence the only *formal* organizational role with respect to the jurisdictional regime for shipping based on free access and national enclosure has been and is likely to be a very modest role in the dispute settlement area.

International organizations, and particularly the U.N. specialized agency concerned with shipping (the International Maritime Organization or IMO), have, however, developed an informal role in the jurisdictional regime for the oceans. The IMO under its former title "the Intergovernmental Maritime Consultative Organization" (IMCO) did not begin to operate until 1958 because of a ten-year dispute over its mandate. It soon took over responsibility for formulating, monitoring, and revising international maritime law with respect to vessel safety, pollution prevention, liability, and the facilitation of traffic. It has committees of governmental and industry experts operating continuously on varied problems of international shipping, and a year seldom passes in which it does not approve a new treaty at specially convened conferences. The way in which the IMO's activities are crucial to the development of the jurisdictional regime is that states (especially those with important trading and shipping interests) know that if safety and pollution problems are not managed reasonably well through international legislation, coastal states could extend their jurisdiction over shipping both within and outside the territorial sea and create a patchwork pattern of regulations that would hinder navigation. Therefore the activities of the International Maritime Organization play a crucial role in ensuring the political acceptability of the law-of-the-sea regime for shipping that is based on innocent passage in the territorial sea and free access on the high seas. It is noteworthy that many issues that the IMO must settle are not simply coordination problems; they concern to a significant degree collaboration problems that involve relative costs for states.[33]

While the importance of international organizations in the operation of a particular law-of-the-sea regime has arisen most significantly in the case of deep seabed mining, organizations have also had an impact on the norms and rules for fisheries. Before World War II fishing vessels of all states had free access to most areas of the oceans outside a narrow three-mile territorial sea, and in fact this situation held for the most part until around 1975 when a 200-mile Exclusive Economic Zone was accepted at UNCLOS III.[35] Various regional fisheries organizations such as that responsible for implementing the International Convention on North Atlantic Fisheries were set up to ensure that free access did not necessarily lead to depletion of stocks, but their inherent legal weakness meant that they could not perform their roles very well. In fact, their failures were pointed to in justifying the need for extended coastal state jurisdiction.[36] With the advent of the 200-mile EEZ in the late 1970s a few organizations have sought to manage fisheries outside the EEZs—in part to legitimize free access in these areas. However, the effectiveness is not particularly important to the legitimacy of free access outside the EEZs since such a small percentage of the oceans' fisheries are in the area.

In the case of the coastal seabed zone (the continental margin) it has been regarded as under national jurisdiction since the U.S. Truman Proclamation of 1945. It was legitimated at UNCLOS II in 1958 and was approved in a somewhat different legal form in the 1982 convention. Therefore international organizations have not played an important role in the acceptability of the regime or its operation. Some permanent and ad hoc judicial bodies (including the International Court of Justice) have, however, played important roles in settling conflicts over maritime boundaries, and this is likely to continue.[37]

In the postwar period international organizations, and more particularly the United Nations, have clearly been very important in the development of the law of the sea. Prior to UNCLOS I and III long multilateral negotiations were held in the United Nations before the actual conference sessions, and it is difficult to imagine that the detailed treaties could have emerged without the sustained negotiations in the U.N. context. Also, as Barry Buzan notes, one of the unique features about UNCLOS III was that after 1967 the initiatives that drove the negotiations came from proposals within the United Nations rather than from national actions outside the organization.[38] More important than the

United Nations' facilitating the meetings by the provision of a variety of services, the negotiation of these matters in the U.N. context established the norm that decisions should be made by consensus or a two-thirds majority, and this pressured states to find compromises that could mobilize support from most groupings. It unquestionably gave the Third World or the Group of 77 at UNCLOS the opportunity to obtain the developed countries' backing for extended fisheries jurisdiction (the EEZ) and a free-access/common-heritage hybrid regime for the deep seabed in exchange for their support for a stronger free-access regime for shipping. As Stephen Krasner remarks: "This tactical linkage was the only source of leverage that the Third World had over the resource exploitation issue."[39] The tactic worked as well, for, as Ann Hollick notes, "U.S. willingness to compromise its mining interests clearly stemmed from U.S. concern to secure consensus on a treaty that protected certain navigation rights."[40] Hollick remarks that "Without the United Nations context and the Group of 77 coalition, the role of such countries [the developing states] compared to that of seabed mining states would have been negligible."[41]

In evaluating the influence of the U.N. institutional context an interesting issue is whether the failure of the developed countries to ratify the 1982 treaty because of their opposition to the deep seabed provisions in part XI negates any positive evaluation one could make about the impact of the United Nations on the deep seabed regime. A definitive evaluation on this matter is impossible, but in the long run the U.N. involvement will likely be seen as quite influential. The 1969 moratorium resolution and the 1982 treaty have both deterred the developed countries from permitting seabed mining to date, although commercially profitable exploitation is now viewed as being about two decades off. (In the mid-1970s states thought that profitable exploitation could occur within a decade.) Still, without the constraints posed by the ongoing negotiations at the United Nations and the existence of the treaty, some experimental mining would probably be taking place. Also, it is highly unlikely that the developed countries will be able to impose a pure free-access regime in which they will be free to keep all the revenues from mining. Either a renegotiation of the free-access/common-heritage hybrid will occur or all mining states will be obligated to give a percentage of their revenues to a global development fund. The Third World has shaped and will continue to mold the deep seabed regime through the bargaining structures of the United Nations.

The acceptability of particular multilateral organizational proposals arose as a central issue in the negotiations for a deep seabed regime in UNCLOS III. The developed countries had grave reservations concerning the powers that the developing states wanted to devolve to the International Seabed Authority, and even after a compromise was reached in 1980, it fell apart when the United States and then some other developed countries defected. The developed countries were not assured a veto over important decisions in the ISA Council and in the review conference, and they will very likely have to be assured this in any future negotiations to revise part XI.

On the matter of the importance of multilateral organizations to the operation of the law-of-the-sea regime, it is not immediately self-evident that they are central to the effectiveness of the free-access for navigation. But on second look it is hard to imagine that the high level of free access over the last half century would have occurred if the International Maritime Organization and other bodies such as the *Comité Maritime International* (an organization of national maritime law associations) had not been active in developing treaties concerning matters such as vessel safety, pollution, and liability for damages. If maritime law had not developed on these matters, many coastal states would have sought to regulate such matters on their own, and the free-access regime would have been seriously weakened. A certain order must exist for a free-access regime to endure.

Airspace and Airwaves

Of the jurisdictional issues considered in this article, the legal status of airspace above states for purposes of air transportation can be discussed in the most expeditious manner. It has not been a contentious issue since World War I when the possibility of attack by airplanes created a consensus in favor of national jurisdiction. The consensus was made conventional international law at multilateral conferences in 1919 and 1944. A stable agreement has also been reached that airspace above the high seas be a common property resource to which all states should have access.[42] Since no exploitable economic resources exist in airspace, there are no incentives for trying to revise the regime for airspace above the high seas along the lines of national enclosure or common heritage. In one sense the activities of the International Civil Aviation Organization in promoting safety of navigation through traffic control schemes are supportive of a free-access regime for areas above the oceans, but on the other hand it is difficult to see the relationship as particularly important.[43]

While the airspace above national territories for the purpose of air transport is universally regarded as under states' jurisdiction, this is not the case as far as the use of the airwaves for radio communication is concerned. Differences have existed for a long time as to whether the airwaves above states are a common property resource open to all or whether they fall within states' jurisdiction. Periodic attempts have also been made by some states that regard the airwaves as a common property resource to have a common-heritage regime accepted for the airwaves. One of the most important things about the jurisdictional status of the airwaves is that it has seldom ever been confronted directly; rather it has been addressed implicitly in negotiations on preventing unintentional interference and on the rights of states to send and jam international broadcasts. In negotiations on preventing unintentional interference the implicit jurisdictional debate has been over the priority to assign to free access vs. common heritage (or a priori planning). And in the deliberations on jamming and the right to broadcast into other countries the implicit debate has been over free access vs. national enclosure. Each of these two sets of negotiations over the greater part of this century will be treated in succession. Some international organizations have been involved in both sets of negotiations, and some have been involved in only one.

The international regulation of radio communications first arose soon after the turn of the century, and the central issue was the prevention of interference among transmissions. In 1906 states adopted the first International Radiotelegraph Convention and Radio Regulations and formed the International Radiotelegraph Union (IRU). These accords did not take an explicit position on the jurisdictional status of the airwaves, but the Radio Regulations did take an implicit stance when they declared that states should avoid harmful interference with stations that were already broadcasting on certain frequencies. This first-come/first-served norm implied that the airwaves were a common property resource open to all as long as broadcasters did not interfere with preexisting users. The 1906 conference did several things that were relevant to this implicit free-access regime. First, it "allocated" certain frequency bands for solely maritime communications,[44] and this act of allocating bands for particular services was the first instance of a type of international planning. Second, it stipulated that states should send information on the frequencies their stations were using to the Berne Bureau of the International

Telegraph Union and that the Bureau should disseminate the information on frequencies in use to all member states. Also accepted was that the IRU would sponsor regular meetings to consider the revision of the regulations. Right from the beginning of the multilateral free-access regime, states were concerned with designing some planning schemes and creating organizations to help the regime operate efficiently.[45] In fact, even in these early years some planning and distribution of information by a multilateral organization was clearly necessary for a jurisdictional regime based on free access.

The decade after World War I was a very important one in the development of the regime. In 1919 a system of "allotting" particular frequencies to states for communications between ground stations and airplanes was accepted—a forerunner of what was soon to be done for maritime communications.[46] Then in 1925 and 1926 plans for allotting frequencies for radio broadcasting to states in Europe were adopted under the auspices of the IRU because the problems of unintentional interference had grown so much with the explosion of public broadcasting after the war.[47] Also, by 1927 the number of services such as aeronautical and maritime services to which IRU conferences had allocated frequency bands had grown to seven. States (especially those whose stations had claimed a large number of frequencies) were not prepared to allow planning of the entire spectrum, but ad hoc planning was acceptable—in fact, it was necessary to make the first-come/first-served system work.

What these developments in the decade after the war indicated was that in order to assure minimal interference with communications important to the safety of international carriers (ships and planes) and in order to minimize interference in areas where demand for frequencies is very high in relation to supply, ad hoc planning for certain resources within a multilateral organization was not just acceptable but crucial. Another point to note about the post-1918 years is that the International Radio-telegraph Union and the Berne Bureau became established as central to both the conclusion of new accords and their implementation. They gathered and disseminated information, and they also sponsored an increasing number of meetings on various aspects of radio communications. It is not that states could not have arranged for information-sharing and planning meetings outside of organizations, but the existing bodies were certainly important facilitators.

The interwar years also brought out some very interesting challenges to the implicit free-access regime, and if accepted they could have had some important impacts on the roles of multilateral organizations. In

1921 the United States convened a conference in Washington to consider the creation of a new body that it entitled the Universal Electric-Communications Union. It suggested that the proposed organization be given authority to allot all frequencies to states or even "assign" them to particular stations. At the time this was referred to as "a priori planning," but in fact it contained the same jurisdictional notion as did the concept of the common heritage of mankind proposed almost a half century afterward. This was that the resource in question should not just be the common property resource of all but should be subject to political management by the appropriate global institution. Most states were not willing to accept the creation of a multilateral institution with such encompassing authority when they realized that they could often be in a minority position on issues that affected them.[48]

In 1933 the International Radiotelegraph Union and the International Telegraph Union amalgamated and became the International Telecommunication Union (ITU), and in the 1930s this new body continued the very important regulatory activities of the IRU in ordering states' use of the airwaves—activities that were crucial to the acceptability of a free-access regime. The idea of a priori planning was mooted again in the early 1930s, but interestingly the jurisdictional proposal that was debated more extensively was sovereign ownership over a particular frequency once it had been utilized. Before this an assumption existed that when a state ceased to use a frequency, it could be used by another state. Also, an understanding prevailed that if technological progress made it possible to broadcast on frequencies closer together than in the past, states would readjust their utilization of particular frequencies so as to permit more efficient use of the spectrum. The actual acceptance of this proposal for national enclosure of specific frequencies would have tended to eliminate even the ad hoc planning activities then performed by the IRU or later the ITU. However, a combination of the anticipated inefficiencies resulting from permanent national claims and opposition from states that did not have extensive existing claims killed the proposal.[49]

Immediately after World War II the ITU was reconstituted, and the United States again proposed a priori planning for the frequency spectrum (referred to then as an "engineered spectrum") and proposed that the ITU assume the role of a global plannng agency. The United States at this time thought that it could secure virtually whatever it wanted in multilateral agencies, but other states (especially the Soviet Union) were not so sanguine about their power and hence international planning. The result was the collapse of the negotiations and a reversion to the prewar first-come/first-served arrangement with a new ITU body to register frequencies—the International Frequency Registration Board (IFRB).[50] Of course, the ITU continued (largely through its periodic World Administrative Radio Conferences) to allocate different spectrum bands to approximately thirty radio services, and at the conferences the IFRB played an important role in generating proposals and resolving conflicts.[51] Without a body such as the IFRB to register frequencies, check on possible conflicting use, and assist in the development of both allocation plans for different services and ad hoc allotment schemes for certain spectrum bands, the creation of an orderly system of radio communications would have been much more difficult. In fact, without the existence of the ITU it is hard to imagine how the large number of states in the world would have been able to create the allocation and allotment schemes that are fundamental to an efficient use of the airwaves.

After the 1940s the only real attempt to create allotment schemes for terrestrial (as opposed to outer space) airwaves concerned the drive by the developing countries in the late 1970s and 1980s to secure planning of the high-frequency (HF) spectrum, which is used for very long distance transmissions. They did not explicitly try to have the spectrum declared the common heritage of mankind, but that notion did underlie their strategy. They at least wanted the ad hoc planning that had become accepted in the ITU for certain frequency bands (e.g., those allocated for maritime and aeronautical communications) to be extended to the HF spectrum—and the redistribution of frequencies skewed in their favor. They supported a plan that would distribute high frequencies according to certain criteria and that would delegate a great deal of planning authority to the IFRB. However, those states that were the largest users of and claimants to the high-frequency spectrum (particularly the United States and the Soviet Union) objected to such a multilateral scheme that would certainly deprive them of their large shares of the resource. The somewhat unique first-come/first-served scheme that prevails for the HF spectrum as well as the ability of the Americans and Soviets to overpower most rival broadcasters with their powerful transmitters served their interests better. A 1984/87 conference on the HF spectrum failed to reach an accord, but a planning scheme with an important role for the ITU's IFRB is quite likely to emerge in the future.[52]

Overall the ITU (and formerly the IRU) has been very important in the evolution and operation of the basically free-access regime for radio frequencies. Its constant meetings, information gathering, and information dissemination have greatly facilitated a recognition of national claims and the development of regulatory arrangements that reduce unintended interference among transmissions and promote the efficient use of the spectrum. To have tried to achieve what the ITU has accomplished through a multitude of bilateral negotiations would have been almost impossible. Where a high level of demand exists for a common property resource that is governed by a free-access regime, some planning is required—whether it is viewed as obligatory or not. For the most part serious conflicts have not arisen between developed and developing states with regard to terrestrial telecommunications since, except for the high-frequency band, transmissions do not generally carry far enough to create serious interference conflicts between these two groups of countries. In the case of the controversy over planning the HF spectrum the majority of Third World states opposed an allotment scheme, but such big users as India and Brazil allied themselves with the major developed countries in opposing the scheme. In most negotiations on frequency management large majorities of states have, in fact, rejected giving binding legal authority over the spectrum to an international organization since they have feared and still fear being outvoted on important issues and having to give up existing frequency claims. Common-heritage planning for the entire spectrum has seldom been able to attract a majority of states since they place greater faith in the give-and-take of international bargaining than in authoritative global political agencies.

A final debate regarding jurisdiction over the airwaves concerns the related issues of jamming and banning foreign broadcasts, and in this case multilateral organizations have not succeeded in promoting the emergence of a regime although organizational resolutions encouraged particular practices by some states. The two central issues have been whether states have a right to jam foreign broadcasts and whether states should obtain the consent of other states before they beam transmissions to the latters' populations. Those who argue in favor of a right to jam and of prior consent support states' jurisdiction over airwaves in their airspaces, whereas those on the opposite side are defenders of free access.

Jamming radio broadcasts began back in the early 1930s, and by the time that World War II broke out, all states except for the United Kingdom were involved in jamming to one degree or another. Because jamming was relevant to the major political conflicts of the day and implicitly concerned the public law of the airwaves, it was logical that it be brought to the League of Nations for resolution. While most states publicly supported the free flow of information, no meaningful accord existed on jamming in the League or the international community more generally. Given the actual jamming practices of states during the immediate prewar and war years, one would have to judge that states adhered to the notion that they had a sovereign right to the airwaves above their territories—at least for purposes of blocking "politically threatening" transmissions. In the turbulent 1930s the absence of an accord in multilateral bodies as well as the activities of states gave weight to a notion of state sovereignty over airwaves in their airspace.[53] A weak implicit regime supporting state sovereign control emerged from "the information battlefield," not from international organizations.

In the postwar period the issue arose again very soon because of the commencement of jamming by the Soviet Union in 1948. The West was able to secure a general statement in support of the free flow of information in the 1948 Declaration on Human Rights and then in several General Assembly resolutions. But this did not change the policy of the Soviet Union and its allies who defended their behavior as legitimate actions of self-defense within their sovereign boundaries.[54] Within the ITU the West did not press the Soviets very hard on the jamming question since it wanted the cooperation of the Soviets on a variety of issues dealing with spectrum management. Also, with the explosion of Third World countries that were very concerned about protecting their independence against varied Western intrusions, the ability of the West to mobilize the U.N. or ITU membership against jamming declined. Again, the absence of a clear response by international organizations indicated the absence of a regime.

The context of the debate changed markedly in the early 1970s as the prospects for direct broadcasting satellites for television transmissions (DBS-TV) were mooted as imminent. Both Third World and socialist countries were worried that Western stations would soon be able to transmit TV signals directly to homes within their borders and that the West would consequently be able to exert a strong influence on the political and cultural attitudes of their populations. They advocated that the transmission of DBS-TV signals into a country should be allowed only with the "prior consent" of the receiving state. They secured resolutions in support of their position in the ITU and the United Nations Education, Social, and Cultural Organization (UNESCO) in 1971, and in 1972 a coalition of the Soviet bloc and Third World states passed a U.N. General Assembly resolution supporting the right to jam DBS transmissions. Lengthy negotiations took place in the United Nations between 1971 and 1982 to try to reach a consensus that balanced prior consent and the free flow of information. Most Western developed countries opposed blanket support for prior consent, but a good number were willing to back it if balanced in some way with support for the free flow of information. In the end the Third World and socialist states were unwilling to back down on blanket support for prior consent, and they secured the passage of a U.N. General Assembly resolution supporting their position. Since the early 1980s some de facto movement has occurred toward free access because of the launching of DBS-TV with regional scope (e.g., Panamsat and Asiasat). Once certain states in a region give permission to satellite services, the transmissions can then be picked up within other regional states. States are trying to control the launching of satellites in their regions, but they appear to be fighting a losing battle.[55]

Clearly, the debates over the right to jam radio/TV transmissions and the right to send TV signals into foreign states have not legitimized a regime that establishes the airwaves either as a common property resource or as an area of national jurisdiction. Political changes in Eastern Europe and the former Soviet Union and the growth of regional satellite systems indicate that the notion of the airwaves as a common property resource open to all is gaining some momentum, but no clear consensus exists on the subject. In fact, a large number of states want to preserve the right to control information flows to their populations. While sizable majorities have existed in favor of particular alternatives at certain times over the past sixty years, they have been unable to pressure their opponents to alter their positions because the political (and to a degree, commercial) stakes were too great. Also, technology has changed the parameters of the debate significantly over time.

A jurisdictional regime probably exists for the airwaves, but it is only a partial one. On the matter of establishing states' claims to particular frequencies, the airwaves are basically accepted as being a common property resource open to all. On the other hand, in regard to matters of the rights to transmit TV broadcasts to other states and to jam radio/TV transmissions, states have differed and still do differ on their implicit support for a common property status or a national sovereignty status. What has emerged is a situation wherein the existence of an implicit jurisdictional accord varies according to functional usage.

What is crucial to stress for purposes of this paper is that multilateral organizations have been very important to the implicit free-access regime governing the use of the frequency spectrum. They have established a practice for the making of state claims and have generated plans for the allocation of spectrum bands for certain purposes and the allotment of frequencies in certain bands to individual states. Without such plans that minimize interference and provide for a modicum of equity in the utilization of the spectrum, a basically free-access system would not work. Multilateral organizations introduce an element of common-heritage planning that make an open-access system politically acceptable and technically efficient.

Outer Space

The space age began with the launching of the first *Sputnik* by the Soviet Union in 1957. Soon afterward it became clear that satellites could become an important element in international telecommunications networks and that in the long run the possibility existed for the exploitation of resources on celestial bodies. The efforts to fashion a jurisdictional regime for space activities both explicitly and implicitly have occurred in two international organizations, the ITU and the United Nations, and these organizations have certainly had an influence on the regulatory arrangements.

In 1963 the ITU convened a World Administrative Radio Conference for space communications (a Space WARC), and a split opened between the Western and Latin American states, on the one hand, and the African, Asian, and Eastern European countries, on the other. The former group strongly backed a free-access regime, and the latter supported international planning—what would soon be known as a regime based on the common heritage of mankind.[56] Negotiations also started at this time in the U.N. Committee on the Peaceful Uses of Outer Space (UNCPUOS) on a treaty on the use of outer space, and they led to the approval of the Outer Space Treaty in 1967. By this time states had divided almost completely along developed–developing lines with the former backing free access and the latter international planning. However, in the eyes of the developing countries a regime based on free access was by no means as undesirable as one based on the right of states to establish national jurisdiction over space resources, and they were therefore willing to go along with a regime based on freedom of outer space. Also, they did succeed in having included in the treaty a stipulation that exploration and use "shall be carried out for the benefit and in the interests of all countries, irrespective of their degree of economic or scientific development and shall be the province of all mankind."[57] While the presence of the United Nations greatly facilitated the negotiation and legitimization of this free-access regime, it is hard to imagine that anything else would have occurred given American and Soviet preferences and their near monopoly of capabilities.

After 1967 the developing countries began to press for common-heritage planning with respect to space activities—both telecommunications and the exploitation of celestial bodies. The industrialized nations responded with modest ad hoc concessions in order to maintain a general legitimacy for the free-access regime. The efforts of the Third World with regard to communications were focused in the International Telecommunication Union. Starting with the 1971 Space WARC they secured general commitments to equity in the use of space resources—one resolution providing that "all countries have equal rights in the use of both the radio frequencies allocated to various space radio communications services and the GSO [geostationary orbit] for these services."[58] They also pressed consistently for the allotment of GSO slots and frequencies for space communications to developing countries before the best slots and frequencies were taken by the developed states. The Western and socialist states resisted any blanket approval of planning, but in the end they did agree at conferences in 1977, 1983, and 1988 to give a small number of GSO slots and associated frequencies to the developing countries for direct broadcasting satellites and for a national communications system.[59] Without the frequent ITU meetings and Third World political pressure it is unlikely that the developing countries would have received what they did. On the other hand, the concessions of the developed countries did not constitute major sacrifices. In fact, the Europeans were concerned that future satellite communications of the developing countries might interfere with their terrestrial microwave systems if they were not well planned, and therefore they had a special incentive to agree to certain DBS-TV allotments. In looking at the general evolution of the regulatory arrangements in the 1970s and 1980s it is probably the case that without the continual pressure by the Third World grouping in the ITU, the developed states would not have felt it necessary to make the concessions to allot space resources in order to legitimate the basic free-access regime. They could have much more easily rebuffed the uncoordinated demands of a modest number of developing states outside a multilateral organization.

The other area where the Third World tried to extend common-heritage planning was the moon and other celestial bodies. In the wake of the U.S. landing on the moon in 1969 the developing countries, led initially by Argentina, sought to establish a common-heritage regime.

They feared that the industrialized powers would take all the resources without any benefits flowing to them and would claim areas for "temporary" exploitation that would soon assume a permanent character. During the negotiations that lasted from 1970 to 1979 in the U.N. Committee on the Peaceful Uses of Outer Space the Third World sought to have all celestial bodies declared the common heritage of mankind in the same way that they were doing at the U.N. Conference on the Law of the Sea for the deep seabed. In these deliberations the Western and Soviet bloc states pursued different tactics in trying to undermine the Third World drive to refashion the outer space regime. The West simply interpreted the term "common heritage of mankind" to mean the same thing as free access. In other words, they sought to appropriate this increasingly sacrosanct concept for their own stance. The Soviet Union, on the other hand, fought until the very end of the negotiations to expunge the term from the draft treaty.

In the end the Soviets gave in on the issue of terminology in the 1979 Agreement Governing the Activities of States on the Moon and Other Celestial Bodies (or the Moon Treaty), but neither they nor the Western states made significant compromises on the substantive provisions. Whereas Article 11 declares that "The moon and its natural resources are the common heritage of mankind" and that there should be "an equitable sharing" of revenues taking into account "the needs of the developing countries" and the contributions of the exploiting states, it then goes on to state that "Neither the surface nor the subsurface of the moon, nor any part thereof or natural resources in place shall become property of any State, international intergovernmental or nongovernmental organization, national organization or non-governmental entity or of any natural person." Some ambiguity exists about whether this precludes a common-heritage regime. The treaty also notes, however, that when exploitation is feasible, the parties "undertake to establish an international regime, including appropriate procedures, to govern the exploration of the natural resources of the moon." This phrase definitely makes possible the creation of common-heritage arrangements.[60]

At the basic level the struggle to revise the Outer Space Treaty in the context of negotiating the Moon Treaty could be said to have been won decisively by the industrialized states. However, by securing agreement on the phrase *common heritage of mankind,* the phrase *equitable sharing,* and an understanding that negotiations on operational arrangements will take place when exploitation commences, the Third World states have planted a seed that will permit them to promote planning or the distribution of revenues to benefit themselves. It is true to a large extent, as Krasner notes, that the failure of the industrialized countries to ratify the Moon Treaty indicates that they are "not . . . prepared to accept constraints on their relational power capabilities emanating from nothing more than Third World United Nations' majorities."[61] On the other hand, what the developing states were able to secure in the U.N. negotiations in the 1970s could provide a normative basis for effective pressure at a future date.

Since the heart of the outer space regime is free access, no need has arisen to charge multilateral organizations with the task of promoting its implementation. However, the U.N. Committee on the Peaceful Uses of Outer Space has remained in existence in order to consider any proposals to revise the treaty or to deal with specific legal problems within its context (e.g., liability for damages). The ITU has also continued to deal with space communications on an ongoing basis, but its role is best considered in the context of the effectiveness of the jurisdictional regime.

As with the regime for terrestrial airwaves the International Telecommunication Union is absolutely crucial to the operation of the jurisdictional regime for communications in outer space. Free access interpreted as uncoordinated access simply does not make sense for space telecommunications any more than it makes sense for terrestrial telecommunications. An organization must exist through which states establish temporary claims to exploit the resource or establish rules of the road to prevent mutual interference. Free access or the legal doctrine of *res communis* has been conceived as first come/first served, and if any kind of scarcity problem arises, this jurisdictional approach must be accompanied by some procedures for mutual adjustment of claims—or in other terms, ad hoc planning. In the case of space communications the ITU began to develop in 1963 a system for consultation and planning for GSO slots and associated frequencies among space powers and satellite communications bodies, and it was developed further in the 1970s.[62] As is the case with the oceans, a free-access regime for telecommunications generally demands the existence of a multilateral organization through which states can assure noninterference with each other's activities.

The importance of a multilateral organization to the outer space regime is enhanced by the fact that the developing countries have pressed for a common-heritage regime or at least ad hoc planning that allots them a modest number of GSO slots and associated frequencies. The establishment of such plans can, for all intents and purposes, be done only through a permanent organization in which states regularly meet for purposes of sharing information and making decisions. The 1977 and 1983 conferences on allotments of GSO slots and associated frequencies for DBS-TV and the 1985/88 conference on space communications that alloted one slot for a national communications system were in a sense the tip of the iceberg of ITU involvement in the decision-making process. A multitude of ITU meetings have been crucial to the establishment of the modest planning arrangements that are very important for legitimizing the general free-access regime in the eyes of the Third World.

Conclusion

The views expressed in this article basically fall within the framework of what Robert Keohane has called "neoliberal institutionalism" or what James Caporaso refers to as "the institutional approach" to multilateralism. The approach posits *inter alia* that international organizations have some influence on agendas, state policies, and the outcomes of states' interactions. In addition, it observes significant mutualities of interest among states and sees multilateral organizations as important in overcoming the collective-action problems inherent in realizing these mutualities of interest.[63] This perspective is likely to gain more adherents in the future since so much international political bargaining is now taking place within the myriad of multilateral organizations and since the demand for international regimes is growing under the pressure of increased interdependencies.

With regard to the *creation* of regimes surveyed in this article, it is probable, first of all, that the regimes would not have developed as soon as they did without the presence of multilateral organizations and, second, that they would not have been as strong in the sense of being quite detailed and broadly supported if they had developed outside such bodies. Ad hoc conferences do not provide the kinds of sustained interactions and information sharing that are often necessary for the building of strong communications links and considered judgments of proposed regimes, and the law creation process outside multilateral organizations is slow and often lacks legitimacy. In the case of the law of the sea almost constant negotiations have taken place in the United Nations since the early 1950s, and at the moment they are going on—largely within the Preparatory Commission, which was established when the treaty was signed in 1982. In fact, a de facto or de jure revision of the 1982 treaty will quite likely emerge from the Preparatory Commission in the next decade. With regard to outer space the United Nations Committee on the Peaceful Uses of Outer Space has continued to function since the completion of the 1967 treaty, and it has generated a number of treaties that supplement the 1967 convention. The committee is almost a surrogate U.N. specialized agency for a number of outer space issues. Of course, in the case of the airwaves and the geostationary orbit the International Telecommunication Union has fashioned an implicit and partial jurisdictional regime, and its activities can be viewed as constantly adjusting the character of that regime in terms of the priorities given to different principles.

A point made in the introduction should be reiterated here: that some things about jurisdictional regimes for nonterrestrial spaces make them particularly susceptible to influence by multilateral organizations. First, these areas are now (or were in the past) common property resources. Common property resources by definition require a modicum of norm and rule making by the international community, and in our present era in which all states have a right to be heard on a large range of issues, it is natural that international decision making on international commons should take place within global bodies—particularly those associated with the United Nations system. Second, greater mutualities of interest probably exist with regard to common property resources than in other issue areas since states' interests in the freedom of commerce and communication are often at stake. Third, states' concern with and power over common property resources are often more diffused than in other international issue areas since many states are active in using or exploiting these resources. This is certainly the case with the seas and the airwaves, but in the case of outer space, power is very concentrated. A regime that provides states with a measure of stability in using such resources generally requires the consent of most members of the international community.

Apart from promoting the creation and strength of regimes, multilateral organizations have also shaped their *nature* in the sense that they make international decision making less hierarchical than it is in the "nonorganized" diplomatic world. Large numbers of weaker states are able to form coalitions and take advantage of the voting formulas and the openness of the diplomatic processes in international organizations in order to increase their influence. The developing countries almost certainly could not have secured the movements toward national enclosure and common-heritage planning in the three nonterrestrial areas that they did achieve if it had not been for the existence of the multilateral organizations in which the jurisdictional regimes were explicitly and/or implicitly addressed. The developing countries pressed for a sharing of resources beyond what they could obtain in a free-access regime, and because of the interest of the developed states in securing their support for certain accords and because of their general political interest in mitigating North–South tensions, they acceded to some of the developing countries' demands. That all these concessions would have occurred outside the institutionalized pattern of interactions within permanent organizations with majoritarian voting rules is hard to imagine. Outside multilateral diplomatic settings the developing countries would not have been able to coordinate their policies and political pressure to secure certain concessions.

In thinking about the specific accomplishments of Third World states in using multilateral organizations to further their interests, one must separate their successes in expanding their national jurisdictions and in furthering acceptance of common-heritage planning. Sometimes observers forget that a frequent goal of developing countries with regard to international commons has been to augment their own jurisdictional control, and in this area one of their most significant successes has been realized. In the law-of-the-sea negotiations the coastal developing states led the fight for extended fisheries jurisdiction in a 200-mile EEZ. They prevented acceptance of Western proposals on limits for the territorial sea and a fisheries zone in 1958 and 1960, and they made it clear in UNCLOS III that their acceptance of stronger provisions for freedom of navigation (particularly in international straits) was contingent on the maritime powers' acceptance of their demands for extended fisheries jurisdiction. Outside the U.N. negotiating context it is problematic whether the developing coastal states could have achieved acceptance of the EEZ. It might have emerged with time, but it would have come later—and probably not in the form that it has now. In the case of the airwaves, Third World states have implicitly supported national jurisdiction over the airwaves because they have favored prior consent for international TV transmissions and the right to jam TV and radio broadcasts. Their position and the passage of organizational resolutions have influenced to an extent state practices, but they have not had the leverage to secure acceptance of a regime based on national sovereignty from the developed countries. In recent years the proliferation of regional satellite systems has undercut their insistence on prior consent, and the cost of jamming and political changes in the socialist countries have reduced the possibility that the right of jamming will receive broad international support.

Probably the most high-profile demand of the Third World with respect to nonterrestrial spaces has concerned the adoption or at least partial acceptance of the common-heritage principle. The area where the principle first arose and where its acceptance is seen as having the greatest potential impact is the oceans—and more specifically the deep seabed. One conclusion that one could draw from many developed countries' opposition to the free-access/common-heritage hybrid regime in the 1982 treaty is that the Third World completely failed in the deep seabed issue area. However, this is probably a serious misconception. First, since the 1969 moratorium resolution the developing countries have discouraged the developed states from embarking on even experimental exploitation for fear of alienating the developing countries and perhaps encouraging some serious retaliation. The developed states might have behaved differently if deep seabed mining were commercially viable now, but it is still significant that they have not crossed "the moratorium line." Second, it is almost inconceivable that the industrialized nations will not either renegotiate a modified hybrid regime that will preserve a commercial role for the International Seabed Authority or adopt a revenue-sharing arrangement with the Third World. The long history of the UNCLOS III negotiations and the part XI compromise have established some basic expectations of the sharing of wealth from this common property resource and, hence, a reversion to a complete free-access arrangement is very unlikely.

The Third World also made some modest common-heritage gains in the jurisdictional regime for outer space that could provide a basis for further gains in the future. They have secured accords that set aside certain GSO slots and associated frequencies for themselves, and this has reinforced the notion in the ITU that a simple first-come/first-served formula is not tolerable. A measure of equity must be assured. The Moon Treaty was far from a great victory for the Third World advocates of global planning, but a seed of international equity has at least been planted with the acceptance of the phrase *common heritage of mankind.* In the case of terrestrial telecommunications the majority of developing countries failed from the late 1970s through the 1980s to obtain an allotment scheme for the high-frequency spectrum since they were opposed by the superpowers and a few large Third World states, but they are likely to make some gains in the 1990s. Also, they have achieved some concessions with regard to the allocation of spectrum bands for telecommunications services of concern to them. Overall the success of the Third World in using international organizations to obtain partial acceptance of the common-heritage principle in outer space and the terrestrial airwaves has not been dramatic, but progress has occurred. They have moved the First World in modest ways toward global planning and an acceptance of a degree of equity among nations.

For the most part international organizations are not given explicit roles in *promoting the operation or effectiveness* of jurisdictional regimes based largely on free access. However, they are sometimes given responsibilities in the area of dispute settlement. One example is the tribunal that was included in the 1982 Convention on the Law of the Sea. Of greater import are the roles that multilateral organizations play in providing a platform for the discussion of challenges to a regime and in revising its existing guidelines—the U.N. Committee on the Peaceful Uses of Outer Space being a very good example. In fact, the International Telecommunication Union performs a comparable role with regard to the law of the airwaves.

While these *explicit roles* should not be denigrated, the most important roles of multilateral organizations in the operation or maintenance of jurisdictional regimes are *implicit*. Designing a jurisdictional regime along the lines of a certain principle or even an attempted balancing among them without its having some perceived shortcomings is virtually impossible. This is particularly the case with the free-access regimes that dominate nonterrestrial spaces. Especially in our present era of rampant technological progress and increased international commerce it is crucial to promote orderly use of the resources and a measure of equity. The International Civil Aviation Organization, the International Telecommunication Union, the International Maritime Organization, as well as a variety of other bodies all promote order and a degree of equity in their respective spheres. Relevant to this point these organizations often engage in ad hoc planning and sometimes legitimize a degree of national enclosure of the international property resource in question. For example, states are on occasion given the right to use certain areas or certain resources in a semipermanent fashion. This is particularly the case with regard to the ITU's regulations for the airwaves and the geostationary orbit, but it has also occurred to lesser degrees in other areas as well. Another way that multilateral organizations promote the acceptability of free-access regimes is that they often monitor states' enforcement of multilateral conventions. For example, this is a common activity of different bodies within the IMO.[64] The implicit role that multilateral organizations play in the operation of regimes should not be underestimated. By promoting those principles or values not explicitly recognized in the jurisdictional regime, they make those regimes politically acceptable.[65] The implicit roles of multilateral organizations in sustaining jurisdictional regimes cannot be stressed enough.

The final role of multilateral organizations is a somewhat unique one in that it concerns the *impacts of proposals for multilateral organizations within proposed regimes on the political acceptability of those regimes.* Clearly, many states have been unwilling to accept organizations that would have binding legal powers over the use or exploitation of a common property resource. States have generally been reluctant to subject themselves to the decisions supported by a majority of their fellow states, and this has especially been the case recently with respect to the developed countries vis-à-vis Third World countries. This attitude was best manifested in the past in the deliberations of the International Telecommunication Union on a priori planning, and now it is recognizable in both the ITU's negotiations on the airwaves and the U.N. deliberations on the law of the sea. The developed countries, led by the United States, which is more fearful of Third World majorities than other countries are, are determined that the developing state coalition is not going to dictate all the terms of their access to the deep seabed, the airwaves, or outer space. Traditionally the major industrial powers have been able in those organizations whose regulatory and operational activities have serious economic implications to find ways of achieving influence roughly commensurate with their power.[66] They are often willing to accept discrete plans for particular problems or "ad hoc common-heritage planning" when faced with a truculent coalition of Third World states, but they want to maintain the power to opt in or out of such schemes. The present logjam in the negotiations over the International Seabed Authority is significantly due to the reluctance of the developed countries to contemplate the prospect that they will be unable to veto rules and programs for the ISA favored by the Third World—including requirements that they transfer funds or technology to the ISA. Their opposition to authoritative planning bodies has also been an issue of contention in ITU negotiations over allotment schemes for the airwaves and geostationary orbit.

While states (and particularly the more powerful ones) are very reluctant to contemplate international organizations with authoritative powers to govern particular issue areas, they have accepted an enmeshment in virtually constant deliberations within organizational structures and the generation of more numerous and stronger multilateral regimes. Apart from recognizing the importance of the organizations in the development and operation of the regimes, states are also willing to accept the modified distribution of influence that accompanies working through multilateral bodies. In fact, in the case of the jurisdictional regimes for nonterrestrial spaces, the key impacts of multilateral organizations have been their facilitation of Third World influence on the development of the regimes and their promotion of the political acceptability of the regimes by creating technical regimes that reduce the shortcomings of the jurisdictional arrangements. Noteworthy is that one very important implicit role of multilateral organizations has been assuring that the developing countries secure enough benefits from the basically free-access regimes to maintain a broad political legitimacy for those regimes.

A final point is that the importance of multilateral organizations is a manifestation of the acceptance of two things: the need for multilateral regulatory arrangements in many issue areas in an increasingly interdependent world and the need for the approval of most states in order for regimes to be effective and legitimate. Multilateral decision making, or the participation of all states in diplomatic deliberations and the approval of accords by a majority of participating states, is really more important than the existence of the organizations per se. Multilateral organizations may facilitate the implementation of the principle of universal and equal participation in decision making, but in a larger sense they are manifestations of the growing acceptance of that principle.

NOTES

1. John G. Ruggie, "Multilateralism: The Anatomy of an Institution," in this volume.

2. See Ruggie's discussion of the nonhierarchical character of multilateral decision making. "Multilateralism."

3. For an excellent analysis of voting systems in international organizations, see Stephen Zamora, "Voting in International Economic Organizations," *American Journal of International Law* (1980), 74:566–604.

4. Between 1909 and 1986 the number of intergovernmental organizations rose from 37 to 337, and the number of congresses and conferences they sponsored went up from 100 per year in the first decade of the 20th century to around 3,000 per year in the 1970s. *Yearbook of International Organizations, 1986/87* (Munich: K. G. Saur, 1988), table 2; Ithiel de Sola Pool, *Technologies without*

Boundaries: On Telecommunications in a Global Age (Cambridge: Harvard University Press, 1990), p. 71.

5. For a discussion of the procedural and substantive components of regimes, see Mark W. Zacher, "Trade Gaps, Analytical Gaps: Regime Analysis and International Commodity Trade Regulation," *International Organization* (Spring 1987), 41:174–178.

6. Miles Kahler, "Multilateralism With Small and Large Numbers," in this volume.

7. Jacobson outlines five functions. His informational, normative, and rule-creating functions fall within my creation role, and his rule-supervisory and operational functions fall within my operational role. Harold K. Jacobson, *Networks of Interdependence: International Organizations and the Global Political System* (New York: Knopf, 2nd ed., 1984), pp. 89–90.

8. Ruggie, "Multilateralism," in this volume.

9. Ruggie, "Multilateralism," in this volume.

10. Robert O. Keohane, *After Hegemony: Cooperation and Discord in the World Political Economy* (Princeton: Princeton University Press, 1984), p. 66.

11. Keohane, *After Hegemony*, esp. ch. 6. Also, for an excellent discussion of this school, see the treatment of "the institutional approach" to multilateralism in James Caporaso's article in this volume.

12. Alan James, "International Institutions: Independent Actors?" in Avi Schlaim, ed., *International Organizations in World Politics: Yearbook 1975* (Boulder, Colo.: Westview, 1976), p. 86. Also see Lawrence B. Krause and Joseph S. Nye, "Reflections on the Economics and Politics of International Economic Organizations," *International Organization* (Winter 1975), 29:336–337.

13. Robert O. Keohane and Joseph S. Nye, *Power and Interdependence: World Politics in Transition* (Boston: Little, Brown, 1977), p. 35.

14. Robert W. Cox and Harold K. Jacobson, et al., *The Anatomy of Influence: Decision Making in International Organization* (New Haven: Yale University Press, 1973), p. 428.

15. Jacobson, *Networks of Interdependence*, p. 418.

16. Jacobson, *Networks of Interdependence*, p. 90; Cox and Jacobson, *Anatomy of Influence*, passim; Keohane, *After Hegemony*, passim; Keohane and Nye, *Power and Interdependence*, pp. 54–58 and passim. For a case study of the role of the International Maritime Organization, see R. Michael M'Gonigle and Mark W. Zacher, *Pollution, Politics and International Law: Tankers at Sea* (Berkeley: University of California Press, 1979); and for a case study that includes analyses of the roles of international commodity organizations, see Jock A. Finlayson and Mark W. Zacher, *Managing International Markets: Developing Countries and the Commodity Trade Regime* (New York: Columbia University Press, 1988).

17. C. Fred Bergsten, Georges Berthoin, and Kinhide Mushakoji, *The Reform of International Institutions* (New York: Trilateral Commission, 1976); Zamora, "Voting in International Economic Organizations"; Inis L. Claude, *Swords Into*

Plowshares: The Problems and Progress of International Organization (New York: Random House, 1964), ch. 7.

18. S. Brown, N. W. Cornell, L. L. Fabian, and E. B. Weiss, *Regimes for the Ocean, Outer Space and Weather* (Washington, D.C.: Brookings, 1977), pp. 13– 18; R. P. Anand, *Origin and Development of the Law of the Sea: History of International Law Revisited* (The Hague: Martinus Nijhoff, 1983); E. D. Brown, *The Legal Regime of Hydrospace* (London: Stevens, 1971); W. E. Butler, *Law of the Sea and International Shipping* (Dobbs Ferry, N.Y.: Oceana, 1985). A very rich literature exists on the law of the sea, and only a modest number of works can be cited in this section. The author also benefited from reading book-length manuscripts on UNCLOS III by Robert Friedheim and Edward Miles.

19. The Pardo statement and accompanying memorandum are in U.N. Docs. A/AC.105/C.2/SR.75 or A/6675 (1967).

20. D. P. O'Connell, *The International Law of the Sea, vol. 2* (London: Oxford University Press, 1983), p. 124.

21. Arvid Pardo and Carl Q. Christol, "The Common Interest: Tension Between the Whole and the Parts," in R. St. J. MacDonald and D. M. Johnston, eds., *The Structure and Process of International Law* (The Hague: Martinus Nijhoff, 1983), pp. 647–655. Another author has referred to common heritage as "a rule of joint property that prevents any co-owner from disposing of or using common property of all states without first obtaining the consent of all states as expressed in a convention, treaty, or declaration which has become binding on all states." R. P. Arnold, "The Common Heritage of Mankind as a Legal Concept," *International Lawyer* (1975), 9:158.

22. On the seabed, see Barry Buzan, *Seabed Politics* (New York: Praeger, 1976). On the Moon Treaty and outer space generally, see Carl Q. Christol, *The Modern International Law of Outer Space* (New York: Pergamon, 1982), ch. 7. For a statement of the Soviet position, see Gennady M. Danilenko, "The Concept of the 'Common Heritage of Mankind' in International Law," *Annals of Air and Space Law* (1988), 13:247–65.

23. Anand, *Origin and Development of the Law of the Sea*, ch. 4 and 5.

24. Stephen D. Krasner, *Structural Conflict: The Third World Against Global Liberalism* (Berkeley: University of California Press, 1985), p. 242.

25. Anand, *Origin and Development of the Law of the Sea*, pp. 148–149.

26. Anand, *Origin and Development of the Law of the Sea*, ch. 6 and 7; Patricia W. Birnie, "The Law of the Sea Before and After UNCLOS I and UNCLOS II," in R. P. Barston and Patricia W. Birnie, eds., *The Maritime Dimension* (London: George Allen and Unwin, 1980), pp. 1–26.

27. The 1982 treaty is in U.N. Doc. A/CONF.62/122 (1982). On developments from the mid-1960s through the early 1980s, see Anand, *Origin and Development of the Law of the Sea*, ch. 8 and 9; Buzan, *Seabed Politics;* Ann L. Hollick, *U.S. Foreign Policy and the Law of the Sea* (Princeton: Princeton University Press, 1981).

28. For an excellent analysis of the UNCLOS III negotiating process, see Barry G. Buzan, "Negotiating by Consensus: Developments in Technique at the UN Conference on the Law of the Sea," *American Journal of International Law* (1981), 75:324–348.

29. Buzan, *Seabed Politics;* Hollick, *U.S. Foreign Policy and the Law of the Sea;* James K. Sebenius, *Negotiating the Law of the Sea* (Cambridge, Mass.: Harvard University Press, 1984).

30. Buzan, *Seabed Politics,* pp. 91–109 and passim; Robert L. Friedheim and William J. Durch, "The International Seabed Resources Agency Negotiations and the NIEO," *International Organization* (Spring 1977), 31:343–384; Edward Miles, "The Structure and Effects of the Decision Process in the Seabed Committee and the Third United Nations Conference on the Law of the Sea," *International Organization* (Spring 1977), 31:159–234.

31. A good description of the provisions is in Roderick Ogley, *Internationalizing the Seabed* (Hampshire, England: Gower, 1984).

32. The U.S. rejection and subsequent developments are analyzed in: Mark W. Zacher and James G. McConnell, "Down to the Sea with Stakes: The Evolving Law of the Sea and the Future of the Deep Seabed Regime," *Ocean Development and International Law* (1990), 21:84–89; and Lee Kimball, "Turning Points in the Future of Deep Seabed Mining," *Ocean Development and International Law* (1986), vol. 17.

33. U.N. Doc. A/CONF.62/122 (1982), article 82.

34. For an analysis of the IMO, see M'Gonigle and Zacher, *Pollution, Politics, and International Law.* It also discusses the activities of other organizations in the field.

35. These developments are discussed in Anand, *Origin and Development of the Law of the Sea,* ch. 8 and 9.

36. Charles B. Heck, "Collective Arrangements for Managing Ocean Fisheries," *International Organization* (1975), 29:711–743; William Warner, *Distant Water* (Boston: Little Brown, 1983).

37. The developments are described in: Buzan, *Seabed Politics,* passim. The relevant provisions in the 1982 treaty are: U.N. Doc. A/CONF.62/122, part VI.

38. Buzan, *Seabed Politics,* p. 278.

39. Krasner, *Structural Conflict,* p. 245. Also see Buzan, *Seabed Politics,* pp. 287–288.

40. Hollick, *U.S. Foreign Policy and the Law of the Sea,* p. 380.

41. Hollick, *U.S. Foreign Policy and the Law of the Sea,* p. 380.

42. Christer Jonsson, *International Aviation and the Politics of Regime Change* (New York: St. Martin's, 1987), pp. 26–29.

43. Vicki Lynne Golich, *The Politics and Economics of the International Commercial Aviation Safety Regime* (Ph.D. dissertation, University of Southern California, 1984); I. H. Diederiks-Verschoor, *An Introduction to Air Law* (Amsterdam:

Deventer, Kluwer Law, and Taxation, 1983); Frederick C. Dorey, *Aviation Security* (London: Granada, 1983).

44. "Allocation" refers to decisions to reserve particular frequency bands for particular services or uses (e.g., maritime communications, radio broadcasting, and space research). "Allotment" refers to decisions to give particular states the authority to use certain radio frequencies. "Assignment" refers to decisions to give particular radio stations/transmitters the right to use particular frequencies.

45. George A. Codding, *The International Telecommunication Union: An Experiment in International Cooperation* (New York: Arno, 1972), pp. 92–95; George A. Codding and A. M. Rutkowski, *The International Telecommunication Union in a Changing World* (Dedham, Mass.: Artech House, 1982), pp. 117–118; David M. Leive, *International Telecommunications and International Law: The Regulation of the Radio Spectrum* (Dobbs Ferry, N.Y.: Oceana, 1970), pp. 41–42; John D. Tomlinson, *The International Control of Radio-Communications* (Ann Arbor, Mich.: J. W. Edwards, 1945), pp. 25–26.

46. Codding, *International Telecommunication Union*, p. 114; Tomlinson, *The International Control of Radio-Communications*, p. 54.

47. Codding, *The International Telecommunications Union*, pp. 113, 126, 147, 150, 157–160, 178–179; Codding and Rutkowski, *The International Telecommunication Union in a Changing World*, pp. 267–681; Tomlinson, *The International Control of Radio-Communications*, pp. 179–223.

48. Codding and Rutkowski, *The International Telecommunication Union in a Changing World*, pp. 15 and 262–268; Tomlinson, *The International Control of Radio-Communications*, p. 48.

49. Codding, *The International Telecommunication Union*, pp. 119–150; Codding and Rutkowski, *The International Telecommunications Union in a Changing World*, pp. 189–191; Leive, *International Telecommunications and International Law*, pp. 45–54. On the 1906–39 period, see James Savage, *The Politics of International Telecommunications Regulation* (Boulder, Colo.: Westview, 1989), pp. 66–71.

50. Codding, *The International Telecommunication Union*, pp. 185–245 and 344–365; Leive, *International Telecommunication and International Law*, pp. 55–65; Savage, *The Politics of International Telecommunication Regulation*, pp. 72–77.

51. For an analysis of the most recent general WARC, see G. O. Robinson, "Regulating International Airwaves: The 1979 WARC," *Virginia Journal of International Law* (1980), 21:1–54.

52. The rather unique system for HF spectrum management is described in: Codding and Rutkowski, *The International Telecommunication Union in a Changing World*, pp. 123–125, 252–253, and 274–278; and Savage, *The Politics of International Telecommunication Regulation*, pp. 92–96. The negotiations in the late 1970s and the 1980s are discussed in: Robinson, "Regulating International Airwaves," pp. 1–54; and Savage, *The Politics of International Telecommunication Regulation*, pp. 97–102.

53. Tomlinson, *The International Control of Radio-Communications,* pp. 227–233 and 303–304; Osborne Mance, *International Telecommunication* (London: Oxford University Press, 1943), pp. 36–37.

54. Ranjan Borra, "The Problem of Jamming International Broadcasting," *Journal of Broadcasting* (Fall 1967), 11:358–360; Julian Hale, *Radio Power* (London: Paul Elek, 1975), passim.

55. Savage, *The Politics of International Telecommunication Regulation,* pp. 131–161; James G. Savage and Mark W. Zacher, "Free Flow Versus Prior Consent: The Jurisdictional Battle Over International Telecommunications," *International Journal* (Spring 1977), 42:352–363; Howard C. Anwalt, "Direct Television Broadcasting and the Quest for Communication Equality," in *Regulation of Transnational Communication* (New York: Clark Boardman, 1984), pp. 361–378; Carl Q. Cristol, *The Modern International Law of Outer Space* (New York: Pergamon, 1982), pp. 648–649 and 702–709. Information on recent DBS-TV developments came from interviews with officials and experts.

56. Donna Demac et al., *Equity in Orbit: the 1985 Space WARC* (London: International Institute of Communication, 1985), p. 10; Ram S. Jakhu, "The Evolution of the ITU's Regulatory Regime Governing Space Radio Communication Services and the Geostationary-Satellite Orbit," *Annals of Air and Space Law* (1983), 8:400.

57. 610 UNTS 205 (1967), article 1; Christol, *The Modern International Law of Outer Space,* pp. 13–58.

58. Codding and Rutkowski, *The International Telecommunication Union in a Changing World,* p. 48; E. D. duCharme et al., "The Genesis of the 1985/87 ITU World Administrative Radio Conference on the Use of the Geostationary Satellite Orbit and the Planning of Space Services Utilizing It," *Annals of Air and Space Law* (1982), 7:266–267; Larry Martinez, *Communications Satellites: Power Politics in Space* (Dedham, Mass.: Artech House, 1985), pp. 116–119.

59. Codding and Rutkowski, *The International Telecommunication Union in a Changing World,* pp. 49–50; du Charme et al., "The Genesis of the 1985/87 ITU World Administrative Radio Conference," p. 271; Martinez, *Communications Satellites,* pp. 120–124; Ram S. Jakhu, et al., "The ITU Regulatory Framework for Satellite Communications: An Analysis," *International Journal* (Spring 1987), 42:280–288; Savage, *The Politics of International Telecommunication Regulation,* pp. 110–120.

60. The treaty is in: U.N.Doc. A/RES/34/68 (1979); Christol, *The Modern International Law of Outer Space,* pp. 246–328; *Agreement Governing the Activities of States on the Moon and Other Celestial Bodies* (96th Congress, 2nd session, Committee on Commerce, Science and Transportation) (Washington, D.C.: Government Printing Office, 1980).

61. Krasner, *Structural Conflict,* p. 228.

62. Demac et al., *Equity in Orbit,* pp. 10–12; duCharme et al., "The Genesis of the 1985/87 ITU World Administrative Radio Conference," pp. 166–167;

Codding and Rutkowski, *The International Telecommunication Union in a Changing World,* p. 248. The United Nations also approved a convention in 1975 asking states to provide information on their satellites. Christol, *The International Modern Law of Outer Space,* pp. 213–245.

63. Robert O. Keohane, "Neoliberal Institutionalism: A Perspective on World Politics," in Robert O. Keohane, *International Institutions and State Power: Essays in International Relations Theory* (Boulder, Colo.: Westview, 1989), ch. 1; Robert O. Keohane, "Multilateralism: An Agenda for Research," *International Journal* (Autumn 1990), 45:731–764; James Caporaso, "International Relations Theory and Multilateralism: The Search for Foundations," in this volume.

64. M'Gonigle and Zacher, *Pollution, Politics, and International Law,* esp. ch. 6 and 8.

65. Lisa Martin's paper in this volume ("The Rational State Choice of Multilateralism") notes that in coordination games we can expect fairly strong regulatory regimes but weak roles for multilateral organizations. However, regimes whose main role is coordination can, in fact, include quite strong organizations since constant revision of the rules and monitoring of compliance require very active organizations. This is due in part to the fact that cooperation games are generally embedded to one degree or another in coordination games. For example, regulations concerning maritime safety or pollution standards often impose differential costs on states.

66. Cox and Jacobson, *Anatomy of Influence,* conclusion.

Part 5

❖

THEORETICAL

REPRISE

❖

12. Norms Versus Numbers: Multilateralism and the Rationalist and Reflexivist Approaches to Institutions— a Unilateral Plea for Communicative Rationality

❖

Friedrich Kratochwil

T HIS concluding chapter cannot summarize in detail the various articles treating the problem of multilateralism from distinct starting points and in a variety of contexts. A more promising strategy is to emphasize certain themes that have emerged from our enterprise of looking at international politics through the prism of multilateralism and to relate these themes to ongoing theoretical discussions in the field. In adopting this strategy, I organize my discussion by categorizing the themes under three rubrics.

First, I focus on the *critical* contribution of multilateralism. I argue that a focus on multilateralism provides us with an alternative and a historically important vantage point for investigating international politics. Next I show that multilateralism also helps us in the *clarification* of several important puzzles that have plagued regime theory. To that extent, it represents an important extension of the regime research program. The third rubric is concerned with the *heuristic fruitfulness* of multilateralism. Here I argue that the future direction of research suggested by multilateralism represents a heuristically fruitful problem shift rather than the expansion of the research program by ad hoc extensions.[1]

Multilateralism as Critique: Anarchy, History, and Structure

This volume began by suggesting that multilateralism is constituted by distinct normative principles possessing a generative logic of its own. Conceptual elaboration of this phenomenon is guided, therefore, not merely by nominal definitional exercises such as defining it as cooperation among more than two members, but also by a substantive question in regard to postwar international politics.

Similarly, while it has been common to associate multilateralism with universalist designs, this volume takes great pains to demonstrate that despite universalist potential, multilateralism provides a viable organizational form for arrangements of more limited scope. Thus in the postwar era, multilateralism was geographically often narrowly circumscribed. The difference in this regard between the Pacific and the North Atlantic regions was also noted in several contributions. Nevertheless, in its effects, multilateralism seemed to be as important as the sovereignty it modified. This modification (not abolition) of the logic of sovereignty is precisely what makes multilateralism an identifiable social institution cutting across various organizational domains.

In this context, Ruggie distinguished among general international orders, more (issue-specific) regimes, and formal international organizations, each of which can incorporate differing degrees of multilateral principles. The latter influence the style of decision making among the interacting parties by limiting the otherwise absolute discretion, characteristic of strict sovereignty. Similarly, the temporal limitation of genuine multilateralism to the recent era—correctly distinguished by Morgan from similar phenomena such as classical alliances—could be interpreted as a drawback for general theory building. However, whatever the advantages of an ahistorical (transtemporal) theory of international politics might be, this "limitation" of multilateralism is more than balanced by its importance for postwar politics and by the effects multilateralism had on the changes in the Eastern Bloc and on the current reconstitution of Europe.

Consequently one of the most important contributions of the multilateral focus is the correction of the blind spots of traditional realist theory. As James Caporaso points out in this volume, theoretical frameworks distort by two means, either by marginalizing a set of interesting problems or by making it impossible to raise certain questions at all. In this vein, the predominance of realism in its various forms has made it difficult to explain the not inconsiderable amount of cooperation in general—except in cases that are well captured by the metaphors of games of coordination. It has also made difficult the answer to the question of why U.S. decision makers, enjoying a virtually unchallengeable position vis-à-vis their Western allies and former enemies, would choose such a demanding institutional form. Finally, the research program of realism, concerned with "cooperation" in its generic form, has great difficulties in accounting for the *particular* set of regimes and formal organizations, for neither of them can be derived from the position of the United States as a hegemonic power, from the precepts of a classical balance of power, or even from interest approaches to politics. As a matter of fact, realism in either its traditional or structural form would lead us to expect a world quite different from the one that emerged during postwar reconstruction.

ANARCHY AND ITS IMPLICATIONS

In characterizing the international arena, structural realism utilizes an analogy. Beginning with self-interested actors interacting with each other in a world of scarcity, it obtains the "anarchy" problematique and its concomitant behavioral prescription by logical derivation. This procedure has, in my view, three theoretical implications. First, whether micro theories are really systemic is debatable, even if they account for unintended consequences. After all, sociological theories concerning systemic factors developed out of a dissatisfaction with attempts at explaining social phenomena in terms of radical methodological individualism.

Second, the systemic context that links individual actions in a market is based on institutional features that are exogenous to the micro theory. Nevertheless, they are absolutely essential for the explanation of interactions and their effects. Thus, actors must not only mutually recognize each other as legitimate partners to a transaction, they must also respect each other's property rights and agree on the convention of money for the exchange of their goods. Only through the convention of a universally accepted medium of exchange can actions taken by the actors independently have clearly identifiable systemic outcomes.

Third, the corollary of the two arguments above is that the microeconomic analogy bears out only the technical meaning of anarchy, i.e., the absence of formal organizations acting on behalf of a collectivity. The anarchy in the realist or Hobbesian sense, however, means above all the absence of norms or even the most elementary forms of sociality. Consequently, a persistent equivocation exists in structural realist writings when anarchy is used in these two incompatible senses. To that extent inferences made on the basis of the first technical meaning (absence of central institutions) are often used to prove that in international politics force "is not the ultimate, but first and foremost reason"[2] However, the latter conclusion follows only if we take the second meaning of anarchy, i.e., anomie, as the defining semantic dimension.

In contrast to this predominant mode of realist analysis, multilateralism focuses explicitly on the institutional characteristics of actions and choices. This does not negate the great advantages of economic modes of analysis in those instances when we can take institutional features for granted and get around the great empirical difficulties of specifying utility functions by simple assumption. For example, under conditions of a mutual recognition of rights and the availability of a universal medium of exchange and stable store of value, the transformation of self-interest into a theoretically meaningful concept such as revenue maximization makes sense. It can also be achieved "by assumption" rather than by painstaking empirical research. But to conclude from this rather exceptional case that this method of analysis is also applicable to cases where no such conventions are widely shared, simply because in both cases actors are self-interested, is rather heroic. That people act in order to further their interests is hardly illuminating, and it leads to tautologies unless we specify their preferences *ex ante*.

Granting these points, we also come to understand why the assumptions underlying the construct of *homo economicus* need not be realistic even *given* a perfectly competitive market. Actors who are not maximizers will automatically be eliminated. Neither the existence of irrational actors nor the unrealistic initial assumptions pose a threat to the heuristic power of the theory. Its usefulness lies in its ability to predict. The accuracy of the prediction is guaranteed by a fit between the theoretical structure and its correspondence to real life "in the long run." Through evolutionary pressures the system rewards conforming and eliminates nonconforming behavior. Ontology and methodological convenience get reconciled. Without such an existential link, however, the proposition that correct prediction is the sole appropriate measure of a good theory—most eloquently advanced by Milton Friedman[3]—would be unconvincing, since we often obtain quite accurate predictions from demonstrably false as well as unrealistic theories.

The last argument leads me to the general question of whether neorealism's rational actor model leading to an "evolutionary" theory of cooperation[4] provides an appropriate paradigm for the emergence of international institutions. First of all, as Ullman-Margalit,[5] Duncan Snidal,[6] and Lisa Martin (in her contribution to this volume) have shown, taking a well-specified Prisoners' Dilemma (PD) as the paradigm for collective-action problems in international politics is problematic. Precisely because different problems arise in situations closer to games of coordination or of suasion, the explanation of cooperation in an iterative PD situation is less than a universally applicable template.

Second, even the emergence of cooperation by means of a tit-for-tat strategy in two-person iterative PD games is not convincing unless a whole host of additional or even silent assumptions is made. Since a niceness rule is required for the first round, the dilemma can be solved only if it is assumed away in the first round, i.e., that actors do *not* behave in a strategically rational manner. In addition, cardinal utilities must be assumed for the whole series of games. Otherwise, the players can calculate neither their gains nor their discount parameter. The latter is important since Axelrod shows that below a critical value for w (the parameter), tit-for-tat becomes collectively unstable. No less puzzling than these largely logical difficulties are the problems that arise when we try to give empirical referents to some of the crucial theoretical terms. Here the laboratory setting and the purely logical relationships postulated between the different parts of the model present difficulties in specifying the exact ranges of application.

The issue is not that game-theoretical models are abstract and therefore, by necessity, always simpler than real life. The issue is rather that certain theoretically relevant aspects of the choice situation are either badly modeled or not modeled at all. For example, in order to play tit-for-tat correctly, the players must know where one interaction sequence ends and another begins. Otherwise no appropriate reward or punishment can be chosen in the subsequent round. In real life, the "ongoingness" of interaction muddies the waters considerably, for a noncooperative move might be chosen by a party in retaliation for a former wrong while the other player might interpret the move as one of unprovoked defection.

In a multilateral setting, the informational requirements are even more baffling. As Geoff Garret points out in his contribution to this volume, governments considering a cooperative solution to the PD situation of free trade are unlikely to know the details of another government's past behavior. They might have difficulty in even establishing whether or not the other government has been playing "fair" with them in the past, "given the wide array of subtle neoprotectionist policy options available to governments."[7]

This point then makes institutions necessary for keeping the game going, by providing the participants with the necessary information, i.e., increasing transparency and lowering transaction costs. In addition, these economies are available to the participants only if obvious procedures or indicators are in place that allow for the appraisal and characterization of an action in terms of a simple dichotomy: compliance/noncompliance. In real life, such appraisals are more complicated than perceiving moves in a well-structured game. Of paramount importance is the interpretation of the "facts" and inferences about motivations, i.e., whether a certain move was made out of fear not to be suckered or whether it represented an aggressive defection from the cooperative solution. As Garret shows, we need not only clear and codified rules but also institutions that constitute "a forum in which states can decide what constitutes fair and unfair . . . practices."[8] Second, these institutions must also contribute "an arena in which the behavior can be scrutinized." As Anatol Rapoport[9] argued a long time ago, such situations do not resemble well-structured games, in which the participants face clearly defined options and payoffs. Rather they are "debates," in which the models of problem solving, consensus formation, and communicative action enter as important defining characteristics.

Here the insights of classical noncooperative game theory are of little help since its particular definition of rationality is insensitive to the practical problem of the discrimination of motives. Consider in this context the classical PD situation and its minimax solution. Two distinct motivations, one defensive and one aggressive, are aggregated in its criterion of rationality. In real life, however, failure or success in achieving cooperative outcomes crucially depends upon our ability to ascertain whether an action was the result of insecurity or aggressiveness. Insecurity makes it necessary to take steps that induce cooperation through reassurance and the building of trust; aggressive intent calls for deterrence.

If such difficulties already exist in bilateral situations, the transition from bilateral to multilateral context creates numerous additional puzzles—even if we assume K-groups and other incentives that attempt to explain the emergence of cooperative institutions. Taylor's work provides much food for thought in this respect.[10] So do Caporaso's references above to the social psychological literature that deals with the reasons why group dynamics push toward the universalization of norms and their duty-imposing (deontological) rather than simply utilitarian status.

These considerations also confirm the argument that multilateralism is viable only if the participants accept "diffuse reciprocity" as a maxim, in addition to adopting general nondiscriminatory principles. In this respect nothing is preordained, and solutions to dilemmas need not occur historically despite their "functional" character. Both leadership and crucial historical choices enter as decisive factors for explaining the chain of events and the character of the game that is thereby established.

THE PROBLEM OF HISTORY

The last remarks demonstrate why history and its lessons become so important for understanding politics. History as the record of things considered worth remembering is far from just a way of preserving and retrieving data. The patterns that emerge in historical processes are not limited to either the cyclical return or to the evolutionary trajectory that weeds out unfit exemplars or species. Precisely because political actors are not in the situation of *homines economici,* in an ahistorical, perfectly competitive market, their choices do matter in shaping the game they are involved in. The record of social development is at best that of a "punctuated equilibrium."[11] According to this reasoning, former events constrain later choices, but no single unequivocal trend occurs through simple adaptation. Thus many types of inefficiencies are viable and survive.

But even such a conceptualization of history is too narrow. The biological process of adaptation provides a mistaken analogy to the evolution of social institutions. In the latter case no simple adaptation analogous to natural events occurs. The evolution of social formations is characterized by learning on the individual and organizational level. This learning is more than adaptation. Since individuals and groups are not passive victims of the viability of their genetic makeup, learning occurs through cognitive changes, rather than through random changes in the genetic endowment of the exemplars in a species. Thus, individuals and groups not only learn from *others,* they also can radically alter the environment within which their interactions take place.

Patrick Morgan's paper makes this point eloquently. Beginning with the structural argument of the security dilemma, Morgan shows that the security dilemma of the postwar world was less the result of anarchy than of specific perceptions and historical experiences that gave rise to particular security policies. Similarly the changes brought about by perestroika were not caused by structural changes in the distribution of capabilities or the reordering of the system through armed conflict but were the result of "learning" and a redefinition of "security" itself. Instead of defining it in military terms, increasingly a more "political" conception of security characterized Soviet "new thinking." Of course this does not mean that the former Soviet Union, or states in general, have ceased to pursue their interests. But what these interests *are* is crucially influenced by institutional structures—in the case of the former Soviet Union its desire to participate in the multilateral economic and political framework and also reap some benefit from some form of inclusion into the emerging Europe. Caporaso's argument that multilateralism is neither a purely instrumental nor a consumption good but rather a background variable that provides the context within which states pursue their interests is helpful in this respect.

Thus multilateralism, as defined in this volume, serves as a critique of the neorealist paradigm by providing an alternative conceptualization of international politics and its practices. Its critical contribution is also evident in rescuing history from the phantasmagorical constructions to which we often get treated. This critical function is most clearly visible in pointing to the "gaps" that appear in realist and functionalist constructions of history.

In order to counteract such tendencies and the amnesia it engenders, a hypothetical history is of great help. Ruggie's counterfactual construction of a German hegemony and its likely implications for the organization of world politics makes us aware of the different generative logics inherent in the ordering principles of realism and multilateralism. We also realize the impossibility of deriving the choices of such architectonic principles simply from the "position" of an actor in the system, such as "hegemony," or from the assertion that form has to follow function. Steve Weber's remarks are useful in reminding us of such unjustified analogies.

Furthermore, since Ruggie and most of the contributors to this volume have criticized the rift between theoretical constructs and actual practice in postwar international politics, several further tasks follow from its challenge. One is to provide an alternative plausible account of why American decision makers opted for a multilateral strategy in reconstituting the international system given the rather demanding nature of this organizational form. A second task is the historical reconstruction of a "hard case" that contradicts the logic of realism—e.g., multilateral cooperation in security affairs. Finally, the failure of realism to account for historically important multilateral aspects of international organization necessitates a reconceptualization of the nature of the international game. The papers of Burley, Weber, and Morgan address these three tasks.

INTERNATIONAL STRUCTURES AND THEIR GENESIS

Anne-Marie Burley's contribution in this volume provides a detailed account of the historically important links between the experiences with domestic regulation and postwar planning. Rather than argue from the inherent logic of increasing interdependence or functional necessity, so common in international legal treatises of the sociological school, Burley shows that the growth of international society was the *result,* rather than the cause, of the facilitative institutions of multilateralism. She also demonstrates that the emerging structures were not simply dictated by systemic forces but that the United States as a dominant actor shaped postwar institutions with minimum systemic constraints and coercion of others.

At the same time, Burley rejects the argument that multilateralism was simply a "consumption good," chosen for its own sake. Such a gambit would provide a convenient ad hoc adjustment of rationalist realist analyses.[12] Instead, Burley argues that the institutional framework was advocated as part of building an international environment in which liberal democratic polities, whose state apparati had increasingly become interventionist, could coexist without exacerbating conflicts.

The move to institutions was here deeply influenced by domestic experiences: by the belief that a liberal international order could be obtained only by creating congruent domestic and international institutions, and by a particular conception of the U.S. role in reconstructing the postwar international game. Burley's analysis of the change from the liberal night watchman state to a state with social purposes not only confirms the "embedded liberalism" argument but also lends at least indirect support to the proposition that the organization of international life was driven by the historical experiences of the interwar era. When the old equilibrating mechanisms such as the gold standard had broken down, and the new policies of a more interventionist state had created extremely negative international externalities, the old forms of organizing only "high politics" through security arrangements and leaving other areas to some "functional" logic failed miserably. After all, both the socialist and fascist challenge had shown that dissatisfaction with the "low politics" of welfare could quickly undo the security structures upon which high politics was predicated. On the other hand—and this Burley mentions only in passing—attempts to create stronger functional regimes through coordination and to link them to the security arrangements via the ECOSOC (Economic and Social Council) of the United Nations obviously misfired nearly as badly as Roosevelt's attempts to centralize control over the domestic regulatory agencies.

Steve Weber elaborates on multilateralism in the North Atlantic Alliance. Weber suggests that the choice of the organizational form was not the result of the good in question, or of U.S. preponderance, or of the lack of realizing this preponderance, or of the logic driven by nuclear weapons and the (in)credibility of extended deterrence. Rather, Weber succeeds in disentangling from the complicated history of NATO two themes that led to contradictory policy responses.

One was the political objective of creating a truly multipolar international system. The policies in pursuit of this goal not only encouraged European integration but also came close to bringing about a transformation of the bipolar configuration of the international system into a multipolar one through the development of a European nuclear force. One of the greatest of ironies was that a professional soldier, Dwight D. Eisenhower, pursued policies that were informed by such "political" considerations. His conception of international politics could not have been farther from the preoccupations of maximizing relative and absolute power or from the systemic logic of deterrence.

The other strand of thought, based on the perceived needs of effective deterrence, subordinated these political considerations. It sacrificed the evolution toward multipolarity to the necessities of centralization of command and control over nuclear weapons. This objective, which became predominant with the Kennedy administration's "defense intellectuals," resulted in the reinforcement of the bipolar configuration. European nuclear weapons were not only incredible and dangerous, Kennedy's advisors believed, but in addition, the problem of nuclear sharing proved to be highly divisive for the Atlantic alliance.[13] It led to France's withdrawal from the integrated command structure (but not from NATO itself or any other European or North Atlantic institution). It also resulted in the incongruities of the "flexible response" strategy, which sometimes seemed to entail only a little more than an agreement to disagree. Nevertheless, the commitment to multilateral institutions, to which U.S. and European countries became accustomed, preserved the alliance and prevented the atrophy and rapid decay we observed in the case of the seemingly similar arrangements in the Eastern bloc.

Telling the story of NATO in this form has several advantages. First, it corrects the myopia of progress, the notion that the ascendancy of the deterrence scenario represented the victory of a more coherent political vision of strategic rationality. Despite some important improvements made by unilateral and bilateral arms control measures during the thirty years in which the deterrence scenario dominated U.S. policy, the record is not one of inevitability or progress. For example, the fear of the "missile gap"—soon to be complemented by the fear of a "Hamburg grab" [14]—led to an escalation of the arms race that probably could have been avoided by more circumspect arms acquisition policies and by settling for a minimum deterrence posture.

Second, Weber's narrative casts doubt on the proposition that institutions evolve according to an evolutionary logic, whether it be due to their adaptation to systemic constraints or to "learning" the preordained lessons derived from the logic of deterrence. If we need important historical counterfactuals, several examples come to mind that undermine rationalistic reconstructions of the historical record.

First were the incongruities of flexible response and the unclear mission of tactical nuclear weapons. And there were the strained attempts of squaring the circle by proposing a "no first use policy" for nuclear weapons (which made sense in terms of tactical but not deterrence considerations). Finally, the abolition of the only type of nuclear weapons enhancing deterrence, the Pershing and cruise missiles, did not lead to an increase of tension inviting Soviet adventurism, but rather led to a considerable deescalation of conflict.

Second, the predominance of the "political" scenario, envisaging an emergent multipolar structure, cannot be represented as resulting from the lack of threat perception among Washington decision makers. On the contrary, starting from the prospects of a potential "bomber gap" to the actual development of ICBMs by the Soviet Union, the perception of increasing U.S. vulnerability spurred, rather than dissuaded, Eisenhower from looking for opportunities to help in the creation of an integrated Europe armed with nuclear weapons. In other words, politics always played a decisive and independent role, thereby upsetting any attempt at reducing it to the logic of strategic systems and calculations. This point might be deeply upsetting to those who have come to identify security policy with the study of weapons systems, but it is no surprise to those of us who still consider the mission of strategy to be the conduct of politics by other means.

Finally, Weber's account alerts us to the fact that the newly emergent Europe will perhaps be closer to the original plans than to the deterrence scenario that characterized the past thirty years. The Europe of the 1990s definitely owes its institutional structure to the original American commitment to multilateralism. U.S. pressure for integrative solutions among the European countries combined with the use of American troops in reassuring the French against a rearmed Germany, and the Germans against possible encroachment from the East, were crucial. They solved the long-standing European rivalry that began with the enmity between the Hapsburgs and Valois and continued through the twentieth century. It also served at the same time as insurance against Soviet threats.

Only in one, though decisive, respect does the emergent structure seem to differ from the visions of Kennan and Eisenhower. The future Europe will not be a "pole" akin to those of the classical balance-of-power period. As a matter of fact, if anything can be said of present European politics, it is that a return to the classical balance of power does not find any credible proponents in Europe today. Whatever misgivings one might have about the state of the European integration, the prospects of 1992, or even of German reunification, nobody seems to be interested in returning to playing the game according to the allegedly permanent rules of international politics under anarchy.

What is universally hoped for is the evolution of a structure that links the United States to Europe; increases European cooperation in defense matters, perhaps even out-of-area operations; and establishes a security regime between the newly agreed upon European Union and the states of the former Soviet empire. Here NATO, WEU, the Conference on Security and Cooperation in Europe (CSCE), will have to adjust to the changing realities of international politics and institutionalize multilateral rather than purely bilateral modes of decision making.

The differences from former plans aimed at multipolarity and at making Europe an independent actor in world politics are instructive. Instead of evicting the United States from the continent and making the (former) Soviet Union the predominant power (the old Soviet preferred scenario), or making "Europe" an independent third force, à la de Gaulle, the emerging structures disaggregate the hard shell of a classical pole in the international system and substitute a variety of overlapping (instead of exclusive) multilateral institutions. Within such a set of institutions, a loose security arrangement characterized by minimum deterrence and a "defensive defense," buttressed by mutual inspections and confidence-building measures, could emerge. This would prevent Europe from becoming a "wanderer between East and West," a role so fatal for German policy in the past, while keeping the gains reaped from European integration.

The confidence in multilateral solutions, for both containing a re-united Germany and for preventing the reemergence of either separate competing European nations or a united bloc confronting other powers, is one of the reasons Morgan adduces for the growth of multilateral cooperation in security affairs, this time even *across* the blocs. Noting earlier attempts at cooperation in security affairs, Morgan emphasizes the distinct feature of present-day multilateral efforts that go beyond the arrangements of the European Concert.

The parallels between the Concert and multilateralism are apparent since the participants in both forms must accept the notion of being part of an integrated system where peace and security are indivisible. In the Concert, the *motivation* for cooperation was still, however, largely driven by fear of war and perhaps revolution, exemplified by Metternich and the Czar. As opposed to these types of cooperation, today's attempts at multilateral solutions are based on a more positive idea of freedom and security. As a great proponent of multilateralism and a superb political sloganeer, Franklin D. Roosevelt realized that the multilateral order he envisaged for the postwar era had to be aimed not only at freedom from fear but also at the achievement of all the "Four Freedoms." Inherent in this program was a positive conception of freedom that was to enhance the well-being, as well as the cultural flourishing, of the distinct states in a security community based on diffuse reciprocity.

These historically distinct features lead to Morgan's frontal challenge to the structural realist paradigm and the "cooperation under anarchy" problematique. Starting from the observation that most states do not fear the imminence of attacks, as the success of strategic surprises ironically shows, Morgan elaborates on the notion that nations pursue security policies that go far beyond the attempts at insuring themselves against armed attack. The initial misconstruing of the security dilemma leads to the structural realist preoccupation with anarchy.

As to the paradigmatic contingency of anarchy in international politics, Hobbes himself suggested that the image of a war of all against all is an inappropriate characterization of the international arena owing to certain decisive differences between social organizations and individuals.

The personal weakness of even the strongest man (the susceptibility to being murdered in his sleep) is not present among states. Social organization thus mitigates this condition of anarchy. Accordingly, the preoccupation with the necessary and sufficient conditions of attack elevates the absence of authoritative central institutions to a complete "theory" of international politics.

According to Morgan, the existence of severe conflicts among states, and not the existence of anarchy, is to blame for the lack of cooperation in security affairs. This makes "security" a contestable concept rather than an overarching goal, subordinating every aspect of political life. Furthermore, in this context the issue of state autonomy and its concomitant right to use force arises. Thus, as Morgan puts it, "It is not anarchy that causes the true security dilemma but what states are entitled to do under anarchy." To that extent, Morgan not only expands on the modification of the realist paradigm provided by Jervis and the cooperation under anarchy literature but also challenges frontally the adequacy of the conventional realist paradigm.

The result is quite a different picture of the implications of anarchy for the international system. The factors that make for the institutionalization of cooperation in such an unlikely organizational form as multilateralism are also viewed differently. This revision recaptures the "political" rather than weapons-related aspect of American foreign policy mentioned by Weber. It shows again the importance of the domestic constitution for a definition of national security and suggests that the changes in the Soviet Union and Eastern Europe were not simply redefinitions of security interests within the old logic of deterrence. Already with the advent of nuclear parity, Soviet fears of an attack must have considerably lessened. Nevertheless, policies were still driven and rationalized by the necessities of weapons systems and exchange ratios. This happened because the political process for making security a politically contestable concept and foreign policy goal was never opened up by the sclerotic regimes of Brezhnev, Andropov, and Chernenko.

The upshot of these remarks is not that global peace has finally broken out and that war is unlikely in the future. Rather, it consists in the realization that the allegedly compelling implications of anarchy are not so compelling after all. Consequently, theories of international politics should reflect this greater complexity both of the structures of international politics and of security policies informed by historical lessons.

Multilateralism as Clarification: Normative Hierarchies and the Impact of Regimes

NORMATIVE HIERARCHIES

The focus on multilateralism has also helped us to better understand some of the puzzles left unsolved by regime theory. In defining multilateralism as an architectural principle that generated more particular rules and regulations, Ruggie avoids several mistakes that have plagued regime analysis. One is the idea that rules, norms, and higher order principles have to fit neatly like a hand into a glove. Although we have taken issue with such a conception in another place [15] and have advanced rather strong reasons why such a postulated fit is unlikely to capture the workings of actual regimes, this instrumental relationship still informs much of the regime debate.

In a way regime analysis is driven by the assumption that normative structures are resolutions to a problem. While such a conceptualization is again unobjectionable in and of itself, the devil is in the details. What represents a solution depends on what we consider "rational." The idea of decomposability into instrumentally related subtasks and subnorms results from an implicit conception close to a classical optimization problem. To the extent that all relevant information is given, one optimizing strategy can be devised. But as soon as we leave this synoptical ideal, sequencing of events will influence outcomes. Sacrificing rather than optimizing becomes the appropriate criterion as the decision algorithm is dissolved. Various norms can no longer be neatly fitted into instrumentally construed end–means chains. Higher order goals quickly become nonoperational because no clear-cut logical means–end chain can be constructed. What were subgoals originally now become competing goals. What is accepted as a solution to a problem now has more to do with what is capable of marshaling consensus than what is rational in a technical sense.

These points have been eloquently made in the organization literature, but they have not been taken seriously in much of the regime analysis. The extreme (methodological) individualism of much of regime analysis has not only led to attempts to explain regimes as simple responses to the problems utility-maximizing actors face but also tended to limit attention to the comparative statics of individual norms. This glosses over the theoretical significance of inconsistent or ambiguous norm linkages and the transformation of normative structures. Regimes are treated as being analogous to single norms, and change is largely treated in terms of decay. The underlying heroic assumption is that regimes were "once upon a time" perfectly rational and well-attuned solutions to clearly defined technical problems. Such a Platonic conception of norms as exiting above and outside the practice of actual actors, not requiring elaboration and interpretation, implies that any deviation from the original standard must be classified as decay.

Multilateralism clarifies these points in several respects. First, it abolishes the mythical account of "once upon a time" by showing that the architectonic principles of multilateralism never functioned in the way suggested by the instrumentalist argument of the demand for regimes. But with this bad news also comes the good news that deviations from certain specific norms need not represent decay. What is important is not the particular regulation. Rather what is crucial is whether the adoption of these architectonic principles was able to sustain a process of consensus formation and thereby to continuously reconstitute the international game without falling into the trap of unilateral or bilateralist solutions.

Second, the conceptualization of multilateralism employed in this volume also clarifies that the important aspect of multilateralism as a political phenomenon was neither its universal scope nor the result of dependence on a hegemon for the provision of a collective good. Much of the organizational efforts of multilateralism were geared to setting up institutions that could effectively exclude possible nonparticipants and/or monitor their compliance. These institutions also sometimes authoritatively decided whether deviations were breaches of the fundamental principles or represented acceptable exceptions or exemptions from the particular rules (GATT violations) or whether the observance of particular regulations could not be suspended through new agreements (move from fixed to floating exchange rates).

Third, stressing the importance of the architectonic nature of the multilateral principles allows us to see that the formation of regimes is not really driven by the issue-specific need for regulation. Rather the form this regulation takes is crucially influenced by the generative logic of the deep structure provided by these principles. As Steve Weber showed, NATO's form was not dictated by the function of defense, nor can the particular organizational design be understood apart from the particular historical experiences and beliefs of the relevant American decision makers.

Furthermore, Weber also helps us understand why changes in the institutional structure need be neither harmonious nor the outgrowth of adaptive or evolutionary practices. As one might cause a house to take on quite different forms by moving inside walls or by building additions or closing down a certain wing, so multilateralism need not lose its identity as a constitutive force by changes in norms or even entire segments of the specific regulative rules.

Since inconsistencies among conventional norms and nonconformity of actions with specific norms are an intrinsic part of political life, a sensible theoretical understanding of these problems will have to focus on the role of such shared meanings as legitimacy and diffuse reciprocity. These shared meanings give coherence, identity, and stability to organizational efforts in the face of persistent pressures for change. By understanding the generative force of multilateral principles, we are relieved from the anxieties and confusions that a purely empirically based analysis of issue areas is likely to engender.

IMPACT OF REGIMES

The common confusions in the regimes literature have also impaired a correct assessment of the impact of regimes on decision making. The conventional wisdom in this respect was that multilateral regimes had entered a crisis stage and that they provided little more than window dressing for decisions that were made on essentially different grounds. The increasing use of bilateral deals and restrictive practices seemed to provide convenient proof of the end of multilateralism. However, the traditional way of conceptualizing the strengths of regimes in terms of overt compliance is far too restrictive in providing an accurate account of the impact of regime norms on decisions. A few brief remarks drawing on the arguments presented here are in order.

Let us begin with the issue of whether regimes are causes of behavior. As mentioned in an earlier article,[16] although regimes obviously influence interaction patterns, they do not do so in the fashion of antecedent causes familiar from the natural sciences. The relationship is not one in which a factor *x*. causes (through constant conjunction) *y*. Rather, action *x* is recognized and appraised through the application of a norm as being an action of a particular kind or quality, such as "moves" in a game that have identifiable consequences. The rules of chess or football neither cause the game to be played nor cause any particular move within the play. If we are interested in these questions we need additional information (though this information will be quite different in type). For instance, we must know the schedules that pit various teams against each other at certain dates. We must know the particular strength of the various teams (such as whether they have good offensive or defensive capabilities), which in turn will allow us to understand their strategies and predict particular moves. Note, however, that without knowing the rules that constitute the game, we could neither specify what constitutes strength (such as weight and height in football, a resource that is irrelevant to playing chess) nor even begin to plan strategies or predict particular moves.

This misidentification of the role of rules and norms in shaping behavior as a causal influence is further reinforced by taking regulative rules as the paradigm for all rules. Since regulative rules are injunctions, their influence can be established within the normal framework of causality as intervening variables in the anticipatory calculations of an individual actor. Given these epistemological commitments, regimes seem to exist and influence decisions only if they satisfy this regulatory requirement of being a constraint. However, this misconceives the constitutive function of rules. Even if constitutive rules also have regulative aspects, as Giddens suggests,[17] this distinction is of fundamental importance. Thus the rules of grammar governing the formation of understanding sentences are of course in one sense regulative. They "rule out" the arbitrary linking of words such as "Green tomorrow though seeing furious" as gibberish. But does this regulative aspect of rules really deal adequately with the enabling function that these constitutive norms have for communication? Even if it is possible to show that constitutive norms have regulative aspects, it does not follow that they are the same or that constitutive norms can be reduced to regulative rules. Thus the influence of norms cannot be adequately understood if the model of regulative rules is our only paradigm.

As to the problem of ascertaining regime strength in terms of compliance, Roger Fisher reminded us several years ago that it is useful for purposes of analysis to distinguish between first- and second-order compliance.[18] First-order compliance largely concerns issues of behavioral conformity with prescriptions. First-order compliance conforms to Hart's argument of a "primitive legal order" that consists of direct injunctions or primary rules.[19] However, more advanced legal systems have "secondary rules," which determine how primary rules can be rescinded, modified, or created. Such legal systems also usually institutionalize authoritative procedures for determining responses to infractions of the primary rules, as opposed to having recourse to the legal institution of self-help, such as retortion, the suspension of treaties, reprisal, etc.

Formally, lack of first-order compliance creates obligations to comply with authoritative or quasi-authoritative determinations that a violation of a primary rule has occurred (second-order compliance). It is therefore entirely possible that significant first-order noncompliance is nevertheless not an indication of regime weakness. This would be the case if there is a significant amount of second-order compliance. We would expect this pattern to obtain in instances in which specific rules are under pressure by rapidly changing environments, or in which the higher order principles themselves can have contradictory implications for specific rules. In the former case, first-order noncompliance is one of the major ways of forcing adjustments, particularly in the absence of a legislative machinery. An example for the latter case is the permission of discriminatory practices in order to create conditions for further liberalization.

GATT provides fascinating material for both phenomena. The frequent first-order violations of this regime are not accompanied by a denouncement of, or a refusal to submit to, its settlement procedures and authoritative determinations (second-order compliance). The influence of GATT norms, however, goes far beyond the formal complaint and dispute-settling procedures of GATT itself. A study of thirteen cases of bilateral settlements between the United States and Pacific-rim nations (Japan, Korea, China, Taiwan, Singapore) indicated that eleven settlements were GATTable, i.e., in conformity with GATT or in compliance with emerging GATT law, although they had been initiated by the United States Trade Representative or the Department of Commerce.[20]

Concerning the issue of the inconsistencies of higher order principles and more specific rules, GATT's famous exceptions and escape clauses come to mind. As Goldstein's contribution shows, the resilience and adaptability of GATT was largely due to the fact that important exceptions were accepted from the beginning. These exceptions allowed states to safeguard important interests without reverting to unilaterialism or purely bilateral deals.

Normative inconsistencies—the value opportunism we encounter also in constitutions—are not detrimental to the strength and adaptability of regimes as instrumental logic would have it. Similarly, although exception and exemptions from GATT principles raise the issue of whether the glass is half full or half empty, i.e., whether we indeed have a multilateral trading order or some form of (increasing?) bilateralism, the issue of compliance with regime norms and principles cannot be reduced to simple observable behavioral conformity. By necessity we enter then a debate in which we must appraise pleas and excuses, deal with exemptions, interpret overt behavior in the light of justificatory arguments, and assess their plausibility.

Whereas my arguments this far have been concerned with the criticism of realism and clarification of certain issues in the regime debate, the task of the last section is to show that an institutional perspective as provided by multilateralism is fruitful for the study of politics in general. Furthermore, from the contributions above it should be clear that such a perspective is neither hostile to a rationalist approach (although a redefinition of rationality will be necessary for certain purposes) nor based on a denial of the importance of power in international politics. My contention is that an institutionalist approach enlarges the research program in international politics not only by linking more closely the informal features of organization to formal organizations but also by more clearly identifying the links between domestic and international politics.

Multilateralism as Heuristics: Domestic–International Linkages, Organizational Design, Collective-Action Problems and Issues of Rationality

The function of theories is to provide "powerful" explanations[21] that are susceptible to empirical tests. Theories have, in addition, a heuristic function, i.e., to stimulate research by providing a set of interesting problems. When measured by this yardstick, one of the contributions this study has made is to have raised the question of whether the institutionalization of multilateralist principles has indeed made as great a difference as suggested in the introduction. The observed marked difference between the Pacific and Atlantic region is not captured by the traditional structuralist theories à la Waltz, or by theories of hegemonic stability. However, these different levels of institutionalization represent significant discontinuities in the international system and are, therefore, likely to influence patterns of change.

This argument is only the more obvious corollary of a general proposition: the level of institutionalization and the congruence between domestic and international structures matter for explaining patterns of interactions within the international system. The contributions of Weber, Burley, Goldstein, and Cowhey all deal with this issue although from different points of departure.

The Importance of Domestic–International Linkages and the Competing Principles of Differentiation

Weber and Burley address the question of how images of the international system and of the constitutional order influence the design of international institutions. Goldstein traces how the resistance to liberalization in agricultural products now encountered by the United States has its roots in previous U.S. protectionist policies and the clientilistic network these policies had developed. Beyond explaining the differential patterns of institutionalization in terms of the strong ethnic links to Europe that made a nondiscriminatory, evenhanded U.S. policy vis-à-vis Europe necessary, Cowhey's paper demonstrates the importance of domestic structures for the visibility of multilateral regimes.

Cowhey's analysis, however, goes far beyond the analysis of specific policy outcomes. For him domestic structures, and in particular electoral systems, serve as *signals* to the other actors that the leading power is serious about living up to its commitments. Here again the maintenance of consensus and credibility is crucial for overcoming the impediments that otherwise would hamper cooperative efforts. In drawing on the insights of the principal-agent literature and organization theory, Cowhey stresses issues of transparency and legitimacy as crucial ingredients of multilateral orders. An acceptable relationship between the leading power(s) and secondary powers can be defined through the acceptance of fundamental principles and the possession of domestic institutions compatible with these requirements. Such shared understandings enhance the "productivity of the multilateral order" by clearly defining the rights and obligations among leading and secondary powers. In contrasting U.S. and Japanese domestic structures, particularly the electoral system and the separation of powers influencing the supervision and functioning of the policymaking and policy-implementing bureaucracy, Cowhey is able to assess the credibility of the commitment to multilateralism by these two systems.

Such a perspective makes short shrift of the traditional division between international and comparative politics. It also dispenses with the notion that instrumental or strategic rationality is able to capture the communicative aspects of the commitment to rules and norms that are decisive for the maintenance of consensus and the proper functioning of the "hierarchical contracts" characteristic of regimes. Of course this argument does not imply that rules and norms cannot be conceived as problem-solving devices. It does mean, however, that problem-solving activities informed by those norms involve a variety of operations that cannot all be reduced to the calculus of individual preference maximization, simply "assuming" these preferences as prior and external to the creation of regimes. In other words, the endogenization of preferences, their formation and their normative context, has to be one of the explicit parts of a research program. Each of these two points deserves some further discussion.

Underlying the argument for the need for a systemic focus on international politics is the domestic analogy, which asserts both the radical difference between these two realms of politics and a construal of international politics largely in terms of a negative analogy. Domestic politics is depicted as founded on hierarchy, on central enforcement of rights, peaceful change, and widely shared normative understandings. International politics, on the other hand, is characterized by horizontal ordering, by the lack of central institutions enforcing respective rights, and by the resort to force in the absence of shared values and norms.

Needless to say, the inhabitants of most major American cities would be surprised by this idyllic picture of the domestic order. But be that as it may, most of us are probably prepared to accept the generative logic of Hobbesian sovereignty and its domestic analogy in some measure. Nevertheless, something is decisively odd about this generative logic and its conceptual apparatus. First, sovereignty itself is normatively constituted and presupposes a shared understanding and valuation among the participants of the international game. Second, "sovereignty" is not the only and exclusive principle according to which the "units" of international politics are differentiated.

Ethnicity and "self-determination" often contest the legitimacy of established sovereign states. It was the nationalism that brought about the end of imperial orders whose sovereignty was never in doubt. The dissolution of the Austro–Hungarian empire and the present changes in the former Soviet Union are a useful reminder that the linkages between international and domestic politics are much richer and more complicated than the Hobbesian domestic analogy with its dichotomy of hierarchy and anarchy.

Moreover, the competing principles of basic differentiation make it necessary to develop domestic structures that decisively deviate from the strict hierarchical organization with which Hobbes (and after him most international politics scholars) identify social order. The existence of federal arrangements as well as the careful exclusion of certain rights of autonomy for language or ethnic groups indicates that even domestically social order is usually not produced by centralization and hierarchy. As important are shared notions of checks and balances, of separation of powers, and of "republican" notions of limiting governmental powers through the protection of individual rights, all of which prevent the emergence of clear hierarchies.

These considerations have several implications for the analysis of social order and for a theory of domestic and international politics alike. Above all it becomes clear that social order and the existence of hierarchies is much more contingently related than Hobbesian absolutism suggests. It is also obvious that the impoverished vision of domestic politics, derived from the absolutist preoccupation of control and rule by fiat, leads to an impoverished version of international politics.

Conversely, a rearticulation of new and more fruitful domestic analogies should be of great help in the development of more nearly adequate theories of international politics. Two areas in particular are likely to profit from such a reconceptualization. One concerns the "design" of organizations, the other the solution to collective-action problems in international politics that are poorly explained by neorealism and hegemony.

ORGANIZATIONAL DESIGN AND THE ROLE OF ORGANIZATIONS IN THE INTERNATIONAL SYSTEM

In regard to the "design" of formal organizations, the remarks above suggest that the efficiency gains from hierarchization vary greatly depending upon the environmental conditions of the organization. Shared notions of legitimacy and the acceptance of a certain knowledge base are crucial for the exercise of "authority" upon which hierarchical decision making depends. Notions of legitimacy not only define the scope and domain of an organization's task or mission but also determine the proper exercise of authority within the assigned task. But what is "proper" is also influenced by technical knowledge of how to go about certain tasks and subtasks.

The term *authority* shows the importance of both dimensions in that it distinguishes "having authority" from "being an authority." Having authority is related to the exercise of power within a legitimate domain, while being an "authority" emphasizes know-how or knowledge that commands respect and deference. The latter is particularly crucial for motivating employees who are otherwise likely to resist orders that "make no sense," even if issued by persons *having* authority.

One of the more interesting issues of modern organization theory has been the question of which types of transactions should be internalized and which should be left to the market. However, it is also clear that such calculations will depend upon a variety of factors. Among them are industry structure, regulatory environment, and prevailing decision-making styles. In this context the Japanese *keiretsu* system mentioned by Cowhey as a structural impediment to freer trade might not be "inefficient" as is sometimes argued, particularly since many of its costs will not appear as such in Japanese calculations.

The linkages between formal organizations and the institutional environment not only necessitates an open-systems approach for the study of formal organizations but also complicates causal analysis because equifinality and self-reference enter the picture. Adaptation no longer has a definite meaning since the environment of organizations is no longer stable. This holds even in a logical sense because organizational activity transforms the environment. Without further empirical specification of the interaction, the argument that efficiency is driving this process is little more than an act of faith. Simply showing that institutions solve problems and formal organizations "implement" regimes is hardly illuminating.

Contrary to an evolutionary argument, the emergence of similar organizational forms might have little to do with their alleged efficiency, as Weber and Michels assumed, but might be the result of the legitimacy that certain formal organizational forms have attained. Consequently, formal organizations proliferate, not necessarily because of their superiority, but because of their ability to signal to the rest of the world that some issue is recognized as being important and that something is being done about it. This signaling function is crucial in the process of persuasion in retaining a stable set of expectations amid great uncertainty and has been well captured by Cowhey's argument.

Furthermore, David Kennedy's "move to institutions" argues that formal universal international organizations were created in the twentieth century because of the widespread conviction that formal organizations were necessary for the management of the international system.[22] Curiously enough this conviction existed despite the ends—means reversal upon which it is based and which detracts considerably from its justification in terms of instrumental rationality. In an area in which the legitimacy of the organization is contested, the domain or mission vague, and the knowledge of procuring particular results scanty, the founding of formal organizations is unlikely to show straightforward results of an instrumental nature. Universal, multipurpose IGOs (Intergovernmental Organizations) have therefore always shown a curious organizational design that bolted together various organizational forms familiar from domestic politics.

The assemblies of these organizations concerned with the definition of "problems" are held together by little more than a yearly schedule to discuss and thereby legitimate and deigitimate issues of concern. Precisely because the domains of these organizational efforts are barely specifiable or of unquestioned legitimacy, only the weakest form of institutionalization is possible: the debate. Topics have to be attended to sequentially and all members ought to pay attention. The organizational economies that are available are schedules (forcing an end to debate), consensus procedures, reduction of participants (committees), and limited delegation (to produce, e.g., a draft agreement). "Councils" are formally empowered to make decisions on certain issues and represent some weak form of authority based on some notion of representation. Only seldom is the actual formal, hierarchically organized bureaucracy entrusted with the administration of programs.

Here the contributions of Burley, Kahler, and Zacher provide some additional insight. Burley takes note of the new organizational forms of the New Deal regulatory agencies. They cut across traditional lines of legislative, judicial, and administrative (executive) functions that the Constitution had entrusted to separate branches of government. The success in overcoming the traditional divisions then served as a blueprint for the design of "functional" organizations. However, as Burley points out, the new functional agencies differed from the earlier public unions significantly in that they were not simply implementors of technical tasks but also were conceived analogously to the autonomous domestic regulatory agencies.

Thus the characterization of certain agencies as merely "functional" is misleading. Two distinct types of organization are lumped together within this category. The crucial distinction is related to the domain consensus that underlies both organizations. The agreement to treat "culture and education" as a specific autonomous domain and create an agency for the facilitation of cooperation is quite different from the domain consensus based on shared technologies (signals, schedules, switch equipment, etc.) that underlies international unions such as river commissions and postal and telecommunication unions. The problem of "politicization" of the former organization is considerably greater owing to the politically contestable definition of its legitimate domain, as indeed the controversies surrounding UNESCO and the International Labor Organization (ILO) showed.[23]

Furthermore, having created semiautonomous organizations, problems of coordination are bound to arise even if organizational charts attempt to centralize control over the fast-growing agencies. The nominal success in integrating the "functional" agencies within the U.N. framework by subordinating them under ECOSOC has never worked, because it could not. Imposing rationalistic solutions to areas that are characterized by shifting patterns of consensus on goals as well as on means is to mistake form for substance. It created frustrations not only among member states but also among the members of the "secretariat," which experienced severe cognitive dissonance. The Bertrand report[24] is only the latest in the host of proposals for streamlining and coordinating the U.N. system.

SOLUTIONS TO COLLECTIVE-ACTION PROBLEMS AND THE ISSUE OF "RATIONALITY"

Kahler's "Multilateralism with Small and Large Numbers" addresses the crucial issue of forming a domain consensus in order to create regimes or international organizations. By analyzing the role institutions play in this context, Kahler is able to demonstrate that some of the well-known impediments to cooperation are considerably less severe than both realism and neoliberalism make it appear. Realists postulate that states will use their bargaining strength in bilateral deals and thus multilateralism will fail. Neoliberal institutionalists are skeptical about cooperative ventures owing to the collective-action problems inherent in large numbers.

In showing how "minilateralism"—the creation of core groups and the multilateralization of their agreements—worked, Kahler is able to give a far more coherent account of postwar collaboration than hegemonic stability theory provides, as well as demonstrate the inapplicability of the atomized Hobbesian world as an analogue to international politics. Regime creation takes place in an arena characterized by "institutionalized bargaining"[25] rather than by the possessive individualism of instrumentally rational actors whose goals are simply "given." This initially allowed for the incorporation of important exceptions and derogations from the injunctions of strict multilateralism (GATT) and set off a process of bilateral and minilateral negotiations in the 1950s and 1960s in which the agreements were subsequently extended to other participants. The web of institutions was strong enough in the 1980s to prevent great-power as well as Third World defection from multilateralism, although exceptions and exemptions are often eagerly sought.

Kahler's investigation of UNCLOS III, the Uruguay Round, the Vienna Convention on the Protection of the Ozone Layer, and the Montreal Protocol leads to some surprising and suggestive insights on the role of institutions in mediating the tension between legitimacy involving participation in decision making and efficiency. What is surprising is that the traditional means of achieving this mediation have decreased in importance when compared to new consensus procedures. Delegation to experts, the core tenet of functionalist theory, has seldom been resorted to. Similarly, weighted voting, another device for increasing efficiency, is often avoided even if it is available. Instead the prevailing practice tends toward consensual decision making. While consensus significantly relaxes the requirement of unanimity, it is not the sheer numbers, but rather the quality, of the consensus that matters. Thus negotiations in multilateral fora and even the quasi-normative pronouncement of some General Assembly resolutions do not have their standing on the basis of the virtually "automatic" majorities to which we have grown accustomed. Rather, their authoritative character depends upon the ability to facilitate an agreement among all the important groups and interests. It follows that the appropriate domestic analogy would not be that of one man, one vote. It would be segmented systems in which important group rights are exempted from majority rule through elaborate procedures such as constitutional guarantees of autonomy, or demanding requirements for the modification of the regime. International lawyers have used similar criteria in the assessment of the authority of norms that technically are not legally binding but often have great persuasive weight in actual decision making.

Mark Zacher takes up a similar set of issues, but his focus is on existing multilateral organizations and their role in influencing the creation and implementation of regimes. In this context, the efforts of multilateral organization to formulate new principles governing the uses of the oceans, airwaves, and outer space are scrutinized. This entails an examination of the impact of the new conception of the common heritage of mankind on the traditional structure of exclusive property rights, a conception that was instrumental for the conceptualization of "sovereignty." It also necessitates an examination of the role of international organization in maintaining the existing regimes. Here Zacher deals with a much neglected role of formal international organizations: their "implicit" role. While not created for these purposes, the contributions international organization make in this respect are essential to the functioning of the regimes that we take for granted.

For example, the viability of a free-access regime governing the high seas would be unlikely without the contribution of the International Maritime Organization (IMO) to vessel safety, pollution abatement, and liability rules for assessing damages. In the absence of such regulation the extension of national jurisdiction, with all the concomitant problems of overlapping jurisdictional claims, would have been necessary. Despite its importance, the contribution of the international organization remains "implicit" because the states retain the sanctioning capacity by not letting unsafe vessels that violate IMO standards into their ports. In the case of a fisheries regime, however, no such decentralized sanctioning possibility exists. This makes the extension of property rights the preferred and arguably cheaper alternative to ensure the sustainable yield of fish stocks.

Similarly, the linkage made in UNCLOS III between access (transportation rights) and resource transfer based on the "common-heritage" principle became undone because the need for implementing organizations with law-making authority overtaxed the existing consensus. True, the provisions for exacting majorities required for the revisions of the regime, as well as the compromise on a parallel system of exploitation, assuaged the fears of expropriation. However, the compromises did not inspire enough confidence that the envisaged ISA (International Seabed Authority) would indeed only regulate the nodules instead of simply redefining property rights (see, e.g., the sweeping provisos for technology transfer as a precondition for obtaining mining licenses).

The last point once more raises the issue of a hierarchical (incomplete) contract and the discretion and authority granted to particular agents for implementing a regime. Can the rise of institutions, and more particularly of formal organizations, be explained by the logic of "market failure," or are other approaches needed? Garret and Zacher seem to suggest, although coming from rather different perspectives, that functional or rational-choice explanations are sufficient. Caporaso, Weber, and Morgan are less convinced. Cowhey and Kahler occupy an interesting middle position since their explorations, although done in a way akin to the rational-choice approach, go far beyond its restricted repertoire by stressing the importance of shared cultural understandings.

Whatever our position in regard to these methodological questions might be, one thing seems clear: institutions fundamentally alter our conceptions of rational action. Even in the paradigmatic case of the emergence of formal organizations, the impossibility of engaging in elaborate individual utility calculations forced "rational" actors to agree to a hierarchical contract that significantly altered their conceptualization of the situation in which the action takes place.

The important point here is that the first question actors now have to face is not an examination of their own preferences but "what situation is this and how appropriate are certain alternatives for me in this situation." This change of terminology is not merely one of semantics. It is rather a different way of viewing and appraising a choice opportunity by matching it with an acceptable (legitimate) course of action.

Note that the point is not that real actors often violate this logic (as they violate principles of rationality). The point is rather to understand the role that rules and norms play in the process of deliberation antecedent to an actor's choice. In the absence of well-specified games, and often without a clear conception of their own long-term utility, actors invoke norms as shortcuts to their decision problems. Within this reasoning process, fitting a rule to a situation is to proceed by analogous reasoning and by typological comparison. This means that they proceed neither by inductive inference nor by deductive entailments. As March and Olsen put it:

> In establishing appropriateness, rules and situations are related by criteria of similarity or difference through reasoning by analogy and metaphor. The process is heavily mediated by language, by the way in which the participants come to be able to talk about on a situation similar or different from one another. . . . Although the process is certainly affected by considerations of the consequences of action, it is organized by different principles of action, a logic of appropriateness and a comparison of cases in terms of similarities and differences. The process maintains consistency in action primarily through a creation of typologies of similarity, rather than through a derivation of action from stable interests and wants.[26]

The language of "appropriateness" seems rather strange for explaining international politics and its organizational features. From discussions of the decision makers themselves, however, we know that realist practitioners have used it. Appropriateness guided action, even in crisis situations when supreme interests were at stake. In the Cuban missile crisis, Robert Kennedy was able to influence the decision against a surprise attack of Soviet bases by invoking the negative example of Tojo. Kennedy noted the incompatibility of such exemplary ruthlessness with the self-image of the United States.

Similarly, as the Truman Doctrine and postwar planning show, the preference for multilateral solutions was the result of a particular conception of the appropriate role of the United States in the world. As Kennan put it so aptly in his long telegram, the Soviet challenge was a threat not only to certain U.S. interests but also to her conception of a free political community. This test of national quality could be weathered only "if the American people understood that their security as a nation depended upon their pulling themselves together and accepting responsibility of moral and political leadership that history had plainly intended them to bear." [27]

Kennan further elaborated on the interconnection between domestic and international politics in a lecture at the National War College a few years later:

> For us . . . the problem boils down to one of obtaining mastery over the run away horse of technology . . . of creating here at home a stable balance between consumption and resources . . . , in producing here institutions which would demonstrate that a free society can govern without tyrannizing and that man can inhabit a good portion of the earth without devastating it . . . and then armed with this knowledge . . . point forth to see what we can do in order that stability may be given to all the non-communist world. [28]

Whatever one might think of this way of conceptualizing about the problem of choices and institutions, it is hard to see how one could characterize such a reflective account as nonrational. What is right under these conditions of rationality is process oriented rather than outcome oriented. Higher order norms and principles have a generative capacity, but their influence on specific rules is not that of deductive entailment, and their influence in shaping behavior allows cause for a good many variations. Nevertheless, the principles of multilateralism make it an identifiable and distinct organizational phenomenon of great significance both for the understanding of postwar policy and for a theory of international politics.

NOTES

1. For a discussion of research programs and heuristically fruitful problem shifts, see Imre Lakatos, "Falsification and the Methodology of Scientific Research Programs," in Imre Lakatos and Alan Musgrave, eds., *Criticism and the Growth of Knowledge* (Cambridge, England: Cambridge University Press, 1970).

2. See, e.g., Kenneth Waltz, *Theory of International Politics* (Reading, Mass.: Addison–Wesley, 1979), p. 113.

3. Milton Friedman, "The Methodology of Positive Economics," *Essays in Positive Economics* (Chicago: University of Chicago, 1958), part I.

4. Robert Axelrod, *The Evolution of Cooperation* (New York: Basic Books, 1984).

5. Edna Ullmann-Margalit, *The Emergence of Norms* (Oxford, England: Clarendon, 1977).

6. Duncan Snidal, "Coordination versus Prisoner's Dilemma, Implications for International Regimes," *American Political Science Review* (1985), 79:923–942.

7. Garrett, in this volume.

8. Garrett, ibid.

9. Anatol Rapoport, *Fights, Games and Debates* (Ann Arbor: University of Michigan Press, 1960).

10. Michael Taylor, *The Possibility of Cooperation* (Cambridge, England: Cambridge University Press, 1987).

11. See Stephen Krasner, "Sovereignty: An Institutional Perspective," *Comparative Political Studies* (April 1988), 21(1):66–94.

12. This is very much like the fallback position of utilitarianism, which holds that compliance with rules is the result of an actor's "utility" since it makes him or her feel good.

13. See my discussion in *International Order and Foreign Policy* (Boulder, Colo.: Westview, 1978), ch. 6, sect. 4.

14. This refers to various scenarios in which the Soviet Union would capture a certain salient West German city in a limited incursion, which then would provide the United States and its allies the unenviable choice of either accommodating to the *fait accompli* or of incredibly threatening the initiation of strategic retaliation.

15. See Friedrich Kratochwil and John Gerard Ruggie, "A State of the Art on an Art of the State," *International Organization* (Fall 1986), 40:753–776.

16. Kratochwil and Ruggie, "The State of the Art."

17. Anthony Giddens, *Central Problems in Social Theory: Action, Structure and Contradiction in Social Analysis* (Berkeley: University of California Press, 1979), pp. 82–83.

18. Roger Fisher, *Improving Compliance with International Law* (Charlottesville: University of Virginia Press, 1981), ch. 1 and 2.

19. H. L. A. Hart, *The Concept of Law* (New York: Oxford University Press, 1961).

20. See Michael Ryan, "Achieving Negotiated Compliance with GATT Law: American Unilateralism and the Settlement of Pacific Basin Disputes Regarding Unfair Trade Practices," University of Michigan, School of Business Administration, 1991, mimeo, pp. 16 ff.

21. Theories are powerful if they explain a series of real-world phenomena by

a small number of explanatory variables. The power of a theory is therefore the ratio of the *explanans* to the *explananda*.

22. David Kennedy, "The Move to Institutions," *Cardozo Law Review* (April 1987), 8(5)841–988.

23. For a good conceptual analysis of the "politicization" problem in functional organization and several case studies, see Mark Imber, *The USA, ILO, UNESCO, and IAEA: Politicization and Withdrawal in the Specialized Agencies* (New York: St. Martin's Press, 1989).

24. Maurice Bertrand, *Refaire l'ONU: Un Programme pour la Paix* (Geneva: Zoe, 1986).

25. Oran Young, "The Politics of International Regime Formation," *International Organization* (Summer 1989), 43:349–376.

26. J. March and J. Olsen, *Rediscovering Institutions: The Organizational Basis of Politics* (New York: The Free Press, 1989), pp. 25–26.

27. George Kennan, "The Sources of Soviet Conduct," *Foreign Affairs* (July 1947), 25:566–582, reprinted in Thomas Paterson, ed., *Containment and Cold War* (Reading, Mass.: Addison–Wesley, 1973), p. 33.

28. As quoted in John Lewis Gaddis, *Strategies of Containment* (New York: Oxford University Press, 1982), p. 36.

Index

NEW DIRECTIONS IN WORLD POLITICS
John Gerard Ruggie, General Editor

John Gerard Ruggie, editor, *The Antinomies of Interdependence: National Welfare and the International Division of Labor* 1983

David B. Yoffie, *Power and Protectionism: Strategies of the Newly Industrializing Countries* 1983

Paul Taylor, *The Limits of European Integration* 1983

William H. Becker and Samuel F. Wells, Jr., editors, *Economics and World Power: An Assessment of American Diplomacy Since 1789* 1983

John Ravenhill, *Collective Clientelism: The Lome Conventions and North-South Relations* 1985

Robert Pollard, *Economic Security and the Origins of the Cold War* 1985

William McNeil, *American Money and the Weimar Republic* 1986

Robert O. Keohane, editor, *Neorealism and Its Critics* 1986

J. Ann Tickner, *Self-Reliance Versus Power Politics: The American and Indian Experiences in Building Nation States* 1987

Robert W. Cox, *Production, Power, and World Order: Social Forces in the Making of History* 1987

Jeffrey Harrod, *Power, Production, and the Unprotected Worker* 1987

David R. Mares, *Penetrating International Markets: Theoretical Considerations and Mexican Agriculture* 1987

John A. C. Conybeare, *Trade Wars: The Theory and Practice of International Commercial Rivalry* 1987

Kenneth A. Rodman, *Sanctity Versus Sovereignty: U.S. Policy Toward the Nationalization of Natural Resource Investments in the Third World* 1988

Constance G. Anthony, *Mechanization and Maize: Agriculture and the Politics of Technology Transfer in East Africa* 1988

Jock A. Finlayson and Mark W. Zacher, *Managing International Markets: Developing Countries and the Commodity Trade Regime* 1988

Peter M. Haas, *Saving the Mediterranean: The Politics of International Environmental Cooperation* 1990

Stephen C. Neff, *Friends But No Allies: Economic Liberalism and the Law of Nations* 1990

Emanuel Adler and Beverly Crawford, *Progress in Postwar International Relations* 1991

J. Ann Tickner, *Gender in International Relations: Feminist Perspectives on Achieving Global Security* 1992

Barry Buzan, Charles Jones, and Richard Little, *The Logic of Anarchy: Neorealism to Structural Realism* 1993

Ronnie D. Lipschutz and Ken Conca, editors, *The State and Social Power in Global Environmental Politics* 1993

David A. Baldwin, editor, *Neorealism and Neoliberalism: The Contemporary Debate* 1993

Karen Litfin, *Ozone Discourses: Science and Politics in Global Environmental Cooperation* 1994

Ronnie D. Lipschutz, editor, *On Security* 1995

Peter J. Katzenstein, editor, *The Culture of National Security: Norms and Identity in World Politics* 1966

Edward D. Mansfield and Helen V. Milner, editors, *The Political Economy of Regionalism* 1997

Robert Latham, *The Liberal Moment: Modernity, Security, and the Making of Postwar International Order* 1997

Ronald J. Deibert, *Parchment, Printing, and Hypermedia* 1997

Peter Trubowitz, Emily O. Goldman, and Edward Rhodes, Editors, *The Politics of Strategic Adjustment: Ideas, Institutions, and Interests* 1998